THE FIRST COLD WAR

BARBARA EMERSON

The First Cold War

Anglo-Russian Relations in the 19th Century

HURST & COMPANY, LONDON

First published in the United Kingdom in 2024 by
C. Hurst & Co. (Publishers) Ltd.,
New Wing, Somerset House, Strand, London, WC2R 1LA

Distributed in the United States, Canada and Latin America by
Oxford University Press, 198 Madison Avenue, New York, NY 10016,
United States of America.

A Cataloguing-in-Publication data record for this book
is available from the British Library.

ISBN: 9781805260578

This book is printed using paper from registered sustainable
and managed sources.

www.hurstpublishers.com

Printed in Great Britain by Bell and Bain Ltd, Glasgow

CONTENTS

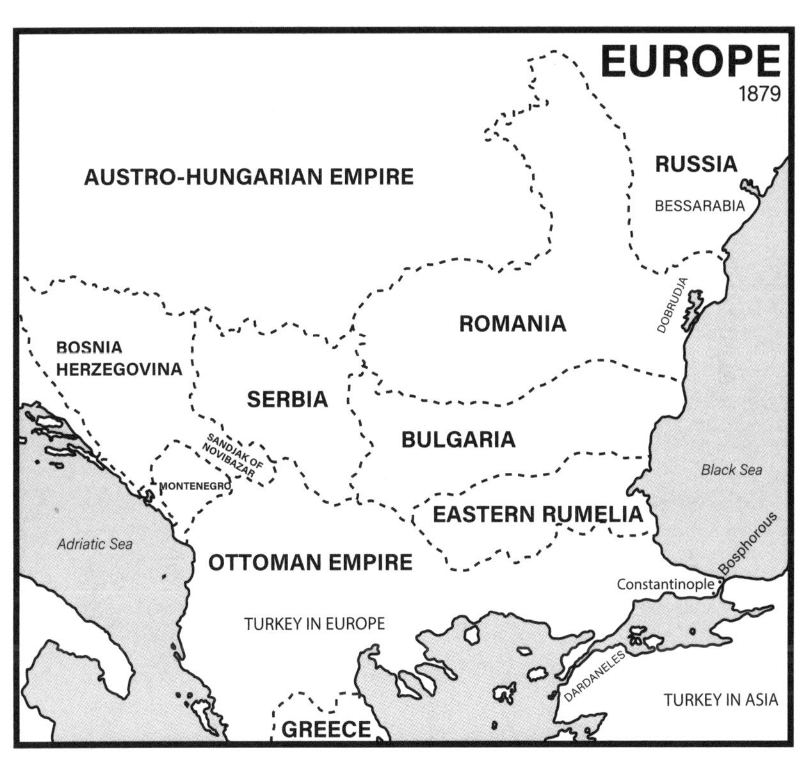
EUROPE
1879
AUSTRO-HUNGARIAN EMPIRE
RUSSIA
BESSARABIA
ROMANIA
DOBRUDJA
BOSNIA
HERZEGOVINA
SERBIA
SANDJAK OF NOVIBAZAR
MONTENEGRO
BULGARIA
Black Sea
EASTERN RUMELIA
Bosphorous
Adriatic Sea
OTTOMAN EMPIRE
Constantinople
TURKEY IN EUROPE
DARDANELES
TURKEY IN ASIA
GREECE

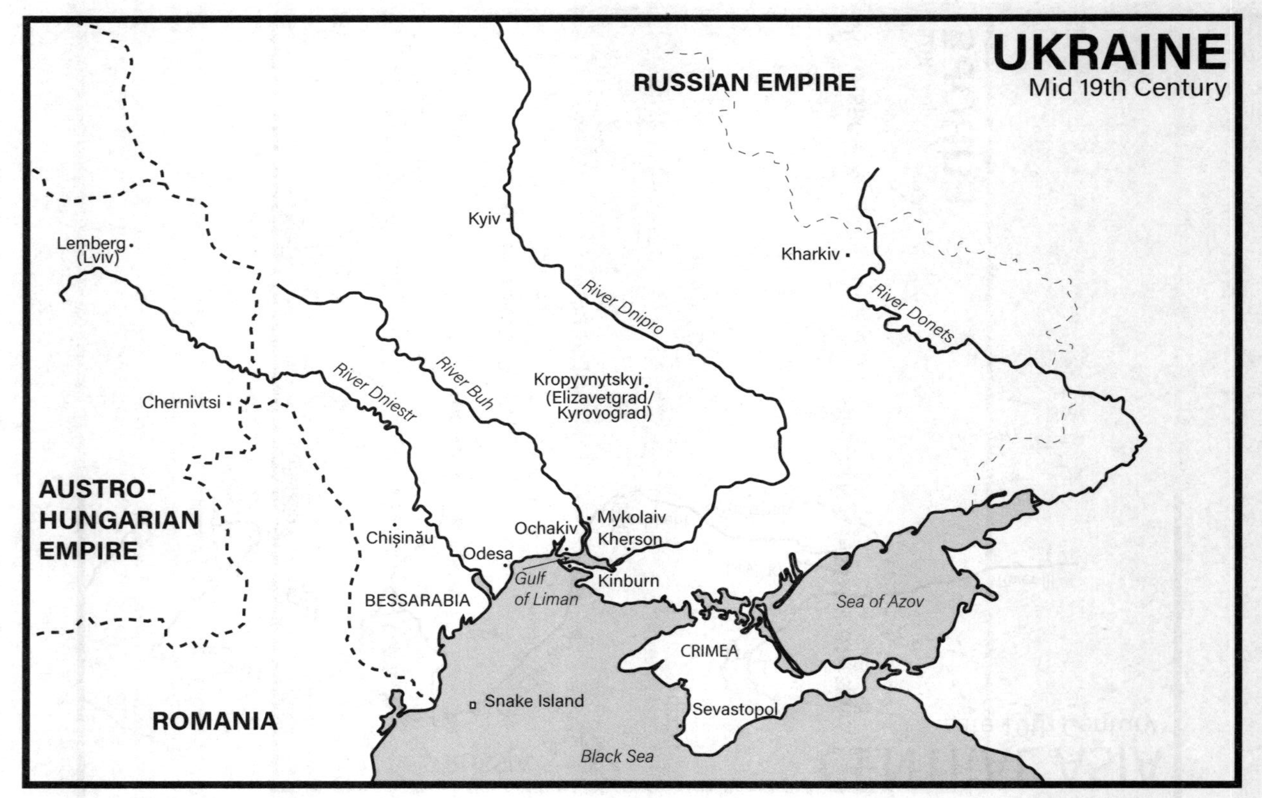
UKRAINE
Mid 19th Century
RUSSIAN EMPIRE
Kyiv
Kharkiv
River Dnipro
River Donets
Lemberg
(Lviv)
River Buh
River Dniestr
Kropyvnytskyi
(Elizavetgrad/
Kyrovograd)
Chernivtsi
AUSTRO-
HUNGARIAN
EMPIRE
Chișinău
Ochakiv
Mykolaiv
Kherson
Odesa
Gulf
of Liman
Kinburn
BESSARABIA
Sea of Azov
CRIMEA
Snake Island
Sevastopol
ROMANIA
Black Sea

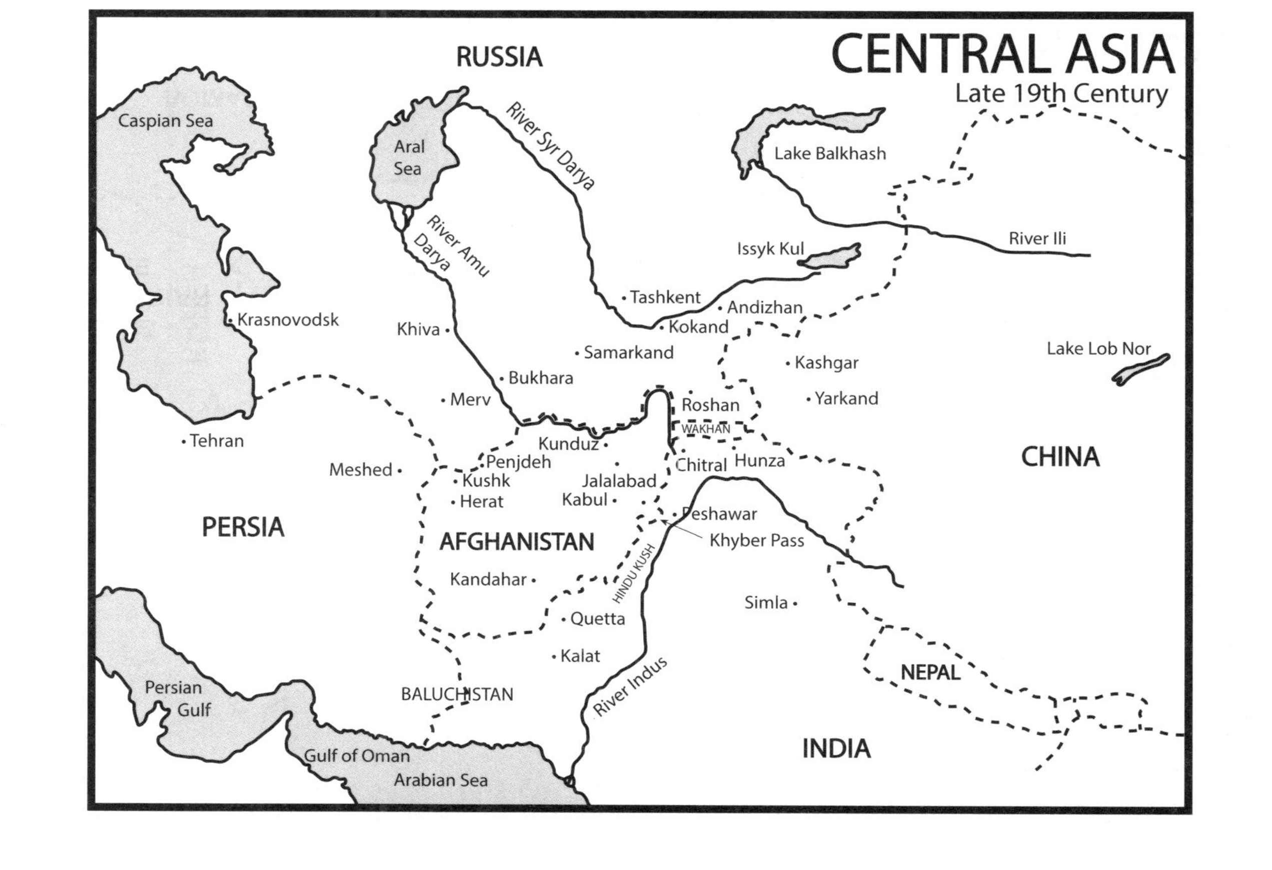
CENTRAL ASIA
Late 19th Century
RUSSIA
Caspian Sea
Aral Sea
River Syr Darya
River Amu Darya
Lake Balkhash
Issyk Kul
River Ili
Tashkent
Andizhan
Kokand
Krasnovodsk
Khiva
Samarkand
Kashgar
Lake Lob Nor
Bukhara
Yarkand
Merv
Roshan
WAKHAN
Tehran
Kunduz
CHINA
Meshed
Penjdeh
Chitral
Hunza
Kushk
Jalalabad
Herat
Kabul
Peshawar
PERSIA
AFGHANISTAN
Khyber Pass
HINDU KUSH
Kandahar
Simla
Quetta
Kalat
NEPAL
Persian Gulf
BALUCHISTAN
River Indus
Gulf of Oman
Arabian Sea
INDIA

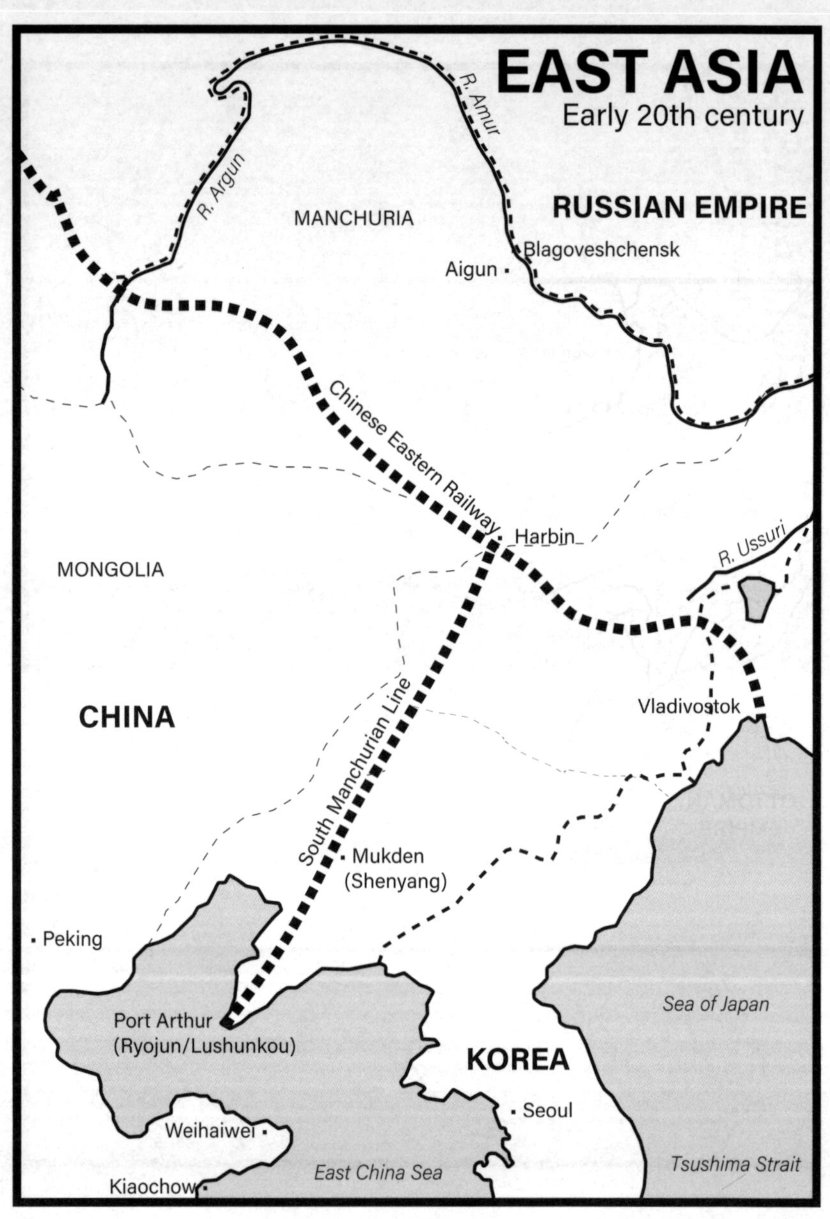
EAST ASIA
Early 20th century
RUSSIAN EMPIRE
R. Amur
R. Argun
MANCHURIA
Blagoveshchensk
Aigun
Chinese Eastern Railway
Harbin
MONGOLIA
R. Ussuri
CHINA
South Manchurian Line
Vladivostok
Mukden
(Shenyang)
Peking
Sea of Japan
Port Arthur
(Ryojun/Lushunkou)
KOREA
Seoul
Weihaiwei
East China Sea
Tsushima Strait
Kiaochow

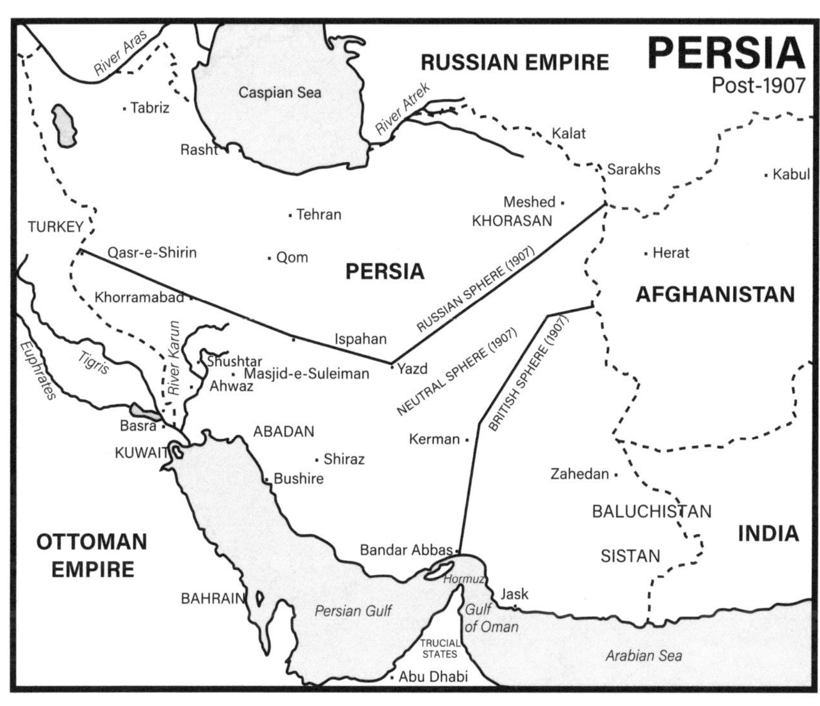
PERSIA
Post-1907
RUSSIAN EMPIRE
River Aras
Caspian Sea
River Atrek
Tabriz
Rasht
Kalat
Sarakhs
Kabul
Meshed
KHORASAN
Tehran
TURKEY
Qasr-e-Shirin
Qom
PERSIA
Herat
AFGHANISTAN
Khorramabad
RUSSIAN SPHERE (1907)
Ispahan
Euphrates
Tigris
River Karun
Shushtar
Masjid-e-Suleiman
Ahwaz
Yazd
NEUTRAL SPHERE (1907)
BRITISH SPHERE (1907)
Basra
ABADAN
Kerman
KUWAIT
Shiraz
Bushire
Zahedan
BALUCHISTAN
INDIA
OTTOMAN
EMPIRE
Bandar Abbas
SISTAN
Hormuz
Jask
BAHRAIN
Persian Gulf
Gulf
of Oman
TRUCIAL
STATES
Arabian Sea
Abu Dhabi

LIST OF ILLUSTRATIONS

ACKNOWLEDGEMENTS

I am grateful to Her Majesty Queen Elizabeth II for permission to consult the Royal Archives, Windsor Castle, and I would like to express my thanks to His Majesty King Charles III. The archivists of the Russian Imperial Ministry of Foreign Affairs, Moscow, were extremely helpful during my research some years ago. I am grateful to the Master of Churchill College , University of Cambridge, for access to the College's Archives Centre.

The National Archives, Kew, are an inexhaustible source for historians and the friendly help provided by the staff makes Kew a delightful workplace. The Bodleian Library, University of Oxford, and Cambridge University Library were essential for much of my reading, and I would like to add my thanks to the staff at the Gladstone's Library, Hawarden, where I spent a fortnight immersed in their collection.

Of all libraries, my home is the London Library, St James's Square. I have spent many years discovering treasures in the stacks and appreciating the Reading Room. While seeking out obscure journals and wondering in what direction to focus, the knowledge and solicitude of the librarians was an invaluable resource.

The former principal of St. Hilda's College, University of Oxford, Miss Elizabeth Llewellyn-Smith CB, offered me a visiting fellowship which enabled me to benefit from contacts with Oxford colleagues and she has subsequently been a constant source of encouragement. I owe particular thanks to Dr Beryl Williams, the eminent historian of late 19th century Russia, who read a draft and offered criticism. David Brummell CB offered wise reflections on his reading.

Lucie Emerson's help was indispensable in copy-editing. Lucie, and Sophie and Martha Sainty, were of great assistance pre-publication and Tom Emerson's stimulating thoughts during research and writing were much appreciated.

Note on dates: Russia was on the Julian calendar until 1918. This was twelve days behind the Gregorian calendar in use in western

Europe in the nineteenth century and thirteen days behind in the twentieth century. The dates cited in the text are as shown in the relevant documents.

PREFACE

Sir Rodric Braithwaite
Former British Ambassador to the Soviet Union 1988–91 and to Russia 1991–2

There has always been something odd about the relationship between Britain and Russia. Situated on the outer flanks of a continent whose history, culture and Christian traditions they share—reluctantly, it sometimes seems—they are geographically too far apart to impinge directly on one another. Russia is not a perennial threat to Britain as it is to the countries of Eastern and Central Europe. They have only been in direct conflict twice. During the Crimean War Britain invaded Russia fairly successfully. In 1919 it sent troops to intervene in the Russian civil war. That was a failure, like so many of Britain's armed interventions in other people's domestic affairs.

The first English visitor arrived in Moscow in 1554 to promote trade. He and his successors were struck by the autocratic power of the tsar, his disregard of any legal restraint, the drunken servility of the aristocracy, the lack of any solid middle class, and the grinding poverty and servitude of those at the bottom. The Russians saw the English as heretics from a distant land of little immediate interest, who treated them too often with infuriating arrogance and condescension. Trade provided mutual advantage, but there was little else of substance.

That changed once Peter the Great had recreated Russia as a major European power. Both countries now played a full part in the games of European Great Power politics. Within a century issues and attitudes had crystallized which still shape the relationship. The British continued to dislike Russia's domestic regime, and said so loudly. They supported Polish independence, to little practical effect because the geography got in the way. Britain and Russia were imperial rivals in the Mediterranean, Persia, Afghanistan and the Far East. There was recurrent talk of war.

The rivalry still casts a shadow even though the British empire no longer exists. Both sides are convinced that the other continually interferes in its internal affairs. Russians still see the hand of the British Secret Service behind their every mishap. They admire one another's high culture, but that does little to mitigate the underlying hostility.

The twentieth century began with Russia still busy in Central Asia, manoeuvring around Afghanistan and Tibet, intriguing in Persia, and showing an unhealthy interest in the Gulf. Many British policymakers and much of the public saw all this as an intolerable threat to their country's imperial interests. They seldom paid much attention to those who believed an understanding was necessary and possible.

But the rise of Germany under the belligerent leadership of Kaiser Wilhelm II threatened both countries. They composed their imperial differences in the Anglo-Russian Convention of 1907 and went on to create a common front with the French and fight as allies in the First World War.

But it was a fragile understanding, which did not survive the revolution and British military intervention. Thereafter the mutual suspicion and hostility revived. They continue to this day, tempered briefly by another common fight against the Germans and the hopes generated by Gorbachev. With Putin they have resumed at full blast.

1

ENGLAND AND MUSCOVY

THE BEGINNING OF ANGLO-RUSSIAN RELATIONS

England was the first European country to establish peaceful relations with Russia; trade relations uncomplicated by territorial or religious disputes. That first contact was in the mid-sixteenth century. It was a dramatic encounter: Muscovy and its culture were very different from any other with which Tudor England was acquainted.

At the height of the sixteenth-century Spanish and Portuguese explorations of the New World, Robert Thorne, an English merchant in Seville, wrote to the king of England, Henry VIII. Thorne was envious of the achievements of the Spaniards and Portuguese. Compared with them, he wrote, the English seemed to be 'without activity or courage'.[1] There was a route to China still undiscovered, a way 'shorter to us than to Spain or Portugal by the north-east'.[2]

Sebastian Cabot, governor of the Company of Merchant Adventurers of Bristol, thought similarly and on his advice £6,000 was raised in London in 1553 and three ships fitted out for exploration of the North-East Passage. On 20 May the *Bona Esperanza*, the *Edward Bonaventure* and the *Bona Confidenza* were towed down to Greenwich for a rousing send-off by the court. Sir Hugh Willoughby, captain-general of the expedition, sailed in the *Esperanza*, Richard Chancellor, the pilot-general, in the *Edward*.

The ships became separated in a storm. Willoughby decided to dock in an inlet off the Murman Coast where he and his men froze to death in the following Arctic winter. Chancellor sailed on, 'and sailed so fare that hee came at last to a place where hee found no night at all, but a continuall light and brightnesse of the Sunne shining clearely upon the huge and mightie Sea'.[3]

Chancellor had landed on the White Sea coast, not far from present day Arkhangelsk. The local governor informed him that the country was called Muscovy and that it was ruled by Ivan Vasilyevich, better known as Ivan the Terrible, although more accurately translated as the Fearsome. Messengers were sent to the tsar in Moscow and, after exasperating delays, Chancellor received an invitation to the court with paid post-horses provided for him. The overland journey by sledge through tundra, marsh and forest was accomplished with the help of 'barbarians' in sheep-skins and in extreme cold.[4]

Chancellor was impressed by the capital:

> Mosco[w] it selfe is great: I take the whole towne to bee greater than London with the suburbes: but it is very rude, and standeth without all order. Their houses are all of timber, very dangerous for fire. There is a faire Castle, the walles whereof are of bricke, and very high: they say they are eighteene foote thick, but I do not beleeve it: it doth not so seeme, notwithstanding I doe not certainely know it: for no stranger may come to viewe it.[5]

After a further wait of twelve days Chancellor and his men were summoned to the court where they were dazzled by its splendour. A hundred courtiers dressed in cloth of gold surrounded the tsar. Then Ivan appeared, dressed in even more gold and holding a sceptre. Chancellor handed over the letter from Edward VI, then king of England, addressed to whatever potentates might be encountered. The king made no bones about what he sought:

> Every man desireth to joine friendship with the other, to love and be loved, and also to give and receive mutuall benefites that our fathers have ever gently and lovingly entreated such as of friendly mind came to them, especially merchants who, wandering about the world search both land and sea to carry such good and profitable things as are found in their countries to remote regions and kingdoms and to bring from the same such things as they find commodious for their owne Countries.[6]

Chancellor could not have arrived at a more propitious moment than 1554 to present English aims. Trade with Muscovy was at that time a virtual monopoly of the Hanseatic League. Ivan had recently quarrelled with the League, which resulted in Muscovy's being cut off from markets at a time when it was trying to import munitions in pursuit of foreign policy aims. At the same time, the appearance of the English clearly promised a potentially lucrative outlet for Russian exports.

The outcome of Chancellor's mission was highly satisfactory. Ivan sent a letter in the 'Moscovian tongue' (with a Dutch translation, as there were some Dutch merchants in Moscow) to the English sovereign, now Mary Tudor, in which he made clear that he had welcomed Chancellor in his country and that he would allow all merchants sent by the English crown to trade freely throughout his country and to enter and leave as they wished. According to Chancellor, Russia could provide tallow, flax and hemp for the navy, plus large amounts of seal oil and furs—sable, fox, beaver and ermine. The letter was handed to Mary and Philip, who declared themselves officially the discoverers of Muscovy. That assertion was false since it was already known to Europeans from other countries, but the intent of the declaration was to buttress an insecure claim to a monopoly of trade with Russia. More importantly, they granted a charter in 1555 to the Merchants of Russia, or the Muscovy Company as it became known in London—the first English joint-stock company. The opening up of trade with Russia also came at an opportune moment for England, which was encountering difficulty in finding export markets for its textiles.

Later that year, the Muscovy merchants equipped the *Edward Bonaventure* for its second expedition to Muscovy, with Richard Chancellor again pilot-general. He received detailed orders as to what he should seek, including the admonition:

> to acquire a perfect knowledge of the people of Russia, so that they should know the laws and customs, manners and behaviours of the people of the countries where they shall traffic, not only of the nobility, lawyers, merchants and mariners but of the common people ... and likewise you shall spie and search as secretly as you may.[7]

On arrival in Moscow the Englishmen were provided with a house and regular food supplies. They presented a letter from Mary Tudor and in return Ivan listed the privileges he would grant, including the right of the English to be within their own jurisdiction and freedom from arrest or imprisonment for debt.

As proof of his new-found enthusiasm for establishing trading relations with England, Ivan decided to send an embassy (short-term missions at that time) to the English court with an appropriate suite. Osip Nepea was nominated to head the embassy and the *Edward Bonaventure* was loaded with valuable merchandise, plus a white falcon for Mary Tudor. It left port in July 1556 but was buffeted by storms off the Scottish coast. Nepea's secretary described how Chancellor did all that he could to save the life of the ambassador and the valuable cargo, but the ship sank. Chancellor and many of his crew drowned, the gifts for Mary Tudor were lost, but Nepea survived.

The ambassador arrived in London naturally much dishevelled after his shipwreck and furious at losing his gifts. To assuage the Russian, he was provided with silk and velvet riding clothes and then given a warm welcome in a procession by the Lord Mayor of London. For the populace this was their first sight of a Russian and vast crowds turned out. Later Nepea was presented at court to Mary, cosseted and taken to a fox hunt.

For all this, Nepea was not a success with those most concerned. The Muscovy Company merchants complained: 'He thinks that every man will beguile him. As the Russians do not always speak the truth themselves, they think that other people are like them.'[8] People were thankful to see the back of Osip Nepea when he embarked on the *Primrose* in the charge of Anthony Jenkinson.

As well as a seaman, Jenkinson, the man chosen to captain the *Primrose* in 1557, was a seasoned traveller, merchant and adventurer who had already been moving to and fro in Muscovy en route for Persia—with the usual aim of reaching China. He was instructed to buy tallow, flax and train oil, but to go easy on the purchase of furs—which were not to English taste—though wisely mink was excepted. Jenkinson's position was rather vague. Something of a half-accredited ambassador, he was given full honours by the tsar at a banquet in the Kremlin and responded accordingly: 'I thinke no prince in Christendome is more feared of his owne then he is nor yet better loved.'[9] He felt differently about the Russians: 'They are great talkers and liars, flatterers and dissemblers. The women be very obedient to their husbands and do not often go abroad. I heard of men and women that drank away their children and their goods in the Emperor's taverns.'[10] The Englishman also noted both that in Muscovy no shame was attached to being drunk and the invasive bureaucracy: 'When a man is hanged he is given no testimony. How they are received into heaven, it is a wonder, without their passport.'[11]

Jenkinson complained about the ingrained mistrust and scarcely veiled hostility with which nearly all Russians treated foreigners. He and later envoys found themselves exposed to rudeness and sometimes violence. From the moment he arrived in Muscovy, the foreigner was under constant observation and all his movements controlled by court officials. Once in the capital he was under even stricter surveillance, a virtual prisoner. Contact between foreigners and ordinary Russians was made as difficult as possible. Despite all the difficulties, Jenkinson's mission in 1557 was highly successful from the point of view of the English merchants. Ivan granted them the monopoly of trade with Muscovy, with any potential rivals having their goods confiscated, as well as exemption from customs duties and the right to set up trading centres wherever they chose. A fresh embassy was dispatched to London with furs for Ivan's 'sister' Elizabeth, now queen, all not surprisingly with a *quid pro quo*. The tsar sought an alliance with England to aid him in his struggle to acquire a Baltic outlet, since Muscovy was to all intents and purposes an inland state. (The significance of the White Sea was not yet recognized.) He proposed that the enemies of one country should automatically become the enemies of the other. Ivan ended by asking Elizabeth for asylum in England, should it prove necessary, as he was locked in a struggle with his own nobles.

The queen had no objection to the extremely rare possibility of having Ivan in England, but it was out of the question that she would become involved in the tsar's conflicts with his neighbours. Ivan flew into one of his infamous rages, threatening to open trade to rivals of the Muscovy Company. To placate him Elizabeth sent another embassy under Sir Thomas Randolph to Moscow. The Company's privileges were not only confirmed but extended. However, the truce was short-lived. In 1570 Ivan again demanded an alliance and fired off insults at the queen:

> And wee had thought that you had been ruler over your lande and had sought honour to you self and profitt to your country, and therefore wee did pretend those weightie affaires betweene you and us; but now wee perceive that there be other men that doe, and not men but bowers and merchaunts which seeke not the wealth and honour of our majesties, but they seeke there owne profitt of merchauntdize: and you flowe in your maydenlie estate like a maide.[12]

To mollify Ivan, Anthony Jenkinson was sent to Moscow once again in 1572, with the rank of full ambassador, but he found that he too had fallen foul of the tsar. Nevertheless, though his life was in danger, Jenkinson waited for six months in Kholmogory (the Muscovy Company's fur trading centre) in great discomfort and braved house arrest in Pereslavl (now Pereiaslav) for seven weeks. Finally he was received by Ivan. The Englishman stood his ground and complained that the privileges of the English merchants had been withdrawn. The tsar agreed to redress the English grievances and Jenkinson was provided with all that he needed for a relatively comfortable journey to Kholmogory. He returned to England for the last time in 1572 with no urge to see Russia again: 'And thus being weary and growing old, I am content to take my rest in mine owne house.'[13] Even so, he lived for a further forty years.

Jenkinson's accounts added much to English knowledge of Muscovy but he never came to know Russia as well as Jerome Horsey, who became an agent of the Muscovy Company in 1572. Horsey was the first of those involved in Anglo-Russian relations to speak Russian fluently and to admire the language. When he presented Elizabeth with a letter from Ivan, the queen commented that the script 'had some affinity with the Greek, and I could quickly learn it'. She urged the Earl of Essex to take up Russian. He replied that he would when he could find the time.[14]

Horsey's writings on Russia have to be approached with caution since at certain times both the Russians and the Muscovy Company accused him of fraud. With this reservation, he undoubtedly came to know the country and its ruler well and did not fear expressing what previous Englishmen had not dared. Writing in a less than tender age, when an English noble could risk losing his head, Horsey related in brutal detail the atrocities committed by Ivan, calling him 'right Scythian, full of readie wisdom, cruell, bloudye, merciles'.[15]

According to Horsey, Ivan took Elizabeth's promise of asylum seriously and, further, expressed a wish to acquire an English wife. She would have been his eighth, the incumbent being dispatched to a nunnery. Lady Mary Hastings, a relative of the queen, was earmarked as a suitable bride by Feodor Pisemsky, who led a Russian embassy to London in 1582. Elizabeth tactfully sent word back that the lady in question was in very poor health and disfigured. There was, however, much more to this resumption of diplomatic contact. The tsar requested a treaty of friendship which would oblige both sides to send military supplies in time of war. Clearly the obligations would fall mainly on the English side. Pisemsky hinted that the English monopoly was at stake. Elizabeth procrastinated and announced that a new embassy would be sent to Moscow under Sir Jerome Bowes. The new ambassador insisted on there being no change in the position of the Muscovy Company. Bowes's failure to show diplomatic flexibility alienated not only the Russians but also his English masters and he was recalled to London.

Ivan died in March 1584. The Anglophobe Andrei Shchelkalov, head of the office of foreign affairs, the *Posolski Prikaz*, gloated, 'Now your English tsar is gone.'[16] The redoubtable Horsey was dispatched to Moscow to repair the damage done by Bowes and to make contact with the new tsar, Feodor Ivanovich, who it was soon clear was uninterested in a political alliance. The Englishman soon established cordial relations with the tsar's powerful brother-in-law, Boris Godunov, who showered Horsey with luxury foods and plentiful drink. More importantly, Horsey was successful in having the privileges of the Muscovy Company renewed.

Elizabeth appreciated wheeler-dealer Horsey's work in Moscow and duly sent him back again in 1586 as ambassador. However, highly placed Russians railed against Horsey's arrogance and the monopoly enjoyed by the Muscovy Company to the detriment not only of all other foreigners but of other Englishmen. The queen was shocked at receiving angry letters about the bad behaviour of English merchants in Muscovy and the 'lewd practices' of Horsey, who was also accused of enriching himself by private trade and, much worse, of having treacherous dealings with Russia's enemy, the Poles. Elizabeth made appropriate noises of support for Horsey but dismissed him. The ex-ambassador stayed on in Moscow as a businessman for a further five years. He left in 1591, claiming that people had been hired to poison him. Horsey went on to serve for thirty years in the English parliament.

Relations between England and Muscovy were strained when Giles Fletcher led an embassy to Moscow in 1588. Fletcher was kept in diplomatic limbo for several months and managed to avoid the usual restrictions, talk to people and study the country. His book, *Of the Russe Commonwealth*, was published on his return to England in 1591 and is the most penetrating and hostile account of Russia in the sixteenth century. The Muscovy Company was horrified and the merchants asked Lord Burghley, the queen's principal minister, to suppress the most offensive passages on the grounds that the Russians would refuse to trade with England if they came to hear of them. The book provided information about Muscovy's government and revenues, 'which is offensive to the Russe that anie man should looke into'.[17] The unabridged version of Fletcher's book was published in 1643. The fear of the Russian reaction to *Of the Russe Commonwealth* was well founded; when a Russian translation was published in 1846, it fell foul of the censor. The full Russian translation was published in 1905 in the midst of the October Revolution.

Whilst all previous English travellers had made clear that Ivan IV could dispose of the lives and property of his subjects as he wished, Fletcher was the first to look into the machinery of totalitarian government:

> The State and forme of their Government is plaine tyranicall, as applying all to the behoofe of the Prince, and that after a most open and barbarous manner ... as well for the keeping of the Nobilitie and Commons in an under proportion, & far uneven balance in their severall degrees, as also in their impositions and exactions, wherein they exceede all just measure without any regard of Nobilitie or people.[18]

The Englishman manifested a certain respect for the common people, seeing the causes of their backwardness in the despotic regime:

> They are of reasonable capacities, if they had those means that some other nations have to traine up their wittes in good nurture and learning. Which they might borrowe of the Polonians [Poles] and other their neighbours, but that they refuse it of a very selfe pride, as accounting their owne fashions to be far the best. Partly also ... for that their manner of bringing up (voide of all good learning and civill behaviour) is thought by their governours most agreeable to that State.[19]

Physically the Russians fared no better at Fletcher's pen:

> As touching the naturall habite of their bodies, they are for the most parte of large sise, and of very fleshy bodies: accounting it a grace to bee somewhat grosse and burley, and therefore they nourish and spread their beardes ... Which may bee thought to come partly of the climate and the numbnes which they get by the cold in winter, and partly of their diet that standeth most of rootes, onions, garlike, cabbage, and such things that breed grosse humors ... At their meales they drinke not until the ende ... taking it in largely, and all together with kissing one another at every pledge. And therefore after dinner there is no talking with them ... To drinke drunke, is an ordinary matter with them every day in the weeke.[20]

Fletcher found the Russians to be of a:

> darke and sallow complexion, their skinnes beyng tanned and parched both with colde and heate: specially the women, that for the greater parte are of farre worse complexions than the men (and) to mende the bad hue of their skinnes, use to paint their faces with white and redde colours, so visibly that every man may perceyve it. Which is made no matter, because it is common, and liked well by their husbandes: who ... delight themselves much to see them as fowle women to become such faire images. This parcheth the skinne, and helpeth to deforme them when their painting is of[f].[21]

The English view of Muscovy and Russians at the end of the sixteenth century was inevitably based almost entirely on the jaundiced views of a limited number of travellers. Hardly surprisingly, those who had never visited the country accepted what they read and heard. Francis Bacon and Sir Philip Sidney regurgitated what Horsey and Fletcher had written, and Shakespeare's audiences laughed mockingly when in *Love's Labour's Lost* the King of Navarre and his courtiers disguise themselves as 'frozen Muscovits', and at what Rosaline calls their 'rough carriage so ridiculous' and 'shapeless gear'.[22] In *All's Well that Ends Well* the Russian language provides the hilarity, with soldiers pretending to be Muscovites. Nevertheless, it shows that audiences in the 1590s could be expected to have a mental picture of Russia.

If in the late sixteenth century there was in England scant and highly partial knowledge of the geography and inhabitants of Russia, it can hardly be expected that there was any more than a nodding acquaintance with its history. Muscovy was on the periphery of the core western European states with the Islamic Ottoman empire. The Russians were Christians, but Orthodox, and not seen as part of the Christendom of the west. Thus the tsar was not included in the diplomatic register of Christian states, *Ordo Regnum Christianorum*.[23]

But remote and strange though it was, Russia was in the latter part of the sixteenth century a state growing in power and with immense potential. Ivan IV conquered and annexed the Tatar khanates of Kazan and Astrakhan in the 1550s, thus becoming the first Muscovite sovereign to rule a multinational state and opening up the way to Siberia. He made conquests in parts of Livonia (today's Estonia and Latvia) and aroused widespread alarm in northern and central Europe. Yet for generations to come Russia seemed too far away to be of real political significance to England. Even so, by the end of the sixteenth century the foundations had been laid upon which the English could build a deeper and more extensive knowledge of Russia. Events in both countries conspired to postpone this development during the next century.

In 1588 the death without an heir of the feeble Tsar Feodor, the only surviving son of Ivan IV, marked the end of the Rurik dynasty in Muscovy. Boris Godunov, the late tsar's brother-in-law, a senior minister and courtier, was highly respected and the obvious choice to succeed. Godunov has been much maligned both during his life and since—by Alexander Pushkin and Modest Mussorgsky among others—as the murderer of Feodor's younger brother Dmitri, but the evidence points to rivals with reasons to traduce him.[24] Tsar Boris was anxious to learn more about England and sent an ambassador, Grigory Mikulin, to London in

1600, probably to enquire about the succession. He also wished to train future diplomats, and four students arrived in England in 1602 and were dispersed to Winchester, Eton, Oxford and Cambridge. None returned to Russia.

In 1604 Boris Godunov was faced by a challenger to the throne who claimed to be Dmitri. Sir Thomas Smith, on an embassy from London, dined with Boris and his son Feodor in July 1604 and reported to Sir Robert Cecil, the secretary of state, that a rebellion had taken place on the borders of Russia with Poland. A widespread rising was already under way when Boris died in April 1605. His son and his wife were murdered and False Dmitri, with Polish support, was crowned in Moscow, only to be assassinated less than a year later by the Moscow mob led by Vasily Shuisky. He held on for four years, confronting yet another False Dmitri.

Thus began the Time of Troubles. Muscovy descended into chaos, with the nobility constantly changing sides, murder rife, starvation the norm and neighbouring states, in particular Poland, pouncing on the defenceless country. Finally, the rich and powerful Romanov family promoted sixteen-year-old Mikhail Romanov in 1612, who was accepted by the traumatized people and the civil war came to an end. The Romanov dynasty was to last for more than 300 years.

Soon after his coronation, Tsar Mikhail sought an alliance with England. Following Elizabeth's death in 1603, James I (James VI of Scotland) had become the first Stuart king of England. Mikhail hoped to appeal to James, a Protestant, to secure Russia—the term that came to be used in the seventeenth century—against further depredation by the Catholic Poles. He naturally also wished to make a political statement about the legitimacy of the new regime.

Years of civil war with the resulting social dislocation had isolated Russia, leaving it in many instances unaware of changes in foreign countries and ignorant as to what alliances had been formed and treaties signed in the interim. Alexsei Ziuzin led an embassy to London in November 1613 where a magnificent reception was laid on for the ambassador, despite understandable reservations at court as to the permanency of Mikhail's position. Ziuzin came on behalf of a war-torn country, still occupied in part by the forces of Poland and Sweden from the Time of Troubles. James was prepared to send an emissary to sound out King Sigismund of Poland's willingness to make peace with Russia, but when Zuizin brought up the subject of a loan for Russia nothing was forthcoming from the English. Although the embassy fell short of Russian aims, it was counted a success by both sides. The following year James sent Sir John Merrick, who had been on missions in Moscow during the Time of Troubles, to the Russian capital with the title of ambassador to lend English support for a peace treaty with Poland, a task in which Merrick succeeded a few years later.[25]

There is some evidence that before this James had entertained the hope of intervening in northern Russia and acquiring the newly founded city of Arkhangelsk. This was to prevent the Swedes and Poles from threatening the accumulated privileges of the Muscovy Company in Russia, and to try to control trade with Persia through Russia. There was even talk of sending Prince Charles, heir to the throne, as a candidate for tsar, or as 'protector' of northern Russia. Merrick quickly disabused any such talk in London.[26]

Political relations between Russia and England were now on an even keel for the first time for three decades, but it was the old subject of trade that was causing problems. The Muscovy Company was making a loss. This was attributable to a general decline in English trade, aggressive Dutch competition, the presence of non-company traders, the move into whaling, and the fact that the Company's main customers were the tsar and the king—'a strong and shameful Monopoly; a Monopoly in a Monopoly; both abroad and at home'.[27] The East India Company withdrew its financial support from the Muscovy Company, which appealed to the Privy Council for support in 1619.

Sir Christopher Cocks was dispatched to Moscow in this year as Mikhail had abrogated the English privileges, placing the merchants in the same position as all foreigners. Merrick continued to represent the Company in Moscow, with promises to the Russians of future political help and bribes to officials. His talk of a league of amity was counterproductive since it placed England in the same situation that had plagued Anglo-Russian dialogue in the reign of Elizabeth and from which she had escaped on Ivan IV's death. With trade now at a low level and no political interest in Russia, James I dropped all diplomatic pretences. After his death in 1625, his son, Charles I, had more than enough foreign and domestic preoccupations in the 1630s and the first half of the 1640s, and Russia was ignored. Mikhail for his part could not but approve of what he knew of Charles's struggle for personal rule.

Tsar Mikhail died in 1645. His son and successor, Alexsei, dispatched an embassy to England—officially to inform Charles I of his father's death, though naturally more to find out what was happening in the Civil War, in which Charles was close to defeat. The ambassador, Gerasim

Dokhturov, was received and entertained by members of the Muscovy Company. He was told that 'among those who trade in Muscovy there is not one person supporting the King, but all support the Parliament'.[28] The Russian persistently demanded to see the king, totally failing to understand the situation. Dokhturov was furious and wanted to return home, but parliament delayed his departure in the hope that he would negotiate with it. Finally he was invited to address both Houses of Parliament, where he delivered a tirade about the disgraceful way in which he had been treated. Despite this, Dokhturov was presented with a letter for Tsar Alexsei in which parliament expressed the wish for Anglo-Russian relations to continue as in the past and even asked for trade favours from the new tsar.

The reaction in Moscow to Charles's execution in 1649 was swift and uneqivocal. Alexsei was appalled and immediately issued a *ukaz*, a decree, abolishing what privileges the Muscovy Company still possessed and expelling English merchants, all to the delight of Russian merchants, who at the same time had their debts in Britain written off. The Dutch, England's main rival for Russian trade, also stood to benefit greatly, and this just when England was about to go to war with Holland.

Although Oliver Cromwell was under no illusions about the chances of establishing cordial relations with Russia, he sent two envoys, William Prideaux and Richard Bradshaw, on trade missions to Moscow in the mid-1650s to try to buy hemp, tar and tallow for the navy, in the hope of re-establishing England's commercial position. The Lord Protector's instructions were singularly inept and both men were given short shrift by the tsar.

After the Restoration of Charles II in 1660, diplomatic relations between England and Russia were resumed, but in a desultory way. Tsar Alexsei expected Charles II to express gratitude for the tsar's opposition to the Great Rebellion and financial support for Charles while in exile. This was not forthcoming. Nevertheless, in accordance with the highly formalized tradition of tsarist diplomacy, Alexsei sent an embassy led by Prince Peter Prozorovsky and Ivan Zhelyabuzhsky to London in 1662 to congratulate Charles on his coronation. Londoners, including Samuel Pepys, enjoyed the sight of the envoys and their attendants driving in great pomp through the streets. Charles gave the Russians a reception unmatched in splendour, and in return received gifts of gold cloth, furs, hawks and horses. Zhelyabuzhsky's main aim, though, was to negotiate a loan. He was unsuccessful.

History has been harsh in its judgement of the Earl of Carlisle. In 1663 he was sent to Moscow as ambassador with a suite of eighty. Carlisle's ostensible assignment in Moscow was to offer Charles II's services as mediator in a dispute between Russia and Sweden, but in reality his instructions were to discuss the restoration of trade privileges. The earl's arrogance and waffling about great affairs of state irritated the Russian court, but it is difficult to imagine that even the most talented diplomat could have been successful. Russia's high-handed attitude towards trade remained an insurmountable stumbling block. Four years later a new Russian commercial code was drawn up with the creation of an official monopoly of major commodities. This prevented any revival of trade with England and there were only two English merchants left in Moscow at the end of the decade. By the end of the seventeenth century the Muscovy Company was reduced to twelve or fourteen members, and diplomatic relations barely existed as England refused to offer Russia effective help against Poland or Turkey.

* * *

The only first-hand English account of life in Russia in the seventeenth century was Samuel Collins's *The Present State of Russia, in a Letter to a Friend at London*, published in 1671. Collins was practising medicine in Holland where he was headhunted in 1660 by a Russian commissar. After a short time in Moscow he was appointed physician to Tsar Alexsei, a post he held for nine years. The doctor greatly admired the pious Alexsei but felt differently about the Russian people. He was even more scathing than his Elizabethan predecessors. He denounced the Russians as a people 'wholly devoted to their own Ignorance' who 'look upon Learning as a Monster', who 'love nothing soft or smooth but their women's fat sides', and who could be compared to a flock of owls, 'more in love with their own Twilight, than with our Noon-day, because the eyesight of their understanding is dazzled with the bright beams of truth'.[29]

Morally, Collins did not find them any better, calling the Russians 'false, Truce-breakers, subtile Foxes, and ravenous Wolves'.[30] Even Russian weddings did not escape the doctor's strictures. Nuptial songs were, he wrote, 'so bedaubed with scum of bawdry and obscenity that it would make Aretine's ears glow to hear them'.[31] Once married, women were subjected to 'severe usage': 'If a man thinks his wife barren, he will persuade her to turn nun, that he may try another; if she refuses, he will cudgel her into a monastery.'[32] 'If a man kill his slave or wife, in correcting them, there is no law against them.' On the other hand, 'A woman that kills her husband is buried alive, put into the ground up to her neck and there suffered to die, which is soon done in winter.'[33]

A certain number of Englishmen, and rather more Scots, were attracted to Russia in the seventeenth century as soldiers of fortune. Alexander Leslie, a Scot, helped train Russian infantry for the Smolensk campaign in 1654. The most famous, though, remains Patrick Gordon, who arrived in Moscow in 1661 at the age of twenty-six. An enthusiastic Catholic supporter of the Stuarts, he rapidly came to be appreciated by Alexsei, undertook missions on behalf of the tsar and rose to the rank of general.[34] The death of Charles II in 1685 and the Glorious and Bloodless Revolution in England that removed his Catholic son, James II, from the throne, as in 1649, was seen as treachery in Russia. Support for the Jacobite cause by Russia was hardly conducive to warm relations between the two countries.

The cumulative result of all this incomprehension was that at the end of the seventeenth century England's moral, political and cultural contempt for Russia was unabated.

2

THE RUSSIAN EMPIRE

PETER THE GREAT

In just two decades—the first of the eighteenth century—Russia moved from being seen as no more than a barbarous backwater to being recognized as a Great Power. This spectacular achievement took place in the reign of Peter I, Peter the Great.

Peter erupted out of seventeenth-century Russia, a country cut off from the Reformation, Renaissance, New World discoveries and the scientific spirit of western Europe. However, many of the policies that he initiated and reforms he introduced had their harbingers in Russia before him. The greatness of Peter lay to a large extent in that he gave shape to the needs and aspirations for change within Russian society that had been emerging in the seventeenth century as a result of greater knowledge of developments abroad. He galvanized his fellow countrymen with his unrelenting demonic energy and ambitions. Peter forced and accelerated the transformation of Russia.

His reign had an inauspicious beginning. In 1682 the sickly Feodor, Alexsei's elder surviving son by his first marriage, died. Peter's elder half-brother by Alexsei's second marriage, Ivan V, would in theory have succeeded, but it was clear that he was mentally incapable and the national assembly acclaimed the sturdy nine-year-old Peter as co-tsar with Ivan. Only a month later the *streltsy*, the corps of musketeers constituting the nucleus of the regular army and the tsar's bodyguard, rioted after being persuaded by the family of Alexsei's first wife, the Miloslavskys, that the Naryshkins, his second wife's kin, had murdered Ivan V. The *streltsy* spared Peter and his mother but set upon lesser Naryshkins and their supporters, torturing and killing. Once the mob brutality they had provoked had calmed down, the *streltsy* were then able to enforce their political demands—Peter was to reign with Ivan and the tsarevna Sophia, his elder half-sister, as regent.

The tough-minded Sophia quickly assumed the title of autocrat, while Peter lived with his mother much of the time in a village outside Moscow. It is said that the boy came upon a dilapidated English sailing boat in a village shed, repaired it and took it to a lake, where he practised sailing and began to build his own boats. Peter came of age at seventeen on his marriage to Eudoxia Lopukhin and was determined to unseat Sophia. When sufficient officials and foreign officers led by Patrick Gordon, as well as the *streltsy*, were won over by the persuasive Peter, the dreaded musketeers executed or exiled Sophia's supporters in 1689. Peter dispatched his half-sister to the Novodevichy Convent outside Moscow and took control.

He immediately embarked on his first attempt to gain an outlet for Russia on the Black Sea, and with it the opportunity to build a navy there with which to challenge the Ottoman empire. In 1695 an attempt to seize Azoz at the mouth of the river Don was a failure and Turkey held on to the citadel, 'the window of the south'. The following year Peter again besieged Azoz, this time successfully, though the conquest was insecure. Peter's reign came to be dominated by his determination to gain year-round access to the sea for Russia (Arkhangelsk was frozen for six months each year) and this inevitably meant that relations with England acquired a political dimension of a quite different order than before.

The centre of shipbuilding, navigation, engineering and gunnery was western Europe. Peter decided to investigate for himself. A second objective, and officially the first of his mission, was to organize an alliance of the Christian powers against Turkey. Hitherto no tsar had travelled abroad except on military campaigns, but in 1697 Peter and his Grand Embassy, 200 strong, descended on Holland and England. General Franz Lefort, a Swiss member of the Russian court, was the ostensible leader of the embassy. One member was 'min Heer Peter Mikhailov', who was learning shipbuilding. The tsar travelled incognito, a way of saying informally rather than in disguise, as Peter was nearly 2 metres tall and solidly built.

William of Orange, stadholder of the United Provinces of the Netherlands and King William III of England since 1690 with his wife Queen Mary II, daughter of James II, was staying at his estate near Utrecht when the Great Embassy arrived in August 1697. Although the king was preoccupied with the delicate negotiations at nearby Rijswijk aimed at bringing peace between England and France and pressing Louis XIV to recognize him as king of England, he invited Peter to meet him. The tsar, speaking Dutch, which he had learned in the 'German' quarter of Moscow, was fulsome in his praise of the king, who only a few years earlier he had seen as a usurper of the rightful king, James II:

> Your Kind Embraces have given me more Satisfaction than the takeing of Azoph [Azoz] and Triumphing over the Tartars, But the Conquest is Yours, Your Martial Genious directed my sword And the Generous Emulation of your Exploits Instilled into my Breast the first thoughts I had of Enlarging my Dominions ... If the Warr continues I and my Armies will readily Observe Your Orders in Warr or Peace.[1]

William was the architect of successive anti-French coalitions and Franco-Russian relations were far from cordial in the years preceding the Great Embassy. The French navy had effectively interrupted foreign trade to Arkhangelsk in 1696.[2] Russia and France had backed rival candidates for the elective Polish throne and Peter feared that the 'French faction' in Poland would serve to strengthen Turkey, an ally of France and thus enemy of Russia. Peter sought an anti-Turkish Anglo-Russian alliance, coupling it with the offer of increased Anglo-Dutch trade to Russia. An alliance was out of the question for William because of the Rijswijk negotiations but an *entente cordiale* emerged during Peter's stay in Holland.

In January 1698, after spending five months in Holland, Peter sailed up the Thames in *The Transport Royal*, the latest model in royal yachts, presented to him by William. The two sovereigns had several meetings in London, on one occasion with Peter in his shirtsleeves. His was clearly a highly unorthodox personality, lacking the refinement of manners expected in western Europe. 'After I had seen him often', wrote Bishop Burnet, 'and had conversed much with him, I could not but adore the depth of the providence of God, that had raised up such a furious man to so absolute an authority over such a great part of the world.'[3] Two mock sea battles were staged in the Solent for Peter, who reputedly said that he would rather be an English admiral than tsar of Russia. (It was William III who persuaded Peter to sit for the portrait of the tsar by Sir Godfrey Kneller that now hangs in Kensington Palace.)

From the English point of view, the tsar's visit was important as it would provide an opportunity to persuade Peter to reinstate the trade privileges the Muscovy Company had lost in 1649 and that had caused its decline. The particular trade the merchants in London had in mind was tobacco from the English colonies, as Peter had repealed the ban on the sale of tobacco in Russia in 1697. However, unbeknown to the Muscovy Company, a group of city merchants led by Peregrine Osborne, Marquess of Carmarthen, and not members of the Company, secured the contract to export tobacco to Russia. An acrimonious dispute between the old and the new traders living in England and Russia developed, as the new traders demanded that they should be allowed to trade freely with Russia, purchasing Russian goods with the proceeds of tobacco sales.

Peter rented the diarist John Evelyn's house, Sayes Court in Deptford, to be close to the naval yards. Here he behaved as a royal hooligan, leaving the house with bespattered walls, smashed floors, ripped curtains, pictures riddled with pistol shots and burnt and broken furniture. The lawns were trampled on and hedges broken to make short cuts with Peter being pushed in a wheelbarrow. The tsar arrived in Oxford in April, visiting the Sheldonian Theatre, a bookshop and the Ashmolean Museum. The museum's assistant keeper described him as 'a very uncouth fellow' with a long black wig and with dirty hands.[4] It turned out that Peter had been recognized and a crowd formed. At this juncture he decided to return immediately to London. Visits to the theatre did not appeal to Peter but he showed great interest in Sir Christopher Wren's Kensington Palace, the new wing at Hampton Court and the incomplete St Paul's Cathedral. Though the visit to England did little to change the previously held view of Russians, for his part the tsar came to see that the wealth and efficiency he so admired in the west could only be transplanted to Russia by the adoption of westernized institutions.

In Peter's drive towards the sea, an opening in the Baltic was clearly crucial for Russia. Sweden, the predominant power in the region, was determined to prevent this. Thus began the Great Northern War, which was to last for twenty-one years and to dominate Peter's reign. Although not involved in the war that broke out in 1700, England knew that it could have an adverse effect on its interests. However, William III and his ministers were preoccupied with the possibility of a new struggle with France over the Spanish succession. In such a conflict, the assistance of the impressive Swedish army would be invaluable. Only a few weeks after Russia, Denmark and Saxony had embarked on the war against Sweden, William III nonetheless offered Peter his 'interposition and best offices' in the dispute with Sweden.[5] It was too late for the king to intervene. Peter's coalition fell into disarray as Denmark collapsed and his siege of the Swedish stronghold of Narva, at the eastern end of the Gulf of Finland, led to a Russian rout by the troops of the Swedish king, Charles XII, in November 1700.

The tsar acknowledged 'this terrible setback' and showed himself amenable to English mediation.[6] Charles XII, flushed with victory, was uninterested and dismissed proposals that he should make peace and become a member of the Grand Alliance against France. As for the Russians, Charles considered them contemptible foes and decided he had first to deal with Poland and Saxony. Here he campaigned for six years. This respite enabled Peter to set about raising, equipping and training an efficient standing army and to attack Ingria, a region on the southern coast of the Gulf of Finland. Narva was taken and, on an almost desolate area at the mouth of the Neva, Peter decided to build a new city designed by western European architects, now that he had access to the Baltic. St Petersburg was begun in 1703.

England decided to send a permanent envoy to Russia in 1704, not as a result of the tsar's military success but because fresh tensions over the tobacco trade had erupted.[7] Charles Whitworth, the envoy, had at one time been employed by the Board of Trade and was aware of the tobacco issue when he was appointed. His instructions were to resolve that particular and sundry other economic grievances of the old and new traders. Whitworth learned soon after arriving in 1705 that the tobacco contractors had grossly overestimated the potential sale of imported tobacco and underestimated the amount of Russian production and of tobacco smuggled into the country. Soon some enterprising Englishmen tried to offload tobacco by teaching Russians how to cut and roll it before it rotted, a skill they could then apply to home-grown tobacco. This provoked protests by the English traders in London and Whitworth was sent orders to 'use your best endeavours and exert your utmost power with your usual prudence & discretion to destroy those materials that are brought hence to Moscow for the carrying on the manufacture … and order the persons concern'd therein forthwith to return home'.[8]

Since he was about to leave Moscow and join the tsar's army campaigning, Whitworth acted quickly. He and his assistants:

> Spent the best part of the night in destroying the severall instruments and materials, some whereof were so strong, that they oblig'd us to make a great noise in pulling them to pieces. There were 11 barrils … which I caus'd to let be let out, and destroy'd five parcels of ingredients … Nor is the least thing left standing … and the very next day my servants burnt

> all the remains of the wood which wee had broke, and my Smith is now working in my house on the rest of the Iron- and Coper-machines.[9]

As Janet Hartley has noted, 'Such were the duties of a diplomat to Russia at the beginning of the eighteenth century in order to serve the national interest.'[10]

The vandalism was an enormous mistake, caused by the failure of the post from London to arrive with modified instructions. Whitworth had been irresponsibly hasty and faced an uphill struggle to extricate himself from the wrath of the tobacco contractors and the Russian authorities.[11] He had had enough of the 'disagreeableness of this post' (his salary was in arrears) and his relations with Peter had inevitably deteriorated.[12] But yet another incident was to rock Anglo-Russian relations.

The tsar had sent Andrei Matveev (whose mother was Scottish) as ambassador to London in 1707 in the hope of persuading Queen Anne, William III's successor, to mediate on his behalf with Sweden and, as a gesture of mutual aid, Peter was prepared to join the Grand Alliance. He was also anxious to ensure that the British would not object if, and when, he secured an opening on the Baltic littoral, by holding out the promise of increased trading opportunities through such ports as Riga. The Duke of Marlborough, fresh from his victories at Blenheim and Ramillies, was targeted as the potential mediator. Peter could offer the duke the pick of titles to the principalities of Kiev (Kyiv), Vladimir or Siberia, a pension for life, one of the largest rubies in Europe and Russia's highest distinction, the Order of St Andrew. Marlborough's view was that it was better to let the king of Sweden turn his armies on the tsar rather than cause trouble for the Allies in the War of Spanish Succession and duly declined the offer.

Then one evening in July 1708, Matveev, shortly after his valedictory audience with Queen Anne, was roughly handled by bailiffs claiming unpaid debts to some fifty creditors and thrown into a debtors' prison for several hours. The London diplomatic corps (except for Sweden) was outraged by Matveev's treatment. Many knew only too well from personal experience that salaries and expenses were often delayed, or never paid, even though the Russian ambassador had been extremely liberal in his spending habits. Peter was furious with the British government (and Matveev) and hoped to embarrass a country that consistently patronized Russians—'a little Demellez, or Broil, with his Czarish Majesty', in the words of Daniel Defoe.[13] Peter demanded (unsuccessfully) the death penalty for the perpetrators. More importantly, the whole question of diplomatic immunity was raised and resulted in the British parliament passing an act in 1708 which gave foreign diplomats, and their servants, immunity from civil and criminal proceedings. The act proved to be useful to future Russian diplomats.

Whatever he had achieved in the early years of the century in the Gulf of Finland, Peter could not regard his conquest as secure until he had defeated Sweden decisively in the field. This he accomplished far from the Neva estuary. Charles XII, as expected, launched an offensive against Russia in 1708, but not in the direction anticipated of Moscow or St Petersburg. Instead the Swedish army moved east and south into Ukraine in the hope of joining up with Russia's enemies—Turks, Tatars, Poles and Ukrainian Cossacks under the hetman Ivan Mazepa. The Russians engaged in a scorched earth policy with the Swedes, who were far from home and unable to acquire supplies. Finally the two armies confronted each other outside the town of Poltava. The Swedes met with a crushing defeat and Charles XII fled south into Turkish territory. This victory in June 1709 meant that Russia was free from invasion in the south and Peter could concentrate on attacking the Swedes in Finland and Livonia.

News of the Swedish defeat at Poltava took London by surprise. Queen Anne's ministers now had to recognize that Peter would be able to make further gains in the Baltic region while unable to do anything to protect Sweden because of the continuing war against France, the War of the Spanish Succession. However, Peter's defeat at the hands of the Turks in 1711, including the loss of Azoz, lessened tensions for the next few years before the Northern Crisis erupted.

The Northern Crisis began when Russian troops moved into the northern German port of Wismar in 1715. Peter's intention was to establish a Russian garrison in Mecklenburg and use Wismar as a base for Russian trade through the Baltic and Elbe. He also planned to bypass the Sound (Kattegat) by cutting a canal from the Baltic to the North Sea. Peter had also arranged for his half-niece, Catherine, to marry the Duke of Mecklenburg. His plan to make Mecklenburg a Russian protectorate naturally alarmed Mecklenburg's neighbour George, Elector of Hanover. George's chief minister, Andreas Bernstorff, was a Mecklenburger whose estates had suffered from the billeting of Russian soldiers. George for his part harboured designs on Mecklenburg. This situation was greatly complicated since the elector, the closest Protestant relative of Queen Anne, had just ascended the British throne in 1714 as George I. It did not bode well for Anglo-Russian relations.

Anti-Russian feeling was already prevalent in Great Britain as a result of Poltava. It was easier to feel sympathy for the Protestant ruler of Sweden than the uncouth tsar of Muscovy. But since Charles XII was known to be encouraging the Jacobite rising of 1715, even his Tory supporters, who included Jonathan Swift, found it hard to see the Swedish king as a hero whom fortune had deserted.

Among George I's Whig ministers the Secretary of State for the North, Charles Townshend, did not share his sovereign's hostility to Russia, but James Stanhope, Secretary of State for the South, became as eager as the Hanoverians to halt the growth of Russian power.[14]

Finally the Northern Crisis ended in 1717 when Peter, anxious not to arouse too much enmity in western Europe, withdrew his forces from Mecklenburg. But what was of far greater and longer-lasting significance than the actual crisis was that yet again the importance of Russia as a power in Europe had been shown. The British had from their first contacts seen the Russians as a brutish people, but what was new was the fear and distrust of Russian power that had been growing over the years following Poltava. Now the first manifestations of widespread Russophobia in Great Britain were seen. Politicians made anti-Russian speeches and journalists, some paid by the government, were quick to climb on the bandwagon by attacking this alien power. In an attempt to counter this, the Russian resident, Feodor Veselovsky (sub-ambassador in London), published two 'memorials' addressed to the British government defending the tsar's policies. His efforts were unsuccessful since Peter was believed to be flirting with the Jacobites (although greatly exaggerated by his enemies), which only contributed to British alarm that the tsar aimed at destabilizing the new Hanoverian regime. There was talk that the Stuart James III—the Old Pretender—son of James II, was to leave Avignon for refuge in Russia, and Peter even suggested that the latter should marry Anna, his elder daughter.

The animosity between Peter and George I could only increase with the conclusion of a Hanoverian-Swedish treaty in 1719 by which the much-coveted (by Peter) duchies of Bremen and Verden, bishoprics ceded to the king of Sweden in 1648 and adjacent to Hanover, were handed over to George I as Elector of Hanover, thus consolidating the pro-Swedish attitude that had been growing in London. Stanhope hoped to build on this an anti-Russian coalition of Hanover (with tacit British support), Sweden, Saxony, Prussia and Poland, and force Peter to relinquish his Baltic conquests. Poland and Prussia refused to cooperate and the plan was dropped. Peter had the upper hand and had made this clear by ordering large-scale Russian landings in Sweden in the same year, ravaging the country to within a few miles of Stockholm. George I signed an alliance with Sweden in January 1720, promising British naval support against Russia. The new Russian resident in London, Count Mikhail Bestuzhev-Riumin (the family was descended from a Scot with the simpler name of Best), produced a new strongly worded memorial arguing the Russian case. The British government would have none of it and broke off diplomatic relations with Russia. The resident was ordered to leave the country.

However, widespread dislike of Baltic entanglements, fear of jeopardizing lucrative trade with Russia and the financial shock caused by the South Sea Bubble crisis in that year prevented the British king from helping Sweden. Instead, George advised the government in Stockholm to make peace with Russia. Abandoned, Sweden agreed and a treaty was signed at Nystad in Finland in September 1721. Peter's conquests were recognized in his extensive gains on the Baltic coast: Livonia, Estonia, Ingria and part of Karelia became Russian. Sweden retained the bulk of Finland. The Great Northern War was over. The treaty was a diplomatic defeat for Britain. The government had induced Sweden to surrender territory to Russia but had completely failed to set limits to Russian territorial and other gains at Sweden's expense. The treaty was not only a blow to British prestige, but also a threat to the foundations of British naval power.

The month following the Treaty of Nystad, in the as yet unfinished capital of St Petersburg, the Senate offered Peter the title of Emperor of All Russia, with the addition Peter the Great. Since then all Russian rulers until the Revolution of 1917 maintained the title of emperor, the form to be found in all official documents. (The use of the title tsar is incorrect, although, even today, in current usage.)

An unmistakable sign of Russia's new standing was the presence of a permanent Russian diplomatic mission in every important European capital, as had been the practice for a number of years by western European countries. Furthermore, the Treaty of Nystad brought into Russia a Baltic population that was to play a significant role in her foreign policy and army. The Baltic Germans, many from the nobility, entered into state service in large numbers. Russia had an insignificant middle or upper class from which to draw its bureaucrats. From then onwards these Baltic Russians, who were incorrupt and efficient, came to dominate many of the highest positions in Russia—families such as Benckendorff, Giers, Lamsdorff, Pahlen, Lieven and Staal, as their Germanic names show, were indispensable.

Inevitably, after the signing of the Treaty of Nystad, Peter retained the power to threaten George I's possession of Bremen and Verden. This was because the Russian emperor was now in a position, should he choose, to support the claims of Charles Frederick, Duke of Holstein-Gottorp, to the adjacent Duchy of Schleswig, while Britain supported Denmark, arch-enemy of the Holstein-Gottorps.[15] Furthermore, Peter's daughter, Anna, was to marry the Duke of Holstein-Gottorp: Holstein was too close for comfort for George I and he detested the ambitious duke. To make matters even worse, the duke was a pretender to the Swedish throne. Then, when Peter, undeterred by the Jacobite failure of 1715, renewed his contacts with James the Old Pretender, he was identified as an unrepentant enemy of Britain. James and his agents in Russia tried to persuade Peter to make use of his forces, now free from the war with Sweden, to invade Britain. This was a constant source of irritation, if not genuine fear, for the British government.

What was far more important, and the cause of much real disquiet in London, was the growth of the Russian fleet. Peter bragged that Russian naval strength would overtake that of Great Britain. George I's government countered by dispatching British squadrons to the Baltic in support of Sweden, attempting to isolate Russia by reaching agreements with Prussia and Denmark and persuading Turkey of the danger Russia posed to her.

In fact Peter had now turned his attention away from the west. Throughout his reign he had cherished ambitions for expansion in Asia. Without a pause, in 1722 he regrouped part of his army and plunged southwards with the aim of dominating the Caspian Sea and defeating Persia. The expedition met with some success but Peter's dream of establishing trade with India was not to be. Nevertheless, it was a further manifestation of Russia's new-found ambitions as a Great Power.

This required a drastic revision of the contemptuous attitude towards Russia long current in the west and in Great Britain in particular. Captain John Perry, a British engineer who had been employed by Peter to supervise the building of a canal between the Volga and the Don rivers to enable ships to sail from the Caspian to the Black Sea, played a part in modifying the British view of Russia. The canal project failed, but Perry continued to work for fourteen years in Russia until forced to leave the country as a result of alienating the reactionary boyars (nobles) who showed 'a dislike to all undertakings which the Tsar by the advice of strangers engaged in'.[16] On his return to England, Perry published *The State of Russia under the Present Tsar* in 1716. He was lavish in his praise of the Tsar-Reformer, while refraining from mentioning the well-documented brutality and vindictiveness for which Peter was infamous. For once, in a British publication, the author had a good word to say about the Russian people: 'As to the common foot soldiers, there are some very remarkable things which render them as fit for service as any in the world.'[17] On the other hand, Perry launched into a diatribe against the superstitious and corrupt nature of the Russian church and condemned those who had frustrated his work. He made clear his grievances against:

> the many and sinister ways the governors and men in power contrive some pretended fault to be charged upon a man and examine him with threats of the knout or battocks; let justice be as it will, every man according to his substance must either suffer stripes or buy off his punishment with money.[18]

However strained official relations were between Great Britain and Russia in the first half of the 1720s, a general admiration for Peter's achievements increased. His reforms, in the military, education and the sciences, the reductions in the power of the church and the proposed Academy of Sciences, all contributed to fostering this view of the new Russia. Even what was known of Peter's role in the torture and death of his son and heir, Alexsei, was glossed over. Still, his country was seen as backward and his people lacking the moral and intellectual abilities of those of western Europe.

Whatever the view of Peter the man, the first emperor of Russia had transformed his country: 'Although in the perspective of Russian history Peter the Great appears human rather than superhuman, the reformer is still of enormous importance. Quite possibly Russia was destined to be westernized, but Peter the Great cannot be denied the role of the chief executor of this fate.'[19]

3

'NATURAL FRIENDS'

Peter I drew up the first law of succession to the throne in Russia in 1722. Each ruling sovereign was empowered to designate as his heir whoever he might choose. Yet when Peter died in 1725 he was intestate. Several candidates emerged—Peter's grandson by his son Alexsei, also Peter; and the late ruler's daughters, Anna, who was now the fiancée of Charles Frederick, Duke of Holstein-Gottorp, Elizabeth and Natalya. Less probable seeming candidates were his half-nieces, Catherine, wife of the Duke of Mecklenburg, and Anna, childless widow of the Duke of Courland (though these marriages were later to have dynastic repercussions).[1]

In the end the ruling elite of Russia, who had been groomed by Peter, led by the former emperor's strong man, Prince Alexander Menshikov, and the Guards' regiments would have nothing to do with Old Muscovy with which Alexsei had been associated. They imposed Peter's second wife, Catherine, a low-born, bawdy Livonian whom Peter had crowned empress. The new empress was hardly surprisingly incapable of playing any role in foreign affairs—despite wanting to—and inevitably they fell to Menshikov and German-born Count Andrei Ostermann. The two men rejected approaches from Britain and France (at the time post-Utrecht allies) and organized a demonstration in the Baltic against George I. The British retaliated by sending yet more squadrons into the Baltic in 1726 and 1727, to signal to Russia British opposition to fresh hostilities in the north and to flag a warning to Russia about any possible Russian support for Charles, the Jacobite Young Pretender. In addition, the Russians continued to support George I's bugbear, the Duke of Holstein-Gottorp, in Sweden and Denmark. The frostiness between Britain and Russia, that threatened at any moment to become one of formal hostility, continued.

When both George I and Catherine I opportunely died in 1727, it marked a turning point in Anglo-Russian relations. Sir Robert Walpole, the (first) British prime minister, and Menshikov in Russia could move towards establishing better relations between the two countries. Catherine's successor, twelve-year-old Peter II, son of Alexsei, reigned only until early 1730 after dying of smallpox, but not before Menshikov had been able to abandon support for the ambitious Duke of Holstein-Gottorp. This gesture was appreciated in Great Britain, where there was increasing opposition to expensive Baltic expeditions to keep Russia at bay.

After complicated machinations in court circles in St Petersburg, the Russian throne was offered to Anna, Duchess of Courland, Peter I's half-niece, daughter of his half-brother Ivan V. A similar Germanized monarchy in Russia now matched that in Britain. The new empress brought with her a strong group of cronies who continued the westernization, though she was herself disinclined to intervene in state affairs.

Far more important than the aborted tobacco trade of the early years of the century was Anglo-Russian trade in naval stores—pitch, tar, hemp and timber—and imports of Russian iron ore to Britain were increasing with astonishing rapidity. If naval stores were essential for the British merchant navy in times of peace, they were still more important in times of war, and Britain was at war for much of the eighteenth century. Trade with the eastern Baltic, now in Russian hands, was necessarily still seasonal but was much less risky than when it had been conducted along the hazardous Arctic convoy route to Arkhangelsk. The vessels were almost exclusively British. They carried manufactured goods from Britain that the westernized Russian nobility in particular appreciated and supplies of the precious metals so essential to Russia's shaky financial structure. They returned laden with naval supplies and the produce of aristocratic estates, including rhubarb, for medicinal uses. The overall balance of trade was heavily in Russia's favour.

There were added political reasons in the early 1730s that spurred the British government into seeking a rapprochement with Russia. London feared that Russia might be won over to the French side, which included the Scandinavian powers (Anglo-French relations were again strained), and exclude Britain from the Baltic. Thus an Anglo-Russian commercial treaty was signed in 1734, according the signatories what was coming to be called most favoured nation status. Sir Robert Walpole refused to accede to Russian demands to guarantee the territories recently conquered from Sweden, but he promised neutrality, or passivity, on

Britain's part in the War of the Polish Succession that had broken out in 1733 between Russia and Austria on one side and France, Spain and Sardinia on the other.[2] Britain contributed to the Austro-Russian candidate's election to the Polish throne in the full knowledge that Poland was weak and essentially under the domination of Russia. The secretary of state, the Duke of Newcastle, told the British ambassador in Paris at the outbreak of the War of Polish Succession: 'What relates singly to Poland is a very remote consideration of His Majesty.'[3]

The mid-eighteenth century was a time of fundamental realignment in Europe, the Diplomatic Revolution. For at least two centuries the struggles in Europe had hinged on the rivalry between the French monarchy and the Austro-Spanish-Burgundian empire of the Habsburgs. From 1740 onwards the pivot shifted from western to central Europe. The duel between Britain and France was fought partly in India and North America, but the outstanding feature of European affairs was the prolonged contest for supremacy in Germany between the upstart House of Hohenzollern in Prussia and the ancient empire of the Habsburgs. This powerfully affected both Britain and Russia.

The Empress Anna, who died in 1740, had nominated as her successor a two-month-old boy, Ivan VI.[4] He was the grandson of Anna's elder sister, Catherine. The intended arrangement was for Anna's favourite, Ernst-Johann Biron, to rule as regent, but he was overthrown, as were Ivan's mother and the entire 'German party'. This *coup d'état* in 1741 was executed by Peter the Great's daughter and last surviving child, Elizabeth, with Guards' support.

The new Empress Elizabeth, the Russian Venus, immediately found herself having to confront Sweden, which had rashly declared war on Russia. With Austrian support, Russia was able to inflict a swift defeat on Sweden that further strengthened her position in the Baltic. Russian expansion seemed irresistible—a natural process begun by Peter the Great that her neighbours were powerless to halt, or even impede.

Russia then became involved in a war fought away from her borders and over issues not immediately related to her own interests. The War of the Austrian Succession was provoked by Frederick the Great's seizure of Silesia from Austria in 1740. Russia joined Austria and Great Britain against Prussia and France, but the Russian auxiliary corps arrived too late to fight in 1748. Britain had paid a subsidy of £300,000 a year for 30,000 Russian troops. Newcastle and the Earl of Sandwich, the strongest supporters of the policy of allying with Russia, were forced to understand the considerable obstacles to any effective use of Russian forces in western Europe—the long lines of communication and the continual financial difficulties of the Russian government.

The disappointment of 1748 did not signal an end to the British hope that Russia's abundant manpower might be used for the defence of British interests in Europe. As Anglo-French relations became more strained, in the early 1750s the possibility of a Franco-Prussian attack on Hanover, Britain's Achilles, heel, loomed even larger. A new subsidy treaty that would secure a Russian force in Livonia to block Frederick II seemed highly desirable. 'The King of Prussia', Newcastle explained, 'fears above all things Russia, and the conclusion of our treaty with her.'[5]

Sir Charles Hanbury Williams was appointed British ambassador to St Petersburg in the spring of 1755, with the principal objective of negotiating a subsidy treaty and renewing the defensive alliance of 1742. The avaricious and corrupt Bestuzhev-Riumin, now chancellor, was delighted by the turn of events and determined to press his advantage, believing that Hanbury Williams had 'in train a large wagon loaded with nothing else but ducats'.[6] He was correct in that Hanbury Williams was also a strong believer in the importance of bribery.

Bestuzhev-Riumin promised to do his utmost to secure the empress's acceptance of a convention in exchange for a subsidy of £100,000 a year, to be raised to £500,000 after the Russian troops had crossed the frontier. However, he would have to be compensated for his efforts. After much haggling he agreed to accept £10,000. 'Such public and private offers made at once struck him', Williams reported, 'and with joy in his face he told me … he would accept and support what I had offered.'[7] The ambassador regarded the private offer as 'the spring which gave motion and success to the public ones'.[8] But the usually indolent, fashion-obsessed empress soon made a mockery of the treaty from the British point of view by adding three vital secret articles, while not touching the main text. The first was to prevent the conclusion of any peace excluding Russia, and the other two, to all intents and purposes, postponed the marching of Russian troops in Livonia until three months after British requisition—this in flagrant contradiction to what was stated in the body of the convention. Britain, however, was now committed to provide the initial annual subsidy of £100,000.

The British government was no dupe. Hanbury Williams later tried to excuse his behaviour in signing the treaty on the grounds that war between Britain and France over North America was imminent and the convention was essential to British interests. The credulous ambassador reported home that the empress's aversion to France and Prussia 'grows daily stronger and her attachment to the King and his allies increases so fast that I will engage ... to put this Court into H. M.'s hands more than ever it was yet in those of any other sovereign'.[9] It was not enough to assuage the fury of George II and his ministers against Elizabeth. The king took great exception to Russia's having been given precedence both in the text and in the manner of its signature, and the Earl of Holderness, Secretary of State for the North, insisted that the article permitting a delay of three months should be removed. In the climate of fear in London that a rupture of diplomatic relations with France would make the Russians yet more intractable, Hanbury Williams was allowed to add £25,000 to the first instalment of the subsidy.

To begin with it looked as though the subsidy treaty (which was never ratified by the British parliament) had fulfilled its aim of scaring Frederick II, who then began approaches to Britain that culminated with bewildering speed in the Convention of Westminster in January 1756. Prussia was guaranteed, to Frederick's astonishment, a British subsidy while he pledged to protect Hanover. The intention was that the new convention would complement the one with Russia. In fact there was miscalculation and contradiction all round. Maria Theresa, the Austrian empress, resented the new arrangement between Britain and Prussia and Britain's refusal to commit to the defence of the Habsburg Austrian Netherlands, thus marking the end of what remained of the Austro-British alliance. Louis XV of France refused to maintain his alliance with Prussia because of the Convention of Westminster and rapidly signed a defensive treaty with Frederick's arch-enemy, Maria Theresa.

Empress Elizabeth for her part was deeply offended when she learned of the Convention of Westminster, of which Hanbury Williams was unaware. The subsidy treaty with Britain was repudiated early in 1756 and, even before the reconciliation of Austria and France by the Treaty of Versailles in May 1756, a Franco-Russian rapprochement began. Despite Hanbury Williams's efforts, in which he was aided by the young Grand Duchess Catherine (to whom he had lent money for her personal use), the ailing Elizabeth authorized mobilization for an attack on Prussia to forestall a similar one on Russia by Frederick.[10] Russia then allied herself formally with France and Austria on 31 December 1756 (old style) by acceding to the Treaty of Versailles.

Britain was isolated as her new ally Frederick was surrounded by enemies who were clearly intending to attack Prussia. The increasingly aggressive French policy in North America and India had to all intents and purposes obliged Britain to declare war on France in May 1756. Then a continental war became a reality in August 1756 when Frederick invaded Saxony, claiming this electorate to be part of an encircling conspiracy of his enemies France, Austria and Russia.

Russia, after declaring war on Prussia later in 1756, inflicted upon Frederick some of his worst defeats during the campaigns of the Seven Years' War: Gross Jägersdorf in 1757, Kunersorf in 1759 and, in 1760, when an Austro-Russian force mounted a raid that enabled them to hold Berlin for two days. In December 1761 the Russian general, Peter Rumiantsev, successfully besieged Kolberg, giving Russia control of Eastern Pomerania. Despite being on opposite sides in the war, Britain and Russia did not break off diplomatic relations. The need for naval stores that only Russia could supply and continued dependence on her as the best customer proved stronger than the political forces that had driven them apart. Britain refused to send a fleet into the Baltic as Frederick demanded, and Russia placed no obstacles in the way of Britain's securing the naval stores required for war at sea and in the colonies against France. The priority attached by Great Britain to trade with Russia rather than political relations had been evident from the time of the first encounters in the sixteenth century, and dependence on Russian raw materials continued to be central to Anglo-Russian relations in the mid-eighteenth century.

The Seven Years' War was a triumph for Britain, despite a disastrous start in 1757, with France threatening to invade. Then came 1759, the *annus mirabilis*, with decisive victories in European waters at Lagos and Quiberon Bay and in North America, and the conquest of Quebec. In the Indian subcontinent Britain's supremacy was established with the battle of Plassey and later at Wandiwash and Pondicherry. Other colonial trophies were seized from near-prostrate France, above all the West Indian islands of Guadeloupe and Martinique. Anglo-French peace negotiations began in 1761, but the entry into the war of France's ally, Spain, only resulted in fresh British victories. Skilful French diplomacy, together with Britain's war-weariness, led to a final settlement in the Treaty of Paris in 1763, which was more generous to France than her military situation justified, but even so marked a serious defeat for France.

The death in early 1762 of the childless Empress Elizabeth, Prussia's implacable enemy, saved Frederick II from an impending crushing defeat. Elizabeth had nominated as her successor her nephew Peter, Duke of

Holstein-Gottorp, son of her sister Anna and Charles Frederick, Duke of Holstein-Gottorp. This grandson of Peter the Great was born and brought up for his first fourteen years in Germanic Holstein: his hero was Frederick the Great. In an egregious switch of strategy, Peter III withdrew Russia from the Seven Years' War. This deprived Russia of enormous potential gains; indeed the Russian emperor refused to accept even what Frederick was willing to give him in return for withdrawing.

Nevertheless, the Seven Years' War had confirmed Russia's place among the Great Powers.

4

CATHERINE THE GREAT

The reign of Peter III lasted for only six months and could well have constituted no more than a footnote to Anglo-Russian relations, but for two decisions he made.

This rabid Prussophile of limited intellect had little to recommend him. Peter was scarred by smallpox, his features were unprepossessing and he was 'hideous' in his wife's eyes. Far more important, as a result of his German upbringing, was his loathing of Russians, their language and religion, and his disdain for the Russian army. The Empress Elizabeth had no illusions about her nephew's depravity, according to his wife Catherine's *Memoirs*.[1] These memoirs (not published in Russia until 1907) must be taken with a pinch of salt, for though Catherine wrote them during her marriage to Peter, she kept rewriting them until a couple of years before her death in 1796:

> She [Elizabeth] knew him so well that for many years past she could not spend a quarter of an hour in his society without feeling disgust, or anger, or sorrow ... she would be unable to speak of him without exhibiting her contempt, and often applied to him epithets which he too well merited.

Catherine claimed that the empress 'curses her nephew and wishes him at the devil'.[2]

Peter broke with Russia's allies of the Seven Years' War when, after making peace with Frederick the Great, he planned to go to war with the Prussian king against Denmark to restore Schleswig to the Duchy of Holstein-Gottorp he had inherited. An issue quite unconnected with Russian interests, this antagonized the Russian nobility and Russia's former ally, Austria, who had no interest in pursuing another conflict. Frederick for his part though was anxious to secure an alliance with Russia that would not only allow him to spread his influence in the German states against Austria, but also would enable him to become Russia's partner in the Baltic.

The situation in early 1762 was complicated because the allies Britain and Prussia—on the opposite side from Russia in the Seven Years' War—were at loggerheads. George III, who had ascended the throne in 1760, hated his first prime minister and the continental commitment that William Pitt (the Elder) represented of maintaining the alliance with Prussia. Pitt had been forced out of office in October 1761 and the new Secretary of State for the North, the Earl of Bute, George's mentor, was determined to end the alliance. The Duke of Newcastle, who remained in office, pleaded with Bute not to make 'two more great and considerable enemies, the Tsar and the King of Prussia'.[3]

When Bute, as a condition for continuing the subsidies paid to Frederick for 1762, enquired what the Prussian king's plans and resources were for carrying on the war, Frederick refused to reveal them to a power he believed capable of passing on this knowledge to his enemies. He was confirmed in this by a mistaken—more probably malicious—report from the Russian ambassador in London, of a conversation with Bute in which the British minister was said to have urged Russia to join with Britain in exerting pressure on Prussia to make substantial concessions to her enemies to bring the continental war to a speedy conclusion. In the end it was Frederick, furious at British tergiversation, who refused to accept any more subsidies from Britain, but the reality was that he had been unceremoniously dumped: 'All these infidelities, having destroyed the links which had united me with Great Britain, have left me isolated without allies in Europe.'[4] In fact it was Britain rather than Prussia who was isolated, and she was to pay a high price in future years for abandoning her vital continental connections now that Russia could count on the support of Prussia.

The second lasting result of Emperor Peter's reign was the introduction of the Emancipation of the Nobility edict, which abrogated Peter the Great's law obliging the nobility to be available for service in the army or civil service for twenty-five years (and there had been no lack of opportunity to see active duty between 1725 and 1762). After 1762 the Russian gentry could retire to their country estates or travel abroad without hindrance. The phenomenon of the Russian Grand Tourist began. A sizeable number of rich and titled Russians descended on London from then onwards and diplomats and other Russians found reasons for prolonged stays. The rich Russian became part of London society.

The reign of Peter III came to an abrupt end in July 1762 with his deposition and brutal murder, in which Catherine connived with her lover Grigory Orlov. Catherine had believed that her life was in danger from her unbalanced husband and his friends who hated her. She was born Princess Sophie Augusta Frederica of Anhalt-Zerbst to the humbler and poorer princely caste of Germany, though her mother, Johanna of Holstein-Gottorp, was a sister of the historically ubiquitous duke, Charles Frederick. On her marriage to Peter in 1745 at the age of sixteen, Sophie converted to the Russian Orthodox religion and was given the name of Catherine by the empress, in honour of Elizabeth's mother. In addition she proceeded to learn Russian, while simultaneously immersing herself in the writings of contemporary *philosophes*, Voltaire, Montesquieu and others, for which she had been prepared by her earlier grounding in French literature. The young grand duchess adapted herself skilfully to the new environment of St Petersburg and became popular in court circles. She participated in political intrigues and plots, carefully covering up her tracks until the largely bloodless and successful *coup d'état* of 1762. Given how many palace revolutions had taken place in St Petersburg in previous years, the accession of Catherine II was not at first recognized in Britain as an event of any great significance. It was true that her position was far from secure for several years. Even when clearly in control, some years later, she never threw off the British view of her as an adulteress, usurper and woman guilty of regicide.

It was obvious from the outset that Catherine was a woman of great intelligence with a natural ability to administer and govern. Along with her determination and sense of destiny went courage and optimism. Self-control, a secretive disposition, skill in discussion and propaganda and an over-weaning ambition sustained her. She felt she had to excel at everything and was what today would be called a control freak. Yet Catherine came to demonstrate that determination could all too easily become ruthlessness; her vanity fed an enormous ego. She had few beliefs or standards of value outside herself and her own overpowering ambitions. Sexually she was voracious with a long list of lovers continuing until old age.

Despite Peter III's meddling, the end of the Seven Years' War had relaxed the tension between Britain and Russia. Catherine II had a much wider grasp of European politics than any of her predecessors since Peter the Great, and recognized that both countries shared certain political interests in the post-war world.

In the early years of her reign the empress was under the influence of Count Nikita Panin, who advocated the 'northern system', that is a system of alliances with Prussia, Britain and Denmark-Norway directed against Russia's neighbours, Sweden, Poland and Turkey. For Britain, having ditched her ally Prussia and with Austria still allied with France, there was only Russia to whom she could look for support. Even before Peter had been murdered, a British envoy, the Earl of Buckinghamshire, had been sent to St Petersburg to seek a defensive alliance and new commercial treaty. He failed to make any progress as the minimum acceptable to the Russians was a subsidy agreement and naval support. The British prime minister, George Grenville, refused to promise any substantial sum of money. However, apart from British parsimony over subsidies, the negotiations were doomed because of the British government's refusal to become involved in the Polish crisis of 1763–4 provoked by the death of its king, Augustus III.

In October 1763, the month of Augustus's death, Count Zakhar Chernyshev, vice president (there was no president) of the Russian War College—the central administration of the army—and a close collaborator of the empress, submitted a memorandum proposing the annexation of Polish Livonia, the palatinate of Polotsk and the parts of the palatinate of Mstislav on the eastern bank of the Dnipro. Chernyshev gave three reasons for the necessity of annexation: (1) Existing questions about the Polish-Russian border had never been resolved; (2) Poland never returned serfs who fled across the border from Russia; and (3) Poland interfered with Russian commerce and illegally collected tariffs from Russians. In conclusion, he emphasized that it was to solve these specific problems that the annexation should be undertaken, and not to acquire territory, of which Russia had plenty. Whether or not Chernyshev was being disingenuous about territorial expansion, Russia had neither Prussia's compelling interest in uniting two separate parts of its territory by acquiring Danzig and Polish Pomerania, nor did she have Austria's anxiety about gaining new territory and revenue to compensate for the recent loss of Silesia, that had also called into question her standing as a great power.

The opportunity was there for Catherine to become the protector and guarantor of the constitution and territorial integrity of the vital buffer state, the Polish-Lithuanian Commonwealth, and she could have made moribund Poland an ally, client and subordinate of the Russian empire. That she preferred a different course of action is clear evidence that territorial gain from Poland, ultimately dismembering the country, was her aim.

With Augustus's demise providing the motivation/pretext, and her interest piqued by impassioned appeals for support from Orthodox 'dissidents' (as the non-Catholic minorities in Poland were officially termed) who suffered harassment and persecution at the hands of the Catholic majority, the Russian empress plunged into Polish politics. She refused to allow Charles of Saxony, Augustus's son, to succeed his father, to prevent the creation of a hereditary monarchy in Poland. This was because France supported the Saxon house. Instead, Catherine imposed Stanislas Poniatowski, a Polish aristocrat who had been her lover during his stay in St Petersburg between 1755 and 1758. In addition to his previous personal relationship, Poniatowski was related to the powerful, wealthy and pro-Russian family of the Czartoryskys. A massive deployment of Russian troops along the border in the autumn of 1763 made clear the empress's determination to support Poniatowski to the full. He was elected king in August 1764, with Russian troops in Warsaw to stave off any opposition. Britain had been asked to support the Russian candidate but refused to cooperate.

From the outset of her reign Catherine had demanded active British support if Russia were attacked in the south by France's ally Turkey, and the so-called 'Turkish clause' became the stumbling block to a political alliance. It was inconceivable that the British government could accept being drawn into a war between Russia and the Ottoman empire, but Prussia and Denmark accepted the Turkish clause. However, given that trade was fundamental in their relationship, both Russia and Britain were prepared to sign a new commercial treaty in 1766. Even then, concessions had to be made by the British government to the Russian point of view, which reduced the value of the new treaty in British eyes. The British envoy in St Petersburg, Sir George Macartney, complained: 'This Court has listened to me with the most provoking phlegm and the most stoical indifference.'[5]

Catherine's attention was now diverted from Poland towards the almost unlimited field of expansion offered by the southern steppes. Paradoxically, though, it was Poland that provided the catalyst as a result of a diplomatic misjudgement by Catherine. The empress had underestimated the strength of Polish Catholicism. She wrote to Voltaire:

> The absurdity of the Crusades has not stopped the churchmen of Podolsky [Poland] ... from preaching a crusade against me, and those so-called Confederate [roughly Polish factions] lunatics have taken the cross in one

> hand, and with the other formed an alliance with the Turks, promising them two of their provinces.[6]

Furious at the Polish Diet's refusal to implement her reform programme, Catherine instructed her envoy in Warsaw to force the Poles to endorse the rights of the dissidents and Warsaw was surrounded by 10,000 Russian troops. Cowed by this demonstration of Russian strength, the Diet grudgingly accepted the conditions and Catherine ordered her troops home.

At this moment Polish patriotism erupted in the south-eastern town of Bar (now in Ukraine, about 300 kilometres from today's Polish frontier), close to the Polish frontier with the Ottoman empire. The rebels declared a confederation in defence of Catholicism; Russian troops moved south where they had little difficulty in dispersing the confederates. However, more Polish confederations sprung up and Catherine again felt obliged to dispatch a large force into Poland. Austria was annoyed, while the Ottoman Porte, fortified with generous French bribes, prepared for war by provocatively incarcerating the Russian ambassador to Constantinople when he refused to agree to an ultimatum to remove Russian troops from Poland.

The Russian empress claimed surprise at Turkey's declaration of war in October 1768. In 1769 Russian troops were dispatched from the north and a Turkish army on the Dniestr fled in panic. The Russians then occupied Jassy and Bucharest. The following year Catherine made a determined but unsuccessful effort to encourage the Greeks to rise against their Turkish masters. The major event of the war, though, was the deployment of the Russian Baltic Fleet under the command of Count Alexsei Orlov (who had never been to sea), ably assisted by the real commanders, Admiral John Elphinstone and Vice Admiral Samuel Greig, two Scots who were formerly in British service.[7] The three squadrons sailed from the Baltic, down the North Sea, around France and Spain through the Straits of Gibraltar, protected by the British navy in the western Mediterranean, and on to the Greek Archipelago. At Chesme on the coast of Asia Minor close to Smyrna, the Ottoman fleet cooped up in the harbour was annihilated in June 1770. Elphinstone wanted to follow up this astonishing victory with an immediate attack on Constantinople, but Orlov procrastinated and the chance was lost.

France would certainly have wanted to intercept the progress of the Baltic Fleet, but for a firm intimation from Britain that she would treat intervention as a *casus belli*. Thus Britain's deeply ingrained and essentially irrational hostility towards France led her to view relations with Russia (outside the Baltic) as part of the larger framework of relations with France. On top of this there existed a condescending, but justified, assumption in Britain that Russia was not a major sea power and would be unable to challenge her on the high seas (the Russian navy had declined since the time of Peter the Great). In March 1770 Lord Charles Cathcart, British ambassador in St Petersburg, declared that it was impossible Russia could 'ever [become] a rival capable of giving us jealousy either as a commercial or as a warlike maritime power'.[8] The following September the Secretary of State for the South, the Earl of Rochford, informed Cathcart that Britain supported Russia's conquests and the latter's demand for free navigation in the Black Sea. He wished to see the natural alliance of Britain and Russia developed to counter a possible Franco-Austrian combination.

One or two signs of uneasiness about Russian expansion at the expense of Poland and victory over Turkey emerged in Britain after Chesme, though in general public opinion was unchanged by the spectacular success of 1770. The extension of Russian frontiers in Ukraine or along the coasts of the Black Sea provoked little interest. The influential writer Horace Walpole in a letter to a friend asked, 'Can one care whether some thousand acres of Tartary, more or less, belong to the Grand Signior, or the Czarina?'[9]

It fell to the Germanic powers to exploit Poland's weakened position. In May 1770 the Austrian envoy to Berlin reminded Frederick II that the acquisition of Pomerania would at long last unite the two major parts of Prussia. Vienna had its own ambitions and had become increasingly nervous about Russian territorial ambitions to the south in Moldavia and Wallachia. Austrian troops moved into Galicia as far as the Vistula and confronted the Poles at Cracow. The Polish confederates blamed King Stanislas and he was duly deposed. Supposedly in retaliation for this unlawful act, Austrian and Russian troops moved into Poland. Frederick II's brother, Prince Henry, was sent to Russia where he found Catherine receptive to the idea of a partition of Poland. By this stage the Russians had abandoned their claims in Moldavia and Wallachia and replaced them with compensation in Poland.

The tripartite carve-up signed in August 1772, the First Partition of Poland, gave Russia Polish Livonia and moved the frontier along the Dvina, the Ulla, the Drut and the Dnipro rivers, thus providing Russia with effective control of the Bielorussian river trade from the Baltic to the Black Sea and the prospect of later projecting her power into Lithuania and the Polish heartland. Prussia took Pomerania so that Brandenburg and East Prussia were now linked. Austria annexed Galicia. The Polish Diet abjectly ratified this rapacious arrangement, by which 30 per cent of the Commonwealth's territory and 35 per cent of its population were lost. Britain stood on the sidelines as Poland was sacrificed. A few politicians, most prominently Edmund Burke, warned that the Partition was 'the first very great breach in the modern political system of Europe'.[10] Horace Walpole mocked Britain's irrelevance as a naval power to influencing events in eastern Europe. The fleet, 'being so formidable will, I suppose, be towed overland to Warsaw and restore the Polish constitution and their King to his full rights'.[11]

William Pitt (the Younger), now Earl of Chatham, told his colleague the Earl of Shelburne in 1773, 'Your Lordship well knows I am quite a Russ. I trust the Ottoman will pull down the House of Bourbon in his fall.'[12] Yet despite the seemingly favourable state of Anglo-Russian relations, negotiations for a new commercial treaty and defensive alliance collapsed in this same year. Britain refused to guarantee Russian conquests in Poland. The Secretary of State for the North, the Earl of Suffolk, blamed Catherine's reluctance to sign a defensive alliance on the overweaning influence of Frederick II at St Petersburg. Once the empress had extricated herself from the war with Turkey—which was dragging on—she would be susceptible to British overtures. The erroneous British idea that time was on her side did not fool Catherine. The risks of concluding any treaty or alliance that would alienate Prussia and Austria were far greater than anything Britain could offer.

Peace talks between Russia and the Porte had begun in 1772. However, Russia arrogantly demanded that Crimea—which included land beyond the peninsula—ruled by Muslim Tatar khans, who were allowed to rule as tributary princes of the Ottoman empire, should become independent of the empire. This was too much for Turkey to accept. It was all too clear that this would be a front for eventual annexation by Russia. But the Partition of Poland and further military success in 1774 had strengthened Russia's position such that Ottoman resistance broke down and the Porte sued for peace. According to the Treaty of Kuchuk-Kainardji, Turkey was to cede Kerch and Enikale, fortress ports at the entrance to the Sea of Azov, and Kinburn plus its hinterland. These provided access to the Dnipro-Bug estuary and hence to the Black Sea. The khanate of Crimea was recognized as an independent state by Russia and all Turkish forts and lands in the region were ceded to the Tatars.

The Danubian Principalities of Moldavia and Wallachia which had been occupied by Russian troops were returned to the Porte, while Russia gained the right to intervene on behalf of the Christian population in the Ottoman empire. Wide commercial privileges were given to Russia in Ottoman territories and her subjects were permitted to trade and navigate in the Black Sea, tacitly the right to operate a fleet there, and to cross the Straits into the Mediterranean. Not only did Russia obtain a firm foothold on the northern coast of the Black Sea; she also gained strategic strongholds on either side of the Crimean peninsula with which to pull the khanate into the Russian orbit. This *de facto* partition of part of the Ottoman empire that ended its hegemony on the Black Sea could not create a durable peace since it constituted a radical shift in the balance of power from Turkey to Russia. What was of lasting importance was that it set the scene for the Eastern Question that was to dominate the nineteenth century.

Her success against Turkey whetted Catherine's appetite (and secured accepted legitimacy of her rule) for further expansion. And she found the man who would be her soulmate in this. Grigory Potemkin had seen distinguished military service in the war with Turkey and had helped to put down the serious Pugachev Revolt that had broken out in Russia in 1773. Potemkin was recalled to St Petersburg later that year. Within two months he had become the empress's adjutant general, a euphemism for official favourite, and head of the new court faction. From early 1774 the empress and Potemkin had become lovers and inseparable. Their passionate affair, and possible marriage, has become the stuff of romantic fiction as well as history.

Potemkin, now governor general of Azoz and New Russia, the territory to the south of Russia's previous borders (now in southern and eastern Ukraine) immediately made good use of his new-found power to conceive the so-called 'eastern system'—though more accurately a 'southern system'—in opposition to the 'northern system' of the head of the College of Foreign Affairs, Nikita Panin. This aimed at annexing Crimea, destroying the port of Ochakov (Ochakiv) that the Turks held on the north coast of the Black Sea, and replacing it with a naval base from which Russia would gain supremacy on the sea and threaten Constantinople. In the Caucasus it would be necessary to build a line of fortifications across the watershed between the Kuban and the Terek rivers from which to launch expeditions into western Georgia to sow discontent among local pashas. Success here would, it was hoped, encourage the Orthodox Greeks and other Christians in the region to rise up against their Ottoman masters.

Although Crimea was now nominally independent, its predominantly Muslim Tatar population was understandably pro-Turkish. In 1776 Russian troops seized Perekop, on the narrow neck of land to the north of Crimea separating the peninsula from Ukraine. A new Crimean khan had been elected in 1775, but his anti-annexation stance made him unacceptable to Russia. Russian troops entered Crimea the following year and installed a sympathetic puppet. This in turn provoked a revolt against the pro-Russian khan. Russian troops came to his aid and reinstated him. Nevertheless, the khan proved unfit to rule and was forced to flee in 1782.

Meanwhile, as Russia was embarking on further expansion in 1775, Britain faced the approach of the American War of Independence. George III wrote to Catherine requesting 20,000 Russian troops for service in Canada under British command. Nothing could more clearly illustrate the isolation of Britain than the desire to see Russian troops operating in a British colony in North America. Britain, with its naval supremacy and small army, had traditionally hired mercenaries. If Russia desired a subsidy, this would be forthcoming. The British ambassador, Sir Robert Gunning, reminded the Russian foreign ministry that Britain had greatly assisted Russia in the war against Turkey in 1770 and a gesture of gratitude would be in order. Catherine refused to help. She could hardly be expected to supply the troops free of charge; she felt she would be lowering herself to the level of a mercenary German prince if she accepted a subsidy (her lowly German origins now long forgotten) and she needed all her troops for campaigns at home. George III did not appreciate the tone of the rebuff: 'Not in so genteel a manner as I thought might be expected. She has not had the civility to answer in her own hand and has thrown out some expressions that may be civil to a Russian but certainly not to more civilised ones.'[13] The British were now alone to fight the rebellion in the Thirteen Colonies with their enemies waiting to take advantage of the conflict.

France was about to join the American colonists in the War of Independence when Sir James Harris, a high-flying young British diplomat, was sent to St Petersburg as minister plenipotentiary and envoy extraordinary at the end of 1777. The Secretary of State for the North, the Earl of Suffolk, instructed Harris:

> Such is the present situation of Great Britain and Russia with respect to the House of Bourbon, and it does not seem too much to say, that their

> *general* situation is sufficiently critical, to make this the proper moment of procuring mutual support, and reverting to the idea of an alliance with each other.[14]

It took some time for Harris to establish himself with the Russian court, but by mid-1779 he had gained easy access to the man who mattered, Prince Potemkin. More than this, the two men struck up a friendship in which Harris milked Potemkin's Anglophilia to the full: 'I told him the moment was now come when Russia must act the greatest part in Europe—and he alone was adequate to direct the conduct of it.'[15] Quite what was in it for Russia was obvious to Potemkin—nothing. There was no advantage to be gained from Russia's sending a naval expedition to help the British. As far as the 'Turkish clause' was concerned, Britain, in a state of war, could not provide any assistance.

Potemkin promised to pave the way secretly for Harris to be accorded the unusual honour for an ambassador of an audience with the empress. With further aid from Catherine's latest lover, Major Ivan Rimsky-Korsakov, he arranged for the Englishman to meet the empress in her private dressing-room. She was sympathetic but vague. When Harris politely enquired whether Catherine would, in Britain's place, give independence to the Thirteen Colonies, she replied with vehemence: 'I'd rather lose my head.'[16]

In the seemingly encouraging climate of time spent with Potemkin talking, drinking, gambling and plotting, the envoy produced two memoranda in 1779 arguing the need for Anglo-Russian cooperation in the American War of Independence. The last thing the French wanted to see was an Anglo-Russian alliance and French representatives at St Petersburg were prepared to stop at nothing to sabotage Harris's excellent relations with Potemkin. A step in this direction was the theft of the British envoy's second memorandum by Prince Potemkin's current mistress, who passed it on to the French *chargé d'affaires* who in turn adulterated it. St Petersburg was a hive of gossip, intrigue and espionage. Bribery was rife and there was nothing surprising about the theft of the memorandum.

However, away from the hothouse of St Petersburg's diplomatic world, events were taking place that nullified Harris's good work. To prevent supplies reaching the rebels in North America, Britain was pursuing a ruthless policy of seizing neutral ships at sea and blockading French and Spanish ports. International law was not clear on the rights of neutral shipping, though it was generally accepted that the neutral flag protected enemy cargo, except war contraband as defined in some commercial treaties. By imposing its naval supremacy, Britain was effectively claiming that might made right.

When Britain seized two Russian ships in the autumn of 1778, Catherine demanded their release. She failed. The empress therefore took it upon herself to challenge the British. London was informed in March 1779 that a Russian squadron would cruise the North Sea to protect the trade of Russia, Sweden and Denmark. A year later she went further and bated Albion with the Declaration of Armed Neutrality. Her stance won support from Sweden, Denmark, Prussia, the Kingdom of the Two Sicilies and the United Provinces, though the Dutch had to pay for their audacity with a declaration of war by the British.

The British government was stunned by the news of the League of Armed Neutrality. The Declaration was not only a serious blow to British prestige but it made clear to all the other powers her friendless state. The Earl of Shelburne, Secretary of State for the South, saw Armed Neutrality as the result of the total neglect on the part of the British government to seek alliances on continental Europe. There was also the fear that Frederick II, now on good terms with France, would use Armed Neutrality as the basis for an offensive alliance against Britain. George III's electorate of Hanover appeared exposed to an attack not only from Prussia but also from France and Austria. This was, however, unlikely, since Catherine had played a leading role with France in negotiating the Treaty of Teschen that in 1779 ended a dispute between Prussia and Austria, with Russia a guarantor of the integrity of the German empire.

With Spain also now at war with Britain over territory in North America, Harris was instructed in 1780 by the new Secretary of State for the North, Viscount Stormont, to press the Russians again for an alliance. By mid-year the attempt had failed. Panin's Anglophobia scuppered any remaining hope of an Anglo-Russian alliance. The British envoy naturally turned to Potemkin, who hated Panin, but the prince prevaricated. There was widespread talk of Harris's offering Potemkin an enormous £50,000 bribe. This seems to be untrue, but there was a great deal of money circulating in St Petersburg diplomatic circles that year. Harris had had enough and wanted to be recalled, but his masters in London would not hear of it. The Englishman had to live with Panin gloating over Britain's snub: 'The Empress is … strongly attached to us; so is Prince Potemkin; but every other member of her Council, every individual of her society, are carried away in that vortex of intrigue and prejudice which seems to have drawn into its circle nearly all Europe.'[17]

In an attempt to explain that Britain's diminished status in Europe would be to the detriment of the balance of power, with only France benefiting, Harris told Potemkin at the end of 1780 that 'our natural friends would then see their error, and, when it was too late, lament their having been the cause of giving additional weight to Courts [meaning France] in interests opposite to theirs'.[18] Certainly it was not inconceivable that successful French support for the American colonists would encourage France to lend support to Russia's enemies, Poland, Sweden and Turkey. The prince replied with a put-down: 'He asked why I was repeating what I had so often said, and whether I thought any doubts remained in his mind of the crisis in which we were.'[19] Harris's relationship with Potemkin deteriorated from then onwards and the ambassador complained bitterly of his increasing isolation in St Petersburg.

From a Russian point of view, the American War of Independence was a welcome distraction from the eyes of the western powers on Russian activity in the south of the empire, and Harris had been aware for some time that Potemkin was far more interested in Russian expansion in the south than in British and continental European matters. The prince was the force behind the 'Greek Project' that fired Catherine's imagination in 1779. So far there had been successful encroachment of the Ottoman empire. The aim now was to destroy it.

The first public manifestation of the 'Greek Project' was Catherine's decision to name her second grandson, born in 1779, Constantine. He was provided with Greek nurses and the long-term aim was to place the grand duke on the throne of a revived Byzantine empire in Constantinople. That could be no more than wishful thinking; serious diplomacy was called for to enact the policy. Catherine found the man who could assist Potemkin and herself in this.

Joseph II, not yet officially Habsburg emperor as his mother, Maria Theresa, was still alive, requested a meeting with the Russian empress in 1779. He wanted to check for himself that the Russo-Prussian alliance was a dead letter. Frederick II had indeed come up with a proposal for a Russo-Prusso-Turkish alliance, a ludicrous idea in Catherine's eyes—she referred to Frederick as 'Herod'. Before leaving for the summit with Joseph at Mogilev in western Russia (where Nicholas II had his headquarters in the desperate days of 1915), the empress instructed her secretary, Count Alexander Bezborodko, to draft a plan for Russo-Austrian cooperation in the dismemberment of the Ottoman empire, the written basis of the 'Greek Project'. Catherine and Joseph struck up an immediate friendship, the young man succumbing to the seductive and dominating personality of the empress, and they began a regular correspondence later in the year, avidly stroking each other's ego. This relationship was cemented with Maria Theresa's death in November.

Catherine demanded from the Austrians not only a full-scale defensive alliance but also the promise of assistance against the Turks who, she claimed, were repeatedly violating the Treaty of Kuchuk-Kainardji. She was able to win Joseph's agreement to a secret exchange of letters by pledging to share with him all gains from any Russo-Turkish hostilities. In the division of Ottoman lands, Russia was to receive the western Caucasus, Crimea and territory between the Bug and the Dniestr. Moldavia and Wallachia were to be joined to form the independent state of Dacia. Joseph was to receive parts of Wallachia, Serbia, Bosnia, Herzegovina, Istria and Dalmatia. What was left of Turkey-in-Europe, the Bulgarian and Greek lands, was to form the new Greek empire, to be ruled by Constantine.

Potemkin was naturally delighted when he learned of the empress's diplomatic success, which coincided with reports of anarchy in Crimea. On his return to Tsarskoe Selo he immediately asked Harris to meet him. Harris found the prince in high spirits, champing at the bit to leave for Crimea, what he called 'the wart' on the end of Catherine's nose.[20]

Despite Russian expansion, the strains over the American War of Independence and Armed Neutrality, the idea that Russia was the natural ally of Great Britain did not disappear. Nevertheless, from 1780 onwards there was developing in Britain a new image of Russia as a power that could not sustain an intimate relationship with Britain, and whose policies might in the future inflict serious harm on her. Charles James Fox in his short-lived Whig ministry of 1782–3 adhered to the policy of his predecessors that saw Russia as a natural ally against France. Under the Tory William Pitt, from 1784 signs of a change became clear. The prime minister assured the new Russian ambassador, Count Simon Vorontsov, in 1785 that Britain's friendship with Russia remained. Yet at that time relations between the two countries were strained because of George III's support as Elector of Hanover for the League of German Princes organized by the redoubtable Frederick the Great and directed against Catherine's friend and ally, Joseph II. The empress dispatched an angry protest to London and privately expressed her contempt for George III, an easy swipe given that his periods of insanity were known by then.

If relations with Britain were becoming somewhat frosty this was the perfect opportunity for the French to benefit, and the new French ambassador to Russia, the Count de Ségur, did his utmost to ingratiate himself with Potemkin with the promise of direct trade relations with France.

Britain was still at war with the Thirteen Colonies and could only observe the formal annexation of Crimea in 1783 by Russian forces under Potemkin. Catherine made a triumphal procession of the peninsula, now called Taurida, in 1787, and Russian landowners, *pomeshchiki*, moved into Crimea, confiscating Tatar lands. Massive emigration of Crimean Muslims to the Ottoman provinces of Anatolia, the Caucasus, and the Balkans ensued. From then onwards, under the brilliant direction of the prince, the natural resources of the peninsula were developed and the naval bases of Nikolaev (Mykolaiv) and Sevastopol created. At the same time Russian agents continued to agitate among the Christian populations of the Ottoman empire, and Russian activity in areas bordering Ottoman territories in the Balkans caused increasing apprehension in Britain and Prussia.

Russia refused to renew the Anglo-Russian commercial treaty that expired in 1786 and instead signed one with France the following year. The British ambassador to Prussia, the Russophobe Joseph Ewart, inveighed against the new treaty: 'The treaty of commerce making France the most favoured nation was concluded with every circumstance calculated to insult this country and was carried on without interruption since 1785.'[21] The claims were incorrect but they led to increased unease and resentment in London now that France was established as a competitor in the Russian market.

War broke out again between Russia and Turkey in 1787 when the sultan delivered an ultimatum demanding the evacuation of Crimea. Russia refused to comply and Turkey declared war. The British ambassador to the Porte made no secret of his pro-Turkish sympathies and it was widely believed by the Russians that his intrigues had played a part in provoking the sultan's action. Catherine disingenuously claimed that British policy was directed by George III and his Hanoverian ministers, but it was Pitt who refused to let Russia rent transport ships, recalled British sailors in Russian service, and would not help in any way the passage of a squadron through the North Sea to the Mediterranean. There was to be no repeat of 1770. Furthermore, the prime minister pushed through an alliance in 1788 with Prussia and the United Provinces (the Netherlands) and was unwilling to abandon Sweden (who had rashly and unsuccessfully attacked Russia) to the tender mercies of Potemkin's troops (the latter to no avail). This Triple Alliance, which had arisen out of incidents in western Europe, was not directed against Russia. Nevertheless, Catherine was furious, or feigned outrage against Britain, openly expressing the hope that George III's insanity and the Regency crisis it provoked would return Charles James Fox to power and divert British policy into more pro-Russian channels. When Prussia aggravated relations with Russia yet more by signing a treaty with Turkey, Catherine feared for her Baltic provinces and blamed George III and Pitt for backing Prussia.

A further deterioration in Anglo-Russian relations took place in 1790 when Britain mobilized a powerful fleet to maintain her claims in North America against Spain. Fallacious rumours were circulated in some British circles that the ships were really intended to be used in support of the Turks against Russia. In addition, Britain was putting out feelers to Poland with the aim of replacing the purchase of naval stores from Russia with similar ones from Poland. A commercial treaty with Poland and expansion of Anglo-Polish trade had become one of the pivots of British policy by the end of the year. The plan was to develop Memel into a rival of Riga and to secure a safe route down the nominally Polish rivers to the Black Sea. Here Russia stood in the way and had for some time been impeding Polish trade along the Dniestr to the Black Sea.

In December 1788 Potemkin's troops took Ochakov, the Turkish fortress on the northern coast of the Black Sea that Pitt believed would enable Russia, assuming she retained it at the peace, to take total control of the navigation both of the Bug and the Dniestr. It would thus be possible for Russia not merely to hamper, or even stop, Poland's trade with Britain via the Black Sea, but to allow France what she denied to Britain—free access to plentiful supplies of naval stores both in Poland and Ukraine. Merely by shifting trade from the Baltic, where Britain had laboriously established commercial superiority, to the Black Sea, where France enjoyed the advantages of her ancient alliance with the Turks and the natural advantage of a relatively short passage to Marseilles and Toulon, Russia could irretrievably harm British trade and national security. Thus the idea of an Anglo-Polish treaty reflected the growing conviction that Russia's newly hostile attitude towards Britain and flirtation with France was a threat not only to the British economy but also to Britain's position as a great power. The upshot for Pitt was clear: Russia must be made to return to the status quo *ante bellum*.

Although eclipsed by the magnitude of contemporary events in France following the 1789 revolution, the Ochakiv crisis of 1791 was a major event in British foreign policy. The diplomat Joseph Ewart had gained considerable influence over Pitt and several other members of the government and Sir Charles Whitworth (namesake of an earlier British ambassador) in St Petersburg urged issuing an ultimatum to Russia. It would, the ambassador claimed:

> reduce Russia to the place She ought to hold amongst the Powers of Europe, and rectify all those Chimeras of Grandeur and Importance which, grounded upon the Idea of Her being a Maritime Power, have formerly given Rise to the Armed Neutrality, and may yet produce Effects still more prejudicial to the Prosperity of His Majesty's Dominions.[22]

But neither Pitt nor the foreign secretary, the Duke of Leeds, was sanguine about the consequences of demanding that Russia should surrender Ochakov.[23]

In fact it was Frederick William, now king of Prussia, who brought matters to a head by proposing that Britain and Prussia should jointly threaten Russia with military action to abandon the territorial gains made since 1787. The cabinet decided on 21 March to throw the full weight of British power behind Prussia. Only Grenville, the home secretary, demurred. It was agreed that a fleet of between thirty-five and forty ships should be sent to the Baltic and a squadron of ten or twelve ships to the Black Sea in May.

Pitt possessed a large Tory majority in the House of Commons and was confident of his considerable influence in the country as a whole. He was stunned when his proposal to force the Russians out of Ochakov met with violent verbal onslaughts in the House of Commons, where Charles James Fox's oratory in particular swayed many members against military action. British trade derived immense benefits from a good understanding with Russia. And if considerations of utility were to be ignored the sacrifice could only be justified by strong moral issues and not by the preservation of Ochakov, which had not been thought worthy of notice in the king's speeches the two following years.[24] Edmund Burke expressed his contempt for Turkey, an Asiatic and infidel power that should be disregarded in the balance of power.[25] In the House of Lords the Whigs were equally appalled. The Duke of Richmond opposed intervention; Lord Porchester denounced the scheme as emanating from the mad ambition of creating an empire in the east; the Earl of Carlisle insisted that Russia was the natural ally of Britain.[26]

By 228 votes to 135 the government won the day in the House of Commons, but the fierce resistance and invective that had been unleashed continued into April. Earl Grey moved eight resolutions as to the inexpediency and folly of the armament against Russia.[27] Fresh declamations issued from the influential Whigs in the House of Commons such as the playwright Richard Sheridan, as well as Fox. At the same time Simon Vorontsov was hard at work urging on the pro-Russian mercantile lobby and paying journalists and pamphleteers to denounce Pitt's project.

In spite of all the opposition Pitt emerged victorious from the further debate on 15 April 1791, by 253 votes to 173. This, he realized, was not enough; he had lost the argument and reluctantly yielded by withdrawing the ultimatum to Russia. Frederick William was forced to leave the Turks to their fate and William Fawkener, a clerk to the Privy Council, was dispatched to St Petersburg in May, on what was obviously mission impossible, to induce Catherine to agree to a face-saving compromise—'As if our blustering would terrify a woman in whom fear of no sort seems to predominate.'[28] The empress ordered Vorontsov to send her a bust of Fox, which she placed between those of Cicero and Demosthenes and displayed to poor Fawkener, telling him that it was in gratitude for Fox's 'eloquence [that] had saved two great nations from a war'.[29]

Pitt's inept plan had failed for several reasons: firstly, because public opinion in Britain was not prepared for a drastic reversal of policy towards Russia; secondly, British dependence on naval stores was exploited by the vociferous and well-connected mercantile lobby; thirdly, the crisis had demonstrated that a naval power could not exert military pressure on a major land power such as Russia.

The crisis ended, in Pitt's words, 'not very creditably, but better so than worse'.[30] Catherine had by the summer of 1791 won enough victories and had little wish to prolong the conflict with Turkey. An armistice was signed in August, and in January 1792 the Treaty of Jassy recognized the Russian annexation of Crimea and of lands between the Bug and Dniestr. Russia, not the Ottoman empire, was henceforth the dominating power on the Black Sea.

A century later, in 1884, the Russian foreign minister, Nicholas Giers, wrote to the ambassador in London, George de Staal: 'After centuries of friendly relations England became hostile to us because the annexation of Crimea enabled us to become a naval power on the Black Sea.'[31]

The indifference with which British opinion had greeted the First Partition of Poland in 1772–3, with the blame attributed to Frederick II, continued for several years. Then had emerged the slow development of anti-Russian feeling during the American War of Independence, Armed

Neutrality, the Ochakov crisis and Catherine's success in the second war with Turkey. There was little sympathy for Poland in Britain, indeed there was contempt for Polish politics and society. 'Poland, where the feudal system continues to take place', wrote Adam Smith in 1777, 'is at this day as beggarly a country as it was before the discovery of America.'[32] The poverty and backwardness of the country seemed to him the inevitable results of its ridiculous constitution and of the excessive privileges of the nobility.

All Poland's well-known defects, though, could not in British eyes, by 1793, provide an excuse for her destruction. A new Polish constitution had been drawn up in 1791 that seemed to bode well for a state wishing to embrace western democratic standards. However, Catherine had different plans for Poland and prepared to invade the country almost as soon as the war with Turkey was concluded the following year. She branded the Polish reformers the eastern wing of French Jacobinism. Prussia and Austria were informed of her intentions but encouraged to leave Russia free to deal with Poland. Russian troops entered Poland in March 1792 and two months later King Stanislas capitulated.

A Second Partition followed inexorably in January 1793, initiated by Prussia who feared that Russia would seize the whole of Poland without compensating her neighbour. Prussia took Danzig and Thorn, while Russia received Lithuania and western Ukraine lands. This action in which Austria, now embroiled in war against France, did not take part, provoked a final revolt by the Poles. Prussia and Russia sent in troops who displayed in British eyes unwarranted cruelty. The insurrection was quelled and Poland was expunged from the map of Europe by the Third Partition in 1795. Russia acquired millions of Poles to her population, including many Jews—a large and hostile population. Yet Europe did not appreciate the enormity of what had occurred.

Anti-Catherine sentiment was rife in Britain, particularly in the press, and gruesome caricatures featured slaughtered Polish women and children with the Russian empress lampooned as the bloodthirsty butcher. But Britain was isolated and powerless because the Second and Third Partitions of Poland occurred under the shadow of the events that followed the French Revolution. France declared war against the Habsburg monarchy in April 1792, a war that by early 1793 had involved Britain. Catherine had long harboured ambivalent feelings towards France. She admired French culture and respected France's international position; at the same time she was distrustful of French attempts to thwart Russian aims in Poland and Turkey. Nevertheless, she recognized that events in western Europe in the first half of the 1790s had served as a cover and distraction from the further partitions of Poland. The empress ordered court mourning after the execution of Louis XVI in 1793, and had already broken off diplomatic relations with France, annulled the commercial treaty of 1787 and expelled all French subjects from Russia. Even so she refused to join the Allies in the First Coalition against France.

Inevitably, the outbreak of the Anglo-French war tended to draw Britain and Russia together against the Jacobins. A new commercial agreement in 1793 helped to consolidate the pro-Russian attitude of the mercantile class in Britain, and in February 1795 Russia renewed the defensive alliance of 1742. It importantly contained a new article in which each country pledged to support the other if their possessions were attacked by a European power anywhere in the world, and for the first time Britain agreed to support Russia if attacked by Turkey, the long-standing 'Turkish clause'. The treaty also recognized the Baltic to be in the Russian naval sphere of influence and that British ships would only enter it if Russia called for assistance. Russian ships were invited to cruise in the North Sea in defence of British interests. Soon afterwards Russian ships sailed into the North Sea with the British Admiral Duncan onboard. Even so, despite the new-found goodwill between the two countries, Catherine refused to commit her troops against France until the Austrian position in Italy collapsed in July 1796. The British government was greatly relieved when she pledged 60,000 men to fight against France the following month. In November 1796 Catherine died aged sixty-seven.

Catherine II wished to be 'the Great' because of her vaunted role in the eighteenth-century Enlightenment and her domestic reforms, but it was the sum of her conquests that earned her the epithet. The annexations resulting from the two Turkish wars and three Partitions of Poland brought Russia the greatest expansion of territory since the mid-sixteenth century, concomitant economic growth and a larger increment of power relative to other states than at any time since Peter the Great (and only exceeded by that of Stalin at the end of the Second World War). She achieved these gains over twenty-eight years and without provoking more than grumbling and supine hostility in Europe, much less fear of a Russian menace to civilization. The diplomatic protests regarding Poland from Britain and France never elicited a possible military riposte because at every stage of her expansion one or more major European states assisted Russia.

5

THE LONG EIGHTEENTH CENTURY

THE DIPLOMATS

The establishment of a permanent Russian diplomatic mission in London in 1707 got off to an inauspicious start with the Matveev incident occurring the following year. Once Peter I felt his honour satisfied by British diplomatic grovelling, the tsar appointed Prince Boris Kurakin to the Court of St James in 1709. The prince met with a cool reception since this was the year of the battle of Poltava and the new-found fear in Britain of Peter's expansionist foreign policy. However, the Russian aristocrat, who had already demonstrated great interest in British politics and the legal system, soon came to be appreciated. It is a measure of his acceptance into British society—something quite unthinkable for earlier Russian envoys—that he was a regular visitor to the Duke of Ormond in Richmond. Similarly, when Kurakin visited the Bodleian Library in Oxford there was none of the shock of the alien that had greeted his master little more than a decade before. During the reign of Peter the Great Russian diplomats came to acquire the same skills and behaviour as those practised in western Europe. They became part of a cosmopolitan, aristocratic society that manifested its distinctive culture, cohesive and homogeneous.

In the years following Kurakin's departure in 1711, and with the strained relations between Britain and Russia, Prussian and Danish diplomats handled Russian affairs, but during the Northern Crisis Peter realized that only a Russian resident could be trusted. Feodor Veselovsky, his choice, had to contend for over three years with the outpouring of anti-Russian pamphlets and newspaper articles condemning the tsar's aggressive behaviour and highlighting his believed support for the Jacobites.

Veselovsky was the first exponent of Russian diplomatic ability to take advantage of the relatively free press in Britain to make the Russian case, but his efforts were not appreciated at home, and his relations with Peter's hated son, Alexsei, sounded his doom. More than just losing his position, Veselovsky's successor, Count Mikhail Bestuzhev-Riumin, was ordered to arrest him. The former resident fled to the continent in fear of torture and interrogation should he return to Russia. The emperor, believing that Veselovsky was still in London, demanded his extradition. The British government refused and insisted on its right to grant asylum to whomever it chose. The former diplomat was living comfortably in Switzerland. Other runaways continued to live in Britain during the eleven years without diplomatic links.

When diplomatic relations were resumed in 1732, the Empress Anna made the exotic choice of Antiokh Kantemir, son of the hospodar of Moldavia (an Ottoman province), the family having sought refuge in Russia some years before. It turned out be an inspired choice, as Kantemir, with his unlikely background and aged only twenty-three, proved extremely able as a diplomat and as a man of letters. Promoted from resident to minister and expressing his great admiration for all things British, Kantemir was soon on good terms with members of the government, Queen Caroline—George II's wife—and Sir Hans Sloane, president of the Royal Society. But like so many of his successors, though he could read English, he had difficulty speaking it and conversed in French, using an interpreter when necessary.

George II expressed his great appreciation of Kantemir to the Empress Anna in 1738 and fortunately the next envoy, Prince Ivan Shcherbatov, proved capable of maintaining the friendly relations that his predecessor had established. Shcherbatov had earlier studied for three years in Britain with the unfulfilled hope of joining the British navy. He spoke fluent English and had been president of the prestigious Russian College of Justice. The Empress Elizabeth recalled Shcherbatov in 1742 as he was associated with the 'Germans' of the previous reign, but his obvious talents had identified him as the best man for London and he returned in 1744 for a further two years.

Given that Anglo-Russian relations were on an even keel for most of Elizabeth's reign and her chancellor, Count Alexsei Bestuzhev-Riumim, an Anglophile, the Russian envoys to Britain—Shcherbatov, Simon Naryshkin, Count Peter Chernyshev and Prince Alexander Golitsyn—could not but enjoy the posting. None were impressive but they were popular with George II and the fashionable society they frequented. Not only were they aristocratic but also necessarily rich, as salaries were paltry. (The British government paid salaries until the 1740s, £400 a year for an envoy, £200 for a diplomat.) Chernyshev spent nine years in London and in general Russian diplomats remained longer in this post than was usual for many other countries, reflecting the smaller pool of suitable candidates in St Petersburg from which to make appointments abroad. The repetition of certain aristocratic names, such as Chernyshev and Vorontsov, illustrates this. The great distance was obviously a further factor.

Catherine II's first ambassador, Count Alexander Vorontsov, had been appointed by her despised husband, which was sufficient to make him unacceptable to her. Worse, members of the Vorontsov family had supported Peter as emperor and one, Elizabeth Vorontsova, was Peter's mistress. Catherine forced the ambassador's uncle, Count Mikhail Vorontsov, out of office as chancellor, but left the 21-year-old Vorontsov *en poste*. Soon the ambassador's inexperience became clear and Catherine removed him at the end of 1763. Nevertheless, even during his short mission Alexander Vorontsov made many lasting friendships in London, from which his brother later profited. The count went on to pursue a successful career at the court of Catherine II and in the early years of the nineteenth century, aged over sixty, he became foreign minister to Alexander I.

George III was not pleased when a low-born diplomat replaced the aristocratic Vorontsov. The envoy's untimely death resolved the matter. As London was a much sought-after posting, Prince Ivan Chernyshev had to lobby hard in St Petersburg before being designated ambassador extraordinary in 1767. He already had a very high opinion of himself and his talents and Catherine added to the ambassador's arrogance by instructing him that no other country should take diplomatic precedence over Russia. This was an inbuilt provocation to the French, and Horace Walpole recounted an incident involving undiplomatic pushing that resulted in wigs going askew. The Chernyshevs were extremely rich and the new ambassador ensured that he and his wife displayed ostentatious wealth in their dress and that of their servants. Countess Chernyshev arrived with £40,000 worth of jewellery, plus vast amounts of silver and other possessions that called for forty-three horses to transport and a special dispensation from the British Customs.

In a way reminiscent of Richard Chancellor's marvel at the rich clothing of Ivan IV and his courtiers two centuries before—though the

Chernyshevs naturally dressed in the current European fashion—London society was awestruck by the Russian display, 'beyond any Publick Minister that has ever been here'.[1] In addition to what the Chernyshevs had brought with them, they engaged in an enormous shopping spree while in Britain. In fairness to the ambassador, it should be added that he was conscientious in his work and, for example, visited Russian seamen in Hull and Portsmouth when the Russian navy was heading for the Mediterranean. He also lent his support to British institutions furthering the arts and agricultural innovation.

Alexsei Musin-Pushkin, who had been ambassador for two years before Chernyshev's descent on London, took over again in 1769 and remained for a further ten years. Inevitably he was a less flamboyant personality than Chernyshev, but in many ways superior with his fluency in English and obvious Anglophilia. But, with Anglo-Russian relations under severe strain during the last years of Musin-Pushkin's appointment with the outbreak of the American War of Independence, Catherine did not feel that she could leave putting pressure on the British government in such hands. His successor, Ivan Simolin, took a tougher stance, but his constant bad temper, womanizing and talk of his being a French spy did not make him popular in either St Petersburg or London. One positive result of his posting was that the house he rented, 36 Harley Street, was purchased by the Russian government and became the permanent embassy.[2]

Count Simon Vorontsov, younger brother of Alexander, had been branded her enemy by Catherine II when grand duchess, when most of the Vorontsov family had supported Peter III. For many years the count led an unsatisfactory life of travel and service in the Russian army against the Turks until the empress came to recognize his talents. While he knew relatively little about Britain when he was appointed to London in 1784, Vorontsov was favourably disposed towards the country. A widower with two children, he came to understand Britain better than any of his predecessors and was steadfast in striving to improve and stabilize Anglo-Russian relations, insisting time and time again that Britain and Russia were 'natural allies'. In this he was sorely tested, although he did not make things easy for himself by supporting Charles James Fox and the Whig Opposition against Pitt's government in 1791.

Vorontsov demonstrated a remarkable ability to mobilize British public opinion during the Ochakov crisis by means of his close links with politicians, the press and business interests in the City, where the Russia Company (as the Muscovy Company had become) was based. He did not limit himself to the capital however, and his embassy produced articles for much of the provincial press, urging readers to write to their MPs and protest at government policy.

Vorontsov's successful public relations campaign was a major factor in forcing Pitt to abandon his aggressive policy towards Russia over the Ochakov fortress.

From 1793 the ambassador had to contend with British disquiet over the Second and Third Partitions of Poland, but there were compensations for him in the form of the extension of the commercial agreement in 1793, followed by the convention of mutual opposition to revolutionary France and Russian cooperation with Britain over a naval blockade. The defensive alliance signed in 1795 was a source of great satisfaction to Vorontsov at the end of his ambassadorship under Catherine II. He remained in his post when Paul I became emperor, but was dismissed in 1800 when diplomatic relations were broken off between Britain and Russia, there being no doubt in Paul's mind where the ambassador's sympathies lay. A consolation for Vorontsov was that he was allowed to remain in England, but the following year Paul took strenuously against him, confiscated his estates in Russia and demanded that he return home. Paul's death in March 1801 solved this problem.

After a brief visit to Russia, Simon Vorontsov was back in London as ambassador for Alexander I and remained in his posting until his retirement in 1806. For many years he had lived in Mansfield Street, London, which on his death became Woronzow Road, and remains so today. His country house while ambassador was Cedar Grove on Richmond Green but he chose to spend his retirement in Southampton to be closer to his daughter, and where he was made a freeman of the city. On his death in 1832, the Russian diplomat, admired not only in his professional field but also in scholarly and scientific circles, showed yet another side to his character in his legacy of £500 for the poorhouse of Marylebone.

Vorontsov's daughter Catherine, with the permission of Alexander I, had married in 1808 George Herbert, later the 11th Earl of Pembroke. Her daughter Elizabeth in turn married the 3rd Earl of Clanwilliam, and another daughter, Emma, in turn became Viscountess Vesci. Catherine, Dowager Countess of Pembroke after 1827, remained at the Pembroke stately home, Wilton House in Wiltshire, and at her behest the dilapidated medieval church at Wilton was replaced by a new one in Italianate style, but in reality with strong Byzantine influences as in Orthodox churches. Something of Catherine's Russian origins remained.

Her son, Sidney Herbert, was born in 1810 at her father's rural retreat in Richmond. He went on to become a Member of Parliament and joined Sir Robert Peel's Conservative cabinet in 1845. Herbert was appointed Secretary at War responsible for the financial administration of the army in Lord Aberdeen's government in 1851. When war with Russia in Crimea threatened in 1853, he urged caution. In October he wrote to his wife: 'The public seems to think that there is nothing to do but to declare war against Russia, just when she is yielding the point in dispute.'[3] Inevitably when war broke out in 1854, Herbert's half-Russian parentage exposed him to accusations of a lack of patriotism and he resigned. A few months later he was reappointed in Palmerston's government. Herbert was one of the few people Florence Nightingale respected and it was he who asked her to take charge of a group of female nurses in Crimea.[4]

Mikhail Vorontsov, Simon's son, was sent to Russia by his father at the age of nineteen where he joined the army and was wounded at the battle of Borodino in 1812. At the end of the Napoleonic Wars he became commander of the Russian army of occupation in France and later was ennobled to prince when he became governor general of New Russia and Bessarabia. It was in Odesa in 1823 that he met Alexander Pushkin, the dissident writer who had been exiled there after falling foul of the censor. Pushkin was to work in Vorontsov's chancellery as a foreign ministry clerk. However, the young man embarked on an affair with his employer's wife, Elise. The furious Vorontsov on learning of the affair requested Pushkin's transfer and the writer was duly dismissed from the foreign ministry.

In fact, Mikhail Vorontsov held liberal views, and advocated the emancipation of the serfs and a constitution for Russia. His taste in architecture also showed him in a different light than Pushkin's view of him as boring and pedestrian. The prince commissioned a British architect, Edward Blore, to design a palace for himself at Alupka on the Crimean coast. One side of the palace combines Russian and Moorish elements, while the other side is Scottish baronial Gothic, and the dining room is Tudor.

Mikhail Vorontsov remained on good terms with his nephew Sidney Herbert during the Crimean War and wrote in September 1854 proposing that they meet in Holland. The letter began 'Dear Siddy'.[5] Prince Vorontsov advised Alexander II to accept the Five Peace Points that ended the Crimean War, just before his death in 1856.

British diplomats appointed to Russia in the eighteenth century reacted very differently to their host country from the Russians in Britain. However much they were impressed by Russia's dramatic westernization and greatly increased status as a power, an underlying disdain and attitude of inherent superiority and over-weening pride was never far away. Early in the century, Charles Whitworth, of the tobacco *debâcle*, wrote scathingly of Russia in his *Account of Russia as it was in the Year 1710* (not published until 1754): 'The Government is absolute in the last degree, not bound up by any law or custom, but depending on the breath of the Prince, by which the lives and fortunes of all the subjects are decided.'[6] The envoy sent home accounts of public punishments including that of a counterfeiter who had 'melted Pewter powered [poured] down his throat' and a woman who was buried alive for murdering her husband and who lived in agony for five days.[7]

More than half a century later, George Macartney similarly wrote a book about his time as envoy to Russia. In *An Account of Russia in 1767*, Macartney adopted a condescending moral stance:

> They have not, nor do they affect to have, that abhorrence of vice and dishonesty, which prevails among other nations: in so much, that many persons retain their employments, though notorious for the most infamous frauds and cruel extortions ... The abject court and adulation, which they pay to minions, ministers, and men in power, are intolerably offensive to every mind that feels for freedom and independence: to an Englishman they are particularly disgusting.[8]

A further reproach to the nobility was what to British eyes was its imitation of all things foreign, especially French: 'abandoning the common sense of nature, [they] adopt fashions and customs totally contrary to their climate and troublesome to themselves. Tho' freezing under the 60th degree of northern latitude, they build their houses like the airy palaces of Florence and Sienna.'[9]

Reflecting a very British attitude to physical activity, Macartney upbraided the Russian nobility for their:

> aversion to all corporal activity and manly exercise ... beyond the smooth velocity of the sledge, or the measured paces of a managed horse: they have no passion for the sports of the field; hunting, shooting and fishing ... Avoiding every recreation attended with exertion and fatigue: they prefer the more indolent amusements of chess, cards or billiards, in all which they are usually extraordinarily proficient.[10]

The diplomat's function was naturally to be the representative of his sovereign in the host country, to negotiate treaties and agreements and to report home in dispatches, the more delicate in cipher, the situation in his country of attribution by remaining close to the court and capable of acting to discredit those opposed to his country. Sir Thomas Wych in the early 1740s was too closely associated with the former Empress Anna's Holstein-Gottorp group at the Russian court to provide a balanced picture. Sir Charles Hanbury Williams's links with the heir to the throne and his wife, Peter and Catherine, was believed to be detrimental to British interests and he came to be considered in London as more enthusiastic about putting over the Russian position than furthering his country's interests. Guy Dickens in St Petersburg fell foul of the Secretary of State for the North, the Duke of Newcastle, in 1753 simply for his lack of assiduity in sending dispatches: 'I cannot conceal from you the King's surprise, that at so critical conjuncture, as the present, when letters from almost every court are full of the march of the Russian troops ... you should continue your silence.'[11]

Not only was there little competition for postings to St Petersburg, the problem was constantly one of finding envoys of the necessary calibre prepared to live in Russia. Edward Finch spent only one year in Russia in 1740 before asking for recall, writing in dramatic terms that he would rather be dead in England than alive in Russia. Sir Robert Keith attempted in 1758 to leave less than a year after arriving in Russia. The Secretary of State for the North would not hear of it:

> You know of what importance it is for us to keep forms with the Court of St Petersburg even at this time, and the necessity of having a person of trust and ability on the spot to be ready to treat the moment a favourable opportunity offers, and at this time you could not be removed without disgusting the Empress.[12]

Joseph Yorke summed up the attitude of British diplomats when he was asked to become ambassador to Russia in 1754. He was sufficiently well connected in London to be able to refuse:

> I have neither strength of mind nor *body* for it ... nothing but an order from the King, under good conditions, should force me into a post which could throw me out of the way of everything, where I should get neither honour nor credit, and from whence I might by some sudden revolution mistake the road, and take a trip to Siberia instead of Middlesex.[13]

Yorke believed, 'I am not good for much, but I am really too good for that country.'[14]

Given that the British government had since the mid-seventeenth century been opening the correspondence to and from foreign diplomats in

London, intercepting post in Hanover and attempting more and more professionally to obtain keys to ciphers used by foreign governments, it was only to be expected that similar means were used by the Russian authorities. However, what was particular to British diplomatic activity in St Petersburg was the accepted venality of the Russian court and extensive use of bribery as a means of acquiring information. The Earl of Hyndford found it necessary in the late 1740s to distribute *largesse* even to unimportant persons. In addition the British government authorized him to 'lend' £5,000 to the Russian chancellor, Count Alexsei Bestuzhev-Riumin, with the promise of a further £5,000 when a convention was concluded. Bestuzhev-Riumin was so angry at what he saw as a paltry sum that the poor British ambassador had to explain to London that this was not considered sufficient. The government then advanced 50,000 roubles to the chancellor who promptly used it to execute a mortgage on his new house. Hyndford explained: 'His politik in this is to prevent the suspicion of his having had any part of this money as a present and to show his enemies that he is very poor, which he really is, and that the Empress may relieve him of this debt.'[15] The wily greedy chancellor was later brazenly demanding further sums of money in 1756 when Hanbury Williams was ambassador. Bestuzhev-Riumin received £10,000 and made it clear that he felt he was entitled to an annual pension of £2,500 from the British government. At the same time Hanbury Williams 'loaned' £10,000 to the Grand Duchess Catherine on the understanding that it would be used 'for the King's service'.[16] In fairness to Catherine, it should be pointed out that she offered to repay the 'loan' when she became empress and the British government declined to accept it.

Sir George Macartney wrote that because of 'the little disgrace of successful villainy and corruption in the highest ranks of people, it is astonishing that any integrity at all should be found among the commonalty'.[17] He held that during his mission to Russia he had 'spent above a thousand pounds of my own money for secret service. This I never mentioned before, nor do I intend to speak of it to the office, though, upon my honour, it is true.'[18] Twenty years later Sir James Harris claimed that no person in his household was too insignificant to escape the temptation of a bribe from his enemies, and that 'when he left his secretary writing, he used to lock him up, not from mistrust of his honesty, but of his leaving the door of the room open'.[19]

Apart from the cost of bribing Russian officials, some of which was not reimbursed by London, there was almost always a financial burden incurred by a posting to St Petersburg. Lord Tyrawley claimed in 1744 that he had paid almost £2,000 to get to Russia and had only the hope of receiving half the sum that he was owed. George Macartney gave as his reason for seeking to be sent to Spain his need to pay off debts built up in Russia.

The Russian climate was another reason that made St Petersburg an undesirable posting. Charles Whitworth thought that the weather in St Petersburg was the worst that he had ever encountered. Hyndford wrote in 1747, 'I have now the spleen for the first time; I long more than ever to change my situation to some warmer climate.'[20] Not only was the Russian weather hard to bear, it was blamed by some British diplomats for their difficulty in marrying before going there. 'Who would marry a man … going to Petersburg?' wailed Sir Cyril Wyche, as would James Harris nearly thirty years later.

Unfairly there was a frequent gripe about having to speak German or French in St Petersburg, more a reflection of British linguistic inadequacy than a justified complaint. The first Charles Whitworth spoke only English, and his secretary read a translation in French and Russian when he delivered a harangue to Peter I about the Matveev incident. Edward Finch bemoaned his lack of German, the foreign language spoken at the Russian court in the first half of the century. The Russian chancellery caused deliberate embarrassment from time to time by using German in documents for the British embassy. By the mid-century German had been replaced by French.

Antoine Pecquet in his diplomatic manual, *Discours sur l'art de négocier*, had warned that women posed a greater danger to diplomats abroad than wine.[21] The suave young George Macartney was recalled to London in 1766, officially because of diplomatic blunders he committed, but another cause advanced was that Catherine II asked for his removal on the grounds of his 'English impertinence', having made one of the empress's ladies-in-waiting pregnant. It appears that the woman in question was duly banished to a convent. The source of this information is Giacomo Casanova, who at that time was pursuing his own romantic liaisons in St Petersburg and was no doubt well placed to know about such matters.[22] When a year later Macartney was reappointed he withdrew. He had by now married Lady Jane Stuart, daughter of the Earl of Bute and Lady Mary Wortley Montagu. The reason given was that Lady Mary refused to allow her daughter to live in Russia, but it is possible she had other reasons for her objection.

Charles Whitworth, a second ambassador of that name, at the end of the century found his position weakened as a result of his affair with Olga

Zherebtsova, the sister of Prince Zubov, an influential courtier in the reign of Paul I: 'Whitworth was warned by [Count Feodor] Rostopchin [the chancellor] of the emperor's displeasure; and indeed at court ... the emperor affected not to speak to him.'[23] There is evidence that undeterred, Whitworth carried on, or attempted to carry on, another affair with Countess Anna Tolstoya, whose husband was an aide to the heir to the throne, the Grand Duke Alexander. Whether the ambassador's pursuit of the countess was for personal or political reasons, or both, is not known.

Despite its westernization and integration into the European state system, Russia was still believed to demonstrate unacceptable behaviour in diplomacy. The death of the British diplomat Joseph Ewart, who had played an important role in hardening the British government's position against Russia in the Ochakov crisis, was attributed to poison administered by a Russian agent.[24]

6

THE LONG EIGHTEENTH CENTURY

WIDER RELATIONS

In addition to the presence of a permanent Russian embassy in London and a British one in St Petersburg, the mutual enlightenment that took place between Britain and Russia in the eighteenth century owed much to people outside the official diplomatic world.

During the early years of the eighteenth century there were few Russians outside embassy staff, its chaplain and interpreters in Britain. The Orthodox church, housed in rented rooms in the Strand, formed the centre of Russian cultural activities. Despite the penury of the church successive priests were prepared not only to officiate but also to act as cultural ambassadors. An outstanding example was Jacob Smirnov, who became chaplain and was involved in the pamphleteering of 1791. He was an accomplished translator and writer, best known for his translation of Pleshcheyev's *Survey of the Russian Empire, According to Its Newly Regulated State.*

The main reason for Russians coming to Britain in the early years of the eighteenth century was the quest for knowledge, intellectual and practical, of which Peter I was the innovator. The first Russian seamen and boat builders arrived from the Moscow School of Mathematics and Navigation. Nobles and commoners, about fifty at any one time, were dispatched at government expense. But the funding was insufficient and many soon found themselves in debt. The despair of many was expressed in heavy drinking and dissolute, unruly behaviour. The scions of noble families fared better financially but their lack of enthusiasm for anything to do with the sea and idleness made many unpopular with their hosts.

Members of the newly founded Russian Academy of Sciences visited Oxford University in the 1720s and established links that they maintained on their return home. The Astronomer Royal and professor at Oxford, James Bradley, attracted three Russian students to his lectures and, given his contribution to modern observational astronomy, it was not surprising that Bradley was made an honorary member of the Russian Academy of Sciences.

Catherine II, three years after becoming empress, instructed the procurator of the Holy Synod to select ten outstanding religious students to study at the universities of Oxford and Cambridge. With her German Lutheran origins, the empress was determined to bring the intellectual level of Orthodox clergy up to the standards of Protestantism in western Europe. Six students arrived and were dispersed among various Oxford colleges. The university was well known at the time for the high life led by students and fellows and the Russians duly succumbed to the temptations. Three returned home in ill health: the three who remained were threatened with the debtors' prison and the Russian government was obliged to pay their creditors and fares home.

Ivan Cherkasov spent fourteen years in England and completed his degree at Cambridge. Alexander Chesmensky, illegitimate son of Count Alexsei Orlov, one of the five famous brothers and victor at Chesme, studied for some months in Cambridge, but both Cambridge and Oxford were becoming less attractive from a Russian point of view. Glasgow and increasingly Edinburgh replaced the ancient English universities for the Russians.

It was due to the presence at the Kronstadt Naval Cadet Corps of John Robison, a distinguished Scottish mathematician, that when he returned home in 1774 he brought with him three Russian cadets who matriculated at Edinburgh University. They were joined a year later by the son of Princess Catherine Dashkova, younger sister of the two ambassador Vorontsov brothers and married to a Guards officer. The princess was already a well-known figure in St Petersburg. Through her uncle, the chancellor Mikhail Vorontsov, she had come to be on good terms with the Grand Duchess Catherine. The future empress recognized the intelligence and ambition of the young Princess Vorontsova, whose extensive connections with the governmental elite made her an excellent source of information, plus the fact that her sister, Elizabeth, was mistress of Catherine's husband. Catherine Dashkova was resolutely on the side of the grand duchess and claimed (incorrectly) to have played a major role in the *coup d'état* that ended the reign of Peter III. Catherine II had no desire to share the glory of her achievement with anyone except the Orlov brothers. The women's friendship came to an abrupt end.

Excluded from the court during the early years of Catherine II's reign, the princess embarked on her first visit to western Europe in 1770, but it was nine years later that she enrolled her son Paul at Edinburgh University (to avoid the usual student pitfalls of Oxford and Cambridge). Not content with this, she decided to live with her son in the New Town, away from the university. This redoubtable mother kept the poor young man on a short leash: 'By way of amusement and exercise for my son I gave a dance every week; I also made him go to a riding school, and an excellent fencing master ... gave him lessons every other day.'[1] Whether by inclination or force, Paul Dashkov was a conscientious student and 'attends his classes with great assiduity and has perfectly melted away all Russian Boorishness in French courtesy'.[2] The flamboyant Dashkova's departure from Edinburgh was not only a social loss but she had also become respected by the academic fraternity. Once home she was appointed Director of the Academy of Sciences, marking the end of her estrangement from Catherine II.

The empress's personal physician, Dr John Rogerson, had studied at Edinburgh University, whose medical school had a well-deserved reputation for excellence. It followed that the most significant number of Russians studied at Edinburgh. The choice of students was fortunate, including one who wrote a doctorate on smallpox inoculation, a subject of great interest to Catherine II.

The early 1760s marked an influx of Russians to study British agricultural methods, which were being revolutionized at that time. The two chaplains of the Russian church were champions of British husbandry and were on close terms with the farmer John Young, who wrote extensively on agriculture. The empress Catherine was persuaded to send seven students to England in 1779 to study variously in Surrey, Kent, Suffolk and Leicestershire. Others followed a few years later, but the problem on their return to Russia was that they were too thinly scattered to have any noticeable impact.

Russians on the Grand Tour were understandably in general less serious and more colourful than their compatriots studying in Britain. The enlightenment most sought after was cultural and social. As they were necessarily wealthy and usually aristocratic, reflecting the Russian penchant for all that was British, they were welcomed.

Prince Grigory Orlov, who had been Catherine II's lover and had figured large in the murder of Peter III, created great interest. 'Orlow the Great, or rather the Big is here ... He dances gigantic dances, and makes gigantic love; but no conquests yet', commented Horace Mann.[3] What impressed London society most were the fabulous diamonds Orlov wore. News of these soon reached the criminal class and a practised pickpocket removed diamonds and gold (worth between £10,000 and £40,000) from the prince as he left Covent Garden one evening. Despite his bulk, Orlov managed to retrieve his valuables. His illegitimate son by Catherine II, Count Alexsei Bobrinsky, was less endowed with jewellery but was a flamboyant playboy, more adept at running up debts and chasing women than anything else, and Simon Vorontsov was glad to receive money to dispatch the young man back home to his estate in Russia.

On her visits to Britain preceding her son's studying at Edinburgh University, Catherine Dashkova had already established her reputation as the most striking female Grand Tourist, and she left an account of her first visit to Britain in her memoirs, later dictated to two Englishwomen. En route for Bath and Portsmouth, among the stately homes where she stopped was Wilton in Wiltshire where she met Lord Pembroke, nearly forty years before her family married into the Herbert family. Horace Walpole's Gothick mansion at Strawberry Hill in Surrey was particularly popular with Russian tourists. Often it was the gardens that impressed more than the interiors. These were studied not only for the pleasure they gave but also as models for gardens the Russians wanted to recreate at home.

On her second visit to Britain, Princess Dashkova ventured further afield to Wales and Ireland and on her return to London was received by George III and Queen Charlotte. However, her sojourn back in the capital took a dramatic turn. The chapel of the Sardinian ambassador was ransacked in June 1780 in what came to be known as the Gordon Riots. The group of men responsible included a Russian officer, Alexander Rontsov, who turned out to be Princess Dashkova's half-brother, the illegitimate son of her father by his English mistress. It was pure coincidence that Dashkova had just arrived in London, but she was tainted by association with the incident that also embarrassed the entire Vorontsov family and the Russian government.

Prince Alexander Kurakin, a descendant of the Russian ambassador early in the century, led a party of friends who, like Dashkova, wanted to see more than was found on the usual circuit of London, Greenwich, Windsor, Oxford and Bath. They visited Leeds, Birmingham, Hull (from where much-appreciated beer was shipped to Russia as ballast) and other rapidly industrializing towns. Leaving for home, Kurakin summed up what had impressed him:

> The English have everything to make them happy and enviable. They are not subjected to the arbitrary will and caprices of one person; they only obey what the law demands ... Their possessions cannot be touched ... They do not fear either the wrath of the sovereign or the hate of ministers or courtesans. They only have to live each according to his pleasure or fantasy.[4]

The British living in Russia in the eighteenth century were far more numerous than the Russians in Britain. The largest group was made up of members of the Russia Company, known after 1723 as the British Factory when the centre of operations was transferred to St Petersburg from Moscow and Arkhangelsk. The Anglo-Russian commercial agreements of 1734 and 1766, conferring most-favoured nation status on British merchants, consolidated British predominance in the new capital. The merchants' headquarters and warehouses dominated the commercial area on the south bank of the Neva, which came to be known as the English Line, Quay or Embankment. (In the Soviet period it was renamed the Embankment of the Red Fleet, but today it is again the English Embankment.)

From about 200 British subjects in the 1720s, the number rose to 1,500 by the end of the century. To begin with men were usually alone, but as time went on more families became residents. However from 1754 the pivot of British community life was the English church. The British Factory bought the dilapidated mansion of Count Boris Sheremetev on the English Line and renovated it as a place of worship. A few years later a subscription library was set up in rooms in the church. Equally in keeping with maintaining a British style of life was the creation of the English Club with a dining room, reading room, billiards and card tables. Despite its name, the club counted members of various nationalities and by the early years of the nineteenth century was English in name only.

British doctors had from the beginning of the Romanov dynasty been much appreciated. Peter I's personal physician was a Scot, Robert Erskine, who travelled with the tsar and on whose death was a wealthy landowner in Russia. But the most famous was John Rogerson, court physician to Catherine II from 1769. The young Scot rapidly established a warm relationship with the empress. She discussed much more than medical matters with Rogerson and he was duly raised to the rank of state counsellor with a generous salary attached. It was said that he passed on, at a price, information to the British ambassador, Sir James Harris. Princess Dashkova held that the doctor saved her son's life, but others were more sceptical and had reservations about his predilection for laxatives and bloodletting. Even though the empress seems to have shared such views, remarking to Potemkin, 'I'm afraid that anybody who gets into Rogerson's hands is already dead', Rogerson was in attendance when Catherine died in November 1796 and was rewarded in her will with an estate near Minsk with 1,500 serfs.[5] Nevertheless, he spent the last seven years of his life back home in Scotland.

Catherine II, who knew only too well the dangers of smallpox and had witnessed its disfiguring effect on her husband, was prepared to submit herself to vaccination against the disease pioneered by Edward Jenner. She looked to Britain, where smallpox inoculation was most advanced and Dr Thomas Dimsdale, who had published a treatise on the subject, was enjoined to come to St Petersburg in 1768 to vaccinate the empress and her son. George III worried about the diplomatic implications if things went wrong. They did not and the doctor was soon invested as a baron of the Russian empire, plus a generous pension.

Dimsdale's third wife, Elizabeth, came to be on social terms with Catherine when the doctor returned in 1781 to inoculate the empress's grandchildren, and they were provided with luxurious accommodation at Tsarkoe Selo, Catherine's favourite residence. Elizabeth Dimsdale was relieved that so much was familiar: 'I was much pleased to find that there was a large English Bed with Crimson Silk Furniture and there was an English Housekeeper, she was an exceeding good plain cook … and one of the Empress's Footmen spake English extremely well.'[6] The baroness also wrote of her admiration for the spectacular Amber Room at Tsarskoe Selo, given by Frederick William I of Prussia to Peter the Great and installed at the Russian palace by the Empress Elizabeth.[7] She duly noted the impressive collections of paintings at the Hermitage, which a few years earlier had been expanded by the purchase of the Walpole Collection of Houghton Hall from the impoverished British family. But seduced as she was by her life as a guest of Catherine II, the baroness was shocked by what she saw outside the confines of St Petersburg society: 'The Peasants, that is to say, the greater part of the Subjects, are in an abject state of Slavery, and are reckoned the Property of the Nobles, and considerable People to whom they belong, as much as their Horses or Dogs.'[8]

Elizabeth Dimsdale was not the first Englishwoman to put pen to paper with Russian recollections. From a humbler position as governess to the family of a rich British merchant in the 1730s, Elizabeth Justice had met the Empress Anna in 1733 who impressed her as 'tall and very lusty'.[9]

However, Russian women as a whole displeased her: 'The Ladies are, or can be, just what you please. For, only say, what Complexion you like, and they will instantly put it on; being well versed in Painting.'[10]

Jane Rondeau, wife of the British minister in St Petersburg at the same time, did not publish her *Letters from a Lady, Who Resided Some Years in Russia, to Her Friend in England* until much later in her life in 1775.[11] She had permanent access to court circles where she was well liked. However Rondeau was reluctant to take part in a favourite sport of Russians, from the empress downwards, of sliding down an ice-covered chute stretching from the top of a house to the courtyard below: 'I was terrified out of my wits for fear of being obliged to go down this shocking place, for I had not only the dread of breaking my neck but of being exposed to indecency too frightful to think of without horror.'[12] On another occasion Mrs Rondeau refused to watch the christening of some Tatar women on the grounds that 'they should have had some other robe than that of righteousness'.[13]

From a Russian point of view, as recognized by Peter the Great, it was most important that its sailors and shipbuilders learned their skills in Britain and then applied themselves to disseminating their knowledge at home; but with the decline in the Russian navy after his death, their numbers decreased. Catherine II was determined to upgrade the fleet to carry out her expansionist foreign policy and in 1769 recruited, and promoted to rear-admiral, John Elphinstone, who went on to be one of the heroes of the battle of Chesme. Samuel Greig was another Scot who joined the Russian navy in the 1760s and rose to brigadier by the time of Chesme. His role in the battle was crucial and was acknowledged by the nominal commander, Count Alexsei Orlov. Greig's career flourished and he too became a rear-admiral, dying in service in the war against Sweden in 1788.

Another foreigner who was an officer in the Russian fleet at Liman was Samuel Bentham, younger brother of Jeremy. Samuel had trained as a shipwright in the British royal dockyards but was a polymath with considerable entrepreneurial skill as well. Finding employment at home hard to come by, Bentham was attracted to the idea of working in Russia. He arrived in St Petersburg in 1780 and soon afterwards met Samuel Greig, who told him that the Russians were building warships on the Black Sea. The young man proved a shrewd networker and through Sir James Harris, the ambassador, and the empress's secretary, Count Alexander Bezborodko, he met Potemkin and was awarded a commission in the Russian army, even though it was in the Russian navy that he was eventually to demonstrate his talent. Bentham worked wonders adapting small craft into highly effective fighting ships and became a close companion of Potemkin in the prince's industrial enterprises.

His brother Jeremy visited him at Potemkin's estate, Krichev, in 1785 having recruited Britons (many dubious characters) to work on the prince's numerous projects. The elder Bentham's hope was that this would be a source of income to enable him to work on his treatise on civil law. He bombarded Potemkin with his philosophical ideas but proved a poor supervisor of the British recruits. Jeremy left for home in 1787, while his brother continued to serve the prince. In the war against Turkey that broke out in 1788, Samuel Bentham's role was crucial:

> Even more important than his presence and his courageous command of the division of bomb ketches and fireships in the battles of June 1788 was the backroom activity which he directed at Kherson during the previous autumn and winter; ... without it the Russians might not have achieved in 1788 the mastery of the Liman which enabled them to besiege and capture Ochakov before the end of the year.[14]

It was this capture which had led to the crisis of 1791 that pitted Britain against Russia.

The Anglo-Russian naval connection that had brought Samuel Bentham to Russia dated back to the time of Peter I: the arrival of British architects and gardeners was something quite new in the reign of Catherine II. The empress declared that she would not know how to live in a place where she could neither build nor plant. The baroque architecture of the previous reign was discarded in favour of neoclassicism, and for this Catherine needed architects. A young Londoner arrived in Russia in 1779 with a book on Roman baths to his credit but little more. Nevertheless, Charles Cameron was able to persuade the empress to put him in charge of redesigning Tsarskoe Selo and he immediately recruited Scotsmen to supplement Russian labourers in transforming the palace. His latter-day Roman baths (highly popular in Russia) covered by a long colonnaded gallery (known since as the Cameron Gallery) delighted Catherine. The southern wing became a temple of classicism, while Cameron adopted Chinese, French and Arab styles for other apartments. A later commission enabled him to design a stunning Palladian villa for the Grand Duke Paul at Pavlovsk.

Catherine II's passion for gardens, above all English gardens, provided the opportunity for numerous British gardeners to seek their fortunes in Russia. The most famous was William Gould who designed the winter garden at the Taurida Palace in St Petersburg that the empress had built for Potemkin. The Scot James Meader was in charge of plans for a wooded area above the palace of Peterhof:

> The spot allotted for me is a park through great part thereof is full of fine Trees. Here are fine pieces of Water which want but little help to make them elegant … I am under no restraint either to extent of land or water; the bounds are only limited by the Gulf of Finland.[15]

St Petersburg soon after its foundation had become a tourist destination and inevitably attracted the more adventurous spirits from Britain. Therefore it is not surprising to find the name of Sir Francis Dashwood, of Hell Fire Club fame, who arrived in Russia in the suite of Lord Forbes, charged with negotiating the commercial agreement in 1733. After an initially favourable first impression, Dashwood was scathing about many of the buildings in the new capital: 'They are building two monstrous great wings … and it is called the Winter Palace, it will be very large when finished, but not a piece of much Architecture.'[16] Seven years later two young aristocrats on the northern Grand Tour, Charles Cottrell and Robert Carteret, later Lord Granville, were in St Petersburg, but Cottrell was singularly unimpressed by what he saw outside the capital: 'The Country about St Petersburg has full as wild and desert a look as any in the Indies … you would think God when he created the rest of the world for the use of Mankind had created this for an inaccessible retreat for all sorts of wild beasts.'[17]

Given the sudden increase in interest in Russia that came with the arrival of Catherine II on the Russian throne, British visitors were more numerous. Some kept diaries intended for publication, while others made a stir that caused others to write about them. One of the early travel writers was Sir Nathaniel Wraxall, who set out for Russia with a book in mind. Wraxall was the first Englishman to commit to print a description of Catherine II: 'Though she is now become rather corpulent, there is a dignity, tempered with graciousness, in her deportment which strikingly impresses.'[18] The empress's sexual appetite that shocked so many Englishmen, Wraxall was told, was condoned:

> Even in the weaknesses of her conduct, the empress is at least decorous: compared with her predecessor Elizabeth, she may be termed modest. It is true that General Potemkin has openly succeeded to the place of personal favourite … but in Russia, these violations of female chastity excite little animadversion, and no surprise … The amours of Catherine, are

veiled under the guise of passion, and are by no means destitute of intellectual enjoyments.[19]

There was an element of voyeurism in the frequent British tourists' desire to visit Russian bathhouses. Wraxall defended his presence at 'this exhibition, a sight rather calculated to excite disgust than desire, and to which only curiosity could ever have carried me. The greater part of the women were the most hideous figures that I ever beheld.'[20] Even Elizabeth Dimsdale was tempted to take a look, 'but the heat and effluvia soon satisfied my curiosity'.[21]

If British visitors claimed to be scandalized by Russian behaviour, the Russians had every reason to be shocked by the comportment of a British woman who descended on St Petersburg in 1777. Elizabeth Chudleigh, Duchess of Kingston and Countess of Bristol, both titles disputable, was infamous in London as a bigamist, adulteress and lascivious woman who had featured frequently in the celebrity magazines of the mid-eighteenth century. Her outrageous exhibitionism was the mildest of her characteristics. The House of Lords found her guilty of bigamy but a convenient death enabled her to avoid branding. This amazing woman acquired a great fortune by deception from her first husband and stole liberally from the home of her second. In this way she was able to equip a large yacht with every luxury and set sail to conquer fresh pastures in Russia. As she numbered a former Russian ambassador to London among her admirers, the duchess was presented to Catherine and Potemkin. The dissolute goings-on on the yacht disgusted the respectable British community in the capital, but the empress provided the visitor with a house to which Russian high society was pleased to be invited. The duchess acquired a Russian lover and came to be on friendly terms with Potemkin, who bought from her, or was given, old master paintings and antiques.

After a storm destroyed her yacht the duchess was obliged to leave Russia by land, only to turn up again two years later on the basis of a just-about-polite invitation from the empress. Money was no problem, and the shameless woman installed herself in a mansion which she decorated in the most lavish manner. As though this was not enough, Elizabeth bought several estates in Livonia.

Hot on the heels of the Duchess of Kingston another scandalous Englishwoman (though not dishonest) arrived. Lady Elizabeth Berkeley, the estranged wife of the Earl of Craven, set out for Russia with a young lover in 1786. In St Petersburg she was invited on several occasions to dine with Potemkin at his Taurida Palace, but it was Crimea that most impressed her. She was carried away by her 'beautiful dream' of establishing 'a colony of honest and industrious people of my country' and acquiring two estates herself.[22] Potemkin would not be drawn into discussion of these outlandish schemes. In her book, *Journey through the Crimea to Constantinople*, Elizabeth Craven had some harsh words to say about the young male British aristocrats and *nouveau riche* on the northern Grand Tour, but none are recorded as behaving as imprudently as she and the Duchess of Kingston.

There was less scope for wild behaviour among those who visited Russia for work reasons. William Richardson, yet another Scot, was employed by the British ambassador, Lord Cathcart, as tutor to his sons from 1768 to 1772. Twelve years later Richardson published in letter form his *Anecdotes of the Russian Empire*, part of which describes ceremonies he attended in St Petersburg and part a highly critical analysis of Russian society. He felt he was obstructed: 'They entertain suspicions of your design ... or that you are carrying on treasonable correspondence; or, still more atrocious, that your purpose is to publish a book ... How unlike England!'[23] One letter is entitled 'The Slavery of the Russian Peasants', another 'National Character of the Russians'. Serfdom is soundly condemned:

> Exposed to corporal punishment, and put on the footing of irrational animals, how can they possess that spirit and elevation of sentiment which distinguish the natives of a free state? Treated with so much inhumanity, how can they be humane? I am confident that most of the defects which appear in their national character, are in consequence of the despotism of the Russian government.[24]

The prison reformer John Howard visited Russia in 1781 and 1789 as part of his study of prisons and hospitals in various countries. During his first stay he gave an account of what he witnessed in the Peter and Paul Fortress in St Petersburg:

> The axe and the block—the machine (now out of use) for breaking the arms and legs—the instrument for slitting or lacerating the nostrils ... the *knoot* [knout] whip—and another called the *cat* ... The *knoot* whip is fixed to a long handle a foot long ... and capable of being changed by the executioner, when too much softened by the blood of the criminal ... I saw two criminals, a man and a woman, suffer the punishment of the *knoot* ... The woman was taken first; and after being roughly stripped to the waist, her hands and feet were bound with cords to a post ... Every stroke seemed

> to penetrate deep into her flesh… The woman received twenty-five, and the man sixty.[25]

Howard wrote harrowing descriptions of conditions in British prisons but he and other Englishmen considered the knout a far worse, and an unacceptably cruel, punishment. On the other hand, he was favourably impressed by the educational Smolny Institute for Young Noblewomen, founded by Catherine II.

When Howard returned to Russia eight years later his focus was on hospitals and lazarettos. Those in Moscow he found squalid and inadequate but in the south of Russia, particularly in the Kherson and Nikolaev (Mykolaiv) regions, they were even worse. The reformer had decreed that there should be no pomp surrounding his funeral and no memorials constructed, but when he died of typhus a year later at Kherson, a stone pyramid, later a cenotaph, was erected by Alexander I to mark the Englishman's burial place. This became a place of pilgrimage for later British travellers.

A Cambridge academic, the Archdeacon William Coxe, dedicated his *Account of the Prisons and Hospitals in Russia, Sweden and Denmark*, published in 1781, to John Howard. Coxe arrived in Russia for the same reason as William Richardson, a tutor to the aristocracy. In Coxe's case his youthful charge was George, Lord Herbert, heir to the Earl of Pembroke (and future husband of Catherine Vorontsova, daughter of the Russian ambassador). Although Coxe only spent six months in Russia he made good use of his time in garnering material for a book. Catherine II granted him an audience and later answered written questions. However the ambassador, Sir James Harris, bombarded for information by Coxe, found him tiresome. The book, *Travels into Poland, Russia, Sweden, and Denmark*, was published in 1784 and a copy presented to the empress, as this was clearly not another British broadside against Russia and Russians. Coxe returned to Russia in 1784, this time as tutor to Samuel Whitbread, son of the brewery founder, to gain information for a further volume. For the following twenty years he amplified from many sources and rewrote his original work. The final product, four volumes, was justly an enormous publishing success in Britain and translated into various languages. Coxe was optimistic in his assessment of material and social progress in Russia, lauding Peter I's and Catherine II's reforms. However, ending his chapter on 'The State of Civilization' he wrote:

> It cannot at the same time be supposed that national manners should suddenly be changed … it may be perceived, that, though they are proceed-

ing towards civilization, they are still far removed from that state; that a general improvement cannot take place while the greater part continue in absolute vassalage; nor can any effectual change be introduced in the national manners, until the people enjoy a full security in their persons and property.[26]

7

THE WARS OF THE FRENCH REVOLUTION AND NAPOLEON, PART I

1793–1807

By the 1790s the idea of Russia as a 'natural ally', dominant in Britain for more than a generation, had become less popular. Armed Neutrality, Ochakov (Ochakiv) and the Partitions of Poland undermined the naively confident assumptions of the 1760s and 1770s. And to Russia, Britain was beginning to appear unwilling, even unable, to provide the support she required. An Anglo-Russian alliance, even if it could be obtained, would be less useful to Russia than one with a major continental state such as Austria or Prussia. However, the full development of these changing attitudes on both sides was delayed by the wars against revolutionary France and then Napoleon, which were to dominate the history of most European countries for more than two decades.

The breakdown of the Old Order in France was watched with fascinated horror or approval in Britain, but with little apprehension of the challenge it would pose to society and traditional forms of government throughout Europe. William Pitt had no desire to meddle in the internal affairs of France; he needed a period of peace and stability to reap the benefits of his fiscal reforms.

French aristocratic émigrés advocated and sought to organize armed intervention in France from across the north-eastern frontier in the Austrian Netherlands and the Southern Netherlands.[1] It was in their name that the Austrian emperor, Leopold II (brother of Marie Antoinette), and King Frederick William II of Prussia issued the Pillnitz Declaration in August 1791, ostensibly expressing concern at the plight of the French royal family after their unsuccessful 'flight to Varennes'. The tone of the declaration was interpreted as threatening in Paris, by a government weak from internal strife and fearful of an attack from the Rhineland, as well as the Austrian Netherlands. From a small power base in the autumn of 1791, the Girondins, revolutionaries originating in Bordeaux, sought to attack Austria in the Southern Netherlands with a pre-emptive strike. By the following spring they were in control. France declared war on Austria in April 1792.

The conflict began slowly and unevenly. The Girondins had mistakenly believed that Prussia's old hatred of Austria would bring her into the war on the French side, but Frederick William was more intent on reversing the course of events in France than maintaining old enmities. For this was the time of hopes by both Austria and Prussia of a slice of the Polish cake. In 1792 Prussia entered the war alongside Austria. The French army was severely weakened by mass emigration of its officers and the indiscipline of its troops: it suffered several humiliating defeats in its attempt to penetrate the Austrian Netherlands. Worse, in July a Prussian army under the Duke of Brunswick was marching on Paris; but the duke was taking his time and his advance was halted in September at Valmy by a newly disciplined French force. The encounter was desultory and militarily inconclusive but it nevertheless marked a turning point.

The revolutionary levies had stemmed the legendary Prussian brigades; the ideals of revolution were now to be carried abroad. In November 1792, with the defeat of the Austrian army at Jemappes, the revolutionary columns poured into the Southern Netherlands and Antwerp fell—a blow to Britain, who attached great importance to the freedom of shipping by having the southern North Sea Ports in friendly hands. The Dutch Republic to the north was menaced and the opening of the river Scheldt to the French could only aggravate British fears. An invigorated France was declaiming that her 'natural frontiers' stretched to the Rhine, that is, encompassing the Austrian Netherlands and the southern part of the Dutch Republic.

Catherine II, with her empire a long way from any expansionist danger, felt secure. She took what measures she could to keep the revolution out of Russia by expelling French citizens, but ignored all pleas to provide active support for the war against France. The empress refused to be diverted from her preoccupation with the Ottoman empire and Poland. The distraction of the Second Partition of Poland provided the French with the breathing space they needed: 'The price for the survival of the French Revolution was, in a very real sense, the destruction of the Polish state.'[2]

The British government watched the bloody course of events in France—the September massacres and the execution of Louis XVI and Marie Antoinette in January 1793—with dismay. To the last, Pitt strove to avoid war. But he had underestimated the fanaticism of the Jacobins, who has seized the reins from the Girondins. They were flushed with victory abroad and elated by the carnage of foes at home. On 1 February 1793 the new republic declared war on Britain and the Dutch Republic. There was a widespread and confident belief in Britain that the war would be short, the revolutionary armies crushed, and that Britain would not need to be one of the principal participants: Pitt still held that the role of Britain would be that of paymaster. By the end of August 1793, Britain had agreed to finance Austria, Prussia, Sardinia, Hesse-Cassel, Spain and Naples—the First Coalition. The turmoil in France, and the seemingly overwhelming forces at the disposal of the coalition, presaged an easy task for the allies. However, the coalition's early victories were dissipated by their dilatory behaviour and the French moved on to the offensive.

Pitt, like his father, believed that Britain's true interests lay outside Europe and that the war provided the opportunity to plunder colonies from France and to cripple French commerce. Small gains were made in the Caribbean and the Cape of Good Hope secured. At the same time Britain possessed certain spheres of interest in the Austrian Netherlands, the Baltic and the Mediterranean, which made it increasingly clear that her war aims had to be expanded. But only a land power, or powers, could defeat France. British support for Austria was crucial but Austria had demonstrated only a half-hearted defence of the Netherlands in 1793 and had been forced back across the Rhine by the end of the year. A British expeditionary force under the Duke of York, George III's second son, was dispatched to the Netherlands in 1794 to assist the Austrians and the Prussians. It was swept back after the retirement of its allies and evacuated.

In April 1795 Prussia made peace with France. She switched her troops from the Rhine into Poland and Bohemia, to which the Austrians reacted by keeping 60,000 men on their northern frontier. Other German states followed the Prussian example. The defeated Austrian Netherlands became the Batavian Republic, allied to France, and Spain deserted the coalition. The following year the young Napoleon Bonaparte won stunning victories at incredible speed in Italy against the Austrians, destroying that country's former primacy in the peninsula.

In early 1796 the previously blinkered Catherine II became seriously concerned at the extent of French military successes. Only then did she send a token squadron to reinforce Britain's North Sea fleet. The dispatch of 60,000 men ordered by the empress in the autumn lifted allied morale, but she died in November.

Paul I, son of Catherine the Great, had waited a long time to succeed the mother he had hated since he was a boy and who had treated him with unconcealed disdain and increasing aversion. It is most probable that his father was Sergei Saltykov, and not his purported one, Peter III. Strangely, though, Paul strongly resembled the ugly former emperor and shared many of his repellent habits. Though not clinically insane, it has been claimed that he suffered from an obsessive-compulsive disorder.[3] Paul had rightly feared that his mother would disinherit him and name his son Alexander as heir.

Once emperor, Paul was determined to instigate a whole raft of reforms in Russia and, as might be expected, one of his first acts was to reverse Catherine's foreign policy. William Pitt wrote to the Secretary of State for War and the Colonies, Henry Dundas, on learning of the empress's death: 'I am afraid much good is not in any case to be expected from the new Emperor. It is difficult to say whether one ought to regret the most that she had not died sooner or lived longer.'[4]

Paul recalled all Russian forces outside the country and cancelled the recruitment order made earlier in the autumn. The French Revolution was obviously repugnant to him and he detested the brutal assault on the Old Order in Europe it had made, particularly on the institution of monarchy. However, legitimacy mattered less to him than good order and he chose to believe that Bonaparte would restore this. Hence he refused to come to Austria's aid. Rather, he backed the preliminary peace signed at Leoben between France and Austria and tried to mediate a more permanent agreement. France was in no mood to countenance such interference and Bonaparte annexed the Southern Netherlands and imposed recognition of France's predominant position in northern Italy at Austria's expense in the Treaty of Campo Formio in October 1797. The First Coalition was at an end.

The coalition had failed because there was no overall agreement as to aims and strategy among its members. Few countries had taken the French threat seriously and had not appreciated the important changes in warfare that 'the nation in arms' had created. With Austria and Prussia looking nervously over their shoulders at what Russia was doing in Poland and with Britain more interested in colonial warfare, it was doomed to collapse.

Britain remained at war with France during 1797. In October 1796 a financial crisis occurred in London with the banks suspending cash payments; the British government felt bitter that its allies had accepted subsidies without fulfilling their obligations. Admiral Jervis's victory over the Spanish fleet at Cape St Vincent in early 1797 brightened a gloomy winter, but then mutinies at Spithead and the Nore paralyzed the fleet. Even though mastery at sea seemed to guarantee that Britain would not have to face a direct attack from France, Ireland remained a target for Bonaparte. Lord Malmesbury, the former James Harris, was sent on an unsuccessful mission to Paris in an attempt to negotiate a peace settlement. British relations with Prussia were strained as a consequence of that country's desertion of the First Coalition and they had soured with Austria because of Campo Formio and Austria's defaulting on Imperial loans raised in London. Russia was needed as a British ally if France was to be defeated.

However, Paul was preoccupied throughout 1797 with his social and administrative reforms and believed that Russia was in no condition to fight a war for the moment. When he gradually came to realize that it was impossible to live in peace with aggressive France, it was not in response to British urgings, nor continued French conquests in western Europe. French expansion in the Mediterranean in 1798 provided the provocation that caused Paul to shift from a peaceful stance to war.

There was good reason for Russia to be hypersensitive about French advancement here, as its presence in Italy and the Adriatic potentially threatened Russia's burgeoning Black Sea trade and impinged on the principalities that Paul had at the outset of his reign promised to protect (today's Romania and Bulgaria). The Ionian Islands were of strategic importance to Russia in the eastern Mediterranean. Yet it was not only balance of power considerations that precipitated the Russian emperor's conversion to the belief that war with France was necessary.

Paul had, since a young man, been attracted to the chivalric idea that the Knights of St John of Malta—originally a medieval crusading order, now in decline—represented. He had not only welcomed the knights into Russia, displaced from Poland in the Second Partition that his mother had instigated, but financed them. In gratitude, notwithstanding his Orthodox religion, he was elected Grand Master of the order in November 1798. However, earlier that year Bonaparte on his way to Egypt had captured Malta. Paul felt compelled to assist those knights who had remained in Malta in expelling the French, a latter-day crusade, and this he could not do alone.

French attention had shifted from Europe to Egypt in 1798. Invading Egypt would compensate for the loss of Caribbean islands to Britain, pre-empt the Austrians from expanding in the Mediterranean from Venice, protect French commercial interests in the Levant, provide a foothold for any future partition of the Ottoman empire and serve as a base from which to attack British India. The ruling elite in Egypt was crushed at the Battle of the Pyramids and French control established in Cairo. Then, at the beginning of August, a British fleet under the command of Admiral Horatio Nelson arrived off the Egyptian coast and annihilated the French fleet at Aboukir Bay—the Battle of the Nile.

Lord Grenville, the British foreign secretary, put forward a plan for a new all-powerful alliance which would defeat France and dictate a satisfactory peace. Austria, newly belligerent, was prepared to join, as were Naples and Portugal, Prussia remaining obstinately neutral. Nevertheless, what emerged as the Second Coalition was a hurried reaction to Bonaparte's Egyptian expedition and it again lacked agreement over political aims and overall military strategy. Even so, Britain had won wholehearted Russian participation because of the French taking of Malta, while Nelson's victory at Aboukir Bay further encouraged Paul. Charles Whitworth, the British ambassador in St Petersburg, wrote home: 'It would be impossible for me to give you a reasonable idea of the zeal of His Majesty the Emperor for the good cause and of his extraordinary desire to contribute by all means in his power to its success.'[5] Anglo-Russian relations were more cordial than they had been for two decades.

The war of the Second Coalition, like its predecessor, began badly when the king of Naples led a premature campaign that ended in disaster. The Russians and the Austrians under the inspirational General Alexander Suvorov successfully campaigned in Italy and Switzerland, while the Austrians moved forward in Switzerland, pushing the French out of Italy. Nelson evicted the French from Naples. By the summer of 1799 the French had been forced back along the Rhine and the allies appeared to be on the point of invading France. The strategy, such as there was one, was for the war to be waged on two fronts. To this end Britain invited Russia to join an expeditionary force commanded by the Duke of York to restore the independence of the Dutch Republic, now under French control. This would also defend Britain in the event of a French invasion attempt. The duke has been unjustly maligned in the nursery rhyme, 'The Grand Old Duke of York', which depicts him as an amiable dolt. He served twice in the Low Countries, where there are obviously no hills:

'Nor did the Duke take his army forward and then reverse the process, whether up a hill or not.'[6] It is debatable, though, whether the duke merits the enormous column erected in his memory in London.

The expedition proved to be a fiasco. Poor coordination of Russian and British units, unexpectedly fierce resistance from Dutch and French troops, and inclement weather condemned the expedition to failure. Amid mutual recriminations between the Russian and British commanders and with the onset of winter, the British command negotiated an armistice. The allied forces were evacuated at the end of 1799. The only result on the credit side was the destruction of the Dutch fleet; on the debit side, the destruction of all good feeling between the British and the Russians.

The unbalanced Paul vented his spleen unjustifiably on his own generals and units—1,800 Russians had been killed or wounded in the first encounter, three-quarters of total allied casualties were Russian and the French took 5,000 Russians prisoner. George III, the Duke of York and the Russian ambassador, Simon Vorontsov, intervened in an attempt to stem the punishments and demotions with praise for the courage of the Russian soldiers. The chastisements were reduced but Paul insisted that the Duke of York should have no further contact with Russian troops. The shabby British treatment of Russian soldiers when they left the Low Countries and were installed in makeshift camps in the Channel Islands only served to aggravate Anglo-Russian relations. Paul petulantly ordered Vorontsov to reclaim Russian medals previously awarded to British military leaders.

The British government tried hard to maintain the alliance with Russia, with earnest urgings from George III, Charles Whitworth in St Petersburg and the British ambassadors in Vienna and Berlin arguing for continued Russian support against France. However, a second major blow to the coalition was the almost simultaneous collapse of the allied campaign in the east, where the planned invasion of France from Switzerland had to be abandoned. The fault lay squarely with the Austrians, who, with their usual ambivalence between the need to work with the Russians to defeat France, their determination to contain supposed Russian expansion and their aim for territorial gains, poisoned the alliance. Abandoned by the Austrians, the Russians were defeated at Zurich in September 1799, although Suvorov's daring escape with some of his troops over the Alps somewhat lessened the blow.

The emperor's fury and rancour at being betrayed by the Austrians knew no bounds. He withdrew from the Second Coalition in November

1799 and ordered troops to the frontier with Austria. Simon Vorontsov in London was alarmed by the emperor's increasing hostility towards Britain and confided to his friend Lord Grenville: 'Back home everything is decided by passion and violence.' The ambassador was 'weary of serving a Court which behaves in such a strange manner'.[7] The Austrian ambassador to Russia, Count Coblenz, though not responsible for the behaviour of his government, was placed under house arrest and isolated from the diplomatic community. Charles Whitworth, who loathed Coblenz, nevertheless defended his fellow ambassador. Secretly Paul requested the recall of the British ambassador in February 1800. Whitworth wrote to London, 'The Emperor is literally not in his senses.'[8]

Paul's erratic behaviour as an ally influenced the British government's decision to continue its alliance with Austria, her traditional and clearly relatively more reliable ally. This choice, rather than Paul's resentment over Malta, or the failure of the Netherlands expedition, was the fundamental cause of the Anglo-Russian breach that became apparent at the beginning of 1800. Although they were a small minority in the British parliament, the Whig Foxites and the press they influenced expressed hostility towards Russia that became increasingly explicit. She was attacked as a dangerous, unreliable and potentially overbearing ally. The *Morning Chronicle* wrote that

> the Prince of Hesse would be a more powerful Ally to this country, since he could keep up the force for which we are to pay, and give us value in blood for our money ... the British Empire ... needs not to be propped up, like that of Rome in its dotage, by profuse largesses to northern tribes.[9]

The value of Russia as an ally, it was widely believed, had been overestimated. The up-and-coming young Tory politician, George Canning, was impressed by the courage of the Russians but critical of the incapacity of most of their leaders and the poorness of their organization. Like many others, he believed their successes earlier in the year had been possible only with Austrian help.

As diplomatic relations with Britain and Austria had been severed, Paul turned to Prussia, Denmark and Sweden. A modest defensive alliance was concluded with Prussia, an act unacceptable to London, but the Scandinavian countries were seeking ties with Russia to secure the Baltic and their maritime interests against those of Britain. Neutral rights had so far played no role in Anglo-Russian relations during the war as Paul had continued Russian naval support for the British home fleet, and the commercial treaty of 1797 not only favoured the rights of British goods but omitted any mention of the sensitive rights of neutral ships.

When Russian vessels were withdrawn and the fleet sailed home, British seizures of neutral shipping became the major issue. Paul made a formal protest to the British government that was rejected. In retaliation he closed the British trading factories in St Petersburg and impounded British ships and their cargoes; but worse was to come. Nelson, in charge of the siege of French-held Malta, asserted (despite opposition from the government in London) that once regained, Malta should not be handed back to the knights, that is to Paul. In September 1800 Nelson took Malta, securing Britain a forward position in the Mediterranean from which she could watch Russian naval movements and threaten the Russian presence on the Ionian Islands. The enraged Russian emperor took yet more drastic steps against British mercantile interests and effectively ordered Prussia to invade Hanover. The British reaction was to dispatch a squadron under Sir Hyde Parker and Nelson which bombarded Copenhagen, destroyed the Danish fleet and was continuing towards St Petersburg in early 1801.

With no substantial allies now left Paul lacked any negotiating position. Increasingly embittered, and with a new-found infatuation with Napoleon, he wrote three letters to Bonaparte proposing a meeting at which they could discuss the prospects for a general peace and ways of putting pressure on the British, who, Paul was now convinced, were the stumbling block to a lasting settlement.[10] The Franco-Russian rapprochement resulted in an extraordinary planned joint invasion of India overland. This hare-brained scheme, seemingly proposed by Paul in January 1801, although sometimes attributed to Napoleon, was for 70,000 Russian and French troops to land at Astrabad on the Caspian Sea and march towards India via Khiva, Herat and Kandahar.[11]

To this end the Russian emperor ordered 20,000 Don Cossacks to march to Orenburg, then Bukhara, through the Khyber Pass and on to the Ganges. Here they would destroy British factories and perhaps stir up discontent against the British. The thinking behind the expedition was that, though Russia could not oppose British naval supremacy in Europe, Britain could not at the same time defend India. The expedition stood no chance of success—the climate, terrain, long distances and hostility in the khanates were all against it. However, it prefigures an orientation of Russian policy that was to become all too familiar later in the century.

Paul had alienated the most powerful men in Russia and exiled his potential supporters, so there was no shortage of volunteers willing to help rid the country of this tyrannical ruler. Paul had demoted generals to privates for no apparent reason, summary punishment of court officials was meted out, equerries were flogged in front of diplomats, the import of books and journals banned, and Russians were forbidden to travel abroad. Anyone whom the emperor encountered when out in his carriage had to prostrate himself or herself and round hats were banned. Failure to comply brought immediate arrest. Charles-François Masson published a long list of such outrageous examples in the second volume of his memoirs, *Secrets sur la Russie*, only a year after Paul's death.

With the aristocracy living in a state of increasing fear, rumours of plots to remove Paul began to circulate in 1799. A conspiracy developed the following year under Count Nikita Panin, the vice chancellor, but he was exiled to his estates and Count Peter Pahlen, military governor of St Petersburg, led the plot together with the Zubov brothers, favourites of Catherine II, and General Count Leo von Bennigsen, a German in Russian service who had been exiled by Paul. Even beyond the inner circle of the aristocracy and Guards officers, there was awareness that something was afoot.

Part of the reason for the conspiracy was Paul's disastrous conduct of foreign policy. He had dragged Russia into a conflict with Britain that offered no advantage. But it was above all his treatment of the nobility, the army and the state administration that made his demise inevitable. Alexander, Paul's eldest son, had himself suffered from his father's arbitrary behaviour and there were rumours that Alexander was in danger of being replaced as heir, maybe even that his life was threatened. Pahlen tried over a period of months to persuade the young man to support the conspiracy. He succeeded in gaining tacit approval for the deposition of the emperor but the grand duke insisted, disingenuously it would seem, that his father's life should be spared.

On the night of 11/23 March 1801 the conspirators struck. Pahlen knew what would happen: 'Gentlemen you cannot make an omelette without breaking eggs.'[12] A group of officers led by Bennigsen and Prince Zubov entered Paul's bedroom and in the scuffle that followed the emperor was struck down and strangled. It was announced that he had died of an apoplectic fit and no one made any effort to dispute this. History has been written according to the the assassins' accounts.

Napoleon Bonaparte and his foreign minister, Count Charles-Maurice de Talleyrand-Périgord, believed, or found it convenient to believe, that the British government had paid money to the plotters to assassinate Paul.

Charles Whitworth in St Petersburg was liberal in his disbursement of monies from the Secret Service and was notoriously bad at accounting for what he had spent. He was a good friend of Panin and was the lover of the sister of one of the conspirators, Olga Zherebtsova, also attempting (and maybe succeeding) in having an affair with a woman close to the Grand Duke Alexander. On learning of Paul's death Whitworth wrote: 'I shall, as long as I live, celebrate as a festival the day on which I learned of the death of that arch-fiend Paul.'[13] But, however much Paul's demise pleased the British government, there is no conclusive evidence that Whitworth, who had left Russia nearly a year before Paul's death, was directed, or decided for himself, to use British funds as bribes to the conspirators. Evidence indicating that Britain was not involved in the coup is that in March 1801 the British fleet was sailing towards St Petersburg to coerce the emperor into reversing his anti-British policies.

Like his ambassador, George III welcomed the news from Russia. The king wrote at the end of 1801 that the favourable events of the year 'included the assassination of Tsar Paul'.[14] Early that year the king had suffered a second serious attack of madness that had led to his being restrained and there was again talk of the need for a regency. This time George's recovery was swifter than in 1789 and the king was able to hold a Privy Council. However much his eldest son and heir, George, Prince of Wales, wanted the king declared incapable, one man's ambition did not hold sway. On 26 March, three days after Paul's death, George III was present at the queen's drawing room ceremony. The important difference between Britain and Russia was that in one case the periodic insanity of the monarch made no difference to the pursuit of national policy in a constitutional democracy; in the other absolutism meant that a deranged autocrat had to be murdered. The standard work on Paul I was, and remains, Nicholas Schilder's *Imperator Pavel I*. With a horrible irony that he did not realize, this was one of the last books read by Nicholas II in exile in Ekaterinburg just before his execution by the Bolsheviks.

As Paul had done on the death of Catherine II, Alexander I reversed—this time with justification—his father's foreign policy. With the British fleet at the time of his accession heading for the Russian capital, Alexander had little choice but to come to an understanding with Britain. Thus British ships and crews held in Russian ports were immediately released.

George III wrote a polite welcoming letter to the new Russian emperor to which Alexander replied in the high-flown language (even for the time) for which he came to be known:

> I feel greatly flattered by these renewed assurances of Your Majesty's Friendship, which I have ever so highly appreciated. I entreat Your Majesty to believe that my sentiments are reciprocal as to personal esteem and earnest desire to draw as close as possible those happy amiable relations which now subsist between Great Britain and Russia. In the present posture of Affairs there is indeed no other hope to terminate the misfortunes which afflict Humanity but by a faithful perseverance in this System of Union. … I trust that Your Majesty will not doubt the sincerity of my prayer that the divine providence may yet preserve for many years an existence so essential for the Prosperity and Happiness of Your People.[15]

The final sentence of Alexander's letter was more down to earth: 'Your Majesty has been rightly informed that I was much attached to the English language. I have always cultivated it with earnestness and pleasure as the language of a Nation which I so highly esteem.' George, in his letter, had included a swipe at the accepted use of French in diplomatic communications, but there is no evidence that Alexander ever felt at ease in English and later letters in the Russian archives show officials struggling to communicate in English on behalf of the emperor.

Diplomatic relations were resumed in May 1801, the plan to invade India abandoned and Lord St Helens appointed British ambassador. A convention was rapidly reached in which the British accepted the rights of neutral ships to enter ports blockaded by them and Russia recognized the right of the British navy to inspect the cargoes of ships flying a neutral flag. Trade between the two countries was resumed and essential Russian imports entered Britain. The Russian nobility for their part could again receive the British manufactured goods they had come to appreciate.

Despite the rapprochement between Britain and Russia, Alexander resented Copenhagen and admired much of what Napoleon was achieving for France. St Helens reported home in September: 'The members of the Emperor's Council, with whom he is particularly connected, … have been … zealous in promoting the intended peace with France.'[16] The events of the following month confirmed the ambassador's suspicions. Russia and France signed a treaty which formally restored peace between the two countries. The French recognized Russia's interest in the eastern Mediterranean and conceded the principle that Alexander should be consulted over reshaping the boundaries of the German states.[17]

George III, also Elector of Hanover, had been rightly outraged when in 1801 Prussia, who had long coveted the electorate, had annexed Hanover as part of joining Paul's League of Neutrality. The king wrote to the Russian emperor in October 1801 to protest, but received a long-winded and meaningless reply that did nothing to allay his fears that Russia had moved over to France.[18] However, the following month Frederick William III of Prussia ordered the evacuation of the electorate, fearful of British retaliation.

The Anglophile Count Nikita Panin, in charge of foreign affairs at the beginning of Alexander's reign, found himself at odds with the young ruler and was replaced by Prince Victor Kochubey, a man more in tune with the emperor's emerging policy of disengagement with the war and desire for domestic reform. Alexander was a well-educated pupil of the Enlightenment and an admirer of his grandmother. This sensitive man promised much, but he was highly secretive and capable of being a different person depending on whom he was talking to. One thing was already clear; he was a complex man.

Britain also wanted to end the war with France. War-weariness had set in; there were serious financial problems and an Irish crisis. Lord Addington, who had replaced Pitt as prime minister, and the foreign secretary, Lord Hawkesbury, recognized that Britain's superiority at sea was not enough to strike a fatal blow at France. Peace preliminaries between Britain and France were signed in March 1802 leading to the Peace of Amiens. France was to withdraw her garrisons from the Papal States and Naples, while Britain gave up all her overseas conquests made during the war with the exception of Ceylon and Spanish Trinidad. Egypt was returned to the Ottoman sultan and Malta handed back to the knights. This did not in any way represent a reconciliation and the British government was only too aware that with French hegemony on the continent and with Napoleon's boundless ambition, it was only a matter of time before France reneged on the peace.

As predicted, Napoleon behaved with scant regard for the terms of the Peace of Amiens and Britain declared war on France in May 1803. The French *Grande Armée* was arraigned at Boulogne, poised for invading Britain, and French troops invaded and occupied Hanover. Alexander for his part was equally disturbed by Napoleon's ambitions in the Black Sea, so important to Russia. In addition, at this time Russia was advancing into the Caucasus, where eastern Georgia (an independent Christian kingdom until 1795, when it was occupied by Persia) had been absorbed in 1801. The adjacent territories of Samegrelo in 1803 and Imereti in 1804 became part of the Russian empire.

Napoleon, aware that Russia was becoming increasingly hostile towards Britain, invited Alexander to mediate between Britain and

France. The Russian emperor completely misjudged the situation by calling upon France to make enormous sacrifices, Britain few. The French emperor was scathing in his dismissal; the British also. Later in 1804 he accused the Russian ambassador in Paris of plotting against him. More serious was the capture of the Duke d'Enghien, a member of the French royal house living in neutral Baden, the home of Alexander's wife. The duke was taken to Paris, tried and executed for treason. Alexander was enraged at what he saw as proof of a new Jacobin spirit in France. An inflammatory statement appeared in the French *Moniteur*: 'If, when England prepared the assassination of Paul I, the Russian government had discovered that the organizers of the plot were no more than a league from the frontier, would it not have seized them at once?'[19] No allusion could have been better calculated to wound the Russian emperor than this reference to the circumstances of his accession. It was a rhetorical question he could not forgive.

The man now chosen by Alexander to take charge of foreign affairs was the seemingly strange appointment of the Polish Prince Adam Czartorysky, who had arrived in Russia as a hostage to the good behaviour of his family and had won Alexander's confidence. The prince advocated an anti-French alliance with Britain, if only because of the need for subsidies to bring the armies of the remaining independent states into the field. One of the emperor's friends from his youth, Nicholas Novosiltsov, described by Alexander in a letter to George III as 'Mon Chambellan et Ministre Adjoint de la Justice', was sent to London on a secret mission.[20] The envoy had meetings not only with Pitt (again prime minister) and the Tories but also with Fox, the Whig opposition and the Prince of Wales. The Russian ambassador, Simon Vorontsov, resented being sidelined and Novosiltsov's arrogance and tactless dealings with Pitt's enemies conspired against this botched attempt at personal diplomacy.

Novosiltsov's instructions represent the earliest draft of Alexander's general plan to establish a new order in Europe and the moralistic phrases which puzzled and irritated Pitt and his ministers in 1804—these appeared in a new guise ten years later. For the sceptical prime minister had no desire to transform a war against France into a crusade for ill-defined 'sacred rights' in which he did not believe. When in February 1805 the dispatches from London reached St Petersburg, it was obvious that Novosiltsov had failed in his mission and the two countries were not ready to conclude an alliance.[21] Even so, an Anglo-Russian subsidy agreement was signed in April, though Britain was at first unwilling to ratify the terms which her ambassador had been forced to accept by Russian ministers.

The previous November Russia and Austria had reached an agreement to send troops to fight in Italy, and two months later Sweden allied with Russia. Napoleon, now emperor, as insatiable as ever, had been tightening his grip on northern Italy and crowned himself King of All Italy in May 1805. The following month he went even further and annexed Genoa and the Ligurian coast to metropolitan France, while in the same year dismantling the Holy Roman Empire and creating the Confederation of the Rhine in Germany with total disregard for Russian interests. Not content with this, he was also establishing bases for expansion in the eastern Mediterranean, the Balkans and clearly had Constantinople in his sights. It was thus the actions of the French emperor that created the Anglo-Russian alliance of July 1805 and Alexander's whole-hearted commitment to war against France.

The British promised an annual subsidy of £1.5 million for 100,000 men that Russia would put into the field, while the controversial questions of Malta and Italy were omitted. A few days later the Austrians, even more alarmed than the Russians or the British at French activity in Italy, joined the alliance, though Prussia still remained resolutely neutral. The Third Coalition was in being. Nevertheless, what had started out as Alexander's first sustained diplomatic initiative to inspire an ideological challenge to Bonapartism was reduced to a hurried instrument for waging a particular campaign.

In British history 1805 is above all the year of the victorious battle of Trafalgar against the combined French and Spanish fleets. However, everywhere else on land it was marked by fresh triumphs of Napoleon. As ever, victory at sea could not undermine the French emperor's hold on continental Europe. The French army was rushed from Boulogne to the upper Danube where it annihilated the Austrians at Ulm before moving eastwards to rout an Austro-Russian army of 86,000 men at Austerlitz in December. Alexander fancied himself as a general and was determined to show himself head of the Russian army. There he pursued a disastrous strategy, contrary to the advice of the experienced General Kutuzov. At Austerlitz his army broke and fled across the marshes, the Russian emperor humiliated in the eyes of the world. Alexander barely escaped captivity and was led sobbing from the battlefield.

Austria once again sued for peace, while Frederick William of Prussia accepted Napoleon's occupation of Hanover and the north German ports and continued his vacillating attitude towards the French and the coalition members. Napoleon tried to lure the Prussian king into acting against Austria with the enticing bait of Hanover. The cession of Hanover to Prussia was achieved in December 1805 with the expected outrage in London. Thus Prussia was forced to join Napoleon's blockade, or Continental System, against Britain, to which the latter responded by declaring war on Prussia.

Then, Berlin learned that the French emperor was rumoured to be offering to return Hanover to George III. Although Prussia was clearly putty in the hands of Napoleon, Russia rashly dispatched an ultimatum to the French emperor. He replied by means of a swift campaign against isolated Prussia, whose army was crushed at Jena-Auerstedt in October 1806 and one Prussian fortress after another surrendered. Russia had promised to send contingents to support Prussia but they had not arrived in time.

Russia was at this juncture not only alone on the continent in being at war against France but was waging it on two fronts, as the Ottoman empire flaunted treaties signed with Russia during the reign of Catherine II. Russian troops moved south and the sultan declared war on Russia. Alexander's bitterness at British inactivity in 1806, and failure to provide all the subsidies he sought, was intense. In December the British ambassador in St Petersburg, now the Marquess of Douglas, reported: 'At Court this morning his Imperial Majesty again urged, in the strongest of terms, the expedience of a diversion on the enemy in the north of Europe by a powerful expedition to the coasts of France or Holland.'[22] The British government refused. The ambassador informed the foreign office: 'I must not conceal from Your Lordship that the silence of His Majesty's Government respecting a military diversion on the coast of France has not produced a favourable impression either on the ministry or the people of this country.'[23] A similar Russian demand was to be repeated 136 years later.

In addition to these reasons for deteriorating Anglo-Russian relations, the British government exacerbated matters by refusing to guarantee a loan of £6 million that Russia sought to equip new armies. There was also bickering over the 1797 commercial treaty that was about to expire. The British government wanted to extend it for a further three years: Russia insisted on one. In the end two years was settled on. And then was there was the perennial problem of Hanover. Russia was asked to press Prussia for restitution of the electorate to George III. The Russian minister of foreign affairs, now Baron Andrei Budberg, told Douglas that the emperor would do so if Prussia agreed. Given Prussia's well-known position, this was hardly helpful. Budberg made clear in bitter terms Russia's disenchantment with Britain: 'Russia has little for which to be grateful to her Allies'; to which, according to Budberg, Douglas 'only replied with vague utterances'.[24]

Alexander had been secretly seeking peace terms with France, while encouraging Prussian resistance to Napoleon. When the French emperor learned of this double-dealing he swiftly moved an army into Prussian Poland, taking Warsaw and Thorn. Alexander had dispatched troops into East Prussia in November 1806 but was now forced to pull them back. Skirmishes took place between Russian and French forces and the Russians won a minor encounter at Pultusk, only to suffer a major defeat at Eylau in February 1807.

Austria had witnessed the collapse of Prussia in October 1806 and was fearful that intervening against Napoleon would spell still further disaster. She remained on the sidelines. Britain for her part seemed even more insular than ever, refusing to provide subsidies, and had shifted to a colonial strategy. Russia faced France alone on the continent. In June 1807 Napoleon defeated the Russian army under General Bennigsen at the battle of Friedland. However, even after the retreat across the river Niemen, the French were a long way from being able to threaten the Russian heartland, and Russian manpower resources were far from being exhausted.

Yet other considerations convinced Alexander that an armistice with France was necessary, as was argued by Bennigsen, his younger brother Constantine, and prominent figures in the rising peace movement in Russia. Napoleon was master of western and central Europe and could strike again. In addition Russia could well pay the price of the Partitions of Poland as it would not take much for Napoleon to persuade the Poles, who, for good reason, had no love lost for the Russians, to cooperate with him and invade the western borderlands of the empire. Russia was without allies with Austria and Prussia defeated, while Britain had no troops on mainland Europe and was unwilling to grant loans, let alone subsidies. On top of all this the treasury was bankrupt and it would take time to get the army back on a war footing.

Alexander dispatched General Prince Dmitri Lobanov-Rostovsky to open peace negotiations with Napoleon.

8

THE WARS OF THE FRENCH REVOLUTION AND NAPOLEON, PART II

1807–1815

Napoleon proposed that the two emperors should meet in the theatrical setting of a raft in the middle of the river Niemen at the town of Tilsit on the border of the Polish lands of Prussia and Russia on 25 June 1807. Alexander supposedly opened the encounter with the words: 'Sire, I hate the English no less than you do and I am ready to assist you in any enterprise against them.'[1] Such a statement does not ring true as the Russian emperor was never direct in his conversation. Be that as it may, Alexander was bewitched by Napoleon and agreed to cooperate with him in forcing a settlement upon Britain. That was quite enough, for the French emperor had no desire to pursue a lengthy and costly campaign in Russia against an army that was defeated but not broken. Hence, in the Tilsit agreement Russia was to lose relatively little territory. She was to withdraw from the Principalities, cede the Ionian Islands and a military outpost in Dalmatia, while she gained a fragment of Prussian Poland. The main loser was Prussia. Russia was to accept French mediation in the war against Turkey and, if this failed, France would enter the war on her side.

Most importantly Russia was to halt all trade with Britain and summon her to make peace, surrendering the colonial conquests. Failing this Russia was to join the Continental System and declare war on Britain. The idea that Britain would accept a Franco-Russian settlement was ludicrous. The Tilsit peace was not an alliance of equals for Russia was clearly the junior partner. Napoleon was ever more powerful.

Alexander believed that he had struck as good a deal as possible in his dealings with the French emperor, but Tilsit was seen as another humiliating defeat by most Russians and there was talk of plots against the emperor. Among his severest critics were members of his family—his mother Maria Feodorovna, his brother Constantine and his favourite sister, Catherine. 'I will tell you I shall not resign myself to this peace', wrote Catherine. 'We shall have made huge sacrifices and for what? ... He [Napoleon] ... is a blend of cunning, personal ambition and pretence.'[2] Others who opposed the French alliance, or at least the way Alexander had carried it out, included Czartorysky, Kochubey, Novosiltsov, Baron Budberg and Simon Vorontsov. The Russian merchant class was unhappy about the break with Britain.

If Tilsit displeased many influential Russians, it aroused feelings of contempt in Britain, as illustrated by a cartoon of 1807 showing Napoleon embracing Alexander on the raft. A crown topples from the latter's head as he exclaims, 'Zounds, Brother, you'll squeeze me to death ... besides, I find my side of the raft is sinking very fast!' as waves lap over his feet. Another depicted the Russian bear being ridden by a tiny Napoleon, licking his boots, being led by a chain attached to its nose, muzzled while blowing a French horn, or asleep in a cradle which Napoleon rocks. Any popularity and respect previously enjoyed by Russians and their ruler in Britain sank to the lowest level in living memory. Russian desertion was seen as exposing Britain to greater peril from Napoleon, and all sections of the British press, irrespective of party, denounced Tilsit as an act of weakness and treachery. The Tory *European* magazine in 1808 reproached Alexander because he 'should so far degrade himself, as to become a partaker of the spoils arising from the misfortunes of his friend and ally' (i.e. the king of Prussia).[3] The Whigs viewed the Franco-Russian peace as confirmation of the low opinion of Russia which many of them had already formed, and that hardened after the death of Fox in 1806. The *Morning Chronicle* declared: 'Without system in her councils, or Statesmen in her Cabinet; without a military genius in her army, or freedom and public spirit in her people; Russia, in spite of her extensive territory, will never be a first-rate power in Europe.'[4]

For now Russophobia was rapidly developing among the Whigs and Radicals. It was an ideological hostility formulated by the likes of Samuel Whitbread, William Cobbett and Leigh Hunt. They feared potential Russian domination of Europe and opposed the political ideas and social traditions for which Russia stood. Their attitude was far more uncompromising, far less pragmatic, than that of the Tories. Their attacks were directed at Russia itself, the Russian people and Russian life, while those of the Tories tended to be concentrated on a weak and unprincipled ruler.

George Canning, who at last had achieved his ambition of becoming the new Tory foreign secretary in March 1807, was particularly circumspect in his reaction to Tilsit, claiming that Alexander had been overreacting to defeat on the battlefield; he would return to his friends.[5] Canning believed that there was a pro-British party at St Petersburg, despite the influence on the emperor of the violently Anglophobe chancellor, Count Nikolai Rumiantsev, and hoped for a change of policy which an open rift would thwart. The French émigré, the Count d'Antraigues, who had entered Russian service in a cloak and dagger way, now lived in Richmond upon Thames and was in the habit of passing on secret documents to the foreign secretary.[6] The French aristocrat reflected one of Canning's major successes during his first period in office, a great increase in British intelligence operations.

D'Antraigues received from Czartorysky a letter which he passed on to the foreign secretary. Canning found it 'very curious in its account of the state of St Petersburg, and [it] gives a picture of the Emperor's weakness that is almost incredible'.[7] He wrote to his wife on 29 August:

> It is very satisfactory in one, as it proves that the course which I had taken with Russia, that of *managing* the Emperor's personal feelings, but at the same time shewing that we are not afraid of him, is the most likely to succeed in bringing him to reason ... I must get acquainted with his friend Czartoryski.[8]

Sir Robert Wilson, a British officer who until Tilsit had been attached to the Russian army, was sent for by Alexander the day before his departure. Wilson wrote that the emperor said he was aware that Britain suspected the Treaty of Tilsit to contain articles hostile to British interests. He assured Wilson that this was not the case. The emperor had perhaps sacrificed the interests of his own country, but he had agreed to nothing unfavourable to Britain. On the contrary, it was his earnest desire to remain on a friendly footing with this country. Baron Budberg was more explicit, telling Wilson that the peace with France could not last, that the war must inevitably be renewed. The continuance of a good understanding between Britain and Russia was of the utmost importance: 'In other words, the British government realized that it had to live with the Franco-Russian partnership.'[9]

Despite all the Russian protestations, when the foreign secretary learned from his intelligence service that under the terms of Tilsit Napoleon was planning to capture the Danish fleet, he dispatched a

British fleet to bombard Copenhagen and seized the Danish fleet. Later it was learned that a Russian squadron was sailing northwards from the Mediterranean. Canning gave orders that it should not be allowed further north than Portugal, except to a British port. Force proved unnecessary; the fleet wintered on the Tagus. Canning was correct in the precaution as Russia broke off diplomatic relations with Britain on 7 November 1807, in terms which George III believed might have been dictated by the Paris *Moniteur*.

As a result the Russian ambassador, Count Maxim Alopeus, and the whole mission had to leave London. The foreign secretary wrote to the king:

> M. Alopeus has upon the whole conducted himself in his mission with great moderation & propriety, & as he appears really to feel deep interest in the restoration of harmony between the two countries, & may by possibility have the means of being of some use in promoting this object after his return to St Petersburgh, it might be desirable that that he should receive some expression of Your Majesty's approbation of his conduct; & whether your Majesty would be graciously pleased to permit Mr. Canning to present M. Alopeus with a snuff box in your Majesty's name.[10]

Similarly, the British ambassador was obliged to leave St Petersburg in late 1807. The man appointed in 1804 had been Lord Granville Leveson-Gower. Reservations were expressed at this choice by Simon Vorontsov in London on account of the young man's—he was thirty-one—propensity for gambling: 'A gaming ambassador will come to no good in Russia. It is the national vice and the Emperor hates it.'[11] Sir John Warren, Leveson-Gower's predecessor, had bankrupted himself in Russia but the new ambassador did not repeat the error: 'I have never gamed here unless playing at a game of skill about once a month.'[12]

In a way reminiscent of so many previous British ambassadors, Leveson-Gower complained bitterly and at length to his friend Lady Bessborough about life in Russia: 'It is impossible to describe to you how bored and wearied I am with being introduced to 2 or 3 hundred people with whom I have repeat the same conversation.'[13] 'If the Public Business in which one is occupied was not extremely interesting, I believe I should not survive the Ennui of this place.'[14] The high cost of living in the Russian capital was intimidating:

> It is the Custom of the Russians when their Houses are completely out of order, and the furniture all broken, to travel and let their house to some

> Foreigner. The proprietor of this House has followed the Custom of the Country, and I find that the Hinges of the Doors are all coming off, that the Chairs are all patched up, and, in short, that I must be ruined in providing furniture.[15]

Despite all his complaints about Russia, Leveson-Gower had met a Russian woman, Princess Sergei Golitsyn, whom he wished to marry, and he felt it necessary to consult his family. For this reason he asked to be recalled in 1806. (He was not the first British ambassador to become involved in an affair in Russia. The second Sir Charles Whitworth's womanizing was legendary.) The man who succeeded Leveson-Gower in 1806, the Marquess of Douglas, also fell for a woman he met in St Petersburg.

Quite how much his affair with Princess Golitsyn influenced Leveson-Gower in accepting a second posting to St Petersburg is clearly unknown, but once there—and these were the months preceding the battle of Friedland—he spent much time with his mistress. However, the peace between Russia and France and the break in diplomatic relations between Britain and Russia that ensued led to the obligatory departure of the British ambassador and, inevitably, the end of his relationship with Princess Golitsyn.

What Napoleon had done at Tilsit by curtailing Russian action in central Europe was to allow Alexander to pursue Russian expansionist objectives elsewhere. Rumiantsev and other like-minded people in the administration did not see France as the main enemy but rather Britain with her expansionist colonial bent. Secret clauses to the Tilsit agreement (discovered soon afterwards by the British)[16] laid the foundations for an attack on India, the longstanding aim of Napoleon. The British government duly instructed the governor general to warn all countries between India and Persia.

Following on from the annexation of western Georgia in 1801 Russian authority had been extended in the Caucasus. This greatly alarmed adjacent Persia and Turkey to the south. The Porte (the Ottoman foreign office) had provoked Russia into war in 1806 over the perennial problem of the Principalities and closed the Straits to Russian warships. After Tilsit Alexander was forced to accept French mediation, but the problem was that both France and Russia wished to despoil the Ottoman empire and the war continued. Persia for her part had declared war on Russia over Georgia in 1804 and this conflict was continuing fitfully.

Persia had first sought help from London but the British government, having secured its position in India following a successful war against the Mahrattas Confederacy in 1803–4, was in 1806 more concerned about maintaining the Russian alliance than about Russia's advance at the expense of Persian interests. The shah of Persia then turned to France and a Franco-Persian alliance was signed in May 1807 in which France promised to guarantee Persia's territory, send advisers and *matériel*, maintain its war against Russia and support Persia in a thrust towards India. As ever, Napoleon was lavish in his promises of help and in guaranteeing Turkey and Persia from Russian encroachments, but, even at the zenith of his power in 1808, he was incapable of threatening India or assisting the Turks in the Balkans. In any case, Persia's main aim was to secure an alliance with Britain against Russia. However, the British government with Canning at the foreign office refused to acquiesce, hoping to win back Russia as an ally.

Persia demonstrated the basic irreconcilability of French and Russian aims. A further example was Napoleon's creation of the Grand Duchy of Warsaw from the Prussian territories of Poland in 1807, that is, placing a French satellite state that could easily be turned into a weapon against Russia. To assuage Alexander, the French emperor urged him to invade Finland, part of Sweden, which remained a British ally, in order to enhance Russian power in the eastern Baltic. After a brief and successful campaign, Finland and the Aland Islands were incorporated into Russia in 1808 as the Grand Duchy of Finland but this undermined Alexander's subservience to France. Most importantly, such a sop to the Russian emperor was not enough to mask the damage being done to Russia by the commercial war against Britain which interrupted a highly beneficial economic relationship. The Continental System not only sapped Russia's commitment to France but at the same time was harming Napoleon more than Britain. It contained the seeds of its own destruction.

It was also in 1808 that Napoleon's 'Spanish ulcer' started oozing. Bourbon Spain had proved a disappointing ally to the French emperor and he decided to take drastic measures to control Spanish resources and direct foreign policy. The country was invaded and his brother, Joseph Bonaparte, was installed as king. This provoked an insurrection and the French army faced determined guerrillas. These assorted juntas appealed to Britain for support, and in August 1808 Sir Arthur Wellesley landed in Portugal with an expeditionary force. More than this, Britain pledged to underwrite any European revolt against Napoleonic hegemony and accepted that she would have to commit troops to fight on the continent.

The first cracks in the French imperial edifice were visible. Despite all her victories, French casualties had been high and experienced troops were becoming rare (while Russia still possessed enormous reserves). And Spain made it clear that there was deep-seated resentment in the conquered countries.

Aware of the danger Spain posed to his empire, Napoleon summoned Alexander to a congress in Erfurt, a small town in Thuringia (east-central Germany), in September 1808 with the intention of forcing the Russian emperor to restate his commitment to the French alliance. Alexander's mother again implored her son not to have any truck with Napoleon who, she believed, was going to topple before too long. Alexander felt obliged to attend. On his way he met Baron von Stein, the Prussian chief minister and a relentless foe of Napoleon, who urged him to take the lead in a coalition against France. But the Russian emperor was still convinced that the time was not ripe.

Napoleon's prime concern at Erfurt was to use the threat of the power of Russia to keep the Austrians quiet while he disposed of the Iberian troubles. Alexander, no longer in thrall to the French emperor's charisma, refused to commit himself to support France in the event of Austrian aggression, making only vague verbal utterances of 'common cause' and steering clear of any commitment in Spain. Napoleon thought that he had once again manipulated Alexander into continuing his subservience, but the latter wrote to his sister Catherine: 'Bonaparte thinks that I am nothing but a fool. *He who laughs last, laughs longest!* And I put all my faith in God.'[17]

As Napoleon feared, the Austrians were determined to go to war with France. The foreign minister, Count Philipp zu Stadion, and the new empress were violently anti-French and were behind the rapid rearmament being undertaken. Count Clemens von Metternich, the Austrian ambassador in Paris, was becoming increasingly hostile to the French emperor's pretensions and reported mounting domestic opposition to Napoleon that further encouraged the war party. The Austrians at the same time were overly optimistic about French problems in Spain. Russian foreign policy post-Erfurt was directed at preventing a Franco-Austrian war, as it was obvious that effective help from abroad was highly unlikely and that a defeated Austria would become a French satellite which would leave Russia alone against Napoleon in continental Europe at a time when she was unprepared for war.

No amount of advice from abroad could stop the suicidal Austrian war party from declaring war on France in April 1809. Britain provided a subsidy and mounted a diversionary attack in the northern Netherlands but these were of little use to the Habsburgs. France won an impressive victory at the battle of Wagram in early July and an armistice was signed a week later.

Alexander had duly declared his support for France when hostilities had broken out but had procrastinated over providing the French with military support. The French ambassador in St Petersburg could see all too clearly that the sympathy of most prominent Russians was with Austria. The Russian emperor, when asked by the French ambassador if his army was marching on Olmütz, replied with deliberate vagueness that she would march in the direction of Olmütz. Russian military correspondence was intercepted by the Poles of the Grand Duchy of Warsaw and demonstrated to the French emperor how little support he was receiving from Russia. His faith in the alliance was destroyed and in the peace treaty that followed the war Napoleon vented his displeasure with Russia and infuriated Alexander by rewarding his ally with only the acquisition of a small region in eastern Galicia.

In 1810 Napoleon divorced his wife Josephine, who had failed to provide him with a son, and he had for some time been on the look-out for a suitably royal replacement. A Russian grand duchess would constitute an appropriate bride and Alexander had two unmarried sisters, Catherine and Anna. Their mother, the Dowager Empress Maria Feodorovna, was determined to prevent any union with the upstart Frenchman, 'a man of vile character', and she wisely did not believe that a marriage would save the alliance with France.[18] Anna was declared too young and Catherine hastily chose to marry Prince George of Holstein-Oldenburg. Since he had rebuffed Napoleon, Alexander had no grounds for feeling disappointment at the French emperor's choice of a Habsburg bride, the Archduchess Marie-Louise. Nevertheless, he was irritated to learn that Napoleon was not only marrying a Habsburg but was also seeking a new political ally in Austria.

The insatiability of the French emperor was increasingly clear after Tilsit. He had annexed to France the Kingdom of the Netherlands, Hanover, the Grand Duchy of Berg, Hamburg, Bremen and Lübeck (a threat to Russia's position in the Baltic), taken over Austrian territory in Poland and occupied the Duchy of Oldenburg. This was in breach of Tilsit but especially provocative to Alexander as the heir to the dukedom was now his brother-in-law (Oldenburg was annexed in January 1811). But what fundamentally doomed the Franco-Russian alliance was the Continental System.

The aim of the blockade was to strangle the British economy and Alexander duly adhered to his commitment to Napoleon at Tilsit to close Russian ports to British ships and to sequestrate British property. Despite this, British goods continued to enter Russia through Finland, and even Afghanistan, and the widespread use of neutral ships, in particular American, was a convenient means of avoiding the ban. Even so, Russia was deprived of imports and those that entered the country rose dramatically in price. From 1802–6 imports were worth 40.8 million silver roubles, to 20.6 million from 1808–12. Russian exports meanwhile slumped from an average of 54.1 million from 1802–6, to 34.1 million in the period 1808–12. The paper rouble plummeted from 50 silver kopecks in 1808 to 23.5 in 1811, and the silver rouble lost one-fifth of its value against the pound sterling in the period 1807–12. Customs revenues collapsed.

To make matters worse, trade with France did not compensate for the loss of exports to Britain. Napoleon for his part was at the same time evading the blockade by issuing licences for French merchants to trade with Britain and by his annexations on the North Sea coastline was damaging Russian trade in the region. On 31 December 1810 Alexander withdrew from the Continental System by introducing a new tariff which discriminated against French in favour of British commerce.

The Franco-Russian alliance was intrinsically unsustainable as Russia could not in the long term accept the French-run Grand Duchy of Warsaw on her doorstep, the Continental System was harmful to her economy, and French and Russian aims in the Balkans were at odds. Plus, in the most general sense Russia could not stomach French domination of continental Europe indefinitely. The incompatibility of French and Russian interests was glaringly obvious and both sides accepted the inevitability of war.

Napoleon realized that a decisive victory over Russia was necessary if Britain was to be brought to her knees and was actively planning an invasion of Russia from the summer of 1811. He successfully intimidated Austria and Prussia into supporting him, or at least not opposing him, and within the next twelve months assembled an enormous army in eastern Prussia with over 600,000 men, of whom about 300,000 were French, 190,000 German, 90,000 Polish and 30,000 Italian, with a further 50,000 second-line forces.

Alexander understood only too well what was impending but in 1812 the war against the Ottoman empire was dragging on. The Turks had proved tenacious enemies, urged on to resist Russia by Britain. However, in the winter of 1811–12 Field-Marshal Kutuzov forced the Ottoman army to surrender and a hurried peace treaty was signed the following May, the Treaty of Bucharest. The British minister in Constantinople, Stratford Canning, a cousin of George Canning, exerted himself greatly in urging the Porte to make peace on favourable terms as war between Russia and France was looming and the Russians would need to redeploy their army northwards. At the same time, he was passing on information to Russia about the shifting attitudes of the Turks. The result was disappointing for Russia.[19] Turkey ceded Bessarabia, but the sultan held on to the Principalities which had been occupied by Russia, annexation being the key war aim. In the Caucasus Russia fared better, securing important territories, and continued in its quest for an enshrinement in law of the power to defend Christians in the Ottoman empire. Serbia's struggle for independence, supported by Russia, failed but Serbia was granted rights of autonomy within the Ottoman empire. This was not important in itself but was to set a precedent for Russia's policy towards the Greek revolution in the 1820s.

As late as spring 1812 neither Napoleon nor Alexander had entirely given up on a peaceful resolution of their differences, but the minimum conditions demanded on both sides rendered it impossible; war between the two empires had become inevitable. In May the French emperor travelled across Germany into eastern Prussia escorted by the cavalry of the Guard. By the end of the month he was at Posen where he took command of the *Grande Armée*, initially divided into three armies, and moved in to the Grand Duchy of Warsaw. One aspect of Napoleon's genius as a military leader lay in the speed with which he moved armies and the spectacular set-piece battles at which he excelled as commander, and in 1812 he saw himself poised for a quick knockout blow. The Russian armies were divided, with 130,000 at Vilna (Vilnius today) under Field-Marshal Mikhail Bogdanovich Barclay de Tolly, the First Army; 50,000 further south under General Peter Ivanovich Bagration, the Second Army; and reserve armies of 40,000 at Volhynia under General Alexander Tormassov and 35,000 in Moldavia under Field-Marshal Kutuzov—a total therefore far below that of the French forces. Barclay de Tolly and Bagration hated each other, which did not bode well.

The Russian emperor was not going to be drawn. He had arrived in Vilna on 26 April, officially to prevent his commanders from making provocative moves in response to the massing of the French in eastern Prussia. No one in St Petersburg believed this fiction, knowing that several regiments had marched westwards over the preceding weeks. He was still at Vilna when the French crossed the Niemen into Russia at Kovno on 23–24 June. Though Napoleon had invaded Russia, Alexander decided on a final plea: 'If Your Majesty will order a withdrawal of your troops from Russian territory, I am prepared to regard what has passed as though it had never happened, and an agreement is still possible between us.'[20] After leading the *Grande Armée* so far, the reply was as expected.

Alexander abandoned Vilna and retired to Drissa, a major fortified camp, where he arrived twelve days later. Here he was determined that his forces would turn and fight. However, his generals knew that Drissa lacked adequate defences and could easily be outflanked. By this stage the emperor reluctantly realized that his presence as supreme commander in the field was a burden for his generals. They were able to persuade him that his duty was to maintain the morale of the population. With his retinue he duly headed towards the upper Dnipro and the long road to the old capital Moscow, with the intention of continuing to St Petersburg.

So far Alexander had not taken steps to sound out Britain, although it was obvious that once war broke out Britain would become his ally. In early July 1812 Russia and Britain were without diplomatic representation, but Alexander by this stage needed to reach an understanding with London if he was to receive a much-needed subsidy. From Drissa he wrote to the Prince Regent. Clearly the emperor had to express his *mea culpa* for Tilsit, claiming that he had been constrained to ally with Napoleon. All he had sought was 'to avoid Russia the suffering of war'. Now, 'the possibility of reversals does not frighten me ... The actual circumstances are going to bring together Russia and England.'[21] Having written in French, he apologized for not having time to draft the letter in English: 'The subject is so important that I dare not express myself in English. My French is much better.'[22]

In his reply the prince made no bones about the past breach: 'My desire is not to recall events which have latterly separated Powers whose true interests must ever dictate between them the closest friendship and alliance; I am rather disposed to look forward.'[23] There was a pointed reference to the Peninsular War: 'By supporting this war, Great Britain prevents half the resources of France from being turned against Your Imperial Majesty ... the defeats of the French in the Peninsula will paralyse their efforts in the north, and effect the most powerful diversion in favour of Your Imperial Majesty's arms.'[24] On 18 July diplomatic relations were re-established and Robert Stewart, Viscount Castlereagh, now foreign secretary, dispatched Lord Cathcart to St Petersburg with £500,000 in his baggage.

The Russian First Army had abandoned Drissa on 17 July, retreating towards Vitebsk, which they hoped to reach before Napoleon. Bagration, the Russian commander of the Second Army, wanted to launch a diversionary raid towards Warsaw but Alexander dismissed this proposal, insisting that, while the First Army retreated, the role of the Second Army and Cossacks was to harass Napoleon's flank and rear:

> In pressing this strategy Alexander was sticking to the basic principles which had guided Barclay's thinking from early 1810 and which in the end were to bring glory in 1812. Whichever Russian army was threatened by Napoleon's main body must withdraw and refuse battle ... But this strategy was only fully realizable by the autumn of 1812 when Napoleon's armies had been hugely depleted and their immensely long flanks were vulnerable to the Russian armies brought in from Finland and the Balkans.[25]

As in the summer of 1812 the French armies vastly outnumbered those of Russia, and the defenders wisely refused to turn and fight at Vitebsk. Therefore the French continued in pursuit to Smolensk, on the road to Moscow. Napoleon himself remained at Vitebsk for a fortnight from the end of July. His army was shrinking although it had not fought a major battle. At Vitebsk one-third of the men were missing—victims of hunger, thirst, disease, fatigue and the weather, which had turned very hot again, with the men marching in stifling dust.

While the Russians dithered and Barclay de Tolly and Bagration continued their personal feud, by 14 August the French approached Smolensk, two weeks' march from Moscow. Yet again he was not able to draw the Russians into battle. They retreated further towards Moscow with the French in pursuit. But one thing was clear to Napoleon; the Russians could not surrender Moscow without a fight. Alexander had now entrusted overall command of the Russian armies to Kutuzov because of the friction between Barclay de Tolly and Bagration. The old field marshal continued the retreat to Borodino, 120 kilometres from Moscow. Here the Russians would have to make a stand if Moscow was to be saved. By this time the French forces were even more depleted by illness and much equipment had been abandoned: 135,000 French faced 120,000 Russians in the battle that took place on 7 September. Napoleon's forces prevailed but with the loss of 40,000 men, while the Russians lost about 50,000.

The victory was not, however, decisive; the Russian forces were able to retreat in good order but Kutuzov decided against any attempt to make a stand against Napoleon. The French entered Moscow on 15 September only to find that most of the population had fled and the city was in flames—probably on the order of the governor general, Count Feodor Rostopchin. The French emperor was faced with a devastated city and still Alexander had not sued for peace. Partisan groups and peasants harassed his troops, whose food supplies diminished yet further. Napoleon had not realized that Alexander could not alienate the army and the nobility and thus put his throne at risk. It was only by mid-October that the French emperor acknowledged that Alexander had outwitted him. By remaining for six weeks in Moscow waiting for a reply from the Russian emperor, the position of his troops deteriorated yet more and winter set in. The epic retreat of the Napoleonic army from Moscow is well known. By the time it reached the Prussian frontier (and it was not a particularly harsh winter) on 14 December it numbered fewer than 40,000 men.

Despite his defeat in Russia, Napoleon still believed that military victory would be his once more; his war against the real enemy, Britain, would continue. No one would have predicted at the beginning of 1813 that the year would see the beginning of the end of the Napoleonic empire. The news of the French disaster in Russia was received with amazement and wild rejoicing in London and the temptation to open a new front in northern Europe—in Hanover or Holland—was strong; but Wellesley, now Viscount Wellington, a friend and close ally of Castlereagh, insisted that Britain's military effort should continue to be concentrated on the Peninsular War. In any case, Britain lacked sufficient troops that could play a meaningful role in defeating Napoleon on the continent. What she could supply was money and munitions.

Alexander now manifested a messianic determination to liberate Europe as well as Russia. His own army was now being rapidly rebuilt and reorganized but he also needed allies with armies to destroy French hegemony on continental Europe. And there were now signs that the rot had already set in for Napoleon by the end of 1812. Field-Marshal Count Hans von Yorck, commander of the Prussian contingent in the *Grande Armée*, defected and signed a convention with Russia. The insurrection gathered momentum when another Prussian general agreed to let the Russians advance to the Oder river while his own forces retired. Russia immediately appealed to Britain for subsidies. The newly arrived Russian ambassador to Britain, Count Christoph Lieven, approached Castlereagh, who was prepared to pay for 10,000 men at that time stationed in Finland on condition that they were to be dispatched to fight in Germany.[26] As well as the subsidy, a shipload of ammunition and military clothing was prepared.[27]

British money was wasted on the German legion which proved militarily worthless, but politically it was productive as seed money to further the insurrection in Prussia. King Frederick William III of Prussia signed a military alliance with Russia in February, the Treaty of Kalisch, and the following month declared war on France. Nevertheless, Castlereagh was irritated by Alexander's evasiveness as to what territorial compensation for Prussia had been agreed at Kalisch, as the British government feared that Alexander might sign a final peace with France without consulting Britain. It was exasperating because Britain was not only fighting in Spain but was at war with the United States over maritime disputes. Nevertheless, without demur, Britain agreed to provide a subsidy of £1.33 million and a further £3.3 million in the form of federal paper money (guaranteed by the British, Russian and Prussian governments, to pay interest and be redeemable immediately after the war). Converted into paper roubles the total sum was expected to cover all the projected costs of the forthcoming campaign in Germany until the end of the year. Predictably, exchange costs, discounting and the slow flow of cash reduced it somewhat.[28]

The spring campaign 'was a race between Napoleon and his enemies as to who could mobilize reinforcements and get them to the German theatre of operations most quickly'.[29] As Dominic Lieven has written in his magisterial *Russia Against Napoleon*, 'the greatest hero of the Russian war effort was not a human being but the horse'.[30] Nowhere is this better demonstrated than in the 1813 offensive when Napoleon's cavalry could not withstand the fast, ugly Cossack horses sowing confusion among them. Berlin was liberated in early March but the French emperor checked the advance with victories at Lützen and Bautzen. Even so the Austrian chancellor, Clemens von Metternich, cautiously watching events, now saw that it was opportune to extricate Austria from its alliance with France by proposing an armistice in early June. Napoleon eagerly accepted this and the summoning of a peace conference, as did the allies on their side, hoping to improve his military position during the lull in fighting.

At Alexander's headquarters at Reichenbach in late June, Austria, Russia and Prussia signed a secret convention which guaranteed that

Austria would enter the war if minimal conditions were rejected by Napoleon. He succeeded in having the armistice extended but French weakness was apparent—the previous month Wellington had won impressively at Vitoria in Spain—and Austria finally declared war in August. The numerical superiority and higher quality of the allied armies was considerable, and by mid-October they won a decisive but costly victory at Leipzig—the Battle of the Nations—in which Alexander played an active and brave role. This defeat destroyed Napoleon's influence in Germany and, as he retreated across the Rhine in late 1813, his Grand Empire collapsed and his satellites deserted him. The allies proposed a peace. Napoleon would remain emperor with France retaining her 1790 frontiers. He refused the Frankfurt offer.

The year 1813 saw the Russian emperor win international acclaim as the man who led allied armies to free Germany. Meanwhile, Britain had driven the French out of Spain and subsidized the allies but had necessarily remained on the sidelines in continental Europe. With the impending defeat of Napoleon it was now crucial for Britain, the one power which had been constantly at war against France since 1793, to play a leading role in the final peace settlement. And the continental powers, war-weary at the end of 1813, realized that Britain would continue the war and they would inevitably be involved. At the same time, if France was to be persuaded to accept a peace, then it had to be made clear to Britain that she would have to return to France many of the colonies she had seized during the war. Dealing with Britain was going to be difficult for she was by far the most powerful of the allies—she dominated the seas and possessed the strongest merchant navy and the largest financial and commercial resources.

Despite this position of strength, events were moving on in continental Europe without British participation or control. The Dutch rose in revolt in November 1813 and the whole question of guaranteeing Dutch independence became much more urgent, and with it the issue of protecting Britain from the threat that Antwerp in hostile hands was always felt to be. Then there was the question of the Grand Duchy of Warsaw and whether France, with or without Napoleon, would accept her 'natural' or 'historic' 1790 frontiers. The French insisted that peace negotiations would have to include the return of many of their colonies and the question of maritime rights, the latter anathema to the British government, which could impose its veto.

Meanwhile, in December 1813 Alexander, against the wishes of his allies and some of his own advisers, was determined to press ahead and defeat Napoleon in France. With such high stakes and the three British ambassadors not competent—Lord Cathcart in St Petersburg now a ponderous old general; Lord Aberdeen in Vienna young, inexperienced and easily flattered by Metternich; and Sir Charles Stewart, Castlereagh's half-brother in Berlin and a swashbuckling soldier—the cabinet decided to send Castlereagh himself to negotiate with the allies who were in dispute among themselves as to the potential spoils and manifesting their ingrained hostility towards Britain for her supposed arrogance and exploitation of the war for her colonial and financial profit.

The war, however, was not over and the representatives of the allies had to content themselves with beginning peace talks in February 1814 at Langres in eastern France, where the foreign secretary met Alexander for the first time: 'I think our greatest danger at present is the *chevalresque* tone in which the Emperor Alexander is disposed to push the war.'[31] As John Bew notes, 'The onward march of Alexander's Imperial army provided a strong visual testimony to the potential rebalancing of Europe under the sway of a resurgent Russia.'[32] More talks took place at Châtillon but it was obvious that the Russian emperor was determined to head for Paris and he abruptly suspended the talks. The Russian army, after resting on the Rhine, was now reinforced, plus the Austrians and Prussians, and advanced.[33] There were some setbacks, but on 31 March Alexander led the victorious allies into Paris, his apotheosis.

For the first fortnight of April Alexander enjoyed predominance in European affairs as principal spokesman for the allies and *de facto* ruler of France. But the question of what regime would replace Napoleon had now to be faced. The Russian emperor had opposed the idea of a Bourbon restoration, holding the exiled Louis XVIII in contempt, but with Britain insisting on the king's return, he gave way—a Russian puppet was avoided.

The allied leaders, Castlereagh and Metternich, were based in Dijon in early April awaiting the end of all hostilities and when they arrived in Paris on 10 April they learned that Alexander had concluded the Treaty of Fontainebleau without consulting them. Although it basically only covered Napoleon's abdication and future exile to Elba, it was far from satisfactory, with the island all too close to France. Nevertheless, it was preferable to Napoleon's seeming desire for asylum (expressed years later) in England.[34]

Louis XVIII arrived in France on 3 May and Wellington, back from Spain and with his headquarters in Toulouse, became British ambassador.

In this new situation a confident Castlereagh could lead the negotiations for a lasting settlement. France grudgingly lost some colonies captured by the British and managed to withstand British pressure to abolish the slave trade, but it was an astonishingly generous settlement for a country that had waged war throughout Europe for so long. The first Peace of Paris was signed at the end of May, but there were many far more controversial subjects to be settled over the dissolution of Napoleon's empire that would be better debated outside France. Therefore a congress was to be held in Vienna in July.

Alexander to all intents and purposes invited himself to London for preliminary negotiations, where he expected to be feted as in Paris. The Prince Regent, the British government and public held him in high esteem, but Castlereagh, the only one to have met the emperor, warned the prime minister: 'When I recommend you to dilute the libation to Russia, I am the last to wish it should be less palatable. The Emperor has the greatest merit, and must be held high, but he ought to be grouped, and not made the sole feature for admiration.'[35] Alexander's taste for the spotlight dissuaded the Austrian emperor from being 'grouped' and fortunately for serious discussion, the chancellor Metternich attended. Frederick William of Prussia was happy enough just to be present.

The now widowed Russian Grand Duchess Catherine, Duchess of Oldenburg, Alexander's favourite sister, had been in London since March and had already alienated most of British society. The Russian ambassador's wife, Dorothea Lieven, who was no sluggard in wanting to impose herself, wrote that 'The Grand Duchess had an immoderate thirst for authority and a very high, and possibly excessive, opinion of herself ... I never saw a woman so given over to the need to stir, act, put herself forward and eclipse others.'[36] All went wrong from the outset. The grand duchess had booked a room in the Pulteney Hotel in Piccadilly where the Prince Regent called on her the following day to welcome her. However, he arrived before the grand duchess had finished dressing and they met on the staircase where she refused to receive him. Each took an instant dislike to other and throughout the following month the prince's hostility grew. 'Handsome though he is', Catherine wrote to her brother, 'he is a man visibly used up by dissipation and rather disgusting. His much-boasted affability is the most licentious, I may say obscene, strain I have ever listened to.'[37] Alexander had already been briefed unfavourably about the regent by Lieven who described the prince as 'little capable of dealing with serious matters'.[38]

Catherine met members of the opposition and announced that she intended to visit the Princess of Wales, the regent's estranged wife. At this Lieven threatened to resign if she went ahead: the grand duchess demurred. But, undeterred, she visited Princess Charlotte, whose relations with her father the Prince Regent were strained. The saga of diplomatic disasters continued.

Catherine had been obliged to cross the North Sea with the high admiral, William, Duke of Clarence, third son of George III, and put up with his obvious advances. She assured her brother: 'This only I know for certain, that I shall not become Mrs Clarence.'[39] Sailor Billy, in no way put off by the unfriendly grand duchess, volunteered his ships for Alexander's crossing, something the emperor could not refuse.[40] Surprisingly though, the emperor, who had manifested a clear taste for public appearances in Paris, wrote to Clarence saying that he wished to travel incognito.[41]

Even though he was being imposed on by Alexander's self-invited visit, the Prince Regent was prepared to lay on full honours for the emperor. For his part Alexander began well, exclaiming at Dover, 'God be praised; I have set my foot upon the land which saved us all.'[42] It all turned sour though when it became clear that the emperor was more interested in popular acclaim than in pleasing his host, plus the nefarious influence of the grand duchess, with her venomous barbs about the Prince Regent, served to aggravate the situation. The prince expected Alexander to stay at St James's Palace, where rooms had been prepared for him. These were spurned and the emperor joined his sister at the Pulteney Hotel. Crowds had gathered to witness his arrival. He stepped out on to the balcony to acknowledge the rapturous reception of the populace. The regent knew only too well that he was more likely to be hissed than cheered when he went out.

Over the next few days the relationship between the prince and the emperor deteriorated yet further. They kept each other waiting and, when they did meet, scarcely spoke. Alexander went out of his way to talk to leaders of the Whig opposition. One, Lord Grey, was annoyed and embarrassed by this attention, describing the emperor as 'a vain silly fellow'.[43] The Russian emperor caused more offence when he remarked on seeing the regent with his mistress, Lady Hertford, 'Just look at those two fat people.'[44] Metternich, on the other hand, charmed all whom he met, something that stood him in good stead in the years that followed.

A visit to Oxford, where Alexander stayed at Merton College, admired Christ Church and New College, attended a banquet at the Radcliffe

Camera and received the degree of Doctor of Civil Law at the Sheldonian Theatre, passed without incident. However, the final banquet at the Guildhall in London marked the culmination of royal Anglo-Russian estrangement. After disagreement as to who should ride in which coach, Catherine, faced with the prospect of singing, dampened the festivities by reminding the Prince Regent that music always made her feel ill. Throughout the evening he treated the two Russians to 'a haughty silence'.[45] (The only person on whom Alexander made a favourable impression was the Quaker William Allen.)

Diplomatically and socially the three weeks Alexander spent in England proved a disaster. He appeared unaware of the effect of his boorishness. He had antagonized the Prince Regent, later King George IV, for life, Castlereagh deeply distrusted him and politicians of both parties were now very wary of him.

The painting at Petworth House in Sussex of the seemingly friendly departure of the Russians in the presence of the Prince Regent presents a less accurate view than George Cruickshank's cartoons ridiculing the emperor. It was the British government who determined relations with Russia, but the hostility towards Russia on the part of the regent was now an additional factor which clouded future Anglo-Russian relations. In St Petersburg they were well aware of the British opinion of the emperor. Count Karl Nesselrode, the foreign minister, explained Alexander's feelings to Lieven. He was worried about:

> all the indications that the Prince Regent has become very hostile to Our August Master … a reflection of his weaknesses … The Emperor hopes that this personality cannot determine the policy of the British Cabinet … His Imperial Majesty instructs you to find out what is the real cause of this regrettable estrangement.[46]

As the ambassador had already told his masters that the Prince Regent enjoyed decorations and honours which came with colourful uniforms, Lieven was instructed to send details of 'everything of this kind that would please His Royal Highness, find out what would be to his expensive tastes and flatter his vanity. Already the Russian uniform that had been chosen was being made up as quickly as possible and with all the required magnificence.'[47] In addition the regent was to be offered the honorary command of a Russian regiment. The emperor, it was insisted, had never intended to insult the prince and had no reason to blame himself. He later wrote to the regent telling him that he was choosing some special Asian horses to send as a present.[48] (Whether the corpulent regent would be able to mount such horses seems doubtful.) Alexander's generosity seems excessive for someone who claimed he had nothing for which to reproach himself.

The Congress of Vienna that opened in September 1814 had to deal with outstanding territorial arrangements and draw up a new constitution for Germany. Discord among the powers immediately became evident. Castlereagh wanted France and Spain to participate but Prussia vetoed this. However, it was the question of Poland that was to prove the most contentious and pit Britain against Russia. Alexander, who so far had wrapped himself in inscrutable mystery as to his plans for Poland, demanded that Castlereagh see him, and held forth for two and a half hours:

> Very early on in the interview the Emperor opened his views with respect to Poland in considerable detail … his plan namely to retain the whole of Duchy of Warsaw, with the exception of a small portion … which he meant to assign to Prussia, erecting the remainder together with his Polish Provinces formerly dismembered into a Kingdom under the dominion of Russia … That it was a sense of moral duty which dictated the measure and that it could not but prove grateful to the British Nation.
>
> I represented that most certainly the British Government would view with great satisfaction the restoration of Poland to its independence as a Nation, but that they took a broad distinction between the erection of a part of Poland into a Kingdom merged in the Crown of Russia, and the restoration of the whole or greater part into a distinct and independent State.[49]

The following day Nesselrode called on the foreign secretary and repeated Alexander's intention of keeping the entire Grand Duchy of Warsaw. Castlereagh objected to such blatant Russian aggrandizement which would effectively replace French hegemony with that of Russia, but with half a million Russian troops occupying it, the emperor saw no reason to budge. Indeed, he complained that Great Britain had become his principal enemy and petulantly avoided Castlereagh at balls. The possibility of war was openly discussed on both sides.

At the same time that Alexander was throwing his weighty around Vienna (and engaging in non-stop womanizing), his minister of finance, Dmitri Guriev (Nesselrode's father-in-law), was trying to raise much-needed money in London. Lieven had been attempting unsuccessfully ever since his arrival to procure a loan. The British government would only consider a public loan as tantamount to a subsidy, something the

Russian authorities wished to separate. The ambassador explained to St Petersburg that the British government wanted to abolish income tax at the end of hostilities and this meant less money to lend. In late 1814 Lieven approached Harman and Co. Bank with a request for £600,000 to £1 million. He was offered a maximum of £120,000 which he turned down as derisory.[50]

The minister of finance then sent an appeal through General Sabloukov, the general's Russian-born father-in-law, to the London merchant, John Julius Angerstein (best known as the man whose art collection formed the nucleus of the National Gallery in London). The Russian ambassador was extremely irritated at being bypassed via this unofficial channel. Angerstein took it upon himself to see the prime minister, Lord Liverpool, and request a private loan for Russia. He reported to Guriev that 'the business has failed notwithstanding the greatest and best of my endeavours'.[51]

Lieven pointed out, not for the first time, that part of the reason the British government and the City of London were reluctant to lend money to Russia was the high Russian tariff. Samuel Thornton, governor of the British Factory in Russia, had made it clear to the ambassador that Anglo-Russian relations would not improve unless 'British merchants were treated on the same footing as Russian ones'. Even Castlereagh brought up the subject of the British complaint when negotiating with the Russians: 'The Secretary of State again brought up the question of our commercial relations ... and he reminded me of the promise Your Excellency had made on behalf of His Majesty.'[52]

The foreign secretary tried to follow his mentor Pitt's example by wooing Austria and Prussia with a view to creating a bloc to combat any future French or Russian expansionism. However, both these countries were set on incompatible territorial gain. In the end the prolonged deadlock was broken by Castlereagh, with firmness, patience and hard work. Prussia was to be compensated for the loss of her Polish territories by part of Saxony and Russia ceded some of the former Duchy of Warsaw to Prussia and Austria. Castlereagh, though, failed to save Poland from Russia.

Only days after the foreign secretary returned to London in March 1815, news arrived of Napoleon's escape from Elba. The powers instinctively drew together and began mustering their forces, though when Alexander put himself forward as the Allied generalissimo, he immediately encountered British objections. Castlereagh and the now Duke of Wellington both insisted that Wellington had to be in charge. The latter

> took a far less exalted view of the Tsar than most of his contemporaries, and was less in thrall to the Russians, who, as he put it, to his brother, 'have neither wealth nor commerce, nor anything that is desirable excepting 400,000 men, about whom they make more noise than they deserve'.[53]

Wellington left Vienna for Brussels where he established his headquarters and embarked on persuading the allies to provide at least 150,000 men. As usual the British government was expected to foot the bill while being accused of parsimony. Only about a fifth of this number took part in the decisive battle of Waterloo on 18 June that finally ended Napoleon's domination of Europe, and the march across France into Paris that followed. Alexander's men had not even begun to cross the Rhine and the subsequent collapse of Napoleonic resistance was so swift that Wellington was left with a free hand to ensure that a moderate government competent to negotiate with the allies was in place.

The final peacemaking in Vienna dragged on for almost five months. France had to retire behind its 1790 frontiers, pay an indemnity and support an army of occupation. Alexander, who had now embarked on his religious phase, was now more cordial to Castlereagh, but when the emperor brought his new-found piety into international politics in his proposal for a Holy Alliance of the four powers, he encountered suppressed hilarity on the part of the British government. The foreign secretary reported that Alexander had:

> developed his whole plan of universal peace, and told him that the three Sovereigns had agreed to address a letter to the Prince Regent to invite him to accede. Wellington happened to be in the room when the Emperor called, and it was not without difficulty that he went through the interview with becoming gravity. Foreseeing the awkwardness of this sublime mysticism and nonsense, especially to a British Sovereign, I examined with Prince Metternich every practical expedient to stop it.[54]

Nevertheless, the Prussian and Austrian monarchs signed, despite their reservations, which put Castlereagh into 'what may be called a scrape', since the only thing wrong with the alliance was its 'excessive excellence', and it would be unwise to antagonize Alexander: 'The fact is that the Emperor's mind is not completely sound.'[55]

The second treaty drafted by Alexander was easier for the British government to stomach, although Castlereagh thought that the text committed the allies too strongly to upholding the existing regime in France and successfully toned it down. The most important article was the formation of the Quadruple Alliance of the victorious powers which was acceptable to the British government. The signatories agreed to meet at fixed intervals to ensure that the peace treaty was respected. Castlereagh widened this provision such that the powers would consult on matters of common interest. Such was the creation of the congress system, the 'New Diplomacy'.

9

THE NEW DIPLOMACY

1815–1825

Castlereagh had recognized that Russia would from 1815 rightly demand to play a greater role than ever in European affairs and that Russia might well replace France as the main danger to the European equilibrium—the disagreement over Poland at Vienna had augured deep differences of ideology and geopolitics. The foreign secretary, with his years of personal experience of dealing with the European powers, was convinced that peace could only be maintained if diplomacy were conducted in a spirit very different from that in the past. He 'wished, in fact, to make permanent the European Council which had grown up in the course of the final struggle against Napoleon'.[1] He told the House of Commons in February 1816:

> If the Councils of the Sovereigns had not been brought together ... he was sure that the Councils of Europe would have been disturbed to such an extent by doubts and misapprehensions that those great exertions whose successful issue was now before the world, would never have been made.[2]

To perpetuate this new system, the New Diplomacy, imposed no new obligations but provided Britain with the opportunity for her to continue the work of reconciliation of the previous two years. Castlereagh instructed his ambassadors that they should discourage:

> that spirit of petty intrigue and perpetual propagation of alarm, upon slight evidence and ancient jealousies, which too frequently disgrace the diplomatic profession ... You must not however suppose that I counsel you to become the dupe of designing men or shut your eyes to those circumstances which may affect the interests of your own Court.[3]

Although Castlereagh treated Alexander's Holy Alliance with amused tolerance, there was much in common with it in the high-minded view of international relations expressed in the dispatch.

This New Diplomacy had first been put into writing when the foreign secretary claimed tongue-in-cheek that he took 'advantage of a bad day to spare the pheasants'.[4] It was not surprising that the Whigs and Radicals expressed their antipathy to the absolutist state of Russia, but the Tory government, for all Castlereagh's avowed aims and emollient language towards the Russian ambassador, was seen as at least wary of Russia. Christoph Lieven reported home in February 1816:

> The colossal power of Russia, her intimate links with all the cabinets of Europe, the habitual glory of her armies and the bent that is attributed to the Empire for war, offer to Lord Castlereagh many reasons to be fearful and suspicious of us ... Perhaps it was Austria who first sowed the seeds of distrust of us.[5]

Here the ambassador was correct in his suspicion of the hand of Metternich.

The continuing personal animosity of the Prince Regent towards Alexander I was a cause of concern to the Russians. Lieven told Nesselrode: 'I did not realize how great was the bitterness felt by the Prince Regent until I learned of what he had said several times about the Emperor.'[6] 'Excellency', he told the vice chancellor, 'you will no doubt be surprised to hear me attribute personal jealousy of the Emperor ... his military and political reputation ... all this shows him as a redoubtable rival of the Prince Regent. Such, Count, is the weakness of spirit that characterizes this Prince.'[7]

There was a great deal of talk of intrigues perpetuated by Russian diplomats and agents in Madrid, Paris, Naples and elsewhere that provoked the suspicion and hostility of their British colleagues. Supposed Russian activity in Spain in particular, it was claimed, had led to a secret treaty by which Russia would acquire Minorca in return for the sale of her fleet to Spain. According to Lieven, the king of Spain had approached Alexander about problems in Spanish territorial waters and asked to build some ships in Russia. Instead, Russia offered some of her old ships.

William Cathcart, 1st Earl Cathcart, in St Petersburg was among those nervous about Russian hostile activity. But the foreign secretary refused to be worried. He wrote to the ambassador: 'My object is to calm and assure that everything that can shake the general Alliance [and] interrupt the harmony of the Courts of London and St Petersburg, whose interests I conceive when well understood ought to render their connection indissoluble.'[8]

In view of the atmosphere of frostiness between Britain and Russia that had been developing throughout 1816, Alexander decided to send his younger brother, the Grand Duke Nicholas, to Britain in an attempt to patch up relations with the Prince Regent. The visit began inauspiciously in November 1816 when the regent kept the grand duke waiting for twenty-five minutes. Lieven protested at the insult. The prince then hastily invited Nicholas to dinner the following day and, in the best tradition of diplomatic tit for tat, the ambassador instructed the grand duke to arrive a quarter of an hour late. The young man made a favourable impression on London society during his ten-day visit, before being dispatched to Scotland in early December for a three-week stay in Edinburgh and Glasgow (at least less cold and grey than St Petersburg in December), followed by short stays in English cities. He was then entertained by the Prince Regent in Brighton. The British government footed the bill for the visit that did little to improve relations between the two countries and their rulers.

The three substantive subjects of disagreement between Britain and Russia were disarmament, the new Russian tariff and Persia, on all of which Castlereagh bent over backwards in his dealings with the Russian government. Britain, Prussia and Austria had already reduced their armies (though Britain kept quiet about her own naval forces) and the Russian emperor was invited to do the same. The foreign secretary showed understanding of the Russian position. 'There is much weight', he wrote to Cathcart,

> in the Russian remark that their army does not admit of such management, and that the military machine, once let down, can only be restored in Russia after long time, labour and expense ... As the Emperor likes an army, as he likes an influence in Europe, and is under an impression of some alarm with respect to the political effervescence of the times, I do not expect him very rapidly to part with the troops he has formed.[9]

Trade, the binding factor in Anglo-Russian relations before the Napoleonic wars, posed problems. Although commercial matters had not played a part in the negotiations of 1814–15, with the restoration of peace they inevitably came to the fore. The Corn Laws of 1815 protecting British agriculture deprived Britain of potentially large and profitable trade in grain with Poland and Ukraine. British lumber merchants faced discrimination in the Baltic. Most importantly, Russia still had the quasi-monopoly of the import into Britain of tallow, flax, hemp and linseed. The balance of trade, British exports to Russia being mainly cotton yarn and sugar, remained firmly in Russia's favour.

The new Russian tariff promulgated in 1814 had provoked outrage in British mercantile circles. Lord Walpole, the British consul general in St Petersburg, considered that it 'showed a most marked hostility to Gt. Br., and absurd jealousy of her Commercial System'.[10] He warned the governor of the Russia Company in London of the detrimental effects of the new tariff and the British press was only too willing to publish alarming articles on the subject. Whether this was the reason or not, Russian import duties on a number of items were lowered in 1818, though that on lump sugar, an important commodity, was raised in 1821 to strong British protests. No less inimical to cordial commercial relations was the way in which the customs system was administered. The inefficiency and corruption of Russian officials were widely attested. Cargoes were forfeited for technical violations of obscure regulations and rates were changed with little warning. British property owners in St Petersburg complained that they were paying higher tax rates than Russian owners. All too often the good offices of consuls failed to gain any redress.

Persia had first assumed a position of significance in British eyes when Napoleon's Egyptian expedition in 1798, and the subsequent activities of his agents, had given rise to fears that India was vulnerable overland. An Anglo-Persian alliance was followed by a treaty in November 1814 in which Britain promised to lend Persia military or pecuniary assistance in the event of an unprovoked attack by a European power, this in return for a promise of aid by Persia against an invasion of India or Afghanistan. The danger from France was removed in 1815: thus the engagement was directed against Russia. Since the turn of the century Russia had been following a policy of quiet expansion in Transcaucasia at the expense of the Ottoman empire and Persia. The Treaty of Gulistan had been imposed on Persia in 1813 confirming Russian acquisitions, but Britain in her treaty with Persia the following year included the right to mediate in disputes between Russia and Persia and called for definition of the Russo-Persian boundary by negotiation among the three powers.

In accordance with the 1814 treaty Britain was keen to exert her right as mediator in 1816 and not let Russia get away with all that she claimed about securing her frontier with Persia, the lack of good maps making this difficult. Persia sent an ambassador to St Petersburg who pleaded with

Cathcart for British intervention over disputed territory. Nesselrode would have none of it. He could 'not add anything to the legitimate reasons that had decided His Majesty to decline any foreign intervention in the negotiation of his Empire's interests in Persia'.[11] The Russian government's aim was to force the Persians to cut loose from Britain. (This marked the beginning of serious Anglo-Russian rivalry over Persia that was to continue for the rest of the century and that the Anglo-Russian Convention of 1907 did not resolve.)

In March 1818 Castlereagh proposed that the first of the periodic conferences envisaged in the Quadruple Alliance Treaty should be held in the near future. Alexander had already been pressing for a conference and welcomed the resumption of summit diplomacy. For Metternich a congress was a welcome diversion from routine. The Prince Regent was tempted by the prospect of a continental trip but was dissuaded from attending the Congress of Aix-la-Chapelle.

The Russian emperor, eager to be seen as the protector of small states, wanted to invite Spain and lesser European states, but he ceded to British and Austrian objections, although he did succeed in insisting that French plenipotentiaries should be invited as he had now taken up the mantle of champion of the restoration of France to great power status. Given that Castlereagh and the Duke of Wellington agreed on the need to end the military occupation of France, the matter was expeditiously dealt with. Alexander was also fully aware that a strong France would constitute a useful counterweight to the combination of Britain and Austria, whose relations had been warm and close since 1815.

So far Britain could go along with the Russian emperor's agenda, but a major source of Anglo-Russian disagreement arose over Alexander's attempt to extend and strengthen the Quadruple Alliance. He proposed a new pact in which the powers would guarantee one another's territorial possessions and political systems as they existed. This would have established a closely knit organization of Europe, a protective union against revolution, and would have permitted a virtually unlimited right of intervention by the powers in each other's internal affairs. Alexander also lent his support to a Prussian proposal to create a European army with Russian forces at the centre, based in Brussels and with the Duke of Wellington as commander in chief. 'A more ingenious device for keeping us in hot water could not have been invented', was Castlereagh's scornful reaction.[12]

However wary the foreign secretary was of the Russian emperor's grandiose ideas, back in London the cabinet, in particular George

Canning, President of the Board of Control for India, was alarmed that Castlereagh had been seduced by the charm of a post-war European get-together and would allow Britain to become entangled in further unwanted commitments. Knowledge of the Russian emperor's drive to organize Europe according to his vision served to elicit increasing insularity in the cabinet, already worried about parliamentary opposition. Castlereagh had to walk a tightrope. In this he was successful at Aix-la-Chapelle; he asserted the British government's view that the Quadruple Alliance was essentially the instrument to prevent the recurrence of French aggression and not the basis for a European super-government. He had also maintained the goodwill of Alexander, who believed that the protocol that resulted affirmed the spirit of the Holy Alliance.

The Russian emperor was already personally aware of the melodramas current in the British royal family, since he had met many members in London in 1814. Frequent updates followed in dispatches from Christoph Lieven. In addition, no one was better informed about royal gossip than his wife Dorothea, Countess Lieven, a social celebrity much appreciated by the Prince Regent, despite his anti-Russian feelings. Her husband satisfied the less glamorous insatiable appetite in St Petersburg by passing on the latest political news.

The Prince Regent's dispute with his erratic wife, Caroline of Brunswick, provided plenty of juicy royal news: 'The estrangement and the hate of the Prince Regent towards His Spouse have even increased since the Departure of this Princess ... No details of Her private life have escaped the knowledge of the Prince.'[13] The rumour of a possible second marriage of the prince to Princess Sophia of Gloucester and the reaction of his current mistress, Lady Hertford, were viewed with a pitiless eye: 'The lack of charm and grace that she [Sophia] possesses and her narrow-minded spirit, made her little feared by the Marchioness [Hertford].'[14]

When the regent's poor daughter Charlotte had at last met a marriageable man whom she liked, her father was obstructive: 'The aversion that the regent feels towards his daughter has been shown in the continual delays he has caused to the celebration of this marriage.'[15] The minor German princeling in question, Leopold of Saxe-Coburg-Saalfeld, had served in the Russian army in 1813–14 (for want of other employment) and his sister Juliana was married to Alexander's younger brother Constantine. Thus the Prince Regent was suspicious that Leopold might harbour pro-Russian sentiments and it was one of the reasons for his reticence.

There was no shortage of unsavoury tales about the other dissolute sons of George III, but it was with the king's fourth son, Edward, Duke of Kent, that Alexander became involved. Even before the death of Princess Charlotte and her stillborn child in November 1817, the Prince Regent's younger brothers had embarked on a frantic race to produce legitimate heirs. Early in 1816 the Duke of Kent, a brutal man who, despite his royal position, had been dismissed from the army for cruelty, suggested to Count Lieven that Princess Katherine Amelia of Baden, sister of the Russian Empress Elizabeth, might be a suitable match for him. 'Following arrangements established between the Duke of Kent and me', the ambassador wrote to Nesselrode,

> he is off ... [to Baden] to meet Princess Amelia ... I have the honour to inform Your Excellency that, in conformity with the authorisation that I have received from our August court, and after the request of the Duke of Kent to pay for his journey, I have paid him a thousand guineas.[16]

As if this was not enough, the duke asked Lieven 'to procure for him a bear skin from Russia'.[17] The duke found the princess odious and aged forty-one. End of episode.

The following year the duke tried to ingratiate himself with Alexander I with an unctuous letter accompanied by the gift of a book. But he was back to more serious matters a year later as he was now in pursuit of Prince Leopold's widowed sister Victoria, knowing that Leopold was popular in Britain and therefore a useful ally. As Edward was heavily in debt (living in Brussels which was much cheaper than London) and his eldest brother, the Prince Regent, refused to help him, the Russian emperor was asked for more financial assistance to which he acquiesced. In January 1819 came another request for money, to which the emperor replied that the 'financial difficulties confronting my Empire prevent me from being able to fulfil my sincere desire to satisfy your requirements'.[18] He simply could not 'at this moment find such a sum as that Y.R.H. asks'.[19] However he relented a couple of months later on learning that the duchess, whom Edward had married in 1818, was pregnant and that the duke lacked the funds to travel to England for the birth: 'If an advance of 100,000 florins could comply with the wishes of Y.R.H., You will find a credit for this sum attached, of which the reimbursement will be entirely at Your convenience.'[20] The Duchess of Kent for her part twice wrote asking for financial help for her son by her first marriage. But Alexander refused to be drawn.[21] (Despite these rebuffs, the duchess in 1827 wrote to Alexander's successor again asking for help for her son.)

The baby girl born to the duchess on 24 May 1819 had as godfathers the Prince Regent and the emperor of Russia. After much tergiversation on the part of the regent the girl was baptized Alexandrina Victoria, or, as the duke wrote to Alexander, 'Alexandrine Victoire, the first name being given to perpetuate in Her the memory of the August Sovereign who for a long time has overwhelmed the Father and Mother with his goodness'.[22] The child was known for a few years as Drina, a diminutive of Alexandrina, despite the regent's dislike of Alexander. Less than a year later the Duke of Kent was dead.

Queen Victoria seems to have heard that Russian money had played a role in her birth. She told Lord Rosebery in 1894: 'She did not know if she was Alexandrina Victoria or *vice versa*. Quite true that George IV wished her to be Georgina, and that the Duke of Kent insisted on Alexandrina as the Russian Emperor had been so kind.'[23]

From 1819 to 1821, events underlined the precarious nature of the links between Britain and the conservative powers, above all Russia, and demonstrated the difficult path Castlereagh felt compelled to follow in order to preserve the unity of the Quadruple Alliance.[24] In parliament and in the press he received repeated warnings that few of his fellow countrymen were prepared to accept continental commitments, apart from consolidating British security against France.

The ideological gulf between Britain and her partners was illustrated in 1820. Alexander had been keen to intervene in Spain for the previous three years, and his ambassador there bombarded St Petersburg with dire warnings of the dangers posed by Spanish liberals who demanded a return to the 1812 constitution that had been replaced by the restrictive one accompanying the Bourbon restoration in Spain in 1815. When in March insurgents forced the king to restore the 1812 constitution, Alexander insisted that it was the duty of the five allies (now including France) to stamp out the flames of revolution.

The Russian response to events so far distant from its frontiers aroused suspicion in London, where the last thing the government wanted to see was a Russian peninsular campaign and the establishment of Russian naval bases in Spain to serve its Mediterranean fleet. Castlereagh had little difficulty in convincing the allies of the folly of the Russian proposals.

The revolt in Spain was not the only one to take place in 1820. Britain had been shaken by the Cato Street conspiracy in London, aimed to liquidate the cabinet. This failed, but in France Louis XVIII's nephew, the Duke of Berri, was assassinated. In mid-July a liberal revolution, similar in character to the rising in Spain, broke out in Naples, Austrian territory. The following month a military revolt took place in Portugal, where a revolutionary junta replaced the regency.

In Castlereagh's opinion the rising in Naples had less justification on the grounds of misrule than in Spain and Portugal, but he believed that it was also more dangerous and Austria was entitled to intervene, although Britain would only provide moral support. However, Metternich dared not act without Russia and had to agree to Alexander's demand for a further full congress. But so strong was the feeling in London against military involvement in continental affairs that Castlereagh could only send an observer to Troppau in the autumn of 1820 and the French followed suit.

Although the British and French representatives were excluded from most of the discussions at Troppau, the foreign secretary knew roughly what had been decided and was furious at the arrogant stance of the eastern powers who were claiming a right of coercion against any revolutionary state. In early December he laid into Lieven:

> It is impossible not to consider the right which the Monarchs claim to judge and to condemn the actions of other states as a precedent dangerous to the liberties of the world. There is a very great danger in allowing such a system to be established ... and although the individual principles of the Monarch guarantee the benignity of their own views, nevertheless no man can see without a certain feeling of fear the lot of every nation submitted to the decisions and the will of such a tribunal.[25]

As John Bew writes, 'Castlereagh made it clear that Britain was not to be associated in any way with what had been agreed at Troppau.'[26]

More evidence of Alexander's increasing conservatism and unpredictability came after the outbreak of a mutiny in the Semenovsky regiment in St Petersburg in 1820, in reality a protest at conditions, but which the emperor preferred to regard as part of a revolutionary conspiracy throughout Europe. At the Congress of Laibach in January 1821, which Castlereagh refused to attend, the arch-conservative Metternich had no difficulty in convincing Alexander of the existence of an international revolutionary committee.

The close collaboration of the conservative powers was shattered in April 1821 when the Greek population of the Morea rose in revolt against its Ottoman rulers. The vulnerability of the Ottoman empire had been evident for many years and it soon became clear that the Turks would not be able to bring this latest threat to their authority speedily under control. The Russians had in the past shown themselves quick to turn any Ottoman weakness to their advantage and there existed in 1821 many outstanding disputes between the two empires. Nevertheless, there was a danger that the Russians might become involved through sympathy for their Orthodox co-religionists in Greece.

Castlereagh's response to the Greek revolt was to urge restraint in both St Petersburg and Constantinople. He warned the Porte that Britain would not support Turkey were it to provoke a war with Russia, who was becoming more bellicose. In St Petersburg the Ottoman countermeasures against the Greeks were seen as totally disproportionate and unacceptable. Diplomatic relations with Constantinople were broken off. Furthermore, Russian maritime trade was suffering from Turkish efforts to prevent supplies reaching the Greeks and Russian feelings were outraged by Turkish atrocities, such as the hanging of the Greek patriarch of Constantinople. The presence of the strongly Turcophile British ambassador, Lord Strangford, in the Ottoman capital and a short-lived revolt against the Turks in their Danubian Principalities then reopened the question of respective Russo-Turkish rights in the region.

Alexander had been at first genuinely shocked by the draconian repression of the Greek insurgency by Turkey, but under prodding from Metternich he came to see the problem as one of maintaining the status quo, even if it involved supporting a Muslim sultan. Appeals from the Orthodox Greeks fell upon deaf Russian ears and in 1822 the emperor sidelined the Ionian born Count Ioannis Capodristrias, in Russian service since 1809 and joint foreign minister with Nesselrode since 1816, who advocated Russian intervention on behalf of the Greeks.

Then, in April 1822, the appalling slaughter of over 20,000 Greeks in Chios horrified Europe. In August of that year George Canning succeeded Castlereagh on the latter's suicide. The new foreign secretary had long been recognized as having a brilliant mind and great political skills but was heartily disliked and distrusted by many of his contemporaries, although he was never vilified to the extent that Castlereagh was. While Greece was the most urgent problem facing the powers at the next congress in Verona, at which Britain had agreed to participate, Alexander insisted that Spain should top the agenda, even though the Spanish question had lain dormant for two years. To British eyes this highjacking of the congress was a cover for Russia's frustration at her inability to intervene in the Greek crisis, and the means to reaffirm the validity of the Quadruple Alliance by intervention in a region where there was less conflict of interests among the eastern powers.

The Duke of Wellington represented Britain at Verona and duly refused to approve any plans for military action in Spain. The true victors at Verona were the French (despite British dissent), who were authorized to take military action against the Spanish liberals if the situation in Madrid deteriorated to a point where intervention was felt in Paris to be necessary for the wellbeing of Europe. However, something more than virtuous inactivity was necessary if the British position was to be respected. Hence, the prime minister, Lord Liverpool, spoke in praise of the Spanish liberal constitution in the House of Lords in early February 1823, and ten days later Canning warned Lieven that Britain would never allow France to recover its previous influence in Spain and would oppose it in any struggle that ensued. This was strong diplomatic language, but in private he admitted that Britain had neither the military nor the financial resources to engage in another peninsular conflict as a decade of retrenchment and savage cuts in the service establishments had destroyed Britain's power to fight a continental war.

The Russian ambassador sent a stream of dispatches home complaining about Canning's objections to intervention in Spain and the foreign secretary's boasting of his aversion to the congress system. Lieven tried to ingratiate himself with Wellington from whom he knew he would receive a different interpretation of government thinking, and he reported an audience with George IV in which the king expressed his opposition to Canning.[27] Nevertheless, it was the government who made policy and in April Liverpool issued a more forceful warning that British neutrality did not imply an unwillingness or inability to fight if necessary. But British threats failed to prevent the French military occupation of Spain. The Spanish crisis was a major rebuff for Canning who henceforth was determined that he would be the master rather than the victim of events.

Although the foreign secretary was as unwilling as his predecessor to interfere in Greece, Canning was faced with considerable pressure from philhellene feeling in Britain to aid the Greeks, with the best known, though not the most effective volunteer to fight in the Greek forces, being Lord Byron. In 1823 the British government recognized the Greek rebels as belligerents, though this was more to do with protecting British shipping than a political stance, and in 1824 the Greeks received the first of a series of British loans which in effect made the City of London the financier of the revolution. While British public opinion was largely behind the Greeks, for Canning the Ottoman empire was a barrier against the advance of Russian power in the eastern Mediterranean. Therefore the government did not want to risk alienating Russia with whom relations had deteriorated further over Spain. Canning was forced to intervene.

In January 1824 Alexander proposed as a solution to the Greek question the establishment of three autonomous Greek principalities. This both disappointed the Greeks, who saw it as a means to deny them independence and unity, and aroused the suspicions of the powers, above all Britain, who saw the scheme (unfairly) as a camouflage for Russian control of Greece. The emperor also invited the powers to a conference in St Petersburg (insisting that Russia was the power most concerned) to discuss a possible settlement, but Canning would only allow the British ambassador there, Sir Charles Bagot, to attend if diplomatic relations were re-established between Russia and the Porte, that is, if the Russian threat of war was lifted.[28]

Although irritated that only Britain of the powers invited was making this demand, Alexander went along with the condition, nominating, but not sending, an ambassador to Constantinople, and the conference opened in June 1824. It lasted for only two meetings as both the Greeks and the Turks refused to accept the idea of autonomous principalities. In addition, negotiations over the Russo-Turkish disputes about Moldavia and Wallachia that Strangford was conducting in Constantinople dragged on until the end of the year. Russia had been strikingly unsuccessful in 1824 and Alexander laid the blame squarely on Canning.

Certainly, as Lieven realized, the foreign secretary had used the Greek question as part of his policy of ending the congress system: 'Not only satisfied at having isolated England from the Continental Alliance, all the efforts of the Secretary of State have been aimed at provoking dissension among the members of this union.'[29] However, the Russian emperor was by now an exhausted, depressed and sick man and gave up. Nesselrode wrote tersely to the ambassador in London: 'His Imperial Majesty sees any further discussion between Russia and England over relations with Turkey and the pacification of Greece as terminated.'[30] On being told this, an unrepentant Canning commented: 'I have not a word to say. H.M. the Emperor of Russia is the master of his own determination.'[31]

The Russian diplomatic retreat over Greece strengthened Canning's position and in February 1825 he demanded not only that there should be more than just the nomination of a Russian ambassador in Constantinople but he also made great play of the rejection of the Russian plan.[32] As Britain had refused to participate, inevitably the second phase of the discussions in St Petersburg was futile. Nesselrode, now completely in charge, and already embittered by the grudging and uncooperative attitude of Britain, was in addition disappointed by that of Russia's continental allies who would offer no support.

George IV also had become increasingly dissatisfied with his foreign secretary's policy towards Greece. The king liked to escape from London to Royal Lodge in Windsor Park where he was surrounded by 'the Cottage Clique', with whom he could lament the new liberalism and the attitudes sympathetic towards self-determination that were spreading so quickly. That the Clique included the Lievens, who were frequent guests, was more because he was an admirer of Dorothea Lieven, rather than her husband's position. She had been Metternich's mistress a few years before, and this added to her key status in taking part in the 'Cottage Plot' of spring 1825. Dorothea knew that Metternich was in Paris and, with the connivance of the Duke of Wellington, no fan of Canning, the plan was for the Austrian chancellor to make a secret trip across the Channel and work out a new programme for the Quintuple (France now being a member) Alliance with George IV and then return to France without so much as a nod towards the foreign secretary.

Meanwhile Canning, who had bought off the king's current mistress's son, got wind of the plot. He made it clear that he would expose it and thus broke its back, saying that he would have resigned and declared in the House of Commons that he had been driven out by the Holy Alliance: 'If after such a denunciation and the debates which would have followed, the Lievens and Esterhazys [the Austrians] did not find London too hot for them, then I know nothing of the present temper of the English nation.'[33]

One might well have concluded that Dorothea Lieven had made herself a liability to Russian diplomacy by plotting against Canning, but on a rare visit to her homeland, ostensibly for family reasons (she had not been there for thirteen years), her political acumen, intimate knowledge of British politics and *entrée* at the highest level led both Nesselrode and Alexander to enter into serious discussion with her. As the emperor now took little interest in foreign affairs, his abhorrence of Canning and British policy mattered little, but in a remark to Nesselrode, Alexander indicated that he had changed his mind over cutting off discussion with Britain: 'Could we not profit by her return to England to re-approach that

Cabinet?'[34] The vice chancellor went much further and sent the countess back to London as a 'living dispatch' with the message that should Britain be willing to restart talks about Greece, 'it will not be repulsed, and that we shall always be ready to welcome its ideas'.[35] Canning welcomed the overture. He knew now that if Britain made advances to cooperate over Greece, he could drive a wedge between Russia and Metternich, thus continuing the disintegration of the congress system by separating two of the conservative powers.

In September the foreign secretary made it clear that he was willing to mediate between the Porte and her Greek subjects because other events had taken place in addition to the Russian offer of cooperation. The sultan had called upon his nominal vassal, Mehemet Ali, the pasha of Egypt, to assist him in suppressing the Greeks, and the pasha duly dispatched his son, Ibrahim, who proceeded throughout 1825 with the ruthless and effective subjugation of the Peloponnese. Despite pleas by Greek leaders, Canning refused to consider making Greece a British protectorate on the grounds that this would effectively mean declaring war on the Porte. The subject was Greece, but the foreign secretary was at the same time anxious to prevent the ever-present threat of a Russo-Turkish war materializing. Russia would be the likely victor with repercussions for the balance of power. Canning's success in convincing Russia to work with Britain rather than her continental allies was illustrated in a dispatch from Lieven to Nesselrode in October 1825: 'In any case England is the Power which needs to be treated tactfully at the moment. Because if a crisis erupts her influence will be preponderant.'[36]

Alexander had left St Petersburg in mid-September for Taganrog, a small town on the Sea of Azov, to provide a warmer climate for his ailing wife, Elizabeth. By mid-November it was the emperor's own health that was giving most cause for concern. Despite the protestations of his personal physician, Sir James Wylie, he refused to accept any medication or allow himself to be bled. When Alexander finally submitted to treatment, little could be done and he died on 1 December 1825.

During his reign Alexander I had made Russia a more powerful and influential European power than ever before, but the last decade of his life represented a watershed, characterized by the growing contrast between Russia's external glory and internal stagnation. Much of the educated elite had become disillusioned by the failure of the regime to effect transformation of her political and social structures—the continued existence of serfdom and the absolutism of the monarchy. By the time of

Alexander's death, belief in peaceful reform to bring Russia closer to western European forms of government had largely faded. The divorce between the ruler and much of the powerful educated classes that was to plague Russia for the rest of the century was made clear within days.[37]

10

NICHOLAS I

The location and unexpectedness of Alexander's death in the south of Russia presented serious logistical problems when the news reached St Petersburg eight days later. It also gave rise to rumours of suicide, a substitute corpse, murder, even of no death at all. In this febrile atmosphere it was assumed that the Grand Duke Constantine, commander-in-chief in Poland and next in line after Alexander, would succeed to the throne. His younger brothers Nicholas and Mikhail and the Guards regiments duly took the oath of allegiance. Then news arrived from Warsaw that Constantine had sworn allegiance to Nicholas. On 13 December the younger brother issued his accession manifesto to the state council.

There is considerable evidence that the Grand Duke Nicholas had been designated to succeed Alexander. For a start Constantine had divorced his first wife, contracted a morganatic marriage to a Catholic Polish countess in 1820 and found full satisfaction for his limited ambitions in Poland. Two years later Constantine was known to have expressed his intention of renouncing the throne, a decision that was formally accepted by Alexander in 1823, when a manifesto declared Nicholas to be heir. However, all this was kept secret, even from Nicholas, the most bizarre of oversights. Some have claimed that Nicholas was in fact aware of his elder brother's renunciation but was reluctant to appear to be usurping the throne, as a message from Constantine abdicating was necessary before the younger brother could declare himself emperor, and this took several days to arrive.

It was this apparent sidelining of the rightful heir that spawned rumours of mischief in high places. Led by a group of young officers who expressed naive monarchism—the belief in the vital necessity of having the 'true' ruler on the throne—some 3,000 rebel troops took to the streets of St

Petersburg. The governor general of the city was shot dead: Nicholas marshalled 9,000 loyal soldiers and the Decembrist uprising was put down. Five ringleaders were executed and many more rebels exiled for life to Siberia.[1] Thus began a new era in imperial Russia, that of active political protest.

The new emperor, a handsome man, nearly 2 metres tall and nineteen years younger than Alexander, was convinced that the Decembrists were inspired by alien, western heresies that owed much to the French Revolution, and could be counteracted only by adherence to orthodoxy, Russian traditions and loyalty to the dynasty. Russian paranoia was fuelled by reports from the ambassador in London that Russian dissidents in the British capital were party to the Decembrist plot.[2] Henceforth as emperor, Nicholas sought to separate Russia's spiritual and intellectual life from that of western Europe with his mantra Orthodoxy, Autocracy and Nationality.

In *The Long Hangover: Putin's New Russia and the Ghosts of the Past*, Shaun Walker wrote of Russia in 2017 that President Putin believed that 'the new Russia should be a continuation of the Tsarist empire, with its triple ideology of Orthodoxy, Autocracy and Nationality'.[3]

Nicholas I defined his duty as that of military commander of Russia. It followed that he was reluctant to trust the cosmopolitan nobility as a class, was even more wary of the intelligentsia, but also even of the regular institutionalized bureaucracy. Only months after his accession he created the Third Section, the secret police which spread its tentacles of surveillance throughout Russia with an enormous network of spies and informers. Strict censorship and other controls were exercised over education, publishing and all manifestations of public life. After a while even the emperor himself could not control the vast bureaucratic police apparatus that he unleashed in 1826.

With his firm conviction that Russia must be ruled by a God-fearing autocrat, Nicholas I was 'the perfect despot': few liked him, but for sheer dedication to duty he won admirers and apologists both during his lifetime and later.[4] Alexander Pushkin, after initially being favourable, wrote that Nicholas I extolled 'the joys of autocratic power and the pleasure of the knout'.[5]

In Britain, Canning's reaction to the news of Alexander's death was expressed in his usual laconic manner: 'One element of the discord is removed by the removal of the principle of the Holy Alliance from the question of intervention' (i.e. Greece).[6] He gave scant recognition to the late emperor's good intentions: 'I am persuaded that though there were moments of enthusiasm, and paroxysms of ambition, the fixed purpose of his mind was not so much to liberate Greece, as to do that work as the blessed instrument of the Holy Alliance.'[7] The foreign secretary rightly believed that the new ruler would be Russian rather than cosmopolitan and thus could well be useful in breaking up what remained of the Holy Alliance.

When Canning learned at the end of 1825 that Lord Strangford, now ambassador in St Petersburg, had been recommending to Nesselrode a collective threat by the powers to Turkey, the envoy was subjected to the full ire of his master: 'By what part of your Instructions Your Excellency thought yourself at liberty to hold out this Intimation to the Court of St. Petersburg, I am at a loss to imagine.'[8] Two months later Strangford was still exceeding his instructions:

> You kept things secret from me ... We were able to speak to the Ottoman Porte the language of friendship and admonition without appearing to be one of a confederacy. You have inevitably changed Mr Stratford Canning's position in Constantinople, and have cut from under his feet the ground on which he was standing.[9]

The rebuke was long and bitter: 'We are again travelling in the old track of the discussions of last year from which we had so happily extricated ourselves. The Instructions which I have therefore now to give to Your Excellency are comprised in a few short words—"to be quiet".'[10] (It seems surprising that Strangford managed to hold on to his position until 1828. It was known in London that he had arrived from Constantinople with debts and in the Russian capital claimed a large sum for new ceremonial clothing that was hardly likely to be appreciated in London.)

However wary the foreign secretary was of Russia, diplomatic protocol demanded the sending of a message of commiseration and congratulation to the new emperor. Canning decided to entrust the mission to the Duke of Wellington, known to be the most prestigious man in Britain in Russian eyes, as the king's representative. But the duke's instructions of February 1826 went further than mere diplomatic niceties.[11] It was an opportunity to reopen negotiations with Russia over Greece. The instructions envisaged the use of force by Britain and Russia to create an autonomous Greek state tributary to the sultan and guaranteed by the powers. At the same time Russia had to be warned that 'a war with the Porte on any other account than that of the Greeks would be a war of ambition and conquest'.[12] After relatively brief discussions in St Petersburg the essentials of an Anglo-Russian agreement were reached and a protocol signed in April 1826 in which the two powers agreed that Britain should offer to mediate between the Greeks and the Turks (which the former had already requested). The sultan was to have a say in the nomination of Greek rulers but nothing was said about boundaries. Article III importantly provided that the agreement should not be dissolved even if Russia went to war with Turkey. It was not what the Greeks wanted as it failed to give them independence.

Wellington had been convinced that signing the protocol was necessary as he believed Russia was on the point of declaring war on Turkey. Canning was not impressed by the duke's diplomatic skills, as he could not approve the tacit recognition that Russia might be forced to coerce Turkey. But the old soldier was correct in understanding that Nicholas was more interested in the general claims of Russia against Turkey rather than in the Greek question. The Russians were harking back to various long-standing issues, the complete evacuation of the Principalities by Turkey, and the release of Serbian deputies covered by the Treaty of Bucharest of 1812.

In March 1826 Russia delivered an ultimatum to the Porte to fulfil her Bucharest obligations. Stratford Canning, on instructions from his cousin, pressed the Porte to comply, to avoid providing Russia with the excuse for war with Turkey. This he successfully achieved and at Akkerman on the estuary of the Dniestr a convention was reached between Russia and Turkey in October 1826.

The last months of 1826 and the first ones of 1827 brought no real solution to what was a precarious peace in the Middle East. Count Ioannis Capodistrias, Alexander I's former foreign minister (who was born in Corfu), had been elected president of Greece in April 1827, but Ibrahim, son of the pasha of Egypt, was still wreaking devastation with his atrocities in Greece and with the help of a Turkish force sent by the sultan, Athens was taken in June. Reinforcements were also reaching Ibrahim from Egypt and a squadron of Turkish and Egyptian ships was lying in Navarino Bay (on the west coast of the Peloponnese peninsula, today Pylos).

Canning, who became prime minister in April 1827 on Lord Liverpool's retirement after a stroke, wanted to turn the protocol of April 1826 into a treaty and, despite Wellington's opposition, succeeded in July 1827 with the Treaty of London. The terms included the purely nominal subjection of Greece to the suzerainty of the Porte and the expulsion of the Turks from Greece. Canning had demonstrated extraordinary skill. He had brought France whole-heartedly to the British position by convincing the Hellenophile King Charles X and prime minister Count Joseph of Villèle of the need for Greek independence and prevented Russia from being able to engage in her own projects. At the same time he preserved the integrity of the Ottoman empire.

Nevertheless, the Porte had to be pressed to respect the terms of the Treaty of London and to sign an armistice with Greece. This would be done by 'a friendly demonstration of force' by the three powers.[13] Their Mediterranean squadrons under Admiral Sir Edward Codrington were dispatched to blockade the Morea and several Greek islands. Canning died in slow agony in August 1827, so failed to witness the *dénouement* of the Greek struggle for independence. For the following month the Ottoman Egyptian fleet reached the port of Navarino. The allied admirals foiled attempts of the Ottoman fleet to put to sea, to which Ibrahim retorted by redoubling his atrocities.

To remonstrate, the Franco-British-Russian admirals sailed into Navarino Bay under orders not to provoke hostilities but, 'if necessary and, when all other means are exhausted', they were authorized to use 'cannon-shot'.[14] The Turks, however, fired on the British frigate *Dartmouth* and the French flagship replied. The ensuing battle raged and by nightfall on 20 October the Turco-Egyptian fleet had been destroyed in the last major battle to be fought entirely by sailing ships.

Codrington had cut the Gordian knot tied by the diplomats and to all intents and purposes had guaranteed a successful end to the Greek struggle for independence. At the same time, the news of Navarino was received with amazement throughout Europe and with consternation by the new Tory government led by Viscount Goderich. Lord Aberdeen, the new foreign secretary, was appalled, and considered that Codrington had exceeded his instructions and that as a result of his actions had gravely compromised the Porte's ability to resist future Russian encroachment. George IV described the victory as 'untoward' and, feeling obliged to honour Codrington with the Grand Cross of the Bath, as Nicholas had decorated the allied admirals with the Order of St George, wrote, 'I send him the ribbon though he deserves the rope.'[15]

The pro-Turkish attitude taken by the Goderich and then the Wellington-led ministry from January 1828, encouraged the sultan to persist in his resistance to concede defeat in Greece. Mahmud II, as caliph of all Muslims, proclaimed a jihad against the European powers. More concretely he closed the Bosphorus to international shipping, a move certain to provoke Russia, whose entire Black Sea trade had to pass through the Straits, and denounced the Convention of Akkerman. Some members of the cabinet, notably the Canningite Henry Temple, 3rd Viscount Palmerston, secretary at war, and William Huskisson, President of the Board of Trade, were anxious to maintain cooperation with Russia, but as a result of disagreement inside the government there was a policy of drift. Palmerston reported: 'as usual much discussion and entire difference of opinion'.[16]

The suspicions and obstruction of Wellington's cabinet, its refusal to put pressure on the Turks to accept reasonable terms, did as much as warlike pressures in St Petersburg to make a new Russo-Turkish struggle inevitable. The foreign office could do no more than lecture Lieven:

> That the conduct of the Turkish Govt. has recently been unconciliatory, and its language haughty and imprudent, His Majesty's Govt. readily admit, but they do not consider them as putting an end to all hope of an amicable adjustment, still less as requiring them to sanction or engage in that extensive plan of attack upon the Ottoman Empire.[17]

Nesselrode irritably informed the ambassador: 'We feel very bad about disagreeing with a man like the Duke of Wellington, but his policy does not give us any alternative.'[18] All the fruits of the prudent diplomacy of Castlereagh and Canning were carelessly dissipated within a few months by their successors.

Russia's long-expected declaration of war on the Porte came in April 1828, but it proved anything but an easy victory for the Russian troops. Nicholas, who insisted on heading the campaign personally, showed that despite his military training he was an inept commander. The following year, however, Russian troops were able to march down the Balkan peninsula to Adrianople (now Edirne). The seizure of the city, and the fact that Russian armies were now within striking distance of the Turkish capital, offered Russia the possibility of attempting the conquest of the city and the destruction of the Ottoman empire.

A special committee appointed by Nicholas discussed this question. It concluded however that the benefits to Russia of the continued existence of the Ottoman empire outweighed those of its destruction and that the preservation of her neighbour, albeit weakened, should be the aim of Russian policy.[19] Although the work of the committee did not influence the terms of the Treaty of Adrianople, which was signed in September

1829, the agreement reflected the Russian 'weak neighbour' policy. A seizure of Constantinople and the Straits would provoke a general partition of the Ottoman empire which would inevitably lead to a general European war.[20]

Nesselrode succinctly expressed the Russian position: 'We started off from the principle that the Ottoman Empire, obliged to align itself with us, provided us with the most advantageous position in the Levant.'[21]

Some foreign observers realized that Russia was not as powerful as she claimed and that her policy was fluid, and not as carefully planned and aggressive as it was portrayed by pamphleteers in Britain and viewed by George IV himself. Lord Heytesbury, the newly appointed British ambassador to Russia, had followed the campaign at the headquarters of the Russian army throughout the war (equipped with ciphers which he was told to screw securely to the wall or floor wherever he was) and correctly reported home that Russia now wanted influence rather than territory in the Balkans. Heytesbury himself suffered from the lack of food and clean water and noted the poor morale of the Russian officers: 'Russia possesses fewer and less formidable means of aggression than any other of the Great Powers ... The long continuation of the delusion was due to military display and to the high tone assumed by Russian agents in foreign Courts.'[22] The ambassador had been able to employ a spy who obtained copies of confidential Russian documents which indicated Russia's military and financial weaknesses.[23]

Despite the Treaty of Adrianople being a moderate peace, Russia had gained much. The provisions of the Convention of Akkerman were reaffirmed and Russia now acquired a protectorship in the Principalities and special commercial privileges in the Ottoman empire. Serbia received the autonomy promised in the previous agreement and Turkey was compelled to pay an indemnity. Article X provided that Greece should become an autonomous tributary state in accordance with a protocol that was signed between Britain, France and Russia in March 1829. Russia, the bastion of legitimacy, had been the deciding factor in the Greeks gaining a degree of independence from their legitimate ruler.

The proposed settlement of the Greek question in the protocol of March 1829 drew the frontiers of the new state. Wellington and Aberdeen wanted the country to be as small as possible as they assumed it would be a Russian satellite. But events were slowly moving in favour of complete independence for the Greeks of the Morea and most of the islands. If, as was plain, the Greeks could not be brought once more under direct Turkish rule, their complete independence was not more objectionable than their limited autonomy. Even Wellington increasingly believed there was no point in putting the Greeks under a suzerain who could not protect or control them. So did Metternich, who was prepared to accept an independent Greece since such a state seemed more likely to resist Russian influence than an autonomous principality.

Meanwhile, it was becoming more and more urgent to restore order in the new state and equip it with stable and effective government. Capodistrias, as the presumed puppet of Russia, was suspect to the British and French governments. By February 1830 Britain, France and Russia, who all wanted a monarchy, had agreed to offer the throne of Greece to Prince Leopold of Saxe-Coburg, George IV's widowed son-in-law, even though Wellington and Aberdeen considered the prince 'the least desirable of all the candidates', but were prepared to accept him.[24] George IV, who had never forgiven Leopold for his support of his estranged wife, 'could not but deeply regret the selection made by France and Russia … [and] without entering into a detail of reasoning, the King considers Prince Leopold not qualified for this peculiar station'.[25] If Leopold, the 'Marquis Peu-à-Peu', as George IV called him, were to accept the throne, he would lose his large pension, title of field marshal, his British nationality and all property he owned in Britain. However, the British government was prepared to go along with Leopold's candidature as France and Russia were pressing for it. Rows between the ailing king and his ministers ensued, but given 'the terror his Prime Minister causes him', Wellington prevailed.[26]

Leopold was in constant contact with Lieven in London, and wrote to Nicholas, who replied with warm encouragement.[27] As the British government was so unenthusiastic about the prince's candidature, Russian support naturally had to be discreet. The prince, now feeling confident of his backing by France, Russia and Austria, was not prepared to accept the nomination without improvements to the protocol and upped the ante by demanding more territory and a large loan for Greece. Capodistrias, self-interestedly wanting to remain president, warned the prince that the Greek people opposed him as a British puppet.[28] In the end the Russians became so irritated by Leopold's pretensions that they were not disappointed when he withdrew his candidature in May. George IV, for his part, was now furious with the prince for not going to Greece. The king's knowledge of his approaching demise brought their niece Victoria closer to the throne and increased the ambitious Leopold's chances of participating in a British regency.

The question of finding a sovereign for Greece fell into abeyance in the summer of 1830 as major crises erupted throughout Europe. Word of a revolution in France came as no surprise. Nicholas told his chief of staff, General Count Igor Dibich, that the political situation in France was becoming increasingly volatile and, 'as painful as it is to say it, it is the folly of the King which is the cause of this'.[29] Therefore, when the revolution came at the end of July and insurgents seized the Hotêl de Ville and took control of Paris, the Russian emperor was in no way disposed to defend Charles X, who had suspended the constitution with his ordinances, censored the press and dissolved the newly elected chamber. On 2 August, Charles abdicated in favour of his grandson, the nine-year-old Duke of Bordeaux, but already his cousin, Louis-Philippe, Duke of Orléans, had become lieutenant general of the kingdom and was rapidly recognized as king of the French.

Nicholas was furious at Louis-Philippe's accession to the throne and refused to recognize the new regime. 'The [Duke] of Orléans will never be more than a vile usurper', he wrote.[30] The emperor engaged in some sabre-rattling about mobilizing if revolution spread but, in the face of recognition by the other powers, he capitulated in October, though he could not bring himself to address the king of the French as 'My brother', using the demeaning 'Sire'.

There was no such equivocation in London. Wellington was not one to lose his head for ideological reasons. 'There is need for anxiety and there is need for watchfulness', he told Princess Lieven, 'but there is no need to exasperate France by making her think there exists a tribunal sitting in judgement on her.'[31] Recognition of the July monarchy was the only solution and Anglo-French relations were set to improve for much of the decade.

Unlike the July Days in Paris, where the outcome was decided within a few days and did not pose any threat to Anglo-Russian relations, the Belgian revolution that broke out in late August was to provoke an international crisis that lasted for more than a year and shattered the nascent Anglo-Russian entente of the late 1820s. The Congress of Vienna had chosen to disregard the ill-feeling and differences between the northerners, the mainly Protestant Dutch, and the southerners, the Catholic Belgians, in creating the United Kingdom of the Netherlands under the Dutch William I. The king's overhasty policy of assimilation became increasingly unpopular in the south. After an opera performance in Brussels, the largely bourgeois audience left singing a catchy revolutionary song. Within a few hours a mob had formed. This was followed by rioting throughout the southern provinces. Local contingents were formed and confronted the Dutch army, which after several days of fierce fighting withdrew.

This time, unlike his reaction to the July revolution, Nicholas considered that war was more than a possibility to preserve the integrity of the United Netherlands. William requested military support from the Russian emperor, and this legitimate monarch's son and heir was also married to Nicholas's sister Anna. 'The dispatches I have received ... are of such a nature that we must, without delay, make preparations for our entry into the field ... It remains to be seen if the knowledge of our formidable preparations will prevent the war', Nicholas wrote in October.[32] Nevertheless, he would only act in concert with the other powers and nothing was forthcoming from them.

A provisional government, the National Congress, was set up and sat in Brussels from November 1830 to July 1831. A constitution, in many respects the most liberal in Europe at the time, was drafted, and as it would be necessary to gain the support of the powers, it was decided to establish a monarchy. The British government, although at first distressed to see the buffer state of enlarged Holland disintegrate, recognized that a country crippled by internal strife could no longer be effective.

The foreign secretary in the newly elected Whig government from November 1830 was Viscount Palmerston. This former Canningite devoted his considerable energies to ensuring the creation of a strong independent Belgium, seeing a new danger in that the French would attempt to take over their new neighbour. When the National Congress wished to offer the throne to the second son of Louis-Philippe, Palmerston saw his worst fears materializing and led opposition by the powers. In his place he proposed Prince Leopold of Saxe-Coburg. The Belgians and the prince were agreeable (the chances of a regency in Britain were greatly diminished) and on 21 July 1831 Leopold entered Brussels and was sworn in as king, although the struggle for the formation of the Belgian state was not completed until nearly a decade later.

What enabled Palmerston to impose the creation of an independent Belgium in the face of strong Russian legitimist opposition was the Polish uprising of November 1830 that prevented any Russian armed intervention in western Europe.

The causes leading the Poles to revolt were numerous and complex as they were the result of centuries-old antagonisms, to which was added resentment by patriotic Poles of the settlement of 1815. The trial for treason in 1828 of the leader of the Polish Patriotic Society and his associates, who Nicholas believed were implicated in the Decembrist uprising, marked a turning point in Russo-Polish relations. Although the sentences handed down were not harsh, Polish national honour was affronted.

Nationalist army officer cadets had been following the July Days in France and learned that the Polish army was expected to march with the Russians to crush the revolution and prevent the Belgians from acquiring independence. Among them developed a loosely knit band of conspirators who, on the night of 29 November, broke into the Belvedere Palace to assassinate the Grand Duke Constantine, while another attacked the Russian cavalry barracks. The grand duke escaped but the head of police and a general were killed. Constantine was not unaware of subversive movements in the capital but he had wrongly counted on the loyalty of the Polish army, his own creation. In addition the grand duke was indecisive and loath to intervene. 'Not a single Russian will meddle in this matter. The Poles have begun it ... Let them settle it among themselves', he told his *aide-de-camp*.[33] Lacking firm leadership from highly placed Poles, armed gangs roamed the streets of Warsaw lynching Russians and Polish collaborators.

Nicholas showed none of his brother's hesitation when he heard of the uprising on 7 December: 'I will never give way before force ... What choice is left to me if the Poles in their blindness persist in their treason and madness?'[34] He refused to meet a member of the Polish National Council, instead sending him a note demanding unconditional surrender before any negotiations could take place. In Warsaw the parliament, or Sejm, declared a state of insurrection and, on 25 January 1831, the dethronement of Nicholas as king of Poland. A new Polish government was formed under Adam Czartorysky, previously a foreign minister of Alexander I, and Michal Radziwill. That same day a Russian army marched into Poland. Despite General Dibich's poor generalship, a cholera epidemic and the loss of many Russian lives, a major battle was won at Ostrolska by Russia in May. Dibich conveniently died, as did the Grand Duke Constantine shortly after. Nicholas was free to pursue his own Polish policy. It would be decisive, firm and merciless.

Under General Ivan Paskevich, and with more than twice the number of troops as the Poles, defeat of the uprising was inevitable. Nicholas's younger brother, the Grand Duke Mikhail, led the Imperial Guards into Warsaw in August 1831. The struggle was over in the following month and the tattered remnants of the Polish army crossed into Prussian territory, many never to return. About 8,000 senior officers, politicians and artists who would become exiles in Paris and London could plot and heap abuse on Nicholas and all things Russian. (Leopold of the Belgians took many of the officers into his army, to Russia's fury, and Russia did not recognize the state of Belgium until 1852.)

Nicholas was king of Poland. The Polish army of Constantine was abolished and Poland became an indivisible part of the Russian empire. Russia had helped to free the Greeks, unwillingly contributed to the Belgians becoming independent by not intervening, but destroyed what little independence the Poles had possessed.

Palmerston, sympathetic though he was to the Poles, was unresponsive and cautioned against any British involvement. To champion the Polish cause would have jeopardized the tenuous relationship between Britain and Russia. Furthermore, to have Russian forces bogged down in Poland strengthened the foreign secretary's hand in dealing with the stubborn Dutch over Belgium. And to be on good terms with Nicholas would give Britain leverage over the French and thwart any potential ambitions in Belgium. He could, on the other hand, have made the legal case that the Vienna accords required consultation with the signatories before punitive action was taken and that the Polish constitution specifically decreed that only Polish troops should garrison the kingdom. Instead, Palmerston sent a dispatch to Heytesbury in St Petersburg in March 1831 which contained a mild remonstrance to the Russian government, going on to say that the British cabinet was 'more than ever desirous of keeping up the closest relations of friendship' with Russia.[35]

Nesselrode retorted that Poland was a Russian internal matter in which neither Britain nor France had a right to interfere, and compared Poland to Ireland, a clearly false comparison as Ireland had been part of Great Britain for many centuries, but one that Russia continued to use. France remained more proactive and proposed joint mediation, but Britain declined. When in 1832 the repressive Organic Statute for Poland was published, Britain did not raise any objection.

The reaction to the Polish uprising in the British press and public opinion was much more vigorous. The relative propinquity of Poland meant that news arrived relatively quickly and from the first rumours which reached London in December 1830 until the fall of Warsaw was announced the following September, hardly any issue of the metropolitan press failed to include some more or less well-authenticated report or editorial commentary. From the very beginning the Poles were accorded unanimous sympathy.

Even the ultra-Tory *Morning Post* agreed that the Poles were a worthy cause.[36] Early on *The Times* held that the Poles must prepare themselves to resist 'the whole force of the Empire' and made the point that an independent Poland would be good for British trade.[37] When the Russian army was engaged in brutal warfare in the summer of 1831, *The Times* led the attack on French and British governments' failure to support the Poles:

> How long will Russia be permitted, with impunity, to make war upon the ancient and noble nation of the Poles, the allies of France, the friends of England, the natural, and, centuries ago, the tried and victorious protectors of civilized Europe against the Turkish and Muscovite barbarians?[38]

The fall of Warsaw did not dim *The Times*'s ardour: 'Polish courage, Polish revenge, and the unquenchable hatred of the Poles to their barbarous conquerors remain as powerful as ever.'[39] Incessant animadversions to Russian cruelty during the war were followed by diatribes about the repressive measures that followed—the closure of the University of Warsaw, the abolition of school instruction in Polish and French, the confiscation of property of exiled patriots, the introduction of Russians into public office, and the transfer of the contents of Polish libraries and museums to Russia:[40] 'The Russians are abhorred in Poland, and ... [there is] little chance of permanent tranquillity under their barbarous tyranny.'[41]

An enduring influence of the Polish revolution in Britain was its humanitarian appeal in an age when the power of political propagandist activity by well-integrated groups had already been demonstrated by, for example, the Catholic Association of Ireland over the question of Catholic emancipation. Public meetings were held at which money was raised for Poland, well-attended banquets attracted radical politicians who spoke of the new-found liberties of France, Greece and Belgium. The Literary Association of the Friends of Poland propagated knowledge of Poland and published a monthly magazine *Polonia*. Pro-Polish agitation also took the form of pamphlets, vituperative speeches in the House of Commons and numerous petitions directed to King William IV and the House of Commons.

However, the most important result of the Polish uprising was the new stereotype of Russia that emerged. Britain had come to accept Russia as a fellow European power in the eighteenth century. Now, the widely held view in Britain was not of a civilized but expansionist state, as under Catherine the Great and Alexander I, but a barbaric oppressor. It had elements in common with the English view of Russia in the sixteenth century, of a state which did not conform to the accepted standards of a European power. Expansionist and savage came to be the widely held views of Russia in the British parliament, the press and informed opinion. There was now a new political alienation of Russia in addition to the geopolitical rivalry that already existed between the two powers. All Russian actions, even the most innocent, now came to be regarded with suspicion and a howl of moral outrage greeted any move which could be in any way interpreted as demonstrating ambitious and ruthless intent. Poland had contributed the essential element of the noble victim of tyranny to rapidly crystallizing British nineteenth-century Russophobia.

11

THE EASTERN QUESTION

While the press and Radicals in parliament railed against Nicholas's treatment of the Poles in 1831, Palmerston continued to say little beyond expressing the mild hope that the Russian emperor would be lenient in his treatment of his Polish subjects. The foreign secretary was thus accused of being a Russian tool and made matters worse for himself in Radical eyes by agreeing that Britain should pay the interest due from Holland to Russia on the loan Russia had made to Holland during the Napoleonic wars. Palmerston defended his action by referring in the warmest terms to the debt owed by Europe to Russia for her part in overthrowing Napoleon.

To preserve the peace of Europe, Palmerston claimed that he saw Russia as a natural ally: the interests of both and of Europe would be served, he argued, by these two powers 'availing themselves of every occasion of cultivating that friendship, & of cementing the union between the two countries', and 'as neither country has any selfish interests to pursue, the motives of their union cannot be misunderstood'.[1]

In July 1832, to illustrate his continued wish for good relations with Russia, the foreign secretary sent John Lambton, Lord Durham, Lord Privy Seal and son-in-law of the prime minister Earl Grey, on a mission to St Petersburg. Durham, known as Black Jack Lambton or Radical Jack, was a surprising choice politically. A rich mine-owning aristocrat, he was a champion of left-wing causes and hardly somebody to appeal to Nicholas I. But he had alienated practically all the British cabinet with his overbearing manner and ill-temper and Grey sought a reason to rid himself of his turbulent son-in-law. The ostensible reason for the mission was to find out where Russia stood on the Belgian question, but what was foremost in Palmerston's instructions was for the envoy to make clear that Britain's position over Poland had not changed and also to find out what the policy of Russification entailed.[2]

The vain Durham was won over by the charm offensive of Nicholas who persuaded him he was the champion of the Polish peasantry against the aristocracy. The Russians conceded nothing. The emperor and Nesselrode were well aware that with the new Whig government preoccupied with the passing of the Reform Act extending the franchise, there was little to fear from Britain. And Palmerston was well aware that Russian acquiescence in deterring France from meddling in Belgium was necessary.

The cordial relations with Russia that Palmerston had striven to establish were severely shaken in 1833 by an adventurer born in the Ottoman province of Macedonia in 1769 to Albanian parents: Mehemet Ali. He had joined the Turkish army and succeeded by his military prowess and ruthless massacres to make himself pasha of Egypt, that is, viceroy of the sultan of Turkey. When the Greek revolt broke out, the sultan, Mahmud II, called upon Mehemet Ali to assist him. The pasha sent his equally brutal son, Ibrahim, to put down the Greeks for which the sultan rewarded Mehemet Ali with the governance of Crete. This was not sufficient in the eyes of the pasha who then dispatched Ibrahim and his army to seize Palestine, Lebanon and Syria, all part of the Ottoman empire. The Turkish forces were defeated and Constantinople lay at the mercy of Mehemet's Egyptian army.

Mahmud II appealed to the great powers for support. Britain and France refused so he turned to Russia. With great alacrity Nicholas, partly because he considered Mehemet Ali a front for French activity in Ottoman Algeria and the French army a danger to Russian ambitions, dispatched troops, and Mehemet and Ibrahim retreated from Anatolia. The Russian emperor was now in a position to call the shots and imposed the Treaty of Unkiar Skelessi in July 1833. Turkey and Russia agreed not to make any moves in foreign affairs without consulting each other and in a secret clause the sultan agreed to modify Turkey's traditional policy of excluding all foreign warships from the Dardanelles in peacetime by allowing Russian ships to enter whenever they pleased.

The British ambassador to the Porte, Lord Ponsonby, was given a copy of the official treaty and through a spy a second copy that included the secret clause. These he forwarded to Palmerston who immediately replied that if Russia attempted to intervene forcibly in Turkish affairs, Britain would feel obliged to feel at liberty as though no treaty existed.[3]

In fact it was not so much the secret clause that alarmed the foreign secretary as the provision by which the two powers agreed to consult each other on their foreign policy that meant 'the Russian ambassador becomes chief Cabinet minister of the Sultan'.[4] It constituted a threat to British influence in the Levant and her access to India.

Palmerston came to rue the day in January 1833 when the cabinet rejected Mahmud's plea: 'There is nothing that has happened since I have been in this office which I regret so much as that terrible blunder of the English government. But it was not my fault; I tried hard to persuade the Cabinet to let me take the step.'[5]

Unkiar Skelessi crystallized Palmerston's changed view of the Ottoman empire. During the Greek struggle for independence he had supported the rebels and believed in the inevitable collapse of their Turkish masters. More generally he felt contempt for Islam: 'The Mahometan faith tells him to commit criminal violence in this life, & promises a reward, the enjoyment of vicious indulgence in a life to come.'[6]

However, from 1833 Palmerston was determined above all to do everything to prevent the collapse of Turkey. Although he was sceptical of the possibility of indigenous reform in the Ottoman empire, it had to be propped up to prevent further Russian encroachment. Fear of Austria's conniving with Russia in the partitioning of the empire exacerbated the problem.

The events of 1833 necessitated a British rethinking of its policy towards Mehemet Ali. The pasha posed a danger in that he was supported by France in Egypt. On the other hand, he could be useful in opposing Russian designs on Turkey. No wonder that Palmerston reflected that the Eastern Question was becoming more and more complicated and that it would continue to bedevil relations among the great powers.

Nevertheless, suspicious though he had become of Russian aims, the last thing that the foreign secretary sought was open hostility towards Russia. In the summer of 1833 he twice defended Russia in the House of Commons from yet more attacks over her treatment of Poland. He admitted that atrocities had been committed but believed that the extent had been exaggerated. Nicholas, he said, was 'a man of high and generous feelings'.[7]

It comes as something of a surprise then that while he was defending Russia on the important question of Poland, Palmerston provocatively irritated Nicholas over the nomination of a new British ambassador to St Petersburg to replace Lord Heytesbury who wished to retire. The foreign secretary proposed the extremely able diplomat Sir Stratford Canning and the appointment was cleared with William IV, who was very much in favour of it, and it was announced in the *London Gazette*. The convention in continental Europe was that a government enquired as to whether a certain nomination was agreeable to the host country before going ahead with its choice. Palmerston refused to conform, holding that it was the business of an ambassador to act as vigorously as possible in the interests of his own country. The Russian emperor and Nesselrode were furious on learning of the nomination, believing that Durham had assured them during his mission, when the nomination was already being mooted, that it would not be carried out.

It has been claimed that Stratford Canning had slighted Nicholas when on a mission to St Petersburg in 1825, but a more plausible explanation was that the Russians believed that during his recent mission to Constantinople, Canning had stirred up anti-Russian feeling in the Porte. The now Prince and Princess Lieven were outraged that someone they knew was *persona non grata* in St Petersburg was being proposed. The princess, who had had a close, though probably platonic, relationship with Grey, pressed the prime minister to make Palmerston withdraw Canning's name. The foreign secretary did not appreciate anyone going over his head on his turf and was not for turning. But neither were Nicholas nor Nesselrode. Princess Lieven, who for so many years had been a celebrity in London, and had influenced British politicians and the Russian emperor and vice chancellor in St Petersburg, had now overstepped the mark and realized that this deadlock could well put an end to her own stay in Britain. Lord Heytesbury had now left St Petersburg so Britain was represented by a *chargé d'affaires*. Princess Lieven was summoned to the Russian capital where she did little to further her cause, as the powerful Russian nationalist faction led by Count Alexsei Orlov distrusted her for her influence on the imperial family. The count spoke openly of Prince Lieven's incapacity and insisted that the time had come for his recall.

On her return to London Palmerston maintained, at least publicly, friendly relations with the princess, visiting her at her home in Richmond and entertaining the Lievens at Broadlands, his residence in Hampshire. Dorothea Lieven meanwhile wrote unflatteringly about the foreign secretary to Nesselrode and attacked Palmerston's reputation with anyone who would listen. The *dénouement* was inevitable. As Britain only maintained a *chargé d'affaires*, Nicholas could not countenance keeping an ambassador in London. In May 1834 the Lievens were ordered to leave London.

William IV, who as Duke of Clarence had been accused of trying to seduce the princess many years before, was one of many who were delighted to see the Lievens depart, and *The Times* exulted in an offensive article about her intrigues and meddling in British politics. The princess never forgave Palmerston and claimed he had engineered Canning's nomination to drive her from Britain. This view was understandable but incorrect since the foreign secretary could not have foreseen the consequences for the Lievens when he gazetted the appointment of Canning to St Petersburg. Princess Lieven's tactics had simply proved counterproductive. Palmerston wrote to this brother William:

> I am very sorry on private grounds to lose old friends and agreeable members of society, but on public grounds I do not know that their loss will be great ... The Lievens are to keep house at Petersburgh for the suckling Czar, and the great Czar and his wife are going to their evening parties. It is a splendid existence ... but I believe the Lievens would both give their ears to stay here.[8]

In the month following the Lievens' departure, Lord Grey resigned as prime minister and was replaced by William Lamb, Viscount Melbourne. The new prime minister and William IV could not agree about the formation of a government and in November 1834 the Tory king dismissed Melbourne. Palmerston, whose relations with the sovereign were frosty, told his brother: 'We are all out; turned out neck and crop ... This attempt to reinstall the Tories cannot possibly last.'[9] He was correct. Sir Robert Peel's ministry, with the Duke of Wellington foreign secretary in a Whig-dominated House of Commons, was in an untenable position and soon fell. One weakening factor to this precarious administration that illustrated the diplomatic significance of the British envoy to Russia had been the nomination of the Marquess of Londonderry, Castlereagh's younger half-brother. The Whigs and Radicals in the House of Commons were outraged as Londonderry had referred to the Poles as rebellious subjects. They asserted that the marquess would inevitably succumb to the blandishments of the Russian emperor. *The Times* agreed that Londonderry was unfitted for the position due to his 'want of sympathy with the known feelings of Englishmen in favour of the oppressed liberties and trampelled rights of Poland'.[10] He stood down.

At the general election that was called in April 1835 the Whigs were returned with a sizeable majority and Melbourne was back as prime minister. Palmerston, however, lost his seat. Melbourne and Lady Cowper, the prime minister's sister and Palmerston's long-time mistress, lobbied hard for him and Palmerston was soon back after an unopposed election. For the next few years he was preoccupied with Spain, Portugal and the deteriorating relations with France. With Russia he continued in his efforts to remain on as good terms as possible.

The first manifestation of this desire came with Palmerston's choice of the now Russophile and newly created Earl (a step up) Durham as ambassador extraordinary to St Petersburg in July 1835. Once in Russia the ambassador, as expected, again lent a sympathetic ear to Nicholas. This came after the emperor had enraged the ambassador's Radical friends at home with a tirade in Warsaw in which he said that he would answer any Polish complaints by bombarding the city. Durham's assurances of Russian good intentions towards Poland were received with due scepticism in London.

Despite the understandable reservations as to his probable usefulness, the ambassador proved a success. He was hard-working despite suffering chronic ill health and proved perceptive, producing reports that were of great value to Palmerston. Durham travelled the country to investigate the state of the Russian army and concluded that only a fifth of the total could be employed abroad.[11] This was no more than an interesting fact as the Russian army could not directly threaten Britain as long as the latter's fleet commanded the seas. It was the growing Russian fleet in the Black Sea and Baltic squadron that mattered. The ambassador took pains to show that defects in Russian equipment, seamanship, rigging and slow gunfire rendered its fleet less impressive in reality than on paper. He relayed Nesselrode's confession that in case of war the British navy would promptly destroy that of Russia. (British naval estimates were nevertheless increased in 1836, though Palmerston insisted it was for reasons of general policy.)

The most important of Durham's dispatches was his estimate of Russia's status:

> The power of Russia has been exaggerated. In fact her power is solely of a defensive kind. Leaning on and covered by the impregnable fortress which nature has endowed her—her climate and her deserts—she is invincible, as Napoleon discovered to his cost. When she steps out into the open plain, she is then assailable front and rear and flank.[12]

An example of Russia's unwieldy outreach had occurred in 1834 in Russian North America when the captain of a British vessel of the

Hudson's Bay Company was prevented at gunpoint from entering the Stikine river (in today's Alaska, but at that time on the border of Canada and Russian North America) to trade with the Indians of the hinterland.[13] Baron Ferdinand von Wrangel, governor of the Russian-American Company which administered Russian territory, claimed that the British traders were intent on swopping ammunition for furs with the Indians who would use the arms against Russian traders. Nesselrode was prepared to admit that Wrangel's men had acted incorrectly but refused any financial compensation for the British company.

A further maritime skirmish occurred in 1835. The Russians had blockaded the eastern coast of the Black Sea, ostensibly to prevent armaments reaching the Circassian people of the north-east Caucasus.[14] A British ship, the *Lord Charles Spencer*, was intercepted in international waters and no arms were found. Durham duly protested. Nesselrode wrote at great length about the necessity for quarantine regulations, pointing out that, if the British captain had understood Russian, any misunderstanding would have been avoided. But he felt obliged to denounce the actions of the captain of the Russian warship and agreed to pay compensation.[15] Though this particular incident was minor, Circassia was a tinderbox as far as Anglo-Russian relations were concerned.

Russia had been waging war against the largely Muslim Circassian tribes in the inaccessible areas on the east coast of the Black Sea since 1817. This provided a first-class opportunity for anti-Russian propagandists in Britain, according to whom Russia was once more crushing a people struggling to be free and in the process strengthening her position in the Caucasus and thus her ability to move against the Ottoman empire. The conflict on the Russian side proved to be the source of some of the most exciting works of Russian literature. The young Leo Tolstoy fought with the Russian army in one of the campaigns against Iman Shamil, the Muslim ruler in Chechnya and Dagestan, and in *Hadji Murad*, he portrayed the struggles against the wild peoples alien to the northern Slav Russians. Alexander Pushkin's *Prisoner of the Caucasus* and Mikhail Lermontov's *A Hero of our Time* capture the romantic view of the warfare of the 1830s without reflection as to its international repercussions.

As usual, Lord Ponsonby, the Turcophile British ambassador in Constantinople, wanted action with the presence of a British man-of-war in the Black Sea and had to be told firmly that this was out of the question. But the ambassador was not the only one at the embassy to the Porte actively seeking the means to hold Russia back in the Levant. He had on his staff a young Scot, David Urquhart, who was soon to become the leading Russophobe propagandist in Europe. Urquhart had visited Circassia in 1834 and Ponsonby passed on to London the young man's proposal that the Circassians should declare their independence and ask Britain for help in maintaining it, an idea given understandable short shrift by Palmerston, and which led to Urquhart's recall.

Unshackled from an official role, Urquhart, on his return to Britain, published a pamphlet he had drafted with Ponsonby in Constantinople, *England, France, Russia, and Turkey*. In an unproven assumption that Russia's major purpose was the acquisition of Constantinople and the Straits, he claimed that although Russia had not been able to accomplish her purpose in 1829 and 1833, in 1835 she had not abandoned her intention. Ponsonby kept his *protégé* up to date with events in Turkey such that Urquhart was able to found in 1835 a periodical, *The Portfolio*, a weekly philippic against Russia containing purloined copies of Russian diplomatic documents. It naturally attracted much attention, particularly in diplomatic circles, and at least at the outset received advice and information from Palmerston's undersecretary and William IV's private secretary, a friend of Urquhart's mother. Nicholas and Nesselrode protested to Durham, a sympathetic listener who feared that it might 'produce the very dangers it denounces'.[16] To begin with Palmerston took the view that there was not much the government could do to control the publication, but other members of the cabinet were worried by the increasing invective of *The Portfolio*. Melbourne wanted to see Urquhart dispatched back to a posting to the Porte on the grounds that he could do less damage there. The foreign secretary went along with this but the young *attaché* was soon at loggerheads even with Ponsonby and Palmerston dismissed him from the diplomatic service in late 1837.

This was too late to undo the damage to Anglo-Russian relations done by the *Vixen* affair. In 1836 anti-Russian British shipowner friends of Urquhart had fitted out the *Vixen* which sailed to Constantinople where it picked up salt (a prohibited commodity under Russian regulations) for the beleaguered Circassians. On 24 November the schooner was sighted by the Russian flagship of the blockading fleet and forced into port. There ensued a long, drawn-out dispute in which the Russian authorities accused the British crew of violation of customs regulations and of the ship's papers not being in order.

Nesselrode used the official *Journal de St Petersbourg* to set out the Russian position and in a dispatch to the ambassador, Count Pozzo di

Borgo, in London, claimed that there was more to the *Vixen* affair than a simple shipping incident: 'In effect it is a fresh attempt by the political faction composed of English revolutionaries & the débris of the Polish insurrection, who constantly seek to provoke a clamour in Parliament against Russia.'[17] A week later Durham delivered a protest drafted by Palmerston which held that the schooner had not been in Russian territorial waters and provocatively questioned Russia's claim to sovereignty over the Caucasus.

Nevertheless, the ambassador sympathized with the Russian case and complained that he did not think it right that irresponsible shipowners should be allowed to raise important political issues and leave the British government to face the consequences.[18] In the end Palmerston came round to Durham's view that the incident should be played down. Nesselrode denied all liability but offered to make an *ex gratia* payment to the shipowners as a contribution to friendly relations with Britain, an offer accepted with gratitude by the British government. Palmerston was strongly criticized by the Radicals for his conciliatory attitude over the *Vixen*, and in *The Portfolio* Urquhart, who had hoped to provoke an Anglo-Russian crisis, denounced the foreign secretary as a Russian agent.

Fundamental to Palmerston's policy was as ever the aim of maintaining a strong enough Turkey to deter Russia from embarking on expansion in the Levant. To this end an Anglo-Turkish convention was signed in 1838 with the aim of furthering reforms in the Ottoman empire and increasing British trade. The foreign secretary was suspicious of Russia but wished to avoid confrontation; in this he was aided by the clear Russian desire to maintain good relations with Britain. For Nesselrode was alarmed by the improving relations of Britain, France and Austria. The Russian economy was in a parlous state while it was clear that vast sums of money were being spent on expanding the fleet that the emperor and the minister of the navy, Admiral Alexander Menshikov, sought. It was reported that 'The Emperor's Nautical passion is not shared or admired by his subjects, who place little confidence or affection in their Navy.'[19]

Durham left St Petersburg in 1837, dispatched to distant Canada, and the next British choice, the Marquess of Clanricarde, did not provoke the ructions of Stratford Canning's nomination, even though the marquess's wife, Harriet, was the daughter of George Canning (to Palmerston's wry satisfaction) and known to be an imperious woman who pursued her late father's supposed enemies and betrayers with political virulence. Her husband had a reputation as a womanizer, proven gambling cheat and blackguard. Despite his inauspicious reputation in the face of Nicholas's stress upon moral character, Clanricarde ably carried out his master's instructions to further good relations with Russia and came to be on friendly terms with the emperor who, if not convinced of new-found British goodwill, was keen to send his eldest son, the Grand Duke Alexander, the future Alexander II, to England as proof of his desire for friendly relations.

There was, however, disquiet at the proposed visit in April 1839:

> The Russian ambassador in London apprehends that the language which will be held in Parliament ... may be so grossly offensive to the Imperial Government as to render the Grand Duke's sojourn in London unpleasant—that His Imperial Highness may be insulted by the populace—and that the Polish refugees may meditate an attack on his person.[20]

The young Queen Victoria was also reluctant to entertain the grand duke and lamented the increased court ceremony that such a visit entailed. She was instructed by the emollient prime minister, Melbourne: 'You must be very civil; that the Emperor makes so much of the opinion of England and of personal opinion.'[21] All reluctance disappeared on Alexander's arrival: 'I went over to the Closet, where I made the Grand Duke sit down ... I like the Grand Duke extremely; he is so natural and gay and so easy to get on with.'[22]

The exuberant twenty-year-old queen gave a ball for Alexander in Buckingham Palace on 10 May and the following week she accompanied him to the theatre, concerts and a reception: 'I really am quite in love with the Grand Duke.'[23] Another ball was held in Windsor Castle at which a new dance, the mazurka, was introduced: 'The Grand Duke asked me to take a turn, which I did (never having done it before).'[24] When the time came for Alexander to leave, Victoria wrote how he 'took my hand and pressed it warmly ... He said, "Words fail me to express all that I feel"; and ... that he hoped to return again, and that he trusted that all this would only tend to strengthen the ties of friendship between England and Russia.'[25]

The politicians and King Leopold were dismissive of the young woman's gushing and both Melbourne and Leopold wrote crusty letters to the queen. However, Palmerston considered the visit a success in so far as it would 'promote ... the relations of amity so happily subsisting between this country and Russia'.[26] He gave a dinner for Alexander and took him to the races at Newmarket, where, in honour of the heir to the Russian throne, an annual race was henceforth to be known as the Cesarewitch (the nineteenth-century form of tsarevich), as it remains today. The grand duke had donated £300 to the Jockey Club.

Dealing with the grand duke was a welcome distraction for the foreign secretary who was confronting a major crisis in the Near East, the second Mehemet Ali crisis. The Ottoman sultan, Mahmud II, knew that he was dying and was determined to regain Syria from his brazen and recalcitrant vassal, the pasha of Egypt. The latter for his part, also a man facing old age, had not abandoned his long-standing aim of establishing a permanent position for his family. In 1838 he sounded out the powers as to their reaction if he declared himself independent of the sultan. Their reaction was unanimous—they were against. This included France, who was the most pro-Mehemet Ali power, with her investment in cotton production, support for Egyptian industrialization and help with the training of the Egyptian army and navy. Mehemet Ali was also a major player in the Islamic revival movement and thus a threat to Russia because of the Muslim rebels against Russian rule in the Caucasus.

Provoked by Mehemet Ali's demand, Mahmud was determined to settle accounts with his vassal once and for all. Palmerston was prepared to promise aid to Turkey if Mehemet Ali declared independence, but he refused to support the sultan in the reconquest of Syria. This was not enough for Mahmud. A Turkish army crossed the frontier into Syria and within weeks the pasha's son Ibrahim had defeated the Turks. Mahmud died; the Turkish fleet surrendered to Mehemet Ali. Near panic prevailed in Constantinople with the Ottoman empire seemingly on the point of collapse. Russian expeditionary forces at Sevastopol were placed in a state of readiness while the British and French fleets were sent to the Dardanelles.

In such a situation there was a grave danger that Russian and western European forces would converge on the Straits and spark a European war. Metternich proposed a conference of the powers in Vienna to which Palmerston agreed, but Nesselrode would have nothing to do with an idea instigated by the Austrian chancellor, a man with a known talent for complicating any problem. In a note to the five powers the Russian vice chancellor expressed his opinion that they should offer their 'good offices' to mediate a direct settlement between Turkey and Egypt. He believed that they were unanimous in wanting a peaceful settlement of the Eastern Question.

But pro-Mehemet Ali France refused to go along with the proposal since she feared that Turkey's claims to Syria, then occupied by Mehemet

Ali, would be supported by the other powers. To Nesselrode's dismay, Palmerston seemed to interpret the Russian note as the first step to a full conference. In spite of its demise, however, it opened the way to the diplomatic paradigm the vice chancellor favoured—a bilateral agreement with Britain.

To begin with Palmerston was as reluctant as ever to believe that Russian policy was not aggressive. At the end of June he had claimed in a dispatch to the British ambassador in Paris that the western powers had prevented Russian aggression because Russia might have made a secret agreement with Mehemet Ali and then played off one side against the other to weaken Turkey and justify intervention. If such a plan had existed, it had been foiled. Yet much as Palmerston preferred to work with France, the French would not cooperate. In view of Russia's conciliatory attitude and her failure to invoke Unkiar Skelessi, he was prepared to listen to the Russians.

The Russian desire to improve relations with Britain was further demonstrated in September 1839 by the sending of Baron Filipp Brunnov, a talented young diplomat, a *protégé* of Nesselrode and a man of similar German Protestant origin, on a special mission to Britain. On his first meeting with Palmerston the envoy found the foreign secretary in a receptive mood. From the start Brunnov made it clear that if Russia felt obliged to send a fleet to Constantinople to defend the new sultan against his vassal, this would not imply a Russian protectorate over the Ottoman empire. In return, Britain and France would have to accept the closure of the Straits to warships as a principle of European public law. This was agreeable to Palmerston but not to the powerful pro-French faction in the cabinet and it ran counter to the general Russophobic feeling prevalent in parliament and the press. Brunnov therefore left London a fortnight later without having arrived at any formal agreement with the British government. He wrote: 'The Anglo-French alliance is already dead ... England is still not with us: but neither is she with France ... England is widow. To marry her much skill and patience are needed, for she is a handsome and capricious woman.'[27]

Marriage became more than a metaphor when, less than a month later, Brunnov was once more in London, this time as Russian ambassador, a post (with the interruption of the Crimean War) he was to hold until 1873. This time, accompanied by the vice chancellor's son, Dmitri Nesselrode, he had instructions to secure a treaty signed by all the great powers if possible. The main Russian effort was now to support

Palmerston, who in mid-December married the now conveniently widowed Lady Cowper. A few days later the newly wed foreign secretary invited Brunnov and the Austrian plenipotentiary, Baron Philipp von Neumann, to Broadlands for Christmas.

The rapprochement with two of the northern powers, Russia and Austria, bore fruit and the three men agreed, subject to the consent of their governments, to expel Mehemet Ali from Syria by force if necessary, while Egyptian independence would be recognized. However, Palmerston rashly told the French ambassador, Count Horace Sébastiani, what had been decided. Not surprisingly, Sébastiani rallied the pro-French members of the cabinet who refused to endorse the agreement. Fortunately though for the foreign secretary, France had declared war on Algeria at the end of the year—a welcome distraction.

Nesselrode believed that as long as Palmerston could stand up to the Francophiles in the cabinet, Prussia would send a delegate and France would not want to be left out. At one point Clanricarde in St Petersburg reported finding the Russian vice chancellor in 'high spirits' after reading an article in the *Morning Chronicle* in which the negotiations were 'so well expounded to the British Publick, he no longer entertained the least doubt that Russia and England would come to an agreement satisfactory to themselves and Europe, and perhaps ultimately France'.[28]

A change of government in France made this less likely when Adolphe Thiers became French prime minister and hardened his country's support for Mehemet Ali. After six months of waiting for France to join with the other powers, news from Constantinople that the French intended to negotiate between Turkey and Mehemet Ali convinced Palmerston that Britain had to act with the northern powers without France. Further pressure was coming from St Petersburg. Nicholas was irritated by having to deal with a parliamentary government: 'All this is wretched and I see absolutely no end to this chatter. I am losing patience and, if everything is not finished within a month, then I will think of other measures.'[29]

Palmerston was also frustrated. As the cabinet still hesitated he offered his resignation to Melbourne, reminding him that he had been overruled in 1833 over the sultan's appeal for help against Mehemet Ali. This time he would resign rather than see the Ottoman empire *de facto* divided into two independent states, one a satellite of Russia, the other a French dependency with British influence obliterated. Melbourne, hitherto lukewarm about expelling Mehemet Ali from Syria, knew only too well that if Palmerston resigned the government would fall. The foreign secretary thus won the day.

Hence, on 15 July 1840, a convention, often called the First Treaty of London, was signed by representatives of the four great powers and Turkey which would guarantee the security of the Ottoman empire; Mehemet Ali could have Syria for his lifetime subject to Ottoman suzerainty but would be recognized as hereditary ruler of Egypt. If he did not comply after ten days and return the Turkish fleet to the sultan the powers would cut sea communications between Egypt and Syria and he would be dismissed by punitive action as viceroy of Egypt. The Straits would henceforth be closed to all foreign warships in peacetime. Palmerston had, by cooperating with Russia, successfully undone the Treaty of Unkiar Skelessi.

Nevertheless, the Russian emperor felt he had achieved his aim. Nicholas congratulated Nesselrode and Brunnov. Lord Bloomfield, number two at the British embassy, found the vice chancellor 'overjoyed' that whereas 'England had formerly found great fault with his policy in the Levant', now, 'whatever he might be called upon to do, would be done in the name of the four powers, in the general Interest of the Alliance and with no selfish object'.[30]

After the expiry of the ultimatum the sultan deposed Mehemet Ali and Ibrahim was driven out of Syria by a combination of the British fleet, plus an Austrian flotilla, attacking garrisons and cutting off communications with Egypt aided by Syrian tribesmen stirred up by Turkish agents.

While Nicholas maintained his contemptuous attitude towards France, delighting in her isolation, his vice chancellor was deeply worried by the furious French reaction to the convention and danger of war that was evident. Palmerston typically was unfazed by French sabre-rattling and demonstrated the diplomatic bravado for which he later became famous: 'The frantic Rage which pervades the whole of the Press and all the good citizens of Paris shews how much France needed such a lesson', namely that 'Her word and her wishes are not to be Law for Europe.'[31]

At the same time he had to confront fellow members of the deeply divided cabinet over collaborating with the autocratic powers, and for the first time the young queen was demonstrating her suspicions of Russia. Victoria was still in thrall to the views of her uncle, King Leopold of the Belgians, and now the recently widowed son-in-law of Louis-Philippe. In a letter of September 1840 to his niece he held that the treatment by the four powers 'towards France was, and is still, harsh and insulting. I don't think France, which these ten years behaved well, deserved to be treated so unkindly, and all that seemingly to please the great Autocrat.'[32]

He followed with a history lesson to his niece about Russian aggressive policy in the late 1820s, continuing:

> Russia is again in this snug and comfortable position, that *the special protection of the Porte* is confided to its tender mercies ... the wolf and the sheep ... The Power which ruined the Ottoman Empire ... is to be the protector and guardian of that same empire; and we are told that it is the most scandalous calumny to suspect the Russians to have any other than the most humane and disinterested views![33]

Victoria's foreign secretary was less willing to be supportive of the French position. In a memorandum to the queen he wrote:

> It is very natural that the French Government after having failed to extort Concessions upon the Turkish Question, by menaces of foreign war, should now endeavour to obtain those concessions by appealing to fears of another kind, and should say that such concessions are necessary in order to prevent revolution in France.[34]

The French were only too aware that they had been checkmated over a major issue. Thiers had already shown signs of recognizing this when he sent François Guizot to London as ambassador in the spring of 1840. Guizot was a highly respected historian, a member of the French Academy who had held various positions in government since the Restoration. The ambassador repeatedly told Thiers that France ought to compromise, but in vain. Then, in October 1840, Louis-Philippe dismissed Thiers and appointed Guizot as foreign minister in a new government. The choice was justified but complicated by the fact that Guizot had been the lover of Princess Lieven for the past three years. After a bitter separation from Prince Lieven in 1835, the princess had refused to return to Russia, supposedly on health grounds, claiming that it had a 'climate made for bears'.[35] She moved to Paris where she embarked on a passionate affair with the Frenchman, twelve years her junior. Her great political influence over him was in no doubt and was to last for twenty years.

Guizot had been *persona non grata* at the Russian embassy during his time in London because of his well-known liaison with Princess Lieven, a woman who had fallen foul of Nicholas and many others in high places because of her refusal to return to Russia followed by her affair. Brunnov therefore viewed Guizot with suspicion and fear now that he effectively headed the French government.

Although the Russians did not have the easy access that the British now had to the French government under Guizot, they did possess close links with the other northern powers and Brunnov learned from his Austrian colleague that Guizot (himself a Protestant) was proposing an agreement between the western Catholic powers to increase their presence in Jerusalem. Without saying anything to Britain, he was clearly trying to drive a wedge of discord between Catholic Austria and Orthodox Russia in the new alignment.[36] At the time the vast majority of pilgrims to Jerusalem were Russians, the Holy Lands being seen as an extension of their spiritual motherland.

Later in the year the Russian government was further alarmed by the efforts of the pious King Frederick William of Prussia to create an Anglo-Prussian Protestant bishopric of Jerusalem. Brunnov made clear Russian determination that the bishop 'could never accept anyone preaching in the place that had always been the exclusive preserve of Greek and Latin rites', that is the Church of the Holy Sepulchre.[37] Aberdeen tried to assure Brunnov that, although the Archbishop of Canterbury was an enthusiastic supporter of the project, the British government would ensure that Orthodox privileges would be respected. The seeds were already being sown of a dispute that was to play a major role in causing the Crimean War.

Nicholas wanted to cement the new-found good relations with Britain with a military alliance. Brunnov presented it but did not press. Palmerston, for good reason, with suitable verbiage about constitutional objections, was able to turn it down politely. Nesselrode knew that such an idea came from his master, a soldier and not a diplomat, and let the matter drop. He was now devoting himself to repairing relations with France and it was clear that Russia wanted to come to an agreement with the other powers. Nevertheless, arriving at the final solution was tortuous in the first half of 1841.

Despite pressure from Leopold and Queen Victoria, the foreign secretary refused to allow Guizot the kudos of a declaration stating that it was at the request of France that they had persuaded the sultan to give Mehemet Ali the hereditary governorship of Egypt (which his family ruled until 1952). France had been humiliated but had been brought back into the concert of the great powers. In July 1841 she joined with the northern powers and Britain in signing the Treaty of London, the Straits Convention, in which they agreed that no foreign warships should enter the Dardanelles while Turkey was at peace.

Palmerston suffered a barrage of hostile criticism in Britain because of his policy of working with Russia. David Urquhart had a field day accusing the foreign secretary of being a Russian pawn. The more moderate *Times* thought the new-found warmth in Anglo-Russian relations too good to be credible. It 'implied the sudden oblivion of all those differences which have for so many years divided the cabinets of St Petersburg and St James' and 'contradicted the whole *Tenour* of Russian policy and Russian history'.[38]

In Russia the emperor was ambivalent. He had helped to further the Straits Convention but this did not mean that he regarded it as viable and nationalists regarded the agreement as a gross mistake for which they held Nesselrode responsible.

Thus there was little conviction in either Russia or Britain that the convention would hold. For, on top of this scepticism about a lasting agreement concerning the Ottoman empire, in Asia conflict between the two powers had been mounting since the mid-1820s.

12

PERSIA AND AFGHANISTAN

Persia was central to Anglo-Russian relations in Asia in 1816, and here Russia had the upper hand following its protracted war against its southern neighbour.

With Persia *de facto* a Russian protectorate, Nesselrode had made it clear that year that Russia would not stand for any interference in her dealings with Persia and, with her long southern frontier bordering that of Persia, she had justification for this assertion. But with Britain and Russia post-Waterloo allies, the British government was not unduly disturbed, as the threat of Franco-Russian use of Persia as a springboard for the invasion of India no longer existed. Moreover, Britain was now confident of her position in India, having established beyond doubt her domination in the subcontinent between 1813 and 1818. The king of Delhi still theoretically enjoyed suzerainty over India and the princes who had submitted were left largely free to govern as they wished within their borders. Nevertheless, all of them acknowledged effective British control of the whole of India as far north as the Sutlej river.

A striking example of the low British priority accorded to Persia came in 1826 with the renewal of war between Russia and Persia, neither side having accepted as final the frontier fixed at the end of the previous war. Responsibility for the fresh outbreak of hostilities is debatable, but there is no doubt that Persia was technically the aggressor, even though Russia had done much to goad her into attacking. George Canning, the foreign secretary, had to decide whether, even though the British government could stick to the letter of an 1814 Anglo-Persian treaty and leave the Persians to their fate, it was in British interests to prevent the Russians strengthening yet more their power base in Persia. Charles Williams Wynn, President of the Board of Control for India in the cabinet, argued that Russian provocation had been such that the Persians had no alternative but to fight. The foreign secretary was not convinced: 'I am sorry—(or rather I am happy)—to say that I cannot agree with you in thinking that the Casus foederis has occurred, under the last of the incredibly foolish treaties of which I enclose copies.'[1]

Canning believed that the decision of the shah, Shah Fath Ali, to go to war against Russia was timed to take advantage of Russia's preoccupation with the struggle for Greek independence and internal problems following the Decembrist uprising. Yet this was not a propitious moment for Britain to alienate the Russians because of ongoing Anglo-Russian cooperation over Greece. Not only would the Persians be refused aid but Britain would take steps to loosen ties with Tehran. British representatives had over the years become used to disbursing subsidies to high-level Persians susceptible to taking an anti-Russian stance (as did the Russians for the opposite reason).

After some initial successes the Persians were forced to sue for peace with Russia. In the Treaty of Turkmanchai in 1828 Persia lost Erevan and Nakhchivan, had to pay an indemnity, sign a commercial agreement with Russia and allow Russian subjects to be exempt from Muslim law in Persian territory. The terms could have been much harsher were it not for Russia's impending war with Turkey. Russia had defeated Persia but the infidel was resented. Nesselrode sent Alexander Griboedov, a well-known playwright, as minister to Tehran. During the holy month of Muharram in 1829 Griboedov provided sanctuary in his legation for some Christian Armenians and refused to hand them over to the shah, knowing their certain fate. For his pains, the mullahs urged a furious crowd to storm the legation, where the minister was hacked to death. Britain's influence in Persia was severely diminished by her refusal to aid the Persians in the war but the Russians were also deeply resented.

The British government in the late 1820s was naturally preoccupied by Greece and then Russian expansion in the Near East. However, the belief in a new threat to India from Russia was being expressed by a number of articulate and influential polemicists. In 1809 Mountstuart Elphinstone had visited Kabul and made a study of Afghanistan which he described in his *Account of the Kingdom of Caubul* in 1815. He later became the East India Company resident in Peshawar and was at pains to keep in touch with events in Afghanistan. Henry Pottinger published *Travels in Beloochistan and Sinde* in 1816. Sir John Malcolm's *History of Persia, from the Most Early Period to the Present Time* (1815) was essentially an academic work. But it was Lieutenant Colonel George de Lacy Evans's *On the Practicability of an Invasion of British India*, published in 1829, that was most influential.

The essential message of these writers was that as the Russians were known to be active in Central Asia (as were the British), their aim was not the gargantuan task of invading India but of destabilizing British rule there. A Russian force from east of the Caspian Sea to Khiva could sail up the Amu Darya (usually known as the Oxus at that time) to Balkh from where it would march to the Khyber Pass.[2] Russia had been seen to be weakening Turkey and Persia in recent years, confirming an expansionist pattern apparent since the end of the seventeenth century. As there was no power capable of resisting Russian armies between her own frontiers and India, Britain had to reinforce her influence in the intervening territories to constitute a barrier to further Russian advance.

Most of the cabinet showed little interest in these publications. Only the Duke of Wellington and Lord Ellenborough, President of the Board of Control for India, were receptive to the arguments exposed. The government would not take any action against Russia but Ellenborough set about gathering geographical, military and commercial intelligence on all the countries surrounding India. Lord Heytesbury in St Petersburg employed a spy to acquire top-secret Russian documents, but Ellenborough took little notice of the accompanying dispatches given the ambassador's known Russophilia.

The new Whig government in 1830 had been outraged by Russian suppression of the Polish uprising at the end of the year, although noticeably less alarmed by the growth of Russian power in Asia. Had Russia therefore kept a low profile in Transcaucasia and Central Asia in the early 1830s, the British government would certainly have continued to focus on Europe and the Near East. Instead, Russia was complicit in Persia's aim to compensate for her losses in Transcaucasia by recovering her prestige elsewhere. Persia's traditional enemy, Afghanistan, was the obvious victim. (Central to all relations between Persia and Afghanistan is that Persia was a Shia state while Afghanistan was Sunni.) It was well known that Tehran would in particular like to regain Herat, which had belonged to her in the heyday of the Safavid empire. And it was realized on the banks of the Neva that if Persia gained possession of Herat she could probably also take Kabul and Kandahar. In such a situation Russian influence would penetrate Afghanistan without any effort on her part, whereas a heavy strain would be thrown on Great Britain to meet the demands of the new situation. If, on the other hand, Britain intervened to save Herat, she would be seen as thwarting the natural and just ambitions of Persia and drive her to lean on Russia for support.

Mahomet Mirza, one of Shah Fath Ali's ambitious grandsons, launched an attack on Herat in 1833 but returned quickly to Tehran a few months later on learning of the death of the shah. Not for the first time, a struggle for the succession to the Peacock Throne ensued. In this Britain and Russia cooperated and Mahomet Mirza became shah, entering Tehran accompanied by a force under Sir Henry Lindsay Bethune and the Russian and British ministers. Nevertheless, Russia felt she still had the upper hand. Nesselrode assured Count Carlo Pozzo di Borgo, the ambassador in London, that 'Our relations with Persia in 1834 provide us with convincing proof of the constant consolidation of her relations with Russia.'[3]

But with Palmerston at the foreign office, Britain was now making up for three decades of underestimating the importance of Persia. Soon after taking office, the foreign secretary appointed a new minister to Tehran, Sir John McNeill, who already knew the country well, and before taking up his post published *The Progress and Present Position of Russia in the East*, in which he advanced the view that Russian foreign policy was based on a preconceived design for subversion and conquest in Central Asia. Palmerston agreed:

> I take Nicholas to be ambitious, bent upon great schemes, determined to make extensive additions to his dominions; and labouring to push his political ascendency far beyond the range of his Ukases, animated by the same hatred of England which was felt by Napoleon, and for the same reasons, namely that we are the friends of national independence, and the enemies of all conquerors. We are an obstacle in his path.[4]

For the foreign secretary was well informed about Russian intrigues in Tehran and exploded when he saw the Russian ambassador in May 1837. 'Your Minister is provoking the Shah into undertaking missions that will ruin him and will lead to disaster ... Lord Palmerston wants war', reported Pozzo di Borgo from London.[5] The foreign secretary was right. Mahomet Mirza marched on Herat in July 1837. To the British government the attack could not be justified being based 'upon some antiquated and obsolete claims of a former Dynasty of Persia on Afghanistan', but what really mattered was, as Palmerston had suspected, that the attack was embarked on with the obvious encouragement of the Russian minister to Tehran, Count Ivan Simonich, who was present in Herat and was said to be directing, telescope in hand, the siege and distributing larger sums of money from the Persian indemnity paid after the previous war with Russia. Also present in Herat was McNeill, counselling the shah to abandon the attack, but more important to the Afghan resistance to Persia was Lieutenant Eldred Pottinger of the East India Company's political service who arrived in the city to gather intelligence in August 1837. Pottinger did much to increase British prestige by supporting the Heratis, while that of Russia plummeted. The siege dragged on until September 1838 when Mahomet Mirza was forced to abandon it in the face of the starvation of his troops and a possible Anglo-Russian clash.

The foreign secretary was not seeking war, as Pozzo di Borgo, who lived in dread of Palmerston's outbursts, had claimed. Nevertheless, whatever the hyperbole being thrown around, Palmerston clearly did fear that Russian activity in Persia would all too soon be extended eastwards: 'That poor old Pozzo is in his dotage ... is the Emperor's affair not ours ... [but] as you say Russia fears above all things a war with England.'[6] Instructions had already been sent to the new governor general of India, Lord Auckland: 'To watch more closely than has hitherto been attempted the progress of events in Afghanistan, and to counteract the progress of Russian influence.' He was given a free hand as to:

> the mode of dealing with this very important question, whether by despatching a confidential agent to Dost Mohammed, the emir of Kabul, merely to watch the progress of events, or to enter into relations with this Chief ... as well as the adoption of any other measures that may appear to you desirable to counteract Russian influence in that quarter.[7]

As was usual in the Indian service, it was a military man in the service of the East India Company, Captain Sir Alexander Burnes (his father was a cousin of Robert Burns) who was sent to Kabul in 1836, in theory on a commercial mission. Burnes had already travelled up the Indus in 1831 to Lahore, the capital of the Punjab, ruled by the powerful Sikh Ranjit Singh, where he had been well received. He went on to visit Bukhara and Afghanistan and in Kabul met the emir, who favourably impressed him. His book published in 1834, *Travels into Bokhara; Being the Account of a Journey from India to Cabool, Tartary and Persia. Also, Narrative of a Voyage on the Indus from the Sea to Lahore*, was a bestseller. The emir was delighted to renew his old acquaintance in September 1837 as he sought British help to recover Peshawar, which had been part of the empire of his ancestors. (Afghanistan in the 1830s was a group of independent khanates, of which the most important were Kabul, Kandahar and Herat. In the two former the rulers were of a new dynasty, while in the third a restoration of the old ruling elite had occurred. The fourth khanate, Peshawar, had been seized by Ranjit Singh who was now an ally of the British.) In return for recognition as emir of Kabul and the receipt of a subsidy, Dost Mohammed would send an army to rescue Herat from the Persians and would become the devoted ally of the British. The emir agreed to Burnes's recommendation that he might attempt to hold Peshawar by paying tribute to Ranjit Singh.

While the negotiations between the emir and Burnes were proceeding, a Russian 'commercial agent' reached Kabul in December 1837. If the Burnes mission was symptomatic of British fears of Russian aggression in Central Asia, the presence of a Russian agent was indicative of similar apprehension on the part of the Russians concerning the British. Captain Yan Vitevich (there are various spellings of his name) was sent by Simonich in Tehran, of whom he was the *protégé*, bearing two letters, one from the Russian emperor and the other from Simonich, plus a considerable sum of money from the latter's reserves. Nicholas's letter was unexceptionable. He wrote of his friendship for the emir and the people of Kabul, and of his happiness to assist its traders entering his dominions. It indicated that the Russians would be happy to continue the diplomatic contact now made.

To demonstrate his new-found goodwill towards the British, Dost Mohammed passed a copy of the Russian emperor's letter to Burnes, who was furious:

> Herat is besieged and may fall; and the Emperor of Russia has sent an envoy to Kabul to offer Dost Mohammed Khan money to fight Ranjit Singh!! … Captain Vitevich … arrived here with a blazing letter, three feet long, and sent immediately to pay his respects to myself. I, of course, received him, and asked him to dinner.[8]

Burnes had done what he could to reach a compromise agreement with Dost Mohammed, though he woefully lacked any political authority. For Lord Auckland in Calcutta refused to countenance acceding to any of the emir's proposals; in particular he was not prepared to imperil his relations with Ranjit Singh. The ruler of Kabul ended negotiations and Burnes left in April 1838. It is therefore no surprise that Dost Mohammed turned to Vitevich, who proffered Russian support to enable the emir to take Herat, Kandahar—held by a brother—and Ghorian from Persia.[9]

The Russians were left in no doubt that the British government knew that Simonich was egging on the Persians in Herat and was involved in the

Vitevich mission. Their ambassador in London played the innocent with Palmerston: 'I replied to him that not only was I unaware of the facts and the suppositions of which he spoke, but that I was persuaded of the lack of substance of all the news that was circulating.'[10]

The new Russian ambassador to Tehran, General Alexander Duhamel, had not long been in Tehran before a study of earlier Russian instructions convinced him that Simonich and Vitevich had acted according to instructions in pursuing an aggressive policy:

> Count Simonich was incautious and made mistakes, I do not deny that; but at bottom he kept to the direction given to him by the Imperial Ministry. Besides, the late Rodofinikin [director of the Asiatic Department, who died in July 1838] gave Vitevich to understand that our government was inclined to lend to Dost Mohammed two million in cash and two million in goods. It is sufficient to run through the instructions given by the Ministry to Vitevich to be convinced that at that time we intended to take an active part in Afghan affairs. Why should we have sent an officer to Kabul if this mission was not to lead to any results?[11]

Although Duhamel himself favoured Russian intervention in Afghanistan, he was instructed to recall Vitevich. Twelve days after his arrival in St Petersburg the Pole shot himself dead in his hotel room. Lady Clanricarde, wife of the British ambassador, believed that the emperor's men were responsible for the 'suicide'.

Vitevich made a convenient scapegoat. In 1872, more than thirty years later, Count Filipp Brunnov, who as a young diplomat in St Petersburg in 1838 had drafted the instructions sent to the embassy in Tehran, wrote:

> Witewitch [Vitevich], of Polish origin was without doubt a badly chosen agent for a secret mission to Kabul. He hoped that he would be able to cause trouble between Russia and England. The Afghan chief took advantage of this disposition to make our agent servile to his plans ... Could he have foretold that the Chief of Kandahar would have given a copy of the treaty of guaranty that the representative of Russia in Tehran had signed?
>
> Cte Simonich had signed the convention without prior approval and it was not sanctioned by the Emperor Nicholas. But it has to be admitted that its very existence provided the English Cabt with grounds for recriminations that Lord Palmerston exploited to the full.[12]

The British government succeeded in obtaining from the Russians a repudiation of the work of their minister to Persia and their agent in Afghanistan, together with the all-important statement that Russia would not engage in political relations with Afghanistan. Matters could have been left there. They were not.

The Burnes mission to persuade Dost Mohammed to do British bidding having failed, Auckland decided to intervene with an ultimatum to the emir to submit. The governor general also concluded a treaty with Ranjit Singh and Shah Shuja, the former emir of Kabul then living on a British pension in India. Much has been written about the First Afghan War, and William Dalrymple's *Return of a King: The Battle for Afghanistan* brilliantly recounts the events of the period. The aim was to place on the throne of Kabul a ruler who would be amenable to British authority and who would prevent aggression on the north-west frontier of India. Shah Shuja fitted the bill, despite being for good reason unpopular in Afghanistan, cruel, weak, inadequate, and who had been of dubious loyalty during his British-supported reign earlier in the century. The British Army of the Indus invaded Afghanistan in 1839, reinstated Shah Shuja, only to abandon Kabul in 1841. Powerful Afghan tribes had risen up against the invaders. After a year of slaughter in and around Kabul, Burnes, now British resident, was murdered, as was Auckland's envoy and minister on behalf of the government of India, Sir William Macnaghten. In the retreat from Kabul in January 1842 the loss of British and Indian life probably exceeded 12,000. Later in the year the British Army of Retribution retook Kabul.

The First Afghan War was a disastrous defeat for Britain, as was felt at the time and has been the view of most historians since, including Dalrymple. For others it was seen as a tactical defeat and geopolitical victory which from a long-term point of view had established Britain as the power with a claim that a friendly northern neighbour in Afghanistan was essential for the defence of India.

As far as Russia was concerned, official expressions of sympathy for Britain were forthcoming, but more convincing was the view of the imperial ministry of foreign affairs which recorded triumphantly that the British had been forced to abandon the 'tyrannous and exorbitant policy to which they had committed themselves, of founding in the heart of Asia a powerful State, of which they should be the masters'.[13]

The Russians for their part also suffered reversals in Central Asia. There had been the failure in the siege of Herat which was raised in June 1839 and constituted a British victory over Russia. For, although Britain could not send an army to Herat, she did send warships into the Persian Gulf and troops were landed on an island opposite Bushire.

Britain had from early in the nineteenth century become active on the south-western coast of Persia, the Persian Gulf, with its ports on the all-important route to India, and already from the mid-eighteenth century a British resident had been present at Bushire. This reflected the fact that for a long time India had been the primary trading partner of the Gulf and the source of supplies such as foodstuffs and wood. The main exports of the Gulf were pearls, dates and horses, which found a ready market in India. However, maritime traffic en route for India in the early years of the nineteenth century was disrupted by piracy, slavery and the arms trade.

These concerns led Britain to establish control over the Gulf. In 1819 the fleet arrived from India off Ras al Khaimah on the Omani coast and opened fire. The town fell and the expedition turned to other pirate ports. Ten pirate vessels were destroyed at Bahrain after which the bulk of the force returned to India, having subjugated many of the Gulf sheiks.

Preparations for treaties began in 1820 and each sheik was required to sign a preliminary agreement before becoming party to the General Treaty of Peace. These agreements provided for the surrender of vessels and that pearling would be permitted for a certain number of months a year. One by one the Arab rulers signed the General Treaty for the Cessation of Plunder and Piracy. Thus from the truce established came the name the Trucial States of the south coast of the Gulf.

Renewed treaties were signed in 1835 and 1853 when the Permanent General Treaty of Perpetual Maritime Peace came into force. But there was no occupation. British supremacy in the Gulf rested on indirect rule—diplomacy and a powerful maritime presence. (Today the former Trucial States form the United Arab Emirates, the UAE.)

A second setback for Russia occurred in the Central Asian khanate of Khiva. There had been rumours reaching London of an impending Russian expedition against the khan of Khiva in 1836. Then in 1838 Pottinger in Herat passed on information that the Russians had finally decided to send an expedition, this being backed by reports from the British ambassador in St Petersburg. Russian caravans were being harassed and Russian subjects kidnapped into slavery and forced to convert to Islam:

> Every means of persuasion has now been exhausted. The rights of Russia, the security of her trade, the tranquillity of her subjects, and the dignity of the state, call for decisive measures, and the Emperor has judged it to be the time to send a body of troops to Khiva to put an end to robbery and exaction.[14]

Britain was preoccupied with Afghanistan. The moment was opportune.

Palmerston warned the Russians that the loss of Khivan independence would be considered injurious to British interests. Occupation of Khiva would give Russia access to the lower Amu Darya and Britain might consider the command of the upper course of the river necessary 'as a measure of precaution and defence'.[15] In November 1839 General Vasily Perovsky, governor of the Russian province of Orenberg, led a campaign against Khiva, a march of more than 1,300 kilometres in a particularly severe winter. The expedition covered only half the distance to Khiva and was obliged to limp back to Orenberg with heavy loss of life.

The struggle for conquest, or at the least influence, in Central Asia involved not only government officials, diplomats or military men of the countries concerned but an important number of explorers, adventurers, evangelists or soldiers with only a tenuous connection to their governments, which therefore had very limited control over them. The largest British group was made up of the 'politicals', military men usually employed by the East India Company in Calcutta. Secondment to undertake missions on the northern and western frontiers of British India came to be known as 'shooting leave' and was welcomed by enthusiastic young men. As far as the Russians were concerned they were spies, and most did engage in what was little short of espionage. Much less is known of the Russians who took part in topographical explorations and reconnaissance missions than the British because of the inherent secrecy of the Russian regime (few names appear in the archives) and the lack of published material. On the other hand, the role played by British men was closely followed in parliament and in the press at home. Above all the opening up of Central Asia in the early decades of the nineteenth century provided plentiful material for its participants to recount in popular publications—or, if they had not made it home, for others to write up. As corroborative evidence was not usually available, the authors often had more influence than was merited.

In 1823 a young recruit to the 6th Bengal Native Light Cavalry, Lieutenant Arthur Conolly, had arrived for his posting in Calcutta. He represented a new breed in the East India Company service, an evangelical with a mission to convert Muslims to Christianity and to see slavery abolished. To begin with Conolly concentrated on learning Asian languages, but on returning to India in 1829 after home leave he decided to travel via Russia and Georgia to Persia and to attempt to reach Khiva. This proved impossible. Despite his disguise as a local trader he was kidnapped and only avoided death or slavery with the help of some Persian merchants. Once freed he pressed on the further 500 kilometres east to Meshed. From there he was able to cross into Afghanistan and arrived in Kandahar from where he could reach the relative safety of the Indus.

Conolly's journey using routes along which a hostile Russian army would be likely to advance on India provided him with the material for his lively and popular account, *Journey to the North of India, Overland from England, Through Russia, Persia and Afghanistan*.[16] Nevertheless, what he has come to be remembered for is being the first to use the phrase 'The Great Game' to describe the struggle between Britain and Russia in Central Asia in the nineteenth century.[17]

After observing the siege of Herat another 'political', Colonel Charles Stoddart, had been sent on a mission to the emir of Bukhara in 1838 to reassure him that British action to replace the emir of Kabul, Dost Mohammed, in no way meant that in Bukhara he had anything to fear from his southern British neighbours. He was a poor choice and immediately gave offence to the emir, a man of a suspicious nature, and refused to conform to local and Muslim customs. For this Stoddart was arrested and thrown unceremoniously into a pit, the Black Hole, tormented by snakes and vermin, as well as starved.

Before the failure of Perovsky's expedition to Khiva, Lieutenant James Abbott of the Army of the Indus had been dispatched in 1839 under orders from Palmerston to travel from Tehran to Khiva to negotiate with the emir on behalf of the Russians, a dexterous British move, it was hoped, to rob Russia of the main pretext for action against Khiva which was that the emir was in the habit of taking Russian traders as slaves. On arrival Abbott learned that two Europeans suspected of being Russian had been tortured with red-hot skewers in an effort to make them confess to attempting to overthrow the regime. While he had good reason to fear for his life given this information, Abbott tried to persuade the emir to release the slaves.

A deal was done. Abbott was told to leave for St Petersburg with a number of Russian slaves as a token of Khivan goodwill. The rest would be freed if Russia abandoned all military operations against the khanate. With a small Khivan escort Abbott arrived in the Russian capital where he was well received and extracted a promise that military operations against Khiva would be abandoned. In fact the Russians already knew their expedition had failed. As far as the emir was concerned, all this served was to persuade him that both Russia and Britain were his enemies.

The British government had become worried as Abbott had not been heard of for some time, so another British officer, this time from Herat, was sent in 1840 in search of him. Lieutenant Richmond Shakespear, accompanied by loyal Herati troops, all in native dress, made the hazardous journey across the desert to Khiva. After the usual long drawn-out negotiations the emir believed that Britain would sign a treaty of alliance with the khanate if the slaves were freed. All 416 slaves were allowed to leave with Shakespear. Thus, on arrival in St Petersburg Shakespear was feted and cordially received by Nicholas I. Meanwhile, Abbott made the journey back to British India where he served until 1877. He was knighted and a town was named after him, Abbottobad, today in Pakistan. (It had its brief moment of international fame in 2011 when Osama Bin Laden was captured and killed there.)

Conolly and Stoddart were less fortunate than Abbott and Shakespear. All this time Stoddart languished in the Black Hole in Bukhara, hoping for an expedition to rescue him. It came in the person of Arthur Conolly, who was sent under orders from London to Kabul in 1840 to urge the Central Asian khans to resolve their long-standing differences and unite against Russia. Neither the emir of Kokand nor of Khiva was interested. Conolly proceeded to Bukhara. The bloodthirsty emir believed that after visiting his enemies Conolly was conspiring with them to attack him; so Conolly joined Stoddart in the pit. The British government then did nothing to help the situation by sending a letter to the emir describing Conolly and Stoddart as private travellers. After months of starvation and torment in the foul dungeon the two men were publicly beheaded in June 1842. The loss of two adventurous officers was not in itself important compared with events in neighbouring Afghanistan, but the fate of Conolly and Stoddart riled the British government. Ministers for many years to come cited them as proof that Britain had interests to defend in Central Asia.

Both Britain and Russia were stymied in 1842 but it was clearly only a lull in the struggle for Central Asia—horizons were widening. As Brunnov in London wrote to Nesselrode at the end of 1841: 'Let us play for time.'[18] And Palmerston warned:

> It seems pretty clear that sooner or later the Cossak [sic] and the Sepoy, the man from the Baltic and he from the British Isles will meet in the centre of Asia. It should be our business to take care that the meeting should be as far off from our Indian possessions as may be convenient and advantageous to us. But the meeting will not be avoided by our staying at home to receive the visit.[19]

13

A FRAGILE FRIENDSHIP

After the years of diplomatic combat with the rumbustious Lord Palmerston, the Russian emperor and his advisers were greatly relieved when the exhausted Whig government fell in August 1841 and was replaced by a Tory administration with Sir Robert Peel prime minister and Lord Aberdeen foreign secretary. It was well known that the new prime minister thoroughly disapproved of Palmerston's fractious style and imperious ways in the conduct of foreign affairs, plus his air of having a prescriptive right to the office. Lord Aberdeen on the other hand was an urbane, melancholy, conciliatory and scholarly man who had been active in foreign affairs since 1814 and foreign secretary in the late 1820s. However, although he was much more knowledgeable about international matters than Peel, the prime minister did not allow his foreign secretary free rein. Aberdeen did not object and the two worked amicably together.

Aberdeen's main objective on assuming office was to renew the entente with France, but he was frustrated in this by having to deal with a number of other pressing problems—ending the Opium War with China, boundary disputes with the United States and instability in Spain. It was not until 1843 that he could make friendly overtures to Guizot, with whom he had excellent relations since meeting him three years earlier. Princess Lieven, who had been corresponding with Aberdeen for nearly a decade, impressed upon the foreign secretary her lover's determination to rescue Anglo-French relations from the estrangement of the 1830s. The two men did in fact establish something of a mutual admiration society that greatly helped to pave the way for better relations. Clear evidence of this came in 1843 when Queen Victoria and Prince Albert visited Louis-Philippe at the Château d'Eu in northern France, although disagreement over proposed Spanish royal marriages cast a shadow over the burgeoning entente.

Nicholas I, as ever, held Louis-Philippe in contempt, a ruler as the result of revolution, of a country demonstrating clear signs of internal instability. He did not wish to see Russia's recently improved relations with Britain over the Near East wrecked by a Franco-British rapprochement. Nesselrode as usual pursued a similar aim but with more subtlety. Knowing that Peel was in favour of making abolition of the slave trade part of general European law, he was not dismayed when France scuppered the plan: he followed it up with a proposal for a treaty on trade and navigation with Britain. However, the nationalists in the administration blocked him in furthering this, and in Britain Peel came up against the protectionist Whigs. Only a minor agreement resulted.

Nesselrode's position had been constantly undermined by his foes in St Petersburg and now, more seriously, by the emperor who, from his longstanding personal conviction and the influence of nationalistic advisers, was again claiming that the status quo in the Ottoman empire could not be maintained. It had to be divided among the great powers, essentially Russia and Austria on the European side of the Straits. Metternich was not receptive and stood firm against a carve-up.

The vice chancellor then suggested to his master that the emperor's energies would be better spent looking to Britain. The latter had reacted with horror at the proposal made to Austria and there were clear indications that, after Queen Victoria's visit to Louis-Philippe, Britain was pulling away from Russia and was seeking a bilateral agreement with France over the Ottoman empire. Nicholas decided to follow Nesselrode's advice and head for London.

There was talk in both St Petersburg and London in the early months of 1844 about such a visit, but which country issued the formal invitation is not clear. Lord Bloomfield, the number two at the British embassy, reported that on 23 January at a ball the emperor had mentioned that he had last been in England in 1817, so enjoyed his stay, and would like to be invited again. Brunnov claimed that it was in London on the same day that at a dinner at Aberdeen's, Peel expressed the hope that Nicholas would soon visit his country. Two months later at a public dinner the prime minister expressed a desire for better relations, which was taken as a tacit invitation. The emperor procrastinated with good reason as his favourite daughter, the Grand Duchess Alexandra, was pregnant and dying of consumption, so he was loath to leave Russia.

Then suddenly, on 24 May, Bloomfield, who had tried in vain to find out about the emperor's intentions—Nesselrode being kept equally in the dark about them—learned that the emperor was about to leave immediately. A letter from Nicholas informed the queen and British ministers that the emperor would arrive two days after his courier reached England. Part of the reason for this behaviour, alien to that of a British monarch, was that the emperor was in the habit as military commander of descending without warning to check on the army. On top of this was his fear of assassination (understandable as his father had died in this way), particularly in Britain where there was a large community of Poles who bore grievances against him.

Queen Victoria later admitted that she was at first 'extremely against the visit', her reluctance being in no small measure because of Nicholas's long-standing conflict with her adored uncle, Leopold, King of the Belgians. Baron Stockmar, a long-time friend of Leopold before becoming an adviser to Victoria, believed that the queen only agreed to receive Nicholas in order to put pressure on the emperor to establish diplomatic relations with Belgium.[1] A further reason for her reluctance was that she was heavily pregnant.

When it actually occurred, the emperor's behaviour from the outset raised eyebrows.[2] He refused to stay at Buckingham Palace, preferring the Russian embassy at Ashburnham House in Westminster (shades of Alexander I in 1814). There, on arrival, he wrote a letter to Prince Albert after midnight which he asked to be delivered immediately to the prince. Even his fellow countryman Brunnov was surprised to learn that his master had rejected the bed offered at the embassy in favour of a straw-filled leather pallet (repeating the ritual later with daily fresh straw to astonished servants at Windsor Castle).

After attending mass at the Orthodox church in Welbeck Street the following morning, Nicholas lunched with the queen at Buckingham Palace. 'The Emperor', wrote Victoria, was:

> 'en grande tenue', with high boots. He kissed my hand & I embraced him … The Emperor's appearance is very striking, though 48 he is still very handsome & his body very fine with a very good figure. His features are quite classical and regular … He kept on making all sorts of fine phrases & kissing my hands.[3]

But the perspicacious young monarch continued: 'There is an expression in the eyes of the Emperor that is extraordinary and not at all what one would expect, his behaviour is excellent, dignified and not proud—but he makes me think, as I said to Albert, that he is not happy, nor at ease.'[4]

A round of courtesy visits to members of the royal family followed and the necessary paying of respects to the Duke of Wellington. On the Monday, Nicholas inspected the building work at the new Houses of Parliament and the recently completed Regent's Park Zoo. There was time though for shopping for jewellery and silverware in Bond Street before meeting the dowager Lady Pembroke, daughter of the former Russian ambassador Simon Vorontsov, and the Duke of Devonshire. A reception for the entire *corps diplomatique* followed, at which it was noticed that Nicholas surprisingly shook the hand of the Belgian minister, Sylvain Van de Weyer. Victoria noted her guest's roving eye: 'His admiration for beauty is very great … when he drove out with us, looking for pretty people. But he remains very faithful to those he admired *twenty-eight* years ago; for instance Lady Peel, who has hardly any remains left.'[5] More serious was a call upon the prime minister at his home in the Privy Gardens before inspecting the telegraph at Paddington Station, from where the emperor and his entourage boarded the train to Slough. There Prince Albert met the party and took them to Windsor Castle where Nicholas was to be Queen Victoria's guest for several days.

The queen did her best to make him feel welcome and ordered several rooms to be 'freshened up', and 'to look as well as they possibly can. We have hung up some Russian pictures, including those of the 2 Grand Duchesses & the Empress … this house has such wretched accomodation'.[6] The man used to the grandeur of the Winter Palace and Tsarkoe Selo assured Victoria that he found Windsor 'absolutely charming' and took her son Bertie in his arms:[7] 'The Emperor praised *my* Angel very much, saying: "C'est impossible de voir un plus joli garçon; il a l'air si noble et si bon", which I must say *is very* true.'[8] Her earlier reservations melted in the face of such flattery of her husband.

The social whirl continued the next day at the Ascot races where Nicholas mixed freely with those in the paddock and upped his popularity by announcing that he would provide an annual prize worth 500 guineas for as long as he ruled. (This did not last his reign and the race was renamed the Gold Cup during the Crimean War.) More to Nicholas's taste was a military review on the Wednesday where he could disport himself in a magnificent uniform—confessing to Victoria that he felt 'so "*gauche*" *en frac*, which certainly he is quite *unaccustomed* to wear'.[9] Here he distributed medals to veterans of the Afghan War. At a second visit to Ascot on the Thursday, this time with the queen, there was a somewhat desultory anti-Russian demonstration. A much larger protest at a meeting in Holborn the same day confirmed Victoria in her fear of a Polish attempt to assassinate the emperor.

Nicholas's final day was spent in London where the Duke of Devonshire laid on a breakfast at Chiswick House, a Whig bastion, with the politically interesting idea of decorating the room as a Turkish tent. At the opera in the evening, the queen recalled, 'I was obliged to take him by the hand and make him appear; it was impossible to be better bred or more respectful than he was towards me.'[10]

As an exercise in royal summitry the visit was an unclouded success—Albert was pleased 'that I not only *see* these great people but *know* them'.[11] And Victoria had taken full advantage of her week with the Russian emperor, sizing him up in a manner that would do credit to any highly experienced statesman:

> He is stern and severe—with fixed principles of duty which nothing on earth will make him change; very clever I do not think him, and his mind is an uncivilised one; his education has been neglected; politics and military concerns are the only things he takes great interest in; the arts and all softer occupations he is insensible to, but he is sincere, I am certain, sincere even in his most despotic acts, from a sense that that is the only way to govern.[12]

But the main purpose of Nicholas's coming to Britain was political. Although he overestimated Victoria's influence in international relations, he did appreciate that in a parliamentary democracy it was above all with her ministers he had to deal. To this end he lost no opportunity to engage in frank discussions with his British hosts during his stay at Windsor, spending time not only with Aberdeen, Peel and Wellington but also with Palmerston and Melbourne.

Nicholas wished to explore the possibilities for improving Russia's relations with Britain in view of France's growing involvement in the Near East, especially Egypt, and most of all the future of the Ottoman empire. He told Aberdeen:

> Turkey is a dying man. We may endeavour to keep him alive, but we shall not succeed. He will, he must, die. That will be a critical moment. I foresee that I shall have to put my armies into movement, and Austria must do the same. I fear nobody in the matter, but France.[13]

There had to be contingency plans should it become necessary to partition Turkey:

> Turkey must fall to pieces. Nesselrode denies this but *I* for my part am fully convinced of it … I don't claim one inch of Turkish soil, but neither will I allow that any other shall have an inch of it … I shall therefore do all in my power to maintain the *status quo*. But nevertheless, we should keep the possible and eventual case of her collapse honestly and reasonably before our eyes.[14]

Nicholas was convinced that he had made a staunch friend of the young queen and that he had dispelled the many suspicions harboured by British politicians. He reminded them:

> Years ago Lord Durham was sent to me, a man filled with prejudices against me. Merely by contact with me, his prejudices were all driven to the winds. And this is what I hope to bring about with you. I hope to dissipate those prejudices by personal intercourse. For I highly prize England.[15]

However, he completely failed to realize that Peel and Aberdeen viewed him as an unreliable eccentric and believed there had been no more than an exchange of views on questions of mutual interest, and no written record was kept on the British side. Nor did the emperor appreciate that no British government could make commitments that would bind a future government.

Nicholas had totally miscalculated, for not only was his visit politically ineffectual, but he had misread British policy towards the Ottoman empire. The British government was ready to agree on the need to plan ahead for the possible partition of the Ottoman empire, but only when that need arose, and that was not yet the case. The emperor instead of dispelling anti-Russian feelings had rekindled old suspicions.

Nesselrode was at Kissingen when he met Nicholas on his way home from London and was immediately aware that his master had blundered and damaged the cordial Anglo-Russian relations he had so long and meticulously built up. The vice chancellor was thus only too pleased to be sent to London with orders to obtain a written agreement. He arrived in August and spent two months in discussions with Peel and his old friend from the days of the Napoleonic Wars, Aberdeen, plus some railway trips round England, a stay in Brighton, visits to the opera and horticulturists. Brunnov at the embassy took care of diplomatic affairs and the talks with Peel and Aberdeen were informal. It is clear Nesselrode was mixing business with much pleasure.

The vice chancellor wisely adopted the position that he had come to clarify what the emperor had said. With Aberdeen's approval he was able to draw up a memorandum based on the conversations between the emperor and the foreign secretary: 'Russia and England are convinced that it is in their mutual interest that the Ottoman Porte remains independent and in possession of all the territories that constitute this Empire. This political combination of them is the best in the interest of conserving peace.'[16]

If, in spite of all their efforts, the Turkish empire did break up, they would 'get together to ensure the establishment of a new order destined to replace that of today'.[17] The British government did not believe that it had departed from its policy towards the Ottoman empire. On the contrary, if Nicholas's word could be relied on, it had gained a substantial victory by securing Russia's formal adherence to that policy. It was a decade later, in totally changed circumstances, that the memorandum assumed an importance that had never been envisaged in 1844.

Although commerce had always played a major role in Anglo-Russian relations, it was not touched upon during Nicholas's or Nesselrode's stays in Britain, despite the increasing friction over trade in the 1840s. With the free trader Peel at the head of the British government and the young William Gladstone at the Board of Trade, in 1843 it was inevitable that highly protectionist Russia would face pressure to reduce her trade barriers. Peel's budget of 1842 reimposed income tax but reduced duties on raw and manufactured goods. Three years later, when the financial situation of the country had greatly improved, he abolished all duties on raw materials except timber and tallow, removed all export duties and abolished duties on several hundred imported articles.

The relaxation of some Russian tariffs and prohibitions from 1836 to 1838 inspired rising expectations in Britain, as two thirds of Russian exports went to Britain and export taxes remained high. Peel told Brunnov that he hoped the British example would encourage Russia to move in the same direction, and wrote a personal letter to the ambassador in May 1845 in which he argued forcefully against Russian protectionism—a model free trade exposé and damning indictment of Russian practices. British tariffs had been lowered during the previous year, but:

> There has been no falling off of Revenues. Diminished duties have not led to diminished Receipts—but quite the Contrary ... If the Government of Russia will adopt the same policy the same Result will follow. The Government will receive increased Revenue. There will be only one party a loser, namely the smuggler and illicit Trader ... But your high duties are not a protection ... All those Duties which would be cheerfully paid if

> they were moderate and enabled the lawful Trader to compete with the unlawful one … You sustain this loss without any Countervailing benefit to your own Subjects, who are deluded by a false Reliance on a protection with which because of your immense frontier, you do not, and cannot afford them.[18]

Russian manufactured goods were higher priced, inferior in quality and in limited supply in Russia. The *Journal de St Petersbourg* accepted that Russia possessed too few capitalists, they 'conduct trade according to their own ideas and plans, who import and export merchandise at their own pleasure'.[19] However, even the free traders among them did not believe that a system of private enterprise would lead to industrialization comparable with that of Britain. They were convinced that Russia would remain dependent on imported manufactures and its economy agrarian. Bloomfield wrote in 1844: 'Almost every large landed proprietor in Russia has capital engaged in manufactories; they have suffered much from the superiority of our goods in the market of Central Asia and latterly also in China: complaints against their own produce are general both at home and abroad.'[20] Basically Russia was mired in the eighteenth-century social order, with the aristocracy, the pillar of state and autocracy, using a serf-based economy incapable of meeting the challenges coming from rapidly industrializing countries with flourishing middle classes, above all Britain.

Andrew Buchanan, secretary at the embassy in St Petersburg, bombarded the Russian administration with examples of counterproductive practices, making clear that export duties above all were preventing expansion of the market: 'Jute, linen, tallow, cow hides, smoked fish, all those are products that Russia depends on selling to England and this country provides the means of transporting them … The value of exports to England are greater by more than two million pounds sterling than imports from this country.'[21] The problem was not only caused by the duties but by the damning fact that commerce from Russia 'is actually a Monopoly in the hands of a few Individuals'.[22]

Sugar, as ever, was a contentious Russian import, to which now was added an expanding British commodity, printed cotton; but Nesselrode insisted that Russia would not be pushed around by Britain and would maintain 'a certain liberty of action in matters of tariffs, and only consult our own interests and convenience'.[23] Free trade, giving Russia the same status as other countries, and facing the same competition, was not enough. He wanted reciprocal agreements with Britain that would favour

Russia alone and these were clearly not part of British commercial policy in 1845.

A striking example of Russia's dependence on British industrial skill was the construction of the new iron suspension bridge over the Neva in St Petersburg, the contract having gone to the company Curtis and Kennedy in Liverpool. The bridge was to be shipped arch by arch during the summer months of 1845 when navigation was open, but the works fell seriously behind schedule—to Nicholas's anger. However, nowhere is Russia's falling behind industrially better illustrated than in the development of railways, which played such a large role in British industrialization from the late 1820s. In Russia the minister of finance, Count Egor Kankrin, failed to see the usefulness of railways at all, although Nesselrode was fascinated by the possibilities they opened up. Significantly, the first Russian railway line was opened between St Petersburg and the imperial palace at Tsarskoe Selo in 1837, a 'toy' railway only 17 kilometres long and without any economic or social impact. The line between Moscow and St Petersburg took from 1842 until 1851 to complete. Lack of railway communication was to be a major factor in Russia's defeat in the Crimean War.

In 1846 it was obvious that Anglo-Russian relations had deteriorated since 1841. After Nicholas's visit there was the reawakened British suspicion of Russia. In Russia the nationalists, with the emperor behind them, were increasingly dissatisfied with Nesselrode's policy of maintaining good relations with Britain and held that there were basic divergent interests between the two countries in the Near East. This Orlov camp, named after Count Alexsei Orlov, felt confirmed in its hostility when the entente cordiale with France was renewed with a visit by Louis-Philippe to Britain in 1845, grander and more successful than that of the Russian emperor.

Onto this background of fragile friendship between Britain and Russia came two substantial events that presaged the jettisoning of any future cooperation. First came the fall of Peel's government in June 1846 over the repeal of the Corn Laws and the return of a Whig government with Lord Palmerston as foreign secretary. This was followed by the Austrian annexation of Cracow. Neither Britain nor Russia were directly involved and only became embroiled because of their relations with the direct participants.

The Polish city of Cracow had been granted free city status under the Vienna Treaties but had been constantly under threat from the three partitioning northern powers. After the rising in Russian Poland in 1830, Nicholas had decided that Austria must eventually annex Cracow. With rumblings of an international Polish plot to take over Cracow and a feeble rising in the city in 1846, the Russian emperor pushed his fellow powers to oblige Austria to incorporate the city into its empire. Palmerston, realist as ever, recognized that there was nothing Britain could do and he was not going to risk an overt clash with Austria and Russia. He dispatched a limp protest to the northern powers without any intention of impressing them but rather to strengthen his reputation in Europe as a friend of liberalism. Fourteen years before he had defended the Russian action in Poland; in November 1846 at the Lord Mayor's banquet he condemned the seizure of Cracow.

While from a Russian point of view Palmerston was an anti-Russian liberal, when David Urquhart was elected to the House of Commons in 1847 as an independent with support from the more extreme wing of the Radicals, the new member proceeded to call for the impeachment of Palmerston, citing among other reasons that he had been employed as a Russian agent by the Lievens when he was secretary at war in 1828, his failure to act when the *Vixen* was seized upon and his collaboration with Russia against France over Mehemet Ali in 1840. The attempt at impeachment obviously failed but, without holding the views of Urquhart, there was by 1848 a powerful lobby of politicians in parliament calling for a tougher line against Russia. Diplomats, in particular Stratford Canning and Henry Bulwer, voiced similar feelings; businessmen claimed that Russian tariffs were a major cause of the economic depression in Britain. The influential *Foreign Quarterly Review*, previously moderate in its opinion, became hostile to Russia and throughout the country anti-Russian sentiments, with the Polish cause still a rallying cry, were increasing.

The Europe-wide revolutions of 1848 had a multiplicity of causes. International tensions had inevitably built up under the Vienna system but were not the fundamental reason for the dramatic events. The uprisings emerged from a wide variety of sources and there was no coherent movement or single social phenomenon behind them. They were a reflection of changes that had been taking place in European society from the French Revolution and throughout the first half of the nineteenth century—liberalism, radicalism, socialism, nationalism, economic factors and technological change.

Internal discontent in France led to the fall of Louis-Philippe in February 1848. The king and his family fled to England and by the end of the year France was a republic under Louis-Napoleon, nephew of Napoleon I. For Nicholas a republic was even more repugnant than the detested Louis-Philippe but he reacted with caution. 'I give you my word', he told the commanders of the Imperial Guards, 'that not one single drop of Russian blood will be spilt on account of these worthless Frenchmen.'[24] Nevertheless, Palmerston warned the emperor that he was glad to learn that Nicholas was not going 'to take any steps which by indicating intended hostilities against France might have the effect of bringing on a European War'.[25]

When Metternich fell in March, insurrection spread throughout the Austrian provinces of northern Italy. The Magyars of Hungary led by Lajos Kossuth declared their autonomy of the Habsburg empire, the Czechs also. Successful revolutions broke out in most of the German states. Austrian influence in Germany collapsed and the Diet of the German Confederation was replaced by a liberal parliament. The foreign secretary kept up his urging of restraint on the part of Russia, flattering Nicholas that

> nothing can be wiser or more dignified than the determination which His Imperial Majesty has taken to maintain a neutral attitude with regard to events which are passing in other Countries and to confine himself to such defensive measures as in his judgement he may deem necessary for the protection of his Dominions.[26]

Similar exhortations followed.

The march of revolution eastwards seemed irresistible and was now close to Russia, but Nicholas realized that he could not intervene directly in Prussia or Austria except at their request. And this was not forthcoming. His only scope for action was in the Danubian Principalities, Moldavia and Wallachia, Ottoman territory but with a right of protection of the Christian population by Russia (the Treaty of Adrianople) which effectively dominated the administration and was extremely unpopular with the people of the Principalities. An anti-Russian uprising took place in Wallachia in the spring and the revolutionaries of Bucharest appealed to Britain for support. An anti-Russian British consul was not sufficient to convince the foreign office to intervene. Russian troops marched into Moldavia in July, occupied the principality and then moved on to defeat the uprising in Wallachia. Public opinion in Britain was outraged by the invasion but the government was determined to continue its policy of trying to influence moderation on the part of Russia. It diplomatically pointed out in September that 'it will be misinterpreted in Europe by those who are always disposed to put an unfavourable construction upon the acts and conduct of the Russian government', and 'HMG is sure Russian troops will be out very soon.'[27] They were not, but Palmerston was prepared to believe, or at least chose to believe, that Russia was not intending to annex the Principalities.

Anglo-Russian relations during this year, when the two countries were the only ones to avoid revolution, had been soured by events but had remained on a surprisingly even keel given the very different political philosophies. Russia for the most part had adopted a defensive stance internationally, although at home the Third Section had become even more repressive and clamped down more aggressively than ever on any suspected dissent.

While most of the uprisings of 1848 were put down by the German and Austrian authorities, the Hungarians led by Kossuth and counting many Poles, including General Jozef Bem who had taken part in the 1830 uprising, plus Italians and ethnic minority groups in Hungary, held out for independence from Austria in the spring of 1849. The new young Austrian emperor, Franz Josef, appealed to Russia for help. Brunnov warned his government that there were likely to be protests from the British government, but in the event the Russians had little to fear, as Palmerston had no desire to see Britain's traditional ally Austria humiliated and her international position weakened. Palmerston simply told the ambassador to 'End the business quickly', while the soldier Duke of Wellington advised, 'Make sure you have sufficient numbers.'[28] Brunnov glowed with delight that Russia could not have asked for more from Britain. Nesselrode was more circumspect. He had long battled with Palmerston: 'Palmerston's welcome to our communications about Hungary is very satisfying. God willing that it will continue like that till the end.'[29] It would take only a few months for this amity to turn sour.

In June, 190,000 Russian troops marched south and in mid-August Hungarian resistance was at an end. This was followed by the flight into Ottoman territory, mainly Wallachia, of about 5,000 soldiers of whom 800 were Poles. Nicholas did not go along with the brutal Austrian reprisals against the Hungarian revolutionaries, but he was determined to recapture his Polish subjects who might constitute the kernel of a future Polish uprising. Austria wanted the Hungarians back. Turkey refused to be bullied or to extradite these men who had claimed political asylum and the Poles constituted a welcome anti-Russian force. Palmerston, plus the vociferous British press and public which lauded the courageous Hungarians, and were suspicious of Russian action in the Principalities, provided loud support for the Turks.

In early October the foreign secretary, in response to appeals from the Porte, sent the Malta squadron to Besika Bay, off the Dardanelles, to be joined soon afterwards by a French fleet. Nicholas at this juncture announced he had come to an agreement with the Porte. The Polish refugees could remain but in Ottoman territory a long way from Russia. To Stratford Canning in Constantinople, who had been hoping for the chance of a showdown with Russia, this was a great disappointment. Palmerston ordered the fleet to withdraw and made great play of the fleet's only having penetrated so far for reasons of weather and that it should have sought shelter elsewhere. Such an error would not reoccur. The Russians believed differently. Nesselrode claimed that the British and French had infringed the 1841 convention and were afraid that they would be confronted by the Russian fleet from Sevastopol. Brunnov gloated that Russia had shown who dominated in relations with Turkey. A conflict with Britain had seemed possible: 'We have been able to avoid that and we have been successful in all our endeavours, winning everywhere against English sympathies which are alien to our own.'[30]

The British prime minister, now Lord John Russell, a much less combative figure than the foreign secretary, tried not very convincingly to pretend that Anglo-Russian relations had not been severely damaged by the events of 1849. He hoped that the unfortunate recent events would not have a lasting effect on relations. 'In his opinion', he told Brunnov, 'Russia and England, which alone have resisted the upheaval that has shaken Europe, have more than ever the need to be on good terms.'[31]

14

TOWARDS CRIMEA

The creation of the independent state of Greece had shown what could be achieved by the powers acting in unity against the Ottoman empire. However, the fledging country posed a mounting challenge to France, Britain and Russia that erupted in 1850 and exacerbated the fragile relations between Britain and Russia that had survived the revolutions of 1848–9.

Palmerston had supported the Greek struggle for independence but his relations with Greece were strained from the start. He had backed the choice of Prince Otto, the seventeen-year-old son of the king of Bavaria, as absolute monarch, and the awarding of a loan from Rothschilds to enable Greece to pay for the Turkish assets she had acquired. Britain, France and Russia, the protectors of Greece, guaranteed the loan.

Otto proved an unfortunate choice. Instead of setting up an efficient administration that would restore order and put an end to the chaotic conditions, the king's German advisers, the Bavarokratia, allowed anarchy and banditry to prevail. Taxes were not collected and the Greek government failed to pay the interest due on the debt. The three powers were obliged to pay it. Although there was general frustration with recalcitrant Greece, Palmerston was hindered in pressing for reform by the Russian refusal to join him. Nicholas stressed Russia's close links with her co-religionists and was only too willing to encourage Otto to reign as an absolute monarch. Hence the Greek government looked favourably on St Petersburg. On the other hand there were factions in the country who sought support from France and Britain.

Since the British fleet was in the Dardanelles in 1849 to make clear that Britain would support Turkey in not extraditing the Hungarian and Polish refugees to their home countries, this provided an opportune moment to settle accounts with Greece. Palmerston dispatched the fleet to the

Piraeus. For, apart from the debt problem, Britain claimed that two men holding British passports had been ill-treated by the Greek government. George Finlay, a Scot whose garden had been seized without compensation, was one. The other was a Portuguese Jew, David (though usually known as Don) Pacifico, who had been born in Gibraltar. Anti-Semitism was rife in Greece, as Anselm Rothschild had found to his cost when he visited Athens in 1847 to discuss repayment of the loan. Don Pacifico exploited this to the full in his claim for the burning down of his house in Athens in 1847.

In January 1850, the commander of the British fleet, Admiral Sir William Parker, demanded that compensation had to be paid to Don Pacifico within twenty-four hours. When this was not done one of the ships of the Greek navy was seized. As there was still no action by Greece, a blockade was imposed on several Greek ports. By the end of the month Greek merchant ships were seized. Russian ships were stopped and some detained.

This high-handed behaviour naturally enraged the French and Russians. Nesselrode pointed out in a long and furious dispatch in February 1850 that Britain had done nothing about the claims for three years. Why had it suddenly become urgent? This was bullying by a strong power of a weak one, an attempt to humiliate Greece in the eyes of the world. And why had Russia as a co-protector not been consulted? 'Greece is a state created by Russia and France as much as by England and they are therefore entitled to protest most solemnly about the pretension of the Gouvt. of England in dealing with this affair without the participation of the two signatory Cabinets.'[1] Brunnov was told: 'The Emperor instructs you Baron to make clear to the English Gouvt. that it must immediately cease pursuing this course of action which is quite out of proportion to the complaints.'[2]

With typical bravado Palmerston was scathing in his dismissal of the Russian protest and would brook no interference. He held that it was ridiculous to claim that a country had to consult other countries before acting. In any case, Greece was an independent state and could be called to account for its actions. Furthermore, he had noted in Nesselrode's dispatch that Russia was aware of the British claims. The foreign secretary's only concession was to agree that Don Pacifico's claim was exaggerated.[3]

For all his bluster Palmerston had not only Russia to contend with but the queen, Prince Albert and Lord John Russell, the prime minister. Britain agreed to French mediation and suspension of the blockade. Agreement was reached in April and, in what superficially looked like a *volte-face* by Russia, she advised the Greeks to pay the claims and to proclaim throughout Europe how she had been ruthlessly pushed around by Britain. But the Russian reason for wanting to end the crisis was to be able to reassert Russian influence in Athens. Publicly, though, Russia adopted a holier-than-thou stance. People could not forget 'the pain being imposed on Greece'.[4] Russia was not in a position to help the Greeks but she had had enough of the contemptuous attitude of Palmerston and 'the lack of respect that he shows towards us'.[5] Britain had to be reminded that their common Orthodox religion gave Russo-Greek relations an importance beyond the political. Moreover, it was not only Russia but France and Austria also who feared that Britain was trying to overthrow the Greek state as created by the three powers and install a British protectorate.

At the same time as Russian complaints mounted against Palmerston's aggressive handling of the claims against the Greek government, so opinion in Britain turned against him. Lord Stanley, a Tory, moved a vote of censure on the government in the House of Lords in June. It was carried by 169 to 132. Yet only a few days later the Radical MP John Roebuck moved a resolution in the House of Commons declaring that Palmerston's foreign policy was aimed at maintaining the peace and friendly relations of European countries and at the same time preserving the honour of Great Britain. Greece was the ostensible subject of the debate but the foreign secretary called upon members to look beyond this minor dispute. Neither rational arguments from the likes of Richard Cobden, who rightly pointed out that Palmerston had done nothing to liberate the Greeks from the tyranny of King Otto, nor William Gladstone, the chancellor of the exchequer, who spoke for three hours on the need for observing a code of morality in international affairs, won the day. The debate lasted for four nights and resulted in the greatest triumph of Palmerston's parliamentary career—he had never been an impressive speaker in the House of Commons. Hyperbole was the order of the day. He quoted from Shakespeare—'Hath not a Jew eyes?'—made oblique unfavourable references to the queen and spoke of 'the immeasurable superiority, the stern serenity, of the people of England ... soaring in our inapproachable greatness'. The almost five-hour-long speech ended with the famous declaration that

> as the Roman in days of old, held himself free from indignity when he could say Civis Romanus sum; so also a British subject, in whatever land he may be, shall be confident that the watchful eye and the strong arm of England will protect him against injustice and wrong.[6]

After the cheering stopped the government emerged triumphant with a majority of 46.

It was the summation of mid-Victorian confidence, aiming to reach the literate middle class who read newspapers, rather than the limited circle of the House of Commons. Palmerston was the first modern politician, a man who recognized that the support of such men, as well as the narrow aristocratic class, was increasingly important in forming government policy. This was beyond the understanding of Nicholas I, who could not comprehend that his excellent relations with the queen and Prince Albert counted for so little in his dealings with the British government.

The strained Anglo-Russian relations were aggravated the following year when the question of the Polish and Hungarian refugees in Turkey again flared up. Turkey decided to allow the men to leave the country despite protests from Russia and Austria. The United States offered to take all of them but a few preferred Britain, one of whom was Lajos Kossuth. He embarked upon a speaking tour and was feted as he headed for London to thank Palmerston personally for all that he had done for the refugees. This provoked an objection by the queen and alarm among most of the cabinet who feared the diplomatic embarrassment that an official welcome by the foreign secretary would cause.

Palmerston cocked a snook at the warnings to begin with and then capitulated. In the end he circumnavigated the ban by receiving a deputation from two London boroughs thanking him for all that he had done for the Poles and Hungarians. While the foreign secretary did not go along with the deputation's condemnation of the emperors of Russia and Austria, a journalist was present and the occasion was reported in the press, to the fury of the queen, Prince Albert and most of the cabinet. For Russia it was a blatant insult and Kossuth should be expelled. Lord John Russell pointed out that Britain accepted political refugees of varying political complexions, including recently Metternich and Guizot.[7]

Palmerston's overweening confidence in his indispensability to the government and popularity in the country led to his forced resignation in December 1851. Louis-Napoleon had become president of France in 1848. The country was in disarray after the fall of Louis-Philippe and the new president promised to restore security. He was initially supported by Britain, but when in December 1851 he carried out a *coup d'état* and declared himself president for life, it posed a problem. The official British position was to adopt a strictly neutral stance and Palmerston had duly informed the British ambassador in Paris of this. However, prior to this he had congratulated the French ambassador to Britain, Count Alexandre Walewski, illegitimate son of Napoleon I, on the coup and informed the British ambassador to France of his view. The foreign secretary then drafted a further modified explanatory dispatch to Paris. The queen wanted to make a correction, only to learn that Palmerston had already sent it. Victoria demanded that Russell force the foreign secretary to resign.

The Russians could not hide their delight. Brunnov enjoyed setting out Palmerston's diplomatic crimes for the delectation of his masters, describing him as an international bully seeking British domination of Europe. And of all the countries with which he dealt, 'Ours was the one to which he most directed his fire. Without a glimmer of regret at the turmoil he provoked, his spiteful nature was the cause of squabbles he caused without his attaching any serious importance to them.'[8] The bottom line was that Brunnov could claim that he could not send Nesselrode a better Christmas present than news of Palmerston's dismissal. The ambassador was sure that Anglo-Russian relations would improve in the future.[9]

The legitimist Russians made much of the 1815 treaty that excluded the Bonaparte family from ever ruling in France, but Nesselrode reasoned that to reject Louis-Napoleon as life-long president would only serve to incite the Frenchman to pursue aggressive policies contrary to the interests of Russia. Certainly there were widespread fears that Louis-Napoleon would be tempted to attack Belgium in an attempt to regain France's 'natural frontiers' as far as the Rhine. This scare passed and the president declared that 'the empire means peace'. Nevertheless, the clearly ambitious president embarked on a different means of reuniting France after the divisions of 1848–9. He was determined to re-establish France's rights on behalf of the Catholic religion in the Holy Lands.

The dispute over the respective rights of the Orthodox, Catholic and Protestant churches in the Holy Lands had been building up in the 1840s. Under the influence of Louis-Napoleon it was ratcheted up several gears. The Catholic right in France had for a long time been seeking a crusade against the Orthodox church in this region and Louis-Napoleon had the man at hand to put this policy into operation—a senior diplomat, the Marquis Charles de la Valette. The marquess was dispatched to Constantinople as ambassador in 1851. Once *en poste* Valette demanded the reassertion and enforcement of concessions made to the Catholic church in 1740, that is, that all shrines and churches should be placed in joint Catholic and Orthodox possession. The Turkish ambassador in London complained bitterly to Brunnov of the concessions extracted, 'humiliating for the dignity of the Ottoman Empire and compromising for its independence'.[10] All this had taken place with an alarming rapidity that prevented the powers from intervening. What was more, the French were active in the Ottoman province of Tripoli in North Africa and appeared to have ambitions in Tunis. It was clear how weak and vulnerable to outside pressure the Turks were. This impression was further emphasized a few months later when the sultan was forced to allow a French man-of-war to pass through the Dardanelles. Since Valette, a diplomat, was on board it was not technically a breach of the Straits Convention but it was provocative and intended to strengthen the domestic position of Louis-Napoleon. In November 1852 the Porte granted Catholics the right to hold a key to the Church of the Nativity in Bethlehem. Increasingly confident and boosted by his success in exacting concessions from Turkey, the prince-president held a plebiscite that overwhelmingly approved his request to become the Emperor Napoleon III.

The death in September 1852 of the Duke of Wellington, who the Russians so admired, and the genuine regrets and encomia that were sent from St Petersburg had eased tensions between Britain and Russia, although the Russians could not comprehend that French ambassador Walewski took pride of place next to Prince Albert at the funeral of the victor of Waterloo over Walewski's father. Britain then accepted the second French referendum creating the Second Empire while at the same time expanding her own army and navy due to uneasiness over potential French imperial ambitions. Nicholas was aware of and understood British fears but lamented what to him was cowardice on the part of the government towards France, the new empire.

The Russian emperor was not going to stand by and let the newly energized French take over in the Levant. It was time for a showdown with this obstreperous people. Thus in December 1852 Nicholas ordered the mobilization of Russian troops in Bessarabia for a strike on Constantinople and a similar campaign in the Danubian Principalities. The war envisaged was against Turkey to demonstrate to the French which country was the most powerful in the Near East. The Ottoman empire was to be partitioned with Russia making major gains and appropriate sops made to Britain and France. As Nesselrode noted, 'It is to be feared that sooner or later war is inevitable given that the new French emperor is ambitious and looking for trouble.'[11]

In Britain Lord Aberdeen had become prime minister at the end of 1852 after a year of political disarray. He was able to form a coalition government whose arrival was welcomed by Nicholas, who still believed in the 1844 agreement and trusted Aberdeen. The prime minister in February 1853 held that the Turkish 'barbarians hate us all, and ... we ought to regard as the greatest misfortune any engagement which compelled us to take up arms for the Turks'.[12] Nevertheless, the continued existence of the Ottoman empire was vital to the balance of power. Talks took place in St Petersburg between the emperor and the British ambassador, Sir George Hamilton Seymour, in January and February 1853, in which:

> His Majesty appeared to expect an early dissolution of the Turkish Empire, and proposed in such a case, to act in perfect concert with the British Government. Lord Aberdeen does not think there is anything new in this demonstration of the Emperor. It is essentially the same language he has held for some years, although perhaps the present difficulties of Turkey may have rendered him more anxious on the subject.[13]

Meanwhile in London, Brunnov held several meetings with Aberdeen and reported home the prime minister's contempt for Turkey. The Russian was well versed in British politics and knew that in the cabinet there were those whose fear of Russian designs on the Ottoman empire was greater than their objections to decadent Turkish rule, in particular Palmerston, now home secretary. However, the ambassador exaggerated Aberdeen's power and ignored the increasing suspicion of Russia being voiced in the press, particularly by the industrial class, as trade with Turkey was worth much more than that with Russia. Brunnov bears a heavy responsibility for encouraging Nicholas at this stage to believe that France was the country Britain feared more than Russia.[14]

Austria had recently with Russian backing extracted a peace treaty over Montenegro that had demonstrated Ottoman weakness. This strengthened the view in St Petersburg that the Turks would always give way if they were bullied enough. Nesselrode suggested to his master therefore that a special envoy should be sent to Constantinople to secure satisfaction for Russia's demands on behalf of the Orthodox church in the Holy Lands.

Nicholas took up the idea enthusiastically and Prince Alexander Menshikov was dispatched to Constantinople. His instructions ordered him firstly to insist that the Turkish foreign minister, the Grand Vizier Fuad Efendi, was excluded from negotiations and, more importantly, to secure a Russo-Turkish convention, a *sened*, re-establishing Orthodox privileges in the Holy Places. It was necessary to make clear that the giving of a key to the Church of the Nativity the previous year to the French in no way altered the previous position there. If it seemed opportune, the envoy could propose a Russo-Turkish defensive alliance which would bind Russia to protect Turkey against French hostility. Above all he was to threaten to break off diplomatic relations if his demands were not met: 'The fact that the Tsar had even thought they might succeed suggests how far removed he was from political reality.'[15] The Russians felt obliged to communicate these instructions to the British government as they were afraid that the French would get wind of them and cause trouble, but Brunnov took care not to reveal their full extent. Seymour in St Petersburg realized what the ultimate Russian intention was and warned the already sceptical Lord John Russell, now foreign secretary, what the mission sought.

Menshikov was a disastrous choice for the mission. He was not a diplomat but a military man with a fearsome reputation since participating in the 1812 campaign and a strong Orthodox churchman. It was not only the prince's own limitations that boded ill. His letters of credence were in Russian only and he insulted the Turks by appearing in civilian rather than military dress. The aim was to intimidate the Turks; they procrastinated. In this they were now being supported by Stratford Canning, now Viscount Stratford de Redcliffe, who had returned to Constantinople in April as ambassador despite the reservations of both Aberdeen and Lord Clarendon, now foreign secretary, who feared Canning's combative manner and anti-Russian bias would exacerbate matters.

Brunnov continued to report home that all was well in relations with Britain: 'The French insinuations have not in any way unsettled the confidence that HMG's Government places in the generous policy of Our August Master towards the Ottoman Empire.'[16] But by early April 1853 he was forced to admit the disquiet being manifested by the cabinet and the press criticism of Aberdeen for his passivity in the face of Russian provocation. The wily ambassador even managed to provide the prime minister with further information about the Menshikov mission and extracted a promise to try to persuade his colleagues that there was nothing to fear from the Russian action. By this time though, Stratford de Redcliffe had reported home and made clear the full extent of the Russian demands. Aberdeen's faith in Russia was shaken and he threatened to resign. Brunnov convinced him once more that Russia could be trusted, but he admitted that the prime minister appeared at the end of his tether.

The Turks were by now enjoying increasingly active British and French backing to stiffen their resistance to Menshikov's demands. The Russian envoy's arrogance and scare tactics as negotiating tools proved counterproductive. The Porte submitted to the Russian demands concerning the Holy Places; Menshikov responded with an ultimatum on 5 May threatening a rupture of negotiations on 10 May, if the Turks did not sign a revised *sened* dealing with the wider issues:

> The events of 5–9 May were crucial for breaking the Gordian knot of British and 'European' trust of Russia and for making the Anglo-French alliance, which was Napoleon III's dream. By the time the ultimatum played itself out, London and Paris were ready with similar and virtually coordinated responses ... The Russian leaders and diplomats had been fooling most statesmen with the recent diplomacy and themselves to boot with their political mythology.[17]

When the Turks refused Menshikov's demands he announced that Russia would break off diplomatic relations and departed. His mission had failed. It was 'a deplorable end ... a moral failure that we cannot accept', complained the Russian chancellor.[18]

Nicholas reacted by resorting to military means. He wrote to his long-standing close collaborator, General Paskevich, at the end of May:

> The consequence [of Menshikov's failure] is war. However, before I get to that, I have decided to send my troops into the [Danubian] principalities—to show the world how far I would go to avoid war—and send a final ultimatum to the Turks to satisfy my demands within eight days, and if they don't, I shall declare war on them. My aim is to occupy the principalities without a war, if the Turks do not meet us on the left bank of the Danube ... If the Turks resist, I shall blockade the Bosphorus and seize Turkish ships on the Black Sea; and I shall propose to Austria to occupy Herzegovina and Serbia ... I must go by my own path and fulfil my duty according to my faith as befits the honour of Russia.[19]

The emperor was prepared to go to war but Paskevich persuaded him that it would be sufficient for Russian troops to occupy the Principalities. On 28 June Nicholas announced the imminent departure of his troops and Russian units began to cross the Pruth. Then on 6 July Prince Mikhail Gorchakov, commander of the army of occupation in the Principalities, entered Bucharest. But, in addition to the hardening positions in London and Paris, Austria was refusing to support Russia. The Russian occupation of the Principalities, by threatening Austrian trade down the Danube, struck at the real interests of the Habsburgs more than of the Ottoman empire.

An effort to find a way out of the dilemma was made by Austria. The foreign minister, Count Karl Ferdinand von Buol, proposed a meeting in Vienna of British, Prussian and French ambassadors to seek a diplomatic solution. This culminated in the Vienna Note of 28 July. The ambassadors agreed on a formula which provided that Turkey should grant Russia certain rights of protection over the Orthodox Christians, though these would fall short of the original demands. Stratford de Redcliffe feared that this would give Russia a foothold in Turkey that would threaten Turkish independence. Disclosure of a secret Russian memorandum, which showed the full extent of Russia's designs on the Ottoman empire, confirmed this. The Vienna Note, drafted on behalf of Turkey, was accepted by Nicholas who saw it as a diplomatic victory, though it was really only a means of letting him off the diplomatic hook. France and Britain agreed. Then the whole fragile edifice collapsed when the sultan rejected it.

In Britain a clamour for war was building up in the press. Yet it was all too clear that the cabinet was divided. Palmerston, though home secretary, was working up public opinion into a war mood through his speeches in parliament and his directives to the *Morning Post*. In fact he was less bellicose than Lord John Russell, who was more vocal in cabinet in expressing his disagreement with Aberdeen's appeasement policy, his supposed willingness to be dictated to by Russia. However, William Gladstone at the exchequer was urging peace. The prime minister was, as ever, trying to keep the temperature down. He believed that the Turks wanted war but his position changed dramatically in early September when he surrendered to the hawks. The secret 1844 memorandum of Nesselrode, leaked to the press, 'interpreted' the Vienna Note as obliging Turkey to take account of Russia's active solicitude for her co-religionists in Turkey; that is, it was a claim to exercise a general protectorate over the Orthodox church and its adherents. This constituted the most extreme interpretation of the meaning of Menshikov's demands.

Shocked by the revelation, Aberdeen, who had so far insisted that there should be no breach of the 1841 Straits Convention, led the cabinet in deciding to send the fleet to Constantinople. The reason given was that the riots in the Ottoman capital in early September protesting at Russian occupation of the Principalities and calling for war with Russia endangered the lives of foreigners and the sultan himself. With French agreement, two warships were sent from Besika Bay to Constantinople. Brunnov remonstrated with the prime minister about this provocation, claiming that 'Muslim fanaticism, if it is awakened, is the common enemy of all Christian Powers.' Aberdeen replied frostily that, if the Russians removed their troops from the Principalities (hardly a possibility at the time), the warships would be withdrawn.[20]

The Russians realized that Turkey was tottering on the brink of declaring war but believed that with winter approaching the Porte would not want to enter into a war. Russia for her part sought time and counted on having until the following spring to prepare for hostilities. Nicholas and Nesselrode went to see the Austrian emperor, Franz Joseph, in Olmütz at the end of September and produced a watered-down version of the Vienna Note, less aggressive towards Turkey. It was too late. On 29 September the sultan ratified the decision of the Grand Council for war with Russia. On 10 October Prince Mikhail Gorchakov was presented with an ultimatum demanding Russian evacuation of the Principalities. Stratford de Redcliffe tried to persuade the Turks to accept the modified note and hold back. They did so for a fortnight. Then on 23 October, Turkish batteries fired on a Russian flotilla on the Danube. Four days later Osman Pasha crossed the river with a Turkish army and fighting broke out in the Caucasus, where it was hoped a successful campaign against the Russians would encourage the Persians and Muslims of the Black Sea area to support them. By mid-November, after being held up by bad weather, the British and French squadrons were in the Bosphorus.

Nicholas was a man obsessed by his belief in his duty as protector of the Orthodox Christians under Turkish rule; his and Russia's God-given mission. The more the West expressed its opposition to Russia's occupation of the Principalities, the more he was inclined to gamble everything on a grand alliance of the Orthodox, even threatening to support Slav revolts against the Austrians, if they should join the West against Russia: 'Religious conviction made the old Tsar rash and reckless, risking all the gains Russia had made in the Near East over many decades of fighting and diplomacy.'[21] Reluctantly, Nesselrode, the emperor's military advisers and Russian diplomats accepted that war with Britain and France was inevitable. The chancellor bemoaned 'the inconvenience ... for us of a war against England and France'.[22] Clear evidence of this is in instructions to Brunnov in London in mid-November to remove all Russian assets deposited in the Bank of England.[23] This was quietly executed without attracting British attention.

Confirmation that war was imminent came with the battle of Sinope on 30 November. Russian warships under Admiral General Pavel

Nakhimov struck and annihilated an Ottoman squadron anchored in the bay of Sinope, a port in northern Anatolia. The Turks lost over 3,000 men, their leader Osman Pasha was captured, the fleet destroyed. This was a perfectly legitimate operation given that Turkey had declared war on Russia, but in Britain it was viewed as an act of treachery by Nicholas. The press was even more inflamed and almost unanimous in its demands for war to protect Turkey and British interests in the Eastern Mediterranean. Aberdeen's lofty view that public indignation should not determine government policy was not shared by his colleagues. He pathetically asked Brunnov whether he had received letters of recall.

As was expected, Russell called for strong-arm tactics. Palmerston, though, with suspicions that the Turks might have used Sinope as an entrapment of Britain, held that 'something ought to be done to wipe away the Stain'.[24] As home secretary he ostensibly tendered his resignation on a domestic matter, though no one was under any illusion that the real reason was Aberdeen's refusal to help the Turks.

Nicholas wrote a long, pleading letter to Queen Victoria in early December (before the news about Sinope had reached London). There was sincerity in his expression of admiration and affection for the queen: 'It is to the justice of Your Majesty's Heart that I appeal, it is to her wisdom that I appeal that she should decide between us.' He wished ardently to maintain good relations. Would she want to see the noble flag of England fly alongside the Turkish croissant to combat that of the Christian flag of St Andrew? He knew that Victoria had written about her fears for a general conflagration but he could not accept a humiliation. Above all he had a duty to protect his fellow co-religionists in the Turkish empire.[25] Earlier in the year the queen had tersely written: 'England should not sanction the claim.'[26]

The French were not as agitated as the British by the Russo-Turkish hostilities, but it was they who demanded of London that Russian warships and troop transports in the Black Sea should be intercepted and forced to return to port in Sevastopol, tantamount to a declaration of war. The weak British government was in no position to object, and on 4 January 1854 British and French fleets entered the sea. A similar order was not delivered to the Turks. Brunnov asked for his passports on 4 February and the Russian ambassador was also recalled from Paris. A fortnight later the British and French ambassadors in St Petersburg left for home.

Gladstone was uneasy about the legality of sending the fleets into the Black Sea, but the foreign secretary, Lord Clarendon, reverted to demanding an end to the occupation of the Principalities. This ultimatum, delivered simultaneously by the British and French governments, appeared in *The Times* on 28 February, a day after it was delivered. Aberdeen believed that there had been opportunities to avoid war. That was history. War was declared on Russia in London and Paris on 28 March 1854.

15

WAR

None of the participants in the Crimean War had wanted war but all bore some responsibility for it. The weakness and mismanagement of the Ottoman empire, the frequent duplicity of its ministers, provided the background to the struggle, and the Porte's rejection of the Vienna Note was one of the decisive steps towards its outbreak.

Napoleon III's insecurity in the early 1850s had led him to adopt policies that would above all be popular in France. There was already an international dispute over the Holy Places; the French emperor saw making strident claims for the Catholic church in the Holy Lands as the opportunity to ingratiate himself with the conservative Catholic right and clergy who resented his revolutionary background. He was also seeking the means of establishing an alliance with Britain and had to go along with her policy towards Russia, even though there was little enthusiasm among the French people for war.

Russophobia had been an important aspect of British public opinion for a generation, and Nicholas I's interventions in the early 1850s, on top of his harsh reaction to the revolutions of 1848, were all too easily seen in Britain as an attack on the balance of power in Europe and the Near East. With the belligerent and popular Palmerston back in the cabinet and the press in full cry over the Russian occupation of the Principalities, followed by the battle of Sinope, war hysteria was rampant. Aberdeen's strenuous efforts to avert war were doomed to fail. The placing before parliament in March 1854 of Nesselrode's 1844 memorandum had convinced waverers of the necessity of combating Russian designs on Turkey. Queen Victoria's convictions were, for religious reasons, anti-Turk, but by the end of March 1854 she had changed her position, for Nicholas 'has told so many falsehoods and acted in such a dishonest manner that no reliance can be placed in him'.[1]

The Russian emperor's deeply held religious belief that it was his mission in life to liberate Orthodox Christians from Muslim rule, combined with his arrogance as an autocratic ruler of three decades, made him blind to realistic considerations as to the practicalities of going to war against the maritime powers. He harked back to his elder brother's victory in 1812, failing to understand that this would be a very different sort of campaign against the superior armies and fleets of France and Britain. His intransigence in the face of warnings from Nesselrode and other advisers, and his willingness to risk all in a war against the Turks, places much of the responsibility for what followed on Nicholas I.

The initial aim of the Franco-British campaign in early 1854 was to demand the evacuation of the Principalities and for Russia to recognize the integrity of the Ottoman empire. Austria and Prussia, the other major powers, had agreed in April to cooperate only if either of them was attacked, or if the Russian army threatened Constantinople. This strengthened Russia's position. In the same month French and British armies landed at Gallipoli to protect Constantinople from a possible Russian attack. Soon afterwards, to ensure supplies, they established themselves north of the port of Varna, on the western shore of the Black Sea, and the Russian Black Sea port of Odesa was bombed by western fleets. With the presence of a Franco-British force in the Black Sea, Constantinople was safe from attack by sea, but its land defence was less certain.

Nicholas was already furious that Austria had not come to his aid—he who had saved the Austrians in 1848–9. Worse, the Austrian chancellor, Count von Buol, demanded that Russia should evacuate the Principalities. While this in fact strengthened Russia's position, as she could then free troops from Moldavia and Wallachia, this in no way assuaged the Russian emperor's rage at Austria. The latter, exposed to Russian attack in a way that Britain and France could not be, near bankruptcy and facing internal dissent, was anxious to end the war as soon as possible and to this end Buol and the French foreign minister in July put forward the Four Points as the war aims of the anti-Russian powers. Russia was to renounce her special rights in Serbia and the Principalities and these would be replaced by a general guarantee of the powers; free navigation of the Danube; revision of the Straits Convention of 1841; and renunciation by Russia of any claim to a protectorate over the Orthodox Christians in the Ottoman empire. Under pressure from the French, Britain accepted the points and they were given final validity as allied war aims in an exchange of notes between Britain, France and Austria on 8 August 1854. Nicholas was outraged. He rejected the Four Points and threatened war on Austria, while she for her part mobilized and then cancelled the order.

Even before the Four Points had been drawn up, the British government proposed to the French that it was necessary to impede Russia's ability to attack Turkey by destroying her Black Sea fleet at Sevastopol. Armies would be landed to the north of the port while the fleets bombarded from the sea. In September, after landing at Evpatoria, the allies defeated a Russian army at Alma. A month later the siege of Sevastopol began, but the Russians had been provided with enough time to block the harbour by scuttling their fleet and preparing their defences on the northern side under the leadership of the three Russian heroes of the Crimean War: Admirals Kornilov and Nakhimov and General Totleben, the engineer.

The allies were setting up camp on the southern side of the port, supplied from the narrow inlet of Balaklava and later Kamiesh Bay. In mid-October it was decided that the time had come to bombard Sevastopol. The first day's fighting was inconclusive. Several days later the Russians changed tack and decided to attack Balaklava to cut the British off from their supplies. On 25 October an Ottoman army and the British Heavy Brigade defeated the greater part of the Russian cavalry, but the day is best known in British history for the Charge of the Light Brigade near Balaklava in which 113 men were killed, 134 wounded and 45 taken prisoner. The Russians suffered 180 dead or wounded. It was reported at the time, and then immortalized in Tennyson's poem, as a glorious disaster. Orlando Figes argues that:

> the charge was in some ways a success, despite the heavy casualties. The objective of a cavalry charge was to scatter the enemy's lines and frighten him off the battlefield. ... The real blunder of the British at Balaklava was not so much the Charge of the Light Brigade as their failure to pursue the Russian cavalry once the Heavy Brigade had routed them and the Light Brigade had got them on the run.[2]

According to Hugh Small:

> The Charge was not a blunder; Lord Raglan's order was a blunder, but the Light Brigade were not told of and did not obey Raglan's order. The men substituted their own order, to charge the Russian cavalry and put them to flight. They succeeded spectacularly. The surviving troopers were initially jubilant at their success; and when Lord Cardigan, who had objected to the charge from the start, told a group of them that, 'Men, it was a mad-brained trick, but no fault of mine', a voice from the ranks replied, 'Never mind, my Lord, we're ready to do it again.'[3]

The deeply flawed British conduct of the Crimean campaign has been recounted many times—the failure in particular to equip the troops for the harsh Crimean winter, the incompetence of the commanders, above all Lord Raglan. The reporting by William Howard Russell of *The Times*, the first embedded war journalist, played an important role. Through the use of the new telegraph it was the first war in which the press was crucial. Florence Nightingale's struggle to improve the sanitary conditions of field hospitals where cholera was rife made her a permanent British national heroine. The Jamaican-born Mary Seacole separately played an important role in caring for the wounded. All aspects of the war are brilliantly described and analyzed by Orlando Figes in *Crimea: The Last Crusade*.

The Russian defeat at Inkerman in November, urging from Nesselrode and Nicholas's brother-in-law, the king of Prussia, warned the Russian emperor of the dire consequences of letting his resentment against Austria persist. This pressure gave Nicholas little choice but to accept the Four Points at the end of November 1854. However, this was too little too late, as, under British pressure, their scope and implications had been drastically changed. Evacuation of the Principalities was not sufficient, as at the beginning of December an alliance, to which the French attached more importance than the British, had been signed between the Franco-British belligerents and the Habsburg empire for the defence of the Principalities.

The secretary of state for war, the Duke of Newcastle, was dismissed in December 1854, the first casualty of the increasing public indignation that followed the fate of the Light Brigade. The Radical MP John Roebuck moved a resolution demanding that a Parliamentary Committee of Enquiry be set up to investigate the conduct of the war. This resolution was carried by 305 votes to 157. Aberdeen resigned. Palmerston was the obvious choice for prime minister. A month later Raglan was deservedly fired.

After the previous year's ignorant optimism it was clear in 1855 that the war, in which the French were playing the preponderant role, had to be carried on with greater vigour, and fortunately for the maritime powers, Piedmont-Sardinia under King Victor Emmanuel joined the alliance. The same realization was true of Russia but complicated for Nicholas by his fear that the Austrians would invade Poland, maybe supported by the Prussians. At this vulnerable moment, with the danger of an allied landing at Evpatoria to cut off Crimea from the Russian mainland at the 'neck', Perekop, he ordered an offensive. This was quickly repulsed.

Even though the French had assumed the leading role in the war, public opinion in France was still far less enthusiastic in its backing of the government than in Britain. In February 1855 Napoleon III astounded not only the British but his own ministers by announcing that he intended to go to Crimea and take personal command of his army. Edouard Drouyn de Lhuys, the foreign minister, warned what might result if the emperor were killed, or taken prisoner. His replacement by his disagreeable cousin, Prince Jerome, Plon-Plon, would be a disaster for France, to say nothing of the minister's losing his job. The British government feared that Napoleon might negotiate directly with Nicholas, using the advantage of his sex over Victoria. The French emperor abandoned the idea for the time being.

It was common knowledge throughout Europe that Nicholas was in failing health. 'I hear that someone who saw him recently says that he is much altered in appearance', Queen Victoria wrote in December 1854.[4] The defeat at Evpatoria, combined with rash behaviour in reviewing the troops in extreme cold, provoked terminal pneumonia. Nicholas died on 2 March 1855 of 'pulmonic apoplexy after an attack of influenza'.[5] There was talk of suicide that persisted into the twentieth century, which accounts by those around him show to be untrue. His doctors recognized that Nicholas's 'spiritual suffering broke him more than his physical suffering'.[6] He died of a broken heart.

The Times declared that the death was an act of divine intervention. Palmerston was singularly, and predictably, unmoved:

> The death of the emperor of Russia may or may not produce important changes in the state of affairs ... It is possible that the new Emperor may revert to the peaceful policy which he was understood to advocate in the beginning of these transactions, but it is possible, on the other hand, that he may feel bound to follow the policy of his father ... At all events the changes at Petersburg should not for the present slacken the proceedings and the arrangements of the Allies.[7]

The British population understandably hated Nicholas. One voice was raised with a good word—Queen Victoria's: 'Although the poor Emperor has died our enemy, I have not forgotten former happy times ... There is something striking in this death of a great and powerful autocrat but the poor Emperor had his good and great quality.'[8]

Even with her generous sentiments, the queen's energetic support for pursuance of the war was in no doubt. She was knitting for soldiers in

Crimea to make clear her position. Palmerston proposed that it would be advantageous for the queen to invite the French emperor to Osborne. Victoria viewed Napoleon as an adventurer but was charmed by him. He for his part agreed to put his recurrent desire to go to Crimea to rest. For the British government the main reason for the visit was to ensure that military strategy was aligned between the two countries. Fortunately, Napoleon and Palmerston were in agreement that the taking of Sevastopol was not the only objective. The aim was to conquer Crimea, taking advantage of their superior infantry skill and rifle power.

In the event only an attempt to cut off Sevastopol from its supply bases by taking the port of Kerch was made. However, the French commander-in-chief, General François Canrobert, decided to withdraw his forces from the attack, forcing the British to abandon the expedition. This aggravated the already tense relations between the British and the French. The war dragged on.

While fighting continued in Crimea, negotiations had been taking place in Vienna from mid-March 1855 chaired by Buol. Although the Russians had by now accepted the Four Points and agreed that Serbia and the Principalities should remain under Ottoman rule and that navigation of the Danube should be controlled by an independent commission, the French proposal that the Black Sea should be neutralized was rejected by the Russian plenipotentiary.

Napoleon informed Walewski, the French ambassador in London, that he would go along with the Austrian draft. The British government rejected it. Three days later Napoleon, with the memory of his recent protestations at Osborne of his devotion to the Franco-British alliance, capitulated to British pressure. The negotiations had led nowhere; the alliance with Austria was worthless. The war had to continue until Russia was defeated.

Throughout the summer of 1855 the siege of Sevastopol dragged on. By far the clearest exposition of what the defenders were living through under bombardment is Lieutenant Leo Tolstoy's *Sevastopol Sketches*. Then, on 8 September the French successfully stormed the Malakov fortress and turned their heavy guns on Sevastopol itself. Prince Mikhail Gorchakov ordered the evacuation of the city. It was a French victory while the British were driven back from the Redan fortress.

The fall of Sevastopol was not a decisive victory and was soured for many of the British in Crimea and at home by the fact that the French had done better at Malakov than the British at Redan. There was also bad news from the Caucasus where the Russians had taken the Turkish town and fortress of Kars, along with capturing the British general, William Williams. Having taken Kars, the new Russian emperor, Alexander II, seized the opportunity of this success to put out peace feelers to the French and Austrians.

The French had vindicated their military honour, but the financial burdens of a war that had never been popular were all too clear. Napoleon did not stress the economic factors with his ally who wanted to continue the war. Palmerston was aware of the lukewarm attitude in France and the view in Berlin and Vienna that it was now time to begin peace talks. Bullish as ever though, he wrote to his brother, William Temple, that after the fall of Sevastopol and the expulsion of the Russians from Crimea, 'our danger will then begin, a danger of peace, and not a danger of war'.[9] Gladstone, now in opposition, reluctantly admitted that the British public did not want the war to end and in government the war party was in the ascendant.

Palmerston sought punitive terms against Russia and, furious with the French and Austrians, continued to plan for a continuation of the war the following spring. On the other side Alexander II was threatening to reopen hostilities in 1856. Yet by the end of 1855, the threat of the French making a separate peace and the impossibility of Britain's waging the war alone made peace talks inevitable.

It was Austria who made the decisive move. An ultimatum was presented to the Russian government at the end of December 1855 demanding unconditional acceptance of terms agreed by France, Britain and Austria. Russia accepted most of the demands but refused to cede any territory. Alexander was hawkish but was under pressure from Nesselrode and practically all senior figures in the government to accept the Austrian terms. Prince Mikhail Vorontsov, son of Simon Vorontsov, the Russian ambassador to Britain half a century before, and uncle of Sidney Herbert, the British secretary at war, warned that a long drawn-out war could only weaken Russia yet further. General Pavel Kiselev, the Minister of State Domains, feared even harsher peace terms and revolt in Poland and among the peasantry. Prince Vasily Dolgorukov, minister of war, pointed out Russia's evident military weakness, and the senior diplomat, Baron Peter von Meyendorff, believed a continuation of the struggle would lead to national bankruptcy. Alexander had only been emperor for a matter of months; whatever his own inclination, he ceded to his experienced advisers.

A clear indication of France's dominant position was Napoleon's insistence that the peace talks should be held in Paris and not Brussels which Palmerston had suggested. The congress opened on 25 February 1856 and an armistice was signed the following day. What dominated the proceedings were not the major issues that had already been thrashed out, but the differences in the stances of France and Britain. Lord Clarendon, the foreign secretary, who represented Britain, was holding out for a maximum weakening of Russia. In this he was not only opposed by the pro-Russian Walewski representing France but by King Victor Emmanuel of Piedmont-Sardinia, who had earned a place at the table as a result of contributing troops in the war. Where Napoleon showed himself to demand more than Britain was in his wish to include discussion of the status of Poland, to weaken Russia's hold on the country. The British government would not hear of it and the French emperor ceded.

The Crimean War had been fought to protect the Ottoman empire from Russian aggression and the peace treaty of 30 March declared that the powers would respect the independence and the integrity of the empire and jointly guarantee its strict observance. The sultan for his part would promise to protect his Christian subjects. The Principalities would no longer be a Russian protectorate but return to nominal Turkish suzerainty as Romania. The Danube was to be placed under the control of a European commission, coupled with the cession by Russia of southern Bessarabia (the first time Russia had lost territory) and thus the loss of her control of the mouth of the Danube.

Nevertheless, by far the most important provision of the Treaty of Paris was Article XI which stipulated the compulsory neutralization of the Black Sea—imposed at the insistence of Great Britain. The waters and ports, whilst open to the mercantile marine of every nation, were 'formally and in perpetuity interdicted to the Flag of War, either of the Powers possessing its coasts or of any other Power'.[10] This rendered the maintenance or establishment of naval installations along its coasts unnecessary. As was intended, this was a one-sided provision against Russia since Turkey would be able to maintain such installations on the shores of the Bosphorus and the Sea of Marmara as before.

What was particularly relevant to future Anglo-Russian relations were the Black Sea clauses to which the British government attached so much importance. These did much to provoke Russia's embarking on a policy detrimental to Britain. The restrictions of 'the sovereign right of a great power over its coasts and territorial waters were, in their severity, without precedent in the annals of European diplomacy'.[11]

The Russian threat to Turkey no longer existed but her resentment against Britain and Austria did. For the next fifteen years, Alexander II would have as his principal aim in Europe the freeing of Russia from these shackles.

(A parallel is to be found fifteen years later, with the loss of Alsace-Lorraine by France to Prussia which led to the *revanche* that was not overcome until 1918, just as in that same year the limitations on German sovereignty imposed by the Treaty of Versailles also had far-reaching consequences. Lessons were not learned from 1856.)

The Treaty of Paris did not mark the end of the peace settlement. A Triple Treaty signed only two weeks later by France, Britain and Austria was designed to perpetuate the Crimean coalition and to prevent Russia from escaping the restrictions imposed on her. The Russian government knew only too well that the treaty was directed against it, although the country was not mentioned. It served also to increase Alexander's anger against Austria who had not come to her aid in the war. This duplicitous neighbour was now trying to prevent a future Russo-French alliance that clearly would be detrimental to Austria in Italy and to the benefit of France.

After the disastrous war which had exposed the backwardness of a system that had seemed so strong to outward appearances, an agonizing process of reassessment, reform and modernization had to be undertaken. The new emperor therefore had need of a new man and a new course, with Nesselrode blamed for the Crimean defeat. The new man, however, was not young but approaching sixty, and twenty years older than his master.

Prince Alexander Gorchakov had been a classmate of Pushkin at the fashionable *lycée* of Tsarskoe Selo. At the age of nineteen he entered the diplomatic service and attended the Quadruple Alliance congresses of the early 1820s. Most of his postings were to the German states but he had spent two years in London and claimed a familiarity with British society that convinced few. In 1856 this tall, slight man, speaking perfect French and with his 'gold-rimmed spectacles and the carriage and manners of a long-past age' became vice chancellor.[12] Sir Horace Rumbold was one of many to comment on Gorchakov's 'almost childish vanity ... no flattery could be too fulsome for him'.[13]

Gorchakov's talent was that he mirrored Alexander II's own feelings and was able to translate them into diplomatic action as effectively as circumstances would permit.

The growing reluctance of France to follow an anti-Russian line was made clear in the diplomatic dispute over Serpents Island and Bolgrad in the summer of 1856. Gorchakov had to rely on the weapons of the weak, chicanery and the exploitation of divisions among the victors, to subvert the Treaty of Paris. Russia had nothing to lose by the attempt.

Serpents Island was an outcrop with a lighthouse near the Danube delta on the Black Sea. Russia landed a handful of men there in May 1856 and claimed ownership on the grounds that she had previously been in possession of it but forced to abandon it during hostilities. (It is today known as Snake Island and is in Ukraine. The Russians took it briefly from Ukraine in the spring of 2022, but it was retaken by defiant Ukrainians a couple of months later.) However, the island had been included in Ottoman territory in the Treaty of Paris and a Turkish garrison was already there. Walewski did not think the island worth disputing but Palmerston objected to the Russian pretensions. A great deal of British shipping, including a gunboat, was deployed around the island. Typically, the British prime minister gave orders for the Russians to be ejected. The two senior British diplomats in St Petersburg, at the time, Lords Granville and Wodehouse, were more circumspect and the queen agreed with them.

Gorchakov disingenuously affected surprise at the diplomatic contestation over such an unimportant matter as a lighthouse. He felt confident of Walewski's support. What he failed to appreciate was that Napoleon III was coming round to the British view. Even so, Palmerston for the moment backed down.

Another dispute had arisen over execution of the Treaty of Paris that provided Gorchakov with a further opportunity to hone his diplomatic skills and weaken Franco-British bonds. The new Russo-Moldavian frontier in Bessarabia was designed to remove from Russia all contact with the navigable portions of the Danube. The new line was to pass south of a village called Bolgrad. Commissions from France, Britain and Russia were on the spot but the maps available were inaccurate. The Russians were able to point out that a New Bolgrad existed, insisting on its importance.[14] This would naturally provide Russia with access to the Danube. Palmerston was as usual on the *qui vive* for any indication of Russian encroachments and became embroiled in the long drawn-out wrangling in which Gorchahov looked to Walewski for support. This time Palmerston was not going to cede. King Leopold of the Belgians had been proposed as arbiter by France and Russia. Clarendon found Palmerston 'very jaunty and won't hear of arbitration—says the Emperor is sure to yield if we stand firm'.[15]

The prime minister was correct in believing that the French were prepared to give in to the Russians. They had offered Russia New Bolgrad, though without access to the Danube, and territorial compensation if she gave up Serpents Island. France also hoped for lucrative railway concessions in Russia. In return Russia would not oppose future French territorial expansion in Italy at Austria's expense.

The French emperor was, as ever, equivocal, torn between his wartime ally and Russia. In early December 1856 Gorchakov realized that France would not back him over the disputes, however much Walewski and the French ambassador in St Petersburg wished to do so. The British government was prepared to assuage Russian sensibilities with some territorial compensation that was grudgingly accepted, but Russia was obliged to give up Serpents Island and cede New Bolgrad to Moldavia.

Where she was able to strengthen her position was in Crimea. For many Russian officers who had served in the war and the Russian government the Crimean Tatars became synonymous with the hated Ottomans. They were seen as traitors to Russia and an easy scapegoat for the empire's defeat. At the end of the war a second massive emigration of Muslim Tatars took place between 1860 and 1861 to the Ottoman Caliph. Slavic peasants from the neighbouring provinces took over the land vacated.

A long way from the Crimean peninsula Persia came to be involved in the war. The adventurous young shah, Naser al-Din Shah, saw the conflict as a fresh opportunity for Persia to capture much-coveted Herat while British attention was distracted from Afghanistan. The British government got wind of Persia's plan and dispatched a new envoy, Charles Murray, to Tehran. Murray was heavy-handed in his treatment of the Persians but worse, he became the centre of a diplomatic scandal on being accused of having an affair with the shah's sister-in-law. British honour, it was claimed, was at stake and diplomatic relations were broken off. This played into the hands of Naser al-Din Shah who immediately ordered troops to Herat.

After a siege of many months the citadel fell in October 1856. Palmerston immediately, and certainly disingenuously, incorrectly leapt to the conclusion that Russia was behind the attack. Soon afterwards the British Indian fleet arrived at Bushire with 15,000 men and sepoys. The Persian forces were then routed in Fars province and hastily withdrew from Herat. A peace treaty was signed in March 1857, but British punitive actions continued under General Sir James Outram who arrived from Bombay and the port of Mohammara (today Khorramshahr) was bombarded. A further humiliating treaty was signed at the end of the year. Persia had to renounce any claims on Herat, or any other part of Afghanistan. Gorchakov protested at Britain's heavy-handed conduct but was in no position to do more than this in 1857.

Shifts in the evolving relations between Britain and Russia and France and Russia had already been seen in a different form in August 1856. Alexander II had become emperor in March 1855 during the Crimean War. (It was customary for the British court to go into mourning on the death of a foreign sovereign, but Queen Victoria was advised, based on the precedent of the Emperor Paul's death, that this was not warranted in the circumstances.) Inevitably the new emperor's coronation had been delayed until after the end of hostilities and took place in August 1856. Foreign countries were expected to send high-level special ambassadors to attend—it had been the Duke of Wellington for Nicholas I's coronation in 1826. The queen did not feel that it was necessary in 1856 for anyone to be sent but deferred to her ministers who wished to send a special envoy.

This time Granville George Leveson-Gower, 2nd Earl Granville, a senior member of the cabinet, former foreign secretary and son of an earlier British ambassador to Russia, was chosen, but was obviously a much less prestigious figure than Wellington. Granville was shocked at the 'no expense spared' coronation in a country whose finances were known to be in a parlous state: 'The present estimate of the expenses is £1,000,000. Nicholas's coronation had cost half this sum, Alexander's cost £150,000 and poor Paul's £50,000 which, even allowing for inflation, shows a determined effort on the part of the defeated sovereign to demonstrate his status as being undiminished.'[16]

The atmosphere in Moscow, where the celebrations customarily took place, reflected the strained relations between Britain and Russia. Granville found his mission fraught. He had several long conversations with Gorchakov:

> He is was in a state of great irritation with Her Majesty's Government ... He is an immense talker and indiscreet with a fair degree of cleverness ... He repeats himself very much, flies from one subject to another, and always sings a chorus about his own frankness, his sincerity and his being a *paysan*.[17]

Later, Granville was presented to Alexander II:

> He is handsome ... He does not give the idea of having much strength either of intellect or of character, but looks intelligent and amiable ... His Imperial Majesty is not supposed to have that power of will which will enable him to deal with the mass of corruption which pervades every class in this country.[18]

The emperor predictably expressed the desire for better relations with Britain: 'There was a distrust of himself which he did not deserve ... He had thought it right to conclude a peace which had caused much irritation in Russia. No such feeling, however, had been or would be allowed by him to influence future conduct.'[19] Granville could only reply that his government desired the same. 'This is not proved by the facts', Alexander replied in a peremptory manner when they met for a second time.[20] The British statesman was annoyed by the emperor's rudeness towards him in front of several foreign diplomats and complained to Gorchakov: 'I should play an undignified part if I were to submit to insults; on the other hand, if my Embassy ended in a sudden departure, the termination would be ridiculous, and the future relations of the two countries embittered.'[21]

At the same time, Granville felt that there were faults on the side of his own government:

> My position as a complimentary Ambassador, and at the same time as a member of a Government which was doing and saying very irritating things to the Court to which I was accredited, was anomalous ... Palmerston and Clarendon in my opinion have been too scolding lately. They are at everybody.[22]

France on the other hand chose as her special envoy the Count of Morny, half-brother of Napoleon III and a flamboyant member of Parisian society. Granville complained about French 'obsequiousness [that] has been great as to everything connected with the conditions of the Peace, and the Russians have spared no attentions to detach them from the English alliance'.[23]

Morny took it upon himself to rent two Moscow palaces and to have brought down from St Petersburg vast amounts of furniture and silver from the embassy there. Granville sourly remarked of the Frenchman's hospitality: 'An ornamented dinner, excellent bonbons and bad wine. Our wine, *par parenthèse*, is quite excellent.'[24] Morny's ostentatious display knew no bounds: 'The carriage of Count de Morny has six windows, the wheels are gilded and the interior is a real work of art with embroidery and ornamentation.'[25] The emperor and empress attended a ball he gave and were clearly impressed, as the count received Russia's highest distinction, the Cross of St Andrew. Morny was very pleased with himself and told his half-brother: 'I believe that they will have no reason to regret having sent me to Russia.'[26] (He was later accused of stealing silver and other valuables from the French embassy in St Petersburg. The Russians were aware of this and Morny's mistress problem through deciphered French telegrams.)

While Morny was successfully ingratiating himself and his country with Alexander and Gorchakov, Britain, who had re-established diplomatic relations with Russia in April 1856, was making no similar effort. The new ambassador to Britain, Count Mikhail Chreptowicz, appointed in September, complained of the continued hostility towards Russia. Palmerston treated him to a bad-tempered list of British complaints against Russia about the destruction of Kars and Ismail—a fortification on the west coast of the Black Sea—and why it had taken the Russians so long to send an envoy to London. The British press maintained its wartime attacks on Russia. Chreptowicz was shocked, like most Russians, by the power of the free press but encouraged to learn that some newspapers (not *The Times*) would print paid-for articles. Palmerston's *Morning Post* was receiving funding from the French embassy, but the *Morning Chronicle*, *Morning News* and newspapers in Scotland and Ireland were prepared to publish articles offered to them. Chreptowicz asked for the enormous sum of £2,000, which he received.[27] Such efforts had little effect. The British government and public opinion remained hostile to the power seen as the main cause of the Crimean War. Unlike France, Great Britain was not prepared to assuage the feelings of the defeated great power.

16

RUSSIA IS NOT SULKING

SHE IS CONSOLIDATING

Whatever long-term aims Alexander II entertained in Asia, he had in 1856 to confront Russia's diminished status in Europe and the need for internal reform that had become ever more obvious during the Crimean War.[1]

The France of Napoleon III was a revisionist state determined to efface finally the defeat of 1815 and to expand her frontiers. Russia was a revisionist state with the aim of overturning the humiliating clauses of the 1856 Paris Treaty. France sought to acquire territory with help from her ally Piedmont-Sardinia from Austria, Russia's enemy, and so wished to further the rapprochement with Russia begun at the end of the Crimean War. On the other hand, Great Britain showed little sign of seeking to ameliorate post-Crimean tensions. In a dispatch marked 'Very Secret' Gorchakov spelt out Russia's position, noting that good relations with Britain were only possible:

> If the English Gouvt. renounces keeping us in the position that the Treaty of Paris has placed us in, above all in the Black Sea, the renewal of our old relations in all their sincerity could be expected ... This is dependent on the abandon by the Cabt. of St James of a state of affairs that is incompatible with the dignity of a Great Power ... 'We shall bide our time', but also the word 'remember' [all in English] will remain inscribed at the fore [*fronton*] of our foreign policy.[2]

This complaint was repeated time and time again in future years.

Baron Brunnov was back in London as Russian ambassador in 1858 after being number two in the Russian delegation to the Paris Congress. As he now became the most junior (i.e. recent) ambassador—being now seated beneath even Denmark—this particularly hurt his pride. His bitterness emerges in many of his dispatches during his first year, which recount with evident glee the discomfiture of the British government at seeing Russia and France on good terms. As usual Britain blamed Russia for events in 1859: 'They accuse us of spoiling their relationship with France', he reported.[3] The vice chancellor agreed. This was what Gorchakov sought.

But no one in any of the European capitals was in any doubt that the Russian government was preoccupied with the emancipation of the serfs; as Gorchakov admitted: 'Our role must be passive. Our internal reforms necessitate it.'[4]

Russia was a poor country with a population of about 60 million inhabitants of whom 50 million were peasants. In 1859, of these 10.7 million were male serfs living on estates belonging to the hereditary nobility; 12.8 million were settled on state lands. The serf could cultivate a small part of the owner's land for his own use for which he had to make a payment in cash or labour to the owner. The larger part of the land was farmed by serfs for the benefit of the landowner or the state.

On the other hand there were fewer than half a million industrial workers in Russia in 1855. Furthermore, most exports were produced in foreign or predominantly foreign-owned firms. The deplorable state of Russian roads continued to shock foreign residents and visitors. Railway building was in its infancy, with only 1,000 kilometres of track. Even so, the major cause of Russian backwardness was serfdom.

The young emperor was aware that he had to lead the process of emancipation and wanted to see it done on his terms. Lord Granville had written in 1856: 'The Serf Question is admitted by all to be of a very difficult character.'[5] This British observer was fearful for the internal stability of Russia: 'It is more than likely that popular movements will take place, and it is frightful to consider the immediate results of a revolution in a country organised as this is at present. No country in Europe will furnish so fair a chance of success to Socialism.'[6]

To begin with Alexander envisaged that the process of emancipation would be gradual. However, during the protracted work of the Editing Commission charged with drawing up the required legislation, it became clear that the liberation of all serfs in one act was necessary. Alexander II signed the emancipation manifesto on 19 February 1861 (os). This was the most spectacular achievement of his reign but it represented only the beginning of a series of major reforms concerning the judiciary, local government and army reform in the first half of the 1860s, although in this process Alexander's personal role was less active, but decisive.[7]

To begin with the Poles also benefited from the reforms in Russia. After the ruthless Russification under Field-Marshal Prince Paskevich that had followed the 1830 uprising, on his death in 1856, Prince Mikhail Gorchakov, cousin of the vice chancellor, became viceroy. Alexander instructed him to dismantle some of the worst aspects of repression of the Poles—such as the ubiquitous use of spies—and to grant an amnesty for those *émigrés* who wished to return and permission for the use of Polish in churches and schools. Nevertheless, there was no question of sanctioning any form of Polish political autonomy. On his first visit to Warsaw as King of Poland in May 1862, the emperor addressed the Polish notables and made his position clear: 'I will not change anything; what was done by my father was done well. My reign will be a continuation of his.'[8]

Such a policy could not satisfy the Poles. They saw a defeated Russia in 1856 and in 1859 the Franco-Piedmontese successes against autocratic Austria. Various societies under sundry guises of being cultural or agricultural attracted the nobility, in particular Count Adam Zamoysky, military officers and students, where political organization was discussed.

The Polish population of Great Britain who enjoyed the freedom of life there was seen in St Petersburg as a dangerous threat to the maintenance of Russian rule in Poland. Gorchakov placed an agent of the infamous Third Section in London, in addition to the numerous spies who regularly, and increasingly, were requested to report to the Russian capital. One asked for £120 to help him track down a Polish plot, to which the emperor had no hesitation in noting his agreement.[9]

This reflected that 1860 marked the thirtieth anniversary of the Polish uprising. Already in June demonstrations were taking place in Warsaw to commemorate the insurrection. The following month a well-placed London spy wrote: 'I have not left a stone unturned to find out the aims of the Polish *émigrés*, expressed in speeches at the meeting of the Polish Literary Society of London.'[10] As evidence of his position in London, he informed his masters that he had placed an article in the *Daily Telegraph* arguing that any Polish hopes of challenging the Russian position in their homeland were fanciful.

With the clear evidence that Russia was reforming, as the emancipation of the serfs in 1861 proved, the Polish *émigrés* in London were not going to be discouraged by obvious plants in the British press. Clarendon assured the Russian ambassador that the British government was blameless as regards Polish activity in Britain. It was Napoleon III who was stirring up trouble with the aim of separating Poland from Russia.[11] Gorchakov noted on the dispatch that by now he no longer had any confidence in the French emperor, to which Alexander added, 'Me neither.'[12]

The British government stood firm in its refusal to become involved in 1862. Palmerston, the prime minister, told Brunnov that the Russian government had been behaving correctly and with moderation: 'The Prime Minister reproaches the Poles for having stirred up the movements, without an aim and without hope, and which will end in fresh disasters for their country.'[13]

At the same time, the Russian dissident Alexander Herzen's monthly *The Bell* (*Kolokol*), published in London, inveighed against the iniquity of Russian rule in Poland. Herzen, the illegitimate son of a rich Russian landowner, had from the moment he left Moscow University in 1834 found himself in conflict with the authorities with his advocacy of socialism and agrarian collectivism. In 1847 he emigrated to Paris, then Geneva, but was bitterly disappointed by the failure of the revolutions of 1848 in continental Europe.

In 1852 he settled in London and founded the Free Russian Press which published works critical of the system of government in Russia. These were smuggled into Russia where they found a wide readership. (When Leo Tolstoy was in London in 1861 he visited Herzen several times, although he was more interested in hearing Charles Dickens speak and in Matthew Arnold's educational ideas.[14]) Herzen was optimistic when Alexander II ascended the throne that emancipation of the serfs would come about. When this happened in 1861 he gave a 'monster fête':

> The Free Russian Press in London and the editors of *The Bell* will celebrate on the evening of April 10th at Orsett House, Westbourne Terrace, the beginning of the emancipation of the serfs. Every Russian of whatever party who sympathises with the great cause will receive a fraternal welcome.[15]

When, however, news arrived in London of the violence erupting in Warsaw, Herzen became a vociferous critic of the Russian emperor, although a moderate compared with his fellow countryman, the anarchist Mikhail Bakunin, who was also in London. Despite Brunnov's and his employees' best efforts, seditious pamphlets proliferated protected by British freedom of the press and were exported to Poland. Instructions came from St Petersburg that surveillance of Poles had to be stepped up and their names transmitted to the viceroy, now the reformist Grand Duke Constantine, in Warsaw.

In July 1862 an assassin narrowly missed killing Constantine and the moderate Polish leader, the Marquess Alexander Wielopolski, but the grand duke maintained his conciliatory stance, despite urgings from St Petersburg to impose martial law. In the knowledge that it was known young men who were at the centre of the disturbances, Constantine believed that their removal would be sufficient to calm matters. The conscription levy that he ordered on New Year's day 1863 was intended to apply mainly to those belonging to secret revolutionary circles. Someone leaked it. All the recruits escaped and the second Polish revolution began.

Count Otto von Bismarck had become Prussian ambassador to Russia in 1859 and during his two-year stay impressed both Emperor Alexander and Gorchakov with the similarity of his views to theirs. At the beginning of 1863 he was now minister-president of Prussia, which like Austria also ruled a substantial part of Poland dating back to the Partitions of the late eighteenth century. On the outbreak of the rebellion in Poland Bismarck immediately dispatched General Gustav von Alvensleben to St Petersburg to draw up a convention according to which Russia and Prussia would work together to suppress the rising. This provided Alexander with the necessary confidence to deal with the Poles as he thought fit. Bismarck thus not only ensured the defeat of the Poles but also gained the useful friendship of Russia in his coming struggles with Austria and France. (Payback time began three years later.)

The Russian emperor and his vice chancellor knew only too well that the traditional sympathies of both French and British public opinion and governments were with the Poles. However, neither country was in a position, nor wished to go to war with Russia. Britain was fully occupied with problems arising out of the American Civil War. France was at least partly committed to her intervention in Mexico on behalf of the Austrian Archduke Maximilian.

Nevertheless, in Britain there was a fear that Napoleon would lead Britain into intervention in Poland. In February 1863 Queen Victoria did not mince her words to Lord Granville, the minister of education: 'The Queen is terribly alarmed at the French language and proposals regarding Poland, and thinks we must, on NO account, let ourselves be dragged into what *may* be a war with Germany!'[16] Her prime minister was in agreement. Palmerston proposed an international congress to discuss Poland based on the Treaty of Vienna. This had a sound juridical basis but anything that harked back to the ignominy of 1815 was guaranteed to receive a firm veto from Napoleon III. The foreign secretary, now Earl Russell, reassured the sovereign in May: 'Your Majesty's Ministers have no wish or intention to go to war for Poland.'[17]

In contrast to the situation in 1831, the Poles possessed no regular army and had to fight as guerrilla bands. The bloodshed spread from the Vistula to the Buh (formerly Bug), from the Dvina to the Dnipro (formerly Dnieper). Russian troops killed Polish insurgents and innocent peasants willy-nilly. There were three months of widespread slaughter. The British press, led by *The Times*, denounced Russian atrocities.

Brunnov suffered to see his country's reputation at such a low ebb. The British government, he wrote,

> believes Russia has her back against the wall. For four months it sees our administration in Poland, in spite of the military forces it possesses, completely incapable of subduing the disorder ... The moral incapacity of our government, at the centre of our power in the Kingdom Poland, emboldens the Cabinets of London and Paris.[18]

Note of Alexander II: 'I believe the same.' The ambassador received £500 to finance pro-Russian publications, of which £15 went to an agent called Kamensky, charged with secret relations with newpaper editors.[19]

Western pressure did achieve something. After three months of carnage Alexander promised a general amnesty at Easter 1863 on condition that the rebels laid down their arms. The Poles replied that they did not trust the Russian emperor and the fighting dragged on. For during the first few months of 1863, Alexander and Gorchakov had surprisingly feared intervention by Britain and France. The Admiralty in St Petersburg with impressive secrecy dispatched a considerable fleet to Halifax, Nova Scotia, seen as a jumping-off ground for attacking British shipping in the Atlantic should Britain declare war. (One of the seamen was the composer Rimsky-Korsakov.)

Far less professional was the attempt by some young Polish *émigrés* to organize a naval expedition from Britain to Poland. The supposedly secret Polish Legion drilled at Woolwich, chartered a ship and bought ammunition from the firm of Whitworth. Brunnov soon learned of its existence and protested to Russell. Customs officers were ordered to board the *Ward Jackson* and refuse clearance. The British captain simply weighed anchor, with the protesting officers on board. The ship reached Malmo. The inglorious conclusion was that the adventurers were hospitably received. The Swedish authorities seized the ship and removed the explosive cargo.

One of the leading opposition Tories, Benjamin Disraeli, was scathing of the government's failure to prevent the suppression of the Polish uprising: 'Johnny [Russell] seems to me to have got into such a muddle in every part of the world ... a policy of meddle and muddle.'[20] But Disraeli was less than whole-hearted in his support for the Poles:

> He [according to himself] entered into the generous feeling of sympathy which pervaded England during this year of 1863 on behalf of the Poles, whom the oppression of Russia had goaded into insurrection. But he knew history too well, and was too open-minded, to suppose that the right was all on one side ... I hear the Polish affair is virtually extinct ... Gortchakoff ... has become the most popular and powerful Minister of the day.[21]

In April 1864 Palmerston informed the queen that 'H.M.'s government has no wish to revive the discussion with Russia on Poland.'[22] For Russia the final trials of insurgents in August marked 'the last act of the Polish insurrection'.[23]

What was not recognized at the time was that the opportunity to force Russia to improve the lot of the Poles had been in 1856, at the end of the Crimean War, when Russia was on her knees and at the mercy of the other powers. She had regained her international confidence by 1864, and not only Prussia but Austria also had an interest in preserving the status quo in Poland.

Not only did the Polish revolution of 1863 lead to the further subjugation of the Poles to Russian rule. It also led to further confirmation of the mutual hostility and suspicion that existed between Russia and Britain, the end of the rapprochement between Russia and France and strengthening of the ties between Russia and Prussia. Moreover, inside Russia there was a closing of the ranks, not only in the face of the outside world but against radical critics of the system of government at home. Even the excesses inflicted on the defeated Poles by the 'Hangman Muraviev' went unchallenged in public, though many Russians deplored the atrocities in private. There was bitterness also that Britain and France had attacked Russia over Poland but were doing nothing about repression of Christians by the sultan in the Ottoman empire. The upsurge in militant chauvinist emotion led by the journalist Mikhail Katkov in his *Moscow Gazette* (*Moskovskie Vedomosti*) created a favourable climate for imperialist adventures, where these could be undertaken without immediate collision with other European powers.

Compared with the serious disagreement over Poland in 1863, Anglo-Russian bickering over the throne of Greece in 1862–3 was of minor importance. The intensely unpopular King Otto was overthrown in 1862. The Protecting Powers who had created Greece in 1830, France, Britain and Russia, recognized the right of the Greeks to expel their king and choose another, but they reaffirmed their ban upon any member of their own royal families ascending the throne. The Greeks nevertheless voted overwhelmingly in a plebiscite for Prince Alfred, Queen Victoria's second son, partly inspired by the hope that a British-born monarch would bring with him constitutional government.

Victoria, in deep mourning for the Prince Consort, who had died in December 1861, reacted not so much in response to the proposed flaunting of the protocol of 1830, but as a mother: 'The Queen said she could not understand why people seemed to think that there was the possibility of her wishing Prince Alfred to accept the throne.'[24] Her son was destined to rule the Grand Duchy of Coburg, he might ascend the British throne if his elder brother died, his children could not be brought up Greeks and he was too young.[25]

Alexander, always on the lookout for Britain trying to extend her influence, was not going to accept a British puppet of any kind. He proposed his nephew, the Duke of Leuchtenberg, a grandson of Nicholas I. Russell wrote politely to Brunnov enquiring as to the position of his imperial highness: 'Is he considered in Russia a member of the Imperial Family?'[26] It was not just the exclusion clause that interested the foreign secretary. He made it clear that Russian consuls were suspected of provoking 'disaffection for the Sultan', extending the question of a minor throne into the major Eastern Question.

The Russian reply was that Leuchtenberg was a member of the royal family but could in no circumstances reign in Russia, so should not be disqualified. Napoleon III, not to be left out in a dynastic squabble, came up with yet another candidate. As one after the other the candidates were weeded out for various reasons, another name was thrown into the ring, eighteen-year-old Prince William George, younger son of the King of Denmark and brother of the Princess of Wales, who did not excite either British or Russian suspicions. In October 1863 he was declared George I of the Hellenes, founding a dynasty that ruled until 1965. The new king went on to marry the Grand Duchess Olga, daughter of Alexander's brother Constantine, to the Russian emperor's delight.

Denmark itself was at the centre of the second major European crisis of the 1860s. Though neither Britain nor Russia was directly involved in the dispute over the duchies of Schleswig and Holstein in 1863–4, both were weakened by Bismarck's aggression in the duchies which had long-term repercussions for their relations.

It was in the knowledge that Russia was beholden to Prussia for her support over Poland that Bismarck was able to act as he chose. He was clear in his aims. On a visit to London in 1862, according to Disraeli, he had said at a reception at the home of Baron Brunnov: 'I shall seize the first pretext to declare war against Austria ... subdue the minor States and give national unity to Germany under Prussian leadership.'[27] For the moment though, Bismarck had need of Austria and formed an alliance with her with the object of taking the duchies. The death of King Frederick VII of Denmark in late 1863 provided this opportunity when his successor, Christian IX, immediately incorporated the duchies into Denmark.

A few days after the Danish claim Prussia and Austria dispatched a joint note to the Danish government which claimed the Danish moves as illegal. The ultimatum was rejected. In February 1864 Prussia and Austria invaded the duchies. By August Denmark had been defeated. Prussia in effect annexed Schleswig and Austria had an army of occupation in Holstein, far from her borders in a territory useless to her.[28] (Kiel was to prove an important acquisition in the building of a German fleet to rival that of Britain in the early twentieth century.)

Based on earlier treaties concerning Schleswig and Holstein, the great powers had the right to intervene. Russia also had a traditional connection. Alexander II announced that he, as head of the House of Holstein-Gottorp, was reclaiming hereditary rights in the duchies.[29] This specious argument was given short shrift by Bismarck. Feelers were put out to Britain that Russia would be prepared to act in concert with her in return for repeal of the hated Black Sea clauses.

The initial British position had been to press the Danes to revoke the November 1863 constitution. 'We cannot', wrote the foreign secretary, Russell, 'give active support to a Government which puts itself so manifestly in the wrong.'[30] At the same time he warned Prussia and Austria against invading Schleswig. As over Poland, his blusterings were ineffectual. Public sympathy was with the Danes led by the Prince of Wales. Queen Victoria, on the other hand, was staunchly pro-Prussian. Palmerston and Russell believed that they could bring the Prussians to reason through threats and diplomatic pressure. The upshot was that Britain, like Russia, did nothing. Prussia had a freehand in the duchies.

These two powers were again outflanked by Bismarck in 1866. The minister-president had needed Austrian support over Schleswig-Holstein in 1864. Now he turned on Austria, making much of disputes with his neighbour over the duchies. On 10 June he presented a text to the parliament of the German Confederation (*Deutscher Bund*), which would exclude Austria.[31] This provoked Austria into declaring war on Prussia, a number of German states and Italy (with whom Bismarck had previously allied). In the seven-week war that ensued the Austrians were routed and accepted defeat after the battle of Koniggratz-Sadowa in July.

In order to forestall any intervention by France or Russia (Britain would clearly not want to take part in a German civil war), Bismarck pushed the Prussian king, Wilhelm I, to make a rapid and moderate peace with the Austrians. The Treaty of Prague resulted in the dissolution of the German Confederation, Prussian annexation of many of Austria's former allies in the Confederation, the permanent exclusion of Austria from German affairs and reparations by Austria. This left Prussia free to form the North German Confederation the following year, incorporating all the German states north of the river Main.

Alexander II and Gorchakov were not sorry to see Austria defeated. The old resentment of 1854—Austria's refusal to come onside in the Crimean War—still rankled and had been exacerbated by the support of Catholics in Austria for the Poles in 1863. The Russian emperor had reiterated his support for Prussia before hostilities broke out. Through the use of deciphered Prussian telegrams, though, he knew of Bismarck's plans in detail—but then the minister-president had made them clear to all several years before. There was a feeling of relief in St Petersburg in August that Russia had backed the right side.[32]

In fact, by excluding Austria from Germany Bismarck turned her towards the Balkans and thus towards potential conflict with Russia there.[33] Britain was engrossed in the question of suffrage reform and the Irish Fenian problem to which was added a change of government in June 1866, and showed scant interest in Germany. Neither power grasped what had taken place over the previous two years: 'The scale of Bismarck's triumph cannot be exaggerated. He alone had brought about a complete transformation of the European international order.'[34]

Queen Victoria and Alexander II had enjoyed a youthful flirtation on his visit as hereditary grand duke in 1839, and throughout the 1840s personal relations between the Romanovs and the Saxe-Coburgs of Britain had been cordial. Naturally the Crimean War had inevitably led to a breach. Signs of a thaw emerged in 1861 when Queen Victoria wrote to Alexander asking for photographs of the whole Russian royal family. The emperor reacted in a typically masculine way, noting he would 'Get my wife to do it.'[35] When at the end of that year the Prince Consort died, Alexander's warm letter to Victoria went beyond basic royal condolences.

Her second son, the seventeen-year-old naval cadet Prince Alfred, visited Russia the following summer. The queen did not want it to be other than instructive travel and no special attention was to be paid to Affie. This was alien to Russian protocol and Alexander insisted on the prince's being accompanied by a Russian officer. The young man made a favourable impression and the emperor assured Affie's mother that his only regret was that the stay had been too short. That same summer two of Alexander's children, the Grand Duke Mikhail and the Grand Duchess Marie, spent six weeks at St Leonards-on-Sea.

A year after the marriage of the Prince of Wales to Princess Alexandra, her younger sister, Dagmar (Minnie), was betrothed to Alexander II's eldest son, Nicholas, despite Russia's refusal to aid Denmark over Schleswig-Holstein. The 21-year-old grand duke had already met and fallen for Dagmar; the wedding was to take place in St Petersburg in the spring of 1865. On New Year's Day celebrations to inaugurate this auspicious year began. The new British ambassador to St Petersburg, Lord Augustus Loftus, filled his letters with descriptions of balls and banquets, of men and women whose clothes suggested a setting for an oriental ballet. In February all changed. The hereditary grand duke fell ill with bronchitis and it was advised that he should leave for Nice. The date of the wedding was postponed and a younger brother and his sister accompanied him south to Nice.

Unlike his three broad-shouldered, strapping brothers, Nicholas had been plagued with ill-health since a child. He was thin and delicate, with a flushed face. The telegrams received at the Winter Palace were alarming. Naturally the imperial family took the four-day journey by train to Nice in early April and Princess Dagmar hurried from Copenhagen. The grand duke died days later and bequeathed Dagmar to his younger brother, Alexander.

Queen Victoria wrote from Osborne that she, above all, understood bereavement:

> It is because of our acquaintance, which dates from twenty-six years ago, that I permit myself to address these lines to Your Majesty. They come from a heart broken by a misfortune which has destroyed all my existence; but because of this my Heart understands only too well the sufferings of others.[36]

Even so, in all the public grief shown by Alexander and his wife, given their son's past health, it could not have come as a total surprise.

When invitations to the new heir's wedding in the autumn of 1866 were sent to the courts of Europe, a difficulty arose in Britain. Queen Victoria set her face against the Prince of Wales's acceptance. He had wanted to visit Russia the previous year when his sister-in-law Dagmar was engaged to Nicholas, but his relations with his mother were strained and she had vetoed it. This time the prince was determined to attend the marriage:

> That you should like to see Russia and, above all, to be present at the marriage of dear Alix's sister, and that Dagmar should see her kind brother-in-law's face at such a trying time, I think perfectly natural. I own I do *not* much like the idea ... I think the Government overrate the importance of it, in a political point of view.

She ended her letter less than graciously: 'If you are still very desirous to go now, I will not object to it.'[37] Certainly the queen had a point in believing that her 25-year-old eldest son's reputation for womanizing and the high life did not indicate him as someone whose presence in Russia would contribute to improving Britain's standing in Russian eyes.

The Anglophile Brunnov was delighted when the Prince of Wales asked to see him to be briefed about his forthcoming visit. The ambassador chose to see it as a gesture of respect towards his sovereign as well as pleasing public opinion in both Russia and Britain. Rather condescendingly and unnecessarily given the prince's reputation, he said he would accompany the prince to the Russian frontier, 'to protect my English Traveller a little lost from home ... You will find him docile and pleasant! He wants very much to go on a bear hunt!'[38]

But the ambassador sought more than the presence of the Prince of Wales at the marriage. Lord Stanley, the foreign secretary, informed the queen of a visit by Brunnov:

> After some expressions as to the anxiety of the Emperor of Russia to stand well with England, mentioned that the Emperor would in his ... belief, be greatly flattered and pleased if he were to receive the Garter from Your Majesty ... Such ... a compliment as showing a disposition on the part of England, to renew with Russia those cordial relations which were interrupted by the Crimean War.[39]

That was too much for the queen. She replied to her minister with a list of precedents which, she claimed, proved that giving the Garter was unnecessary. Stanley tried to assuage Russian feelings by telling Brunnov that the queen was constantly opposing all that her eldest son wished.

On his return from St Petersburg the Prince of Wales, who had greatly enjoyed the lavish hospitality offered him and the frozen hunt when seven wolves were bagged, invited the ambassador to Marlborough House where he expressed his humiliation at not being able to offer the Garter which, he had hoped, would have done something to efface the memory of the Crimean War. Not only this, his suite had been presented with Russian decorations; he had nothing to offer in return. In a long letter to Gorchakov after the meeting Brunnov made clear that the poor relations existing between mother and son were the reason for the insult. Alexander noted on the letter: 'It has to be said that the Queen has not been very pleasant', and not mincing his words: 'I think she has been for a long time slightly unbalanced [*traquée*].'[40]

It was not the end of the Garter affair. Napoleon III invited the principal crowned heads of Europe to the International Exhibition in Paris in 1867. Alexander made the journey. The Prince of Wales went to see the prime minister (not his mother) and protested that it was outrageous and a serious lapse of courtesy that the Russian emperor had not been invited to Britain. The queen was at Balmoral so a visit by Alexander was out of the question, although his intention to go to France was no spur of the moment decision:

> But His Royal Highness cannot but bear in mind the friendly and magnificent reception which he met with on his late visit to Russia; and on personal grounds would deeply regret that occasion should not be taken of his Imperial Majesty's near neighbourhood to our shores to show him some mark of attention. His Royal Highness urges also, and in this Lord Derby cannot but express his entire concurrence, that a very unfavourable impression may be produced on his Imperial Majesty's mind by the contrast between the flattering reception which he will undoubtedly be met with at Paris, and the total lack of any recognition from this country.[41]

In the end the Prince of Wales emerged the winner from the duel with his mother. She grudgingly agreed to accord the Order of the Garter to Alexander II, diluting any special recognition by offering it at the same time to the emperor of Austria—and unaccompanied by a signed letter: 'The Queen *feels* compelled to take *as much* care of her health as she can, and *quiet* is the principal thing she requires.'[42] Any desire to improve relations with Russia was conspicuously absent from the queen's behaviour.

Alexander had more serious concerns in the mid-1860s than snubs from Queen Victoria. In early April 1865 he had ordered a solemn requiem in the Kazan Cathedral for the assassinated Abraham Lincoln. He, the emancipator of the serfs, had refused to arbitrate in the American Civil War, though his sympathies were for the north which had offered its ports to Russia against possible British action during the Polish uprising. A year later Alexander was himself the target of an assassination attempt in the Summer Gardens of St Petersburg, narrowly prevented by a young hatter's apprentice. The would-be assassin was hanged but it was obvious that subversive movements were developing in Russia.

There were also those abroad who sought to assassinate Alexander II, and it was not surprisingly a Pole who fired on the Russian emperor, Napoleon III, the King of Prussia and Alexander's two sons in the Bois de Boulogne during the visit to the International Exhibition in May 1867. A horse was hit and its blood spurted all over the Russian grand dukes, but narrowly missed the target: 'The Czar and his two sons sat as unconcerned as if being made a target for patriotic pistols was an everyday incident in their lives.'[43]

From then on, it was not only a matter for the Russian emperor of dealing with the dangers posed by foreign countries. There were also those created by his fellow countrymen with which Alexander II had to contend.

17

MANIFEST DESTINY IN CENTRAL ASIA

A defeated power in Europe after the Crimean War, Russia looked elsewhere for compensation for her battered prestige. Central Asia, where she was not in direct conflict with any of the European powers, was the obvious sphere of expansion. Russia had of course been active in the region earlier in the century, above all in the 1820s and 1830s, seeking influence in Persia and Afghanistan. This had led to acrimonious diplomatic tussles with Britain but it had not proved possible to establish a predominant role in either of these countries, nor take control in the khanate of Khiva when it was attacked in 1839.

Nevertheless, advances had been made in the 1840s during the lull in Anglo-Russian rivalry, and the mouth of the Syr Darya river on the north-east coast of the Aral Sea was occupied. A line of fortifications was established along the Syr Darya and in 1853 the Kokandese fort of Ak-Mechet, 300 kilometres upriver, was seized and renamed Perovsk.[1] Further progress was arrested on the outbreak of war in 1854, but plans for advances in Central Asia were being forged during the Crimean War. General Duhamel—of earlier note in Persia—wrote that it was Russia's duty to show 'how she can attack England in her only vulnerable point, in India'.[2] General Stepan Khrulev urged 'the dispatch of a corps of thirty thousand men to Candahar ... The English cannot introduce a large army into that mountainous country. Death will face them in every defile.'[3] Thus a key element of all plans was to foster fear in the British that an invasion of India was possible, even likely. Although such an idea was devoid of serious logistical appreciation and topographical knowledge—like the earlier plans of Paul I and Napoleon I—it found currency in Russian military circles. From 1856 it became seen as an instrument of political vengeance for defeat in Crimea whereby feelings of backwardness and weakness would be exorcized.

It was not only among the military that territorial expansion in Central Asia was being urged. The educated elite in Russia had for a long time cherished the belief that the country had a 'civilizing mission' to fulfil—the age of manifest destiny—the expansion of a more advanced power at the expense of tribal states, inevitable and beneficial to mankind, the *Kulturträger*.[4] The Panslavist professor of history at Moscow University, Mikhail Pogodin, asserted that 'Leaving Europe alone, in expectation of more favourable circumstances we must turn our entire attention to Asia, which we have almost entirely left out of our considerations although it is precisely Asia that is predestined primarily for us.'[5] Another mid-nineteenth-century historian, Sergei Solovyov, preached that given the lack of natural barriers across the entire Eurasian steppe up to the Hindu Kush, Russia should fill the power vacuum before the British or another power did so. Later in the century, when the Great Game had been largely played out, the distinguished historian Andrei Snesarev did much to disseminate the view that it was Russia's historic mission to reach the warm waters of the Indian Ocean.

Such was the justification for Central Asian policy in imperial Russia. Soviet historians, such as Nicholas Khalfin, argued that above all Russia was obliged to make up for lost markets in Europe after the Crimean War and in the United States as a result of the Civil War.[6] Furthermore, Russia in the late 1850s was set upon a course of capitalist development, and control of Central Asia with its vast potential market and as a source of raw materials was indispensable for its success. Nicholas Ignatiev at the ministry of foreign affairs held that 'Asia is the only field left to our commercial activity and for the development of our industry, which are too weak to enter into competition with Britain, France, Belgium, America and other states.'[7] Brunnov in London, even more aware of British strength based on her powerful trading position, insisted in 1860 that 'the security of our commercial relations, of which the importance increases from day to day ... encouraged by the solicitude of the Imperial Government is developing our resources and extending its operations'.[8]

The importance of Central Asia economically was rapidly demonstrated during the American Civil War. Russia depended upon American cotton imports for its textile industry, and when the Union blockaded Confederate ports she sought alternative sources in the steppe. In 1860 Central Asia accounted for only 6 per cent of Russia's cotton, but it was known that that the fertile Fergana valley in Kokand was suitable for growing cotton. By 1862, 40 per cent of Russia's raw cotton imports came from Central Asia, a rise that was followed by a threefold increase between 1863 and 1867.

But it was not only the Moscow textile millionaires, like the Khludovs, who had commercial aspirations. It was Pervushin with his lead mines, Kolesnikov in gold and coal mining, the large trading firms of Pupyshev and Bykovsky and others applying for concessions for fishing, salt and sulphur, who influenced policy. The *Daily Telegraph* reported in 1872: 'The merchants of Russia desire to extend that trading intercourse with Turkestan which has always been considerable. They argue, that where the caravan can go the railway and tramway can be laid.'[9] There was already talk of a railway line from Orenburg into Central Asia. And, as if to clinch the claim of Russian alarmists post-Crimea that Britain was set on further expansion in Asia, Palmerston's government had waged a successful war on Persia in 1856. He had made it clear to the queen that the enemy in sight was not Persia: 'People will understand that Herat is an advanced post of attack against British India and that whatever belongs nominally to Persia must be considered as belonging practically to Russia.'[10]

Previously Russia had enjoyed the right to place consuls wherever she chose in Persia; now Britain insisted on a similar right. Russia in 1857 was not in a position to object, but the struggle for predominance in Persia between the two powers could only increase.

Britain's dispute with China that erupted in 1856 was a further example of Palmerston's high-handed bullying of weaker states, but it did not threaten Russian interests. On the contrary, Russia was prepared to horn in on the benefits that could be gained from intimidating the Celestial Empire. Following the defeat of China by Britain in the Opium War, the Treaty of Nanking in 1842 had opened up Shanghai, Canton and other cities to foreign trade. The treaty did little to stem the trade in opium, despite the Chinese government's objections. Free trade, not humanitarian arguments, prevailed, as far as the British government was concerned. Minor incidents between British merchants and the Chinese were common. Then in 1855, after Palmerston returned to office as prime minister, the incipient conflict escalated. The governor general of British Hong Kong used the seizure of the *Arrow*, a pirate ship flying (albeit out-of-date) British colours, as the basis for shelling the city of Canton. Looting, arson and general mayhem ensued. War was declared on China in October 1856.

Unlike the war with Persia, that with China, in which France participated, dragged on for four years but with little actual fighting. Palmerston's government fell during this period in the face of widespread criticism of his China policy, but after a brief Conservative government he was triumphantly returned to power. By this time the British mission led by Lord Elgin, with a force of British and French troops and the diplomatic backing of Russia and the United States, had forced the Chinese emperor to accept permanent foreign envoys in Peking.

Russia played her hand cleverly and disingenuously. Count Nicholas Muraviev, governor general of eastern Siberia since 1847, had from the outset advocated a forward policy. Russia and China did not, for the most part, have a clearly defined common frontier and many of the peoples of the region were neither Russian nor Chinese. Muraviev believed erroneously that as a result of the Opium War the British fleet would be used to establish claims on the coastal regions. Emperor Nicholas I had accepted the establishment of the military outpost of Nikolayevsk and favoured establishing a stable frontier with China but he was not prepared to confront China. The governor general pressed on and, despite the Crimean War, had made the Amur region effectively part of the Russian empire by 1856.

During the Franco-British conflict with China the Russian government offered its services in 1858 as mediator between the two western powers and China. For this it naturally required a handsome reward. Thus, in the Treaty of Aigun the Chinese government agreed that the river Amur should form the frontier between the two empires as far as its junction with the Ussuri river, and from that point should pass eastwards.[11] When Peking then tried to revoke this concession, Russia sent an envoy, who took advantage of the arrival of Franco-British troops to extract even better terms than those of Aigun. By the Russo-Chinese Treaty of Peking of November 1860, the frontier was to follow the Amur to the junction of the Ussuri, then follow the Ussuri to its source and across the thin strip which separated it from the Pacific. At the bottom of this strip a city, significantly called Vladivostok, Ruler of the East, which became Russia's main Pacific base, was founded in 1860. At the same time the treaty recognized Russian sovereignty in the area of Lake Balkash and Lake Issik Kul in Central Asia on the border of Chinese Turkestan.

The dispute with China in the late 1850s, seen initially by the British as an issue unconnected with Russia, although recognized by Russia as linked, demonstrated that both countries were contenders for power not only throughout Central Asia but also in East Asia.

Western Asia was also seen by the expansionists as a region where Russia had to secure her southern domains and check suspected British designs. The newly appointed governor of the Caucasus, Prince Alexander Bariatinsky, feared the support the British might give to the rebellious mountain people of the region against whom the Russians had been sporadically at war for many years. Certainly David Urquhart and his associates had increased their aid following the neutralization of the Black Sea in 1856. The Russian conquest of the Caucasus was a matter of cleaning up unfinished business, necessary for the firm establishment of a frontier which would provide a powerful operational base from which Russian forces could descend on Turkey, Persia and the road to India. It would also free up Russian troops for deployment elsewhere.

In 1859, after the long and heroic struggle by the Circassian mountain people against overwhelming odds, their leader Shamil, with the tiny remnant of his tribesmen, was encircled and surrendered to Bariatinsky, who received him with full military honours. Shamil was established in comfort in St Petersburg and given an estate, but the proud Circassians were subjected to treatment which was a mild foretaste of Stalin's behaviour in the Caucasus. They were told that they could go to new lands assigned to them in Russia or emigrate to Turkey. Nearly a million chose emigration. By 1864 the whole of the Caucasus and Transcaucasia was absorbed into the Russian empire and Britain and Turkey were deprived of their most valuable potential allies within the Russian empire. And the conquest of the Caucasus left large Russian armies unemployed and longing for further action.

In the late 1850s the Russians were making the running in the Great Game in Central Asia, with their activity comprising putting out feelers in several directions, in addition to the campaign in the Caucasus and involvement with China. Persia, with its long northern frontier with Russia, was, as ever, at the centre of preoccupations in St Petersburg. The shah had been defeated by Britain in 1857, but Russia was not prepared to lessen her efforts for influence in that country while recognizing that the Persians were past masters at playing one power off against another and little confidence could be placed in any commitment. In 1858 a mission led by Nicholas Khanykov and ostensibly sponsored by the Imperial Geographical Society, but with government funding, was sent by Egor Kovalevsky, head of the Asian Department. The instructions were for scientific exploration of Khorasan in the north-east of the country—which deceived no one. Khanykov was invited to Tehran by the shah and visited Herat, both notably far away from the Khorasan. Dost Mohammed in Kabul was given a letter from the Grand Duke Constantine expressing the hope that 'you will be open to people drawn there [to Afghanistan] by a noble and disinterested spirit of enquiry'.[12] Whether he believed Constantine or not, the wily emir refused to receive the Russian as it would clearly jeopardize his relations with Britain. Whatever the ostensible scientific and military reconnaissance results, politically the mission was a failure.

A second mission was dispatched to Eastern Turkestan, to Kashgaria, a province nominally under Chinese rule. An insurrection by the Turkic Muslim tribes of the region, it was claimed, was threatening Russian Kazakhs over the frontier. In the best tradition of nineteenth-century adventurers, a Russian Kazakh, Chokan Valikhanov, was disguised as the leader of a merchant caravan and sent to Kashgar to assess the situation. After an arduous and dangerous journey he reached the city, where he acquired much valuable information for his masters about this hostile territory which he published in the journal of the Russian Geographical Society. Britain was not at this time interested in Kashgar, but a few years later its importance was recognized, and by the time Valikhanov's account was translated into English a decade later, Anglo-Russian rivalry was rampant in Chinese Turkestan.

The third mission was led by the 27-year-old Nicholas Ignatiev, newly employed by the Asiatic Department after serving as military attaché in London after the Crimean War (before his triumph in Peking). He was sent to Khiva and Bukhara with instructions to strengthen Russian influence and eliminate British interference. In neither khanate was he able to extract any worthwhile concessions. The value of his expedition lay in the influential report he wrote:

> The most important and essential result of our mission to Central Asia in 1858 consisted in dispersing the fog shading the khanates from the eyes of the Russian Government … Information obtained by our mission and the conscientious destruction of the former mirage, provoked a sudden shift in the character of our relations with these crafty and treacherous neighbours, and contributed to the establishment of a more correct view of the meaning and basis of their power, of their real strength, and in particular, of that position which we must, and may, occupy in Central Asia.[13]

In the mid-nineteenth century the three Central Asian khanates of Khiva, Bukhara and Kokand (today in Uzbekistan) ruled the vast region of desert which stretched from the Caspian Sea in the west to the Pamirs in the east. The city of Samarkand was part of the emir of Bukhara's domains while the great walled city of Tashkent, the richest in Central Asia, was at the time part of the khanate of Kokand: Khiva was to the west. The rulers and the great majority of their subjects were Sunni Muslims. All three khanates were in a state of almost continuous war with one another and with the nomads who presented a threat to their security. And these states lay just south of the region of established Russian settlement in the steppe.

Alexander II in the years immediately after the Crimean War was young, inexperienced and sovereign of a newly defeated country. Not surprisingly, he was circumspect in these years as regards expansion in Central Asia, ambiguous and unsure how much Russia could dare without provoking Britain, hence vacillating. His hope was that the enterprise of Russian merchants and manufacturers would, if the government negotiated attractive trading conditions, carry Russian influence deep into Asia in a manner that was inexpensive, profitable and acceptable to the British. Gorchakov was concerned only about relations with the European powers and straightforwardly opposed advances in the khanates for fear of friction, if not war, with Britain. Yuri Gagemeister at the Russian finance ministry for his part pleaded the impoverished condition of the country and the need for industrial development as the reason for not authorizing expenditure on expeditions. However, the appointment of the aggressive Nicholas Ignatiev as head of the Asiatic Department in 1861 presaged an active policy of conquest and annexation. The new war minister, Dmitri Miliutin, was placed somewhere between, favouring moderate advance southwards.

But what was to play a determining role in Russian policy towards Central Asia was the lack of any collective responsibility for decisions. Each senior minister was independent and accountable only to the emperor. Even when a special commission of ministers reached a decision, an individual minister then had the right to an audience with the emperor in which he could put forward his arguments. A common decision could be voided almost as soon as it was made. Thus the three major ministries—foreign affairs, finance and war—all too often sabotaged each other's aims.

Nevertheless, it has been argued that this was not the case and that Russian officers on the spot were tightly controlled by St Petersburg. Certainly there were some in the foreign office who held that the idea of unchecked Russian expansion in Central Asia was a good cover story that masked the reality. According to the distinguished historian Beryl

Williams, 'it is now recognised that Central Asian leaders like Kaufman and Cherniaev did not act as independent agents. The [Russian] foreign office was usually the last to be told of advances but actions were often cleared before-hand by the Tsar or the Ministry of War.'[14]

Russia gained in self-confidence as regards Central Asia as a result of the dent to British prestige caused by the Indian Rebellion (Mutiny). The pacification of the Caucasus achieved in 1859, followed by the emancipation of the serfs in 1861, provided further boosts. Then, the successful suppression of the Polish uprising in 1863 convinced the expansionists that Russia had nothing to fear from Britain by advancing into Central Asia. What also has to be taken into account was the prevailing colonial *Zeitgeist* among the European powers and the United States. Unable to stem military action in Kokand in the early 1860s by military commanders who claimed to be filling gaps in the frontier and increasing alarm in Britain, a reluctant Gorchakov issued a lengthy circular in November 1864 justifying Russia's forward policy:

> The position of Russia in Central Asia is that of all civilized states which are brought into contact with half-savage, nomadic populations ... In such cases it always happens that the more civilized State is forced, in the interests of the security of its frontier and its commercial relations, to exert a certain ascendency over those turbulent unsettled tribes who are the most undesirable neighbours.[15]

In 1863 a special committee of ministers advocated consolidating the existing southern frontier with the khanates by closing a gap, 800 kilometres wide, in the middle. This would entail seizing several small towns and forts situated in the northern region of Kokand, the khanate closest to Russia. A reconnaissance mission from western Siberia in 1864 led by Colonel Mikhail Cherniaev proved a simple and straightforward operation. He linked up with another detachment moving south-eastwards from the Syr Darya line and the town of Suzak and the holy city of Turkestan were taken. Cherniaev now exceeded his instructions and went on to capture Chimkent in September, provoking the emir to issue a jihad against Russia.

Emboldened by this victory, the headstrong and fearless Cherniaev mounted an unsuccessful and costly 'reconnaissance' of Tashkent in October. Despite the humiliation of forty Russian heads being exposed, the colonel was promoted, awarded three medals and named governor of Turkestan in February 1865. The now General Cherniaev was only too aware that if Russia was to exert influence in Central Asia, especially to protect her frontier with Kokand, then Tashkent had to be taken. But he was not the only person who recognized the importance of the city of 100,000 inhabitants and centre of trade for the region. The covetous eye of the emir of Bukhara was fixed on Tashkent, and in the spring of 1865 the emir began preparations for military operations against the khan of Kokand. Cherniaev decided that he had to pre-empt the emir and capture Tashkent to drive a wedge between Bukhara and the rest of Kokand.

At the ministry of foreign affairs, Peter Stremoukhov, the new more moderate director of the Asiatic Department who had replaced the ambitious Ignatiev, distrusted Cherniaev and advocated leaving Tashkent outside the orbit of Russian conquest. Gorchakov for his part unreservedly demanded an end to military operations. Despite orders to the contrary, in May 1865 the general decided to take Tashkent by storm. The following month the city surrendered. Disobedience was forgotten. Alexander II described it as 'a glorious affair' and decorations were liberally distributed.[16] 'General Cherniaev has taken Tashkent', noted the minister of the interior, Peter Valuev, 'and nobody knows why ... There is something erotic in everything that happens on the distant frontiers of the empire.'[17] The question then had to be faced as to what to do with Tashkent—whether or not it should be formally annexed. Gorchakov, as usual, feared British protests and Miliutin the expense of a military administration. The official line was that the occupation was temporary.

Cherniaev thought differently and clashed with his superior, the governor general of Orenburg, who denounced his 'wilfulness ... and petty tyranny' which 'amounted to clear violations of the military service'.[18] The general, in no way dismayed, ignored the complaints against him and led a series of successful operations towards Bukhara. This was too much for his masters and Cherniaev was recalled. However his successor, Dmitri Romanovsky, showed himself to be equally independent by continuing offensive actions against Bukharan troops. Then, in yet another example of how little orders from St Petersburg sometimes counted, the governor general of Orenburg reversed his earlier decision and ordered Romanovsky to go further and take the city of Bukhara, despite orders to seek peace with the emir.

It was clear to the government that reckless commanders based on Orenburg were not capable of administering Turkestan and could provoke unnecessary problems, not only with the khans, but with foreign powers. In 1866 the Tashkent region was annexed to the Russian empire and in July 1867 General Constantine von Kaufman, a Baltic German (who had trained as an engineer with Feodor Dostoevsky), was appointed governor general of the new province of Russian Turkestan, with plenary powers over administration, the military, finances and diplomacy. When he entered Tashkent on horseback accompanied by Cossacks with bared sabres, most Uzbeks realized that Russian rule would be permanent.

The response of the British government to the Russian expeditions in the late 1850s and the first half of the 1860s was singularly muted. This was due in part to avoid a replay of Palmerston's vociferous reaction in the late 1830s to Russian activity in Central Asia. After the Afghan War, the Crimean War, the Persian campaign and the Indian Rebellion there was little desire to risk military adventures as a check to Russia. The mood in the 1860s—there were four governments during the first five years—was for coming to a deal with Russia. Sir John Lawrence, a former chief commissioner of the Punjab and old India hand, like his elder brother Henry with whom he had virtually ruled the Punjab in the late 1840s, became viceroy in 1863 and advocated a closed border policy for India, better known as 'masterly inactivity'.[19] In 1867, even after Bukhara was taken by Russia, he believed that an understanding should be reached with Russia.

The leading exponent of the opposing school was Sir Henry Rawlinson, who had fought in the Afghan War, was president of the Royal Geographical Society and the Asiatic Society, a member of the India Council, and a Member of Parliament from 1860. Rawlinson led the forward school and had for three decades preached that Russia was expansionist, inherently hostile to Britain and had designs on India. In an article in the *Quarterly Review* in 1865 he despaired that 'The progress of Russia in Central Asia attracts less attention than it deserves. Step by step she approaches our Indian frontier; one by one the independent nations or tribes which separated her dominions from our own, fall beneath her sway, or sink into a condition of dependence on her.'[20] The relative positions of Britain and Russia had changed to Russia's advantage. He dismissed critics who argued that opposition to Russian advance was impossible, indeed would only provoke that country to move faster.

The foreign secretary, now Earl Russell, was bestirred into a half-hearted protest after the fall of Tashkent. On 16 September he sent a personal letter to Brunnov from Balmoral that could not fail to reassure the Russians. He knew, he claimed, that Gorchakov:

> wished as much as ourselves to leave undisturbed the *status quo* in Central Asia ... I think the object of the Russian Govt perfectly legitimate, & I am

> always for the regular civilised Power against the irregular & barbarous states ... But what I wish in Central Asia is such a complete understanding between Russia & Great Britain that no unfounded jealousies may spring up. I cannot be concerned for the Emir of Bokhara who puts our subjects to death [a reference to Stoddart and Conolly].[21]

The death of Palmerston in October 1865, the 'old shark' as he was known to them, was welcomed by the Russian government as removing their most redoubtable adversary. Even the British press, including *The Times*, normally more hostile to Russia than a Liberal government, was understanding of the taking of Tashkent. The *Morning Herald* believed that 'the present position of Russia in Central Asia is nothing more than the logical consequence of her legitimate pretensions, and a mission which has peace for its first purpose and commerce for its second is one which this country, of all others, is bound to recognize and accept'.[22]

The second reason for the lack of British fear of Russian advances in Central Asia was reliance on Afghanistan as a barrier between Russia in Central Asia and India. Dost Mohammed had been allowed to return to Kabul as emir in 1842 on the assassination of Shah Shuja. He had good reason to be anti-British after his treatment in the Afghan War and had allied himself with the Sikh leader Ranjit Singh against the British with the aim of taking Peshawar for Afghanistan. After the defeat of the Sikhs in 1847 and the incorporation of the Punjab into British India, he judged it prudent to retreat. An inveterate expansionist, Dost Mohammed conquered Balkh to the north of Kabul in 1850. Four years later he extended his domain southwards to Kandahar and later recovered Kunduz and Badakhshan.

After ignoring him for a decade, the British had good reason to woo the emir of Afghanistan, and an offensive and defensive alliance, backed up with generous subsidies, was signed in 1854 with Sir John Lawrence, then Commissioner for the Punjab. In 1857 the emir had joined with the British in repulsing the Persian attack on Herat and during the Indian Rebellion he had refrained from supporting the insurgents. When the Russian Khanykov the following year had asked for an audience with Dost Mohammed it was refused. He made it clear that he was an ally of the British and did not want to run the risk of another *débâcle* like that caused by Vitevich twenty years before.

When the ever-aggressive Persians moved against Kandahar in 1862, the old emir placed himself at the head of his army and drove the attackers back. Some months later, now confident, and with British acquiescence, Dost Mohammed took Herat, his lifetime aim. He died a few weeks later.

Dost Mohammed had named his third son, Sher Ali, as his successor but an elder brother, Mohammed Afzai, with help from the latter's son, Abdur Rahman, captured Kabul. By 1868 Sher Ali was able to retake the capital and Abdur Rahman retreated north across the Amu Darya to bide his time. Afghanistan was a British ally, but generations of internal strife with frequent regime change made its loyalty far from certain.

In that year Britain came to appreciate the threat posed by Russian conquest in Central Asia. Kaufman in April learned that the emir of Bukhara was amassing a force in Samarkand—inside his khanate—with the aim of driving the Russians out of Turkestan. The Bukharan troops overwhelmingly outnumbered those of Russia but were inferior in armament, training and discipline. Kaufman occupied the city without resistance. From there he advanced and routed the main Bukharan force at the battle of Zerabulak. In the peace settlement of July 1868 Bukhara was absorbed into the Russian empire, the emir forced to pay an indemnity and Bukhara opened to Russian commerce. The emir was allowed to retain his throne, for what that was worth. When Gorchakov ordered Kaufman to return Samarkand to the emir, he refused: 'I could not commit such sacrilege against the prestige, honour and rights of Russia.'[23] He travelled to St Petersburg and convinced Alexander that Russia had to retain Samarkand.

The logistical problems the Russians faced, if they were to maintain their hold over Kokand and Bukhara and take Khiva, were enormous. The march from Orenburg to Turkestan was long and through difficult terrain in appalling heat. A shorter link from European Russia would be created if a port on the eastern shore of the Caspian Sea could be established so that men and *matériel* could be shipped down the Volga and across the Caspian. Already in 1865 the British were aware that Russia was increasing her military vessels in the sea. It came as no surprise therefore when at the end of 1869, a small Russian force arrived on the eastern shore at Krasnovodsk with instructions to build a permanent fortress there. The whole enterprise was to be secret, above all from the British, but in a region where spies were readily available and cheap, London and Calcutta soon learned of the project. It would enable the Russians to be closer to Khiva in the case of an expedition but, more importantly from a British point of view, would pose a threat to Afghanistan by bringing the Russians within striking distance of Herat, the strategic key to India.

It is striking that John, now Lord Lawrence, the principal proponent of confident 'masterly inactivity' in previous years, had by 1867 decided that negotiations with Russia were necessary to resolve frontier questions:

> The Government of India on the one hand could look on without anxiety or apprehension at the proceeding of Russia on her southern frontier, and welcome the civilising effect of her border Government on the wild tribes of the Steppe and on the bigoted and exclusive Governments of Bokhara and Khokand; while Russia, on the other hand, assured of our loyal feeling in this matter would have no jealousy in respect to our alliance with the Afghan and neighbouring tribes, or our negotiations to repress Persia in her designs upon the tracts which border on her eastern frontier.[24]

Little attention was paid to the viceroy's advice. He became more worried as the Russians advanced. They must be given to understand that they must not be permitted to interfere in the affairs of Afghanistan or of any of the states contiguous with the Indian frontier: 'An advance on India, beyond a certain point, would entail on her a war, in all parts of the world, with England.'[25]

The new Gladstone government formed in December 1868 was favourably received by the Russian government. The prime minister made friendly noises to the Russian ambassador and said that 'he could not doubt the friendly intentions of the Emperor towards England'.[26] In a speech in the House of Commons in June 1869 Gladstone insisted that the British government understood Russia's need to protect her southern frontier. More used as the Russians were to a hostile House of Commons, the speech was published in the official *Journal de St Petersbourg*. Clarendon, the foreign secretary, who had been dealing with Russia since he was a young man in St Petersburg in 1820, was less sanguine and took Russia to task. While understanding the problems caused by the men on the spot, he told the British ambassador, Sir Andrew Buchanan, that

> Abstinence from aggression, would on every account promote the true interests of Russia, whose territorial possessions need no aggrandisement; and if the giving effect to this policy depended on the Russian Government alone, I should not doubt it being maintained; but I was sure, judging from our own Indian experience, that such would not be the case, and that Russia would find the same difficulty that England had experienced in controlling its own power, when exercised at so great distance from the seat of Government as to make reference home almost a matter of impossibility ... Such in the main had caused the extension of our Indian empire;

> and there was reason to apprehend that such was the course into which Russia, however unwillingly, was about to be drawn.[27]

In March 1869 Clarendon held talks with Brunnov and advocated the recognition of a neutral territory between Britain and Russia 'which should be the limit of those possessions, and be scrupulously respected by both Powers'.[28] St Petersburg concurred in the proposal and said that Alexander had always held that the two powers should not be contiguous in Asia. For Russia, Afghanistan was an appropriate neutral zone. Later in the year Clarendon met Gorchakov in Heidelberg to develop the proposal and the chancellor reiterated that Afghanistan was entirely outside the Russian sphere of influence. Clarendon recalled:

> The conference lasted 3 ½ hours, and we agreed that it *must* lead to a right good understanding between the Lion and the Bear ... I am glad I went, as we certainly arrived at agreement upon several points. Perhaps, however, the crafty man was only practising upon my youth and innocence.[29]

Unfortunately Clarendon was seventy, in poor health and no longer the redoubtable diplomat of earlier years. (He died some months later, from overwork and too many cigarettes, according to Brunnov, and was succeeded by Lord Granville.) For Clarendon had weakened the British position by holding that Afghanistan would not fulfil the conditions of a neutral territory such as the two governments desired because its frontiers were ill defined, and that this uncertainty as to the limits of Afghanistan was sure to lead to disputes between the Russians and the Afghan chiefs. He proposed the Upper Amu Darya, which was south of Bukhara, territory belonging to the khan of Khiva. Gorchakov demurred, since a portion of the country south of the Amu Darya was claimed by the ruler of Bukhara and might lead to disputes between Britain and Russia.

Direct negotiations between the two governments were suspended, but a representative of the Indian administration, Thomas Douglas Forsyth, was sent to St Petersburg in November 1869 by the new viceroy, Lord Mayo. The viceroy was dissatisfied with the position taken by Clarendon. He had been convinced by Henry Rawlinson that Afghanistan had to be accepted as constituting a neutral zone. It was a defined independent state and in the north-east the remote and mountainous regions of Badakhshan and Wakhan, where Russian outposts lay closest to British India, had to be included within its frontiers. The talks were protracted, consisting largely of trying to agree as to what exactly constituted the frontiers of Afghanistan. Agreement was reached that everything in the actual possession of Sher Ali would be considered Afghan territory, and Forsyth left the Russian capital convinced that the Amu Darya had been recognized as a frontier and that Badakhshan and Wakhan were included in the emir's territory.

However, before too long Gorchakov realized that Forsyth had gone beyond what Russia could accept. In a dispatch to Brunnov he insisted that the boundaries of Afghanistan in the time of Dost Mohammed were not the same as those of Sher Ali: 'This important distinction is the measure of the difference between our views and those of Lord Mayo.'[30]

Gorchakov had promised to instruct Kaufman to report on the Afghan boundary question, but when the British showed impatience with the lack of news, they were told that communication with Tashkent was the problem:

> In the first place, all the data we have to rely on respecting those regions are very vague and uncertain. The little native testimony that there is, [is] unworthy of credence. The maps are problematic, hypothetical, and often contradictory. No country offers less resource to the inquirer into its historical and geographical conditions, past or present.[31]

More revealing was a later dispatch to the ambassador: 'In the middle of all the incertitude in which we find ourselves, the Imperial Cabinet has adopted the most favourable stance. I mean, that it is important above all to play for time.'[32]

Granville had realized that the Russians were procrastinating and that the moment had come to pursue a firmer line. In October 1872 he set out in detail the boundaries of Afghanistan as seen by the British government. Both the contents and presentation of the dispatch angered Gorchakov who declared it an unacceptable ultimatum. He therefore showed no inclination to reply.

The chancellor now had good reason to feel confident and able to stand up to the British government. Russia had the previous year abrogated the Black Sea clauses in the face of British objections and in 1872 had met with success in Kashgar. In the late 1860s a former Kokand officer, Yakub Beg, had carved out an independent state, nominally under Chinese suzerainty, based on Kashgar. He showed himself to be friendly towards the British in India, causing dismay in St Petersburg, as eastern Turkestan was important for access to China. In 1870 Yakub Beg was attempting to extend his influence to Kulja. The following year Russian forces occupied Kulja, which put them in a strong position to attack Kashgar. Yakub Beg was obliged to accept a treaty ceding commercial rights to Russia, though without Russian occupation. It was known that Yakub Beg was playing a double game and a British mission obtained a similar treaty in 1872, signalling the British intention of resisting Russian claims to Kashgar. The fact was that the Russians could easily put an army in Kashgar and the British could not.

Already in the autumn of 1872 there had been rumours in Britain of a Russian expedition to Khiva. 'After a considerable pause, Russia is once more on the march in Central Asia', reported the *Daily Telegraph*, in colourful terms:

> The assailant has actually set out from the seashore and may be imagined as making his way by the Caspian to the Oxus [Amu Darya]. When envoys from the lone star of the desert sought the Viceroy of India, asking for help or counsel, it was plain that the Khan really believed his sovereignty imperilled, and dreaded the coming of Muscovite troops into his oasis.[33]

The Russians had well-founded grievances against Khiva, which still maintained a slave market where Russian captives were brutally treated and engaged in raids into Russian-controlled territory. Kaufman persuaded his easily convinced masters in St Petersburg of the 'unnatural, abnormal and ... intolerable order of relations with the Khanate of Khiva to us'.[34] The governor general was therefore authorized in January 1873 to lead a punitive expedition to seize Khiva's capital and subject the khanate to Russian influence. Given that he marshalled 13,000 men who were to converge on Khiva from Tashkent, Krasnovodsk, Mangyshlak and Orenburg, it was clearly more than influence that was sought.

The desert wastes proved a much greater obstacle than Khiva's army. Men, horses and camels died in the extreme heat but Kaufman pressed on. The Orenburg detachment under Colonel Mikhail Skobelev had already bombarded Khiva when the general arrived but he withdrew to enable Kaufman to make a triumphal entry. The khan, Mohammed Rahim, was forced to submit; all slaves were freed and a large indemnity imposed. By the Russo-Khivan treaty of August 1873 Khiva became a Russian protectorate with the khan the 'obedient servant' of the Russian emperor, conducting foreign relations only with Tashkent's consent. As if this was not enough, Kaufman went on to annex more Khivan territory, despite the objections of the foreign ministry. The Russian frontier was now on the right bank of the Amu Darya and Russia controlled the east coast of the Caspian and the Ust-Urt plateau.

In anticipation of the British reaction to the conquest of Khiva, Alexander II had sent Count Peter Shuvalov on a mission to London in January 1873.[35] Brunnov had protested time and time again against the rapid expansion in Central Asia and had told his masters that he could no longer continue repeating empty and unconvincing assurances about a civilizing mission and commerce as being Russian aims. In late 1872 he had an acrimonious exchange with Gorchakov and, given that he knew he was coming to the end of his career, he urged the chancellor, whom he thought complacent about British acceptance of Russian expansion, to rein in the commanders in Central Asia or risk serious confrontation with Britain.[36] Brunnov was seen in St Petersburg as too much inclined to sympathize with the British point of view—apart from during the Crimean War he had been in London since 1840. And he was now old, 'very infirm and feeble', senile even.[37] A more robust defender of Russian policy in Britain was needed.

Count Peter Shuvalov was one of the most talented men in the upper echelons of Russian government. The son of a major landowner, he possessed good connections at court and a reputation for mildly liberal principles. Born in 1827, he had begun his career as a cavalry officer in the Crimean War and then become governor general of the Baltic provinces, but it was Alexander II's decision to appoint him head of the Third Section in 1866 that propelled the count to prominence. Shuvalov rapidly restored the falling credit of the department after the assassination attempt on the emperor that year and he successfully held his own against intrigues from across the political spectrum. However, in the early 1870s he fell foul of Alexander II's mistress, Catherine Dolgoruka. The powerful young woman wanted Shuvalov out of St Petersburg: the emperor complied.

Given his ability, it was a felicitous appointment to London from the Russian point of view. From the outset, the count proceeded to charm his way through London society and his lively dispatches, with much more information than Brunnov was capable of eliciting, were much appreciated by Alexander and Gorchakov.

Shuvalov admitted that a small expedition had been sent to Khiva, which in no way allayed British suspicions. What enabled him to permit Russia to have a free hand there was that he informed the British government that Russia had dropped her objections over Badakhshan and Wakhan being part of Afghanistan.

Queen Victoria was incensed on learning the news about Khiva in 1873 and in no way placated by the Russian climbdown over Afghanistan. Granville tried to mollify the sovereign:

> The Russians had cause for complaint against the khan of Khiva, which were thought just, that Lord Northbrook [the viceroy] strongly advised the Khan to make reparation to the Emperor. The Khan declined to follow this judicious advice—and the expedition against Khiva was resolved upon & announced without any objection being raised by England.[38]

The queen was again reminded that Britain had pursued a policy of gradual conquest in India and was not in a position to object when the Russians behaved similarly.

It was natural that Russia should wish to feel secure in the future but the problem was that Alexander's assurances through Shuvalov that Russia was not planning further annexations were worth little, since the emperor was:

> neither strong enough nor able enough to ensure his policy, when moderate, being carried out … A probable renewal of expeditions in Central Asia is also a matter of great difficulty—It is the opinion of the Government which Lord Granville knows is entertained by Lord Lawrence [the former viceroy], and which he believes is shared by Lords Derby and Salisbury [leaders of the Opposition], that it would be unnecessary and impolitic for England to go to war with Russia as to any operations on the side of Affghanistan, but the taking of Merv would excite considerable alarm in this country.[39]

South of Khiva was the region occupied by the Teke Turcomans, troublesome and daring horsemen who had nominally owed allegiance to the khan of Khiva. After his subjugation, they were to all intents and purposes independent, and at the heart of the region was the oasis of Merv. Occupation of Merv by the Russians would mean that they were only 300 kilometres from Herat and on the easy route to India. British India could therefore be threatened and Afghanistan placed at the mercy of the Russians. As if this was not enough, Russia would dominate Persia on her Khorasan frontier.

In 1874 Shuvalov, now ambassador, had to deal with the new Disraeli-led Conservative government. Lord Derby, the foreign secretary, was far less easy to reassure than Granville. He demanded to know what the Russians would do once they had dealt with the incursions of the Teke Turcomans into Russian territory. Shuvalov replied that it would probably be necessary to reach Merv to be able to impose a lasting settlement: '"Oh non", exclaimed Derby several times, "il ne faut pas aller à Merv."'[40]

Reassurance for the British government, however, came the following year, when the Russian emperor himself told Lord Odo Russell that 'He had no idea of occupying or taking Merv, or any other portion of Central Asia that might lead to a misunderstanding between Russia and England; the friendship and confidence of England was worth more to him than territorial aggrandizement, & he gave me his word of honor.'[41]

18

THE END OF THE CRIMEAN SYSTEM

Changes took place in the ever-unstable Balkans in the second half of the 1860s that weakened the Crimean system. In 1866 Prince Cuza in Romania was overthrown and, contrary to an international convention of 1858, a foreign prince was chosen as ruler. Russia failed to extract any tangible advantage from the Romanian revolution, only a clear lessening of the moral validity of the Treaty of Paris. In that same year a revolt broke out in Crete against the Turks. Gorchakov supported the rebellion in the hope that it would encourage similar rebellions in the Balkans. However, by 1869 the rising was suppressed and Russia gained nothing. Similarly, Russia had emerged empty-handed from the events that brought about the reorganization of Germany in 1866 with Austria's defeat by Prussia.

In 1866 Alexander II and his chancellor had hoped to secure the long-sought-after abrogation of the Black Sea clauses in exchange for their support for the destruction of the German Confederation: Bismarck had settled matters as he wished.[1] Russia's only gain was a mission to St Petersburg by General Edwin von Manteuffel with instructions to reassure Alexander that Prussia sympathized with the Russian view of the Black Sea clauses. That Austria made a similar gesture was of little importance, as both Britain and France had declined to associate themselves with the offer. Britain remained determined to defend the Treaty of Paris in its entirety and Napoleon III was loath to offend the British government.

He did, however, increasingly antagonize his continental neighbours, above all Prussia. The French emperor was a frustrated man in 1867. He believed that Prussia owed him a debt for remaining neutral in the war against Austria the previous year. As compensation—*la politique de pourboires*, as Bismarck called it—he held that the Prussian chancellor had promised his ambassador in Berlin, Count Vincent de Benedetti, that France could annex Belgium. But the ambassador warned Napoleon that, unless France was really prepared for the use of force, she would need to move very carefully. She did not.

The failure of his Mexican policy, with the execution of the Archduke Maximilian, led Napoleon to be yet more determined to find a source of French compensation in Europe. He turned his attention towards the Grand Duchy of Luxemburg which the king of Holland wished to sell. Bismarck goaded Napoleon on and then prevented France from taking even this '*bicoque*', or shanty. Napoleon then made a feeble attempt in early 1870 to woo Russia away from Prussia. He completely failed to understand the deep-seated grudge felt by Russia for the Crimean War, French support of the 1863 Polish rebellion and events in Romania.

It was an incendiary situation created by the French emperor's lamentable record in foreign affairs and it was clear that the peace of Europe was at the mercy of any fresh incident that might arise.

This duly happened. In June 1870 the dispute over the candidature for the vacant Spanish throne came to a head. France opposed the Prussian king's nomination of Prince Leopold Hohenzollern. In the face of French resistance the prince's father renounced the throne on his son's behalf on 12 June. It was a triumph for France but it was not enough for the French parliament and public opinion which demanded that the king of Prussia publicly associate himself with the withdrawal. Napoleon dispatched Benedetti to Ems to extract this assurance. Wilhelm became increasingly irritated by the ambassador's insistence and, contrary to normal practice, he decided to make public the details of his conversation with Benedetti. He sent a telegram setting out what had been said to Bismarck to release to the press. As is well known, the Ems telegram was doctored by Bismarck such that it omitted how courteous and correct the king had been with Benedetti. It insinuated that the ambassador had been snubbed and that all relations with France were terminated.

France mobilized and on 19 July declared war on Prussia. The pent-up feelings of resentment in France at her poor showing in Europe in recent years exploded. The Austro-Hungarian ambassador, Prince Metternich, summarized the situation: 'Here they absolutely want war, very great agitation, the cause popular, the outcome dangerous.'[2]

In June 1870, Alexander II, a nephew of King Wilhelm of Prussia, while taking a cure at Ems had received a visit from the king and Bismarck. The Prussian chancellor was satisfied that he had Russian support for

Prussia confirmed. Gorchakov, on his way home from Wildbad where he had been for a cure, happened to be in Berlin on 13 July and Bismarck was able to firm up Russia's commitment to Prussia to remain neutral in a war against France. Bismarck, who on a personal level hated Gorchakov, was entirely satisfied with the conversation, held hours before he edited the Ems telegram later in the day. How sincere the Russian chancellor was when in Berlin he urged the French government to be satisfied with what they had achieved and to recognize the conciliatory spirit of the Prussian king is open to grave doubt.

On arriving back in St Petersburg and to the French declaration of war, Gorchakov immediately set about ensuring that the Austrians would not attempt to attack Prussia from the rear in revenge for the humiliation of 1866. Russia was taking the high moral ground of a country which had nothing to gain from a Franco-Prussian war. The Russian chancellor set himself up as the leader of countries who would declare their neutrality in the conflict. He was assured by the British ambassador, Sir Andrew Buchanan, that Britain would remain neutral as long as Belgium was not invaded. With Britain onside, Italy and the minor countries would follow suit. In this situation Austria-Hungary would not dare intervene. Events proved him right.

France was swiftly defeated on the battlefield by Prussian troops and troops from the North German Confederation. Napoleon III and his army surrendered at Sedan on 2 September 1870. When the news hit Paris of Napoleon's capture the Second Empire was overthrown in a bloodless *coup d'état*. While the new republican government was amenable to the payment of reparations and the loss of colonial territories, Jules Favre on behalf of the Government of National Defence declared that France would not yield any territory. The republic renewed the declaration of war and pledged to drive the enemy out of France. Under these circumstances the Germans felt obliged to continue the war. Bismarck decided to put pressure on the enemy by attacking heavily fortified Paris. The siege of Paris began on 19 September.

This was the moment for which Russia had been waiting since 1856.

The signatories of the 1856 Treaty of Paris were France, Prussia, Austria, Italy, Turkey and Britain and they had collectively imposed the humiliating Black Sea clauses on Russia, creating a festering resentment from the outset. But now, in the autumn of 1870, France was prostrate: Prussia could be counted on to support Russia: Austria had more than once indicated that she attached little importance to neutralization of the

Black Sea: Italy was preoccupied with domestic matters, above all the incorporation of Rome: Turkey was known to be allowing warships into the Black Sea. The problem was Great Britain.

Gladstone's newly formed government was neither unforewarned nor unprepared for Russia's taking advantage of the fall of the French Second Empire. Buchanan had expressed the view in June, 'that on the first favourable opportunity, Russia will claim the abrogation of the stipulations of the Treaty of Paris'.[3] This he had repeated throughout the following months.

Palmerston, the man who above all had insisted on the Black Sea clauses, had admitted in 1856 that he did not believe the neutralization of the Black Sea would last for more than ten years, seven according to some. 'Well at all events they will last my life', said the satisfied old man who died in 1865.[4] Gladstone had served in Palmerston's wartime government but had never evinced the rabid Russophobia of the old statesman. He believed at the end of the Crimean War that, popular though it was in Britain, 'the stipulations were politically absurd, and therefore in the long run impossible'.[5] Granville, who had become foreign secretary on Clarendon's death in June 1870, was equally frank: 'I have frequently said in public that with the exception of ourselves and the Turks, all the co-signatories of the treaty of Paris had expressed views in favour of modifying the article.'[6]

Gorchakov thus seized this propitious moment in 1870 to throw off the shackles of 1856. On 31 October he dispatched a circular to the signatories of the Treaty of Paris. In it he announced that Russia would no longer consider herself bound by the demilitarization clauses of the Treaty of Paris. He justified this decision by pointing out, correctly, that the treaty had been repeatedly infringed in the Danubian Provinces. He argued that it could not be expected that some of its provisions should remain intact while others were disregarded.

The Russian chancellor staked his whole career on the success of the undertaking. Walking with his deputy, Baron Alexander Jomini, Gorchakov declared: 'If my calculations have deceived me, and if I have raised a storm which will prove to be too dangerous for Russia, the Emperor can always disavow me if he deems it necessary for the good of the country. I will gladly sacrifice myself.'[7]

In London and Vienna, as was expected, a storm of indignation greeted the circular. Buchanan in St Petersburg expected to be asked to demand his passports. But the dispatch sent to him had a docquet open at the end to friendly discussion. Nevertheless, Granville protested in strong terms against the Russian announcement. The issue in the opinion of the British government was 'not whether any desire expressed by Russia ought to be carefully examined in a friendly spirit by the co-signatory powers, but whether they are to accept from her the announcement that, by her own act, without any consent from them, she has released herself from a solemn covenant'.[8] Gorchakov replied that the Russian emperor's decision was irrevocable. The circular had no other motive but to remove a stain on the honour of Russia and to establish more amicable relations with Turkey. That the usually suave chancellor was less than confident, the ambassador noted with satisfaction, could be seen by the fact that his legs and feet shook with a nervous tremor when listening to the British dispatch.

The Russian press, which was to all intents and purposes under government control, was unanimous in welcoming the declaration and claimed that the country was prepared to go to war if necessary. In Britain, where public opinion played a large and independent role, the press was almost at one in demanding an ultimatum to Russia to withdraw the circular. Gladstone was outraged by the unilateral Russian action but told Granville on 22 November: 'I will frankly own that I am much disgusted with a good deal of the language that I have read in the newspapers about immediate war with Russia. I try to put a check on myself to prevent the reaction it engenders.'[9]

Though privately Gladstone did not consider the Russian declaration a *casus belli*, he did not try to cool the bellicose mood of the country because of the pressure it would put on Russia. He told Granville: 'I have had half an idea that it might be well that I should see Brunnow.'[10] The prime minister knew that it was widely known that he had been a dove like Aberdeen in 1853, and he wished to disabuse the Russians: 'This I do not conceive to be true, and possibly I might undeceive Brunnow a little.'[11] The ploy worked with the aged ambassador, who was convinced that Britain was prepared to go to war: 'Russia and England are like two locomotives moving at speed towards each other. If this happens, a crash is inevitable. The men in power in England are not strong enough to resist the pressure of public opinion pushing them.'[12]

For Brunnov, the situation in early November 1870 was comparable with that in late 1853, when war between Britain and Russia looked likely and he had taken the precaution of removing money from the Bank of England. He pointed out that in 1870 the Russian ministry of finance had raised capital for railway construction in London. This would be cut off if war were declared. The ministry of the marine had placed orders for arms in Birmingham: 'A simple order of the Privy Council would be enough for these arms and machines to be sequestered.'[13] The ambassador was seen in St Petersburg as having overreacted and was rebuked by Gorchakov: 'It seems to me that the apprehensions you feel, and the responsibility you have borne during your long and successful career, make you rather more pessimistic than the situation warrants.'[14] It had been necessary for Russia to hit hard to be listened to.

The Russian chancellor knew that Bismarck would support Russia. Even though the Prussian chancellor had been irritated by the Russian attempt at a *fait accompli* whose timing was unfortunate, from his point of view it was nevertheless of paramount importance not to alienate his only friendly great power while the war with France was continuing. Russia sought a conference to ratify the renunciation and Bismarck was prepared to go along with the proposal. Lord Odo Russell, an undersecretary at the British foreign office, was to visit Bismarck in Versailles to discuss pending issues, a meeting planned before Gorchakov's circular and now all the more important. The envoy insisted that Britain was prepared to go to war unless the Russian circular was withdrawn. Bismarck had to mediate. The chancellor agreed that a conference had to be convened and he proposed St Petersburg.

The British government agreed in principle to the calling of a conference, but on condition that there should be no assumptions as to what it would decide. And to hold it in St Petersburg was unacceptable—Vienna, Florence or London were possible choices. Gorchakov rather patronizingly replied that he would not object to London to satisfy British national sentiment. The decision was followed by weeks of intensive diplomatic preparation. This suited Bismarck, who sought time to push on with the hostilities in France. By mid-January France was defeated and in the Palace of Versailles on 17 January 1871 the creation of the German empire was declared.

The previous day the conference had at last been convened in London. So far none of the powers had shown any concern for the sixth signatory of the Treaty of Paris, Turkey, the power who, apart from Russia, was most directly affected by the Black Sea clauses and in whose interest it was to maintain the status quo. The Turks raised their voice as proceedings began. Brunnov was furious: 'They are playing a double game. Their calculation is clear. They show themselves conciliatory towards Russia with the aim of wrecking the conference.'[15] (Note of Alexander II on the telegram: 'If this is true it is too despicable.') Ali Pasha, the grand-vizier, knew well that there were many Members of Parliament who were hostile to abrogation and the Turkish ambassador in London was actively courting support among them. Nevertheless, with all the other powers seeking a successful outcome of the conference, the Turks were forced to cede.

Under the terms of the convention finally accepted by all the plenipotentiaries on 13 March, Russia was permitted to resume her sovereign rights in the Black Sea. In exchange the sultan was authorized 'to open the said Straits in time of Peace to the Vessels of War of friendly and allied Powers, in case the Sublime Porte should judge it necessary in order to secure the execution of the stipulations of the Treaty of Paris of the 30th March 1856'. Russia's long struggle was over. Alexander II reacted as would be expected: 'The Emperor is said to be personally overjoyed at the success of his policy and is reported to have ordered a "Te Deum" to be sung in the chapel of the Winter Palace.' A trustworthy source reported that

> His Majesty went to the Cathedral of St Peter and St Paul in the fortress ... and there prayed for some time with signs of deep emotion at the grave of His Father, saying to his attendants as he left, that he trusted the shade of the Emperor Nicholas would now be appeased.[16]

From the point of view of the British government it had succeeded in making nullification of the Black Sea clauses, at least formally, the result of an international decision and not the action of Russia alone. But the Russian circular of 31 October had not been withdrawn but rather neatly and effectively bypassed. Russia had won a diplomatic victory and Gorchakov's prestige and reputation were at their height. It was though a rather hollow victory, gained by beating at a door that was already open, or at least half-open. (For many years to come financial constraints and the lack of a consistent Near Eastern policy were to prevent Russia from rebuilding a Black Sea fleet of any consequence.)

As was to be expected, the Liberal government was lambasted by Disraeli in the House of Commons over the protocols of 13 March 1871. The 1856 Treaty of Paris, he asserted, had prevented the Near East from disturbing the general peace. It was deplorable that this safeguard, the only tangible outcome of the Crimean War, should now be thrown away. The government held its own in parliament and Gladstone and Granville felt vindicated, but the result of the London conference was to weaken the government's position in the country. It was widely viewed as having caved in to Russia.

Russia was beholden to Prussia in 1871, and Bismarck recognized that the powerful position of the German empire could provoke a new danger by a combination of two or more neighbouring powers, '*le cauchemar des coalitions*' as he called it. Royal meetings, mainly in Berlin, followed. Alexander was in the German capital to see his uncle, the now kaiser, in September 1871. A little later Franz Josef assured Wilhelm of Austrian friendship and Alexander put aside his old antagonism by visiting Vienna. In the autumn of 1873 the *Dreikaiserbund*, the League of the Three Emperors, was formally created with appropriate pomp. In reality it was no more than a monarchial assertion of the intention of the three governments to return to the relationship that had existed among them for most of the period between the Napoleonic and Crimean wars. It was not solid, as the two junior partners had very divergent aims in the Balkans, and it was further weakened by the increasing personal jealousy of Gorchakov towards Bismarck.

While the royal families of Germany, Austria-Hungary and Russia were engaged in exchanges of political friendship, those of Britain and Russia were negotiating more personal links. Prince Alfred (Affie), the Duke of Edinburgh, and second son of Queen Victoria, was heir to the Duchy of Coburg—the ruling duke, Ernest, brother of the Prince Consort, being childless and likely to remain so. (The Prince of Wales had renounced his rights to Coburg, as ruling the duchy would be incompatible with reigning in Great Britain.) Affie had met Alexander II's only surviving daughter, the Grand Duchess Marie, in 1868, and appeared impressed by the young woman. His sister-in-law, the pro-Russian Danish-born Alexandra, Princess of Wales, and her sister Dagmar (Minnie), married to the tsarevich Alexander, encouraged Affie to pursue the grand duchess. Such a marriage would be a snub to Germany.

The prince was a captain in the Royal Navy based in Malta where he kept a mistress and led a rather dissolute life. Thus his mother was keen to see him settle down to avoid further 'scrapes', but she was far from convinced, when he announced in 1871 he wished to marry Marie, that he had chosen the right woman. Queen Victoria feared that Marie's head would be filled with 'half oriental Russian notions'. Her family was arrogant and 'false' and there was the question of religion. Indeed, it would be 'the first departure since 200 years nearly from the practice of our family since the Revolution of 88! We must be very firm—or else we may pack up and call back the descendants of the Stuarts.'[17]

When Vicky, Affie's elder sister, the crown princess of Germany, learned of the plans she was predictably opposed to the marriage and reacted in a distinctly over-the-top manner at the idea of having a sister-in-law belonging to the Russian Orthodox church. 'The murder is out', she wrote to her mother.[18] Granville, ever the emollient diplomat, assured the queen that 'A Russian princess would be a more desirable marriage for the Duke of Edinburgh than an English subject, a Catholic Princess, or a daughter of the King (dispossessed) of Hanover.'[19]

The queen though was not only concerned about religion. She had not been given the opportunity to meet the young woman. It was said that Romanov men did not make good husbands. Did their women make good wives?

The Russian royal family was similarly opposed to the marriage. On a personal level, Alexander was loath to see his only surviving daughter, to whom he was devoted, and who was the most eligible bride in Europe, leave Russia to live in a hostile country. His wife, who had never been to Britain, said that (apart from English nurses) she did not care for the British, whose ways were peculiar. Maria Alexandrovna was convinced that her daughter would never be happy there. Marie's brothers also opposed the marriage, reflecting the widespread Anglophobia felt in Russia. (The Mariinsky Theatre in St Petersburg and Marie biscuits are named after her.)

In addition, there were good practical reasons why such a marriage was not in Russian interests. Gorchakov set out the Russian position. It was above all a question of money. The grand duchess possessed a considerable fortune to which her father would add upon her marriage. The British government expected this to accompany the bride to Britain: Russian law stated this must remain in Russia but a concession could be made to allow Marie to have the use of interest on the capital. Then there was the question of the education of children in the case of the grand duchess's predeceasing her husband. Under English law, but not Russian, the father would have the right to decide on their domicile. According to Russian law the duke would not stand to inherit his wife's fortune if she predeceased him, but Alexander was prepared to donate 250,000 roubles in such an eventuality.[20]

With only a few weeks to spare before the wedding, planned to take place in St Petersburg, an agreement was reached between the two governments and the British parliament increased Alfred's £15,000 a year income by £10,000. Marie would receive £6,000 a year if widowed.

In the end the Russian emperor, who himself had to fight to marry the woman of his choice, yielded to his daughter, who was determined to marry Affie, and now gave full rein to his generosity. Above all he showered her with magnificent jewellery that had belonged to Catherine the Great. There were also presents and distinctions for the Duke of Edinburgh, who was made honorary chief of a Guards regiment. The Prince and Princess of Wales travelled to St Petersburg for the wedding and Alexander offered Bertie the colonelcy of a regiment. Victoria decided it could not be accepted as it would mean a departure from precedent and be unpopular in Britain. The prince had already ordered the uniform. Affie's position was different.

Prince Arthur, the Duke of Edinburgh's younger brother, was best man and Affie's elder sister, Vicky, and her husband the German crown prince, despite their misgivings, were also present at the wedding in the splendour of the Winter Palace on 23 January 1874. The Orthodox service performed by the Metropolitan came first, then an Anglican ceremony was conducted by Dean Stanley, as stipulated by Queen Victoria. The dean's wife, Lady Augusta, was amazed at the mixture of magnificence and squalor of the palace, with avenues of flunkeys and portraits of 'frowning old Tsars'. Dust, dirt and stenches abounded.[21]

After their honeymoon the young couple came to England where the queen met the first (and only) Romanov to marry into the British royal family:

> I took dear Marie in my arms and kissed her warmly several times. I was quite nervous and trembling, so long had I been in expectation of Marie … Dear Marie has a very friendly manner, a pleasant face, beautiful skin and fine bright eyes, and there is something very fresh and attractive about her. She speaks English wonderfully well.[22]

The queen's unease vanished. She approved of her new daughter-in-law, and in April Windsor and Buckingham Palace began preparations to receive the new duchess's father.

Alexander's visit started inauspiciously. His yacht went aground off Dover, ruining the first day's plans. The luncheon was cancelled. The queen, who had taken great care to have the grand staircase lined by the Yeomen of the Guard and lavish floral arrangements, fretted as her family, dressed in their finest clothes, had to wait. The royal kitchens were in rare turmoil. Alexander arrived at 10.30 p.m.:

> I stepped out to greet the Emperor, who was driving with Marie, Bertie and Arthur … Then the Emperor presented his immense suite to me in

> the Waterloo Gallery. I wore my Russian Order ... The Emperor was very kind but is terribly altered, so thin, and his face looks so old, sad, and careworn ... It is just thirty-five years that I took leave of him here, at Windsor, in June![23]

The following evening at a state banquet in St George's Hall the emperor's mood was nostalgic and he reminisced about the people he had met in England in 1839 and his father's visit in 1844. When Victoria assured him of her affection for his father, Alexander replied:

> 'Oh! il le savait'... and continued that he did not see any reason why our two countries should not be on the best of terms, and that if he saw any difficulties 'si vous me permettez, je vous écrirai directement,' which I quite acquiesced in ... And I put my hand out across the Emperor and took Marie's, she herself being nearly upset.[24]

Alexander rode in Windsor Great Park, drove with Queen Victoria to Virginia Water and dined with the Prince of Wales in London. The newly widowed ex-French Empress Eugenie was visited at Chislehurst and the French pretender, the Count of Paris, acknowledged at Claridge's Hotel. The same evening the emperor was taken to the Crystal Palace for a choral concert at which he heard 'Home, sweet home' and made his devotions at the Russian chapel in Welbeck Street. The Lord Mayor of London and Corporation entertained Alexander at the Guildhall, and warm words expressed that 'this visit may tend to cement the friendly relations now existing between the two countries'.[25] At a grand review at Aldershot the emperor saluted troops newly returned from the Ashanti War. The press dropped its habitual Russophobia. Alexander was impressed by the vast crowds, kept so effectively in order by unarmed police.

Warmly worded letters followed between the two sovereigns, but even inside the royal families relations deteriorated. Affie treated his wife badly, rapidly returning to his wayward ways and a few years later becoming a solitary alcoholic. The Duchess of Edinburgh was considered haughty; she shocked her mother-in-law by breastfeeding in public the child born in October 1874, detested the English climate, deplored the cooking, and resented the fact that not only the Princess of Wales but Victoria's unmarried daughters took precedence over her.

The marriage of the Duke of Edinburgh and the Grand Duchess Marie provided a fillip to Anglo-Russian relations in 1874, but just as it fell apart, so, much more importantly, did relations between the two countries sour.

1. Catherine the Great, Empress of Russia (1729–96). She became empress in 1762 on overthrowing her husband, Peter III. Catherine was inspired by the ideas of the Enlightenment and under her rule Russia experienced a renaissance of culture and in the sciences. Her expansionist foreign policy in the Russo-Turkish wars saw Russian territory extend to the Black Sea, including annexation of Crimea, and by the Partitions of Poland.

2. *The Allied Sovereigns at Petworth*, 24 June 1814. Relations between the Russian and British royal families were strained, and not as shown in the painting.

3. Alexander I, Emperor of Russia (1777–1825). The grandson of Catherine the Great, Alexander became emperor in 1801 on the assassination of his father, Paul I. He ruled during the Napoleonic wars and was one of the victors in 1815 at the Congress of Vienna. Alexander was the driving force of the congress system that followed.

4. Princess Dorothea Lieven (1785–1857). A charismatic woman, she became an influential figure in international diplomatic, political and social circles. Her husband, Christoph Lieven, was Russian ambassador to Britain 1812–34.

5. Nicholas I, Emperor of Russia (1796–1855). A younger brother of Alexander I, this authoritarian ruled from 1825 to 1855 with the guiding principles of Orthodoxy, Autocracy and Nationality.

6. Count Karl Nesselrode (1780–1862). Foreign minister under Alexander I and Nicholas I.

7. Alexander II, Emperor of Russia (1818–81) (seated). He is shown with Prince Alfred, Duke of Edinburgh (1844–1900) (right standing)—second son of Queen Victoria—who was married to Alexander's only daughter, the Grand Duchess Marie (1855–1920), and the Grand Duke Alexsei of Russia (1850–1908) (left standing) in 1874.

8. Prince Alexander Gorchakov (1798–1883). Foreign minister under Alexander II, Gorchakov was successful in abrogating in 1870 the hated Black Sea clauses of the 1856 Treaty of Paris.

9. Count Peter Shuvalov (1827–89). He became ambassador to Britain in 1874 and played a major role at the 1878 Congress of Berlin. After the assassination of Alexander II in 1881, Shuvalov was appointed minister of the interior and was responsible for the repressive 1882 May Laws.

10. Cartoon, published in *Punch*, 30 November 1878, commenting on the predicament of Sher Ali, Emir of Afghanistan, who was wooed by Britain and Russia and then sacrificed.

11. General Constantine von Kaufman (1818–82). He became governor general of Turkestan in 1867, a post he held until his death in 1882. Kaufman was a leading figure in the expansion of Russia in Central Asia.

12. Alexander III, Emperor of Russia (1845–94). His reign from 1881 saw the reversal of the reforms of Alexander II, as well as the creation of the Franco-Russian Alliance, 1894.

13. Prince Alexander of Battenberg (1857–93). The son of Prince Alexander of Hesse and by Rhine, he became Prince of Bulgaria in 1879 following the Congress of Berlin. Alexander, a favourite of Queen Victoria and despised by Alexander III, abdicated in 1886 and died aged 36 in 1893. His brothers Louis and Henry married into the British royal family.

14. Nicholas Giers (1820–95). Foreign minister under Alexander III, Giers, a man of peace, was internationally respected.

Spotkanie ekspedycji B. Grąbczewskiego z angielską ekspedycją kapitana Younghusbanda w pustyni Raskemu, w listopadzie 1889 r., gdzie znaleźli się razem przedstawiciele 21 narodów (str. 127).

1. Kap. B. Grąbczewski, Polak, 2. kap. Younghusband, Anglik, 3. preparator Conrad, Niemiec, 4. 6 kozaków — Rosjanie, 5. Kozak Matwiejew, Mordwin, znający język mongolski, 6. Tadżycy, 7. Sartowie, 8. Kirgizi, 9. Kandżuci, 10. Wachańczycy, 11. Żołnierze armji angielskiej z indyjskiego plemienia Gurków, 12. Kaszmirczycy, 13. Baltistańczycy, 14. Tybetańczycy, 15. Hindusi, 16. Mongołowie, 17. Kirgizi z Sarykji, 18. Kirgizi tybetańscy, 19. Kaszgarczycy, 20. Toglicy Pachpu, 21. Sarykoltowie

15. The meeting of Francis Younghusband and Bronislav Grombtchevsky in 1889. The two men representing rival powers met in the Pamirs and dined together. One of the iconic encounters of the Great Game.

16. Count Vladimir Lamsdorff (1845–1907). Foreign minister under Nicholas II 1900–06, the reclusive minister gradually lost influence to a clique of the emperor's friends.

17. Baron George de Staal (1822–1907). A Russian diplomat and ambassador to Britain 1884–1902, Staal was a staunch advocate of Russia's improving relations with Britain.

18. Count Sergei Witte (1849–1915). The foremost Russian statesman of the late nineteenth and early twentieth centuries. Witte was the force behind the Trans-Siberian Railway and the industrialization of Russia.

19. Count Alexander Benckendorff (1849–1917). Ambassador in London from 1903 until his death in 1917, he played a major role in the rapprochement between Britain and Russia that led to the Anglo-Russian Convention, 1907.

20. Count Alexander Isvolsky (1856–1919) (centre). Russian diplomat and *protégé* of the Dowager Empress Maria Feodorovna, Isvolsky was foreign minister 1906–10 and a major player in the negotiation of the Anglo-Russian Convention, 1907.

19

WAR IN THE NEAR EAST

After two decades of relative calm in the Balkans following the Crimean War, a crisis erupted in 1875. The Orthodox Christian Slavs in the Ottoman provinces of Bosnia and Herzegovina rose against their masters. For generations these peoples had suffered the misgovernment and economic difficulties that afflicted the whole Ottoman empire, but in July 1875 increasing taxation and a year of bad harvests provoked a widespread revolt. The severity of the Ottoman repression of the insurrection aroused the strong sympathy of neighbouring Slav Serbia (*de facto* independent of the Ottoman empire from 1835) and Montenegro (semi-autonomous under Prince Nicholas). It was a tinderbox.

The Serbian ruler, Prince Milan, confronted with popular clamour, feared for his throne if he proffered no help. By October frequent clashes were occurring between the Serbian army and the Turkish forces assembled across the frontier to suppress the revolt. However, the most important result of the rebellion was the response that it aroused in Russia, and the divergence between her and the other great powers which soon became apparent.

The foreign policy of Alexander II and the Russian foreign ministry was increasingly under attack by many nationalist groups and individuals, but the place of prominence was occupied by the Panslavs. Although this term was used to designate men and women of widely varying beliefs, the Panslavs all reacted strongly against the relatively passive role that Russia had played in Europe since 1856. They called for the resumption of an active policy in which Russia would exploit her position as the greatest of the Slav nations. In the reign of Nicholas I, Slavophil ideas claimed that the westernization taking place in Russia was antagonistic to the fundamentals of Russian life. But Slavophilism had remained an intellectual, cultural and philosophical movement without political aspirations and had taken little interest in the Slav world outside Russia.[1]

The goal of the Panslavs of the 1870s was very different. In addition to Russian leadership of the Slavic peoples, their aim was the liberation of such people from foreign, that is, Habsburg and Turkish, rule. In 1858 the Moscow Slavic Benevolent Society was founded with the clear aim to assist the Christian southern Slavs of the Ottoman empire in freeing themselves from Muslim rule. This organization, in which Mikhail Pogodin, professor of history at Moscow University, was the ideological moving spirit, brought to Russia students from the Balkans, chiefly from Bulgaria, and carried on activities of a publicist and educational nature. Branches were later opened in St Petersburg and Kyiv and the Slavic Ethnographic Exhibition in Moscow in 1867 attracted widespread attention. The movement was also supported by influential individuals in the Russian court, the emperor's youngest brother the Grand Duke Mikhail, the heir apparent the tsarevich Alexander, and the Empress Maria Alexandrovna. It was only to be expected that Panslavs were to be found in the upper echelons of the military, including the colourful hero Mikhail Cherniaev of Tashkent fame.

Nevertheless, it was above all through the talented writers who embraced Panslavism that the movement spread beyond the confines of the capital and Moscow and won widespread support among the population. Of the two who commanded the widest public attention, Rostislav Fadeev, a retired soldier and author of *Opinion on the Eastern Question*, published in 1869, argued that the eternal enmity of the Slav and Teuton meant that the road to Constantinople lay through Vienna. Nikolai Danilevsky, in his *Russia and Europe* in the same year, called for a great Slav federation with Constantinople as the capital. Although comment on internal matters was censored in Russia, that on foreign affairs possessed a degree of freedom, and two of Russia's foremost journalists, Igor Aksakov and Mikhail Katkov, were redoubtable Panslavist publicists. Such was the climate in Russia in 1875 in which Alexander II had to confront the Balkan risings.

The Russian emperor warned the Serbian government against military intervention on behalf of the rebels. Gorchakov naturally was in agreement, but backing also came from Dmitri Miliutin at the war ministry, Mikhail von Reutern at the finance ministry and the key ambassadors in Vienna and London. Panslavism was unacceptable to Alexander, not only because of its disturbing effect on international relations, but also its revolutionary implications. It would entail a probably republican federation including autonomous units both in Poland and Ukraine. As Gorchakov sensibly wrote, it was difficult to believe in a sincere sympathy of the non-Russian Slav races for autocratic Russia. Against them was ranged the brilliant, headstrong and unscrupulous Nicholas Ignatiev, ambassador in Constantinople since 1864, who believed that Russia should follow a policy towards the Porte independent of the other powers. He disliked Austria-Hungary, Britain even more. His aim was to see the collapse of the Ottoman empire and insurrections among the Balkan Slavs were a step in that direction.

British ultra-sensitivity to any suspicion that Russia was meddling in the Ottoman empire was long-standing, and obviously Alexander II was well aware of this. Throughout 1875 he strove to assure the British government of his desire for good relations between the two countries. The new problem was that Benjamin Disraeli had replaced the conciliatory William Gladstone as prime minister following the general election of 1874 and the Conservative defeat of the Liberals. Disraeli, now at the top of what he called 'the greasy pole', was determined to pursue a vigorous and assertive foreign policy.

Britain was a world power, and within a year of assuming office the flamboyant prime minister had, with two dramatic gestures, set the tone of the new administration. He began by purchasing the khedive of Egypt's 44 per cent holding in the shares of the Suez Canal, whose importance to the route to India Britain had only belatedly recognized. Disraeli gave the cabinet little chance to object and with speed and secrecy raised an advance of £4 million from Rothschilds. This delighted the queen and was evidence to Russia of the increased vigilance of the Conservative government as regards India.[2] It was followed up by the Royal Titles Bill, according to which the queen was henceforth to become Empress of India. Proposals to adopt the imperial title had been in the air since the Indian Rebellion, but with the advance of Russia in Central Asia in the early 1870s, a counterblast to the perceived threat of a Russian invasion, or subversion in India, would reaffirm British power and determination. Alexander II was duly irritated. His contempt for Queen Victoria, whom he saw as an upstart monarch trying to rival himself, a long-standing emperor, was confirmed. (The fact that his uncle, Wilhelm I, had previously been king of Prussia and then emperor, kaiser, after 1871 was overlooked.) Peter Shuvalov mocked the queen's now signing herself 'VRI'. He even claimed royal linen was being changed to incorporate her upgraded status.

Disraeli believed that Britain had to reverse the decline, as he saw it, of British prestige in previous years under a Liberal government. Britain did not possess an army strong enough to combat the continental powers in war, but the prime minister was not prepared to see these states—essentially the *Driekaiserbund*—call the tune. Things did not begin well. In the 'War in Sight' crisis of May 1875, France appealed to Britain and Russia for support in the face of Bismarck's apparent threat of a preventive war against her, and it seemed to provide the prime minister with the chance to revive Britain's role on the continent. But Disraeli failed to act. It was Gorchakov, in what was to be his last personal triumph, who was able to defuse the crisis by impressing on Germany how much she still needed Russia's friendship.

Nevertheless, the real danger to European peace arose from events in the Balkans. With supreme confidence Disraeli wrote in November 1875: 'I really believe "the Eastern Question", that has haunted Europe for a century and wh. I thought the Crimean War had adjourned for half another, will fall to my lot to encounter—dare I say to settle?'[3]

Austria-Hungary (as it was after 1867), the Central European empire with aims to expand southwards into Bosnia and Herzegovina after its exclusion from Germany, could not stand by and watch the unrest on her southern borders. On 30 December 1875 the Austro-Hungarian foreign minister, Count Julius Andrassy, took the initiative in concert with the Russian and German ambassadors in Vienna. In a Note addressed to the powers he outlined the minimum reforms that should be demanded of the Porte and acted upon by all the powers. Lord Derby, the moderate, imperturbable foreign secretary, advised accepting the Note. Disraeli on the other hand was reluctant to be seen to be following the lead of the northern courts and disliked the actual proposals. In the end he had to give way as the Turks asked Britain to support the Note. Given how moderate the demands were this was hardly surprising.

The leaders of the uprisings in 1875 looked to Serbia and Russia for support. Egged on by Ignatiev, Serbian nationalists called upon the government in Belgrade to dispatch troops to defend the Christians in Bosnia and Herzegovina and by April 1876 the war party there had the upper hand. The official Russian position was maintained but nothing could be done to contain the national surge of sympathy for the Christian Slavs. The Slavic Benevolent Society collected funds throughout Russia and volunteers streamed into Serbia to aid in the liberation of fellow Slavs. In May the redoubtable Cherniaev arrived, without an official Russian blessing, to take command of the Serbian armies. The Russian empress, Maria Alexandrovna, paid for special hospital trains to be sent to the Balkans. Russian governors general disregarded the ministerial ban on organizing Balkan appeals and collected medical supplies, uniforms and boots for the volunteers. Some joined the Serbian army for personal reasons. The mother of Count Alexei Kirillovich Vronsky in Leo Tolstoy's *Anna Karenina* tells a friend that she is grateful for the war as it will take her son's mind away from the suicide of Anna Karenina.

That month the northern courts decided to address another note of protest and exhortation to the sultan, plus calling for a two-month armistice in hostilities against the Serbs, but this time including the implied threat of coercion that would follow if the Turks did not comply. Britain, France and Italy were invited to sign the Berlin Memorandum. The latter two were prepared to do so but Britain refused. As there had been no prior consultation, Disraeli's rejection of the Memorandum was understandable. Even so, the queen was alarmed that the Turks would interpret the British position as freeing them to continue as before. Her secretary wrote to Derby: 'The disaffected Christians who are beginning to hate the English as their enemies naturally turn for assistance to Russia ... We have no intention of making the state of the Ottoman Empire a cause for quarrel with Russia.'[4]

However, the prime minister was clear in his mind that, although Russia was not behind the Balkan uprisings, she above all stood to gain from successful Slav nationalism. The long-standing British policy of sending out a signal of support for Turkey was followed. Warships were dispatched to Besika Bay, just outside the Dardanelles, ostensibly as a result of the revolution at the Turkish court and the murder of the sultan, but which the Turks inevitably interpreted as a sign of British support.

Disraeli was inherently suspicious of Russia. What better way though to find out about the Russian position in June 1876 than by entering into discussion with the Russians? It is also possible that the prime minister was not being Machiavellian but felt that Britain was isolated in the new Eastern Crisis. For whatever reason, Disraeli delivered a speech on 9 June that was surprisingly conciliatory towards Russia. That same evening at a dinner given by Baron Rothschild the prime minister began a conversation with Count Peter Shuvalov, a fellow guest: 'Neither I nor my Government distrust a Great Power which is governed by wise men and on conservative principles.'[5] He was sure that Russia 'does not wish to precipitate matters and is waiting for the nature of things to let Turkey disappear from the map of Europe'.[6]

Shuvalov, exceptionally for an ambassador, communicated directly with Alexander II and related *in extenso* his conversations with the prime minister and foreign secretary. Disraeli was frank in admitting that he had no faith in the Ottoman empire's carrying out effective reforms. The Serbs and the Montenegrins might as well go to war against Turkey:

> We think blood-letting to be necessary and will consult together. If the Christians get the upper hand, we shall only have to register accomplished facts: if Turkey crushes the Christians and the repression becomes tyrannous, it will be the turn of all the Great Powers to interpose in the name of humanity.[7]

The foreign secretary, on the other hand, tried to put over a less brutal view of the situation in the Balkans and outlined various proposals for granting autonomy to the Christian states. However, Alexander II's numerous annotations to Shuvalov's dispatches show him highly sceptical of the British government's sincerity in wanting to come to any understanding. When the ambassador, who was far more inclined to believe the men with whom he had good personal relations in London, reported that on 24 June, 'English agents are claiming that we are exciting Serbia and Montenegro to go to war and that our Consulates are the headquarters', the emperor ironically annotated: 'What can one do with such people?'[8] A few days later his exasperated reaction to what he saw as yet more equivocation by Derby was: 'All that proves to me once again the duplicity [*sic*] of the English Cabinet!'[9]

The Russian emperor was not only kept well informed about the British position through his ambassador's official discussions. Shuvalov had also become a close friend of Lady Derby, wife of the foreign secretary. The rumour in London society was that they were having an affair. Mary Derby was a highly intelligent woman with an all-consuming interest in politics; Shuvalov, with a reputation as a successful ladies' man, cultivated his relationship with this highly placed woman. (She was formerly stepmother to the Marquess of Salisbury, now secretary of state for India.) It was well known that her husband confided in her what had taken place at cabinet meetings. The ambassador made frequent references in his communications home to 'a sure source' or 'a confidential route' which his master knew to be Lady Derby. In November 1876, for example, he wrote a long letter to the foreign secretary's wife in which he insisted that 'we do not want Constantinople'.[10] He sent a copy of the letter which began, 'some more words dear Lady Derby following our interesting conversation of this evening', to St Petersburg. Alexander II noted: 'very good'. That same month Lady Derby asked Shuvalov what he thought of a recent speech of Disraeli, 'knowing that it could not be good, but she wished to know how bad it was'. The ambassador reported that he replied that if Britain wanted war, then so do we. Alexander noted: 'Well replied.'[11] According to Shuvalov, Disraeli and Derby were 'haunted by the ghost' of the spurious Testament of Peter the Great.[12]

Increasingly the British government had become aware that the Russians knew what had been discussed at cabinet meetings. Lady Derby was alleged to be the source. She was accused of treachery as a result of having an affair with the Russian. No proof of this relationship exists. Neither is the case against Lady Derby as the source of the cabinet leaks proven. Given that the Russians deciphered British telegrams to and from St Petersburg, this provided them with a reliable source of insider information without needing recourse to the foreign secretary's wife.

The desultory talks between Britain and Russia had come to an inevitable end in late June when Serbia declared war on Turkey. Then, the following month, sensational news arrived in London, where so far public opinion had been largely uninterested in events in the Balkans, transforming the situation. The Liberal *Daily News* published a terrifying account of barbarities committed by Turkish irregular troops, the Bashi-Bazouks, upon the Bulgarian peasantry as reprisals for a widespread revolt that had broken out in the spring. It was alleged that 25,000 men, women and children had been slaughtered and there were grisly details of accompanying outrages. The ultra-Turcophile British ambassador in Constantinople, Sir Henry Elliot, protested to the Porte about the use of irregular troops but he toned down some reports from consuls on the spot and suppressed others. In fact, during the early days of the rising in Bulgaria, the rebels had massacred Muslims, but this was not reported at the time, and the figure for the dead was 12,000 and not 25,000. Even so, it was the perception at the time that determined events.

So far the Liberal opposition in parliament had been muted in its criticism of the government's dealing with the Eastern Question, but in September Gladstone, officially in retirement, somewhat belatedly intervened—for already in August the non-party Eastern Question Association had organized a meeting in Hyde Park calling for help for the insurgent Slavs. He published his famous pamphlet, *Bulgarian Horrors and the Question of the East*.[13] It sold 40,000 copies in the first week, 200,000 within a month, and became one of the most feted examples of nineteenth-century polemics. Gladstone's phraseology encapsulated the high moral values of the Victorian age. He had only a superficial grasp of Balkan terminology but understood the effect of fulminating against the Bashi-Bazouks, their Zaptiehs and their Mudirs. He castigated the Turks who had indulged in 'abominable and bestial lusts' and enacted scenes 'at which Hell itself might blush ... Let the Turks now carry away their abuses in the only possible manner, namely by carrying off themselves ... and their Pashas, one and all, bag and baggage.'[14]

At a public meeting a few days later he called for the Russians to drive the Turks out of Bulgaria: 'I, for one, for the purposes of justice, am ready as an individual to give the right hand of friendship to Russia when her objects are just and righteous, and to say, in the name of God, "Go on and prosper!"'[15] However, there was a widely held view in political circles that the former prime minister was willing to surrender the hard-won gains of the Crimean War and that he was providing the Russian emperor with a pretext for war against Turkey.

Disraeli, from the summer of 1876 the Earl of Beaconsfield, could no longer insist that the reports of atrocities were 'coffee house babble' and that brutality was endemic on both sides in the Eastern Question. He was understandably furious with Gladstone, whom he detested and saw as an ambitious hypocrite: 'The document is passionate and not strong; vindictive and ill-written ... Indeed in that respect, of all the Bulgarian horrors, perhaps the greatest.'[16] The Prince of Wales deplored 'the present agitation over the so-called Bulgarian atrocities' which, he was convinced, merely emboldened Russia to increase her demands on the sultan.[17] Shuvalov believed that the heir to the throne was the most hostile to Russia: 'He encourages the belligerent aspirations of the prime minister.' Alexander II noted, 'I fear he is becoming mad.'[18] The Russian emperor approved his ambassador's decision to avoid gatherings where he was likely to meet the Prince of Wales. Unsurprisingly, in the royal family the Duke of Edinburgh, Alexander II's son-in-law, and his wife Marie sympathized with Russia. The queen sent a stern warning to her second son not to meddle in politics. This was somewhat disingenuous, considering how involved she was herself. The Princess of Wales, sister-in-law of the tsarevich, took the opposite stance from that of her husband.

While Gladstone and Disraeli indulged in verbal warfare, the war in the Balkans continued. Gorchakov and Andrassy had come to an agreement in July not to intervene in the war, and to cooperate over the inevitable changes once it was over. The aged Russian chancellor, whose grasp of Balkan geography and Turkish military strength in the region had never been great, assumed that the Serbs would be victorious. When it became clear that the Serbs and the Montenegrins would be defeated, he could not avoid the pressures of Panslav agitation in Russia for support of Russia's co-religionists.

Thus, although Russia was not a participant in the war, Panslav feelings in the country after the Serb defeat could not be ignored. Ignatiev, as ever, was pressing for a declaration of war on Turkey. However, the powerful ministers Dmitri Miliutin and Mikhail von Reutern still argued that Russia was unprepared for war and could not afford one. Even the chief of staff, General Obruchev, was for peace. Nevertheless, Russia could not sit back and accept Turkey's victory over the Serbian Slavs. Alexander issued an ultimatum to the Turks on 31 October to accept an armistice of six weeks followed by negotiations. The Turks asked for six months. Under pressure from Beaconsfield the Porte agreed to an armistice under the Russian terms followed by a conference of the six powers who had signed the 1856 Paris treaty.

In what seemed at the time, even to Gladstone, an inspired choice, and has met with the approval of most historians since, the Marquess of Salisbury, secretary of state for India, was invited by Beaconsfield to represent Britain at the conference. Robert Gascoyne-Cecil was no Turcophile and, as a High Anglican, he sympathized with the Christians in the Balkans. At the same time, with his ministerial responsibility for India, Salisbury was only too aware of the Russian threat posed by expansion in Central Asia.[19] He asked for precise instructions as to how far the Turks could be coerced and was told to demand administrative autonomy for the insurgent provinces, but not to threaten that Britain would allow Russia to occupy Bulgaria if this failed. Salisbury was unenthusiastic about his nomination—'seasickness, much French and failure—this futile mission of mine'.[20]

After a whistle-stop tour of European capitals, Salisbury, his wife, two of his children, and staff arrived in Constantinople in early December 1876, where the first person he met was Ignatiev. The Englishman had been warned about the Russian ambassador's reputation as a consummate liar and schemer, and they were the representatives of two countries with opposing views on the Balkans. Nevertheless, the two plenipotentiaries struck up an immediate rapport. The European quarter of Constantinople, Pera, was infamous for brigand attacks, but the count and the marquess strolled its streets unaccompanied, arm-in-arm. It was only to be expected that the British ambassador, Sir Henry Elliot, and his wife felt sidelined by the arrival of the senior cabinet member who had usurped the ambassador's place as British representative at the Porte. Worse, not only did the Salisburys find the Elliots 'stiff, extra proper, not over good-looking', but they also enjoyed the company of the young, attractive Countess Ignatieva as well as her clever, charming husband.[21] More importantly though, Salisbury failed in his attempt to have Elliot recalled. To the prime minister this would have looked like caving in to Russian pressure.

The British plenipotentiary won a major concession from Russia in an agreement whereby Bulgaria would be split into two provinces. When Salisbury noticed that a frontier agreed on with Ignatiev at a previous meeting had mysteriously moved overnight, he challenged his Russian colleague. The Russian ambassador replied good-naturedly that the marquess was quick-witted. Ignatiev was a man with whom Salisbury could do business. This was seen differently in London. The prime minister complained to Derby about Salisbury: 'He is more Russian than Ignatieff.'[22]

On the major question before the conference, the demand for reforms in its Balkan states, the Porte refused to comply. The Constantinople Conference dragged on into January 1877 with Salisbury becoming more and more convinced that Britain should not spill blood shoring up this ramshackle empire. It was on its last legs and incapable of carrying out reforms, even if it accepted to do so. In addition, he was sure that there were other means of securing the road to India. Inevitably, in late January 1877 Turkey refused the powers' final watered-down terms, confident in the belief that Russia could not defeat her if war broke out. In such an eventuality—when push came to shove—the Porte believed that Britain would come to her aid.

The failure of the Constantinople Conference caused 'general chaos' in St Petersburg according to Baron Alexander Jomini, senior counsellor at the ministry of foreign affairs, while in Constantinople Ignatiev railed against the 'confusion and incompetence' at home.[23] The usual arguments from the finance ministry that the country could not afford a war were advanced, while at the same time the up-and-coming deputy to the chancellor at the ministry of foreign affairs, Nicholas Giers, believed that circumstances would eventually force Russia into a war with Turkey. Gorchakov, as ever, remained anxious to avoid a war. A cynical diplomat wrote:

> They cry from the official housetops their complete military powerlessness, their administrative disorder. What is most comical of all, the

> Chancellor does not worry in the least about the Turks or the Bulgars or reforms for the Christians. All his attention is concentrated on the successful rise of General Ignatiev, whom he wishes at any price to keep reined in.[24]

This was unfair. For while Gorchakov was sincere in his protestations of being determined to avoid war, the chancellor was devoting his energies to taking steps to assure Russia's position in the event that hostilities could not be avoided. He had to know what would be the attitude of the Habsburg monarchy should Russia feel obliged to act. Already in mid-January 1877 he was instrumental in agreeing a military convention with Austria-Hungary, which provided for Austria to observe benevolent neutrality in case of a Russo-Turkish war. In return she was to be allowed to occupy Bosnia and Herzogovina at a time of her own choosing. Russia's hand was now greatly strengthened. Any chance of Britain's coming to an agreement with Austria that could stymie Russian action had been scuppered.

Shuvalov continued to protest his country's peaceful intentions but the British government was not persuaded. 'I doubt if either we or Shouvaloff have now any hold over events—the fatal resolution has been taken at St Petersburg', Salisbury believed.[25] He was correct. And there could be no stronger indication of Russian plans for independent action against Turkey, even if minimal reforms were undertaken, than sending the arch-hawk Ignatiev on a special mission to the capitals of Europe in February 1877. After Vienna, Berlin and Paris the emissary intended to visit London, ostensibly to see an oculist. Shuvalov at once warned that the effect of Ignatiev's visiting London would have the same disastrous effect as sending Elliot to St Petersburg. Gorchakov, though, argued that through a man possessing an unrivalled knowledge of the Turkish situation, a full explanation of Russian aims would reassure the British government. Turkey was to demobilize. There was no mention of Russia, with her 500,000 men now under arms doing similarly.

Derby and Salisbury urged a postponement of the visit. Shuvalov, who detested Ignatiev for obvious policy reasons, but also ones of personal rivalry in the ministry of foreign affairs, went further and took the boat to Paris in an effort to persuade his colleague that a visit to London was inopportune. But Ignatiev was backed by the emperor and duly arrived in London on 17 March.

Noblesse oblige, Salisbury, to Beaconsfield's dismay, invited Ignatiev to stay at his home, Hatfield House. Here the Russian made a terrible impression, living up to all the British preconceptions of him as a dishonest intriguer by trying to persuade members of the opposition invited to dinner to sabotage government policy. The prime minister, an increasingly sick man suffering from gout, asthma and bronchitis, was none the less game to indulge in social cold war and gave a banquet for the Ignatievs, to which the Prince of Wales invited himself. Beaconsfield's account dwelt on diamonds rather than diplomacy. Madame Ignatieva's 'paled' compared with those of Lady Londonderry who, not to be outdone by Russian bling, staggered under the weight of her family jewels.[26] At an after-dinner concert, Gladstone was introduced to the Russian envoy, who held forth with such fluency that the usually loquacious former prime minister could not get a word in.

Despite all the ill-feeling he generated and ingrained suspicion of him in Britain, Ignatiev's mission did achieve its aim. After much wrangling in cabinet, with the prime minister arguing that Russia should be obliged to demobilize before any agreement was signed, largely at Salisbury's insistence it was decided to accept a modified version of the Russian proposals, or what came to be called the London Protocol. The document was signed on 31 March on behalf of the six powers. It was a conciliatory and basically toothless document.

It omitted the requirement for Turkey to carry out the specific reforms agreed as necessary by the powers at the Constantinople Conference. In its place the Porte was invited to put into effect as rapidly as possible the reforms; what these constituted was not stated. It was to demobilize, except for such troops as were indispensable for the maintenance of internal order—a massive loophole. The powers affirmed their common interest in the amelioration of the lot of Christians in the Ottoman empire. If this condition was not met, the powers reserved the right of deliberating in common as to what they might do.

The Turks were intransigent. In addition they were aware that Sir Henry Elliot had finally been persuaded to be transferred from Constantinople. But the choice in early April 1877 of Henry Layard, well known as an archaeologist for his discovery of Nineveh and equally as an ardent Turcophile, led the Turks to feel that they could, as ever, rely on British support in the last resort, while the Russians were correspondingly confirmed in their belief of British duplicity. The nomination effectively neutralized the British signature of the London Protocol. On 9 April the Porte formally rejected the Protocol.

There is not much doubt also that the Turks calculated that Russia at the last moment would hesitate and draw back from war. The country's financial difficulties were common knowledge and the British government believed that this could serve to restrain Russia from embarking on a war.

But in March Russia was already in the grip of war fever, and the Turkish rejection of the Protocol stiffened the feeling that national pride was at stake. Gorchakov told the German ambassador that the Turks had gone mad and warned the British ambassador, Lord Augustus Loftus, that if it came to war, the main responsibility would rest with Britain. Beaconsfield held his ambassador in contempt, referring to him as 'Pomposo'. For some years Loftus had not been privy to the confidences of those at the highest level in St Petersburg and his dispatches were ignored in London. However, Loftus had asked in early 1876 to be moved to a less demanding post. If Britain had sought to understand Russian public opinion and be aware of the strength of nationalist fervour in the country, then there had been plenty of time to place an ambassador in St Petersburg who would have been able to report accurately and be listened to at home. In London, Shuvalov was ably putting forward the Russian view to the British government, the opposition and the press.

In Russia the Panslavic press in St Petersburg and Moscow was relentlessly calling for intervention, reflecting a view widely held by the intelligentsia and all-important bureaucracy that the status of Russia as a great power was at stake. Alexander II was lured into war.

At the beginning of April he reluctantly responded to the collapse of negotiations by joining the army in Bessarabia, and three weeks later declared war on Turkey to great public enthusiasm. His eldest son Alexander, his brothers the grand dukes Nicholas and Mikhail, and Ignatiev, plus notoriously nationalist Panslav officers joined him. The emperor himself declared that he wished to serve as a nurse. This was clearly ridiculous, but an indication of his mental state. Gorchakov, too feeble for camp life, remained in Bucharest, largely excluded from discussion on the conduct of the war. The campaign was confidently expected to be a swift victory that would finally erase the ignominy of the Crimean War. It began well, with the Russian army crossing the Danube at the end of June. The British fleet was again ordered to Besika Bay, exacerbating the already acute tension existing between Britain and Russia.

To this state of affairs between the two governments was added an incident that caused the already highly excitable queen to become even more hostile to Russia. Colonel the Hon. Frederick Wellesley, son-in-law of Beaconsfield's *bête noire* Lord Augustus Loftus and great-nephew of the first Duke of Wellington, had been military attaché in St Petersburg since

1871, living a life mainly of society parties and bear hunts, while at the same time his dispatches contained the long-standing British gripes about the high cost of living and dishonesty of Russian servants. Wellesley had close relations with the royal family and had only become a full colonel at the beginning of 1877; this new rank combined with being nominated an *aide-de-camp* to the queen. He had for some time been highly rated by the queen and Beaconsfield, who both read his dispatches. What they did not know was that the Russians were deciphering these documents and made sure the colonel was provided with doctored, as highly favourable as possible views of the Russian military. Even so, the attaché sent home disparaging reports about the Russian army. On one Alexander wrote, 'I compliment him as he is always well-informed.'[27] Wellesley found himself ostracized by the imperial family and wrongly blamed the leaks on the French embassy.

Hence, Wellesley was not invited to join Russian army headquarters, the French and German attachés being already there. Alexander wrote on Loftus's deciphered dispatch to Derby proposing that the attaché should accompany the emperor: 'I will not accept him.'[28] However, although Alexander relented, his brother, the irascible Grand Duke Nicholas, the commander-in-chief, who was aware that the attaché had made critical comments about the Russian mobilization, confronted Wellesley. He angrily informed him that the only reason his presence was tolerated was because of express orders from the emperor himself: '"I warn you … that I shall have you strictly watched, and that if you say or do or write anything of which I do not approve, I will turn you out of my army", and as he uttered these words the Grand Duke snapped his fingers in the air.'[29]

This incident was reported home and Queen Victoria was furious. Derby called in Shuvalov and told him:

> I need not say that the Queen has been deeply hurt at the manner in which one of her officers, proceeding by the Emperor's own person, on behalf of her Government … has been treated. He should receive the treatment naturally to be accorded to an officer and a gentleman in the service of a friendly power.[30]

The upshot was profuse apologies from the ambassador, who admitted that the grand duke had been too severe but was only giving 'paternal' advice to the young colonel. Shuvalov was irritated by such an unimportant matter being attributed political significance in London at such a sensitive time.

Now that he was posted to Alexander's headquarters, Wellesley, with the queen's personal blessing, took full advantage of this elevation to volunteer as an unofficial channel of communication between the Russian emperor and Beaconsfield, bypassing Derby, who was strenuously working to avoid war with Russia. This was, to say the least, unorthodox diplomacy. Wellesley was sent back to the emperor's headquarters with a secret communication to warn Alexander not to open a second front. That would mean war with Britain. The Russian emperor was assured that the British cabinet was united in its determination. This was a ridiculous assertion, as Alexander knew only too well from Shuvalov's dispatches and decrypts of British ones that the cabinet was riven on the subject. But Alexander was left in no doubt that the queen and Beaconsfield would prevail if he failed to heed the warning not to take Constantinople. The mission of a junior officer convinced Alexander that the course to follow was to press forward as quickly as possible and thus avoid the need for a second campaign.

Nevertheless, after its success in June, the Russian army by August found its route forward blocked at the fortified town of Plevna. The Ottoman defenders under Osman Pasha repulsed three Russian attacks, the assailants suffering heavy casualties. The Grand Duke Nicholas, clearly incompetent in both strategy and tactics, wanted to withdraw across the Danube, but Alexander and Miliutin forbade him. The tsarevich, commanding two corps, was ordered to defend the river Lom and proved no better than his uncle: 'The truth is that the Tsarevitch … indulged in unaccountable movements and wild manoeuvres … It was certainly much less owing to his brilliant generalship than to the strategical blunders of the Turks that he had kept intact the line of the Lom.'[31] With 300,000 men bogged down, Russian morale was low.

Thus Alexander reluctantly agreed to hand over command to the Hohenzollern Prince Carol of Romania—the Romanians having supplied troops to Russia. The prince's *aide-de-camp* was Prince Alexander of Battenberg, a nephew of the Russian emperor. The twenty-year-old German prince added his criticism of the Russian army. He wrote to his father in St Petersburg of the 'hair-raising incidents' which occurred daily, the 'carelessness of the High Command', the 'universal disorder' and the jealousy between the grand dukes. He ended by saying that it was providential it was the Turks against whom they were fighting, for against any other enemy all would have been lost long ago.[32] There was a sufficient number of journalists observing the campaign for the war to be described as 'the breakfast war' in Britain, where newspaper readers read daily reports of the bloody fighting in the trenches of the southern Balkans.

It was not until November that the tide turned in favour of Russia. On the Transcaucasian front, where the Russian and Turkish armies were also engaged, the stronghold of Kars fell and at the end of the month the heroic Osman Pasha surrendered at Plevna. The road to Constantinople was open. The Russians advanced steadily south and occupied Adrianople in January 1878. The sultan now sued for an armistice which was signed on 19 January. Shuvalov telegraphed on 13 February that the British fleet had been ordered to Constantinople. Alexander noted on it: 'I have ordered my brother to stop the march of our troops both on Constantinople and on Gallipoli.'[33] Russia had clearly intended to take the Ottoman capital.

This ended one war but threatened to cause another. In answer to Russian protests, the British government replied that the fleet was heading for the Ottoman capital to protect British subjects and their property. Alexander indignantly wanted to do the same for his subjects but was persuaded by Gorchakov to make this advance contingent upon a British landing. However, his brother, the earlier defeatist Nicholas, provocatively moved his headquarters to San Stefano, a suburb of Constantinople on the European shore (today Yesilkoy). On 19 February Russian and Ottoman representatives signed the terms of a preliminary peace. The danger of war between Britain and Russia was acute.

On the same day Derby asked the sultan to agree to the occupation of the eastern shores of the Straits by a British army, and Layard was ordered to arrange the secret purchase of four of the ships in the Turkish navy to prevent their seizure by the Russians.[34] Alexander noted on the decrypt of the telegram he received: 'All that is so important that it is imperative that you telegraph my brother [Nicholas] as information that has come our way without divulging the source.'[35] Consternation broke out in the foreign office when the Russian ambassador accused the British government of trying to buy Turkish ironclads. Derby lied: 'I said that no proposition had been made to the Porte to buy vessels except for the three unfinished ships in this country.'[36]

The ambassador in Constantinople replied:

> Your Lordship asks me whether I can suggest how these secret matters became known ... General corruption and treason exist here, mainly attributable to the skilful and unscrupulous organization of Count Ignatiev

> ... The fact that the instructions to me ... for the purchase of ... ships of the Turkish Government became known to the Russian Government admits ... of only two explanations ... either the contents of Your Lordship's telegram were allowed to transpire in London, or Russian agents possess the key to our cypher.[37]

The British government had still not suspected the Russian government of systematic decipherment of telegrams. Alexander angrily reacted to the clear dishonesty of the British government by again threatening to occupy Constantinople.

The British fleet was at Constantinople and the entire population of the country was gripped with patriotic fervour directed against Russia. The term 'jingo' of course dates from this time.

Alexander had taken heed of British determination: Beaconsfield's brinkmanship worked. The Porte accepted Russian occupation of San Stefano and the Russian advance stopped there. A year later Alexander II admitted to the British ambassador, now the Marquess of Dufferin, that Russia could not have held Constantinople, but 'the exigencies of war might perhaps have made it advisable for him to occupy it'.[38]

However, Russia had defeated the Turks and the peace treaty dictated by Ignatiev, signed at San Stefano on 3 March, made this clear. Its provisions, based on the preliminary peace terms of 31 January, represented the fullest practical expression ever given in Russian foreign policy of the Panslav ideal. The political autonomy of Bosnia and Herzegovina was recognized. Serbia and Montenegro were to become independent states and in addition were to receive considerable territorial rewards. An enormous Bulgarian state under Russian protection was to be created. Russia was to receive southern Bessarabia and the important Transcaucasian fortresses of Batum and Kars.

The conditions of the peace of San Stefano aroused strong opposition not only in Britain but in Austria. It violated previous international agreements and both powers firmly rejected the creation of 'Big Bulgaria' which, they believed, would constitute a Russian satellite and dominate in the Balkans. Alexander thus had to face the possibility of another war. Russia had already suffered severely from the unexpected length and difficulty of the war with Turkey, her ever-shaky finances had been desperately strained and she was not on good terms with any of the Balkan states affected by San Stefano.

Talk of an international congress began in February 1878. The emperor was wary. He wrote to his brother Nicholas:

> I confess that I do not altogether trust the Turks' ready acceptance of all our conditions, and see in it a trap prepared by England and, probably, by Austria, both of whom may well have promised to plead on Turkey's behalf at a European conference ... We have accepted the idea conditionally.[39]

Gorchakov was equally hawkish and railed against Beaconsfield who was seeking to deprive Russia 'of every practical advantage and all legitimate gain for the sacrifices of a war which he, more than anyone else, helped to make inevitable'.[40]

Lord Derby, weary after four years of struggling to rein in the wilful Beaconsfield, finally resigned at the end of March 1878. Shuvalov, with whom he had forged an excellent working relationship, and who for his part had also had to contend with aggressive and at times erratic superiors, naturally regretted the foreign secretary's departure and his replacement with the Marquess of Salisbury. The new foreign secretary did not go along with the flamboyant Russophobe style of the prime minister, but he had been secretary of state for India and knew only too well that Russia's expansionist policy in Central Asia reflected an overall challenge to Britain. On 1 April he issued a circular defining the British position as regards San Stefano, insisting that all aspects of the treaty would have to be reconsidered.

For Salisbury understood that, although Russia had been weakened by the war, Britain for her part had lost a great deal of prestige by the obvious divisions within the government and the hesitations of her Near Eastern policy. Beaconsfield's often wild words had so far been conspicuously divorced from deeds. War between Britain and Russia had still looked probable throughout March 1878 and a force of Indian troops was ordered to Malta. Then in April nearly 700 officers and men of the Russian navy were sent to the United States to acquire and man ships that could be used for privateering against British merchantmen in case of war. Despite all this bellicose posturing Alexander II knew that another war was beyond Russia's military and financial strength and he had come around to Miliutin's position that he had to be careful not to provoke one.

The upshot was that Russia was forced to accept the invitation of Bismarck to a congress in Berlin, at which the powers would examine the Treaty of Stefano.

20

THE WAR WON

THE PEACE LOST

In the second half of May 1878 Ignatiev was forced to resign as ambassador to the Porte, his hawkish stance rejected by his masters. It was Shuvalov's conciliatory views that now accorded with those of a resigned Alexander II, and because of Gorchakov's poor health, the Russian foreign ministry lacked vigorous leadership. After a briefing in St Petersburg in early May, Shuvalov was sent back to London to try to arrange peace terms acceptable to the British government.

The protocol of 30 May signed in London laid down in general terms the frontier between the new southern and western frontiers of Bulgaria and provided for dividing the San Stefano Big Bulgaria along the Balkan mountains. The frontier between the two new Bulgarias was not defined. This represented a considerable concession by Russia and Salisbury insisted on acceptance of the agreement, although Beaconsfield and the queen, as might have been expected, did not think enough had been gained. Certainly the 30 May agreement was a good deal less than a complete settlement of all the questions at issue between Britain and Russia and still left scope for violent disagreement between them.

Salisbury however scored one outright diplomatic triumph that month. Taking advantage of the extreme weakness of the Porte, Britain forced upon the Turks the Cyprus Convention which compensated London for the Russian gains in the war. In return for a pledge that Britain would guarantee Turkey's Asiatic territories, the Ottoman empire ceded the strategic Mediterranean island of Cyprus, close to the Suez Canal on the sea route to India. Also, in preparation for the forthcoming congress, Britain came to an agreement with Austria that her delegate would cooperate. The three interlocking bilateral agreements ensured that the major issues of the Congress of Berlin were a foregone conclusion even before it had been formally summoned. And it was thus Britain, not Russia, who held the best cards.

On 13 June 1878 the third great European congress of the century, the most glittering summit since the Congress of Vienna in 1814, opened in Berlin under the presidency of Prince Bismarck, the self-styled 'honest broker', who wanted to push on the work of the congress as fast as possible and to exert strict control over its proceedings.

Beaconsfield and Salisbury were to attend as the British plenipotentiaries. Queen Victoria was opposed to her prime minister's travelling to Berlin because of his age (he was seventy-three) and serious health problems. The Prince of Wales disagreed, insisting that he was 'the only man ... as he would show Russia and the other Powers that we were really in earnest'.[1] Beaconsfield himself was determined that nothing would prevent him from playing the part he had always dreamed of as a principal actor on the European stage. Only he was capable of dealing with Bismarck as an equal. 'He will have interviews with all the chief statesmen, so that there will be no mistake as to the designs, and the determination of this country', reported Beaconsfield.[2]

The prime minister's lack of qualifications for the role he sought to play was clear. It was twenty years since he had been abroad, his knowledge of geography was vague, his interest in it minimal and his memory sometimes failed him. He intended to speak French, the lingua franca of European diplomacy, but was persuaded by Lord Odo Russell, the British ambassador in Berlin, to speak in English whereby his eloquence as 'the greatest living master of English oratory' could be appreciated. The stratagem worked, thus avoiding the embarrassment of having a speech in 'grocer's French' imposed on the multilingual foreign plenipotentiaries.[3] Beaconsfield intended to 'exhibit his full powers' and then leave it to Salisbury to 'complete all the details of which he is consummate master'.[4] The foreign secretary saw his chief's role differently: 'What with deafness, ignorance of French and Bismarck's extraordinary mode of speech, Beaconsfield has the dimmest idea of what is going on, understands everything crossways and imagines a perpetual conspiracy.'[5]

The Russian delegation was headed by Gorchakov, now in his eightieth year, wheelchair-bound, a shrivelled 'little insignificant old man' but determined to end his career in a blaze of diplomatic splendour:[6] 'I don't want to go out like a spluttering lamp, but rather like a falling star.'[7] Vain as ever, he detested his younger and more able colleague Shuvalov and was anxious to acquire kudos for any Russian successes himself, while at the same time saddling his irksome colleague with the odium for any concessions. According to Shuvalov the chancellor still showed 'flashes of dialectic brilliancy, but he was no longer capable of sustained argument or negotiation'.[8]

The other senior plenipotentiaries were younger and in more robust health. Count Andrassy represented Austria-Hungary, determined to maintain the Habsburg empire's interests in the Balkans. The Ottoman Greek, Caratheodory Pasha, was a man in fear both of the sultan and Henry Layard in Constantinople. William Waddington, the French foreign minister, had only a bit part, as did Count Corti of Italy.

As was expected, the hard slog of negotiation fell to Salisbury and Shuvalov but it was Beaconsfield's presence that dominated the proceedings. He had let it be known that he had ordered a special train to be available to take him and the British delegation home should the Russians reject the British demands. He was thus able to talk 'thunder' to Gorchakov, but it was known that Shuvalov, rather than the chancellor, knew what concessions Russia would be able to accept and what her red lines were.

There was much international theatre played out in Berlin during the sessions and much over-eating and smoking to be indulged in after hours. Bismarck was the master of ceremonies but the star performer was Beaconsfield, and the two men found they liked each other. The autocratic chancellor most unusually put himself out to visit Beaconsfield and several times invited the prime minister to dine with his family: 'In a quarter of an hour you knew exactly how you stood with him.'[9]

The prime minister's major victory over Russia came on the first question on the agenda, that of Bulgaria. He set out to intimidate Shuvalov by telling him that the Russian proposal to forbid the sultan to garrison the frontier of southern Bulgaria with Eastern Rumelia (the name given on British insistence to the southern half of the former Big Bulgaria) was unacceptable to the British government. Days passed with no word from St Petersburg, but the prime minister remained confident. Beaconsfield's threat of breaking up the congress was real. An ultimatum had been sent to Russia. Then on the evening of 21 June came news: 'Before I went to bed, I had the satisfaction of knowing that St Petersburg had surrendered.'[10] Bismarck expressed his admiration for Beaconsfield's ability to get what he wanted: 'Der alte Jud, das ist der Mann.'[11]

Austria, who had supported Britain in the struggle over Bulgaria, received her reward in the second phase of the congress when Salisbury proposed that she should receive the mandate to occupy Bosnia and Herzegovina and the Sanjak of Novi-Bazar. Bismarck and Beaconsfield bludgeoned the helpless Turks into submission and the provinces were handed over with a sublime disregard both for Turkish rights or the claims of Slav nationalism. Serbia, Romania and Montenegro were all given formal independence but otherwise the results were deeply disappointing to them. Serbia gained only a triangle of territory to the south-east of her existing frontiers and her disillusionment drove her into a rapprochement with the Habsburg empire. Romania was forced to cede Bessarabia to Russia, which brought the latter back to the Danube, the former receiving in return the marshy non-Romanian territory of Dobrudja.

There remained the claims of Russia to the conquered Turkish Anatolian territories on the Asian side of the Black Sea which had a frontier with Russia. They included Batum on the coast (today Batumi in Georgia) and Kars and Ardahan inland (today both in Turkey). At first Beaconsfield had considered these territories to be a matter of importance to Britain, but, after acquiring Cyprus, he was disposed to compromise. Gorchakov felt strongly on the subject and confronted Beaconsfield, to Salisbury's dismay: 'But Lord Beaconsfield can't negotiate: he has never seen a map of Asia Minor.'[12] Shuvalov for his part alleged that Gorchakov could not indicate even approximately the positions of any of these towns. Hence, it was not surprising that the two septuagenarians found themselves in a muddle over their respective maps of the area. Frederick Wellesley, who was part of the British delegation, opined that both being blind and confused they had in fact 'inadvertently exchanged their most secret maps' prepared for them by their military chiefs.[13] In the end a compromise was reached by which Batum became a free port, preventing Russia from making it a naval base, and a portion of the surrounding territory was restored to the sultan. He for his part promised to institute reforms that would protect Christians in his empire. The reparations that Russia had imposed on Turkey at San Stefano remained, effectively preventing the bankrupt Ottoman empire from being able to finance reforms.

The Congress of Berlin marked the apotheosis of Benjamin Disraeli. He and Salisbury returned home to a tumultuous reception. On his arrival in London the prime minister coined the famous phrase that he had brought 'Peace with Honour' that would be repeated, with less good cause, sixty years later. The jubilant queen offered him the Order of the

Garter, which he accepted on condition that it was given also to Salisbury, but a marquisate or dukedom for himself and a barony or viscounty for his brother and nephew were both declined. The crowning moment came in early August when the two statesmen were presented with an address at the Guildhall. Beaconsfield grandly replied that under the new settlement everyone had benefited and no one was humiliated. Nevertheless, it was 'a great check to the restlessness and military authority of Russia' and a lesson for extremists. The wisdom of the congress had made Russia 'relinquish the greater portion and the wealthiest portion of her conquests'.[14] A year later he told Salisbury that the joint themes of Conservative foreign policy were 'the maintenance of our Empire, and hostility towards Russia'.[15]

For Russia the Congress of Berlin was a bitter blow, despite the fact that she had made gains with the establishment of semi-autonomous Bulgaria, the re-annexation of southern Bessarabia and the acquisitions in Asia Minor. Though exercised independently, the combined efforts of Britain and Germany, it was felt, deprived her of the greater rewards that were her due for the hard-won victory over the Ottoman empire on behalf of the Christian Slavs. Britain and Austria, who had not fought, had made unfair gains. A flood of accusations was levelled in Russia against the country's diplomacy, the major blame for the failure in Berlin being attributed to Gorchakov and Shuvalov:

> The chancellor, a decrepit old man who, with tenacious ambition refuses to give up his position; the other two ... not knowing the East and indifferent to the destiny of Christians under Turkish domination. ... The verbosity of the old chancellor, his boasting, his total ignorance of everything produced ... [a] painful impression.[16]

Even so, it was Shuvalov more than anyone else who became the scapegoat for the Russian failure at Berlin, largely, he suspected, through Gorchakov's briefings against him. Alexander accused the count of being Bismarck's dupe, as it was well known that the two men had become friends. He refused to be convinced that it was only thanks to the German chancellor that the congress had not broken up in war. Shuvalov returned to his post in London in the autumn of 1878 but he had lost all influence in St Petersburg and knowing this, he went on long leave in May 1879 and was never again (except for a brief interlude two years later) to hold office.

But, if the Congress of Berlin destroyed Peter Shuvalov's career, the repercussions were ultimately fatal for Alexander II. Russia was already in 1878 a country of seething popular discontent that was rendered immensely more serious by the national disillusionment with the Treaty of Berlin. The vociferous Slavophiles interpreted it as a betrayal of the Slavic cause. At the same time, it enraged liberals, who angrily noted that the Bulgarian state was to have a constitution, whereas Russia still lacked one. Overall hostile reaction to the Treaty of Berlin breathed new life into the activities of the emerging nihilists, who viewed Russia's diplomatic defeat as an opportunity to open a revolutionary campaign in Russia.

By emancipating the serfs in 1861, followed by the creation of the *zemstvos* (local councils), reform of the law courts and a lessening of press censorship in the mid-1860s Alexander II had destroyed the foundations of the Russian system of government. Condemnation of the administration was possible, hence Russian public opinion had a chance of forming.

At the same time the assassination attempt against Alexander in 1866 had provoked stringent measures by the Third Section under the (then) reactionary Peter Shuvalov that stifled any nascent activity of discontent, but by 1869 there were signs of its revival. Groups of revolutionaries were being formed in many parts of the empire, composed mainly of young intellectuals of the upper and middle classes. Then, in 1873 the Russian government had unwisely ordered all Russians studying at foreign universities to return. Thus further reinforcements were provided for the revolutionary groups.

The term nihilist had first been coined by Ivan Turgenev, no revolutionary himself, in his 1862 novel, *Fathers and Sons*.[17] His protagonist Eugene Bazarov was a young man who rejected the old order and sought to bring about political change in Russia by educating the people, but it rapidly came to denote those who were implacable enemies of the state—the Russian revolutionaries of the 1870s.

The time seemed propitious. The peasants had not received the land they expected after emancipation and many of the lesser nobility were impoverished by their lack of workers. The young revolutionary leaders ordered their followers to 'go to the people' and in 1873–4, thousands of young men and women invaded the countryside dressed as peasants in an attempt to convert these people to their political ideas. These *narodniki* met with little success. The peasants, the real *narodniki*, proved apathetic, even hostile. Shuvalov's police were active in successfully breaking up many of the groups and sending the leaders for trial.

Undeterred by this failure, the revolutionaries attempted a second 'going to the people' in 1876. This time they went as those they hoped the peasants would respect—petty officials, teachers, artisans and shopkeepers—but again with little success. It was obvious that more effective means had to be found of undermining the status quo. Thus there emerged in St Petersburg a highly centralized revolutionary organization, Land and Liberty, *Zemlya i Volya*, that even had its 'disorganizing section' in addition to a political directorate and propaganda network armed with a secret printing press. Such was the body that now began to pit its forces against the emperor and his government.

In December 1876, on the eve of the Turkish war, a small nihilist demonstration had been organized in St Petersburg. It was easily dispersed but many arrests were made and the first mass trial of revolutionaries was staged. Another took place the following autumn, the trial 'of the 193'. As the accused were tried by the new independent courts the sentences were lenient. Alexander could not accept this and a number of those acquitted were exiled.

In January 1878 one of the young radicals, Arkhip Bogoluibov, who had been gaoled, failed to acknowledge with due deference General Feodor Trepov, a high official of the Third Section. For this he was flogged in contravention of the accepted code of Russian behaviour among the educated classes. To avenge this outrage, a young female revolutionary and prison veteran, Vera Zasulich, gained an interview with Trepov. She shot the general point-blank but failed to kill him and made no attempt to escape. The government, certain of the outcome, decided that her case should be tried by jury. She was acquitted to public applause. Nevertheless, the police tried to rearrest her, but she was spirited away and reached Switzerland. (She later came to live in London.) The government in impotent fury decreed that in future such cases would be tried in military courts. It was a declaration of open war against the revolutionaries.

The growing ferment was not confined to the capital. In Odesa the revolutionary ringleader was court-martialled and hanged. A few months later a prominent revolutionary, Sergei Kravchinsky, killed General Nicholas Mezentsev, head of the Third Section, with a sword in broad daylight in a St Petersburg street. Further acts of violence followed in 1879. Prince Dmitri Kropotkin, governor general of Charkov, was killed and again the assassin was able to escape—the connivance of the urban populace in assisting assassins was obvious.

Alexander II was extremely unpopular. Part of the reason was events in the Near East from 1877. Revelations of corruption in the supply services of the Russian armies due to the inefficiency and peculation of the grand dukes Nicholas and Mikhail commanding the forces provoked widespread discontent and disgust. The Russian defeat at the Congress of Berlin had then further increased public hostility to the government. To this was added widespread opposition to the police system. When the government turned to the *zemstvos* for support against the insurgents, the reply was that until the public received greater freedom to express its views, no help was forthcoming.

However, the emperor's personal unpopularity stemmed above all from his relationship with Princess Catherine Dolgoruka. He began an affair with the beautiful eighteen-year-old lady-in-waiting to his wife in 1866 and was infatuated with the young aristocrat. She began secretly visiting the Winter Palace several times a week before being installed in a house on the English Quay.

Within the imperial family there was outrage. The health of the empress was failing and she was only too aware of her husband's infidelity. The tsarevich Alexander abhorred moral laxity and was horrified at seeing his father making a fool of himself. He was soon the bitter enemy of Catherine and her friends, as were the grand dukes (all of whom kept mistresses but not in their palaces) and grand duchesses. Moreover, it was not long before the princess began to exercise a political influence and became the rallying point for a group opposed to the Panslavists and the tsarevich in particular. The previously all-powerful Peter Shuvalov at the Third Section refused to pay court to Catherine Dolgoruka and had unwisely opposed some of her friends in a doubtful railway speculation. (It was for this that he had been suddenly appointed ambassador in London in 1874 against his wishes.) The results of his dismissal were not long in emerging. The efficiency of the police organization deteriorated: this at a time when the government was entering into its mortal combat with the revolutionary movement.

Four years later when the terrorist campaign was in full swing, Alexander, fearful for the safety of Catherine, brought her into the Winter Palace where they lived in semi-isolation, therefore with limited awareness of events around them, the emperor cynical, bitter, disillusioned and close to nervous collapse. This refusal to face the worsening situation inevitably served to exacerbate public contempt for, and hatred of, the emperor. In April 1879, Alexander, while walking alone, was fired on several times outside the Winter Palace. This time the would-be assassin was caught and executed. To many he was seen as a martyr.

The government stepped up its repressive measures against the revolutionaries. Governors general with emergency powers were appointed for the whole of Russia, under whose direction military courts began to operate. Within a few months fifteen revolutionaries were sent to the gallows and the governor general of St Petersburg expressed the well-founded conviction that the number of active revolutionaries was small. It was the calm before the storm.

In fact Land and Liberty was passing through a crisis, with its members profoundly divided between those who advocated terrorist methods and those who preferred the earlier policy of peaceful propaganda. In the summer the schism crystallized. Land and Liberty was dissolved and replaced with two new organizations, the Black Partition, which favoured peaceful methods, and the more important faction, the People's Will, *Narodnaya Volya*, for whom Jacobin-like terrorism was necessary before social revolution. In September its leaders Alexander Mikhailov, Andrei Zhelyabov and Sophia Perovskaya, an aristocrat, created the Central Executive Committee of the People's Will which formally condemned Alexander Romanov to death. From now on every effort was directed to his assassination. The revolutionaries resolved to discard revolvers and daggers as obsolete and uncertain weapons and to turn to dynamite and bombs.[18]

An attempt was made to blow up a train in which Alexander was returning from Crimea in November. The imperial train was ambushed outside Moscow. However, last-minute changes had been made to the emperor's journey and it was a baggage train sent behind the one in which he was travelling that was destroyed. The second attempt took place within the Winter Palace in February 1880 when Prince Alexander of Hesse and his son Alexander of Battenberg were visiting the emperor. The palace was shaken by a violent explosion that wrecked the dining room in which it was expected that the emperor and guests would be eating. But the three Alexanders were running late in their talks; catastrophe for the royal family was avoided. Not for others though. Ten servants and nineteen Finnish Guards were shattered to pieces; many more were seriously injured. The enquiry that followed revealed the most momentous stupidity on the part of the security services and the incredible cunning of the Executive Committee. Structural works had begun in the palace basement in the autumn. A workman with a fake passport was employed who daily brought in small quantities of dynamite and other material in his pockets. His work so impressed the builders that he was made foreman. The man escaped to continue his revolutionary activities in southern Russia.

Nicholas Giers, the effective head of the foreign office, did no more than send a servant to enquire about the explosion at the Winter Palace when he heard it *en route* for a dinner engagement at the French embassy. If Alexander's 'best and most honourable' minister was not concerned for the fate of the emperor then the indifference of the populace to this further terrorist attack was only to be expected.[19] As the German ambassador observed, 'One is tempted to regard as moribund a social body which fails to react to such a shock.'[20]

The British embassy was following closely the dangerous internal state of Russia. Thomas Michell, the locally employed consul fluent in Russian, translated revolutionary publications as they appeared and were sent to London. The *chargé d'affaires*, Francis Plunkett, reported that

> another printed nihilist proclamation has been secretly distributed here and is couched in language more violent than usual. It says that the attempt made on the life of the Emperor on Monday last by order of the Committee failed, either the next or some future attempt will succeed. After much hostile criticism of the Emperor's conduct, it says the only chance for him is that he should abdicate, or hand over his power to popular assemblies. The greatest mystery is now made respecting the movements of the Emperor.[21]

Sympathetic messages had been sent to Alexander from Queen Victoria and the British government each time the emperor's life had been threatened. London was in no doubt that his life was hanging by a thread.

The Russian empress was supported by her children, in particular her daughter, the Duchess of Edinburgh. They were disgusted by Alexander's treatment of his wife, who died in May 1880. He then waited only a month before secretly marrying Catherine, contrary to the custom of the Orthodox church which imposed a year's mourning. The marriage was morganatic but the children were legitimized and Catherine given the title Princess Yurievskya, a reference to her Rurikovich ancestors, direct descendants of St Vladimir. Alexander saw no reason why she should not now become empress. The tsarevich was appalled. The emperor and his eldest son had been estranged since the arrival on the scene of Catherine and the young Sasha was increasingly outspoken in his criticism of the senior Alexander. He did little to suppress palace talk of forcing Alexander II to abdicate in his favour.

Alexander II, who had been purblind in the face of the terrorism ravaging the country until the February 1880 attack, urged on by his mistress, seconded by his brother, the Grand Duke Constantine, and the respected former interior minister, Peter Valuev, agreed to seek a way of conciliating the people. They put forward proposals for advisory constitutional bodies, something that they had first suggested in the 1860s. In a rare inspired choice, an Armenian soldier, Count Mikhail Loris-Melikov, a former hardliner, was chosen to head the new Supreme Executive Commission with a mandate for reform at all levels. He spent the second half of 1880 drawing up plans for constitutional reform, a peaceful transition from autocracy to semi-constitutional monarchy.[22] The hated Third Section was disbanded, press censorship relaxed and some repressive measures rescinded.

During this period the government appeared to be winning the battle against the terrorists. Numerous arrests were made; sixteen members of the People's Will were tried in October 1880 and three executed. Deportations followed apace. The terrorist organization shrank dramatically. At the same time desperation and doggedness to achieve their major aim led those still at liberty to redouble their efforts. A combat unit focused its attention on Alexander's movements in St Petersburg.

On Sunday, 13 March 1881, Alexander received Loris-Melikov to give his personal approval to the recommended constitutional changes. They were to be made public the following day. At the same time the count, who was in possession of sound information that the revolutionaries were planning to strike again in the immediate future, pleaded with his master not to attend the usual Sunday parade.

Alexander was undeterred, and after the inspection he paid a visit to his cousin the Grand Duchess Catherine to tell her of the impending constitutional changes. It had long been his practice not to announce his return route until the last moment, and the one chosen by the emperor that day avoided the road that had been mined in anticipation of his passage. But he was a doomed man. An underground explosion had failed but the revolutionaries were circling in.

The inevitable happened. While driving in his sleigh along another road between the wall of the Summer Garden and the Catherine Canal, a bomb was hurled at the imperial sleigh, downing two horses of the escort, wounding one of the Cossack escort and a passing baker's boy. Alexander was unhurt. His coachman had orders from the family to waive all ceremony when his master was in danger. However, the emperor amazingly insisted on stepping out to enquire after the wounded. He turned around, saw the assassin and ordered him to be removed. Suddenly another young man threw a bomb at his feet; an explosion followed that was heard all over the city. When the smoke cleared, Alexander was seen covered in blood, his legs shattered. He murmured: 'Quick home, carry me to the Palace to die.'[23] Alexander II had won the war against Turkey but lost the peace in Russia.

Queen Victoria wrote in her journal: 'Feel quite shaken and stunned by this awful news. May God protect all dear ones! Poor, poor Emperor, in spite of his failings, he was a kind and amiable man, and had been a good ruler, wishing to do his best for his country.'[24] She did not express surprise.

21

DÉTENTE

After the danger of war between Britain and Russia in 1878, and the acrimonious disputes that had taken place in Berlin, a thaw in relations was evident in 1879. Beaconsfield sent a racy, confidential handwritten letter to Gorchakov in February:

> I am going to send Yr Highness a friend of mine, (ambassador) whom, I think, you will like. You must have known his mother, & probably made love to her, in those dangerous days of your English residence. She was one of the three beautiful Sheridans, & perhaps the most fair ... I have fulfilled the promise I made to Yr Highness in Berlin, & have not only labored to maintain peace, but to lay the foundations of a sincerely good understanding between our two Empires, but I will frankly tell you I am hard tired. My friend, when he arrives, will speak to you on these matters.[1]

The Russian chancellor was guarded in his, also handwritten, reply, exceptionally in English:

> Your friend Lord Dufferin will be welcome. I shall be more than happy to see him as he is entrusted by Your Lordship to Communicate to me all your efforts for the maintenance of peace and the foundations of a sincerely good understanding between our two Empires. The achievement would be worthy of your superior intelligence. For my part I entertain entire confidence in the words we exchanged at Berlin. But I must candidly avow that the conduct of your agents abroad does not confirm our mutual hopes and I am sure you will not grudge me for this frankness is the highest proof of esteem and that you allow this appeal to your personal power and loyalty.[2]

The choice of Dufferin was in some respects surprising as he was a member of the Liberal party that had shown no support for Beaconsfield, though the prime minister must have known that this would be a point in his favour with the Russians.

Gorchakov behaved as Beaconsfield had expected and paid a *non-protocolaire* visit to the ambassador's wife, Hariot Dufferin, before she had been presented at court. He was:

> a charming old man of eighty-four, full of the grossest flatteries, expressed in the most delightful manner. He was surprised at my youthful appearance ... Then he told me he relied on me to help him to keep the peace, and to make friends, that he always enquired when he heard a new Ambassador was coming, whether he had a pretty wife, and that if the answer was 'No!' he always said, 'Alors il perd son meilleur argument'. He was in England in 1816–17 [in the 1820s, and Gorchakov was eighty-one, not eighty-four], and remembers all the people so well. They say here that he is getting feeble, but he certainly appeared most vigorous.[3]

More important for Gorchakov than the arrival of a pretty ambassador's wife was the defeat of the Beaconsfield government in 1880. Russia was delighted to see Gladstone once more prime minister. Changes were also taking place in the direction of Russian foreign affairs. Gorchakov, who was by now clearly senile, and said to talk only of women and unimportant matters, was finally persuaded to retire at the age of eighty-three in 1881. Nicholas Giers, aged forty-one, emerged from the shadow of the prince. Unlike his predecessor, Giers was not an aristocrat but the son of a frontier postmaster of Swedish descent. Even so, his father was able to offer his children an excellent education. Giers attended the Nobleman's Boarding School in St Petersburg and the *lycée* at Tsarskoe Selo where so many of Russia's leading statesmen were educated. After various foreign postings he returned to the capital in 1863 as head of the Asiatic Department. However, Giers never imposed himself on St Petersburg society. Although he married a niece of Gorchakov, this did not help him financially and he was constantly concerned about paying for the education of his nine children, and clearly lacked the financial means to give the lavish receptions that were associated with his position at the head of the ministry of foreign affairs. Unlike almost every top official in the Russian service Giers was dependent on his salary, but his position was eased when Alexander II gave him an estate in 1879.

With this background the minister was prepared to accept a more subordinate position in relation to Alexander III than his predecessor had enjoyed with Alexander II. Throughout his tenure Giers had also to contend with constant opposition from those who disagreed with his policies, such as Constantine Pobedonostsev, procurator of the Holy Synod, Baron Alexander Jomini and Prince Alexsei Lobanov-Rostovsky at the ministry of foreign affairs, and the influential journalist Mikhail Katkov (who had the ear of Alexander III). Then there were those who sought his position, such as Nicholas Ignatiev, the Shuvalov brothers Peter and Paul, and Baron Alexander Mohrenheim, the ambassador in Paris. The sniping that went on in St Petersburg was well known to foreign diplomats but most of them wisely recognized Giers as a force for peace and stability. Dufferin considered Giers 'one of the most moderate, sensible and straightforward statesmen I have ever known'.[4] For Russia needed a breathing space to recover from the war of 1877–8 and the Congress of Berlin settlement, and to be able to continue with her advance in Central Asia.

Relations between the Russian and British royal families also improved. The Prince and Princess of Wales and obviously the Duke and Duchess of Edinburgh had attended the funeral of Alexander II in March 1881. For all his strongly anti-Russian views in the late 1870s, the prince insisted that he should be there, despite the wishes of his mother, who considered the security risks in St Petersburg too great for him and his wife to attend. 'The Queen has informed D[ufferin] that she looks to him for the safety of the Prince', wrote Hariot Dufferin, 'so I am very nervous about this week, and long for it to be over.'[5] Certainly it would have reflected badly on the Prince and Princess of Wales if the brother-in-law of the new emperor and the sister of the empress, now named Maria Feodorovna, had been deterred from attending due to fear for their persons.

The composure and confident manner of the Prince of Wales impressed all during the lying-in-state of Alexander II when every day for a week members of the Russian royal family had to kiss the putrefying body in the coffin. The transfer of the body to the Peter and Paul fortress came as a relief. Despite the people's former hostility towards the dead emperor, on the snowy March day of the procession they turned out in large numbers. 'I never saw such a mass of people swaying to and fro; they had to be kept back by soldiers', reported Lady Dufferin:[6]

> The greatest precautions were taken all along the route of the procession. An inspector was in charge of each house, the garrets were locked, and the roofs were forbidden as standing places ... As to the procession, it was a great disappointment. On paper it sounded beautiful, but it was so straggling that one never quite knew when it had begun.[7]

It is noteworthy that there was no repeat of Queen Victoria's reluctance to invest Alexander II with the Order of the Garter. The Prince of Wales had brought the decoration with him and presented it to his brother-in-law the day after the funeral. The British royals stayed with Alexander and Maria Feodorovna at the Anichkov Palace, chosen by the new emperor as it was relatively easy to guard. Even there, Alexander could only exercise in the palace backyard, which to the Prince of Wales 'was an area unworthy of a London slum'.[8]

The relaxation in Anglo-Russian relations at the beginning of the new decade reflected the shift in the political centre of gravity in the Near East from Constantinople to Egypt. The significance of the Ottoman capital had been declining in the late 1870s. Beaconsfield referred as often to the importance of the Suez Canal as he did to Constantinople and this became ever more true in subsequent years. The dominance of steamshipping concentrated more and more trade in that direction. The overland route to India was no longer a critical factor in British thinking.

Therefore, when Britain became increasingly embroiled in Egypt in 1879 with the establishment of the Anglo-French Dual Control of the finances of the newly imposed khedive, Russia, after going to war against Turkey only two years previously, sought to bolster the position of the sultan in Egypt, where he was the official sovereign, against further Anglo-French encroachments of his position.

In 1882 the Ottoman ambassador in London, Musurus Pasha, conferred with his Russian counterpart, Prince Lobanov-Rostovsky. Musurus insisted that 'the Egyptian question having been settled by the 1840 Convention was above all a European one ... It is certain that the dangers that now threaten the Khedive come only from the Powers that pretend to protect him.'[9] 'This is correct', noted Alexander III on the dispatch. Nevertheless, there was little practical help that Russia could offer Constantinople in 1882.

The Egyptian crisis that had erupted in 1881 was precipitated by an autochthonous reform movement led by Arabi Pasha directed against foreigners, fifty of whom were murdered in June 1882. The powers most concerned were naturally Britain and France, but the French, for domestic reasons, refused to act. Britain went ahead alone, bombarded Alexandria and landed troops at Port Said. In September Arabi's troops were annihilated at Tel-el-Kebir. A powerless European conference was convened in Constantinople: the British were masters in Egypt.

This effectively ended French influence in Egypt and was to a large extent responsible for the alienation of France and Britain for twenty years. This was not directly relevant to Anglo-Russian relations but was to prove an important factor in the creation of the Franco-Russian Alliance a decade later that weakened Britain's position *vis-à-vis* Russia. It is also interesting to point out that in Britain's unilateral action, in a situation that had been internationally established, she was doing what she had condemned Russia for having done over the Black Sea clauses in 1870.

The Russian government muttered that all the powers ought to have been consulted; *Novoe Vremya* called for a stronger Russian presence in Egypt but, as Bismarck signalled a free hand to Britain (to isolate France), it was considered prudent by Russia to keep a low profile on the subject.[10] There were sufficient mounting causes of Anglo-Russian tensions in Central Asia and criticism of her domestic policies for Russia to avoid provoking yet more over Egypt.

Alexander III's coronation in Moscow in May 1883 provided the occasion for a demonstration of official Anglo-Russian goodwill. Although he had become emperor two years previously, the risk of an attack by terrorists at that time was believed to be too great for the very public ceremonies that accompanied the traditional pageant in the old capital. The determined cull of revolutionaries after Alexander II's assassination had, however, succeeded in decimating those likely to perpetrate a similar atrocity. And the press hostile to the government had been muzzled. In early January 1883, the newspaper *Strana* was shut down on the grounds that 'it persists in pursuing the unhealthy direction which it has chosen—to blame without exception all the acts and all the measures of the government and to seek to represent the general situation of the affairs of the country in the most distressing light'.[11] *Golos* was suspended for six months in February for its 'pernicious attitude, which seeks to distort all government policies'.[12]

The emperor's sister, the Duchess of Edinburgh, and her husband Alfred attended as members of the British royal family and the government, rather provocatively, sent Lord Wolseley, victor the previous year at Alexandria, as its representative. In a letter to the queen, the general wrote:

> I never saw satisfaction and pleasure more clearly depicted by the human countenance than it was on the face of the Czar when, having reached the sacred gate leading into the Kremlin, he dismounted and let us, who rode immediately behind him, file past him ... I need scarcely say that every possible precaution had been taken along the line of route followed by the procession ... Coming from St Petersburg, there were 20,000 men along the line of railway ... It must be a miserable life for a sovereign to lead.[13]

The general found the religious service far too long and thought that even Alexander himself looked bored.

But Wolseley did not confine his report to a description of the lavish ceremonies. He was struck by the refusal of Russian officials to discuss politics, their apparent fear for the future. Alexander's stance was made clear to the queen: 'I have heard that the proclamation issued by the Czar ... has given great dissatisfaction to the peasantry', and it appeared that he had 'no intention of relaxing in any way the despotism of the government ... If able and good ministers are selected the country will become great; if the reverse, the people will be discontented and the nation impoverished.'[14]

22

THE POGROMS

The revolutionaries had succeeded in killing Alexander II. They also unintentionally killed off the liberal reforms for which they had been fighting. The chance offered by Loris-Melikov's proposals for constitutional progress would not recur.

This though was not immediately clear, for a week after his father's murder Alexander III chaired a meeting of the Council of Ministers and announced that the future of the Loris-Melikov reforms had not been decided. Nevertheless, the new emperor ceded to the strongly held views of his long-term tutor and mentor, the Procurator of the Holy Synod and reactionary, Constantine Pobedonostsev, who denounced the introduction of a constitution of a western European type. Russia was strong because of her autocracy, the unbreakable union of emperor and people. At the end of April Loris-Melikov, Dmitri Miliutin and Alexander Abaza, the finance minister, resigned. The Grand Duke Constantine retired. The ubiquitous Nicholas Ignatiev, now back in favour, became minister of the interior. A purge in the higher bureaucratic echelons followed. The age of the Great Reforms had followed its originator to the grave. The political creed returned to the tripartite formula devised half a century before—Orthodoxy, Autocracy and Nationality.

Alexander III was not heir to the throne until the age of twenty-one and during his youth little attention had been paid to his education. Even after the death of his elder brother Nicholas, his political education was scanty. He was described as dull, phlegmatic and ponderous; also a poor linguist, who never mastered Russian spelling.[1] The most distinguished statesman of his reign, Sergei Witte, described the emperor as: 'The most honest man I have ever met: not the most intelligent or cultivated.'[2] Alexander III was nearly 2 metres tall, ursine and heavily bearded: 'The massive build, the slow tempo, the enormous strength, the upward scowl which does duty as a glance, the side gait, awkward bearing, and bovine butting of the head, suggested "bullock" as a term of endearment which his father first conferred upon him in childhood.'[3] Alexander was known for his enormous appetite and predilection for alcohol; much was made of his being a poor rider and fearful of horses. The emperor enjoyed the theatre and played the trombone. (But he did leave a cultural legacy, commissioning Peter Carl Fabergé in 1885 to make the first of the exquisite bejewelled eggs.)

For all his intellectual and physical limitations, Alexander III possessed qualities lacking in his father. He was a Russian Victorian, faithful to his wife and scandalized by the Prince of Wales's promiscuity; he lived modestly at the Gatchina Palace (which was easier to guard than the Winter Palace), shunned the *vie mondaine* of St Petersburg and was a devoted father to his children.

Alexander III's behaviour as ruler of Russia showed a very different man. His father's assassins were quickly rounded up. Nicholas Rysakov, who had thrown the first grenade, broke down under interrogation and named the other members of the People's Will who had taken part. Seven conspirators, including Sophia Perovskaya, Alexander Mikhailov and Andrei Zhelyabov, were tried, and all but one condemned to death by public hanging as regicides. Liberals, such as Leo Tolstoy, pleaded in vain for mercy. The sole revolutionary to escape the death penalty, as she was pregnant, Hessia Helfman, was Jewish.

The pogroms erupted six weeks after the demise of Alexander II. Anti-Semitism was rife in Russia and the new emperor himself detested the Jews, disparagingly referring to them as 'Yids'. But there was no evidence of Jews being prominent in the revolutionary movement that had killed Alexander II. Even so, the Jews were blamed.

The tsars of Muscovy had pursued anti-Jewish policies and during the first half of the eighteenth century there had been a consistent attempt to banish Jews from Russia. However, the Partitions of Poland under Catherine the Great had resulted in almost a million Jews coming under Russian rule. With such a number, banishment was no longer possible. The Russian government then set about limiting Jewish rights within the empire. In 1772 a *ukaz* was issued which made a distinction between Jewish and non-Jewish subjects. The latter could exercise their rights throughout the Russian empire; Jews on the other hand could only exercise their rights in the territory in which they were living at the time of

Partition—in White Russia and Ukraine. That is, the Pale of Settlement was established. And, even within this, Jews were singled out for discriminatory legislation through the imposition of additional taxes levied on them. By the mid-nineteenth century there were about 5 million Jews in the Russian empire.

Nevertheless, a small Jewish bourgeoisie existed, a high proportion of whom resided outside the Pale—a few financiers, a larger number of substantial merchants and entrepreneurs, as well as members of the professions and a few university professors. The Ginzburgs in finance, and Samuel Poliakov, a railway magnate, were influential in St Petersburg. The Ephrussi family in Odesa controlled the lucrative wheat trade in the Black Sea, as described by Edmund de Waal in *The Hare with the Amber Eyes*.[4] The vast majority of Russian Jews, on the other hand, lived harsh, hungry and increasingly impoverished lives.

Most British consul generals and consuls posted throughout the Russian empire felt sympathy for the Russian Jews. The views of George Stanley in Odesa were typical:

> The average Russian has certainly no legitimate cause to despise the Jews, who are his superior in education, intelligence, morality, sobriety, and enterprise ... As to their character for honesty, nearly every foreign business establishment in South Russia largely employs them in confidential situations, and were Jews to leave South Russia trade would entirely collapse.[5]

From March 1881 attacks against the Jewish population of Russia were widespread and deadly; the pogroms—the Russian word for a mass violent attack or massacre—has now acquired a specific meaning. Western Jewish scholars in recent years have made clear that the Russian government did not institute the pogroms. But many of those perpetrating the violence believed that they had the tacit support of the authorities. Certainly, the state did little or nothing to restrain the murderous campaign against the Jews. However, governmental control in Russia was weak; local police forces were to blame for not putting down the attacks and not pursuing the perpetrators. These *pogromshchiki* were generally not peasants but roving bands of industrial workers from Moscow and St Petersburg. Having lost their jobs in the industrial depression, which had just begun, they could not find seasonal work in Ukraine because of crop failures. Joined by railway workers and local riff-raff, this unemployed lumpenproletariat took to the railways, travelling from town to town assaulting and robbing Jews.

The first pogrom erupted in the Jewish quarter of Elizavetgrad (today Kropyvnytskyi) in central Ukraine. At least forty Jews were killed and hundreds more injured; women were raped. Millions of roubles worth of damage was inflicted and about 20,000 Jewish homes destroyed. The pogrom raged uninterrupted for days. Soldiers then made an appearance and the *pogromshchiki* scattered. A few were arrested and lightly punished, if at all.

Next the outrage spread to Kyiv where the British consul, Hugh Wyndham, reported to the foreign secretary that an insurrectionary proclamation had been discovered, 'exciting the people to massacre the Jews'.[6] The *London illustrated News* expanded:

> Suddenly a whistle would be heard, and in a moment men would issue from the crowd and form themselves into a band, and an attack would be made on a house ... Nearly all the largest and finest shops in Kiev [Kyiv] and the principal storehouses ... belonged to the Jews. None were left unmolested.[7]

'Beyond expostulation no effort was made to protect the Jews.'[8]

Nicholas Ignatiev, acting under the express orders of Alexander III, immediately issued a circular,

> claiming that within the last twenty years the Jews had not only been monopolizing trade and commerce, but had also ... been gradually acquiring a considerable portion of the land, in doing which they did not so much aim at increasing the productive power of the country as of exploiting its Slavonic inhabitants, especially of the poorer class.[9]

This was followed by the temporary May Laws which prohibited new Jewish settlements outside towns and *shtetlekh*, banned them from buying property in the countryside and forbade them from trading on Sundays and Christian holidays. However, the real power of the May Laws was the scope they gave to the arbitrariness of local officials, above all the police, to interpret them as they thought fit. These temporary laws, in effect legislative pogroms, remained in operation until 1917.

Warsaw followed in December, where 1,500 shops and houses were destroyed, although British Jews resident there were unmolested. But the most destructive and bloody episode was still to come. At the end of March 1882 a pogrom raged in the largely Jewish town of Balta in Poland. Some 5,000 peasants poured into the town to pillage and, by the second day, all but thirty Jewish homes had been looted and destroyed. Forty Jews were killed, maimed or seriously wounded.[10]

Although the British consul generals and consuls in the different parts of Russia officially reported to the ambassador in St Petersburg, and hence to the foreign office in London, a fair number maintained unofficial contacts with journalists and *The Times* and the *Daily Telegraph* employed permanent correspondents in St Petersburg. The pogroms were widely reported in the British press to national condemnation of the Russian government for permitting, or not effectively stamping out, such barbarism. These reports were not available in Russia. The British ambassador reported that 'it is the custom to efface the articles contrary to them before the papers are delivered to subscribers, and I have seen whole columns of *The Times* blotted out for this reason'.[11]

A meeting of the Victorian great and the good was convened at the Mansion House in London in January 1882, 'to give expression to the feeling excited in this country by the atrocities recently perpetrated on the Jews in Russia'.[12] Among the many famous names present were the Bishop of London, the Lord Mayor of the City, the reformer the Earl of Shaftsbury, Cardinal Manning, the poet Robert Browning, practically all the names of top Anglo-Jewry, beginning with the Rothschilds, and numerous MPs. At the bottom of the list of distinguished men came the women, led by the banker and philanthropist Baroness Burdett-Coutts.

In the many long speeches, due sympathy was expressed for the Russian imperial family for the assassination of Alexander II, and it was insisted that the protest did not arise out of hatred for Russia. Nor was there any desire to attack the Gladstone government in power since 1880. Cardinal Manning was cheered when he asserted that

> The laws of Russia relating to the Jews tend to degrade them in the opinion of the Christian population, and to expose Russian Jewish subjects to outbreaks of fanatical violence … Is there anything that can debase and irritate the soul of a man more than to be told, 'You must not pass beyond that boundary' …? I hold the proofs in my own hand [of atrocities] … (Cheers) And from whom do they come? From official documents, from the Minister of the Interior General Ignatieff (Cheers).[13]

A memorial was to be sent to the emperor of Russia expressing public protest at the recent persecution of the Jews. A copy was also to be sent to the prime minister and Lord Granville, the foreign secretary, 'in the hope that her Majesty's Government may be able, when the opportunity arises, to exercise a friendly influence with the Russian Government'.[14] But the meeting was not only about moral indignation at the pogroms. In addition a fund was set up 'for the purpose of contributing to relieve the distress among the Jewish population of Russia and among the refugees therefrom, which distress has been caused by the recent outrages of which they have been victims'.[15] Donations totalling more than £15,000 were received on the spot, £5,000 coming each from the Rothschilds in London and Paris.

Clearly the resolution to protest to the Russian government was not going to have any effect other than to anger it. Giers duly replied to the Russian ambassador, now Prince Lobanov-Rostrovsky: 'You have done absolutely right in declining the address to the Emperor.'[16] Making the incorrect assumption that it was British Jews who were solely responsible for the resolution, the foreign minister continued: 'We do not know a Jewish nation, and, as English subjects, the Jews of London have no right to interfere in our affairs.' The long-standing comparison with Ireland was dragged out that Russia did not interfere with 'demonstrations in favour of the Irish'.[17]

Novoe Vremya launched into an attack on the British:

> The concern of England, which has beggared the population of India and Egypt, which has poisoned the people of China with opium, which destroyed, like dangerous insects, the natives of Australia, and which, under pretext of abolishing the slave trade, is now exterminating in most wholesale fashion the numerous races of Africa—the concern of a people who do those things is certainly astonishing.[18]

Questions were raised the following week in both the House of Commons and the House of Lords. Gladstone replied that he understood the importance of 'a subject to which no man of ordinary feeling can refer without sentiments of the utmost pain and horror'.[19] Nevertheless, he insisted, the British government had no *locus standi* to protest about the internal affairs of a foreign country. Office had changed everything. The man who had thundered about the Bulgarian atrocities to Christians as prime minister did not feel able to express even disapproval of Russia over the pogroms. Granville sent a dispatch in June mildly asking the British ambassador for information.

If the pogroms had no obvious effect on official governmental relations between Britain and Russia in 1882—Central Asia and Egypt were the dominant subjects—in the long run the legacy of the suffering of Russian Jews in the 1880s was to provide an enormous benefit to British society.[20]

The position of Jews in Britain was very different from that of Jews in Russia. After being expelled from England in 1290, Jews had been allowed back by Oliver Cromwell. By 1880 there were about 80,000 Jews in Britain, living mostly in London. The majority were poor, but not paupers, while a substantial minority were very rich and influential—the Rothschilds, Montefiores, Salomons, Goldsmids, Sassoons and Montagus. Most legal restrictions on Jews had been removed by 1845 and there were Jewish barristers, solicitors and City brokers. Moses Montefiore had been knighted and was on good terms with the queen. The one 'disability' that remained was the oath that had to be taken on the Bible by Members of Parliament and that had been removed in 1858 when Baron Lionel de Rothschild (an Austrian title) had been able to take the seat to which he had been elected some years before. In 1871 his son was raised to the British peerage.

In the wake of the pogroms of 1881–2 and the effects of the May Laws, many Russian Jews saw that emigration, with all the risks that it posed, offered a better chance for the future than remaining in Russia. The image of the new exodus leaving the land of bondage to a promised land came to dominate. Three-quarters of a million Jews emigrated from Russia and eastern Europe between 1881 and 1900.

Modern transport communications made this possible on a massive scale that was not previously possible. Emigration without permission was illegal in Russia. However, the long frontier with Austria-Hungary meant that it was porous and, once over it, there was a railway network into Germany and hence the ports of Hamburg and Bremen. From there steamships left for Britain—Hull, Harwich and above all London, several times a week.

Most Russian Jewish emigrants hoped to continue to the United States: Britain was not their chosen destination. However, for reasons to do with the shipping cartel, it was cheaper to buy a ticket to England and then another to the United States. There were many transmigrants who made it to Liverpool and on to New York. And there were many who, on arrival in London, either did not possess the means to continue, or decided to remain.

The important Jewish community in England was confronted in the 1880s with the arrival of large numbers of poor, Yiddish-speaking Russian Jews. The initial reaction of Anglo-Jewry was to seek to remove the problem. The funds raised at the Mansion House and in the following months were aimed at helping the emigrants to continue on their way to the United States, the colonies, or to repatriate them. Advertisements were placed in the Russian and east European Jewish press to the effect that the streets of London were not paved with gold. Nevertheless, nothing could be done to control the influx.

Anglo-Jewry had been dispersing throughout the country in recent years, and into an increasingly wide range of occupations. The arrival of the immigrants dramatically reversed these trends. Firstly, overcrowded communities of Yiddish-speaking immigrants, noticeable because of their foreign dress, east European habits and patterns of religious behaviour, settled in the traditional Jewish quarters of London and other large cities. Secondly, the immigrants were concentrated in a few largely non-unionized occupations: clothing, footwear, cabinet-making and street trading. And the peaks in immigration coincided with downturns in the economic cycle and higher unemployment in Britain. The indigenous population, both Jewish and non-Jewish, feared that the newcomers were causing job losses, lower wages and higher rents.

There were also widely held apprehensions about imported disease, crime and the infiltration of socialism and anarchism. The established Jewish community did not wish to be tainted in the eyes of the British authorities. The religious establishment was wary of foreign practices in the synagogues. There was also anxiety that Jewish welfare organizations would be swamped by the needs of the newcomers. The London Board of Guardians that oversaw Jewish charities denied relief to immigrants in their first six months.

Gradually though, a more sympathetic attitude prevailed. It was clear that the Jews of Russia were in increasing danger of starvation and physical violence if they remained there. Many British Jewish leaders, including Lord Rothschild and Sir Samuel Montagu, MP for Whitechapel, opposed limitations on immigration. In the tensions in the East End, for instance the great tailors' strike of 1889, communal leaders showed practical support for immigrant strikers.

Above all, strenuous efforts were made by Anglo-Jewry to anglicize the immigrants. There were Jewish denominational schools and London County Council (LCC) state schools, some of which had so many Jewish pupils that the timetables were adjusted to Jewish religious requirements. Relief institutions, such as the Temporary Shelter and Soup Kitchens, ministered to the immigrants' basis needs, and young Jews from the wealthier classes ran clubs and settlements in the Jewish immigrant areas.

At the same time there was a call from some in Anglo-Jewry for the tradition of British Jewish orthodoxy to be maintained. The chief rabbi, Dr Hermann Adler, held that the object was to render the immigrants loyal subjects and steadfast Jews. However, it was obvious that the main aim of the vast majority of the Russian Jewish immigrants was to better themselves economically, to secure independence, even if only as an employer on a small scale—as happened in the clothing trade, where 40 per cent were employed by the end of the century—and to adapt to British ways and follow their Jewish precursors out to suburbia. The enormous contribution to all aspects of British life of descendants of the Russian Jewish immigration of the late nineteenth century needs no elaboration.

23

THE PENDJEH INCIDENT

In 1868, Russia had signed a commercial treaty with the khan of truncated Kokand, which effectively reduced the khanate to vassal status, although it remained nominally independent.[1] The ruler, the dissolute Khudayar Khan, continued to deploy his energies towards improving his lavish palace in Kokand—a city of 80,000 people with 600 mosques and 15 madrasas—and extorting oppressive taxes from the people. At the same time, internal disputes caused turmoil and yet more political deterioration. Unruly Kokanese mobs invaded adjacent Russian territory and an exasperated Constantine von Kaufman, the governor general of Russian Turkestan, invaded Kokand with a powerful force in August 1875. The khanate was placed under Russian overlordship, the khan deposed and the cities of Kokand and Margelan taken.[2] Fresh disorders broke out in the khanate and General Mikhail Skobelev stormed Andizhan in the east, close to the Chinese border, in January 1876. Two months later, Alexander II announced that he had been obliged to yield to the wish of the Kokand people to become Russian subjects. The khanate was declared abolished, and incorporated into Russian Turkestan as the Fergana Province.

Although Russian treatment of Kokand was in many respects understandable, it had taken place when the Conservative government under Benjamin Disraeli had come to power in 1874. The new administration was determined to reverse the policy of Gladstone's administration, which had sought to limit the Russian advance in Central Asia by diplomacy. The immediate task, the prime minister and the secretary of state for India, the Marquess of Salisbury, believed, was to prevent all-confident Russia from establishing a foothold in neighbouring Afghanistan.

Despite the new government's wariness about Russian expansion in Central Asia, it was 'surprisingly fatalistic' about this absorption of a khanate. The Russian foreign ministry in St Petersburg had only been informed after the decision to annex Kokand had been reached on the spot. It was felt that Gorchakov would be worried about the consequences. As it turned out, little interest was evinced in London.[3]

Nevertheless, there was no shortage of distinguished hawks outside the government in Britain keen to warn about the danger posed by Russian conquests in Central Asia. Yet again, Sir Henry Rawlinson, now a member of the India Council, was at the fore. In 1875 he published *England and Russia in the East*, raising the spectre of further Russian expansion. Sir Henry Bartle Frere, a former governor of Bombay, the following year wrote that it was necessary to post a frontier army at Quetta to assure access to southern Afghanistan and to establish agents in Kabul, Herat and Kandahar. An English translation of Colonel Mikhail Terentiev's *Russia and England in the Struggle for the Markets of Central Asia* in the same year claimed that there were no insurmountable problems to invading India from Russian possessions. Afghanistan, therefore, once more came to the fore in British foreign policy.

The new policy was communicated to the viceroy, the Liberal Lord Northbrook, who replied that, since the previous British government had refused the opportunity of coming to an agreement which Sher Ali, the emir of Afghanistan, had proposed in 1873, they could hardly now demand what they had rejected. After an acrimonious exchange of cables Northbrook resigned, and was replaced by Lord Lytton.

The new viceroy was the son of Edward Bulwer-Lytton, the well-known author of many books including *The Last Days of Pompeii*. The younger Lytton had served as a career diplomat in western Europe, and published poetry under the name of Owen Meredith. Yet, whatever literary talents he possessed, the Bohemian younger Lytton had no administrative experience. This in no way diminished Disraeli's determination to send his *protégé* to India, as the prime minister knew that his choice, 'a man of ambition, imagination, some vanity and much will', shared his desire for a vigorous 'forward' policy to replace 'masterly inactivity'.[4]

Before leaving for India, the new viceroy met several times with Shuvalov. The Russian ambassador insisted that Russia wished to come to an agreement with Britain over Central Asia. His proposal would have led, Lytton believed, to the absorption of the states between Russian and British possessions, the partition of Afghanistan and the establishment of a common frontier between the two empires. He was determined to prevent this. On arrival in India, the viceroy demonstrated his flamboyant and assertive style by proclaiming Queen Victoria's recent assumption of the title of Empress of India, and holding a lavish durbar in Delhi in December 1876.

Poor Sher Ali, sandwiched between the Russian juggernaut north of the Amu Darya and the newly restless British in India, had good reason to feel unease for the independence of Afghanistan. His relations with Britain were strained after the Gladstone government's refusal to accept his offer of a defensive alliance, and British interference in his treatment of his sons. Naturally, the Russians were aware of the emir's bitterness. Soon afterwards Kaufman began sending letters to the emir. When Lord Derby, the foreign secretary, protested at this incursion into Afghan affairs, Gorchakov flatly denied that there had been any contact with the emir, either by letter or special agent. Confronted with the text of the offending letters, the chancellor instituted enquiries and then dismissed them as being merely letters of courtesy such as Kaufman was in the habit of writing. The governor general was asked to explain, and it gradually became apparent, as further letters passed between Tashkent and Kabul, that he had acted on his own initiative.

In addition to the reports of friendly correspondence came rumours that the bearers were remaining in Kabul, and were acting as agents of the Russian government. Their alleged purpose was the establishment of offensive and defensive treaty relations with the emir. Derby instructed Loftus in St Petersburg to remind the Russians that Afghanistan was outside their sphere of influence, and to obtain a written disclaimer of any intention to negotiate treaties with Sher Ali. The ambassador failed, and Nicholas Giers, now head of the Asiatic Department, retorted with accusations of encroachments by the Indian army into territory close to Bukhara and, of a British agent working in Khorasan close to the Russian frontier with Persia. Such exchanges continued throughout 1877.

It was realized in London that Russia was engaged in diversionary tactics to distract from the crisis in the Near East, and that the danger of war was in Central Asia rather than in Europe. For General Skobelev advocated a rapid advance on India with 15,000 men from Russian Turkestan. The first stage would entail a political agreement with Sher Ali, combined with the occupation of Kabul by Russian troops. Then, it would be a matter of subverting disaffected elements in British Hindustan, to be followed by 'hurling masses of Asiatic cavalry upon India as a vanguard under the banner of blood and rapine, thereby reviving the times of Timur'.[5] It was not necessary to take seriously such military pipe dreams, but when the gist of them came to the knowledge of Lytton and the British government, they obviously did nothing to improve the extremely strained Anglo-Russian relations.

Lytton had convened a conference attended by Afghan representatives in Peshawar in February 1877, with the aim of persuading Sher Ali to accept a British mission in Kabul, that would replace the Muslim representative of the Indian government, who appeared to take his orders from the emir. (Following the 1857 Government of India Act, the Indian government was made up of British government viceroys and the Raj in Calcutta, while responsibility in London was held by the secretary of state for India. The Indian government had no Indian representatives.) The Peshawar discussions proved fruitless. Sher Ali refused to accept a British mission, citing among other reasons that the Russians would then be able to demand a similar mission. This argument was interpreted by the British government as confirming their loss of influence, since the emir appeared to have come to regard the Russians as being on an equal footing in Afghanistan. Sher Ali was in an extremely difficult position. He wished above all to remain as free from foreign interference as possible, and it looked as though circumstances were going to force him to decide which of the two powers was the least objectionable. It was rumoured that he was going to call a loya jirga (great council) to advise him as to which he should ally himself with.

With both Russia and Britain concentrating their energies on preparations for the Congress of Berlin in June 1878, Kaufman dispatched a letter to Sher Ali: 'Be it known to you that your union and friendship with the Russian Government will be beneficial to the latter and still more so to you. The advantages of a close alliance with the Russian Government will be permanently evident.'

Naturally, it was not long before the Indian government learned of the letter and a draft treaty that accompanied it. Loftus was ordered to demand of Giers (in Gorchakov's absence in Berlin) on 2 July whether a mission had been sent to Kabul. This was denied. This obvious mendacity, Shuvalov admitted to Salisbury, now foreign secretary, was due to the disorganized state of the Russian government during the period of the Congress of Berlin. When confronted by his ambassador in September as to whether a mission had been sent to Kabul, Gorchakov replied with less than conviction, 'No, I believe not.'[6] Yet, in December the chancellor admitted in a letter to Shuvalov that instructions had been sent to Kaufman in Tashkent on 25 April. Not until 28 June, it was claimed, did the imperial government learn that the mission had left Tashkent. It was only after that 'therefore they were prepared to admit to its existence'.[7] Such unconvincing hair-splitting could only render Shuvalov's task in dealing with an angry Salisbury more difficult, and also illustrates the declining powers of Gorchakov.

However, the following January the Russian chancellor rightly claimed that Beaconsfield had accepted, prior to the Congress of Berlin, that the Russians had a legitimate right to send a mission; indeed, the prime minister had written to Gorchakov on 11 September 1878 from Hughenden Manor, 'not an official or even ministerial letter, but one between two gentlemen in confidence', saying that in their place he would have done the same.[8]

Nevertheless, the Russian government insisted that, once the peace conference had been called, orders had been countermanded and its troops had been recalled northwards; the letter to Sher Ali was designated as one of pure courtesy from the emperor. Misunderstandings had arisen because of the international situation. The same old excuses were trotted out, namely, the difficulties of communication between St Petersburg and Central Asia, and the inevitable independence of commanders on the spot.

Major General Nicholas Stolietov had in fact been dispatched to Kabul under orders from his superior Kaufman in June 1878 to negotiate a treaty with Sher Ali. Yet hardly had he arrived in Kabul on 22 July when he was recalled. Stolietov was informed that Russia and Britain had settled their differences and Russia wished to avoid further involvement with Afghanistan. He left Kabul in August 1878 but his aides stayed on until December (something Salisbury only learned three months later from Shuvalov). The British government, post the exertions of Berlin and during the August holidays, was loath to stir up a fresh dispute with Russia. But for Lytton, this was the opportunity for which he had been waiting. In telegrams that 'all but scorched the newly laid cables', he inveighed against Sher Ali's treachery.[9] He proposed the sending of a British mission to Kabul and, if this was refused, an invasion of Afghanistan was necessary. Beaconsfield tergiversated, but finally decided that a mission could be sent to Kandahar, not Kabul, in order to avoid forcing the Khyber Pass.

In a blatant act of insubordination, the viceroy announced on 8 September that a mission under General Sir Neville Chamberlain, a veteran of the earlier Afghan War, and the political officer, Major Louis Cavagnari, would leave Peshawar for Kabul a week later with 1,000 men.

It was blocked by an Afghan force from passing Ali Mesjid in the Khyber Pass. Beaconsfield was furious: 'He was told to send the Mission by Candahar. He has sent it by the Khyber, and received a snub, wh. may cost us much to wipe away. When V-Roys and Comms-in-Chief disobey order, they ought to be sure of the success of their mutiny.'[10] The queen, for her part, also condemned the viceroy:

> Lord Lytton should not have sent the mission, having been forbidden to do so by the Cabinet. Now, of course, we must punish the insult, and support Lord Lytton. Care must be taken that we are quite sure of success, and that there should be no repetition of the misfortunes at Cabul in 1840! ... That she [Russia] is at the bottom of it all, there is little doubt.[11]

Most of the press thought similarly, although moderates, such as Lord Lawrence (whose views no longer carried much weight), did not believe there was sufficient reason for a casus belli. But, even though most members of the cabinet believed that it would be unwise to undertake a war in Afghanistan, as by then fences were being mended with Russia, national prestige was seen as being at stake, and the cabinet decided to dispatch an ultimatum to Sher Ali—accept a British mission, apologize, or war. The hawks in the cabinet, led by Lord Cranbrook, now secretary of state for India, and Lytton, had won the day.

The ultimatum sent to the emir at the end of October gave him three weeks in which he must accept the British terms—a very short period given the state of communications—or be declared an enemy. Sher Ali replied on 19 November, by which time he had learned that the Russians would do nothing to help him. His reply did not reach Lytton until 29 November. The invasion of Afghanistan had already begun on 21 November.

Three armies totalling 30,000 men were dispatched across the passes. In the east, 15,000 men under General Sir Samuel Browne (of military belt fame), who had won the VC in the Indian Rebellion, advanced through the Khyber Pass and Jelalabad was occupied on 20 December. A second central column under Major General Sir Frederick Roberts, another Indian VC, marched through the Kurram Valley and, after heavy fighting, prevailed at Peiwar Kotal. The third column under Major General Sir Donald Stewart marched through the Bolan Pass and occupied Kandahar in early January 1879.

In desperation, Sher Ali again turned to the Russians. After all, Stolietov had assured him only recently that they were prepared to support him. In early December, he fled Kabul with the intention of pleading his case with Alexander II in St Petersburg. The emir reached Tashkent, and was informed by Kaufman that he could not continue his journey.

The reason was clear: Sher Ali was collateral damage in what mattered to the Russians in Central Asia. With Britain on top in Afghanistan, he was abandoned. Gorchakov was frank in telling his ambassador in London that what concerned Russia was improving relations with Britain, and the presence and welcoming of Sher Ali in the Russian capital would be compromising.[12] And in London, the man who had been so enthusiastically wooed by the Russians the previous year was dismissed by Shuvalov as 'nothing more than the unpopular chief of a federation of tribes which he had abandoned in their hour of peril. It is doubtful if he can return to his homeland.'[13]

The brutal clarity of Russian policy was clear in the dispatch from the ambassador. Russia had made overtures of support to Sher Ali, to buy him onside if war with Britain had broken out in the Near East in 1878. Sher Ali became superfluous when this was avoided. Shuvalov pointed out to his government that the emir's reception of the Russian mission had sealed his fate with Britain and provoked her to invade Afghanistan. Russia had overplayed her hand.

It is difficult not to feel sorry for the hapless Sher Ali. One power had conquered his country; the other let him down. He died a broken man at Balkh in Afghanistan on 21 February 1879, having been ejected from Russian Turkestan.

The previous month the Russian correspondence with Sher Ali had fallen into British hands in Kabul, but Salisbury refrained from having it published. Inevitably, knowledge of its existence circulated in London, and Shuvalov informed St Petersburg at the end of the year that the British press had copies of translations of the letters, the leak coming from India. It was not likely that it would hold back on such a scoop. The bombshell came in February 1881, and the full extent of Russia's economy with the truth in 1878 was in the public domain.

It was Lytton, now recalled from India, who used the disclosure to justify in the House of Lords his policy before the outbreak of war. *The Times* reported:

> We obtain a description of the Treaty concluded between SHERE ALI and the CZAR of RUSSIA ... The significance of the document it is hardly possible to exaggerate. By this Russia bound herself to perpetuate friend-

> ship with Afghanistan, undertook to assist the AMEER against foreign enemies ... Russia, in effect, was to be for the future the firm friend and guardian of Afghanistan?[14]

The staunchly Tory *Daily Telegraph*, on the other hand, which might have been expected to adopt the Russophobic stance of the late Beaconsfield government, did not find Russian perfidy in the correspondence. It regretted the theatrical indignation expressed in parliament and sympathized with the Russian government:

> After the signature of the Berlin Treaty Russia found herself in a most awkward position. Taking advantage of the dread produced in SHERE ALI's mind by the menacing policy of Lord LYTTON, she had succeeded in securing the alliance of Afghanistan in what was then believed to be inevitable... The poor earthen 'pipkin', threatened with destruction between the 'two iron pots,' had after much hesitation thrown in his lot with the Power who promised to defend him from the war for which Lord LYTTON had been preparing.[15]

Douglas Forsyth, a former Indian civil servant, in a letter to *The Times* appositely quoted a conversation he had had with Sher Ali:

> 'We Afghans are people of the hills, and, please God, we can take care of ourselves, and give a good account of any foe who tries to enter our mountains,' adding emphatically, 'Whoever be our invader, whether Russian or English, the Afghans will never rest till they get the enemy out of the country.'[16]

The British had only learned this after their initial military success in the Second Afghan War. Successive generations—and the Russians—might well have taken heed.

Negotiations were opened in early 1879 between the British and the new Afghan emir, Yakub Khan, a weak young man whom his father, Sher Ali, had unsuccessfully tried to remove from the succession. Yakub gave in to all British demands in the Treaty of Gandamak of May 1879. There was to be a permanent British resident in Kabul; Britain would take control of the foreign policy of Afghanistan, the Khyber Pass and the border districts of Kurran, Pishin and Sibi. In return Yakub Khan would receive an annual subsidy of £60,000. Defying strong parliamentary criticism, both Lytton and the government in London preened themselves on what they saw as a military and diplomatic success. Beaconsfield congratulated the viceroy on having achieved a 'scientific frontier' of Afghanistan.

However, in the euphoria that prevailed in Calcutta and London, few in positions of power had noted that the new emir possessed very limited authority in Afghanistan, nor that he had agreed a raft of unpopular measures, which his father had steadfastly refused to accept.

In fulfilment of the Treaty of Gandamak, Sir Louis Cavagnari was appointed resident and took up residence in Kabul in July 1879. From the outset, he was regarded with suspicion by the Afghans. Six weeks later, Afghan regiments from Herat ruled by the emir's brother Ayub Khan descended on Kabul claiming that arrears of pay were due to them. A massacre, in which Cavagnari and most of his entourage were killed, followed. Roberts returned to Kabul and wreaked revenge on the Afghans. Trials took place under martial law and hangings followed. Lytton egged Roberts on: 'Every Afghan brought to death I shall regard as one scoundrel the less in a nest of scoundrelism.'[17] Yakub Khan was forced to abdicate (living in India until 1923) and Roberts assumed supreme authority.

The British had eradicated Russian influence in Afghanistan, and this was recognized in St Petersburg. But the arch-enemy had assiduously been formulating expansionist plans of her own in Central Asia.

One reason that Russia did not intervene and try to occupy Herat in the west while Britain was occupied fighting in the east of the country was an acknowledged lack of resources she could deploy from Russian Turkestan.[18] Another reason was that the Near Eastern crisis had demonstrated that the Russian belief that the Indian troops were anti-British was a myth; indeed, they had shown themselves to be enthusiastically pro-British.[19] The Indian frontier was safe for the Raj. A further argument advanced, above all by Shuvalov, was that, by providing Britain with a free hand in Afghanistan, Russia could assert herself freely elsewhere.

The ambassador had been advocating since 1878 an advance into Trans-Caspia, the region east of the Caspian Sea occupied by the warlike Teke Turcomans: 'It is towards Merv that we must advance and occupy permanently ... We must not remain the impassive witness to the conquest of Afghanistan by the English. We must do this blow by blow, for the English are extremely sensitive to anything about Merv.'[20] Alexander II noted on the dispatch: 'I completely approve the idea of Shouvalov about Merv.' At the same time, the ambassador was instructed not to mention Merv, even in private conversations: 'It is better that it remains bathed in the light and shade of our old arrangements.'[21]

Since the aged and ill Gorchakov no longer counted for much in foreign affairs, the ambassador in London felt able to reply, protesting yet again: 'I must insist nevertheless, that in invoking the spectre of Merv, I have made a major contribution during the last parliamentary session of moderating the Ministers and toning down their programme in Central Asia'. Alexander II noted his approval of the Shuvalov view on the dispatch: 'Everything he says is correct.' There was no doubt that despite several further years of denying any intention to take Merv, Russia was heading for the oasis. It was a prize, for which it was worth striving. Merv (today in Turkmenistan, 30 kilometres east of the large Soviet-built city of Mary), was one of the most fertile areas in Central Asia and the site of one of the most important cities along the Silk Road. It was founded around the sixth century BC, becoming perhaps the third largest city in the world in the tenth century AD. It is now in ruins.[22]

Preparations for a Russian expedition to Trans-Caspia in the spring of 1879 were taking place that aimed to push as far as the Akhal oasis, 200 versts (roughly kilometres) from Merv. The attack on the Turcomans was a failure. The headstrong General Lomakin commanded a force of 15,000 troops and a train of about 20,000 ponies and camels, but lacked supplies and water. Only about half reached the Akhal oasis, and then, faced with a much greater number of Tekes, they were forced into a disorderly retreat to their base of Chikishlyar on the Caspian Sea. Lomakin was relieved of his command. Salisbury believed the Russians, despite all their disclaimers, were aiming for Merv, and protested. However, the Russians could rightly claim that the expedition was directed at the Akhal oasis.

Alexander now hesitated. The minister of finance argued that Russia needed peace and tranquillity to combat the spread of revolutionary terrorism at home. Even the chief of the general staff, Count Feodor Heiden, advised against further involvement in Trans-Caspia, but Dmitri Miliutin, supported by the *Turkestantsy*, the officers in Central Asia, convinced the emperor otherwise. Britain, he argued, having 'subjugated Asiatic Turkey, having destroyed Afghanistan, having established close ties with the Turcomans, and trying to win Persia to her side as well … is beginning … to threaten the Caspian region'.[23] Even the usually cautious Giers agreed that strong retaliation was necessary.

The 1879 expedition had demonstrated Russian military administration at its worst, and the commander chosen to avenge the defeat was General Mikhail Skobelev, one of the few Russian military commanders who had distinguished himself in the recent Russo-Turkish war. In the autumn of 1880, his force of 11,000 men and 97 guns headed for Akhal where he laid siege to Geok Tepe, the principal town and mud fortress in the oasis.

Its fall, in January 1881, was inevitable, despite a heroic defence, but there followed a brutal massacre of fugitives, which appalled the British. The British journalist Charles Marvin interviewed Skobelev. According to Marvin, the general bragged:

> We killed nearly 20,000 Turcomans ... The survivors will not soon forget the lesson. I hold it as a principle that the duration of peace is in direct proportion to the slaughter you inflict on the enemy. The harder you hit them the longer they will be quiet afterwards.[24]

Another British journalist present at Geok Tepe was Edmund O'Donovan of the *Daily News*, whose graphic account of the slaughter contributed to the uproar that followed in Europe. It is to be noted that independent Russian journalists were absent in Central Asia.

Skobelev later reduced the number killed to 8,000, but in the face of international outrage, Alexander III, now emperor, dispatched the general to faraway Minsk. There may well have been other reasons for the former hero's disgrace, as he was demonstrating signs of delusions, and was rumoured to be plotting against the authorities. (Boris Akunin, in *The Death of Achilles*, has written a brilliant fictionalized account of the mysterious death of Skobelev the following year, supposedly in a Moscow brothel.)[25]

A month before his death in February 1881, Feodor Dostoyevsky had celebrated: 'Let me exclaim once more; long live the Geok Tepe victory! Long live Skobelev and his good soldiers!'[26] The following May 1881, the Akhal oasis was officially annexed to the Russian empire, and Trans-Caspia declared an *oblast*. What mattered in the long run though was that Turcoman resistance had been broken by the taking of Geok Tepe. In the following weeks, the chiefs in the area around Geok Tepe had surrendered to Skobelev and to all intents and purposes had decided the fate of the rest of Trans-Caspia. The construction by the Russian army of a narrow-gauge railway line from Krasnovodsk on the Caspian eastwards had been begun in 1880, but it actually proved a hindrance to the 1881 expedition, drawing away much supply and personnel. Twenty thousand camels were what mattered. The age of crucial railway lines in Central Asia was yet to come.

A general election had taken place in Britain in March 1880. The electorate, weary of the Great Eastern Crisis and the imperial wars in Zululand and Afghanistan, inflicted a crushing defeat on the Conservative Beaconsfield government. In his Midlothian campaign before the election,

Gladstone pledged to reverse the Conservative government's policy towards Afghanistan (Granville and Hartington were leaders of the Liberal Party in the Commons and Lords respectively). He lambasted Beaconsfield, whose showy imperialism, he held, was as cruel to its overseas victims as it was corrupting to the appetites of its home supporters. Gladstone insisted that 'the sanctity of life in the hill villages of Afghanistan, among the winter snows, is as inviolable in the eyes of Almighty God as can be your own'.[27]

By the time Gladstone took office as prime minister, Abdur Rahman Khan, grandson of Dost Mohammed and nephew of Sher Ali, had become emir of Afghanistan, after spending eleven years on a Russian pension in Tashkent. Lytton had to take a chance, now that Britain had decided to evacuate Kabul: 'No prospect of finding in the country a man strong enough for this purpose. I therefore advocate early public recognition of Abdur Rahman.'[28] For neither political party in Britain was prepared to accept the huge cost and bloodshed that would have been required for a permanent occupation of Afghanistan. With annexation ruled out, the only alternative was to make the best of the situation by establishing good relations with the best candidate available as emir.

However, Abdur Rahman did not exercise effective control over either Herat or Kandahar. In July 1880, 20,000 Afghan irregulars under Ayub Khan advanced from his base in Herat towards Kandahar. A British force of 2,500 men under General Burrows went out to confront the Afghans. In the clash that occurred at Maiwand on 27 July 1880, the British army was defeated with the loss of nearly 1,000 British and Indian lives. The survivors fell back on Kandahar, where they prepared for a siege. To rescue the trapped troops, Roberts set out from Kabul with a relief force of 10,000. His famous march between the two cities, covering more than 500 kilometres in twenty days at the height of summer, before defeating the Afghans, became the stuff of British military legend. 'Bobs' was raised to the peerage as Lord Roberts of Kandahar.

The British government decided to leave Afghanistan now that there was some semblance of stability under a relatively friendly emir. Roberts himself wrote, echoing Forsyth:

> The less the Afghans see of us, the less they will dislike us. Should Russia, in future years, attempt to conquer Afghanistan, or invade India through it, we should have a better chance of attaching the Afghans to our interests if we avoid all interference with them in the meantime.[29]

The Russians were delighted with the Liberal government's policy towards Central Asia. Gladstone made it clear that he believed the Russian threat to British imperial interests was greatly exaggerated. For him, this and European problems dividing governments could be solved as they arose by informal consultation. He praised Russia as the liberator of the Bulgarians, and thought that putting diplomatic pressure on the Turks to reform, rather than making them a bulwark against Russia, was in British interests. Granville, the foreign secretary, told the Prince of Wales, who was about to leave for St Petersburg for the funeral of Alexander II in March 1881, 'that a good understanding and friendly relations between this country and Russia may be of immense advantage to both ... The best course appears to be, to be perfectly frank, not to make undue concessions but to avoid unnecessary complaints and petty acts of ill-will.'[30]

In the more relaxed climate that marked the beginning of the reign of Alexander III, the British government sought assurances in St Petersburg that there would be no forward movement from the Akhal oasis. For two years, only evasive replies were received. Suspicions of Russian plans were rife—'Mervousness', as the Duke of Argyll cringe-makingly called it.[31] The sceptics were proved correct in February 1884. With the connivance of a friendly tribal leader, who, it was claimed, asked for Russian protection (intimidated/bribed as others saw it), Merv was occupied, and annexed by a force under Colonel Alikanov. It was 500 kilometres south of Khiva and a mere 300 north of Herat, 'the gate to India'. Russian troops were now approaching the border of Afghanistan.

If Russian forces centred on Merv encroached on Afghan territory, the British would be likely, as they had promised Abdur Rahman, albeit in not very precise terms, to come to the defence of Afghanistan. The long-awaited confrontation between British and Russian armies in Central Asia would be precipitated. With uncharacteristic diplomatic defiance, Giers claimed that the British government had misinterpreted previous Russian assurances.

The British were in no position to challenge the Russian move, however alarmed they were. Granville tried to play down its significance on the grounds that it had been long expected.[32] On the other hand, the British ambassador in St Petersburg, Sir Edward Thornton, related a terrifying rumour that General Cherniaev, of Tashkent fame and now governor general of Turkestan, had submitted to Alexander III a project for the invasion of India. In March 1884 Cherniaev was dismissed from his post (even though the reported project was clearly pie in the sky). Giers, now in a more conciliatory vein, felt obliged to report that the emperor had been shocked by the dangerous suggestions made by the governor general. In a further and more substantial move to defuse the situation, he resuscitated a proposition, mooted in 1882 and then let drop, that Britain and Russia should negotiate a precise frontier along the indeterminate stretch of territory lying to the south of Merv between the Amu Darya and the Afghan border with Persia along the Hari-Rud river.

This provoked a fierce struggle in St Petersburg. Those who opposed the idea, essentially the deeply entrenched forward school in the Asiatic Department and in the war ministry, were able to delay matters, since only they could provide the technical expertise essential for any delimitation. Hence, as so often had happened, officers in Central Asia pushed ahead with their own plans. The governor of the Caucasus, General Dondukov-Korsakov, responsible for Trans-Caspia, was particularly outspoken in his criticism of the proposed bases of delimitation and, as he was in overall command of the Trans-Caspian region where it was to take place, he was in a powerful position to obstruct progress.[33]

The British press was up in arms about more Russian duplicity in Central Asia, while the Gladstone government was, as usual, restrained. The queen called for a more spirited response. Lord Kimberley, secretary for India, told Sir Henry Ponsonby, the queen's private secretary: 'It will certainly be necessary to deal firmly with questions affecting the North Western frontier of Afghanistan: the particular language however to be held to the Russian Govt. must, I think, depend naturally on the course of the negotiations which are now going on.'[34] In no way mollified by this, the reply came: 'H.M. hears from India that much excitement exists in consequence of the advance of Russia & She thinks firm language should be used in St Petersburgh so as to make them understand that any attempt on Herat will be treated as a casus belli.'[35]

Embroiled as Britain was in Egypt and Sudan in the autumn of 1884—Irish issues were ablaze and parliamentary reform in progress—the government was eager for a binding agreement with Russia in Central Asia and had taken up with enthusiasm Giers's former proposal for a joint Russo-British Boundary Commission. General Sir Peter Lumsden, an experienced officer and member of the India Council, was appointed to lead the British commissioners. He arrived with an escort of several hundred armed men at Kuhsan and then Sarakhs, close to Merv, in October 1884. From Sarakhs, he advanced eastwards and was backed up by a force sent from India under Colonel West Ridgeway to Helmand, and on to

Kuhsan. The work began inauspiciously. Russia procrastinated. St Petersburg came up with a raft of reasons why work could not start—it was too late in the year; the alleged illness of General Zelenoy, who was to lead the Russian commissioners; the fall from his horse of a key Russian officer.[36] The Russians also put forward difficulties as to the exact scope of the delimitation, objected to the presence of Afghan experts on the British side and even raised questions about a possible division on ethnological grounds. Lumsden, with mounting irritation, was obliged to while away the winter at an out-of-the-way base in Central Asia.

The general, with time on his hands, was a prolific telegram writer—his frequent telegrams were sent to Tehran and Calcutta and forwarded to London—and in them for the first time Pendjeh (sometimes written as Pandjeh), an oasis halfway between Merv and Herat, was mentioned, on 26 November 1884.[37] All these telegrams giving details of British activity were deciphered in St Petersburg, so that the Russians could make plans to outwit the British. With Granville urging prudence to Lumsden in his sorties—'That is good' noted Alexander III understandably on one—the commissioner was convinced that the Russians, with furtive Cossack attacks in the vicinity, were trying to pick a quarrel and provoke a conflict with the Afghans over Pendjeh.[38] The tension was mounting but, even in this situation, in the best tradition of Great Game politesse, Granville thought it worth protesting to the Russian ambassador that General Komarov, when close to the British base, did not pay a call on Lumsden but sent a subordinate. Another Russian officer acted with a similar lack of courtesy by riding past the camp with a group of horsemen, without paying his respects.

Within the Russian government the military party was, hardly surprisingly, ascendant at the beginning of 1885 after the string of successes in Central Asia over the previous years. Giers had increasing difficulty in holding his own with the bellicose generals, who welcomed the idea of a showdown with Britain. They were further emboldened when news reached St Petersburg in early February of the massacre of General Gordon and the British garrison, and the fall of Khartoum to the dervishes of the Mahdi. The Panslavic press, led by *Vedomosti*, called for immediate action to take advantage of Britain's humiliation: 'Europe would calmly receive the intelligence that the Heratees, discontented with the rule of the emir, were desirous of following the example of the Mervees and requesting the protection of Russia.'[39]

On 7 February 1885, Gladstone announced in the House of Commons that, for reasons of prestige, it would unhappily be necessary to crush the

Mahdi in Sudan. The prime minister was feeble and unconvincing. In a censure vote on 27 February, the government's majority fell to fourteen. Then, a dramatic and unforeseen crisis in Anglo-Russian relations afforded him the excuse to reverse his previous decision to destroy the Mahdi. These events made clear the close inter-relationship between the affairs of India and the events in Egypt and Sudan. As Lord Kimberley declared: 'Does anyone really suppose that if we did not possess an Indian Empire we should have interfered in Egypt!'[40]

The British government was aware that the Russians were already at Pendjeh in mid-February, having moved south from Merv. To whom Pendjeh belonged was a matter of dispute. The Russians claimed that it lay outside the frontier of Afghanistan and that Afghans had only been there since Merv was occupied by the Russians. Britain insisted that Pendjeh was in Afghanistan.

With Britain reeling from its defeat in Sudan, it was a situation that the Russian military machine could hardly resist. There was no question in St Petersburg that the political masters could pretend otherwise. Komarov telegraphed on 20 March to inform his government that he had held discussions with the Afghans at Pendjeh, and had assured them of his amicable intentions. However, he claimed that, spurred on by a British officer, Captain Yate, the Afghans had moved closer to the Russian camp in a threatening manner, and that 'Their audacity and their arrogance were increasing.'[41] According to the general, the Afghans were advancing. He ordered them to retreat. They replied, according to Komarov's account, that they had been advised by the British not to move. To insist on his orders, the Russian brought his men forward, close to the Afghan encampment, still hoping, he wrote, for a peaceful outcome: 'But artillery fire and a cavalry attack obliged me to accept combat.'[42]

The Afghan force occupying Pendjeh was driven away in a battle in which hundreds of Afghans and a few Russians were killed. The Russian knowledge of the small Afghan force that the deciphered British telegrams had provided proved critical to the success. They had made sure they had a sufficiently large force. Russia announced that Pendjeh had been annexed.

Sir Edward Thornton in St Petersburg thought that war was inevitable.[43] Lord Randolph Churchill, a young Conservative MP visiting India, believed that Indian security was seriously menaced and the advance to Pendjeh a cause for war. Queen Victoria had telegraphed Alexander III in early March to appeal to him personally to prevent the calamity of an armed conflict. Anti-Russian sentiment convulsed Britain, and produced a panic on the stock exchange. Gladstone asserted himself, with a vigour worthy of Disraeli. He spoke in the House of Commons on 20 and 27 April, and he was clear that

> Whose was the provocation is a matter of the utmost consequence. We only know that the attack was a Russian attack ... All I say is, we cannot in that state of affairs close the book and say, 'We will look into it no more'. We must do our best to have right done in the matter.[44]

On 27 April he asked for a vote of credit of £11 million, the largest ever amount raised for military purposes, of which £6 million was earmarked for India. It was announced that all the forces of the empire would be concentrated immediately in readiness to meet the threat from the Russian act of wanton and high-handed aggression. But what mattered above all was Herat. Thornton was instructed to inform Giers that any attempt by Russian troops to occupy Herat would be considered tantamount to a declaration of war.[45]

The Pendjeh incident proved a turning point. There was the realization in St Petersburg that the British could no longer be taunted. The scales were now tilted in favour of Giers. The finance minister, the Grand Duke Vladimir, the emperor's brother, and even the ardent nationalist Nicholas Ignatiev rallied. The minister of war admitted that the Russian army was in the midst of reorganization, the navy and coastal defences unprepared and, not least, the treasury was empty. Alexander agreed that delimitation of Afghanistan's northern frontier would go ahead.

On the British side it was proposed that if Abdur Rahman must give up Pendjeh then he should at least retain the Zulficar Pass linking north and west Afghanistan with Persian Khorasan. The wise and restrained emir accepted this without remonstrance, and said he attached little importance to Pendjeh which would bring turbulent Turcomans under his rule, but possession of the pass was essential to Afghanistan. Above all, he did not want a conflict between the neighbouring empires involving Afghanistan. The Russian government agreed, as Zulficar was a small concession compared with acquisition of Pendjeh closer to Herat.

Gladstone's government fell in June 1885 and detailed consideration of the Afghan frontier delimitation passed to Lord Salisbury's administration. Despite an earlier agreement with Russia as to what exactly was meant by Zulficar—essentially how much territory was to be included in Afghanistan—prolonged and complicated discussions to defuse the crisis ensued. The Russians pressed for a more southerly limit than the British government had promised Abdur Rahman, but by late August a compromise was reached that was incorporated in a protocol signed by Salisbury and the Russian ambassador, George de Staal, on 10 September.

This was only a first step in settling the north-western frontier of Afghanistan. A reconstituted commission led by West Ridgeway (Lumsden had been replaced as he had favoured a declaration of war on Russia in April) and Colonel Kuhlberg on the Russian side began work at Zulficar in the autumn of 1885. Even then, obstruction by the local Russian military continued. A substantial group in military circles hoped that the commission would fail. Deadlock was reached in September 1886, with the joint commission unable to agree on an 80-kilometre stretch between Dukchai and the Amu Darya, and there was much mysterious moving of demarcation posts at night by persons unknown. Ridgeway proved an able negotiator, who convinced Salisbury to make concessions to Russia, much to Staal's relief: 'Lord Salisbury had been convinced that the Imperial Cabinet was not going to move.'[46] There were certainly strong elements in the Russian military party who wished to keep the Afghan frontier undefined, so as to retain the possibility for further action among the Turcomans. A rumour spread in the spring of 1887 that the Russians intended to repeat the tactics of Pendjeh and, while the negotiations hung fire, to take possession of Khamiab. However, Alexander III, of whom Salisbury had contemptuously written in 1885, 'I am more inclined to believe that … the Emperor is really his own Minister, and so bad a Minister that no consequent coherent policy is pursued', intervened in May, and summoned Ridgeway for an audience, throwing his considerable weight behind a rapid conclusion of the frontier dispute.[47]

In July 1887 the last obstacles were overcome and the Russian war ministry agreed to the modified Amu Darya frontier with the Hari-Rud, which gave Russia a southward bulge around Pendjeh, bringing it closer to Herat. Many in both Britain and Russia believed that the agreement would not permanently halt Russia's advance in Central Asia. (In fact, the north-western frontier fixed in 1887 would hold until the Soviet invasion of Afghanistan in 1979.)

In St Petersburg, Ivan Zinoviev, head of the Asiatic Department, and Ridgeway signed the final protocol. The Russian military grumbled, but Staal in London was delighted. To him what mattered was that Anglo-Russian relations had risen from the nadir of 1885: 'We had no reason to complain about the attitude of England towards us in this regard.'[48]

24

THE BATTENBERGS

RUSSIA VERSUS BRITAIN OVER BULGARIA

The Congress of Berlin had decided to create the autonomous principality of Bulgaria, theoretically under Turkish suzerainty but endowed with its own constitution and ruled by a prince. This was the single important gain for Russia at Berlin. The next step, after commissioners had delimited the frontiers in 1879, was to find a ruler of what was widely expected to become a Russian satellite state.

From the Russian point of view it was they who, because of their war against Turkey, had enabled the largely Slav Orthodox Bulgarians to become *de facto* free of Ottoman rule. The Russian government therefore expected due recognition from the liberated people and that the new state would welcome its benevolent, tutoring hand. The fund of gratitude towards Russia, though, was not as great as the Russians believed. The Bulgarians after the war counted on gaining their freedom and did not wish simply to change masters. For a decade this Balkan country was to play an important role in European politics, in particular between Britain and Russia.

The powers had agreed at Berlin that the ruler of the new Bulgaria should not be a member of any of the ruling houses of Europe, which ruled out the ambitions of Prince Carol of Romania, a Hohenzollern. The Russian general Prince Alexander Dondukov-Korsakov had assumed administrative powers in Bulgaria and hoped to be elevated to ruler. But Alexander II had rightly recognized that such a flagrant assertion of Russian aims would be unacceptable to the powers. He was persuaded by his machinating brother-in-law, Prince Alexander of Hesse-Darmstadt, that the prince's second son, Prince Alexander of Battenberg, was the ideal candidate.

Prince Alexander of Hesse-Darmstadt was born in 1823, the third son of the Grand Duke Louis II of Hesse and by Rhine, a minor German princeling who, like so many of his kind, would have to seek fame and fortune abroad. Alexander's chance came in 1841 when his sister Marie married the tsarevich, Alexander of Russia.

At the time of her marriage, the timorous seventeen-year-old minor German princess persuaded her father and new husband to allow her eighteen-year-old brother, Alexander, to accompany her to Russia.[1] On their arrival, Nicholas I appointed Alexander a colonel in the household cavalry, and he soon distinguished himself in campaigns in the Caucasus. In the turmoil of the 1840s, he led a regiment of cavalry to the assistance of the Austrians against the Hungarian rising. As a result he became a great favourite at the Russian court, a member of the tsarevich's inner circle.

This all changed in 1851, when Alexander eloped with the Polish-born Countess Julia von Hauke, a lady-in-waiting to his sister Marie. The marriage was necessarily morganatic as the bride was not of royal birth and therefore any children were debarred from using the title Hesse. In Russia, a furious Nicholas I stripped Alexander of his command and rank. The German prince then joined the Austrian army and fought at Solferino. A few years later, when his sister became empress of Russia, he was restored to his rank and rights in Russia. Ultimately, what was to prove of greater importance, however, was that his brother, now Grand Duke Louis III of Hesse, resuscitated for him a Hessian title that had become extinct in 1314, that of Battenberg, a small town in northern Hesse. Julia became Countess, later Princess of Battenberg, and her children henceforth bore the title of Serene Highness (lower than Royal Highness), princes and princesses of Battenberg. They were Marie, Louis, Alexander (Sandro), Henry (Liko) and Francis Joseph.

On becoming Russian emperor, his brother-in-law bestowed on Alexander and his family an importance and influence far beyond that of their official status. Alexander of Hesse, a man of great charm that he passed on to his descendants, concentrated his energies on furthering the careers of his children. The young Battenberg children spent their summers with their Russian cousins at Alexander's Heiligenberg Castle in Hesse, although the tsarevich Alexander, the future Alexander III, treated his morganatic cousins with unconcealed disdain.

The Battenberg children were at the same time frequent visitors to England, as Princess Alice, Queen Victoria's second daughter, was married to Louis IV, Grand Duke of Hesse, and was thus the niece of Alexander of Hesse. In numerous letters, Alice urged her mother to take an interest in the Battenberg children. The eldest boy, Prince Louis, decided in 1868, under the influence of Victoria's sailor son, Alfred, that he wanted to join the British navy and he soon afterwards became a British subject. Louis impressed the Prince of Wales and was part of the prince's entourage on a visit to India in 1875–6. But it was the second, most handsome of the four sons, Alexander (Sandro), whom Queen Victoria came to adore. Invitations to Osborne were frequent.

Alexander of Hesse, always aware of the need to maintain his Russian connections, was delighted that his second son had fought with distinction in the Russian army in the war of 1877–8. When, in 1879, the choice of a ruler of the new Bulgaria had to be made, Alexander II had thus been persuaded to back the young Alexander of Battenberg, his favourite nephew, confident that he would do Russia's bidding. The tsarevich wanted to see his Danish brother-in-law Prince Waldemar elected, but was overruled by his father.

The British government, seeing the new Bulgaria as no more than a Balkan means to keep Russia in check, and accepting its colonial relationship with Russia, was unperturbed at the election by the Bulgarian assembly, the Sobranje, of Alexander of Battenberg in April 1879. The foreign secretary, Lord Salisbury, accepted Battenberg's assurances that he would rid himself of the Russian officials as soon as was feasible. He described the prince as 'a typical Life guardsman—much perplexed at being a reigning Prince. All his sentiments are unexceptionable.'[2] Salisbury's acceptance of the choice was simply that Alexander 'had the advantage of being a *persona grata* not only in Russia and Austria, but also ... in London, on account of the position of his brother [Louis]'.[3]

Although the British government did not feel any particular attachment to Prince Alexander of Battenberg, his relatives felt very differently. Battenberg's uncle, the Grand Duke of Hesse, assured his mother-in-law, Queen Victoria, that 'he is *not Russian* in heart, and ... he is *not* inclined to act as Russia's tool [marionette]'.[4] The queen surprisingly did not hold it against Sandro that he had served in the Russian army in 1877, and made clear her position to the foreign secretary:

> I ... wish to express my sincere interest in young Prince Alexander of B. and my belief that his professions are perfectly sincere, as he and his brother are singularly honest and good young men, known and liked by

> my dear Alice. Any help and encouragement we can give him would be well bestowed.[5]

Beaconsfield, the prime minister, was unworried about the creation of the new principality, and had told the crown princess of Germany, Queen Victoria's eldest daughter, Vicky, during the Congress of Berlin that without Eastern Rumelia he would give Bulgaria seven years at most.

What does seem exceptionable is that a 22-year-old German soldier should have been parachuted into a Balkan country. Alexander had no knowledge of Bulgaria and was a diplomatic and political novice. It seems amazing that there was so little thought given to the task awaiting the young man, no foreboding of the drama that was to ensue.

From the beginning, everything went wrong. The Ottoman sultan, who had lost Bulgaria at Berlin, showed his hostility when the prince visited him in Constantinople. Then in Sofia, the military governor, Prince Dondukov-Korsakov, for reasons of failed ambition, did not go out of his way to prepare a favourable reception for the new ruler. The new prince's residence had mud walls and a ceiling that was not waterproof. Far worse were the complexities of attempting to rule under the provisions of the Bulgarian constitution. This liberal instrument, hastily worked out in the weeks before the prince's arrival by a Russian commission and the Bulgarian Sobranje, failed to define clearly the boundaries between legislative and executive authority, and gave more power to the assembly and less to the prince than Battenberg had been led to expect, or was prepared to accept. And the Bulgarian politicians were inexperienced, headstrong and devious.

The prince soon demonstrated his impetuous nature. In a letter to Alexander II in September 1879 he wrote:

> The fears I entertained regarding the Constitution have unfortunately been fulfilled even sooner than I expected ... This again proves that the exaggerated liberalism favoured by the Constitution only benefits the unsound and corrupt section of the population and not the decent well-meaning people ... Every day I am more convinced that it is impossible to govern the country under the present Constitution, and I am determined to make this a *sine qua non*.[6]

What was already weakening Battenberg's position in the eyes of Alexander II, who had his men keeping a close watch on the prince's correspondence, was that he was at the same time criticizing the Russians in Bulgaria. 'All the scum of Russia has ... taken refuge here', the prince wrote. There followed complaints about 'the Russian system of bribery' and the 'most imprudent demands' made upon him by the Russians.[7] According to Prince Carol of Romania, Battenberg felt undying gratitude towards Alexander II, but 'he has no words bad enough for the policy which the Russians are pursuing in the country and which he is called up to keep in check'.[8]

For as long as Maria Alexandrovna was empress and Alexander II emperor of Russia, Alexander of Battenberg had powerful protectors and he was sympathetically listened to in St Petersburg when he made the journey there in February 1880. (He and his father were among those present in the Winter Palace when a bomb intended for Alexander II exploded there.) All this changed when his cousin came to the Russian throne in March 1881. Alexander III did not hide his long-standing contempt for his low-born German cousin.

Battenberg attended Alexander II's funeral in March 1881 and attempted to discuss his troubles with the new emperor. It would seem reasonable to assume that Alexander III, so soon after the assassination of his father, and with a plethora of new burdens thrust upon him, was unable to pay much attention to the affairs of Bulgaria, but the naive Battenberg returned to Sofia believing that the emperor had sanctioned his acting as he thought fit.

The young man duly dismissed the Russian-appointed war minister, General Piotr Parasenov, and replaced him with a Finnish-Swedish officer of the Russian army, General Kazimir Ehrnrooth, one of the Russians placed by St Petersburg in 1879, but one in whom the prince had confidence. With Ehrnrooth's support, Battenberg dismissed the Liberal cabinet then in office, formed one of his own choosing with Ehrnrooth as prime minister and asked the Sobranje to suppress the constitution. He demanded full powers to govern as he might choose for a period of seven years; otherwise he would abdicate. On 13 July 1881, the Sobranje agreed. Battenberg then issued a manifesto proclaiming the golden age of Bulgaria that was to follow.

The prince of Bulgaria's *coup d'état* took St Petersburg by surprise, as the Russian government's attention was concentrated on dealing with nihilists at home and events in Central Asia. The conscientious Nicholas Giers, head of the foreign office, nevertheless was called upon to deal with little Bulgaria. He believed that the prince had exceeded his mandate and that, if he assumed too much authority, it would bode ill for Russia. But Russia had come to regret that she had accepted the liberal constitution and sympathized with the prince's frustration. Alexander III was advised by Giers to be supportive of Battenberg, and the emperor wrote to his cousin:

> You can count on me, but I need hardly add that I can only give you my moral support and even that will be restricted, as it excludes interference in the internal affairs of Bulgaria … I therefore feel assured that you will not fail to realize that you are assuming a heavy personal responsibility to the memory of my beloved father, to Russia, Bulgaria, Europe, and I might even say with regard to history.[9]

Nevertheless, the Russian government was by this time beginning to feel alarm over the manner in which the Bulgarian situation was developing, as Battenberg was, despite his assurances, not the pliant Russian puppet he was expected to be. To this were added lurid stories of Battenberg's supposed iniquities as related by the dismissed Parasenov. The Russians insisted on the recall of Ehrnrooth, and two new Russian generals, Leonid Sobolev and Alexander Kaulbars, were appointed minister president and minister of the interior and war. Sobolev was patronizing and appeared intent on making Bulgaria another khanate, similar to the one he had ruled in Bukhara. His lavish bribes to the Sobranje were badly received. There was a row between Sobolev and the Bulgarians over a proposed railway from the Danube to Sofia. In their reports to St Petersburg, the two generals painted the prince in the blackest of colours, claiming that he was in the pay of the detested Austrians who were supporting the Bulgarians. His ingratitude to the imperial family, to whom he owed everything, was unbounded.

Lonely and depressed in Sofia, Battenberg expressed his misery in numerous telegrams to his *aide-de-camp* and friend Captain Polsikov in St Petersburg, all of which were deciphered by the Russians: 'I fear that my enemies in Russia are setting traps for you. I have you, who is all my happiness; that is more than sufficient. I embrace you from the bottom of my heart, my adored friend.'[10]

With Alexander III's coronation set for May 1883, Battenberg decided to use this as a reason for making the journey to Moscow to explain that it was impossible to govern the country while the two generals were there. In fact, the two generals, plus a delegation of their choosing, had also arrived in the old Russian capital and the emperor early on received Sobolev and Kaulbars, while Battenberg repeatedly sought an audience in vain. He pestered Giers, who became increasingly irritated by the young man. Then, unwisely, the prince stormed over to Alexander's quarters and virtually forced himself into the latter's presence, a grievous offence against rigid Russian protocol. He won his point about the rival delegation, and later paid an official visit to the emperor. However, when Alexander came to return the call, the prince, either by intrigue or carelessness, was not there to receive him. From that time onwards, Alexander III did not try to hide his hatred of the upstart Alexander of Battenberg and his desire to unseat him was little short of an obsession. According to the Austrian ambassador in St Petersburg, he saw the prince as 'an untruthful ingrate with a predilection for swindle who, moreover, has most imprudently insulted the Tsar, his benefactor'.[11]

Battenberg was not friendless. Frank Lascelles, the British consul general in Sofia, was sympathetic to his efforts to combat Russian attempts to run Bulgaria as they thought fit, but held that Battenberg had not taken sufficient trouble to gain the confidence and affection of his subjects. Lascelles had little influence in the foreign office: Battenberg's energetic champion with the British government was Queen Victoria, who followed closely Sandro's trials and tribulations, and his knowledge of her support contributed not a little to his stand against Russia. She entered the fray, protesting that Lascelles reported what Gladstone wanted to hear. From her personal knowledge of the prince, she was impressed by Battenberg's boldness. A spoke would have to be put in Russia's wheel if Russia was to be prevented from forcing the prince to abdicate and installing a Russian vassal in his place so as to have a free hand in Bulgaria. The queen wrote to the foreign secretary:

> Standing alone, without help from any of the Powers, he has relieved the Bulgarians from the presence of the irresponsible Russian Generals, he has induced the two opposing political parties to unite, he has been received with enthusiasm in the Chamber and he is aiding his people to render themselves free and independent of Russia.[12]

Frustrated by the foreign secretary Granville's failure to act, the queen passed the baton to the Prince of Wales. He was instructed to write to Herbert Bismarck, the German chancellor's son who was living in London, to say that the queen was most anxious that Germany should either intervene in St Petersburg on behalf of Battenberg, or at least assist him with good advice. Bismarck politely replied that Germany did not interfere in the affairs of the Balkan states. The Prince of Wales was undeterred:

> That is true, but what can we do with this Government? The Queen has tried her utmost to persuade her Ministers to intervene in St Petersburg, but in vain. She is very annoyed about it, but finds it impossible to make Lord Granville do anything. Nevertheless, she feels that something should be done for the Prince of Bulgaria.[13]

While she had not referred to it in her communications with the foreign secretary and her eldest son, Victoria had been told by her eldest daughter, Vicky, the German crown princess, of the possibility of a marriage between Victoria, Vicky's eldest daughter, and Battenberg. (The enthusiasm that the crown princess manifested came essentially from young Vicky, rather than Battenberg.) The queen was excited at the prospect of her granddaughter's marrying her beloved Sandro. When Prince Bismarck got wind of this, he was furious. A Hohenzollern could not stoop to become a lowly Battenberg, and such a union would be unacceptable to Alexander III, with whom he wished to be on good terms.[14]

An attempt to kidnap the prince was made in 1883 by persons unknown. It was frustrated by the courage of the sentry on duty at the palace in Sofia. In the hope of arresting his clearly weakening position with Bulgarian nationalists, Battenberg restored the constitution in that year. This enraged St Petersburg, which saw Bulgaria and the prince slipping from Russian control. In a rare example of a Russian foreign minister's accepting an article in the British press as being impartial, Giers was impressed by an account of the former Liberal minister W. E. Foster's travels through Bulgaria that year, in which he wrote:

> The Bulgarians are well able to govern themselves. That is the chief fact that is impressed upon my mind as the result of my visit. If only foreign Powers will leave them to themselves they will work out a very creditable future for Bulgaria. Their progress has already been surprising, and if they are left alone it will continue ... There is no place in either of the Bulgarias where law and order do not prevail, and where the authority of the police is disputed.[15]

Giers regretfully accepted that 'Bulgaria has no need for Russian assistance. She is more advanced than Russia in many respects ... That should at least make us doubt our power in Bulgaria and make us more prudent, if we are to avoid the alternative of a recourse to arms or a humiliating failure.'[16]

Giers's view was rejected by Alexander III. The Russian emperor was not prepared to let go of Bulgaria. He was determined to bolster Russian influence in the principality and bring about the prince's abdication. The new Russian political agent, Alexander Koyander, sent to Sofia in the spring of 1884, was known to be devoting his energies to persuading pro-Russian Bulgarian politicians to take the initiative in ridding the country of the prince.

However, Battenberg still had the British card to play. His elder brother, Prince Louis, had in 1883 become engaged to Victoria, daughter of the Grand Duke of Hesse and his late wife Alice, Queen Victoria's daughter. Victoria of Hesse was the queen's favourite granddaughter, and her approval of the match was a distinct feather in the cap of the Battenbergs. Not only this, but Henry (Liko), Battenberg's younger brother, became engaged in 1884 to Queen Victoria's youngest daughter, Beatrice, whom the queen had wanted to keep unmarried at her side in her old age. Unlike the rulers of the northern courts (Russia, Germany and Austria-Hungary), the queen did not attach much importance to morganatic descent and believed in the importance of introducing fresh blood into royal families. She therefore welcomed the dashing Louis and Liko. But what mattered above all in making Liko acceptable was that he was prepared to live at Osborne House. In addition to the redoubtable queen, Battenberg now had two brothers in place in Britain to plead his case in his struggle against Russia.

The situation in Bulgaria simmered along in a precarious state throughout 1884. In 1885 it exploded, but not because of events in Bulgaria itself.

The Congress of Berlin had kept separate the two Bulgarian provinces of Bulgaria and Eastern Rumelia, but a movement for national unification of Bulgaria and Eastern Rumelia developed in the latter. On 18 September 1885, a bloodless revolution took place in Philippopolis (today's Plovdiv), the capital of Eastern Rumelia. Gavril Pasha, the Turkish governor general of the province, was deposed, and nationalists, who had organized the movement with the cognizance of at least some of the authorities in Sofia, proclaimed the union of Eastern Rumelia with Bulgaria under Prince Alexander of Battenberg. The prince, foreseeing difficulties with the powers, hesitated before he accepted the union. He realized that his position in Bulgaria demanded that he assume the leadership of the national movement, and knew that, if he had refused, it was extremely unlikely that the Bulgarians would allow him to continue as their ruler.

The effect of the union on the powers was the reverse of what would have been expected a few years earlier. Russia and Britain each executed a political *volte-face*. Russia, the power which had originally planned a Big

Bulgaria in 1878, was furious at unification: the ultimate blame lay with Britain. The Russian government was 'convinced that the English Government is following a course hostile to Russia in protecting the escapade of Prince Alexander and sponsoring the reunion of the two Bulgarias to substitute its influence for ours in this expanded state'.[17] George de Staal, the new Russian ambassador in London, was instructed to make clear to Salisbury that 'we must vent all our fury against the conduct of England ... she will bear a great responsibility for all the chaos that will follow and from which she will not gain any advantage'.[18]

Battenberg was seen as a two-faced British stooge who the previous month had met Giers at Franzensbad and given assurances that he would not take any steps to further the cause of unification. Alexander III ordered all Russian officers out of Bulgaria on 21 September, when it was apparent that Battenberg would accept the role of governing a united Bulgaria. He announced that he would not recognize the unification as long as Battenberg remained in office, and the prince was removed from the Russian army list. This last, a pointless example of personal vindictiveness, produced a deplorable impression of the Russian emperor throughout Europe.

Britain, formerly the opponent of Big Bulgaria, had now come to see that Bulgaria, far from being an outpost for a Russian advance on Constantinople, was on the contrary a barrier to Russian expansion in that direction. Salisbury, now prime minister, proposed accepting the union, but only as a 'personal union' under Battenberg and not as a constitutional alteration to the Berlin Treaty. This sophism reassured Queen Victoria, who was again demanding that Sandro must be backed by the British government against the Russians.

At the same time, Salisbury was wary of the new Big Bulgaria becoming too strong and posing a threat to Turkey, for so long supported by Britain. Another danger of unequivocal support for Battenberg was of a Russian-inspired Panslav rising in Bulgaria, unseating the prince. But not only Russia was opposed to the unification of Bulgaria and Eastern Rumelia: so too was Austria-Hungary, bordering the new expanded Balkan state. The Austrian foreign minister proposed a conference, to which Salisbury could not reasonably object. The Constantinople Conference was duly convened; Britain was let off the hook of either alienating British public opinion, which was strongly pro-Battenberg, or taking on Russia, so firmly anti-Battenberg.

Relief came from an unlikely source—Serbia, Bulgaria's north-westerly neighbour. On 14 November, King Milan of Serbia, on the basis of an insignificant border dispute, declared war on Bulgaria. His own predominance in the Balkans was threatened by Bulgaria's unification and he judged that with the union with Eastern Rumelia, the recall of the Russian officers and the reorganization that was necessarily taking place in expanded Bulgaria, it was a propitious moment to attack.

Because of the disturbed internal conditions in Bulgaria, the powers expected to witness a quick Serbian victory; to the amazement of all, the Bulgarian army not only defeated the Serbs, but also prepared to invade Serbia itself. In this crisis, Austria stepped in to protect its *protégé*, Serbia, and forced the conclusion of a peace based on the status quo ante.

Despite the intense hatred that the Russian government felt towards Battenberg, and its opposition to the unification of Bulgaria, it recognized that Russia could not afford to precipitate a major Balkan crisis over the events of 1885 (Central Asia was a more important problem). Although Bismarck maintained his support for Russia for wider political reasons, Britain and Austria-Hungary were openly delighted to see this blow to Russian prestige and power. A compromise solution was finally agreed upon. Battenberg was recognized as governor general of Eastern Rumelia, in theory only for five years, and the provinces were to remain administratively separate. Battenberg, however, almost immediately violated this agreement and joined the two assemblies. United Bulgaria was created.

Although Bulgarian unification had now been achieved, the Russian government did not let up in its efforts to regain control and to oust Battenberg. Alexander III, who placed the entire question on as personal and emotional a basis as Queen Victoria, was particularly bitter. There was still a deep-seated feeling in high places in Russia that the Bulgarian Slavs supported them and that only the prince and his regime prevented reconciliation. Conspiracies directed against the person of Battenberg and his government therefore received thinly veiled assistance from St Petersburg.

On the night of 21 August 1886, with the connivance of Alexander III and Giers, a band of conspirators, including officers Battenberg had trusted, entered the prince's bedroom in Sofia and compelled him to sign a letter of abdication. They then spirited him and his brother Francis Joseph, who was staying with him, out of the country along the Danube in Battenberg's royal yacht, handing them over at the first Russian port, Reni, to the Russian authorities. 'A common felon could not be worse treated', fulminated Queen Victoria, 'the revolutionists were bribed and instigated by a Russian official agent … surely a breach of the law of nations … Russia has failed, and it seems clear that the Bulgarians and the

Roumelians love their Prince and wish him to reign over them.'[19] Alexander III then ordered Battenberg to take the train to Lemberg (today's Lviv in Ukraine). Battenberg's disappearance and mysterious kidnapping made him a hero in Britain and Bulgaria. Queen Victoria dispatched his brother Louis to Lemberg to bolster his morale and persuade the prince to return to Bulgaria.

A pro-Russian provisional government was established. It proved of only very short duration. After three days, the reins of government were taken over by forces loyal to Battenberg under the leadership of the Bulgarian Russophobe politician, Stefan Stambolov. Thus, only eight days after the kidnapping, Battenberg recrossed the frontier into Bulgaria. Confused and at the end of his tether after seven years' struggle, Battenberg committed a stupendous blunder. Under the impression, difficult to believe today, that Russian support for his return would be forthcoming, he telegraphed the Russian emperor: 'As Russia gave me my crown, I am prepared to give it back into the hands of its sovereign.'[20] This message naturally enraged the Bulgarian nationalists, who had done so much to support Battenberg in his struggle, but it provided Alexander III with the welcome opportunity of accepting it: 'I cannot countenance your return to Bulgaria as I foresee the disastrous results it entails for that sorely tried country.'[21] Not content with this the emperor had his and Battenberg's telegrams published in the Russian press. The prince appointed a regency and left the country.

Battenberg's loyal supporters in Bulgaria, in Berlin (though only the crown prince and princess) and London increased their clamour for his return. Queen Victoria was obsessed by the fate of Alexander of Battenberg for several months. She blamed the former Gladstone government for its refusal to provide active support for the prince against Russia in previous years, and expected better of the new Conservative administration. On learning of the abduction, Victoria dispatched an urgent telegram to Salisbury lambasting 'these Russian fiends'.[22] She lamented:

> the cruel end of the exertions and self-sacrifice of the poor dear young Prince, whose great abilities and bravery (far greater than those of any other abroad) were the admiration of everyone … and now *here* the worst thing which *could* have *happened* for us and Turkey, has *taken place*! Russia is intriguing right and left, and we *must not* tamely swallow *everything* with a mere protest! Russia sets us at defiance! … The most able and independent Prince Alexander of Bulgaria has been driven away, and we must not swallow *that* (meant as a slap in our face) without a *formal protest*, and … we must not accept any Russian candidate.[23]

The queen's exertions were in vain. Battenberg made his position clear to her on 6 September:

> I beg Your Majesty to believe that I have only come to the decision of abdicating after mature deliberation. Three-fourths of all officers are mixed up in the conspiracy ... The people and the soldiers are on my side, but supported alone by them I cannot govern ... I only returned to Bulgaria in order to be able to leave of my own free will.[24]

Russia now had the opportunity of re-establishing her influence in Bulgaria, and Britain feared that she would invade Bulgaria, egged on by Bismarck. Yet the mistakes of the past were repeated. Baron Kaulbars, dispatched from St Petersburg, resorted to the same crude pressure and violent measures that had alienated the Bulgarians in the past. When the newly elected Bulgarian Sobranje refused to accept the Russian choice of a prince and proceeded to elect a new ruler of their own, despite Russian opposition, Kaulbars and all Russian officials were recalled from the country and diplomatic relations severed.

In December 1886, the name of Prince Ferdinand of Saxe-Coburg, 'Foxy Ferdy', was proposed in the Sobranje, and in July 1887 he was voted to replace Alexander of Battenberg. Queen Victoria greeted the choice with disbelief: 'He is totally unfit—delicate, eccentric and effeminate ... Should be stopped at once.'[25] There was nothing she could do. Russia, though, had its own objections to Ferdinand on the grounds of his Austrian connections and Catholicism and his known deals to buy arms in Belgium that he could take to Bulgaria. But neither of the powers could sway the Bulgarians in their choice of this unsavoury character. In the first years of his reign the new ruler was without the recognition of any of the powers and his tenure was precarious due to the constant threat of Russia invading. Nevertheless, the new Bulgarian state under the political guidance of Stambolov successfully threw off the domination of Russia and survived.[26] Russia seethed for years about Britain's denying her rights in Bulgaria.

Alexander of Battenberg was handed a poisoned chalice in 1879. The idea that the young man would be able to rule a newly created semi-autonomous state that Russia considered hers by right to dominate, while at the same time furthering Russophobic designs inculcated in him in Britain, was clearly unrealistic. Queen Victoria's vigorous and highly emotional championing of Sandro as the man whose task it was to wrest Bulgaria from Russian domination only made him yet more vulnerable to

Russian ire. His fall was a disaster waiting to happen. Battenberg tried to appease his powerful master, Alexander III, who from the outset sought his total subjugation or removal. But the crude and heavy-handed manner with which the Russians treated Bulgaria in the first half of the 1880s only served to encourage Battenberg and Bulgarian nationalists to assert their independence of Russia. In such a situation Alexander of Battenberg's downfall was inevitable, his mistakes and ill-judgement only incidental to a situation beyond his control.

On 10 September 1886, a broken Prince Alexander of Battenberg arrived back in Darmstadt in Hesse. He hoped to be given a post in the German army but Bismarck would have none of this as it would displease Alexander III, and the chancellor had suffered enough of 'this never-ending Battenberg business'.[27] Understandably, the prince was depressed. This lifted when he met a Darmstadt opera singer, Johanna Loisinger. They married in 1889. Battenberg had embarked on a new life and decided that a new name would be appropriate. His father had adopted the name Battenberg for his children on his marriage in 1851; his son followed suit by dropping not only the name Battenberg, which had brought with it all his vicissitudes in Bulgaria, but his princely title too. (He claimed he was doing it to protect Princess Beatrice, now that she had become a Battenberg.) Henceforth, Alexander would be known as the Count of Hartenau. The new name came from a small estate his father had owned, named after a family that had died out. Two children were born who faded into German society. Alexander of Battenberg died in 1893 at the age of thirty-six.

His younger brother, Henry, was killed while serving in the British army in the Ashanti expedition of 1896. Princess Beatrice, Henry's widow, lived until 1944.

But it was the family of Louis, the eldest Battenberg son of Prince Alexander of Hesse, which would establish the Battenberg legacy. He had married Victoria, daughter of Louis IV of Hesse and Princess Alice. Victoria's sister, Alexandra (Alix), married Nicholas II of Russia. Another sister, Elizabeth (Ella), married the Russian Grand Duke Sergei, a younger brother of Alexander III. Louis of Battenberg became British First Lord of the Admiralty in 1911, but was forced to resign in 1914 in the face of opposition in Britain on the grounds of his German ancestry. Like the British royal family, he renounced his German princely title and name in 1917 and became the Marquess of Milford Haven. Battenberg was anglicized to Mountbatten, just as Saxe-Coburg became Windsor. Louis's second son, also Louis, went on to become Earl Mountbatten of Burma and the last viceroy of India.

The elder Louis's youngest daughter, Princess Alice of Battenberg, married Prince Andrew, fourth son of the king of Greece. Their son, Philip, born in 1921, although strictly speaking through his father, Prince Philip of Sonderberg-Glücksburg-Schleswig-Holstein, like his maternal grandfather, Louis of Battenberg, served in the British navy. After distinguished service in the Second World War Prince Philip wished, like his grandfather, to become a British subject. On the advice of the home secretary, in 1946 he adopted his mother's anglicized maiden name, Mountbatten.

25

THE TSAR PEACEMAKER

During the first years of his reign, Alexander III was anxious not to make hasty changes to the foreign policy edifice erected by his father. There were, nevertheless, significant differences in their approaches to Russia's international position. Alexander II was unequivocally pro-German, devoted to his uncle, Wilhelm I, and anti-Austrian. His son recognized and accepted the personal tie to his granduncle but no more than that. Alexander III manifested clear hostility towards the newly powerful German empire. In this his influential Danish-born wife nurtured her husband's views. The emperor's dislike of Austria-Hungary was as strong as that of his father.

Essentially the Russian emperor had to accept that the international situation had been profoundly altered by the creation of united Germany; Russia's position in Europe diminished. Bismarck called the tune. For as long as Russia post-1878 remained without allies, she could be expected to be aligned with Germany according to his wishes.

The Russian minister of foreign affairs, Nicholas Giers, for his part believed that Russia, assailed with bitter internal problems and in need of a long period of peace after the exhausting war against Turkey, should take advantage of Bismarck's offer of a new agreement with Russia. The League of the Three Emperors, the *Dreikaiserbund*, had been created in 1873—a personal arrangement among the three monarchs. According to it, Germany acquired almost total security, while Russia was forced into a partnership with hated Austria. Giers recognized that Russia was not in a strong bargaining position. If Russia had refused to join the *Dreikaiserbund*, she would have faced the hostility of both Germany and Austria-Hungary. Russia needed reasonable relations with Berlin and Vienna.

The arrangement fell apart in 1878 after the Congress of Berlin but was revived in 1881 after Alexander II's death as a formal alliance. The main beneficiary of the formal *Dreikaiserbund*, signed for three years, was of course Bismarck. However, as both Germany and Austria had little interest in Central Asia, it provided Russia with the confidence to take on Britain in Asia.

The pro-German policy of Giers was opposed by influential officials in his own department. They argued that the alliance should be seen as an opportunity for broadening its terms. Russia, according to this view, should be given a free hand in Constantinople and the Straits in return for suitable compensations to Germany and Austria. The acting foreign minister successfully fought off opponents to his policy, maintaining good relations with Russia's neighbours. The treaty was renewed with minor modifications for a further three years.

The Austrians disliked any growth in Russian power in the Balkans and after the Battenberg *débâcle* in 1886, the foreign minister, Count Kalnoky, announced that a Russian occupation of Bulgaria would be a violation of the treaties and for Austria was inadmissible. The Russian ambassador in Berlin retorted: 'It is absolutely necessary that we should make Austria disappear from the map of Europe.'[1] The election of the Austrian Prince Ferdinand of Saxe-Coburg as sovereign then served to exacerbate Austro-Russian relations. (It was a matter of regret to the Russians that they were unable to decipher Austro-Hungarian telegrams, unlike their easy access to those of other countries.[2]) The *Dreikaiserbund* was clearly on its last legs. Even so, Giers advocated its maintenance, although Alexander III was unwilling to cooperate with Vienna.

In May 1887, Bismarck argued that since the German position had consistently been that Austria must be upheld, this purely defensive alliance did not preclude a separate Russo-German agreement. The secret Reinsurance Treaty concluded the following month brought the German chancellor the assurance of Russian neutrality should France attempt to reverse the defeat of 1870. In return, Germany agreed to support Russian interests in Bulgaria and the Straits. Although Bismarck in this agreement apparently assured Russia of wide support in the east, he thereafter proceeded to create, through a system of counter-alliances, a general diplomatic situation that would make it impossible for Russia to carry out an active policy either in Bulgaria or at the Straits, and thus benefit from the treaty with Germany.

The Reinsurance Treaty was only one of a wider framework of alliances encouraged by Bismarck in order to meet the collapse of the *Dreikaiserbund* in the east and the revival of *revanchisme* in France—the

Boulanger movement that erupted in 1885—and the danger of a Franco-German war that ensued.

Britain in 1885 was isolated, overstretched and insecure after defeat in the Sudan and the Pendjeh crisis. Relations with Russia had reached rock bottom and Anglo-French antagonism, provoked by colonial rivalry, had greatly increased during the previous years. But, although tensions over colonial matters had recently developed, Anglo-German relations were cordial. Italy had joined the Austro-German alliance in 1882 and in 1887 approached Britain with the request for an alliance covering their mutual interests in the Mediterranean, as Italy now had colonial ambitions in North Africa. Despite inherent British contempt for Italy, with Bismarck's encouragement the Mediterranean Agreement was signed in February 1887. This was directed primarily against extension of French control in North Africa, but only months later, when Austria-Hungary adhered, the Mediterranean agreement was clearly to preserve the status quo in the Near East and thus block Russia. The Russian government was confronted with the united front of the other powers (except France) in the eastern Mediterranean and was boxed in in the Balkans.

The Bismarckian system of alliances and counter-alliances thus brought Europe safely through 1887. It was a complicated pattern, and perhaps unnecessarily complex. Peace was maintained not so much by the existence of the agreements but because none of the powers wished to or was prepared to enter a major war. The preservation of the system also depended on the continuation in office of Bismarck.

Suddenly his ability to control German diplomacy, let alone European, came seriously into question in 1888. First Wilhelm I died in 1888. He was succeeded by his son Frederick III, a liberal holding pro-British views and married to Queen Victoria's eldest daughter Vicky. When the new kaiser died three months later he was succeeded by his son Wilhelm II. It was inevitable that the new German emperor—young, intolerant, aggressive and headstrong—would clash with the man who had been for so long accustomed to directing German policy unhindered. Bismarck was forced to resign in 1890. For his part, Alexander III could not stand the new kaiser who failed to treat the Russian emperor with the respect he expected.

The entire question of Germano-Russian relations was reviewed at the time of the scheduled renewal of the Reinsurance Treaty that year. Wilhelm accepted the advice of the new chancellor, General Count Leo von Caprivi, who insisted that the treaty should be allowed to lapse. Alexander III received the news with equanimity bordering on indifference; for Giers it was a bitter blow. He sought in vain some kind of substitute. Germany's new rulers were bent on attempting to strengthen ties with Britain.

With great reluctance Giers now had to consider a complete change of policy and the formation of an alignment previously pressed by Russian nationalists, that of an alliance and cooperation with Republican France. The diplomatic situation that Bismarck had laboured so long to prevent had thus been created. Russia and France both stood alone. Neither had any outstanding quarrel with the other; each faced dangerous neighbours. Both were colonial rivals of Britain.

Wilhelm II's advisers believed that the ideological issues that separated tsarist Russia and Republican France, so long a pariah in Russian eyes, ruled out the possibility of a Franco-Russian alliance. However, before Bismarck's fall the groundwork had already been laid for cooperation in the financial field. In an ill-advised reprisal for Russian action in the Baltic provinces, the German chancellor forbade the Reichsbank to accept Russian securities as collateral for loans in Berlin. Russia turned to Paris where the necessary funds were readily available. (France was left with much worthless paper after the Russian Revolution in 1917.)

The actual negotiations were slow with Russia hesitant to accept effective obligations towards France, and it was not until 1894 that the Franco-Russian Alliance was signed.

Even before the alliance came into existence the negative repercussions for Britain were clear. Sir Augustus Paget, the ambassador in Vienna, argued in 1891 that the rapprochement 'was an event of the most momentous European importance which may be attended with far more serious consequences'. If nothing else, both powers were likely to pursue a more decided policy 'in antagonism to the policy and interests of the other powers … and … to those of Great Britain especially'.[3] The Lords of the Admiralty argued that Britain could not now defend Constantinople against a Russian attack because of the French squadron in Toulon. British protection of the Turkish capital was possible only if France was Britain's ally, unthinkable in the early 1890s.

Russian contemporaries lauded Alexander III on his death in 1894 as the Tsar Peacemaker, and certainly, with the exception of a few short-lived monarchs in the eighteenth century, he was the only emperor whose reign had been unscathed by war. At the same time he had given a sense of purpose and new self-confidence to Russia in the international arena with the Franco-Russian Alliance. Nevertheless, Alexander III's increasing repression of dissent within Russia and persecution of the Jews in the late 1880s masked the development of a revolutionary movement in Russia more broadly based than that of the 1870s which had resulted in the assassination of his father.

26

THE TSAR PERSECUTOR

After the successful crackdown of the early 1880s the remaining revolutionaries who chose to remain in Russia, or who were unable to emigrate, went underground in the face of the government's repressive measures.[1] As Dmitri Miliutin observed, the leaders of imperial Russia did not search for the causes of the revolutionary movement, but only thought about protective police measures. The police therefore continued to report on new conspiracies, but, in contrast with the 1870s, political trials were rare and barely mentioned in the censored press. The ministries of justice and the interior had streamlined the system of administrative exile: opponents of the autocracy were silently removed from public view. The students chafed under the retrogressive 1884 University Statute; periodic strikes disturbed the empire's calm.

By 1886 the reform tradition of Alexander II was definitely quashed. The symbolic repudiation of the most fundamental of the reforms, emancipation, seen as the seedbed of liberalism, came on its twenty-fifth anniversary, with the prohibition of its observance. The emperor and Pobedonostsev feared political demonstrations but, more specifically, they wished to discourage any interest in the previous reign that might stir hopes of reform. Counter-reforms of the courts and the *zemstvos* were issued between 1887 and 1892 with increased authority assigned to the minister of justice and the governors over the *zemstvos*. The most thoroughgoing backward step, however, was the virtual elimination of the independence of urban institutions.

An attempt to assassinate Alexander III in 1887 could only serve to harden the resolve to maintain autocracy. (Among those condemned to death for their part in the plot was Alexander Ilyich Ulyanov, elder brother of the future Lenin.) Then, in 1888, the imperial train returning to Moscow derailed at Borki station leaving twenty-one dead. The carriage carrying the royal family capsized but all members escaped serious injury. Alexander himself, it was claimed, used his impressive strength to prevent the roof collapsing and took charge of the evacuation of the wounded: 'The disaster was presented as proof of the miraculous grace God sheds on the tsar and the Russian people … It was God's response to "the fervent prayers, which thousands and thousands of sons of Russia daily make for Us wherever there stands a Holy church".'[2] On the other hand, some in the ministry of the interior and police chose to see the accident as the result of a terrorist plot.

Some of the disillusioned populists turned to Marxism. Outstanding among the converts to 'scientific' socialism was George Plekhanov, who broke away from Land and Liberty, emigrated to Switzerland, and in 1883 founded the first Russian social democratic organization, Liberation of Labour, *Osvobozhdenie Truda*. Its programme, based on Marxist analysis, held that the historic destiny of Russia was not different from that of other countries; that is, Russia had to pass through the stage of capitalism before reaching the higher stage of socialism; the traditional land organization of the Russian peasantry contained no elements of the future socialist society; the industrial proletariat, not the peasantry, was the only class capable of accomplishing a social revolution; and terrorism, although a useful subsidiary weapon, was not to divert the leaders from their main task—the creation of a disciplined working-class party which would lead Russia along the path to social revolution. This was the negation of the populists' most sacred principles, and much of the time and energy of the Russian Marxists, mainly in Switzerland, was spent in writing polemics against the populists. Meanwhile the writings of Marx and Engels were translated into Russian, but groups of Marxist socialists were few and their existence precarious within Russia.

During the 1870s political *émigrés* had not been given serious attention by the regime and the Russian police operated abroad to only a limited extent. Spies had been employed by the Russian embassy in London since its establishment, but on an ad hoc basis, some permanent, some casual informers; the main target was the Poles. After 1881 the Russian police system was reorganized under the ministry of the interior, and the Special Section, the Okhrana *Osobi Otdel*, was created, which employed specialized anti-terrorist agents. This political police also exercised the legal right of administrative exile over opponents of the state. In most cases the individual was exiled to Siberia or another remote part of the empire. It became a rather common practice to offer the best-connected radicals the alternative of expulsion to Europe, on the understanding that their illegal return to Russia would constitute grounds for imprisonment. The efficiency of the Okhrana abroad therefore depended to a large degree on the complicity of the local police. In Britain, however, the government and the police remained impervious to the Okhrana's wiles and would not cooperate. In Paris the police were more amenable, which resulted in key *émigrés* crossing the Channel, to the fury of the numerous Russian agents in France.

The most prominent and talented of the Russian *émigrés* in London was Sergei Kravchinsky, known by his *nom de plume* Stepniak, who had shot dead the St Petersburg head of police in 1878. The revolutionary's great skill, attested by those around him, was as a conciliator, working to bring into alignment the disparate groups of Russian revolutionaries spread around Europe. He began by publishing his book *Underground Russia* in 1883, and contributed articles to *The Times* a year later. In 1889 he founded the Society of Friends of Russian Freedom and visited the United States the following year to establish a branch there. Kravchinsky edited the organization's newspaper, *Free Russia*, whose liberal stance, emphasizing economic over political freedom, was denounced by Plekhanov's group in Switzerland. He was successful as a novelist, beginning with *The Career of a Nihilist*, and became a friend of William Morris and George Bernard Shaw, among others. The Russophile Constance Garnett and her sister-in-law Olive welcomed Kravchinsky and his friend and collaborator, Felix Volkhovsky. Constance chose to live in Fitzroy Square at the heart of the French anarchist colony and was at first greatly attracted to Volkonsky, who was fond of recounting his twelve years spent in Siberian exile and who taught Constance and Olive Russian. (Constance became the first important translator of Russian writers.) With well-connected admirers, the Russian revolutionaries could feel at home in London.

A journalist who interviewed Kravchinsky at his St John's Wood house found the furnishings exotic: '"Couches and settees had the places that in more bourgeois homes would have been occupied by stiff-backed chairs"—the man himself was thoroughly congenial: "capable of enjoying a good dinner," and irresistibly charming as he sat sipping spiced tea and languidly smoking a cigarette.'[3] He later moved to the new, highly respectable, Arts and Crafts suburb of Bedford Park in Chiswick.

The Okhrana's western European spymaster based in Paris railed against the reports he received from an agent in London of 'the ease and affluence that the London *émigrés* enjoyed thanks to their "ghastly agitation of the English"'.[4] Russian agents were paid to shadow Kravchinsky; professional cracksmen were employed to burgle the homes of known associates of the revolutionaries; thugs were hired to beat up young women who worked on the stand of the Society of Friends of Russian Freedom in Hyde Park. Money supplied from the Okhrana purse bought an agent who infiltrated the Society.[5]

The Russian government was furious at the very public activity of the London *émigrés* and the lack of support from the British authorities in cracking down on them, in particular after the assassination of General Seliverstov in Paris in 1890, in which the finger was pointed at Kravchinsky. The foreign ministry sent Staal, the ambassador, to deliver a dispatch that came to be known as the Russian Memorandum, which argued that the British government had a duty to take action against the enemies of the Russian state living in Britain. Salisbury expressed lukewarm support for surveillance of dissident Russians, and nothing was done. Alexander III's terse reaction was: 'This is not a very reassuring result.'[6] Kravchinsky died an unrevolutionary death, killed by a train on a level crossing in Chiswick in 1895.

Many Russian *émigrés* in London spent much of their time in the Round Reading Room of the British Museum in what was regarded as the best library in the world. The true extent of the library's popularity with Russian *émigrés* is impossible to establish, despite the museum's excellent archives and the alphabetical lists of ticket holders.[7] This is in part due to the Russian revolutionaries' passion for pseudonyms, coupled with the difficulties in transcribing Russian names, and the consequent problems this poses when attempting to identify individuals in the various indexes and registers. This constant name-changing was of course necessary to throw the Okhrana off their tracks.

Prince Peter Kropotkin, the geographer and anarchist, was admitted to the library in 1881 and became a prolific reader (returning his card only in 1907). The Book of Presents shows his appreciation in his donating not only his own books but also numerous *émigré* journals and socialist and anarchist books. Soon afterwards his wife requested a reader's ticket, but the most famous Russian woman to use the library was Vera Zasulich, the would-be assassin of General Trepov in 1878, who had surprisingly been acquitted of the attempted murder.

In theory Zasulich was researching a book on Rousseau, but she admitted that she found time to enter into lengthy correspondence with friends on the continent. In these letters she describes how impossible London life is; how she can only find peace of mind in the museum, where, though stuffy, she does not mind because she buries herself up to her ears in piles of books, and finds she is gradually overcoming her desire to dash out every hour for a cigarette. Rosalia Plekhanov described meeting Zasulich:

> She wore a shapeless grey dress made out of a piece of linen from the centre and sides of which she had cut holes for her head and arms. This piece of linen was thrown over her and held by a narrow belt while the edges hung loosely all around. On her head was something not quite resembling a hat, but rather a pie, made out of crumpled grey material, while on her feet she wore clumsy wide boots which she had made herself.[8]

Sergei Kravchinsky had already registered with the library in 1884 and sponsored friends for admission. One of them, Vladimir Burtsev, became a reader in 1891. He wrote an excellent reference work on Russian political movements and figures and in 1895, under a pseudonym, published an article titled 'The British Museum', the first full description of the library's holdings of Russian manuscripts.

The museum's trustees were naturally well aware of the controversial Russians using the Reading Room and in 1894 a letter was received from the Home Office warning of the imminent publication of a second edition of Cundhill's *Dictionary of Explosives*, and expressing the desire that the book should not be lent to readers unknown to Reading Room staff. If the *bona fides* of a person wishing to consult the book were in doubt, then the matter should be reported to H.M. Chief Inspector of Explosives. The trustees agreed to take proper care and, when a copy was received some months later, it was not entered in the catalogue.

While life in Russia became increasingly oppressive for those opposed to the autocratic regime, those fortunate *émigrés* in London could, in Leo Trotsky's words, count on the 'sanctuary of the British Museum'.[9]

The dissidents in London had chosen to hold views that made life in Russia impossible for themselves without incurring the wrath of the authorities. Jews in Russia, unless they were able to emigrate, found themselves singled out for yet more particularly harsh treatment in the repression of the late 1880s. The influx of Jewish students and their high scholastic attainments had caused irritation among influential anti-Semites and led the government to issue two circulars in 1887 with, for the first time in Russian history, quotas for Jewish students in higher and secondary schools. Within the Jewish Pale of Settlement the quota was set at

10 per cent of the student body and outside the Pale 5 per cent, except in St Petersburg and Moscow where it was 3 per cent. Since the quotas were considerably below the actual number of Jewish students, thousands of them were henceforth denied educational opportunities above the level of primary education. In 1887 the cities of Rostov-on-Don and Taganrog, hitherto included in the Pale, were barred to new Jewish residents. Two years later a *ukaz* was issued essentially excluding Jews from the legal profession. This marked the beginning of a determined new anti-Semitic campaign, pinning blame on the Jews for Russia's internal problems.

While in *Narodnaya Volya* in the 1870s there had been few Jews, this had changed in the late 1880s, by which time there was a proportionally large number arrested and many were exiled to the far east of Siberia.

Press reports in Britain of the new enactions against the Jews in Russia resulted in a repeat of the reaction to the pogroms of 1881–2. Staal reported home in January 1890 on the political agitation brewing, expressing an unconvincing hope that it would rapidly calm down, as every day he faced a new article in the British press on the subject. A book published in London that year, *The Persecution of the Jews in Russia*, by the Russo-Jewish Committee, further inflamed public opinion. Questions in both Houses of Parliament in July elicited from the government the predictable reply that it was an internal matter outside foreign interference. The Russian ambassador was nevertheless worried and wrote home: 'These delicate situations can only become more common. You might be minded to supply me with information which would enable me to react indirectly against these excitations which, absurd though they are, are damaging to our good name and our interests.'[10]

Inevitably a Guildhall meeting was organized, although Lord Rothschild opposed it—understandable given that he was interested in financing the proposed Trans-Siberian Railway at that time. It was presided over by the Lord Mayor of London, Sir Joseph Savory, 'to express public opinion with regard to the severe "exceptional edicts and disabilities", which are viewed as a "renewed persecution of the Jews in Russia"'.[11] The first resolution, proposed by the Duke of Westminster, declared that the renewed sufferings of the Jews were to be 'deplored'.[12] This was carried by acclamation. A deputation was to accompany a memorial to be sent to the Russian emperor that would also offer help with the famine that had broken out in Russia.

As was to be expected, the letter was returned unopened. Giers informed Staal: 'It is to be hoped that this little lesson will deal with the representative of the City of London in stopping once and for all his taste for such behaviour.'[13] Yet the ambassador continued to bewail the position in which he found himself. From Knowsley, where he was spending Christmas with Lord Derby, he wrote: 'I continue to be preoccupied with the Jewish question which torments me because of the impossibility in which I find myself to influence matters.'[14]

Even the appalling anti-Semitic measures of the late 1880s pale in comparison with the cruelty the Jews suffered in 1891. George Dobson, the veteran *Times* correspondent in St Petersburg, warned in 1890 of:

> new and savage laws about to be decreed against the Jews ... The statement was solemnly denied by Russian officials, as were all other rumours of prospective persecution, but through the indiscretion or venality of local administrators it became known that these denials were lies made out of whole cloth.[15]

It was estimated, taking into account the usual death rate, that there were close to 20,000 Jews living in the capital in 1882, but 8,000 in 1890. More than 11,000 had fled or been expelled in the intervening years. Then, there was a sudden acceleration in 1891. Between May and November almost 2,000 Jews were removed from St Petersburg.

The Chief of Police, General Groesser, who frankly declared that he was above the law, acted entirely on his own initiative:

> The most common pretext, where any was vouchsafed at all—was that the victims did not work at their trades on Saturdays ... General Groesser, so long as he did not incur the wrath of the Czar or offend the Czar's master, the dread Pobiedonostseff, freely did anything that he pleased.[16]

The savage vagaries of Groesser provided extensive evidence of individual examples of random cruelty. One old man was dispatched in chains for no other reason than that he was a Jew: a gold and silversmith who had possessed the right of residence since 1871 was reduced to beggary.

'Can a country be regarded as civilized, or as fit to hold friendly relations with civilized peoples, of which such a story as that can be truthfully told?' wrote *The New York Times* Moscow correspondent, Harold Frederic, in St Petersburg in 1891.[17]

An even greater blow, however, was reserved for the Jewish community of Moscow. Early in 1891 the Grand Duke Sergei, a younger brother of Alexander III, was gazetted governor general of Moscow. The octogenarian governor general, Prince Dolgorukov, 'a very characteristic and likeable type of the best that the ancient Russian aristocracy affords', was dismissed. The Grand Duke was married to Ella, daughter of Princess Alice of Hesse, a granddaughter of Queen Victoria. Sergei was a 'scrawny, hollow-eyed man of thirty-five, everywhere throughout European Courts known to be the least intelligent and respectable Romanoff since the time of Paul, and in Russia familiarly called by a name which involves offences hardly to be hinted at in type'. That he was homosexual was irrelevant, but that Sergei was a stupid stooge of his brother mattered greatly: 'It was to "purify" the city for the entry of this obscene simpleton that the Cossacks and police made that famous midnight descent upon the Jewish quarter in Moscow that ushered in the new persecution.'[18]

A rumour was circulating that the emperor had decided to make Moscow the capital of Russia again and that he sent his brother there to take the appropriate first steps. Whether in preparation for removing the imperial seat to Moscow, or in honour of the arrival of the new governor general, who shared the anti-Semitic prejudices of the court, the administration decided to expel the Jews who had legally settled in Moscow in accordance with the law of 1865.

The edict of expulsion was published on 29 March 1891, the first day of the Jewish Passover. The *ukaz* was ambiguous and the Jewish residents believed that it was to restrict new Jewish artisans from settling in the city. This was not accidental; it was designed to hide the arbitrary and illegal character of the new enactment which had not been submitted to the State Council. The resolution to uproot the 30,000 Jews of Moscow was adopted by Alexander III on the suggestion of the minister of the interior.

At midnight following the promulgation of the decree, the Zaradie quarter, slum and home to the poorer Jewish population, was surrounded by police, Cossacks and firemen led by the Cossack General Yurkovsky.

Then, under Yurkovsky's personal supervision, the whole quarter was ransacked, apartments forced open, doors smashed, every bedroom searched and men, women and children rooted out for examination of their passports:

> The indignities, which the women, young and old alike, underwent at the hands of the Cossacks may not be described ... As a result, over 700 men, women and children were dragged at dead of night through the streets to the *outchastoks* or police stations. They were not even given time to dress themselves, and they were kept in this noisome and overcrowded confinement for thirty-six hours, almost all without food... There was no charge

> of criminality or of leading an evil life against any of them. They were arrested and banished whether their passports were in order, or not.[19]

A police officer who was a Christian convert forewarned his former co-religionists of the coming raid and many chose to flee to cemeteries, or kept moving through the city, for during the night the police would break into Jewish homes in search of new arrivals. As time passed, many reputable Jews, because of failure to wind up their affairs, were caught after the expiration of their period of grace and marched to railway stations in manacles. A Jewish corporal in the army reserve sent a pathetic petition to Alexander III who, it was reliably reported, read the letter. As a result the veteran was imprisoned and the expulsions proceeded with fiercer determination. Unable for lack of time to dispose of their property adequately, many Jews were virtually forced to give it away.

The expulsion of about 20,000 Jews left only about a third of Moscow's Jewry—people with a higher education, first-guild merchants born there, and children of soldiers who had served under Nicholas I—who were allowed to remain, but even these lived under severe disabilities and in humiliating circumstances.

Algernon Swinburne vividly encapsulated the British reaction to the persecution of the Jews during 1890–1 in his poem 'Russia: An Ode':

> . . .
>
> What though sun be less than storm where these aspire,
> Dawn than lightning, song than thunder, light than fire?
> Help is none in heaven: hope sees no gentler star:
> Earth is hell, and hell bows down before the Czar.[20]

27

PERSIA

Persia, along with Afghanistan and Baluchistan, had long been regarded as part of India's hinterland, but not until the last three decades of the nineteenth century did the British government play a major role in the affairs of Persia. The geographical situation of Persia, and the political considerations thus arising from its proximity to India, conferred on the kingdom of the shah a significance far out of proportion to its size, population and wealth.

Lord Salisbury, the prime minister in 1889, summed up the situation. He declared that 'were it not for our possessing India, we should trouble ourselves but little about Persia'.[1] Salisbury believed that the Indian government—the Raj in Calcutta—did not take the Russian threat to British interests seriously enough:

> I do not think they have done wisely to neglect Persian dangers to the extent which they have done. The same circumstances and motives which might carry Russia into Afghanistan might, if she finds it too dangerous to venture, carry her into Persia. A successful occupation of Persia, reducing it to Russian vassalage, using and improving all its vast resources, & preparing them from that base for a further move Eastward, would be a policy that might attract the Russian Govt, and might be very menacing to India.[2]

What was fundamental to the situation was that Persia possessed a long border with Russia in the north, on which Russia could at any time mobilize her forces. Furthermore, the Caspian Sea, once Persian, was now, in the late nineteenth century, Russian, and much of the territory in Russia's Caucasus provinces had also belonged to Persia. The Atrek river formed the north-eastern boundary and in the west the Aras river had, since

1828, separated her from the Russian empire. The kingdom of the shah since 1848, Naser al-Din Shah, was a shrunken one of faded glories; the mainstream of history and economic progress had passed it by. Britain from India could only prevent a complete Russian annexation of Persia by what would today be called soft power, using her deep pockets to finance projects in the country, while Russia was constrained by her endemic financial weakness and technological backwardness, although she had acquired commercial and diplomatic privileges in the 1828 Treaty of Turkmenchai. Russian influence was dominant in the north of Persia; British influence had to be concentrated on the south.

Anglo-Russian rivalry in Persia had ratcheted up from the 1860s as a result of Russian conquests in Central Asia and the increased confidence that this engendered. The first major step by Britain to stem creeping Russian ambitions in Persia came in 1871. A newly appointed grand vizier, foreign minister Mirza Hossein Khan, wished to confer the much-needed regeneration of the country to Britain in the belief that, if she had a major stake in the country, she would protect it. To do this, it would be necessary to create a monopoly through which the construction of railways would be financed, mines exploited and a national bank established. In return, Persian customs revenues and almost all the resources of the country were to be pledged for seventy years. This concession was granted to Baron Julius de Reuter, a German-born naturalized British subject, who, twenty years before, had founded the eponymous financial news agency in London. Reuter set about floating several companies which would manage the vast enterprise.[3]

Naser al-Din Shah could, in such a promising situation, well afford a journey to Europe in 1873 to celebrate the schemes that were to transform his country. For the shah, the golden prospect was dimmed as soon as he arrived in Russia; he was confronted with his hosts' strongly expressed objections to the Reuter concession.

When he reached London the Persian sovereign, dressed in his customary blaze of diamonds, was warmly received by members of the royal family. Queen Victoria presented him with the Order of the Garter, the Prince of Wales ferried him on a hectic round of visits to parliament, Woolwich, London Zoo and the Crystal Palace, and a meeting was arranged with the prime minister, Gladstone. The tsarevich Alexander and his wife were also in London and were annoyed to find themselves sidelined by the fuss made of the Persian. They, however, were at ease with European manners—which was not true of the shah, who raised eyebrows with his unfamiliar habits. Staying with the Duke of Montrose, Naser al-Din Shah had insisted on having two sheep killed each morning in the sight of his suite; he blew his nose on the duke's muslin curtains and offered to buy Lady Mary Beaumont for his harem.

Despite the best efforts of the royal family and government, the visit was a failure, as the City showed no enthusiasm for the Reuter concession. Then, opposition in Persia to the surrender to Europeans of such far-reaching control manifested itself. The combination of what he had learned in St Petersburg, the London Stock Market's reluctance and his subjects' complaints led the shah to cancel the concession on his return home.

In the same year Russia had annexed Khiva and Naser al-Din Shah recognized that he needed British support if Russia was to be prevented from having a free hand in his country. Lord Salisbury became secretary of state for India the following year in 1874, and although he did not seek to establish a British protectorate over Persia, he deprecated the policy of drift. He believed that Britain could 'not give *complete* assistance to Persia' and 'incomplete & hesitating assistance' was dangerous:[4]

> If we took the matter entirely into our own hands, it is possible that we might successfully defend the Persian Frontier & even Merv. The demerit of such a policy would be its exceeding costliness; & that it would precipitate the conflict between ourselves & Russia upon a distant & ill-selected field. But at least it would for the purposes of that conflict place the resources of Persia at our disposal.[5]

As the ensuing years saw no satiation of the Russian appetite for expansion in Central Asia, in 1875 the commander-in-chief of the Indian government urged London to stem Russia's advance by providing Persia with the 'friendship she seeks' and continuing:

> We should do all in our power to prevent Russia from working round our flanks ... By increasing our diplomatic influence in Persia, we shall best be able to prevent that country from giving Russia cause for aggression, but should we be driven to war, the people of Persia, supported by a British contingent and aided by British arms, supplies and officers, would render the task of conquering the country as difficult and exhaustive as the conquest of the Spanish Peninsula was to France.[6]

Even so, Salisbury made no real attempt to cultivate the friendship of the shah, whom he (rightly) suspected of being ready to exploit either Britain or Russia as he thought profitable. Therefore a new policy for Persia was decided upon when Salisbury became foreign secretary in 1878. The breach between Britain and the emir of Afghanistan, Sher Ali, followed by the successful Second Afghan War, did not alleviate British fears that reliance on Afghanistan as a buffer state between India and Russian Central Asia was insufficient. Salisbury looked to Persia as a possible substitute for Afghanistan. Naser al-Din Shah would acquire coveted Herat and Sistan territories in return for which the shah would permit British officers in Herat, would place no obstacles on the construction of a railway from Kandahar to Herat and a road from the Persian Gulf inland, would resist further Russian inroads and undertake internal reform.[7] Negotiations towards this goal came to nothing because of the shah's increasing demands and Russian contrary pressure on him. On his visit to Russia in 1873 the shah had been much impressed by the imperial troops, and in 1879 he encouraged the Russian government to create a Cossack brigade based in Tehran. This highly efficient body was naturally closely aligned to the Russian legation and became a powerful tool of Russian political influence.[8]

Where Britain was successful was in Baluchistan to the south-east of Persia, which was, from the mid-nineteenth century, a British Indian protectorate. (Persia laid claim to all of Baluchistan and exercised limited authority over the western half of this large, undefined region.) Persian encroachment into British Baluchistan was not feared; Russian infiltration was the danger. Major General Frederic Goldsmid had in 1871 led the Boundary Commission to delimit the Baluch-Persian border on the Makram coast of the Gulf of Oman, but there remained the region to the north. In 1876 Salisbury wrote that 'the doctrine of non-intervention in Beloochistan has been carried a great deal too far ... Of course we must bring Khelat [Kalat] into a more orderly state.'[9] The civil war between the khan of Kalat and the confederacy of Baluch had caused such devastation that the government of India acted and re-established a treaty with Kalat which placed the whole of Baluchistan under British control.

The man who executed the forward policy in Baluchistan was a frontier officer, Robert Sandeman. In his expeditions he was able to extend British influence up to the borders of Sistan. At the same time he helped to stimulate interest and concern for the affairs of Persia in Britain.

The Liberal government that came into power in 1880 under Gladstone viewed any extension of responsibility for Persia with distaste and, by the time the Conservatives were again in government in 1885, two months after the clash at Pendjeh, from a British point of view the situation in Persia had deteriorated. During the preceding years Russia had whittled away at the shah's loosely controlled north-eastern territories. On the Khorasan frontier there were Russian incursions into the Atrek and Akhal country. Gross misgovernment sapped the people's will to resist encroachments, and an increasing number of Persian officials were in Russian pay. Would the Khorasan, the Parthia of the Romans and a bone of contention throughout the centuries between Turcoman and Persian, be next?

Naser al-Din Shah himself was well aware of the danger posed to Persia by Russian conquests in Central Asia that threatened Persia, and, in approaching the British government for protection against possible Russian annexations, he took the obvious line of stressing the danger to India arising from the Khorasan's unsettled frontier. Giers asserted that Britain had no rightful interest in Persia's possessions in the Atrek country. Salisbury riposted that the Russians should be told that 'in our view the integrity of Persia is a matter of serious importance to this country'.[10] The Persian minister in London, Malkom Khan, was understandably distressed by the deplorable state of his country and its increasing subservience to Russia. He appealed to Salisbury for help, only to receive a restatement of the prime minister's stance. Communications had to be improved between the Gulf and the northern regions and steps taken to reform the system of government:

> If England in the future was to be of any use in sustaining Persia against the probable encroachments and gradual absorption by Russia, two things were necessary. In the first place, that such strategic precautions should be taken as to oppose the greatest facility for possible English succour; and, in the second place that the corruption that was eating into the Kingdom and bringing it to decay should be attacked with a firm hand.[11]

The Persians found a more sympathetic ear in the secretary of state for India, Lord Randolph Churchill, in 1885. He emphasized the incongruity of protecting Afghanistan but not Persia. Unless the Persians believed that Britain would support them, they would drift along on their lethargic course, which could only end in further and perhaps complete Russianization. The prime minister was not persuaded and dispatched a clear putdown to the minister: 'Reply that the difficulty of supporting Persia against Russia lies in the fact that the regions in which Russian encroachments are likely to be made lie wholly beyond the reach of any material assistance wh H M G could furnish to the Persian govt.'[12]

From 1885 onwards Alexander III took a close interest in Persia now that the Anglo-Russian Boundary Commission was settling the north-western frontier of Afghanistan and there was little for Russia to hope for in pressing southwards from her Central Asian possessions. Persia, with her chaotic, corrupt government, was potentially the territory where expansion at the expense of Britain, and keeping up the pressure on the government of India, would be most fruitful. The Russian decipherment of British telegrams to and from Tehran, previously spasmodic, became systematic. The Russian emperor wrote numerous and usually acerbic annotations in Russian on the telegrams, and a slash with two dots signified that he had read a telegram. Quite often he demanded more information about the telegram's contents, and he noted on most that they should be forwarded to the head of the Russian legation in Tehran.

While the British government remained unaware of the Russian access to its diplomatic correspondence, conventional spying in Tehran continued apace. The *chargé d'affaires*, Arthur Nicolson, in 1886 relayed copies of secret Russian plans which had been acquired surreptitiously from the Russian legation.[13] The most serious document was a memorandum announcing that a sizeable slice of the Khorasan bordering Afghanistan was to be ceded to Russia. Nicolson did not believe that Russia would violate Persian territory by a precipitate and outright invasion, but he warned the foreign office that the Russian legation appeared to be preparing the ground for a diplomatic coup. When confronted, the shah, as was to become repetitive in what was little short of grovelling, had assured the *chargé d'affaires* 'that he was not only anxious but resolved to be on the most trusty and friendly terms with England'. (Note of Alexander III: '?!!!'.[14])

The British government wished to cooperate with Russia and not permit her a free hand over delimitation of the Khorasan frontier: St Petersburg held that Britain had no right to a voice in the matter. General Schepelev of the Russian Caucasus government then arrived in Tehran, ostensibly to discuss minor rectifications of the Khorasan frontier, but rumours attributed a more sinister motive for his journey. Nicolson soon verified the worst suspicions. Russia would assist the shah in his disputes with Turkey—his western neighbour—if, in the event of war with Britain, the Khorasan could to be used as a base for operations against India. An India Office official observed that even if the convention were only partially carried out, Persia would become 'a feudatory' of Russia.[15]

The shah pleaded in a further conversation with Nicolson (surprisingly to a junior diplomat) that he was unable to hinder frontier changes favourable to Russia: 'What was he to do? … His Majesty prefers England …

and he has assured me that he will never enter into an agreement with Russia.' The Russian emperor noted with exclamation marks that Naser al-Din Shah was either playing tricks or was out of his mind. There was certainly mounting evidence in 1887 of a possible advance into Persia by Russian troops based at Merv, and Naser al-Din Shah showed Nicolson a secret agreement of 1881 according to which the shah would permit Russian troops to enter his country 'if necessary'. An irritated Alexander III commented: 'Did he have to give it to the English.'[16] Lord Salisbury was grateful to receive the document and telegraphed in all innocence: 'Express best thanks of Her Majesty's Government for his communication. It will be kept strictly secret.'[17]

While the Russians threatened the shah over his choice of a governor of the Khorasan, the British legation for its part kept up the constant pressure on Naser al-Din Shah to resist Russian demands:

> Shah has sent me [Nicolson] the following message. He was desirous to open his mind without reserve to Her Majesty's Government. He has the most absolute confidence in Her Majesty's Government and in their good will and would sign and follow anything they ask of him, but if he concedes something to England, Russia, he is quite convinced, would immediately make such a request that his authority in the north would be lost. His only friend is England and he now asks her for her counsel. If England would protect him from consequences, if she would give him strength to resist the demands of Russia, he would do all that Her Majesty's Government desired ... I thanked the Shah for this message, the *sincerity of which* [Alexander III commented on a decrypt: '?!'] It would be certain to be appreciated by Her Majesty's Government.[18]

It was not only a matter of stiffening Naser al-Din Shah's resistance to Russian demands; Britain had her own shopping list in Persia. Nicolson successfully gained acceptance of a British concession to exploit mines in the south, although he failed to persuade the shah that a railway should be built there. Nevertheless, the main British aim in 1887 was to see the Karun river—a tributary of Shatt al-Arab, that flows from Shushtar to Mohammerah (Muhammara or Khorramshahr) before joining the Tigris and Euphrates—accessible to navigation. It was Persia's only navigable waterway.

The opening of the Karun had for many years been the aim of British companies operating in the region, but inevitably it had become more pressing in the mid-1880s with heightened Anglo-Russian rivalry in Persia. Foreign navigation of the river was a prerequisite for the economic development of the south of Persia given the challenges of the traditional Bushire–Shiraz route.[19] This, in turn, would further British influence as she could take advantage of her control of the Persian Gulf, and the naval links with India. British trade with Persia was expanding from the 1870s, albeit from a low base—£50,000 in 1875, £170,000 in 1879. Nicolson told Lord Dufferin, the viceroy: 'we should not waste our energies in endeavouring to counteract Russian influence on the Central Government at Tehran. This part of the world is lost to us and we should devote the modicum of attention which we seem disposed to give to Persia to the South alone.'[20]

Lynch Brothers, established in Baghdad in 1841 by the redoubtable Irishman and epitome of Victorian commercial nous, Henry Lynch, was operating a steamer service on the Tigris and the Euphrates to Mohammerah. Gray, Dawes & Co. had been set up in Bushire on the Persian Gulf in 1866 as merchants and shipping agents and they had in 1875 petitioned the British government to secure the opening of the Karun.[21] An Anglo-Swiss firm, Ziegler & Co., concentrated on exporting silk and cotton goods to Persia from its head office in Manchester and came to play a major role in reviving the moribund Persian carpet industry.[22]

Clearly, a more dynamic British representation was called for in Tehran, and a politician rather than a career diplomat was Salisbury's choice. In late 1887 Sir Henry Drummond Wolff was appointed Envoy Extraordinary and Minister Plenipotentiary. Drummond Wolff, an exuberant personality, had begun his career as a clerk in the foreign office but in his early thirties had become a Conservative MP of Lord Randolph Churchill's Fourth Party and became involved in international finance. His powerful political backing at home, friendship with the Prince of Wales and success as High Commissioner in Egypt from 1885 marked him out for a difficult post in Tehran. The Russians also upgraded their legation with the appointment of Prince Nicholas Dolgorouky, but the new minister proved disdainful of the Persians and refused to treat Naser al-Din Shah with the respect the shah believed to be his due. Drummond Wolff, on the other hand, was charming and a great believer in largesse and decorations, to help oil the wheels of diplomacy—to the point of creating his own medal, which he awarded to all and sundry. There was an outcry in the government-inspired Russian press, claiming that the Drummond Wolff mission was intended not only to establish British paramountcy in Persia, but also to launch an anti-Russian, pan-Islamic crusade throughout the east.[23] The British government admitted the importance of the Drummond Wolff appointment, but insisted that hostility to Russia did not follow from it.

It was obvious that a full-scale return to the hostility of the early 1880s in Central Asia was not in Britain's interest in Persia, where its representatives were the junior partners. The joint development of Persia was to be the aim and the British government was now more than ever determined to play an active role. What Salisbury aimed for was a partition of preponderance between Britain and Russia based on economic development. This would serve a dual function. It would mitigate the friction between Britain and Russia by reducing their points of contact, and at the same time strengthen Persia herself by the construction of railways, greater trade and industrial development and the flow of capital. Once the process began, other nations such as Germany and the United States would trade and invest in Persia—not only in the British sphere in the south, but also in the north, thus thwarting Russian designs for sole control. Thus, the question would be transformed from an Anglo-Russian into an international one.

To this end it was important to get the Drummond Wolff mission off to a good start along these lines, and the ambassador in St Petersburg, Sir Robert Morier, was instructed to assure Giers of Britain's intention to maintain Persia's territorial integrity and to disclaim rivalry with Russia. Unfortunately, Alexander III was in early 1888 still obsessed by Bulgaria and irritated by Britain's refusal to cooperate in deposing Ferdinand of Saxe-Coburg. The Russian government was also agonizing as to whether it was possible to expand the war budget, and Morier claimed that the country was about to declare bankruptcy. Its lack of direction, he held, made it impossible to negotiate over Persia.

Drummond Wolff arrived in Tehran in April 1888 determined to conclude an agreement with Russia, to promote British trade and encourage better governance. His aim was to transform Persia into an effective buffer state. Drummond Wolff bombarded Salisbury with telegrams from the moment of his arrival, in which he expounded at length on the discussions he was having with the shah and Prince Dolgorouky, whom he found was 'a man of most amiable character and in every way conciliatory'.[24] The prime minister tried to restrain his envoy, as politely as he could, from making commitments without the authorization of his government. Drummond Wolff's Russian counterpart found the Englishman a congenial interlocutor, but could offer little given the disagreement over Bulgaria and the opposition of the military party in Russia to a pacific policy in Persia. Russia aimed simply to maintain pressure on the shah to prevent him from coming to any agreement with Britain.

Naser al-Din Shah claimed to have been greatly distressed by an article in the French press which circulated in Tehran in November 1888. It held that, under Dolgorouky's guidance, Persia had become a Russian province and the shah a 'simple lieutenant of the Russian Tsar'. From a British point of view, the insulting article proved a welcome gift. Suddenly, Naser al-Din Shah told Drummond Wolff that he was prepared to open the Karun river to foreign navigation, something the envoy had been persistently plugging since his arrival. Work would need to be done on the river to enable the passage of commercial vessels and Drummond Wolff had already enquired in May whether a City friend, Sir George Mackenzie of Gray Dawes, could find the £100,000 necessary to finance the river works and a road from Shushtar to Qom in the north. Soon afterwards Lynch Brothers managed to sail a paddle steamer up the Karun (assisted by subsidies from the British and Indian governments) and inaugurated a regular service between Mohammerah, Ahwaz and Shushtar.

(Ten years later they built a 400-kilometre-long road between Ahwaz and Isfahan. It was not a very profitable commercial deal but it opened a trade route between Isfahan and the Persian Gulf.)

In 1888, George de Staal, the Russian ambassador in London, tried to play down the importance of the opening of the Karun—a river of little importance, not offering much possibility for traffic—and claimed that the British press exaggerated its importance.[25] Giers was less sanguine, pointing out that each country had a sphere of influence—Russia in the north, Britain in the south—and that the opening of the Karun would enable British goods to be brought into the heart of Persia, upsetting the balance: 'The reality is that this line of navigation goes against Russian interests.'[26]

If the Russian reaction to the opening of the Karun was a renewed determination to combat further British success in Persia now that Drummond Wolff had 'stolen a march' on them, 'it was clear that Russia would not rest until she had obtained an equivalent concession'.[27]

Hence, the Russians moved first in 1889, and having sabotaged the earlier British attempt to construct railways, elicited from the shah a promise that no railway nor waterways concessions would be granted for a five-year period. For some time they had planned to connect Persia with their own system based on the Caspian Sea, but could not raise the capital. Even so the British government was alarmed by talk of a concession to Russia. Drummond Wolff was instructed to protest.

In the summer of 1889 the shah again visited Europe. In St Petersburg, Alexander III insisted on the railway moratorium and Morier, who was worried about a Russian charm offensive on the notoriously susceptible Naser al-Din Shah, feared: 'I shall have no means at my disposal to prevent the Shah when here from signing IOUs.'[28] In London, on the other hand, the benefits that would be derived from railway construction in Persia were emphasized. Drummond Wolff accompanied the shah and arranged for him to meet many leading financiers and visit industrial centres, in addition to the Prince of Wales's assiduous personal attendance on the Persian sovereign.

The indefatigable Drummond Wolff also found time while in London to repeat his aims to an increasingly weary Staal:

> His favourite thesis is that of an entente between Russia and Great Britain concerning Persia ... Capital, he told me, is so abundant in England, and would provide good returns, which we could use as much as the English. At the same time we would be free to impose our conditions to guarantee our legitimate influence and ensure the independence of our enterprises in the north of Persia, while England could do the same in the south.[29]

The envoy, with his boundless self-confidence though, sought a more important Russian on whom to press his ideas, namely Alexander III. Drummond Wolff proposed to return to Tehran via St Petersburg. Already Morier, ambassador to Russia for the past five years, had been irritated by the pretensions of the upstart diplomat in Tehran who wanted to take charge of Anglo-Russian relations over Persia, and there was considerable personal animosity between the two men which Salisbury tried to alleviate. By chance, Morier was on leave in Finland in the summer of 1889 and Salisbury telegraphed him to say that Drummond Wolff was 'anxious to be assured that his coming would be agreeable to you'.[30] Morier would have vetoed the visit if he could have done so, but could not—though Queen Victoria was of the same opinion—and Giers wanted the Persian question ignored. But it had been arranged between Wolff's friend the Prince of Wales and the Russian emperor, when on holiday together in Denmark that summer.

Drummond Wolff, in his audience with Alexander III, which took place in Berlin, exchanged with the emperor assurances about both powers being willing to discuss the economic development of Persia, on the basis of their common interests, by the opening of railways, waterways and industrial undertakings. Drummond Wolff reported back to Salisbury but Morier, back *en poste*, managed by his superior diplomatic skill to undermine Wolff and have the agreement downgraded to an exchange of views. There were two different versions of what took place: 'The Emperor's tallies exactly with all the antecedents of the case whereas Sir Henry [Drummond Wolff]'s implies so complete a change from one pole to another on the subject treated that it almost presupposes a kind of miracle.'[31]

Meanwhile the British economic penetration of Persia continued. The British-owned New Oriental Bank Corporation, which operated throughout East Asia, extended its business to Persia in 1888, with an obvious warm welcome from Drummond Wolff. No concession was required and the bank rapidly flourished, establishing branches from Tabriz in the north of Persia to Bushire on the south coast.

While the New Oriental Bank was laying the groundwork, George de Reuter, son of Baron Julius, arrived in Tehran in 1888. The shah assured Drummond Wolff that he would confer on Reuter the right to found a national bank, as compensation for the 1873 abrogation of his father's concession. The necessary capital was easily raised in London from the bankers David Sassoon and J. Henry Schroeder, although the Rothschilds did not feel the enterprise to be potentially remunerative enough to invest in. The Russians were furious: 'The rights attributed to the founder of the bank by this arrangement, even though they are less extensive than those attached to the 1872 concession, are nevertheless very important.'[32]

The Russian *chargé d'affaires* in Tehran argued that the shah's (supposedly) secret agreement of 1881 with Russia prohibited the granting of concessions without Russia's consent. The Amin al-Sultan, the effective foreign minister, and increasingly important as the shah showed less and less inclination for serious discussion, however, upheld Baron de Reuter's claim since this long preceded the understanding with Russia. Moreover, he saw the Reuter banking concession as a 'means of liberating Persia from the dictation of Russia'.[33] Early in 1889 permission to establish a national bank was given in lieu of the original concession.

The Imperial Bank of Persia opened its doors in Tehran in September 1889 and the following year took over the New Oriental Bank. It was given the exclusive right to issue bank notes and in addition was permitted to carry on normal banking business, and exempted from all taxes and import duties in Persia. Not surprisingly, the bank's initial capital of £1 million was heavily over-subscribed within hours of the lists being open to the public.

The Times, in an editorial at the end of 1889, felt that now Britain was in a stronger position in Persia:

> The day of doing nothing, and letting the over-ripe Persian pear fall into Russia's mouth, of discouraging still further by our apathy the already disheartened Persians, seems to have passed away, and in its place has arrived one marked by energetic but not provocative action, by the resolve to uphold our legitimate rights against all comers.[34]

Naturally, the British success in establishing the Imperial Bank provoked a Russian *quid pro quo* to improve on her own position in Persia. This took the form mainly of pressing for a railway concession, while at the same time putting pressure on the shah to prohibit such concessions to others. It was the Russian military party, not Giers and the foreign ministry, that was pushing for lines through the Khorasan east to Herat and south to Sistan. The syndicate of Poliakov and Raffaellevich, which had been formed to build railways in the north from Rasht to Tehran, was unable, to Giers's relief, to raise the necessary finance. For if Russia did not present a united front, neither did Britain. Morier opposed all activity which would alienate Russia; Drummond Wolff, advocating the contrary, was supported by Salisbury:

> If Russia makes her railway through Khorasan the North of Persia is hopelessly lost. Will the South of Persia ... be lost also? The answer to that question largely depends on some line as under consideration. If it is not made, Southern Persia must fall too—Afghanistan so embraced must be indefensible—the advanced Russian posts will be on the Helmund.[35]

At the same time the prime minister cautioned his headstrong minister: 'You may use extreme reserve and abstain from making any proposals to Russian representative or entering into any discussion with him without special authorization.'[36] Alexander III noted on the decrypt: 'Glad that Salisbury put him down a bit.'[37] The Russian *chargé d'affaires* in Tehran was similarly told by his masters to hold back.

After failing to come up with a realistic exclusive railway project, the Russians fell back on demanding that the shah prohibit all railway construction. Naser al-Din Shah had the previous year, under Russian pressure—having given Drummond Wolff a promise of a priority for Britain in railway construction in the south—agreed to delay any railway building for five years. Now the Russians demanded a ten-year restriction. Salisbury was furious: 'We cannot accept as valid so barbarous a measure as consent by the Shah that his subjects shall be permanently deprived of the benefits of railways: nor can we admit that their enjoyment of it is to depend on the will of Russia.'[38] The outcome was that the weary shah decided to bury the railway question for the rest of his lifetime. Giers, who had had more than enough of the subject, was relieved.

In the spring of 1890 Drummond Wolff complained to the senior civil servant at the foreign office responsible for Persia, Sir Philip Currie, that Morier was working against him. He was clearly paranoid. In September British policy towards Persia was shaken when Drummond Wolff had a serious nervous breakdown. The first secretary in the legation informed London that:

> the three doctors ascertain that Wolff is losing strength progressively, the mind is very disturbed ... he is full of the most extraordinary fancies. He believes he is a bishop, who is travelling to London in six hours etc. and he insists on dispatching foolhardy telegrams to the Foreign Office, which are however retained. It is doubtful whether he will be able to travel before the winter sets in and ... he is unable even to manage his private affairs ... It is absolutely necessary that some responsible member of his family should hold himself in readiness to come here.

'It seems that Wolff is nuts!' smirked the Russian emperor (in English) on the telegram decrypt.[39]

When he was well enough to travel, Drummond Wolff left Persia, never to return, although he hoped to regain his posting. A year later he had made a surprisingly rapid recovery and was pressing Staal in London with yet more ideas for railways in Persia.[40]

What had seemed a successful Drummond Wolff scheme in early 1890 turned into a diplomatic disaster for Britain. The envoy had assisted an old City friend, Major Gerald Seymour, in buying a concession for a fifty-year monopoly of the production, sale and export of Persia's entire tobacco crop. The shah was paid £25,000 and the Amin al-Sultan £15,000 on signature. In return, the Persian treasury was to receive an annual rent of £15,000 and a quarter of the annual profits. Major G. F. Talbot, after forming the Imperial Tobacco Corporation of Persia in London, returned to Tehran in early 1891 with staff to organize what was known as the Tobacco Régie. Details of the concession soon leaked out and quickly provoked a popular outcry when the extent of foreign control over the country's tobacco became known. The mullahs, with active Russian assistance, stirred up anti-British feelings. The British consul in Tabriz feared a massacre of Christians. There was a remarkable response, when a leading religious divine called upon all Persians—and most men and women smoked—to abstain from tobacco until the concession was repealed.

'Suddenly', a French observer recorded, 'with perfect accord the tobacco merchants have closed their shops, all the *qualyans* have been put aside and no one smokes any longer.'[41] In December 1891 the shah caved in to public opinion and cancelled the concession, causing great loss of face to the British, and corresponding Russian schadenfreude.

For a year the British legation in Tehran was in limbo after Drummond Wolff's departure, while the Russians pressed ahead taking advantage of the absence of their formidable British adversary. Sir Frank Lascelles, late of Bulgaria, who replaced Drummond Wolff in late 1891, was handed the difficult task. As well as having to deal with the fallout from the Tobacco Régie *débâcle*, Lascelles had to deal with Persia's internal crisis which was acute. In the sensitive Khorasan, where the influence of the central government was almost non-existent, the most alarming events were taking place. Some of the Turcoman tribes, equipped with Russian breech-loaders, were in revolt. The nomads passed part of the year in Persia and part in Russia, where they came under the influence of General Alexsei Kuropatkin, the governor general of Trans-Caspia. Morier wrote that reports of Kuropatkin's doings 'were not pleasant reading for nerves unstrung'.[42]

Before the Salisbury administration fell in 1892, a new Anglo-Russian crisis had erupted over Russian incursions in the Pamirs. As a result, Persian affairs receded into the background during the Liberal government's tenure of office until 1895. In any case, the Liberals attached much less importance to Persia than did the Conservatives, and also were more disillusioned by its government. Lord Kimberley, the secretary of state for India, wrote in 1893 that 'Russia will without actively taking possession of the North Eastern Provinces [of Persia] control them virtually and that the Shah will become the vassal of the Tsar in reality tho [*sic*] not in name. I cannot see what we can do to avert it.'[43]

The young MP George Curzon, who visited Persia in 1889, published a book in 1892 titled *Persia and the Persian Question*. He concluded:

> Russia regards Persia as a power that may temporarily be tolerated, that may even require sometimes to be humoured or caressed, but that in the long run is irretrievably doomed. She regards the future partition of Persia as a prospect scarcely less certain of fulfilment than the achieved partition of Poland; and she has already clearly made up her own mind as to the share which she will require in the division of the spoils.[44]

28

THE ROOF OF THE WORLD

THE PAMIRS CRISIS

The north-western, and most pregnable, frontier of Afghanistan had been established in the Anglo-Russian agreement of 1887 as far east as Khoja Saleh on the Amu Darya. However, there remained undemarcated the mountainous no man's land in the north-east of the country with its treacherous passes. There the Hindu Kush, Pamirs and Himalayas meet, and the Russian, British and Chinese empires converged—a junction of spheres of influence rather than sovereign territories. The region was of little interest to the Afghan emir, Abdur Rahman Khan, as it had no communication with Kabul and was inhabited by poverty-stricken Tajiks and Kyrgyz.

It was, however, of great interest to Britain. The crescent-shaped northern frontier of the British Indian empire had three main lines of approach from the north, that is, from Russian Turkestan: in the east from Kashgar towards Ladakh; in the centre from the Pamirs towards Hunza; and in the west from the Upper Amu Darya provinces towards Chitral. The question posed for Britain was how vulnerable the north-west frontier of India and the Indus Valley were from these three pressure points. Sir Robert Morier in St Petersburg had warned that Russia was actively looking for a hole on her Central Asian southern frontier through which to penetrate into British India.[1]

It was obvious that no amount of activity south of the Hindu Kush could in itself prevent Russian infiltration along the northern slopes of the range. And so, since the territories north of the mountains were beyond the range of effective Indian influence, diplomacy had to be employed to achieve what was impossible by any other means. It followed that what the British government sought was to extend the Afghan boundary 100 kilometres eastwards to meet that of China. For as long as this gap between the Chinese and the Afghan territories remained, the Russians could, on the strength of the 1873 mutually agreed line, deny the emir any rights and move southwards.

Thus, in June 1885, only three months after the Pendjeh incident, that had brought Britain and Russia close to war, and which had proved continued Russian expansionism to the detriment of the British, Colonel William Lockhart of the Indian Intelligence Branch was ordered to see whether it was possible for the British to use the route from Peshawar to Chitral to hold the mountain passes to the north and to do a deal with the notoriously devious ruler of Chitral to support the British. The military survey party was also to explore and map a large swathe of territory from Chitral to Hunza. In his report Lockhart argued that earlier fears attached to the region were exaggerated: snow closed the mountain passes, while in the summer the rivers became raging torrents. There were, however, windows of opportunity for the Russians in the spring and autumn. In those seasons, a small Russian force might be directed across the Pamirs to support a full-scale invasion through the Khyber and Bolan passes. Such infiltration by armed groups could be used to undermine social stability on the North-West Frontier.

Concurrently, a well-respected independent British explorer, Elias Ney, had been designated by the viceroy, Lord Dufferin, to survey the region west of Yarkand under Chinese Qing control. Ney had been based in the Kashgar region of China for six years as the Indian government's representative. He was therefore well qualified to establish the western limit of Chinese territory; to determine the feasibility of the Pamir passes for military purposes; and to confirm the source of the Upper Amu Darya. His account very much corroborated that of Lockhart. Additionally, Ney's contribution was to propose the line to be drawn westwards from the Chinese frontier into Afghanistan. This would separate Russian Turkestan from British India.

The British were not, however, entirely free to decide the frontiers in the Pamirs: Russia had already been active there for some time. As early as 1876 the ubiquitous General Mikhail Skobelev had led an expedition to the Alai mountains, as a result of which the northern portion of the Pamir region was annexed to the Russian empire. Russian agents of various kinds subsequently were busily engaged exploring the headwaters of the Amu Darya and adding to the scant knowledge of the rugged terrain around Lake Victoria (now Lake Zorkul). At the same, time glowing accounts of the benefits of Russian rule were provided to the tribal leaders in the region, whose constant warfare with one another made their control precarious.

Lord Randolph Churchill was a strong advocate of the extension eastwards of demarcation of the Afghan frontier. He had been secretary of state for India in the second half of 1885 during the short-lived Conservative minority administration, but in 1887 he was out of office and a dangerous political loose cannon. Churchill expressed his desire to visit Russia, a country he had for a long time wanted to see. Both the queen and Lord Salisbury, again prime minister, were alarmed at the prospect of this maverick's presence in St Petersburg, and the foreign office made clear that it was an entirely private visit. *The Times* warned Alexander III not to be misled by any assurances of British friendship that might be offered by this 'most versatile and volatile' of politicians.[2] The young lord, accompanied by his wife, ignored the hullabaloo and unashamedly enjoyed himself in Russia. He first met Nicholas Giers, and then the Russian emperor invited him to Gatchina, where they smoked cigarettes and discussed the international situation. Churchill was surprised to discover that Alexander III spoke English perfectly—'Well, I hope you have been long enough in St Petersburg to find out that we are not so terribly warlike as we are made out to be.'[3] Inevitably, the conversation turned to Central Asia:

> [The emperor] said that it ought not be a great difficulty any longer, that the Russians wanted no more, that they had more than they could manage ... that the two Powers must be *limitropes* [have a contiguous frontier]; that we were making a great mistake in still pursuing the neutral-zone policy by insisting on the independence of Afghanistan, which we ought to take and govern ourselves ... He had a great wish to go to England for the purpose of ascertaining the drift of English policy [and] in order to have a full explanation with Lord Salisbury, 'until now an inveterate enemy of Russia'.[4]

Back in London the reports of the apparent Russian seduction of a prominent British politician caused unease in the cabinet whilst eliciting nothing less than fury from the queen. She inveighed against him in a letter to the Prince of Wales, a friend of Churchill:

> I have heard that Lord Randolph C. has returned with the most monstrous political views from Russia which frightens everyone and I am sure would

> shock you … The sum total of his views is to break with Germany and Austria (!!) and have an alliance with Russia—letting her have all she wishes in Europe—the Black Sea, the Mediterranean etc in return for leaving us alone in India!! Now no treaty with Russia ever is kept. We keep our part and they break theirs as you will remember at Khiva and others, and the Czar may and I dare say has very good intentions (though he wishes to be all powerful in Southern Eastern Europe) but he is never able to restrain his generals and the Panslavists and therefore cannot be relied on.[5]

Churchill was ignored.

George Curzon, a young Conservative MP more congenial to the British government, visited St Petersburg later in 1888. Academically brilliant and highly ambitious, Curzon had four years before decided upon a project to study Asiatic problems in Asia itself, in particular those of India and the territories that bordered the Raj. (Some have speculated that he already had his eye on the viceroyalty.)

The Trans-Caspian Railway to Bukhara and Samarkand, essentially a military project, had recently been opened to civilian travellers. George Dobson, St Petersburg correspondent of *The Times*, had already made the journey and published a series of articles about his experiences.[6] Curzon's expedition to observe Russia's administration of Turkestan and to assess the degree of threat that Russian expansion in Central Asia posed to British India also had a journalistic objective, but it was above all an intelligence-gathering exercise. His series of articles were collected together in his book *Russia in Central Asia in 1889 and the Anglo-Russian Question* of 1889.

Russian bureaucratic problems forced the MP to spend a frustrating time in St Petersburg, but while there he formed a favourable view of the Russians he met, no doubt because he found no widespread hostility to Britain openly expressed. Confident that the all-important permissions to travel in Central Asia would be granted, Curzon took the train to the Caucasus and there the documents arrived. He thereupon took a steamboat to the western terminus of the Trans-Caspian. Once ensconced in the fairly comfortable train, with a quantity of luggage incredible today—it included bedding, a rubber bath, tinned meat, chocolate and flea powder—he embarked on his observations. Initially, he found the scenery disappointing: 'A funereal tale of destruction, both to man and beast, engulfed in their whirling crests, might these cruel sand-waves tell.'[7] However, on the second day the train halted at Geok Tepe, scene of the bloody encounter of Skobelev's troops and Teke Turcomans in 1881. In a swipe going beyond commenting on previous incidents, Curzon claimed:

> repellent though they may be to nineteenth-century notions, and discreditable to the Russian character, they do not stand alone in the history of Russian conquest in Central Asia but are profoundly characteristic of the methods of warfare by which that race has consistently and successfully set about the subjugation of Oriental peoples.[8]

On arrival at the capital of Trans-Caspia, Ashkhabad (Ashgabat), the governor general, General Komarov of Pendjeh fame, met the MP. Here there were signs of future Russian designs with the building of a military road to the Persian frontier at Kalat: 'Russian influence, and, it is alleged, Russian roubles, are most assiduously at work.'[9] The Russians refused to allow foreigners to visit the road. Merv, next on the route, remained an open wound with the British from its annexation in 1884. Komarov was anxious to explain the peaceful purposes for which the Russians were developing the oasis—American cotton-seed and large numbers of saplings were being planted—but Curzon tartly remarked on 'the entire district having been made over to the private purse of the Czar—a guarantee that its development will not be allowed to slacken, or its revenues to result in a loss to the exchequer of so economical a monarch'.[10]

Noblesse oblige, at Bukhara Curzon stayed at the Russian embassy. Here was a reminder of an earlier regrettable incident in British history, the murder by the emir of Arthur Conolly and Charles Stoddart in 1842. In 1888, the ruler—a Russian puppet—was kept on a short leash. The railway had already in its brief existence brought about major changes to the economy: 'Native monopoly is challenged in every quarter. There are branches ... of the Imperial Russian Bank, of the Central Asian Commercial Company, and of the Russian Transport Society; and of private firms.'[11]

Curzon devoted the last hundred pages of his book to the Anglo-Russian Question. He was ready to applaud the technical triumph of Russian military engineers in having subdued the desert, laying a railway across hundreds of kilometres of the most unpromising terrain and bringing economic development to Central Asia, but appreciation gave way to apprehension when he turned to an analysis of the political design that lay behind it: 'Is this railway the mere obligatory thread of connection by which Russia desires to hold together ... her loosely scattered and heterogeneous possessions in Asia; or is it part of a great design that dreams of a wider dominion?'[12]

In a detailed examination of the strategic factors governing the defence of India, Curzon concluded that Russia, after long preparation and at a suitable time of the year, could use the Trans-Caspian Railway to place a force of 100,000 men on the north-western and northern frontiers of Afghanistan. Yet, to meet such a menacing concentration, there were in India only 70,000 British and 148,000 Indian troops, of whom only half could be spared for frontier defence, kept in the field for any length of time or adequately reinforced.

However, he did not believe that Russia was bent upon the invasion of India: 'So far from regarding the foreign policy of Russia as consistent, or remorseless, or profound, I believe it to be a hand-to-mouth policy ... of profiting by the blunders of others, and as often of committing the like herself.'[13]

Consoling in its way, such an interpretation allowed no relaxation on Britain's part. In its very capriciousness, Russian foreign policy could be as oppressive as a direct threat of aggression. Behind Russia's provocative behaviour in Central Asia Curzon discerned that 'the tsar's real objective is not Calcutta, but Constantinople; not the Ganges, but the Golden Horn. He believes that the keys of the Bosphorus are more likely to be won on the banks of the Helmund than on the heights of Plevna.'[14] However, although that might be the long-term Russian goal, it did not lessen the present responsibility for defending India: 'Whatever be Russia's designs on India, whether they be serious and inimical or imaginary and fantastic, I hold that the first duty of English statesmen is to render any hostile intentions futile, to see that our own position is secure, and our frontier impregnable.'[15]

Much of what Curzon included in his book had already been published in 1888 in a series of articles; thus his views were already known to the British and Russian governments. They were to be highly influential in shaping subsequent British policy in Central Asia.

A Russian visitor to India in 1890 was far more elevated than the British MPs who wished to see something of Russia and her empire. Alexander III decided to send his eldest son, the tsarevich Nicholas, not on a conventional Grand Tour of Europe, but on a round-the-world trip that would take advantage of modern communications, the steamship and railways. For health reasons, Nicholas's younger brother, George, was to accompany the tsarevich. Several other young aristocrats also travelled as companions. The key person, however, was Prince Esper Ukhtomsky, Nicholas's tutor on Asian culture. The prince was an ardent imperialist whose antipathy to all that was British was well known. The British government was displeased. 'I do not at all like this tour of the tsarevich', the secretary of state for India wrote to the viceroy, but it was impossible to refuse it.[16] Damage limitation was attempted through Morier in St Petersburg putting pressure on the Russian government to accept that Donald Mackenzie Wallace, a former *Times* journalist who had lived for several years in Russia, been a secretary to a former viceroy and was a fluent Russian speaker (although Nicholas spoke good English), should escort the tsarevich when on British territory. His task was to portray the Raj in a favourable light. Queen Victoria had rightly feared the presence of Anglophobe aides.

The large party left St Petersburg in October 1890, Nicholas writing in his diary that he was 'very sad and depressed'.[17] It was not a good beginning, but when his cousin Prince George of Greece joined them, it mutated into a travelling house party. The Russians reached Bombay in December to begin a seven-week tour of India. Official dinners and receptions proliferated. Queen Victoria thought the tour important enough to keep a wary eye on its most minor of aspects and even involved the poor prime minister in the etiquette of seating at dinner in Bombay, for there were political considerations to such matters. Precedence 'should be done as not to give the natives the idea that it is a tribute to his [Nicholas's] superior power'.[18] The grand duke shook innumerable hands, mounted horses and boarded trains to the major cities. There were visits to tombs, mosques, palaces and the Taj Mahal. On a tiger shoot, two of the party each killed a tiger but, to his chagrin, Nicholas killed nothing. The heat was intense and the tsarevich grew irritable. In Delhi he wrote in his diary, perhaps influenced by Ukhtomsky: 'How stifling it is to be surrounded again by Englishmen and to see red uniforms everywhere.'[19] Petulant remarks in a telegram to his mother followed. Hurriedly the empress replied:

> I'd like to think you are very courteous to all the English who are taking great pains to give you the best possible reception ... I quite see that the balls and other official doings are not very amusing ... but you must understand that your position brings this with it ... It is your duty to *dance more* and *smoke less*.[20]

At the end of January 1891, the party moved to Colombo, where Nicholas met his cousin Sandro, who had been elephant hunting. The tsarevich was not tempted and again complained: 'Palaces and generals are the same all the world over, and that's all I am permitted to see. I could just as well have stayed at home.'[21] The Grand Tour continued to yet more British Asian territories, Singapore and Hong Kong. After a few days in China, Nicholas's retinue sailed for Japan. There, an attempt was made to assassinate him:

> The experience left an emotional scar that found an outlet in contemptuous private references ... to the Japanese as 'monkeys'; and his imprudent—one might even say reckless—policy in East Asia in later years that revealed not only a deeply rooted animosity toward Japan but an ugly streak of chauvinism hazardous to the national interest.[22]

Alexander III curtailed the tour immediately and in May 1891 Nicholas stepped back on Russian soil at Vladivostock, the city founded in 1860 in the wake of Russian expansion at China's expense. The city had been destined to become the eastern terminus of the Trans-Siberian Railway. This grandiose project had recently been decided upon and the tsarevich laid the foundation stone in Vladivostock before embarking on the long journey overland to St Petersburg.

With the obvious exception of the attempt on Nicholas's life, the tour fulfilled Alexander III's expectations. His heir had accepted Russia's Asiatic mission and fixed his hostility towards the British Raj.

Away from the rarefied world of distinguished visitors, in Calcutta the Indian government was increasingly concerned with the difficult task of bringing the hill states under British control and maintaining a close watch on the increasingly active Russians. The man most involved in this was Francis Younghusband.

Following on from Lockhart's 1885 exploration, in 1887 Francis Younghusband, a dashing lieutenant in the Dragoons, had been dispatched to investigate further the western regions of China. He distinguished himself in an adventurous journey from Peking, marching westwards across the Gobi Desert to Yarkand. This took seven months and entailed a dramatic winter crossing of the then unexplored Mustagh Pass, before descending through Sind and then the Kashmir valley to Srinagar.

The feat was recognized by the new viceroy, Lord Lansdowne, in 1889. Younghusband was sent to Hunza, ostensibly to investigate reports of raiding activities on British traders and to examine the hitherto unreconnoitred passes east of the Baroghil Pass. More importantly, though, it had become clear to Calcutta that the new ruler, the Mir Safdar Ali Khan, was treating with the up-and-coming Russian star explorer, Colonel

Bronislav Grombtchevsky, who had crossed the Hindu Kush and the Pamirs to the northern border of Kashmir.

After three months of mapping in the mountains, Younghusband was leading his Gurkha escort to the Taghdumbash Pamir when a courier arrived with an invitation from Grombtchevsky to visit him at his camp nearby: 'This was not exactly a surprise ... But it was an exciting event, also delightful in prospect; for two Europeans always find it a joy to meet one another in the depths of Asia.'[23]

It was one of the classic encounters of the Great Game: 'As I rode up a tall, fine-looking bearded man in Russian uniform came out to meet me ... We had a short talk together and he asked me to dine with him.'[24] The two young explorers, who had much in common, unsurprisingly spent an agreeable evening together:

> This dinner was a very substantial meal, and the Russian plied me generously with vodka ... He became very frank about the invasion of India. He said we English might not believe the Russians really intended to invade India, but he could assure me that the Russian Army ... thought of nothing else.[25]

The visit was returned the following day. Grombtchevsky, after several brandies, volunteered that he, like his host, was a military officer in civil employment, with a taste for adventure that few of his fellow officers shared:

> The Tsar had sent for him before each of his expeditions ... Unless some such encouragement was given, no Russian would think of exploring. I told him that with us it was exactly the other way round. Every obstruction was put in the way of exploration, or the whole army would be careering over Central Asia.[26]

'We bade farewell to each other, promising to continue cooperation and keeping up corresponding', the Russian wrote in his diary: 'The British expedition, particularly its courageous chief, impressed me greatly.'[27]

Despite the bonhomie, they were representatives of rival powers. Evidence of the reality of Anglo-Russian hostility came from the Englishman, who ungallantly deliberately misled Grombtchevsky into continuing on a route that he knew to be 'of absolutely no importance, leading from nowhere to nowhere' and extremely dangerous to boot.[28] Gentlemanly behaviour only went so far.

(It says much for Grombtchevsky that he bore no grudge against Younghusband. Out of the blue the Englishman received a letter from the

Russian in 1924 asking for help publishing a book and enclosing a photograph of their meeting. The Polish-born explorer, who had risen high in the Russian military, had fallen foul of the Bolsheviks and was destitute and in ill-health in Warsaw. He died in 1926.)

Younghusband pressed on south towards Hunza but failed to induce the Mir to sign a treaty. In terms of increasing topographical knowledge, however, the expedition was a success, for seventeen passes had been crossed and some of the roughest country in the world traversed. Back in Simla in 1890, Younghusband felt himself in a position to propose that he should lead a new mission to the Pamirs to survey the contentious gap between China and Afghanistan, the Wakhan territory. It looked likely that the Russians would claim that territory on the basis of the 1873 agreement. Younghusband wrote:

> Grombtchevskys were a nuisance, and must be prevented from dropping in of their own sweet will upon the peoples inhabiting valleys on the Indian side of the great main watershed of Central Asia. We did not want to extend across the watershed ourselves, but equally we did not want to have the Russians coming over it to our side and talking to the people about an invasion of India. And our frontier would be all the stronger if Afghan and Chinese territory were to meet on the far side of the watershed on the north and so prevent the Russians from actually touching the watershed. They were then more than a hundred miles from it, and we did not want them any nearer.[29]

In June 1890, under orders from the viceroy, Younghusband, now a major and attached to the Intelligence Department of the Indian government, left Simla with George Macartney, son of a British diplomat and Chinese mother, as interpreter. They were to head to Kashgar to persuade the Chinese to establish military posts on the borders of their claim. On their way to Kashgar, Younghusband and Macartney stopped at Yarkand. There they were unexpectedly joined by Grombtchevsky, who after leaving Hunza had been exploring the northern border of Tibet. The meeting between the Russian and the Englishman was again amicable, but after the British party had left for Kashgar, Grombtchevsky trailed them in order to report to Kashgar the content of Younghusband's discussions with the Chinese at Yarkand.

China had reconquered Eastern Turkestan a decade earlier, but there had been a Russian consul installed in Kashgar for the past eight years, while the Chinese refused to accept a British one. The consul, Nicholas Petrovksy, who had already lived there for twenty years, was known to be the *de facto* ruler of Chinese Turkestan, paying Chinese salaries and flooding the market with Russian manufactures. He would accept no British meddling in Kashgar.

Younghusband was operating in a situation beyond his capacities and was outmanoeuvred by Petrovsky. Russian agents reported that another British officer was en route for Kashgar. The Russian consul was convinced, or pretended to be, that a new element had been added to the situation. (The British were not alone in seeing single travellers as the vanguard of armies.)

In fact, the officer, Lieutenant Davison, had decided without leave to follow Younghusband's route, but had lost his way and most of his equipment. The senior officer decided to take Davison back to India with him. He had failed to gain anything from the Chinese during the nine months he had spent in Kashgar. But Petrovsky had reported Davison's arrival to his superiors in Tashkent with alarming comments. They reacted by sending a detachment of cavalry and infantry under the command of Colonel Mikhail Ionov, with instructions to annex the Pamirs as far east as the Sarikol mountains and as far as the Hindu Kush in the south.

The two Englishmen set off south in July 1891. As they began their ascent of the Pamirs, news reached them that a force of 400 Cossacks had arrived with orders to annex the territory. Younghusband sent Davison westwards to investigate, and himself proceeded south to the Taghdumbash Pamir. On 10 August he reached the village of Bozai-Gumbaz where he found ten Cossacks encamped:

> I marched into their camp … and was introduced to Colonel Yanoff (or Ionoff). I informed him that I was an agent of the Government of India; that I had heard rumours from the natives that he was annexing the Pamirs; that I did not like to report on this to my government on mere native rumour, but should like to know from him personally whether this was the case or not. He replied that it was … He took out a map and showed me, marked in green, a large area extending right down to our Indian watershed, and including much of what was not merely debatable but was clearly either Afghan or Chinese territory. I only said that the Russians were opening their mouth pretty wide. Whereat he laughed and said that this was but a beginning.[30]

Naturally, the Russians invited Younghusband to dinner—excellent food and wine from the Caucasus—during which much useful topographical information was exchanged between hosts and guest and at which Ionov toasted Queen Victoria and Younghusband Alexander III. The Russians left the following morning, while the Englishman waited for Davison. However, as Younghusband was going to bed, forty Cossacks led by Ionov arrived:

> They said they had received orders to remove me from Russian territory. I told them I was not on Russian territory … They said that they had told me the other day that they had annexed all this part. I replied that I could only recognize what was told me by my own Government … Colonel Yanoff [Ionov] said that anyhow I should have to go. I replied that undoubtedly I should as he had forty Cossacks and I had not a single soldier. I would, however, only go under protest.[31]

Davison was arrested and hauled off to Turkestan before being released soon afterwards.

Whitehall was incensed when the news of Younghusband's expulsion and the taking of Davison prisoner arrived in London. For in July 1891 news had already reached London that a Russian expedition had been ordered to the Pamirs plateau to annex the territory. The Russian government at first denied the report, and then made light of it, claiming that a detachment had gone 'to shoot game for rifle practice, and to note and report what the Chinese and Afghans are doing in these regions'.[32]

By the end of the year the Russians were aware, through Morier in St Petersburg, how seriously the British government was taking the Pamirs question. The independent-minded ambassador had throughout his seven-year posting to St Petersburg sought an agreement with Russia over the north-west frontier, but he was not a man to be bullied, and for Britain to have to swallow a second Pendjeh would be a clear step forward towards India on the part of Russia.

Anglo-Russian relations were extremely tense at this time due to rivalry in Persia, and the Younghusband deportation exacerbated matters. Also, a disastrous famine was raging in Russia, in which half a million people died, and there was widespread social unrest. Consequently Russia's fragile finances were even more strained, such that the country was in no position to sustain a full-scale conflict with Britain.

While Morier sought a full settlement of the Pamirs question, he began by demanding an apology for the Ionov incident by describing the colonel's exploits as those of an irresponsible hothead. This provided the Russians with an opportunity to avoid loss of face. George de Staal in London was greatly relieved when an apology was forthcoming: 'The expulsion of the English officers was a gratuitous abuse of force. I shall go even further ... and say that this expedition of Colonel Yanoff ... seems to me denuded of any use at all.'[33]

The Russian ministry of foreign affairs was, in the early 1890s, riven with dissension, and Staal frequently complained from London about receiving conflicting orders from his ministry in St Petersburg. Giers was ill for much of the period, and rival subordinates vied for control. There was also the war ministry that, as usual, argued for a forward policy in Central Asia. Ivan Vyshnegradsky at the finance ministry was determined to prevent war over the Pamirs for financial reasons. The civil–military feud in Russia was known in London.

If Russian policymaking in 1892 was in disarray, the British position was not one of a united front. Morier advocated taking a strong line and insisting on delimitation of a boundary; Lansdowne in Calcutta concurred. But the prime minister, Salisbury, disagreed, arguing 'We are in a corner ... delimitation would lead either to a breach in our pledge to the Amir (of Afghanistan) or a quarrel with Russia.'[34] However, Salisbury was at the head of an expiring administration. In May 1892 the Liberals came to power, with Gladstone once more prime minister and Lord Rosebery foreign secretary, who at first evinced little interest, and admitted that although he had located the Pamir region on a map, his knowledge did not extend beyond that.

Morier now had little difficulty in convincing the new, inexperienced foreign secretary that delimitation was the course to pursue. The Russian foreign ministry and war ministry had decided to 'extend our domination to all the region of these plateaux of Central Asia'.[35] Action by Britain was clearly necessary before another Russian military excursion took place:

> It may result in a conflict between the organised forces of Russia and the scattered detachments both of the Amir and the Chinese in the Pamirs, in which case, if ever a delimitation Commission is appointed, the British Government will take it up from a much worse position than they would if it were now entered upon. There is the likelihood of another Pandjeh business, and of the Commission having to deal with accomplished facts.[36]

Negotiations began in March 1893—hard bargaining with other people's lands—but in the autumn an understanding was achieved. The British reluctantly agreed to make Afghanistan evacuate parts of Shignan and Roshan, and in return Russia accepted the Pamir river as a demarcation line of its frontier, extending in a roughly easterly direction as far as the Sarikol mountains, which marked the Chinese frontier. Sir Mortimer

Durand, foreign minister of the Indian government, was dispatched to Kabul to persuade the emir to abandon his claim to Shignan and Roshan whilst at the same time holding firmly on to Wakhan territory south of the Pamir river. Abdur Rahman grumbled at having to hold Wakhan, but, tempted by a generously increased subsidy from India, he agreed. Accepting suzerainty of Wakhan was indispensable to the British, making possible the continuation of the policy of no coterminous border with Russia. The final terms embodied in the Durand Agreement included an exchange of populations.

Nevertheless, there remained the Pamir boundary east of Lake Zorkul. This was amicably resolved by the Joint Pamirs Boundary Commission in 1895 which left Russia in full possession of all the Pamirs, except for the Taghdumbash, which was the subject of a later agreement between Afghanistan and China. In an unwonted spirit of conviviality between Russia and Britain, the commission named one of the border mountains Mount Concord.[37]

Colonel Thomas Holdich, chief surveyor of the British commission, wrote eloquently of the delimitation of eastern Afghanistan, the Wakhan Corridor:

> Here we … defined a buffer between ourselves and Russia. It is not an impressive buffer—this long attenuated arm of Afghanistan reaching out to touch China with the tips of its fingers. It is only eight miles wide at one part, and could be ridden across in a morning's ride. It presents no vast physical obstacle to an advance of any sort; physical obstacles, however, are not wanting but they lie on the Indian side, and they are rude enough and difficult enough to answer all possible purposes. It is a political intervention—a hedge, as it were—over which Russia cannot step without violating Afghanistan, and the violation of Afghanistan may (or may not) be regarded as a 'casus belli'. … Here, amidst the grassy valleys and glacier-freighted ridges of the world's roof, a boundary was actually demarcated … and here at last was laid to rest the ghost of years of apprehension as to possible invasion of India from the extreme north.[38]

The Durand Line—as the 1895 demarcation is known—thus created the long narrow arm of territory that constitutes eastern Afghanistan today.

29

THE CELESTIAL EMPIRE AND THE LAND OF THE RISING SUN

At the time of Nicholas II's accession in late 1894, Anglo-Russian relations were better than they had been for many years. Since 1892, the Liberal government in Britain had been pursuing a policy of rapprochement with Russia and the Pamirs dispute was close to resolution. This was the calm before the storm.

Three years earlier Russian foreign policy had undergone a reorientation with the beginning of the construction of the Trans-Siberian Railway. East Asia, rather than the Balkans, Ottoman empire and Central Asia, became the focus of imperial attention. Within only a few years, the Far East became the scene of bitter rivalry among the great powers and Japan. In this international *mêlée*, Russia and Britain, the main players in the region (France and Germany were secondary), clashed to reach a new nadir in their relations by the end of the century.

To begin with, Russian expansionist ambitions were pacific. Russia had possessed territory in the Far East since the seventeenth century, but poor communications hindered exploitation of its resources and populating it. Anton Chekhov's famous journey to the convict colony on the island of Sakhalin off the Pacific coast in 1890 took nearly three months. There were good reasons for embarking on the enormous undertaking of building a railway 8,000 kilometres long to the Pacific coast.

However, the Trans-Siberian project had been mired in controversy in the late 1880s, with internecine fighting between the ministries of finance and transport. With the aid of French capital, construction was begun at the western terminus, but it was the arrival of Sergei Witte (who would become the dominating Russian statesman of the next decade) as finance minister in 1892, that gave a new impetus to pushing forward with the building of the railway that the tsarevich Nicholas had inaugurated at Vladivostok, the eastern terminus, the previous year.

The main political aim was to consolidate Russian power in its eastern regions by enhancing their defensive capabilities. According to Giers in 1891:

> The Chinese may not have any hostile intentions against Russia, but Russia cannot be certain that such ideas may not hereafter enter their heads, especially if we are brought into collision with any of the European powers. In this event, the possessions of Russia in Eastern Siberia, cut off as they now are seven months out of twelve every year would be in an exceedingly precarious position.[1]

In addition, the great famine of 1891 had shown the need for a means of transporting grain rapidly across the empire. And the Trans-Siberian would also add lustre to the image of Russia by providing a direct link between Europe and the Pacific: 'The railroad would end the isolation of the East, with Russia acting as cultural mediator between Europe and Asia, regulating their relations to its own advantage.'[2]

In 1895, the importance and role of the Trans-Siberian changed dramatically as a result of the Sino-Japanese War. This conflict was provoked by the rivalry between China and Japan over the Korean Peninsula, an important bridge between China and Japan, and rich in minerals and timber. Japan had been rapidly building up its army and navy after the Meiji Restoration of 1868, and, lacking minerals at home, sought to create an empire elsewhere in Asia. Korea was, however, a vassal state of China and in the early 1890s China tightened her grip on the peninsula, while Japan backed anti-Chinese reformers. Disturbances broke out in 1894, and Japan dispatched troop transports. War was declared on 1 August. China was roundly and quickly defeated to the great surprise of the powers, and forced to accept the Treaty of Shimonoseki in April 1895. China recognized Korea's independence and ceded Formosa, the Pescadores and the entire Liaotung Peninsula—which included the important harbour of Port Arthur—in addition to paying an indemnity and commercial concessions.

Japan had clearly decided to act to obtain a foothold on the mainland to cover herself against possible Russian expansion in East Asia before the Russians completed the Trans-Siberian Railway.

Thus, Russia now had to confront the reality of Japan's presence on the Asian mainland. Prince Alexsei Lobanov-Rostovsky, who had become foreign minister in January 1895, took particular exception to Japan's control of Port Arthur, an ice-free port: 'Such an occupation would also be very undesirable from the standpoint of Russian interests.'[3]

But the event that had also caused changes in Russian foreign policy since the outbreak of the Sino-Japanese war and its conclusion was the death of Alexander III in November 1894, compounded a few months later by that of Nicholas Giers.[4] Alexander III had pursued a foreign policy of avoiding conflict and Giers was internationally respected as a man of peace.

To begin with, Alexander's son, Nicholas II, was overwhelmed by the task ahead of him. 'I know absolutely nothing. The late emperor did not foresee his end and did not initiate me into anything', he complained plaintively.[5] Ill-informed though he was, from 1895 for the next decade Nicholas led his empire into a messianic policy of aggrandization in East Asia. After only a short time as emperor, Nicholas was asserting himself as Autocrat of All the Russias. He was distrustful of officials, especially gifted ones, whom he saw as threats to his personal authority. Although not unintelligent, his capriciousness of judgement and contempt for rule and consistency exasperated his ministers. Nicholas's wilfulness, hasty decisions, unwillingness to heed contrary opinions and his opaque manner naturally frustrated his official advisers. He was pathologically averse to confrontation and only saw ministers individually, to avoid their 'ganging up' on him. However, there was one man whose advice coincided with his instincts and was therefore to be followed: that of his third cousin, Kaiser Wilhelm II.

After the signing of the Treaty of Shimonoseki, Wilhelm assured Nicholas (writing in English): 'I am glad to be able to be of use to you in such an interesting and great question of foreign policy.' He was pleased 'to guard the rear of Russia so that nobody shall hamper your action towards the Far East!', concluding with the observation that 'it is clearly the great task of the future for Russia to cultivate the Asian continent and defend Europe from inroads of the great yellow race'.[6] Later in the year, the kaiser made clear in an interview with the Russian diplomat, Alexander Benckendorff, that he considered Russia to be in his debt. Wilhelm obviously had good reasons of his own to direct Russian energies away from Europe to clear the pitch for Germany.

Japan's victory over China caused consternation in the British government. Decrepit Manchu China was known as the 'sick man of Asia', but with her enormous natural resources, commercial ties with China were important—Britain having by far the largest foreign stake in China with control of almost three-quarters of the trade and shipping. A free trade Open Door China was essential to Britain, and her envoys in Peking had constantly impressed on the home government that it was necessary to be on good terms with China and warned of Japanese ambitions as regards Korea. Nicholas O'Conor, *chargé d'affaires* at the legation in Peking in 1886, had urged that 'We ought ... to go in for an entente cordiale with China, though carefully excluding from its meaning an alliance.'[7] Cecil Spring Rice, in 1893, similarly believed that 'If China herself is dismembered, would Japan be willing to protect her against Russia. Basta.'[8] Giers, in the same year, had written: 'As regards China, ... England will not neglect any means to be on good terms with this Power.'[9]

(Cecil Spring Rice was a talented British diplomat and prolific poet. Today he is remembered as the author of the words of the hymn, 'I Vow to Thee My Country'.)

Lord Rosebery, prime minister, and Lord Kimberley, foreign secretary, had recognized in 1894 that the clashes between the Chinese and Japanese in Korea would inevitably lead to war. Should Britain intervene to hold Japan back? This would mean acting with Russia in some form of armed mediation directed against Japan. But this would result in the disagreeable prospect of the two intervening powers having to administer Korea jointly in order to forestall further Japanese and Chinese clashes. Thus, Britain decided to let the two belligerents settle the dispute over Korea between themselves, as long as Russia did not intervene. Basically, 'the FO is rather Chinese in its sympathies, & yet does not wish to break with Japan'.[10]

In St Petersburg, there were those who advocated coming to an agreement with Japan on spheres of influence in Manchuria and Korea. Others argued that an alliance with China aimed at bringing the sick man into the Russian orbit was called for. A third alternative, favoured by the powerful General-Admiral Alexsei Alexandrovich, Nicholas II's uncle, was to initiate a diplomatic *démarche* of the European powers to counter Japanese encroachments on China.

Desultory sparring about joint or collective action was superseded by the Chinese capitulation. Britain did not find the Japanese terms unreasonable. However, Russia objected strongly to Japan's acquisition of the Liaotung Peninsula. Even George de Staal, who, as ever, sought to find common ground between Britain and Russia, saw British acceptance of Japan's terms as a volte-face: 'The mercantile spirit of England was awakened and dominated all other considerations.'[11]

The British government decided that it had no grounds for interference and adopted a stance of studied neutrality. However, Russia was not prepared to be constrained by the British refusal to cooperate. Cleverly, Russia consulted two other European powers—France and Germany—and they were prepared to play ball with Russia. Identical notes were delivered to Japan on 28 April 1895. In vain, Japan sought backing against European bullying, appealing unsuccessfully to the United States. By early May, Japan had renounced the entire Liaotung Peninsula, only to nurse a dangerous grudge on the subject for several years to come. (Shimonoseki was seen as Japan's San Stefano.)

China, for her part, was fully aware that the triplice of Russia, France and Germany was hardly altruistic: 'Only the Japanese decision to give in to the three-power note had allowed the gap between the Russian and British positions to be bridged, and such an occurrence could not be counted upon in the future.'[12] Rosebery regretted that Britain had not cooperated with the powers, but contrary opinions, led by Kimberley, had prevailed in cabinet and it was decided that there were no grounds for interference. Queen Victoria in a letter to Nicholas II showed that she agreed with the foreign secretary.

Sir Edward Grey in the early twentieth century wondered: 'It would be interesting to know what the statesmen of Berlin, Paris and St Petersburg saw of the future when they decided on joint action to restrain Japan.'[13]

It did not take long for Russia, who had portrayed herself as a defender of China, to exploit her neighbour's gratitude for her own ends. China had been forced to pay a large indemnity. Central government financing was beyond China's means; there was no other choice but to turn to international markets. The Hong Kong and Shanghai Banking Corporation, the HSBC, the leading financier in the region, could not make an attractive offer. Russia had little capital to provide and was a major borrower on European markets. Witte immediately realized that here was an opportunity to begin to displace Britain as the most prominent player in the Far East and to extend Russia's influence in China. Here one sees one of the first fruits of the Franco-Russian alliance coming into play.

France came to the rescue, and by June 1895 a loan of 100 million gold roubles at the favourable rate of 4 per cent had been arranged, with interest payments guaranteed by Russia in combination with French banks.[14] It was a large loan, but only half of the indemnity. Russian banks then produced the funds necessary for the foundation of the Russo-Chinese Bank, the charter of which was granted in December 1895 to the

Committee of the Siberian Railway. Apart from the right to engage in regular banking operations, the new institution was empowered to collect taxes, handle local government business, act as a commission merchant and seek railway concessions. It was an only slightly disguised branch of the Russian treasury. For Witte, the bank was an essential part of the Trans-Siberian Railway scheme, and he assured the emperor that it would prove a useful weapon in aiding the completion of the railway.

Britain did everything possible to prevent the Franco-Russian loan going through, but in vain. Lobanov-Rostovsky, openly Anglophobic, was able gloatingly to claim that its aim was to expedite Japan's retrocession of the Liaotung Peninsula, with derisory financial compensation. Russia had now stolen a clear march on Britain, hitherto so powerful in East Asia. Witte, of course, was delighted to contemplate that, if China defaulted on the loan, Russia would be able to interfere directly in Chinese financial affairs and re-route the Trans-Siberian to Russia's advantage. Even before this eventuality, he drew up plans to shorten the route to Vladivostok by cutting through northern Manchuria, a saving of 700 kilometres.

It was not merely a matter of making savings in railway construction by routing the railway through Manchuria. The Chinese Grand Secretary, Li Hun-Chan, the country's leading statesman, attended Nicholas Il's coronation in Moscow in May 1896, and it took little pressure for him to agree to a military alliance with Russia, in which China was very much the junior partner. The treaty signed in June 1896, denied by Russia, but whose terms were roughly known abroad, provided that any Japanese aggression against Russian, Chinese or Korean territory would be met by the combined forces of Russia and China, and that all Chinese ports would be open to Russian warships for the duration of any war. It did not include the cession of an ice-free port to Russia.[15] (The treaty was not fully disclosed until 1922.)

Russia was granted the right to build a railway line from the Heilongjiang and Kirin provinces of Manchuria to Vladivostok—the Chinese Eastern Railway (CER). Witte claimed that the CER marked one of the most splendid pages in the history of Russia in East Asia, and certainly within a few years the CER had developed into a Russian enclave:

> a semi-independent fiefdom on Chinese soil, with its own cities, government, and police. Also operating mines, ships, telegraphs, and lumber mills, it came to dominate much of Manchuria, especially the sparsely

populated north. 'Witte built up and directed a veritable kingdom in the Far East' one tsarist official recalled.[16]

Lord Salisbury, who had again become prime minister and foreign secretary in June 1895, was relatively sanguine about Russian activity in East Asia. In November, he deprecated unnecessary disturbance and alarm: 'Depend upon it, whatever may happen in that, be it in the way of war or in the way of commerce, we are equal to any competition which may be proposed to us.'[17] The following February, Arthur Balfour, a cabinet minister and also Salisbury's nephew, all but invited the Russians to secure for themselves an ice-free port. The British government had taken its eye off the ball in East Asia, preoccupied with problems with France over Africa and Siam, the Armenian massacres and the repercussions of the Kruger telegram in South Africa. However, it was not Russia who provoked a fresh crisis over the Celestial Empire in 1897 that brought Britain's attention back to East Asia.

Since 1895, Wilhelm II had been determined to establish a naval station in China as one of the bases Germany would require in her *Weltpolitik* as a naval power. A move against Kiaochow in northern China had long been under consideration as part of this policy. The murder of two German Christian missionaries in Shantung province in November 1897 provided a convenient pretext for a reprisal, and the German squadron in Chinese waters was ordered to Kiaochow to demand compensation as a first step towards gaining control of it. Germany was granted a 99-year lease in March 1898.

This suited cousin Nicky in St Petersburg perfectly. Moreover, the Russian emperor's East Asian dreams were now being fuelled by a group of rabid expansionists, under whose influence he had fallen. The most prominent of these were Alexander Bezobrazov and Nicholas's Asian mentor, Prince Esper Ukhtomsky.

Britain suspected Russo-German collusion over the seizure of Kiaochow, namely that it would provide Russia with a *quid pro quo* to follow suit. At the same time, it made sense for Britain to put her oar in before this happened. The minister in Peking, Colonel Sir Claude MacDonald, advocated the acquisition of a fortified coaling station in northern Chinese waters, while Sir Nicholas O'Conor, now ambassador in St Petersburg, believed that it was necessary to demand a clear sphere of influence in China, and possibly seize Chinese territory. For this to be permanent an agreement with Russia would be necessary.

Witte assured O'Conor that Russia intended to develop her economic interests in northern China, while supporting China's political independence for several years to come (clearly until the completion of the Trans-Siberian to Vladivostok). Yet at the same time, it did not take much to suspect that the Russian government might be following the kaiser's example. A Russian squadron was sent to winter in Port Arthur, at the southern tip of the Liaotung Peninsula. Two British warships were sent to anchor in the port soon after the Russian ships arrived.

German seizure of Kiaochow had obviously reignited international tensions in East Asia, and China was having difficulty in paying the war indemnity; an Anglo-German banking group had been negotiating for raising the third portion of the war indemnity. Britain then separately offered China a loan. This was declined. Claude MacDonald reported that Russia had agreed to a £16 million loan to China in return for a Russian rail monopoly in northern China. There was a new urgency for Britain to combat Russian designs.

Despite this, the ambassador in St Petersburg was optimistic, reporting that 'the Emperor is pleased to hear the desire of H.M.'s Government to avoid by an "entente" all misunderstanding in regions where the interests of the two countries are at issue and thinks that the affairs of China would offer an opportunity of putting them into operation'.[18] Sir Thomas Sanderson, permanent undersecretary at the foreign office, agreed, telling Staal that

> there seemed many reasons why we should try to come to an understanding instead of working against one another. He agreed ... if we made an attempt, we should be better treated than by Pce Lobanoff ... He got rather red and said Lobanoff had an almost morbid idea that our interests and policy were rootedly antagonistic to Russia. There was no longer that impression. I am afraid however that your overtures to Witte may not come too much. The opposite current is so strong in the official mind.[19]

In January 1898, Salisbury decided to seize the moment and offered Russia a far-reaching 'partition of influence' in China and the Ottoman empire. He suggested that Britain might dominate the Yangtse valley, Arabia, Egypt and the lower Euphrates area, while Russia should control northern China, the Straits and the Euphrates valley north of Baghdad. Inevitably, after the British loan to China was rejected, and combined with the Russian presence at Port Arthur and later in neighbouring Talienwan, the prime minister's efforts at coming to an agreement with

Russia were scuppered. It became clear that Russia was doing more than wintering a squadron at Port Arthur.

In March 1898 the Chinese government agreed to lease the port and its hinterland to Russia. The British government had no means of preventing this. This the Russian government naturally recognized. Staal reported that Balfour, replacing the sick Salisbury, could only regret what had taken place: 'The taking of the most important fortified place in China … was an important blow to the independence of the Government of China … and completely overthrows the political equilibrium of the Far East.'[20] In sadness, Balfour 'reminded me [i.e. Staal] how he had always been convinced of the need for an entente with Russia, and he would let me judge for myself the pain that he felt in seeing this fail'.[21] An agreement to extend the CER concession to Russia through southern Manchuria followed a few months later. The moment was clearly not propitious for any agreement.

Nevertheless, Russia did not have things all her own way. Japan, which still occupied the port of Wei-hai-wei, was due to remain there until the indemnity was paid. The British minister in Tokyo enquired whether a lease of the port by Britain was possible. Naturally, the Japanese government was pleased to agree to this as Wei-hai-wei on the coast of Shantung, roughly midway between Port Arthur in the north and Kiaochow in the south, would constitute a check on Russia and Germany, although it was a second-class harbour compared with Port Arthur. Britain did not create a fuss about Port Arthur and took Wei-hai-wei. Then, with what seems like straightforward cheek, Nicholas was said to be 'much froissé at our taking Wei-hai-wei'.[22]

Germany, Russia and Britain were all engaged in gaining territorial footholds on the Chinese coast, but Russia went much further. She successfully extracted railway concessions on the Liaotung Peninsula and in the Shing-king province of Manchuria. Mikhail Muraviev, foreign minister after Lobanov-Rostovsky's death in 1896, baldly denied that 'the dismemberment of the Chinese empire was threatened'.[23] The British press mounted a typical attack on Russia after the publication of a Blue Book on the Far East in April 1898. Even Staal had given up on any hope of reaching an understanding with Britain.

Salisbury's pre-eminence in the cabinet had been on the wane since 1895, mainly because of ill-health, and among some British diplomats he was referred to as Old Sarum (the rotten borough in Salisbury that was abolished in the 1832 Reform Act.) Dissatisfaction was rife in the cabinet, but the most open opposition to the prime minister's China policy came from Joseph Chamberlain, the colonial secretary. Hitherto an advocate of an understanding with Russia, in a bellicose speech in May 1898 he condemned British policy as flaccidly letting Russia establish a predominant position in China.

If there were divergent views within the British government, there was a veritable gulf between Russian officials and personal advisers to the emperor. In April 1898, Baron Roman Rosen, Russian minister in Tokyo, signed an arrangement with the Japanese government, according to which both governments pledged to refrain from direct interference in Korean internal affairs. At the same time, however, Alexander Bezobrazov and Vladimir Vonlyarlyarski convinced Nicholas II that Russia could continue to challenge Japan with impunity. An agency managing the properties of the House of Romanov took over the timber concession granted by China to the king of Korea and turned it into a vehicle of Russian expansion. The concession, comprising 5,700 square kilometres along the Yalu river, the entire Manchurian-Korean border, would provide cover for troops disguised as lumberjacks and become the nucleus of an East Asia Company, subordinated directly to the emperor, and not accountable to the ministers of finance or foreign affairs.

Britain had triumphed under Kitchener at the battle of Omdurman in North Africa in September 1898, and two months later successfully concluded a stand-off with France at Fashoda on the Nile. But from 1899 she was diplomatically and militarily weakened by the impending war in South Africa, the threat of a Russian takeover in Persia, and reports of Russian troop movements in Central Asia. The Boer War began badly for Britain in 1900. In a crude opportunistic gesture, Muraviev embarked upon a tour of European capitals with the aim of organizing a coalition in support of the Boers. What he sought, apart from making life difficult for the British government, was not obvious—to weaken Britain in Persia, in Afghanistan, or to force the opening of the Straits? Muraviev failed in his mission, but naturally his efforts aggravated Anglo-Russian relations. The Russian press meanwhile waged a high moral tone campaign against the British conduct of the Boer War.

The sudden eruption of repressed Chinese xenophobia at the turn of the century took all the powers by surprise. The Chinese reaction to defeat by Japan had taken two opposing lines. The first was a demand for modernization; the second a call for the expulsion of foreigners and a return to traditional seclusion.[24] The latter won.

Members of the secret Society of Righteous and Harmonious Fists, who came to be known to foreigners as the Boxers, were given official encouragement and support to act against foreigners. They killed a British missionary and persecuted Chinese Christians in early 1900. In June, Christians were massacred in Chihli province and all foreigners lived in fear for their lives. To protect them, and also the legations in Peking, an international force set out from Tientsin in June, but was strongly attacked and only just managed to fight its way back. To protect the foreign residents of Tientsin, the force occupied the Taku forts commanding the river approach to the city. This act was greeted by the Boxers as an act of war. The Tientsin concession was attacked and the ministers of the foreign powers were ordered to leave the city. A German envoy was murdered and foreigners and Chinese Christians were besieged in the Roman Catholic cathedral. An international brigade fought its way to Peking and relieved the legations in August. By the autumn, the situation from a Chinese point of view was nothing short of disastrous. Peking was occupied by the European powers and was being plundered by their troops. The court had fled and foreign troops roamed Peking rescuing foreigners and inflicting arbitrary vengeance.

With British troops tied up in South Africa and with Russia, as ever, financially weak, Anglo-Russian relations were at the mercy of another power, ever more prepared to exacerbate them. Wilhelm II, the opportunist par excellence, told the Russian ambassador in Berlin, Count Nicholas Osten-Sacken, in January 1900, that 'there was only Russia who could paralyze the power of England and, if necessary, deliver her a mortal blow ... If ever Our August Master were provoked to direct his arms towards India, no one would do anything in Europe.'[25]

The British government was no dupe, however, as regards Germany. Salisbury told George Curzon, now viceroy of India:

> I do not feel the same danger in the case of Russia—for though Russia is far more powerful and quite as unscrupulous, she is less likely to do a coup de tête. As to Germany I have less confidence than you. She is in mortal terror on account of that long undefended frontier of her's [*sic*] on the Russian side. She will therefore never stand by us against Russia; but is always rather inclined to curry favour with Russia by throwing us over.[26]

But however much the Russian government was aware of the kaiser's well-known reasons for keeping them embroiled in East Asian problems, Muraviev was encouraged by Wilhelm's support: 'The tendency of the

Berlin Cabinet to sow disaccord among the Powers ... is not new. We had no reason to lend our support, while maintaining excellent relations with the neighbouring Empire with whom we are united by many traditional and glorious links.' Muraviev's junior colleague Alexander Isvolsky, the minister in Tokyo, opposed the collusion with Berlin and described his superior as 'a man of the most mediocre capabilities'.[27]

The Boxer uprising had provided Russia with a golden opportunity to stake a further claim on Manchuria. The demolition of over 200 kilometres of track of the South Manchurian Railway during rioting and an attack on Blagoveshchensk across the Amur were used to justify sending 200,000 Russian troops into China. By October, the whole of Manchuria was under Russian occupation. Cossack troops even entered Mongolia in order to strengthen the position of the Russian consul. This was the policy advocated by Alexsei Kuropatkin, the war minister, and which was opposed by the new foreign minister, Count Vladimir Lamsdorff (Muraviev having died in June 1900). The new minister, a small reclusive man, who shunned the social life of St Petersburg and was supported by Witte (who later claimed the minister to be more in fear of Kuropatkin than the Chinese), insisted that Russia supported Chinese territorial integrity and would evacuate Manchuria.

However, in January 1901, the full extent of Russian ambitions became apparent. A draft treaty was submitted to China which proposed the restoration of Chinese authority in Manchuria but forbade China to keep troops there, at least until the completion of the CER. Russia would have the right to demand the dismissal of governors and officials whose activities were not compatible with friendly relations. The principle of an indemnity to compensate for the damages caused by the Boxers was established, but with the option for China of paying it in the form of new privileges and concessions to Russia. As a start, China would allow a line to be built from a point on the CER or the South Manchurian Railway to the Great Wall in the direction of Peking.

The Manchurian Protocol, or Convention, although in theory secret, was known to the other powers and was too much for them to stomach. The Chinese were encouraged by the British government, whose minister in Peking, now Sir Ernest Satow, was instrumental in stiffening Chinese resistance to the protocol. France and (reluctantly) Germany lodged formal objections. The other powers concerned for the Open Door trade policy towards China, the United States and Japan, joined in to defend Chinese territorial integrity and the rights of trading nations. Russia climbed down. A further blow was inflicted in November when Li Hun-Chan died, reducing Russian influence in Peking. Witte, obsessed with his economic plans for Manchuria, held that Russian troops should evacuate Manchuria to pave the way for improved relations with the other powers, while Isvolsky in Tokyo warned of increasing anti-Russian feeling in Japan.

Bezobrazov and his coterie considered that they had as much right as officials to make Russian policy, while Witte vainly protested that Nicholas could not reign outside cooperation with the official state bureaucracy. State counsellor Alexander Polovtsov wrote in July 1901:

> In no field of policy is there a principled, well considered and firmly directed course of action. Everything is done in bursts, haphazardly, under the influence of the moment, according to the demands of this or that person ... The young Tsar feels more and more contempt for the organs of his own power and begins to believe in the beneficial strength of his own autocracy, which he manifests sporadically, without preliminary discussion and without any link to the overall course of policy.[28]

There was also a change of direction at the foreign office in London, when Salisbury resigned in 1901 and was replaced by Lord Lansdowne, a former viceroy of India. The 'new course' of Lansdowne resembled the policy of limited colonial agreements through which his predecessor had, from 1886 to 1892, escaped from the isolation of 1885. But Lansdowne intended to go further and faster in a search for general settlements of Britain's disputes with the other powers. In 1901 he was unsuccessful. Germany refused to support Britain against Russian encroachments in China. The kaiser would not accept an alliance confined to East Asia and preferred to wait until the British government felt obliged to commit herself to the Triple Alliance.

This was a moment of reckoning for Britain, financially and diplomatically weakened by the Boer War, and the chancellor of the exchequer, Sir Michael Hicks Beach, was insisting that Britain could not afford to maintain the 15,000 troops sent in as part of the international brigade following the Boxer uprising. Furthermore, relations with Russia came under fresh strain as a result of a possible large Russian loan to Persia. What was left was the possibility for Britain of an agreement with Japan.

Already, by October 1901, talks were taking place in London between Lansdowne and the Japanese ambassador, Viscount Tadasu Hayashi. At the same time the Japanese statesman, Marquis Ito, hoped to resolve disputes with Russia and visited St Petersburg. But no amount of politeness could conceal the fact that Russian aspirations were incompatible with Japanese interests. Hence, in November 1901, a draft Japanese alliance was submitted to the British cabinet, although Lansdowne still hoped that an agreement with infinitely more important Germany would be possible.

Not all the cabinet was of the same opinion. A speech by Joseph Chamberlain that was hostile to Germany provoked strong criticism from the chancellor, Bernhard von Bülow, in the Reichstag, which in turn produced an anti-German outburst in the British press. Talks that had been taking place since 1899 ended. This set a premium on success with Japan. Divided counsels in Tokyo caused some delay; Lansdowne finally secured sufficient minor modifications of Japanese proposals to cajole a wavering cabinet into acceptance. The alliance was signed on 31 January 1902. According to its terms, after an affirmation that they were both Open Door powers, the treaty stated that if either country, in defence of their respective interests, should become involved in war with another power, the other would maintain a strict neutrality and use its efforts to prevent other powers from joining in hostilities against its ally. In peacetime the two powers would maintain a naval force superior to any other power in the Far East.

An important effect of the Anglo-Japanese Alliance was that this constituted a warning to Russia by giving Japan virtually a free hand in Korea. Russia, now less sure of her position, decided to cut her losses in Manchuria. The Manchurian Protocol of January 1901 was dropped and a new agreement re-established Chinese authority in Manchuria as an integral part of the empire. The Russians pledged to withdraw their troops by October 1903 without obtaining economic or political concessions.

When the treaty was made public in Britain in February 1902, public reaction was surprisingly favourable. The official Russian position as expounded by Lamsdorff—who was astounded by news of the alliance—was couched more in sorrow than in anger. Nevertheless, the minister warned that as the treaty had been concluded with rapidity in (attempted) secrecy, it would naturally confirm the Russian public's long-standing opinion that Britain was Russia's natural enemy. It vitiated the efforts by Russia to come to an understanding with Britain. Prince Lev Urussov, Russian ambassador in Paris, was ordered to appear unperturbed by the alliance: 'Our position in Asia is sufficiently strong for us to take on any hostile schemes that may be mounted against us … It is always wise to take things seriously, but I refuse to take this sort of treaty as more than bluster.'[29] Sir Charles Scott, the British ambassador in St Petersburg, recognized that the treaty was a blow to Russia:

> At present I think we must be prepared to find Russia, even if she takes no more active step, for some time exceedingly unconciliatory & disposed to make herself disagreeable to us all round. They can scarcely disguise their discomfiture at our having stolen a march on them in the matter of this agreement with Japan.[30]

(Hostile reaction in Russia to the Anglo-Japanese Alliance lasted long after 1902. Boris Romanov, a Soviet historian, argued as late as 1928 that Britain had sought to use Japan to fight her battles for her; and Alexander Galperin two decades later claimed that Britain, in 1902, was egging Japan on to make war on Russia in East Asia.[31])

Russia retaliated by signing an agreement with France to work together to maintain the status quo in China, and Lamsdorff unsuccessfully attempted to revive the Muraviev plan for a continental combination against Britain. At the same time, Russian ministers, already dissatisfied by Nicholas's mistrust of them, complained more about their treatment. The emperor was known to be encouraged by his wife, the Empress Alexandra, and Bezobrazov reigned supreme.[32]

Inevitably, the brunt of Nicholas's suspicions was borne by Witte. In late 1902, a separate Merchant Marine, previously under the ministry of finance, was created under Witte's foe, the Grand Duke Alexander Mikhailovich, Nicholas II's brother-in-law. A well-funded Bezobrazov was dispatched to Port Arthur in a special train from where to oversee the concessions in Korea and Manchuria. There, he met the war minister, Kuropatkin, who was shocked by the arrogance of the unofficial adviser. On his return to St Petersburg, the minister submitted a report to the emperor: 'However great the commercial advantages of the enterprise may be, it appears advisable for us to sell it to foreigners if we do not wish to maintain a constant source of danger of a break with Japan.'[33]

Undeterred by official opposition, Nicholas created Admiral Evgeny Alexseev viceroy in the Far East in 1903, with full plenipotentiary powers, to the dismay of the ministers of foreign affairs, finance and war. To guide Alexseev, the emperor formed a Special Committee on the Affairs of the Far East, with himself as chairman, thus taking personal control of all questions pertaining to the region. Lamsdorff despaired: 'My opinion is that this policy is likely to lead Russia into a nefarious war ... The situation is rendered still more complicated by the rumours that Your Majesty has invested his own capital in that concern.'[34] The climax of the emperor's new-found firmness (all the time fed by cousin Willy) was the dismissal of Witte, who was still advising the evacuation of Manchuria. With the benefit of hindsight, this had been a long time coming.

Sir Charles Scott in St Petersburg recognized cold official civility and a lack of access to the ministry of foreign affairs, plus a new social exclusion. It was impossible to know what Russia would do next. But if Russian foreign policy was difficult to follow, Scott's position was undermined by a British foreign office campaign against him, backed by King Edward VII. The ambassador's continual defence of Lamsdorff's sincerity also irritated Lansdowne, and *The Times* carped at Scott's unwillingness to protest against the expulsion of its correspondent in 1903.

The Japanese had borne a grudge against Russia since 1895, when they had been forced to climb down after Shimonoseki. Now, strengthened by the Anglo-Japanese Alliance, they opened unofficial negotiations with Russia. They offered a bargain, whereby Japan would gain rights in Korea, while Russia would be compensated in Manchuria. The Russians were dilatory—they believed they had nothing to gain by making concessions, as they were already in control of the vital parts of Manchuria. (Indeed, they not only failed to observe the third phase of the evacuation of Manchuria, but, in September 1903, they had audaciously reoccupied Mukden.) Japan, meanwhile, only had a sphere of influence in half of Korea, which she shared with Russia.

The Russians were arrogant and overestimated the strength of their position. Tokyo became convinced that Russia was prevaricating. Russia's international position became increasingly precarious in the face of the stiffening Japanese stance.

Count Alexander Benckendorff, newly Russian ambassador in London, did not hide from Lansdowne that the foreign policy of Russia at this point was no longer one and undivided. Benckendorff, according to Lansdowne, 'evidently wished me to understand that many things happened for which Count Lamsdorff could not be held responsible'.[35] Benckendorff warned his minister in mid-December 1903 that while Britain recognized Russian interests in Manchuria, the same was not true for Korea, which was not limitrophe with Russia.

Alexseev, for his part, grumbled at the inaction in East Asia, declaring that if Alexander III were still alive, he would give the Japanese a thrashing they would not quickly forget. Kuropatkin unsuccessfully counselled sending troops to East Asia. As for Lamsdorff, he fell into a deep depression. When Nicholas did deign to see his foreign minister in September 1903, the emperor asked him: 'What do you think of the position generally?' Lamsdorff replied: 'It is difficult for me to give my opinion, Sire, as of late I have been in the darkness as to our policy in the Far East and have lost the drift of things.'[36]

By October, confusion in Russian foreign policy was causing great unease in London. Lansdowne complained to the French ambassador that Russia's policy in Manchuria could only aggravate suspicion of Russian motives. The ambassador apologized for his country's ally, as talks were taking place between Britain and France to resolve their outstanding disputes.

At the same time in St Petersburg, a confident Nicholas declared that present events recalled the situation after the Sino-Japanese War. Then, Russia had firmly said 'Back', and Japan had obeyed. Now, they had become yet more demanding: 'All the same, it is a barbarous country. Which is better: to risk war, or to continue with concessions?'[37]

At the official reception on New Year's Day 1904, the Russian emperor sought out the Japanese envoy, Shinichiro Kurino, impressing on him that Russia was 'quite conscious of her own strength', though there was a limit to her patience.[38] As it happened, the patience of the other was also approaching its limit. On 8 February, a Japanese squadron launched a surprise attack, without declaring war, on the Russian fleet at Port Arthur, sinking some ships and blockading the rest by mining the port (a precursor of Pearl Harbor). This, Nicholas claimed, was 'but the "bite of a flea." The serene and even-joyful spirit of the Czar amazed me', recalled Prince Urussov.[39] The Russian press blamed Britain for encouraging the Japanese attack.

So began an unnecessary war, for which Nicholas II was largely personally to blame, and which was to have repercussions beyond the balance of power in East Asia: 'Russia possessed interests in Europe which she could not abandon and to which her Far Eastern policies did great harm. In 1902–3 a wise policy would have retained many of the advantages accrued in earlier years in the Far East without the risk of war.'[40]

The two belligerents appeared unevenly matched. An Asian people from its small islands was defying one of the European great powers with a population three times as great and with a vast territory. But in the area of conflict, the advantage was with the Japanese. The Russian land and sea forces available in Manchuria were less than those which the Japanese could quickly bring into action. Russian land reinforcements depended on the Trans-Siberian Railway, only a single track, to transport the army needed. Soldiers were poorly equipped with modern weaponry. Added to this, Admiral Alexseev and General Kuropatkin, in charge of the armies in Manchuria, hated one another. At home, poor Lamsdorff could only bewail the folly of provoking the conflict.[41] But the minister of foreign affairs was an onlooker.

Despite reports of Russian disarray, the British cabinet had little confidence in the prospects of the Japanese. It was agreed that the Russians would probably win, although ministers differed as to what should be their response. Lansdowne wanted to avert a war which Britain could ill-afford. Austen Chamberlain at the exchequer hoped that a Russian government preoccupied by war would think it worth coming to terms with Britain. Lord Selborne, First Lord of the Admiralty, and the service chiefs, thought that Britain would have to enter the war if a Japanese defeat was imminent. The prime minister, now Arthur Balfour, on the other hand, believed a Russian victory would be to the advantage of the British, as the Russians would cripple themselves in the process and would only be able to sustain their newly won position by permanently diverting much of their strength to East Asia. Without exception, however, British diplomats were now strongly sympathetic towards Japan.

Britain and France had mended their diplomatic fences in 1904 with the signing of the Entente Cordiale, and France was therefore unwilling to aid her Russian ally in the war against Japan. Soon, Japan had command of the seas, and occupied the Liaotung Peninsula in September 1904. To combat Japanese naval supremacy, Russia decided to move her Baltic Fleet (unconvincingly renamed the Second Pacific Ocean Squadron), under Admiral Zinovy Rozhestvensky, to East Asia, as the Black Sea Fleet was unable under international law to pass the Straits. The Baltic Fleet set off from Libau on 16 October in a state of unpreparedness, intending either to coal at sea or in one of France's colonial ports.

On 21 October, the Russian fleet attacked some British trawlers from Hull in the Dogger Bank area of the North Sea, killing two British seamen. Lansdowne immediately demanded an official Russian apology, compensation for the families of the trawlermen, and security against a recurrence of such an action. Edward VII exploded with anger and public opinion was inflamed. The two countries seemed on the brink of war. Lamsdorff came up with only a vague expression of regret—in today's terms he considered the incident unfortunate collateral damage. The tense Anglo-Russian relations were then aggravated when Rozhestvensky claimed that his fleet had been threatened by torpedo boats—possibly Japanese—and the usually reasonable Lamsdorff held that he had indisputable proofs of Japanese schemes to attack the Russian fleet with twenty agents based in Hull.[42] The Russian ambassador in London obviously maintained the same line. He was booed in the street. Lansdowne was having none of it. Britain would use force if necessary to stop Rozhestvensky at Vigo in Spain: British warships were being concentrated in Gibraltar. Lansdowne later admitted that 'it looked to me as if the betting was about even between peace and war'.[43]

Only after a week of vociferously asserting its innocence did the Russian government make an ignominious climbdown. Benckendorff and his colleague in Paris, Alexander Nelidov, proposed that the incident should be referred to The Hague Tribunal (which Nicholas II had been instrumental in creating in 1899), but this was unacceptable to the British government. Lamsdorff had to plead with the emperor to persuade him to accept the establishment of an independent commission of enquiry at The Hague. In early November, Balfour announced that the Russian government had expressed its regret, would detain its fleet at Vigo, punish the guilty, and had guaranteed that there would be no repetition of such happenings. Lamsdorff called on the British ambassador in St Petersburg, now Sir Charles Hardinge, expressing a new-found cordiality. Lansdowne and Benckendorff thanked each other most warmly. A financial settlement of £65,000 for the victims' families was agreed in April 1905.

The Baltic Fleet was allowed to continue on its way, creating international tension whenever it came close to land—but this was of minor importance. The entire international situation was transformed by the course of the war in East Asia. Port Arthur fell to the Japanese in January 1905 after a protracted siege. The Manchu capital Mukden was captured in March. Kuropatkin was demoted. Then the final blow fell in May, when much of the Baltic Fleet was annihilated in the Straits of Tsushima, and the Japanese were advancing deep into Manchuria. Russia was financially exhausted and in a state of revolutionary upheaval.

Theodore Roosevelt, the American president, had since May 1904 offered to mediate between Russia and Japan, but neither party was interested. Then, post-Tsushima, Japan was prepared to enter into negotiations with the enemy. Russia was wary as to how neutral Roosevelt was—and with good reason. The American was known to despise the Russian system of government and the United States was on good terms with Britain, Japan's ally. And the victor was intent on demanding a favourable (i.e. harsh) settlement, a large indemnity—such as France had had to pay in 1870—and territorial concessions. The president called on the Russian ambassador, Baron Rosen, and told him 'to say to the Czar that I believed the war was absolutely hopeless for Russia; that I earnestly desired that she and Japan should come together and see if they could agree on terms of peace'.[44]

While they appeared to be reflecting, the Russian emperor and Lamsdorff were also closely following discussions in Washington, London and Tokyo. London forwarded to Hardinge, in St Petersburg, telegrams from Washington and Tokyo to London. Most of the Russian decrypts are marked as having been read by Nicholas II. Thus, the Russians knew from a deciphered telegram marked 'Secret' that the Japanese were prepared to make concessions over the island of Sakhalin, which they had captured from Russia.[45]

Two months after the Tsushima disaster, Nicholas met cousin Willy at Bjørko on the Gulf of Finland with no foreign policy advisers present. This was an ideal situation for the clever kaiser to exploit. He arrived with a draft secret Russo-German alliance in hand. Germany had supported Russia against the British, who had encouraged Japan to go to war against Russia. France had not backed her ally Russia but had colluded with Britain in the Entente Cordiale. The naive Nicholas signed on the dotted line. Nevertheless, there was no chance that France, Russia's ally, would agree to be part of such a continental bloc. And France was now the stronger partner in the alliance.

Bülow was furious that the kaiser had acted without his knowledge and threatened to resign. Lamsdorff recognized that he would have to extricate Nicholas from the trap into which he had fallen and preserve the Franco-Russian alliance, particularly as Russia needed a loan, which would necessarily involve France. If the treaty came into operation, the long-term goal of German foreign policy would have been achieved at Russia's expense. Lamsdorff pointed out that the Franco-Russian Alliance would be wrecked, and relations with Britain would be harmed to such an extent that Russia would be united exclusively with Germany.

The Bjørko treaty was quickly dropped. It represented the last example of old-style diplomacy, unacceptable in the twentieth century. But not only had Nicholas II been humiliated; Wilhelm II was isolated. He decided to turn to other means under his sole control to bolster Germany's position in Europe to deal with recalcitrant neighbours.

Russia's ally France had for a long time been urging Russia to treat for peace with Japan, but it was the failed cajoling by Wilhelm II of his cousin at Bjørko that finally convinced Nicholas to accept negotiations, grudgingly, while at the same time threatening to reopen hostilities if things did not go as he wished. However, Russia's diplomatic position had been weakened even before her defeat at Tsushima. Secret talks were taking place for a renewal of the Anglo-Japanese Alliance, for which both parties were anxious. These were, of course, known to the Russians through the decipherment of telegrams. Britain wished to extend the scope of the alliance such that, just as the two countries stood together against Russian aggression, the Japanese army would support Britain in India. Talks were hurried along and a new treaty signed in August.

Negotiations led by Roosevelt at Portsmouth, New Hampshire, began in August 1905. Nicholas's first two choices of plenipotentiary declined, and he had to swallow his pride and choose the obvious candidate, Sergei Witte, to represent Russia, along with the ambassador to the United States, Baron Rosen. He gave 'the most precise instructions to Witte that not an inch of territory should be ceded and not a rouble paid as He could not accept such concessions either to his conscience or his people'.[46] Witte for his part admitted to a feeling of patriotic shame: 'It was morally hard to be the representative of the great military power Russia, so horribly and so stupidly defeated.'[47]

After a week of fruitless negotiations, the Japanese delegation led by the senior diplomat, Jurato Komura (though the Russians had asked for Marquis Ito, known to be favourably disposed to them), attempted to break the impasse by dropping its demand that Russia provide financial compensation for Japan's war costs. Instead, it insisted that Russia should cede the southern half of Sakhalin and pay compensation to Japan for the northern half. 'But fancy sharing an island with a convict establishment', Cecil Spring Rice wryly commented to Mrs Roosevelt.[48]

Witte proved a brilliant defender of defeated Russia. He successfully held out against the payment of an indemnity, and Japan only gained the lease of the Liaotung Peninsula with its ports and the South Manchurian Railway. Manchuria was to be evacuated and returned to China: Korea was to be independent, although within the Japanese orbit.

Although not directly involved in the Portsmouth Treaty, its signature influenced Anglo-Russian relations for the better. The treaty, and the now renewed Anglo-Japanese Alliance, drew a line under East Asian quarrels of the previous decade. The Russian threat to India, while still possible, was now less likely, and a weakened Russia would be more amenable to coming to an agreement with Britain on other issues. Charles Hardinge was told to impress upon the Russian government that Britain 'always desired, and still desires that we should live on neighbourly terms'.[49]

In London, Lansdowne assured Benckendorff that 'there was nothing to prevent Russia and Great Britain from resuming the friendly examination of those important questions which you and I were discussing when the war so unfortunately interrupted our deliberations'.[50]

But the removal of East Asia, only one danger zone out of several, was not sufficient to make any Anglo-Russian agreement achievable in 1905.

30

THE ROADBLOCKS TO AN ANGLO-RUSSIAN RAPPROCHEMENT

Lord Salisbury, when he became prime minister for the third time in June 1895, voiced restrained optimism about relations with Russia: 'We have ... the necessity of coping, practically alone, with the alliance of France and Russia ... It may not be possible for England and Russia to return to their old relations. But it is an object to be wished for and approached as opportunity offers.'[1]

There had been prominent politicians and diplomats in both Russia and Britain who, for the previous decade, had been advocating an Anglo-Russian agreement. In 1883 Nicholas Giers had instructed George de Staal, when the latter became ambassador to Britain, to seek a rapprochement between the two countries. Staal did his best. Ivan Zinoviev, head of the Asiatic Department in St Petersburg, favoured an agreement with Britain. Sir Robert Morier in St Petersburg had irritated his colleagues in the foreign office with his constant urging for an understanding with Russia, but, with the acute rivalry of the two countries in Central Asia in the early 1880s, nothing could be achieved. Lord Randolph Churchill and Sir Henry Drummond Wolff were also vocal advocates of settling differences in the late 1880s. The young parliamentary undersecretary for foreign affairs, Sir Edward Grey, in the early 1890s held that an arrangement with Russia should be sought.

Doing anything in this direction was out of the question in 1895–6 because of the Armenian massacres. In 1894, the paranoid Turkish sultan, Abdul-Hamid II, embarked on a murderous policy of persecuting and ridding himself of his Christian Armenian subjects, about a million in number, living in colonies and cities such as Constantinople and scattered over Asia Minor. Late in 1895, Abdul Hamid put a stop to the massacres at the behest of the European powers. When, the following summer, the Armenians demonstrated in Constantinople, the sultan either ordered or acquiesced in yet another massacre. The European ambassadors witnessed the slaughter in the streets and the sultan was obliged to call a halt.

British public opinion was aroused. The aged Gladstone, infused with new life, led a campaign against the 'Great Assassin'; the foreign office was inundated with resolutions from humanitarian and religious organizations; the British people clamoured for action. Salisbury was aware that merely to denounce the sultan was not enough, and at the Guildhall in November 1895 he appealed for international cooperation, issuing dire warnings that Abdul Hamid was destroying the Ottoman empire.

However, Russia, the other great power most concerned with Turkey, refused to cooperate. There was a large number of Armenians living within the empire. From 1883, they had been subjected to increasing efforts to Russify them and destroy their national consciousness. Autonomy for Turkish Armenians would make the absorption of Russian Armenians more difficult. Russia would not play ball.

The question was, what good could Britain do acting alone? There was no possibility of a military landing that would actually help the land-locked Armenians. 'Our ships', as Salisbury admitted, 'will not surmount the mountains of Taurus.'[2] The only course that could be envisaged was a naval demonstration in the Straits aimed at deposing the sultan. The cabinet would not go along with the prime minister—evidence that the predominance of Salisbury in foreign policy was over—as the Admiralty feared that, once the fleet entered the Straits, it might have its communications with Britain and Egypt cut off by France's Toulon squadron.

Salisbury had come to realize that Britain had backed the wrong horse for many years by supporting the irreformable, corrupt Ottoman empire. In a confidential letter to *Daily Telegraph* journalist, Ivan Muller, in August 1896, he made clear that British policy had changed dramatically:

> There is no such thing as a fixed policy, because policy like all organic entities is always in the making. I do not know that I can sum up the present trend of English policy better than by saying that we are engaged in slowly escaping from the dangerous errors of 1848–1856 … Politics is a matter of business; our allies should be those who are most likely to help or not to hinder the interests of which we as a Government, we are the trustees. Now the interests of France clashed with ours on almost every coast; those of Russia in reality only on the Afghan-Perso frontier; those of Austria nowhere.[3]

There was no point in continuing to bolster the Ottoman empire; Salisbury needed to work with, not against, Russia. And 1896 provided the prime minister with the opportunity to confront the Russian emperor personally as to his country's stance on the Near East.

It was hoped by the British government and royal family that the accession of Nicholas II in 1894 boded well. Sir Frank Lascelles, ambassador to Russia, wrote that 'ever since his arrival he had noticed the growth of a more friendly feeling, now strengthened by the sympathy exhibited by the action of the Prince and Princess of Wales'.[4] They had attended Alexander III's funeral. Bertie reported that 'all had gone off well, and been very impressive, but lasted three hours and a half ... I thought so much of darling Alicky and all at St Petersburg.'[5] For now, the Russian emperor was the Prince of Wales's nephew by marriage, and his new wife, the Empress Alexandra, was the favourite granddaughter of Queen Victoria.

A year later, Nicholas assured Lascelles that over Armenia, 'he could not conceive of any difference on that subject between our two countries. Both desired a full enquiry into the alleged atrocities, it was doing too much honour to the Turks to admit that they could be the cause of a quarrel between Russia and England.'[6] But when the Russian press attacked Britain over not cooperating in putting pressure on Japan after Shimonoseki, Queen Victoria protested at the violent and offensive articles about Britain that were appearing in Russia.

Nicholas was crowned emperor in Moscow in May 1896:

> This was in his eyes far from being merely the symbolic act through which he signified to the world his assumption of the responsibilities of government ... Nicholas believed that through his coronation he assumed before God a responsibility for the fate of his empire from which no human being could ever absolve him.[7]

But the coronation led to a disaster. Four days after the enthronement, half a million people, mainly peasants, gathered at Khodynka Field. The huge crowd could not be controlled by the handful of Cossacks and police present. Within seconds, hundreds of men, women and children began to lose their footing, but their cries of panic were lost in the clamour of the orderless thousands behind them.

Emergency squads belatedly arrived at the scene. Sir Nicholas O'Conor, the new British ambassador, reported to Queen Victoria that 'there seems to have been a lamentable want of foresight on the part of the police authorities in allowing such a vast concourse of people to assemble overnight … There are scenes and incidents too terrible and harrowing for the Queen's ears.'[8] The official figure for the dead was 1,429; in fact, probably many more died.

Four months later Nicholas and Alexandra visited Queen Victoria at Balmoral. Security was tight around the Russian emperor and empress, who came to mark the queen's diamond jubilee to take place in 1897 and Nicholas's coronation. Victoria was charmed by the good-looking young couple. The Prince of Wales for his part dragged his reluctant nephew out shooting. Nicholas complained bitterly to his mother: 'After he had left I had an easier time, because I could at least do what *I* wanted, and was not *obliged* to go out shooting every day in the cold and rain … Granny was kinder and more amiable than ever.'[9]

Salisbury hoped to take advantage of the visit to raise not only the subject of the Armenian massacres, but the question of the future of the Ottoman empire. The signatory powers to the 1878 Berlin treaty should decide what reforms were necessary, and force the sultan to accept them. Failing this, Abdul Hamid should be deposed. Britain and Russia would establish a *modus vivendi*, and partition the Ottoman empire. Nicholas was taken aback by this exposition. What would happen to the Straits? 'The Straits were the door to the room in which he lived, and he must have the key to that door.'[10] Nicholas insisted that the Straits and Dardanelles should be in Russian hands, fortified so that an attack, such as had been launched in Crimea forty years before, would be impossible. This Salisbury would not countenance. Any general dismemberment of the Ottoman empire must also involve France, Austria-Hungary and Italy.

By the time the two men met again two days later, the Russians had taken the precaution of preventing too much pressure by the experienced statesman on the young emperor by inviting George de Staal to attend. Nicholas was briefed to tell the prime minister that Russia was not prepared to run the risk of dethroning the sultan, which could well provoke a Muslim revolt in Russia. This was clearly an unlikely outcome, but a Russian rebuff to Salisbury. For by 1896, Russia had the upper hand in Constantinople. The British ambassador, Sir Philip Currie, held that 'the Sultan, who is an object of loathing to all decent Turks … is selling himself to Russia'.[11]

The diplomatic activity of 1895–6 was a failure. Nothing was done to help the Armenians. No agreement was made either for the partition of the Ottoman empire or for the establishment of some form of international control over it. Russia was neither willing to forget her old rivalries and antagonisms with Britain, nor able to act independently. Salisbury, for his part, was now ceasing to believe that it would be possible in the long term to prevent Russia from seizing the Straits, though he hoped that the issue might not arise in an acute form until the Ottoman empire had finally collapsed. From the beginning of 1897, he felt that Britain should withdraw from all responsibilities at Constantinople and concentrate on the defence and development of Egypt.

The following year Salisbury made an offer that he hoped would end friction with Russia over China, but with Russia concentrating on making her position dominant in East Asia, there was no chance of reaching any agreement. Moreover, in 1899 any idea of establishing an understanding between the two countries came to a complete standstill with the outbreak of the Boer War. The Russian press, undoubtedly with official approval, lambasted the British government with 'its hostile and abusive tone', gloating over early military reversals.[12] Mikhail Muraviev's visit to Madrid that year was seen as 'striking proof of the hatred of Russia and France for us, not only of the official classes but of Russian society as a whole ... The Emperor is weak and the Military party are getting the bit between their teeth.'[13]

Nicholas wrote to his uncle, now King Edward VII, in June 1901, protesting at the British conduct of the war (the king rightly suspected that his nephew had been put up to it by his ministers or Boer leaders):

> My Dearest Uncle Bertie,
>
> I often wanted to write to dear Grandmama to ask her quite privately whether there was any possibility of stopping the War in South Africa. Yet I never wrote to her fearing to hurt her and always hoping that it would soon cease ... A small people are desperately defending their country, a part of their land is devastated, their families flocked together in camps, their farms burnt. Of course in war such things have always happened and will happen, but in this case, forgive the expression, it looks more like a war of extermination.[14]

Edward was not prepared to accept such criticism from a young, inexperienced sovereign and, with advice from Salisbury, dispatched a strong remonstrance:

> My Dearest Nicky,
>
> I can quite understand that it was in every respect repugnant to your feelings to write to me relative to the South African War, though great

> pressure has been brought to bear upon you ... I do not know whether you are aware that the war was begun and elaborately prepared for many years previous by the Boers and was unprovoked ... If England had quietly submitted to this outrage no portion of her Dominions throughout the world would have been safe. Would you have submitted to a similar treatment?

There followed a long lecture on the lessons of the Indian Rebellion, the Russian campaigns in the Caucasus and the American Civil War, accompanied by a veiled criticism of Russian governance of its empire:

> It is impossible to see into the future, but we have every reason to hope that the end is not far off, and we entertain no doubts whatever that when peace and order have been fully restored, the territories which belonged to the Republics will enjoy in a full measure the tranquility and good government which England has never yet failed to assure to the populations which have come under her sway.[15]

The British government had become understandably fearful that Russia would take advantage of its preoccupation with South Africa to resume expansionist policies in Central Asia. Problems there, while not at the forefront of Anglo-Russian relations, thus re-emerged. A crisis had blown up in Chitral in 1895, as a result of yet another murder in the royal family.[16] The fourth new sovereign in little more than two years demanded recognition by Calcutta and turned to his southern neighbour in Swat, and a former ruler, for support. However small these hill-top states were, alarm bells rang in British India. The door to northern India was once more dangerously ajar. A small force was sent to Chitral, only to be besieged for several months. Finally, a large British relief column arrived from Peshawar. It was one of the last heroic adventures of the Great Game; the garrison was relieved and the defeated protagonists found a bolthole in Afghanistan.

All this took place only months after the Pamirs settlement, with only the narrow indefensible Wakhan corridor separating British and Russian possessions in Central Asia. This naturally had a close bearing on the Chitral question, with the hawks in London (many of them from the numerous ranks of retired Indian Army officers) and the Indian government pressing for a permanent garrison in Chitral. Nevertheless, despite the arguments in favour of retention, Lord Rosebery's cabinet overruled Calcutta. Less than two months later, the new Salisbury government, with George Curzon undersecretary of state at the foreign office, decided to retain Chitral to prevent a possible Russian seizure of the state.

Three years later, while on 'shooting leave' in the Pamirs, a British official, Ralph Cobbold, learned from a Russian frontier officer that the Russians intended to take immediate possession of Chitral, if the British government evacuated it. Cobbold reported that 'trusty men in disguise are constantly coming between the Russian frontier, Kabul and Chitral, and these are encouraged to gain all the information possible compatible with their own safety'. The Russian officers whom he met 'all look forward to war with Britain with the greatest eagerness'.[17]

The appointment of George Curzon as viceroy of India in late 1898 presaged a more robust policy towards Russia in Central Asia. Lord George Hamilton, secretary of state for India from 1895, admitted to Curzon in 1899:

> I have felt for a very long time past that we must, so far as Russia is concerned, acknowledge the changed conditions that the extension of railroads has made in the relative fighting power of Great Britain and Russia ... and thus any tug of war on land between Russia and Britain must result to our disadvantage.[18]

Curzon was not prepared to accept the contention that Russia was stronger than Britain:

> I should be prepared to meet & contest Russia on any field of conflict in the world: partly because I think her diplomacy blustering & bad, still more, though I admit that She has every card of vantage in her possession, I should not fear to meet her forces military or naval.[19]

In theory, the status of Afghanistan had been agreed by the two powers in the late 1880s, but it was too much for the British government to expect that Russia would not choose to create maximum unease in Calcutta and London. What better year than 1900, with Britain stymied in South Africa, to revive the Afghan question?

In a memorandum of 6 February 1900, the Russian government stated that it regarded 'as indispensable the re-establishment of the direct relations between Russia and Afghanistan concerning matters of the frontier', which had no political character.[20] This need, the Russians held, was because their Trans-Caspian Railway had reached the Afghan frontier.

The Indian government was outraged at this apparent flaunting of previous agreements, which placed Afghanistan entirely outside the sphere of Russian action. But, the Russians had been taking soundings. Abdur Rahman, the Afghan emir, passed on a copy of a letter from Mikhail

Ignatiev, the Russian political agent in Bukhara, to the British. Ignatiev expressed a desire that his letter might be the first step towards the establishment of direct friendly relations between Russia and Afghanistan. At the same time, reports were received in London of a considerable body of Russian troops being concentrated in the vicinity of the Afghan frontier. Muraviev insisted that the troop reports were a gross exaggeration, but Abdur Rahman believed that the Russians were 'only waiting for my death or some convenient time to use them'.[21]

The India Office took the straightforward view that no alteration of the status quo was possible. Britain was in exclusive control of Afghan foreign policy. Even so, Lansdowne was prepared in 1901 to admit the force of Russian arguments in favour of direct communication between frontier authorities on matters of purely local interest. The Russian government's reply was peremptory. The British *chargé d'affaires* in St Petersburg, Cecil Spring Rice, informed the foreign office in October 1903 that 'Russia has notified her intention of sending, when she pleases, her Agents in to Afghanistan.'[22] This, it appeared, she had already begun, with friction between the local people on both sides of the frontier occurring, and a revival of the old habit of boundary pillars near Herat being mysteriously moved.

Curzon characteristically maintained that 'Russia has no conceivable advantage in coming to an agreement with us.'[23] Edward VII, who did not share the viceroy's Russophobia, nevertheless agreed with Curzon: 'The sending of an agent at all is most dangerous and I cannot see how we can allow it. How can we be made to believe that the relations desired will be non-political and solely to deal with local and commercial matters of the Frontier?'[24]

It had become clear that Russia was resorting to her well-tried policy of making Britain nervous about her activities in Central Asia, without actually doing very much. The Russian expert and journalist, Donald Mackenzie Wallace, now in the king's confidence, prepared a paper for Edward in December 1903, in which he claimed that Russia had not seriously contemplated aggressive action against Afghanistan:

> The military authorities pointed out that a military demonstration might easily lead to real warfare, and the Afghans are much more warlike than the Boers, and almost as well supplied with arms of precision, Russia might find herself in a position similar to that of England in South Africa. In that case she would have to increase tenfold her Army in the field, as England had been forced to do, and with the existing means of communi-

> cation this would be a tedious process … It was thought necessary to remind England that in the event of her supporting Japan in the Far East, Russia could easily cause her considerable annoyance.[25]

The tensions were suddenly assuaged in November, when Benckendorff assured Lansdowne that the Russian government wished to come to an agreement on Afghanistan. The reason was clear. In the divided chaotic state of the Russian government during the build-up to the war with Japan, Afghanistan was an unnecessary issue. Nevertheless, the Afghan question was not lost sight of during the war. Following rumours that Britain was preparing to annex or occupy Afghanistan, the new emir, Habibullah, who had succeeded his father in 1901, had demonstrated a vexatious attitude of independence and stallings.

The Indian government felt that it received very little in return for the generous subsidies it provided to the emir. Curzon was furious with Habibullah, and recommended a declaration of war on Afghanistan. This was wisely overruled by London. Instead, an envoy was sent to Kabul in 1904 to renegotiate a treaty with the emir. Curzon, increasingly out of tune with the British government, advocated rejection of the new treaty proposed by Habibullah; the British government, on the other hand, welcomed this rapprochement in Anglo-Afghan relations. In Russia, it appeared with hindsight that it had been a mistake to try to take advantage of British involvement in the Boer War to stir up trouble in Afghanistan when British troops were unavailable. Benckendorff complained to his minister, Lamsdorff, that the 1900 memorandum, and Ignatiev's 'unfortunate' letter, had provoked a pointless renewal of Anglo-Russian tension over Afghanistan.[26]

A crisis over Afghanistan was defused in 1904. However, a new focus of Anglo-Russian rivalry in Central Asia had arisen in the early twentieth century: Tibet.

This inaccessible kingdom bordering north-eastern British India was separated from India by the Himalayas. Since the second half of the eighteenth century, it had been part of the Chinese Qing empire, but by the late nineteenth century, Qing influence was in decline. Here was a Buddhist state, a theocracy with its titular ruler, the Dalai Lama, which banned all foreign contact. Nevertheless, its strategic position made it impossible for Tibet to escape the attentions of Russia and Britain. The danger from the British point of view was not of a Russian invasion of India through Tibet—even the most nervous observers discounted that possibility. What was at stake was possible Russian political control over the centre of the Buddhist world.

The Russian explorer, Nicholas Przhevalsky, had led an expedition to Tibet in 1878, writing that 'Scientific research will camouflage the political goals of the expedition and ward off the interference of our adversaries.'[27] Przhevalsky was turned back by the Dalai Lama's officials. Two further attempts also failed to reach the capital Lhasa, but sufficient information had been gathered about the Qing decay. China's rapid defeat at the hands of Japan in 1895, followed by the seizure of Chinese ports by the European powers, made this abundantly clear to the world.

By the late 1890s the Russians were again active in Tibet. Two explorers, Agvan Dorzhiev and Peter Kozlov, were able to enter Tibet. Dorzhiev, a Buriat Mongol, who had trained as a Buddhist monk, claimed (writing three decades later) that he was establishing links between Russian Buddhist Buriats and Tibetans; he also insinuated to the Tibetans, ignorant of the realities of world politics, that with the decline of the Manchu dynasty, Tibet was to fall either to the Russians or the British: 'If Russia takes Tibet under her protection, the Tsarist government will be benevolent to the Buriats and their religion. And Tibet will avoid the maw of aliens.'[28] Dorzhiev arranged the first Tibetan unofficial mission to St Petersburg in 1898, ostensibly with the objective of raising money for a Buddhist temple in the Russian capital. More importantly, Nicholas II received him in a private audience with Prince Ukhtomsky.

The Russian emperor, intoxicated with ideas of the Russian mission in East Asia, promised to support the Tibetans in their struggle for autonomy, against either the Qing or the British empire. Military instructors plus war *matériel* were dispatched to Lhasa. Dorzhiev met Nicholas a second time in Yalta, where he plied the susceptible monarch with entreaties to become the earthly protector of the Tibetans. The audience was duly reported in the *Journal de St Petersbourg*. A third Tibetan official mission was welcomed by Nicholas at Peterhof in 1901. Negotiations began for a Russo-Tibetan treaty of alliance, but the majority of Russian ministers were sceptical, above all Witte and Lamsdorff, and nothing came of them. Nevertheless, Nicholas showered luxurious gifts on Dorzhiev for the Dalai Lama.

The well-grounded British ambassador in St Petersburg, Sir Nicholas O'Conor, had already, in 1895, felt it necessary to warn the viceroy, Lord Elgin, that 'some time ago some Russian officers had been in communication with the Tibetan authorities ... and impressed upon them [the

Tibetans] the importance of maintaining friendly relations with the Russians who were alone able to protect them against the ambitious designs of the English who evidently coveted Tibet'.[29] It was only to be expected that after several years of reports of increasing Russian contacts with Tibet, the viceroy in 1899, George Curzon—who was convinced Russia was expansionist everywhere—should wish to take action. He argued that now that China had fallen prey to Japan and the great powers had scrambled for possessions there, next in the spiral of Chinese collapse, Tibet, would fall under Russian influence. Here was another zone ripe for a new Anglo-Russian confrontation.

Thus, in 1903, Curzon wanted to send troops to Tibet. The cabinet in London rejected his proposal. Lansdowne held that the distances and terrain meant that there was no chance of an immediate threat to Tibet, and that there were 'many difficult questions pending between Russia and us in connection with Central Asia ambitions'. Britain sought a general agreement covering the region, 'but no such agreement is possible if we irritate her [Russia] unnecessarily about Tibet'.[30] However, the appointment of a Russian agent in Lhasa would be met by a similar British action; one likely to be accompanied by troops.

By mid-April 1903, there were indications that Russia was willing to cooperate. The foreign secretary had received quite straightforward and satisfactory assurances about Tibet (Manchuria was preoccupying the Russian government). Nevertheless, the Russians remained convinced that Britain had designs on Tibet. What was going on had 'the signs of the usual cover-up of the English when they want to mask an enterprise'.[31] Throughout the year, Lansdowne insisted to Benckendorff that it was necessary to deal with 'outrages' and to inspire 'respect in the Tibetans to bring them to an acceptable conduct'.[32] Quite what these isolated Buddhists were engaged in against British interests was not specified. An air of specious fabrication hangs over British Tibetan policy in 1903. Everything had to be done to placate Curzon.

In early 1904, Britain was in a stronger bargaining position as regards Russia. Talks for an agreement with France were proceeding and Russia was now at war with Japan. It was a propitious moment to take advantage of Russia's weakness and deal with Tibet. George Curzon was not a man to let pass such an opening.

The first reason he advanced for action in Tibet was that three letters he had written to the Dalai Lama were returned unopened. Secondly, the St Petersburg press claimed that the Tibetan god-king was on excellent terms with Russia. The viceroy was genuinely alarmed that a secret treaty was being forged, and, characteristically, was personally affronted by the Dalai Lama's lack of diplomatic civility. Even so, he did not look too closely into his sources, which were flimsy—often based on anecdotal evidence, fanciful reports in the Chinese press and Russian wishful thinking.

Curzon was convinced that the Indian government had to dispatch a mission to Lhasa—using force if necessary—to discover the truth about Russian activity, and to place Britain's relations with Tibet on a firm and proper basis—in his opinion to establish permanent control over Tibet. Despite the home government's misgivings about embarking on any further adventures in Central Asia, the cabinet sanctioned the sending of a small escorted mission to Khamba Jong, just inside Tibet on the Sikkim border, where it would endeavour to hold talks with the Tibetans. The viceroy was also successful in having his choice for leader of the mission accepted: Francis Younghusband, now promoted to colonel for the occasion.

The Tibetans refused to negotiate at Khamba Jong; the mission was a failure. A second expedition, strengthened with an escort of 1,200 Gurkhas and Sikhs, marched north. At Guru, warrior monks came out to block the invaders. A sepoy was killed. The British force retaliated, killing nearly 700 ill-armed Tibetans, before continuing on to Gyantse, the designated end of the march. Here a further 400 Tibetans and 5 British soldiers died. The planned negotiations were clearly not possible at Gyantse. Younghusband, backed by Curzon, asked for permission to advance on Lhasa, unless the Tibetans were prepared to parley. The fortress of Gyantse was taken and the expedition continued to the sacred capital.

The Dalai Lama had fled; evidence of Russian presence was scant. The 'rifle factory' turned out to be no more than a small workshop and the feared treaty between St Petersburg and Peking over Tibet had never been signed by the Russian government. (If nothing else, the march on Lhasa provided excellent material for the personal accounts of the participants, including journalists from *The Times* and *Daily Mail*, which poured off the presses in this last flourish of the Great Game.)

William St John Brodrick, the secretary of state for India, argued that British claims to Tibet could be established by 'the mere fact of a British force marching on Lhasa and slaughtering a great number of Tibetans on the way ... It should destroy the city's arsenal ... and withdraw with as large an indemnity as it could obtain.'[33] Such an undignified end to the expedition was dismissed. Younghusband was instructed to negotiate with the Chinese government's representative, the amban. It was agreed that all fortifications between Lhasa and the Indian frontier were to be razed; Lhasa was not to have any dealings with any foreign power without British consent; trade was to be opened up and Tibet was to pay an indemnity.

Within hours of the news of the Lhasa Convention reaching London, the British government had changed its mind. Younghusband was accused of insubordination and repudiated. On his return to Britain he was seen as a popular hero, but was snubbed in official circles and awarded the lowest possible knighthood, and even this, only at the king's personal insistence. Balfour, the prime minister, unbelievably insisted that Britain had to clear her name from any unjust imputation of using the discreditable methods of Russian diplomacy. Younghusband was the scapegoat, while the viceroy was in the clear.

The whole Tibetan crisis was an unnecessary sideshow cooked up by Curzon. For good reason, Russia in 1904 was uninterested in the Land of the Snows.[34] But Tibet remained another unresolved issue of disagreement between Britain and Russia.

The much more serious and long-standing, seemingly intractable, rivalry between Britain and Russia over Persia of the 1880s in no way diminished during the following decade. As the shah Naser al-Din Shah's authority declined in the early 1890s, the prospect that Persia would cease to exist as an independent state increased, while the spectre of the country becoming a Russian protectorate loomed even larger in British eyes. The military attaché, Henry Picot, wrote in August 1895, that efforts towards reform in Persia had taken the form of encouraging commerce and internal development, 'in the vain hope of thereby materially improving the finances, or adding to the stability of the country'. According to Picot, this policy had failed: 'We should have directed our effort at the administration itself: for mal-administration is at the root of all evil from which Persia now suffers.'[35]

A month later, Sir Mortimer Durand, newly appointed British minister in Tehran, was clear in his opinion. Russia had no interest in strengthening Persia. Her policy was to keep a close watch on the 'continuous disintegration, hasten it when possible by peaceful means and by displays of strength, with the aim eventually to obtain political control over the whole domain of the Shah'.[36] The return of the Conservatives to government in 1895 promised a stronger line being taken over Persia. However, the assassination of Naser al-Din Shah in 1896 provided Russia with an opportunity to increase her hold over Persia. The new shah, Muzaffar al-Din Shah, was weak and even more profligate than his father, and this swung the balance even more towards Russian ascendency than before.

It boiled down to a question of lending money to Persia. In 1897, Durand was wary of Persia's contracting foreign loans in return for handing over the customs revenues of the south of the country, where British influence was strong. The Imperial Bank lacked the funds to make a large loan: the British government would not countenance lending money with such poor security, and the Stock Exchange refused to raise funds. Durand bewailed his impotence, declaring that the Russians were 'I fear lending money and will take a heavy price for it'.[37] George Curzon wrote to his school friend, Cecil Spring Rice, *chargé d'affaires* in Tehran:

> I can never get Lord S or anyone in the F.O. to take the least interest in Persia ... Mark my words, in a few years we shall have just the same trouble with Russia over Persia as we have recently had over China. But it will be more acute.[38]

For once though, Curzon was not exaggerating. The Russians, already paramount in the north, were now infiltrating southern Persia. They were engaged in road building; engineers surveyed the region for railways; and, for the first time, detachments of Cossacks appeared in Shiraz. Russian doctors were studying the plague in the Gulf. A detachment of Russians was 'sketching' in terrible heat near Jask.

In addition, with the return to power in 1899 of the grand vizier, Amin al-Sultan, now the Sadrazam, the country's highest office, the Russian hold tightened. 'They have the Sadrazam in their pay', Spring Rice believed.[39] This was confirmed later that year, when Amin secretly negotiated a massive loan with Muraviev and Witte. It was the sum the Persians sought, 22.5 million roubles, or £2,380,952. Repayment was to be guaranteed by the customs revenues of all Persia, except the Fars province and the Gulf coast. If Persia's repayments fell below a specified limit, Russia's agent, the Discount and Loan Bank of Tehran, would have the right to exercise effective control of customs receipts. Meanwhile, Persia could not borrow abroad without Russian consent until the loan was paid off.[40]

In 1900, Russian power in Persia reached its zenith, while Britain was embroiled in the Boer War. Salisbury rightly attributed his country's failure to its inability to lend money: 'I think our trouble with Persia ... arises from a fundamental and immovable cause ... Other nations can lend money: and we cannot. The House of Commons, which never would guarantee the debt of India, would positively refuse any advance to an impecunious Oriental Ally.'[41] The weary prime minister never ceased to complain of the niggardly outlook of the British treasury and the City's lack of interest. Charles Hardinge in St Petersburg saw the Russian loan as a 'disastrous blow to Great Britain'.[42]

The retirement of the aged and exhausted Salisbury in 1902, and the arrival of Lord Lansdowne at the foreign office, signalled a policy more in tune with that of Curzon and Arthur Hardinge, now British minister in Tehran. Hardinge had not been long in his post before negotiations for an oil concession began.

The existence of petroleum in Persia had been commented on by travellers through the centuries, and a substantial body of literature on Persian oil resources was published in the nineteenth century, most importantly by the French archaeologist Jacques de Morgan, who published a paper in 1892 claiming that considerable oil deposits existed in south-western Persia. A former agent of the Reuters news agency, and Persia's commissioner at the Paris Exhibition in 1900, approached Sir Henry Drummond Wolff—old, but as dynamic as in earlier years—with a highly speculative oil concession. Capital was needed to finance prospecting, and Drummond Wolff introduced the Persians to the rich businessman William Knox D'Arcy, who 'had money to burn' and was prepared to finance the project.[43] D'Arcy sent representatives to Tehran in 1901 to negotiate on his behalf, and through bribery and political pressure acquired a sixty-year concession, covering all but the five northern provinces of Persia, to search for, develop and sell all natural gas, petroleum, asphalt and ozokerite. It included the right to construct pipelines from anywhere in Persia to the south coast. The businessman paid £20,000 in cash for his exclusive rights and, in addition, the Persian government was promised 20,000 £1 shares in the company D'Arcy was to form to exploit the concession, and 16 per cent of the net profits.

Arthur Hardinge strongly supported D'Arcy's venture but was sceptical as to its chances of success: 'The soil of Persia, whether it contains oil, or not, has been strewn of late years with the wrecks of so many hopeful schemes of commercial and political regeneration that it would be rash to attempt to predict the future of this latest venture.'[44] Curzon, who considered himself Britain's undisputed Persian expert, poured magisterial cold water on the concession:

> I am not myself a believer in any of these commercial concessions in Persia—Lynch's, D'Arcy's or any others. It may be worthwhile to get hold of them for political reasons. But as long as the Persian government

> and people are what they are, there is no chance of fair play, of progress, or of profit.[45]

It looked, for a time, as if Curzon's prediction would prove correct. Drilling, which had begun in western Persia in 1902, proved unsuccessful.

After five years D'Arcy had nothing to show for the quarter of a million pounds spent in his search for oil.

(In 1908, in one final attempt at Maidan-e-Naftun near Masjid-e-Suleiman, 100 kilometres north-east of Ahwaz, a gusher was struck. In London the Anglo-Persian Oil Company, APOC, was formed to take over the concessions. By 1911, a 200-kilometre-long pipeline was completed to the Gulf coast, and two years later the refinery at Abadan was in operation, BP today.)

Nevertheless, the significance that the Russians attached to the D'Arcy concession was reflected in articles in *Novoe Vremya* in 1902. These recalled that the prohibition on railway construction had been designed to prevent an influx of foreigners and hostile influences.

However, the real diplomatic contest in Tehran between Britain and Russia in 1901 was not over oil; it was once again over a loan to Persia (Russia had a flourishing petroleum industry based in Baku). In February, the Sadrazam asked for an immediate small loan of £200,000, which the Imperial Bank met. As ever, it was not enough. By the autumn, the budget deficit had reached £500,000. Muzaffar al-Din Shah planned a trip to Europe (for genuine health reasons) and his government attempted to borrow £1 million. Arthur Hardinge was obliged to pass on the request to London. An outright refusal would be regarded 'as abdication of our interests in Persia as leaving her no option but to accept without reference to them the Russian Commercial Treaty including possibly secret political terms which Shah refused in July last and harm caused by which may prove irreparable'.[46] The minister urged his government to find at least part of the sum as the loan question 'dominates entire Persian situation'.[47]

As in the past, the treasury opposed the loan. Curzon, on the other hand, wanted the money to be found to avoid Persia's sinking more deeply into Russian debt, but only if guaranteed by the customs revenues of the Gulf ports and Sistan in the south-east, and that no concessions should be granted without the consent of the British government. Despite these safeguards, the viceroy was overruled.

Clearly, the danger was that the shah would, yet again, turn to Russia. To avoid this, Charles Hardinge in St Petersburg was instructed to propose that Britain and Russia might jointly advance money to Persia, secured on the revenues of those parts of the country where each predominated. The Russian government was not interested. Half the sum was then offered by Britain. Russia put pressure on Persia, and this loan was rejected. Meanwhile, fresh negotiations were taking place in St Petersburg between Russia and Persia, and the shah finally received the £1 million he had sought, although the conditions were more onerous than previous ones.

In this highly unfavourable climate of Anglo-Persian relations, Britain turned the other cheek, and prepared to welcome the shah to London. The British government hoped that suitable hospitality would impress Muzaffar al-Din Shah and that City financiers would show interest in raising money for Persia. (The shah was uninterested in discussing politics, visiting factories or the like; all of which he rightly feared would be laid on.) What happened was that the visit degenerated into a diplomatic row involving Edward VII. It was known that Muzaffar al-Din Shah coveted the Order of the Garter, which his father had received from Queen Victoria in 1873. This, even more than his health problems, was the reason for his visit. Arthur Hardinge made clear to the foreign office how much importance the shah attached to receiving this decoration. Lansdowne had the insignia redesigned, omitting the Christian cross. On learning of this, the king was furious and flung the new design to the other side of his cabin on the royal yacht. (In later tellings the document was hurled out of the cabin porthole onto a passing steam pinnacle.[48]) Francis Knollys, the king's secretary, agreed with his master: 'A. Hardinge's reasons for decorations for the Persians are unsound. Persia seems to be falling to pieces. What object can be gained by distributing orders to members of the government.'[49]

Edward VII's passion for correctness as regards decorations was notorious, and he refused to be bullied by the foreign office. For Lansdowne, though, it was a resigning matter. But, if he went, the government would fall. In the end the Garter was awarded to Muzaffar al-Din Shah on his return to Tehran. The result of this indecorous squabble in Britain was that relations between the king and his foreign secretary, who already disliked Edward, were yet more strained. The shah, to whom being automatically given all the honours he felt due to the incumbent of the Peacock Throne was primordial, was even more alienated by his treatment in London.

For no member of the cabinet wished to meet him—one reason being that the visit took place inconveniently during the shooting season. Arthur Hardinge despaired of the British government's inaction. It appeared to regard Persia as an unmitigated bore: 'No wonder the Russians always beat us. They are in earnest and we are not.'[50] The minister's dispatches calling for more financial aid for Persia were considered tiresome.

Despite all, in 1903 Hardinge succeeded in persuading the British government to lend £200,000 through the Imperial Bank. A further £100,000 was advanced in 1904. The sums were not large, and half was contributed by the government of India, but the change in principle was an important one. The minister optimistically maintained that it established a vital precedent by enabling the Persians to negotiate for better terms with Russia.[51]

The duel between Britain and Russia in Persia was not only about loans, but the territorial integrity of the country, which British diplomats in Tehran believed also received too little consideration in London. The blame was placed squarely on Salisbury, who had allowed Russia to establish herself yet more firmly during the 1890s. But in the foreign office in general—as opposed to the view from Calcutta—the belief was that it was impossible to avoid Russian encroachments; the 'buffer state' concept would have to be abandoned in favour of a more tangible hold on south-east Persia and the southern end of the Persian Gulf.

The advocates of this limited policy believed that Russia's advance to the Persian Gulf was irresistible, and hence Britain could not prevent Russia acquiring a warm water port on the Gulf. Not only was there Russia's superior geographical position, but her diplomacy operated outside what were, for Britain, acceptable standards—bribery at the Persian court, state capital was available for infrastructure projects, and Russia had French backing. This minimalist position was essentially that so long as Britain controlled the coastline east of Bandar Abbas, such that Russian warships could always be bottled up and her position attacked by superior British naval forces, it did not matter if Russia reached the northern end of the Gulf.

But in another argument, the emphasis was placed on the importance of the Sistan eastern frontier with British India. Unsurprisingly Curzon insisted that a rail link between Quetta and Sistan was needed: 'The real object of a Seistan railway would not be to attack Russia in Northern Persia, but to save Southern Persia from falling into her grasp.'[52]

Balfour drew up a paper for the Committee of Imperial Defence in 1903, in which he discussed the strategic value of Sistan. He opposed the building of a rail link with India, believing that it would be 'dearly bought if it occasioned the construction of a Russian line from the north'.[53] The Russian government was naturally aware of increased British concern for Sistan. *Novoe Vremya* launched an attack:

> We have already called attention to the endeavours of England to lay hands on Persian Baluchistan, and, if possible, Sistan also, in view of the considerable political and strategic importance of these provinces. With this object we find them constantly full of British Agents, sowing discontent among the tribes, and suborning them ... It is therefore necessary ... we should send Russian Plenipotentiaries... We cannot continue to leave South-Eastern Persia to the mercy of England.[54]

Russia appointed a consul to Sistan. Since there were no Russian subjects anywhere near, and no Russian trade, the step was calculated to demonstrate to the British that they had no monopoly on south-eastern Persia. The Russian consul, Alexander Miller, accompanied by a sizeable and well-armed escort, travelled along the Perso-Baluch frontier in open defiance of British pretensions.

The Persian Gulf, yet more than Sistan, was an area where the British were eager to maintain a monopoly of influence and power. Russia, in 1897, appointed a consul in Isfahan, who regularly visited the Gulf coast and Basra. The Russian government subsidized regular voyages by steamers of the Russian Steam Navigation and Trading Company into the Persian Gulf from 1901, and surveys for railways, which were intended to connect Russian systems in the north with the Gulf, were undertaken. It was obvious that Russia sought a port on the Gulf.

In 1900, Russia made preparations to occupy the port of Bandar Abbas, claiming that it sought only a coaling station for its ships at Basra and Bushire. The British government answered the Russian threat by giving discretionary authority to the naval commander to hoist the British flag at any port. Nevertheless, it was obvious that more than a gesture was needed to prevent foreign occupation. Britain did not wish to obstruct Russia from finding a commercial entrance to her trade in the Persian Gulf, but could not allow the Russians to establish an ascendency in the south comparable with that enjoyed in the north. Lansdowne told the House of Lords in May 1903 that the British government would 'regard the establishment of a naval base or of a fortified port in the Persian Gulf by any other power as a very grave menace to British interests, and that we should certainly resist it with all the means at our disposal'.[55]

Benckendorff in London immediately denied any desire of Russia to obtain a naval base in the Gulf. Curzon felt vindicated in his warnings about Russian ambitions, and declared that Lansdowne's statement was 'our Monroe Doctrine in the Middle East'.[56]

The British were overly optimistic: Russia was not intimidated. Lamsdorff told the Russian ambassador in Paris, Prince Lev Urussov, that despite a disastrous harvest and revolutionary activity in the universities, a 'calm and pacific attitude must be maintained ... That does not prevent us from advancing, without noise, in Persia ... without all the fracas that they adore in parliamentary countries.'[57]

It seemed an opportune moment to show the British flag in the Gulf. The cabinet, although apprehensive, could find no valid reason to oppose Curzon. In mid-November 1903, he set off from India to Muscat with an impressive naval escort. A first durbar was held at Oman, and then on a ship furnished with Indian trappings. With typical hyperbole Curzon declared: 'We were here before any other Power in modern times had shown its face in these waters. We found strife and we have created order. It was our commerce as well as your security that was threatened and called for our protection.'[58] But no amount of gesture imperialism altered the fact that Russian supremacy covered most of Persia. Nevertheless, there were no further encroachments in 1904, as the view in Persia of Russia as a power impossible to defeat faded. After the annihilation of the Russian fleets in 1905, Arthur Hardinge expressed British relief: 'Indeed from one end of Persia to the other, a huge weight has been lifted from men's hearts, and the whole native population breathed again.'[59]

Even so, there was no sign that Russia would give up her supremacy in northern Persia, and her longer-term goal for ascendency throughout the country.

31

TOWARDS THE ANGLO-RUSSIAN CONVENTION

Despite the failure of so many attempts for a rapprochement with Russia, in 1903, with Lord Lansdowne at the foreign office and the strongly Anglophile Count Alexander Benckendorff Russian ambassador in London, there had been talk of resolving long-standing disputes between the two countries, although the Russian emperor and his foreign minister were both reluctant to pursue the subject. Benckendorff wrote in May 1903 of 'English openings'.[1] In August, the ambassador believed in the 'eventuality of more cordial relations with this Power'.[2] Three months later he reported that Lansdowne had spoken of his desire 'to establish normal relations'. The foreign secretary had insisted that, 'distrustful relations had become almost a tradition'.[3] Two years later, the ambassador rightly blamed the outbreak of war with Japan in early 1904 for the breakdown in talks. Russia had failed to seize the opportunity: 'There was a moment but, I believe, it was misunderstood by us.'[4]

The expulsion from Russia of *The Times* correspondent in St Petersburg, Dudley Disraeli Braham, in May 1903, was an irritant to the efforts in London to improve relations. The newspaper was well known for its hostility to Russia, but Braham's reports of the pogrom in Kishinev (today Chisinau, capital of Moldova)—Braham was, as his name implies, Jewish—and revolutionary activity in the country were considered by the hard-line minister of the interior, Vyacheslav Plehve, as unacceptable attacks on Russia. (Leo Tolstoy and Maxim Gorky wrote letters to the press protesting about the Kishinev pogrom.) Braham was roughly treated; conveyed 'from station to station with batches of common criminals'.[5] In a leading article, the newspaper insisted that its correspondent had not given the slightest justification for the expulsion, and 'if there were features in Russian domestic policy which he could not overlook or minimize, his view has been shared by not a few thoughtful and patriotic Russians themselves'.[6] There was no *Times* correspondent present in St Petersburg in 1905.

Edward VII did not play in Anglo-Russian relations as important a role as in relations with France. Even so, the king actively sought an understanding with Russia. Given Nicholas II's contempt for Britain's parliamentary democracy, messages telling him that his uncle personally advocated resolving outstanding problems between the two countries carried a weight far greater than Edward's constitutional limitations warranted. Access to the Russian emperor was difficult for British diplomats in St Petersburg (the imperial family having retreated to semi-isolation at Tsarskoe Selo); the British king had a direct conduit to his nephew. This was particularly important in view of combatting the influence of cousin Willy in Berlin.

Edward asked to see Sergei Tatishchev, financial secretary at the Russian embassy, on the latter's departure in March 1903: 'The King wished to make clear the community of interests. He sought an *entente politique* of the two countries. He knew Russia well, having visited on more than one occasion and he had always come away with a pleasant impression.'[7] Edward concluded, 'If you see the Emperor, "tell His Majesty that you have found me in good health, more alert and vigorous than ever".'

Benckendorff was furious that the king had spoken to a much-distrusted member of his staff—rightly suspected of being the author of articles in the Russian press hostile to the London embassy—but he was later assuaged by an invitation to spend two days at Windsor Castle. Alone with Edward, 'the King began by telling me how much he regretted, that we have still not ended the state of disturbance, if not tension, in the political relations between the two countries'. He was pleased that his efforts to establish better relations with France and Italy seemed to be bearing fruit, 'But the relations to which he attached most importance to improving and making cordial were those with Russia.'[8]

The outbreak of the Russo-Japanese war in February 1904 had, inevitably, put an end to the possibility of further talks on the subject. There had been an upsurge of anti-British hostility in Russia. Nevertheless, soon afterwards Lansdowne asked the king to speak to Benckendorff before the ambassador's departure to St Petersburg to assure Nicholas II that Britain would not intervene. Edward also undertook other measures to ensure that the diplomatic lines of communication would not be broken as a consequence of the war. He maintained considerable influence over senior diplomatic appointments and ensured that Charles Hardinge, whom he knew to favour an agreement with Russia, was appointed ambassador to St Petersburg.

A few days after the signing of the Entente Cordiale in April 1904, the king was in Copenhagen visiting his wife's relatives, and asked to see Alexander Isvolsky, the Russian minister to Denmark and *protégé* of the Danish-born dowager empress. In a friendly conversation, Edward told Isvolsky that the Entente 'gives me hope of attaining by the same methods more important results, that is to say a similar entente with Russia,—an entente which has always been and continues to be the object of my most sincere desires'.[9] Talk naturally turned to the regrettable Russo-Japanese War, with the king lamenting the increasing anti-British feeling it had provoked in Russia, and the serious obstacle this ill-feeling placed in the way of an entente between the two countries. With astonishing exaggeration, Edward declared that 'his government had done all in its power to moderate Japan, which did not want to hear and had asked to be left alone to settle the dispute in its own way'.[10] Lamsdorff did not think any follow-up was possible at that time: 'A time of war is not the right one to enter into negotiations with England, but we have never shown ourselves opposed to a sincere entente, on condition that the cabinet of London puts forward clear and equitable conditions.'[11] Isvolsky, for his part, later grandly claimed that at Copenhagen he had been able 'to establish the bases of the agreement between Russia and England, which exerted so great an influence on the sequence of events in Europe'.[12]

In addition, the king's decision to send Prince Louis of Battenberg to Russia in August 1904 as his representative at the christening of the newly born tsarevich, Alexsei, was a further move designed to improve Anglo-Russian relations. Battenberg, a member of the family once despised by the Russian royal family, was director of British naval intelligence and married to Victoria of Hesse, sister of the Russian empress and therefore also a niece of Edward VII. The king agreed to be one of Alexsei's godfathers and the visit, although private, had political resonance. Edward regarded it as a resounding success and Battenberg reported that Lamsdorff was 'very optimistic as to the ultimate establishment on a lasting basis of a good understanding between the two countries'.[13] It was learned that 'the Emperor has spoken enthusiastically of the King and in a generally friendly way of England'.[14]

The goodwill was short-lived. By the end of 1904, Anglo-Russian relations became even more strained because of the possible passage of the

Russian fleet through the Straits (forbidden by the treaty of 1856) and Russian suspicions that British shipping was being used to transport arms to Japan. However, what nullified the work of Lansdowne, Hardinge and Edward VII to improve relations with Russia was the Dogger Bank incident. After strenuous efforts in both St Petersburg and London, the issue was resolved early in 1905. But by then, the successive defeats in the war with Japan, and Bloody Sunday in January 1905, had dramatically changed Russia's position.

The revolution of 1905 was the result of the social transformation that had been taking place in Russia since the great reforms of the 1860s, and the concomitant opposition to the regime that had developed. The rapid industrialization of the 1880s and 1890s resulted in social changes and tensions. With the rise of a bourgeoisie and proletariat came liberalism among the professionals, and from the proletariat emerged a labour movement with a more radical programme of opposition to the state.

The oppositions began to organize. After the lull caused by the terrible famine of 1891–2, social and political activity critical of the regime was resumed. Liberals formed the Union of Liberation in January 1904, and the following year this became the Constitutional Democratic Party, the Kadets (the initials in Russian). The radicals formed three important parties, beginning as the Social Democratic Party (SD), a Marxist party which later split into the Bolsheviks led by Vladimir Ulyanov, Lenin, who wanted a tightly knit organization of professional revolutionaries, and the Mensheviks who preferred a somewhat broader and looser association. The third major party, the Socialist Revolutionary Party, engaged in a running debate with the Marxists as regards the nature of Russian society and its future. They represented the older populist tradition of Russian radicalism. From the beginning of 1905, strikes with avowedly political aims had broken out throughout Russia. Then on 22 January, the Orthodox priest Father Gapon was at the head of a large, but unarmed, body of strikers in St Petersburg, which, having given full notice of their aims, marched to the Winter Palace to demand implementation of constitutional reforms that had been promised a month before. Confusion set in and the result was a massacre by armed troops. Charles Hardinge reported the events to the king's secretary:

> During the days preceding the catastrophe, and on the day itself there was no direction of any kind, in fact one might say there was no Govt., the only idea that seems to occur to anybody being repression by force, and that only at a moment when all preventive measures would have been too

> late … I am quite convinced that a few London policemen could have managed that crowd.[15]

Nicholas, as ever, remained away from the capital at Tsarskoe Selo. 'I cannot help thinking that the Emperor missed the chance of his lifetime', Mackenzie Wallace wrote:

> His Majesty knew that these thousands of workmen were coming to present him with a petition setting forth their grievances & if he had received at the Winter Palace a small deputation and promised to give them then what has since been promised to them in his name, he would have obtained the undying loyalty and admiration of the lower classes of his subjects … I told Lamsdorff that … events in St Petersburg had made a very deep impression in England and in this case the Emperor had had to pay the price of an autocracy.[16]

Edward VII also asked Hardinge to keep him closely informed of events, and in his frank letters addressed to the king's secretary intended for the king's perusal, the ambassador recounted the mounting violence, painting a depressing picture of Nicholas II:

> I often wonder whether the Emperor realises upon what a volcano he is living. I am told that he never speaks either of the war or the internal state of the country if he can help doing so, but that he seems perfectly happy, interesting himself in all sorts of trivial affairs.[17]

The party of reaction assumed control. The liberal Prince Peter Svyatopolk-Mirsky was replaced as minister of the interior by a reactionary (Plehve had been assassinated the previous year), and the hard-liner Dmitri Trepov, formerly minister of police in Moscow, was appointed governor general of St Petersburg. Then the following month, the procurator of the Finnish Senate was assassinated and the detested Grand Duke Sergei was killed by a bomb in Moscow. The murder of officials became frequent. Anti-British notices were posted across the old capital, and the consul general reported that the British colony there felt under threat and asked for help to leave the city if the situation worsened.

By April, it was clear that the disorders were not going to come to a rapid end. Strikes and demonstrations spread throughout the country. The crew of the battleship *Potemkim* in Odesa mutinied in June 1905 (since mythologized in Eisenstein's 1925 film). 'It fizzled out ingloriously, and only served to show the rotten state of the Black Sea fleet and the complete absence of discipline on board', reported Hardinge.[18] The signature of the Treaty of Portsmouth in August brought home the extent of Russia's humiliation by Japan, and the resentment of the people increased. Nicholas reluctantly announced constitutional reform in the October Manifesto, which promised the establishment of a Duma, or parliament, equipped with real powers: freedom of conscience, speech and association to all subjects. He was also persuaded to appoint Sergei Witte as prime minister, who was obviously the only man with the stature and ability to cope with the crisis facing the government, however much Nicholas disliked him. Edward sent an optimistic telegram for Hardinge to communicate to Nicholas:

> Pray express to him my earnest desire that the best & most durable relations should be established between the 2 countries, & that all important points should be discussed in the most amicable spirit & arranged as soon as possible. I need not assure the Emperor what my personal feelings are towards him.

Nevertheless, the last sentence carried a sting with it: 'You can at the same time convey to him my hope that he may find himself able to grant a more liberal form of government to his country.'[19]

Despite the concessions made in the Manifesto, it was far from clear that this would be sufficient to restore order. The wealthier urban classes were anxious to see an end to the anarchy into which the country had fallen, but the workers and peasants were unconvinced, and the strikes continued. Cecil Spring Rice, in charge of the British embassy in Hardinge's absence, held out little hope that the Manifesto would help to restore order or that the necessary reforms would be instituted. The emperor and Witte were at loggerheads, with Nicholas 'more and more convinced that the party of reaction is growing in strength', while the prime minister was hoping, 'poor man to find that the country will get tired of sedition'.[20] At the same time, the dowager empress was begging her son to refuse to be guided by reactionary counsellors, while the Empress Alexandra vigorously supported repression. The grand dukes, for their part, were said to be discussing the course to be taken, should Nicholas abdicate. The reactionaries among them 'were quite as full of abuse of the Emperor as the extreme liberals'.[21]

'The Government had declared', Spring Rice reported in late December, in his usual bleak way,

> that it will not yield any further and will enforce the law. The opposition says that it will not have the law enforced. The Government then puts as

> many of the opposition in prison as it can get hold of. They might as well intimidate an ant heap by imprisoning the four biggest ants.[22]

In London there was great anxiety about the safety of the British colony in Russia. Most were in St Petersburg, and the British government offered to send a cruiser to evacuate its citizens. Some in the business community were leaving by private steamers, but Spring Rice did not feel that foreign lives were at risk in the capital, or that there was any reason to panic. On the contrary, he pointed out that Irish governesses were out and about to experience the excitement taking place in town. They liked to sit on the upper deck of trams to get a good view of activity in the street: 'I am glad Lady Hardinge wasn't here as I am sure she would have been out on the Nevski.'[23]

In March 1905, reports had reached London of attacks directed specifically against Jews in Russia. The *Jewish Chronicle* published accounts of this violent agitation, and anti-Russian articles in *The Times*, critical of Russia's creditworthiness, were viewed by Benckendorff as having 'Jewish undertones'.[24] Lord Rothschild, unofficial head of the Anglo-Jewish community, and Sir Marcus Samuel, a prominent financier, brought the subject to Lansdowne's attention and suggested that the Russian government should be warned of the disastrous effect which would be produced, were they to tolerate such occurrences. The foreign secretary's response was so reserved that it was tantamount to a refusal to do anything.

The situation turned dramatically for the worse after the issuing of the October Manifesto, which had improved the rights of Jews as citizens. Jewish parades were held celebrating emancipation. Then, the British foreign office was informed at the end of the month by its consuls in Rostov-on-Don and Odesa in Ukraine of serious riots in which Jews were massacred, their property pillaged and burned.[25] Further reports describing the new wave of pogroms arrived from Kyiv, Mykolaiv, Sevastopol and Riga. All pointed out that troops and police, far from stopping the attacks, in many instances actually took part in acts of robbery and murder. The consuls protested to the local authorities and stressed that British subjects were also in danger. They called for the proper guarding of Jewish hospitals which were crowded with the injured, and offered Jews refuge in the consulates. The first telegrams were seen by Lansdowne, who made no comment on them. Only the king, to whom they were forwarded for perusal, noted: 'A very serious situation.'[26] Later, after Rothschild had again protested, the foreign secretary finally agreed to inform the Russian government of the 'most painful impression which the accounts of massacres and plundering of the Jewish communities in various parts of Russia apparently unopposed by the police are creating … on the public mind in England', adding that 'unless effective steps are taken to check and punish such outrages, the sympathy that Count Witte hopes that the English press and public will manifest towards his administration may be seriously affected'.[27]

Spring Rice lodged a protest with the assistant minister of the interior, although he doubted that ministers were in a position to end the violence. He was aware that Witte opposed the pogroms, but was in a weak position. The prime minister was constantly identified with the Jews because of his Jewish-born second wife, and also because of his 'personal relations with Jews in the outside world'.[28] The reason for the outrages lay in the deep-seated anti-Semitism of the people now inflamed by the revolution and the belief that the Jews had helped to provoke the war with Japan. The police and local governors were seeking to divert the frustration and anger of the revolutionary working class against the liberal middle class and the Jews in particular.[29] Intentionally or not, the Russian government encouraged the pogroms. It certainly did have the effect of channelling discontent away from autocracy and towards the Jews.

The official position was that Jews were playing a major role in the revolutionary movement, and it was a spontaneous reaction of loyal workers and peasants that caused the pogroms of late 1905 and 1906. In fact, revolutionaries formed only a small minority of the Jewish population, although their share in the revolutionary movement did exceed their share in the population. As some individual Jews played an important part in the revolution, their role was emphasized. Leon Trotsky and Rosa Luxemburg came to the fore among the Jewish leaders.

Conservative estimates show that at least 650 pogroms occurred between October 1905 and September 1906, and most took place in Ukraine during the two months following the Manifesto. Between the 1903 pogrom in Kishinev and 1906, over 3,100 Jews lost their lives, of whom 800 were in Odesa; 15,000 serious injuries were recorded, to say nothing of the destruction of Jewish business and homes. The pogroms of the early twentieth century were more deadly than those of the early 1880s. In the latter, it was mainly property that was destroyed. The twentieth-century pogroms saw many more Jews killed and less material destruction.

The British government chose to accept the reasons put forward by the Russian government for the pogroms, whatever reservations were held privately. It would be contrary to international usage for a foreign government to interfere in what was an internal Russian question—as in 1882. Despite the refusal of the government to support Russian Jews, the enormous sum of £600,000 was collected by British Jewry to help their co-religionists in Russia, but the Russian government refused to allow British consulates to distribute the money on the grounds that it would fall into the hands of revolutionaries. Charles Hardinge, in 1906, strongly opposed several attempts to intervene on behalf of Russian Jews, and on certain occasions used language that smacked of anti-Semitism. The foreign office refused to pass on protest resolutions adopted at public and religious meetings in Britain condemning attacks on Russian Jews, advancing the usual reason.[30] There was a clear view among British Jews that the foreign office was turning a blind eye to the fate of Russian Jews because of its aim of reaching an understanding with Russia. In fact, Grey sent two telegrams to Sir Arthur Nicolson, the British ambassador, in September 1906 about the death sentences passed on 200 Jews in Poland. 'It would have a deplorable effect if anything of the kind should happen', he wrote in one, and in the other referred to the 'persecution of Jews'.[31] In the same month he wrote to the ambassador: 'I also realize that you can do nothing by representation about pogroms, and I shall not ask you to make any, though we may send you from time to time the apprehensions that are expressed here.'[32]

That Russian Jewry was fragmented only further weakened its position. The bourgeois forces among it united in the Union for Equal Rights, which became a platform for the most prominent figures in Jewish public life and identified with the Kadets. This call for unity was rejected by the 'proletarian' left with the Bund at its head and which advocated class war—nothing should be allowed to divert attention from the overriding issue of the victory of the revolution.[33] Emigration soared, above all to the United States, and a new wave of Jews settled in Palestine, including the family of David Ben-Gurion.

(It is interesting that Arthur Balfour, prime minister until December 1905, had a long conversation in Manchester the following month with a young Russian Jewish lecturer in chemistry at Manchester University. The British politician was greatly impressed by Dr Chaim Weizmann, who convinced him that a permanent Jewish home had to be created in Palestine.)

Throughout the dramatic events of 1905, when the attention of most statesmen and diplomats was focused on the Russo-Japanese War and turmoil in Russia, the indefatigable Benckendorff never let up in his quest for an Anglo-Russian rapprochement.

Indeed, by March 1905, though the Russian position had already shifted, Lamsdorff reluctantly decided that his ambassador should be allowed to open talks in London:

> The ideas set out by Count Benckendorff … concerning a serious rapprochement, so desirable between England and Russia, can only be approved. The Imperial Government is showing clear proof of its spirit of conciliation [but] England and its press concerning the war are making things difficult. The Count is invited to work in the sense of a rapprochement and the removal of misunderstandings.[34]

There was a sound practical reason, apart from the internal situation, to wish to improve relations with Britain; Russia was in desperate need of a loan, having already borrowed heavily to finance the war with Japan. Barings had helped Russia since the 1820s to float both Russian loans and Russian issues on the London market. (Barings had also, in 1902, been involved in a loan for Japan that was heavily oversubscribed.) John Baring, 2nd Lord Revelstoke, was approached by Benckendorff and assured the ambassador that as soon as the war was ended, it should be possible to arrange a loan. Nevertheless, Benckendorff was aware that it was the domestic upheaval in Russia that was the problem. The Jewish Rothschilds were reticent in view of the anti-Semitic reports coming from Russia. (Earlier in the war they had arranged a loan for Russia.)

There were naturally practical considerations surrounding the loan and Revelstoke asked Lansdowne whether the government supported the proposed loan. The foreign secretary encouraged the banker, who duly made the journey to St Petersburg in October 1905. However, French and American markets as well as London were involved, and they would not cooperate, given the continuing turbulence in Russia.

The loan question made clear the wider view of Russia abroad. A depressed Benckendorff bemoaned his country's fate to Lamsdorff:

> A new page is opening with the storm clouds building up on all sides. We have a navy: in reality we no longer have one and the importance in this war of maritime strength is obvious. I fear that nothing can cover this up. But it is necessary to tell you reluctantly, dear Count, that the danger is not only because of our defeats on land and at sea. The danger is the discredit that has befallen our Government. Nobody has any confidence. Everything seems to take place without consulting us.[35]

While Russia was in a parlous state politically and economically, 'the position of England is strengthened ... She goes from one treaty to another while we cannot reply with anything similar ... She is winning the territory that we are losing. But where her interest coincides with ours, that is where we can search for peace.'[36]

After Tsushima, Lamsdorff had for the first time spoken about an agreement with Britain in more than general terms. However, he was still not convinced that the time was ripe. Never a strong minister, he had to deal with an emperor whose anger against Britain—trotting out the old claim, that Britain had encouraged Japan to go to war with Russia—was undiminished.

Lamsdorff, now greatly weakened by two heart attacks in the summer of 1905, lacked more than ever the strength to combat the emperor's Anglophobia and was himself loath to negotiate from a position of Russian weakness. Lansdowne in London also felt that Russia had first to come to terms with her position post-Portsmouth and subdue the internal turbulence. He invited Benckendorff to spend a week at his home in Ireland to reassure the ambassador of his continued support for his efforts. Revelstoke used his considerable influence on the press in Britain, and it became less hostile to Russia. But not only Benckendorff, but other senior Russian diplomats were pressing for talks with Britain. Alexander Nelidov, Russian ambassador in Paris, believed that Lamsdorff should be sidelined, and Roman Rosen in Washington agreed.

Events in December 1905, both in Russia and Britain, marked a turning point and provided the conditions for serious Anglo-Russian talks to begin the following year. Russia's diminished international status had been obvious since her defeat by Japan, but she was unable to negotiate with foreign powers even after Portsmouth because of the internal situation. In December, an insurrection in Moscow was suppressed and a degree of calm descended in the towns and cities as the government asserted itself and the old police regime was restored; although disturbances continued in the countryside, the Caucasus was in a state of civil war, there was a revolutionary movement in Tiflis (now Tbilisi) and a mutiny in Tashkent.

In Britain, the Conservative–Unionist Balfour government, riven by internal dissension, above all over tariff reform, resigned, to be replaced by a Liberal one headed by Sir Henry Campbell-Bannerman, with Sir Edward Grey at the foreign office. Elections in January 1906 provided the new administration with a solid majority in the House of Commons.

The foreign secretary had been advocating coming to an agreement with Russia since the early 1890s, and in 1902 in the House of Commons he had deprecated the perpetual quarrelling with Russia at all points and what he considered a policy of drift by the British government. Now he was in a position to bring an agreement to fruition, his motive, above all, was to change the balance of power in Europe by an agreement with Russia, to resolve Asiatic disputes and to reduce military spending, particularly in India. But there was another major new factor to be considered: the need to create a counterpoise to an increasingly aggressive Germany.

Russia had been for the Victorians the constant enemy of Britain worldwide. For the Edwardians of the early twentieth century, Germany came to be perceived as the principal danger with the dramatic growth of German economic and military strength. It was accepted that Germany was the dominant military power in Europe: Britain held naval supremacy. Germany chose to challenge British pre-eminence at sea.

During the second half of the 1890s a series of Anglo-German clashes in foreign affairs had occurred—over South Africa, the Kruger telegram and the Jameson Raid; the East Asian Crisis, the Armenian affair and the future of Turkey. There was colonial rivalry, growing commercial competition, but above all it was the expansionist *Weltpolitik*, fuelled by nationalist intellectuals, Pan-Germans and Wilhelm II, that provoked grave disquiet in Britain.

The appointment of Grand Admiral Alfred von Tirpitz as state secretary of the Reichsmarineamt in 1897 signalled the first distinct change for the worse in Anglo-German relations. Tirpitz advocated the building of a powerful battle fleet. His motivation was clear—an overriding desire to create a political power against Britain. For him an Anglo-German conflict was in the long-term unavoidable. This dovetailed well with the views of the kaiser, obsessed for many years with the aim of Germany possessing a large fleet with which it could rival that of Britain, though Wilhelm was equivocal as to the necessity of conflict. The First Navy Law of 1898 sanctioned the building of a battle fleet of sixteen battleships to be built in the following three years. A Second Navy Law in 1900 increased the fleet to thirty-six battleships and two flag ships, effectively doubling the navy.

A virulent anti-British propaganda campaign waged during the Boer War could only aggravate tension between the two countries. Joseph Chamberlain, the colonial secretary in 1899, proposed an alliance with

Germany, only to recant a short time afterwards and lead an anti-German press campaign in 1903. Britain retaliated with the introduction of naval reforms and by embarking on the introduction of the dreadnought class of ships—concentrating its battleship strength in home waters, pointed in the German direction.

A further step in the deterioration of Anglo-German relations was the presence of Prince Bernhard von Bülow as secretary of state at the Auswärtiges Amt (Federal foreign office). Bülow enthusiastically supported Tirpitz's naval expansion and was determined to prevent Britain from joining the Triple Alliance—something which in the 1890s had seemed a possibility. For the foreign minister not only believed that an Anglo-Russian war in Asia was inevitable, but that it was to be encouraged. This would not only greatly weaken the British empire; it would do the same to Russia: 'Overall, Bülow believed he had to eliminate Britain's global predominance in order to secure Germany's "place in the sun".'[37]

To the antagonistic Anglo-German relations caused by German naval provocation and general hostility, the proposed Baghdad Railway, part of increased German activity in the Ottoman empire, constituted an incremental factor. From the beginning of his reign, Wilhelm II pursued a clear policy of supplanting British and French influence, hitherto dominant, in Turkey. In 1889, he visited Constantinople and during the following decade German economic and political penetration, the *Drang nach Osten*, continued apace; Germany had no 'colonial' past—clean hands, unlike France and Britain.

The Deutsche Bank and its collaborators soon came to control the railways of Turkey from the Austro-Hungarian border to Constantinople, and from the Asiatic shores of the Straits to Angora (now Ankara). The project was to continue the line through the hills of Anatolia into the Mesopotamian valley, to Basra and on to the Persian Gulf.

The trunk line was built from Constantinople to Konya by 1904, but it had become clear that Germany alone could not finance the extension, and work was stopped. The obvious source of capital was Britain. Three-cornered negotiations for the internationalization of the line were conducted by German, Turkish and British bankers under the watchful eyes of their respective foreign ministries. Lansdowne, who was not anti-German, was in favour, but vituperative press and parliamentary opposition in Britain—fear for the safety of communications with India and of a German presence as far as the Persian Gulf—forced the government to withdraw its support.

For their part, the last thing the Russians wanted was a German presence on the threshold of Persia, and construction of the railway was inimical to its vital economic interests. It was claimed that the new line would offer serious competition to the railways of the Caspian and Caucasus regions; that it would menace the success of the proposed Russian Trans-Persian line, and that it might prove to be a rival even of the Siberian system. Witte, a former railwayman, asserted that the proposals for the internationalization of the line were chimerical and Nicholas II decided to prevent Russian capitalists from having anything to do with the Baghdad Railway. It was clear that under German influence Turkey might experience an economic and military renaissance which strategically, with completion of the line, would enable the Ottoman government to mobilize rapidly along Russia's Armenian front. But in 1906, Russia was powerless alone to block further construction of the railway. At the same time, Germany's flourishing relations with the Ottoman empire were a source of trepidation at the foreign office in London.

Benckendorff told Isvolsky in June 1906 that he agreed with the British that the Baghdad Railway was an opportunity for Russia and Britain to settle Persia in order to keep Germany out.[38]

Inevitably, with Sir Edward Grey and Charles Hardinge at the helm from 1906, their long-standing commitment to a rapprochement with Russia could only be strengthened by such threats to British security from Germany. They were both convinced that Germany was seeking to establish its control over continental Europe, was rapidly acquiring the means by which this could be accomplished, and, in addition, was posing a serious threat to Britain in the Near and Middle East. Most senior members of the foreign office were of the same view. Eyre Crowe, the pre-eminent expert on all matters pertaining to Germany, circulated a memorandum in January 1907 in which he warned of the danger of German militarism and current restlessness: 'The vain hopes that in this matter Germany can be "conciliated" and made more friendly must definitely be given up. It may be that such hopes are still cherished by irresponsible people, ignorant, perhaps necessarily ignorant, of the history of Anglo-German relations during the past twenty years?'[39] In February 1906, Grey had told Spring Rice:

> I am impatient to see Russia re-established as a factor in European politics. Whether we shall get an arrangement with her about Asiatic questions remains to be seen. I will try when she desires and is ready, and till she is ready we do not wish to change the situation in Persia or elsewhere.[40]

The time was still not right in early 1906. The Moroccan crisis that had erupted following the kaiser's descent on Tangier at the end of March 1905 was not at first sight related to Anglo-Russian relations.[41] However, the intention was 'to take the earliest opportunity of driving a wedge into the Entente' and to demonstrate how worthless Britain's fair words of new-found friendship for France, Russia's ally, were.[42] Technically, Germany possessed sound legal reasons for complaint against France. In 1880, the French, Spanish, Germans, Italians, British and Americans had signed a convention at Madrid which virtually guaranteed Moroccan independence. French attempts to establish economic and indirect political control over the sultanate ran counter to the Madrid agreement. And Germany had her own economic interests in Morocco. Wilhelm announced that Germany would support the sultan's efforts for peaceful competition in trade among all nations.

Edward VII described his German nephew's behaviour as a 'political-theatrical fiasco'.[43] It was certainly a maladroit attempt by an agent provocateur to disrupt the Entente Cordiale. Germany called for an international conference on Morocco's future, and refused to negotiate with France alone. The Algeciras Conference of January–April 1906 proved a diplomatic disaster for Germany, who was only supported by a wavering Austria, and a personal defeat for the kaiser. Britain provided firm support for France: Russia was grateful for this. Thus, apart from resolving the problem of Morocco, Algeciras served the additional purpose of improving Anglo-Russian relations.

France and Britain both wished to see the Russian parliament, the Duma—established by imperial *ukaz* in March—meet after the elections in April 1906, before going ahead with the loan to Russia, since lending money to an unreformed weak autocracy would cause anger among their electorates, and withholding the loan was a means of exercising pressure on Russia. In that month the loan went ahead, the largest in European history. It was for a massive £89,325,000, of which France took the largest share and London over £13 million. German bankers refused to raise a loan in Berlin because of 'the general hostility against Russia' post Algeciras.[44] It was not found possible to raise any money in Vienna. Naturally, the loan was denounced by British radicals (and the Rothschilds) and those in Russia who saw it as conferring on the government the ability to act without the consent of the Duma, basically to strangle the democratic movement in Russia. The British embassy in St Petersburg attempted, unconvincingly, to make political capital out of the loan by asserting that, by backing the loan, Britain was helping the Russian government out of the financial difficulty caused by Britain's support for France and Russia, against Germany, at Algeciras. Revelstoke received a decoration from Nicholas II.

Two new major participants in Anglo-Russian relations entered the scene in May 1906, both advocates of an agreement. Alexander Isvolsky became Russian foreign minister and Sir Arthur Nicolson arrived as the new British ambassador to Russia, now that Charles Hardinge had become permanent undersecretary at the foreign office. Vladimir Lamsdorff resigned, forced out, many said, by pressure from Germany for lack of support for Russia's western neighbour—'Delcassisation', according to Spring Rice, in a reference to the French prime minister who had suffered this fate at Germany's hands the previous year.[45] A sick man, Lamsdorff died the following March. Charles Hardinge had, on early acquaintance, described Lamsdorff as duplicitous, but came to view the Russian minister as well disposed towards Britain. By the time Lamsdorff retired, Hardinge was laudatory, although there was no doubt that the Russian minister was never more than lukewarm at most about an Anglo-Russian agreement.

The new man was from a different professional background having, unlike the reclusive Lamsdorff, spent little time working at the ministry of foreign affairs, but in numerous diplomatic postings abroad. He was, therefore, well known to British diplomats. Isvolsky spoke English and had visited London in March 1906. It was agreed that he was a liberal and generally pro-British, which boded well, but also susceptible to flattery, snobbish and conceited, and he was never entirely trusted. Nicolson described the minister: 'He strutted on little lacquered feet. His clothes, which came from Savile Row, were moulded tightly upon a plump but still gainly frame ... He left behind him ... a slight scent of violette de parme.'[46] At first Nicolson found Isvolsky timorous, but within a few months reported that the minister was 'quick & intelligent & a delightful man with whom to do business'.[47]

What Nicolson had come to understand was that Isvolsky found himself in a position very different from that of his predecessors. The ministry of foreign affairs no longer possessed the independence of earlier years, but was part of a new political environment in Russia.[48] Isvolsky was a member of the Council of Ministers headed by Ivan Goremykin, with Peter Stolypin at the interior ministry. He was bound to be intimately involved in domestic issues, something outside his previous experience or that of his predecessors. Concomitantly, other members of the council came to expect to be consulted on foreign affairs. Isvolsky also confronted determined resistance to talks with Britain from some colleagues, many in the Asiatic Department of his ministry: the military, led by the head of the General Staff, Feodor Palitysin, who feared hostile German reaction to any deal with Britain, and the powerful Germanophile/Anglophobe court.

The British government managed to sideline its military in talks with Russia. It was the Indian government that was the opponent of an agreement with Russia, although not the enormous stumbling block it would have been if Curzon were still viceroy. John Morley, secretary of state at the India Office, was, partly for financial reasons to ease the India budget, anxious to reduce Anglo-Russian rivalry: 'For the same reasons that make Germany seek coldness or a quarrel between us and Russia, we ought to do what we can to baulk her.'[49]

Algeciras and the Duma elections had resolved two obstacles to negotiations, but further hitches occurred soon after Nicolson's arrival in St Petersburg. The omens were not good. A new pogrom took place in Bialystok in Poland, which was extensively reported in the British press. A desperate sounding Benckendorff wrote—interestingly from Windsor Castle: 'The King was so distressed in speaking to me ... in the most measured terms, the most friendly but the most serious.'[50] Appropriately, Edward VII expressed the shocked British reaction: 'This fresh outbreak of disorder feeds the harmful suspicion that, if not the Government, at least some of its organs, are not without reproach.' Jews were to be found among the revolutionaries. Nevertheless, 'What must not be done is to treat the Jewish race as responsible for the misdeeds of some.'[51] The king, who had many friends in Anglo-Jewry, had made clear to several other people his repulsion at this fresh massacre of Jews. Questions were asked in the House of Commons, with many new Liberal and Radical members who were foreign policy experts and keen to influence the government.

This was only one cause for delaying talks. Nicholas II was very keen for Edward VII to visit Russia. The emperor, after all, had been to Balmoral in 1896 (though that was during the reign of the previous monarch). It seems incredible that the emperor should have even entertained the idea that the king could travel to a country where assassinations were a daily occurrence in 1906. It makes it all the more surprising as Nicholas was under no illusion as to the dangerous situation in his country. He vetoed a visit by a British naval squadron to Russia at this time. In a telegram in English to his uncle, he wrote:

> To have to receive foreign guests when one's country is in a state of acute unrest is more than painful and unappropriate [*sic*]. You know how happy I should have been to receive the English Fleet in normal times, but now I can only beg of You to postpone the squadron's arrival till another year. Nicky.[52]

One cannot help but wonder whether Nicholas did not want to see even a squadron of the British fleet after losing both his Pacific and Baltic fleets. The foreign office in London was relieved that the visit was cancelled, having been bombarded with letters demanding that an event that could be seen as honouring murderers should not take place. It was not easy to embark on talks in the climate of Bialystok, the king's visit question and the cancelled naval visit.

Officially, talks had begun in early June between Isvolsky and Nicolson. Tibet was to be the first item discussed, essentially because it was the least controversial, but this was overshadowed by yet another event in late July. The Duma had immediately shown itself to be a contumacious rabble in the eyes of the government and Nicholas prorogued it on 21 July. This dissolution of the institution that had betoken political reform in Russia was predictably greeted with indignation among British Liberals.

Worse was to come. It so happened that a delegation of Duma deputies was in London and was being addressed by the prime minister when the shattering news from St Petersburg arrived. Sir Henry Campbell-Bannerman, the prime minister, left foreign affairs to Grey, but, in the unscripted outburst of a man of liberal instincts, he departed from his prepared speech and cried out: 'La Douma est morte; Vive la Douma.' Grey congratulated the prime minister, who, on reflection, felt his stance was justified: 'Mere platitudes would not do. I think what I did say was free from offence yet was, I think, effective for good.'[53] Naturally, Benckendorff lodged a protest at the foreign office, though understanding that Grey had to carry his backbenchers with him. The ambassador was booed in London.

In this inauspicious climate, the foreign secretary told Nicolson at the end of July that negotiations had better be suspended. Benckendorff was further dispirited when *The Times* published an article in early August abusing Nicholas II. Nicolson was dismayed: 'The attitude of our press is most unfortunate, and they have completely misunderstood the position ... Iswolsky's former eagerness has been replaced by silence and apparent indifference. The Emperor is wounded. Two months ago there was every hope, and now very little.'[54] *The Times* was hated by the Russian government, but its influence was indisputable. Peter Stolypin, now prime minister, complained about 'the old stereotyped phrases of fashionable Liberalism poured out without any knowledge of local conditions, and spiced with vague expressions of hostility to the Government'.[55]

Communication between the British and Russian governments was, at this juncture, maintained not by diplomats nor ministers, but the well-placed ubiquitous former *Times* journalist, Donald Mackenzie Wallace, who had accompanied Nicholas as tsarevich to India in 1891, been present at Portsmouth in August 1905, and was later at Algeciras. He was invited to St Petersburg—officially by Arthur Nicolson, though in reality at the instigation of Edward VII—and spent seven months there from July 1906. Wallace had entrée to people and places that were impossible for Nicolson. He spoke fluent Russian, and engaged in 'puffing huge cigars into the red-silk curtains of his bedroom, reading revolutionary pamphlets, visiting Witte, Milioukoff [a professor and former Kadet deputy in the Duma], and the reactionaries, attending secret conclaves of the Social Democrats'.[56] Stolypin provided him with pamphlets of the Socialist Revolutionary Party acquired by the secret police.[57] As Edward VII's personal envoy, Wallace had access to Nicholas II.

Wallace arrived with two letters, one from Edward VII to the emperor and a second from Queen Alexandra to her sister, the dowager empress. A few days later he was invited to the Peterhof Palace outside St Petersburg for an audience with the emperor. Wallace had been warned that since Nicholas had for a long time been irritated by the attitude of the British press and public opinion in general, he would receive a frosty reception: 'During the first few minutes of my audience my apprehensions seemed about to be realized ... He remained standing before me apparently with the intention of bowing me out as soon as possible.'[58] Then suddenly Nicholas unbent, and reflected on their last meeting at Balmoral a decade before, where he remembered that he had had toothache. More small talk ensued about the king's improved health, but it was Wallace who did most of the talking, giving his view of the current situation. However, even Wallace could not overcome the emperor's reticence. 'Yes', Edward VII noted, 'A most interesting account which contains much valuable information.'[59] The king was grateful that there was at least some contact with his nephew.

Throughout August, the revolutionaries were active, killing among many others the acting governor general of Warsaw—the Poles were, to a man, as ever opposed to the Russian government. In St Petersburg, an *aide-de-camp* of the emperor was assassinated. The Socialist Revolutionaries quickly made Stolypin their main target. Bombs were thrown into his house, killing twenty-five people. The prime minister found his children buried under rubble, his daughter's legs mangled, but she survived. The family was then removed to the safety of the Winter Palace. Wallace reported:

> The long list of murders, robberies and all sorts of horrors which are committed daily in the provinces and which are served up to us in the morning papers … produces little more than momentary indignation … From 11th to the 22nd inst: in various parts of Russia, excluding the Caucasus, where the state of anarchy is worst, the following acts are recorded in the police reports: 101 policemen and officers killed, and 72 wounded; private persons killed or wounded, 29.[60]
>
> (Note: 'Very interesting ER.')

As if the events from June onwards were not enough to derail Anglo-Russian talks, yet another British gesture of support for reform caused irritation in St Petersburg. On 6 September, *The Times* published a 'Memorial to the Douma', addressed to the president of the dissolved assembly and signed by a considerable number of the great and the good in Britain—Liberal lords, bishops, Members of Parliament and a group from the Labour Party. Benckendorff protested at 'the painful impression that the Imperial Government should be treated in this way, harmful in every way and damaging to the renewal of good relations between the two Powers'.[61] Worse, a deputation was to take the Memorial to Russia. Isvolsky was furious, fearing that the arrival of a group of men, many of whom were members of the Labour Party, would lead to further demonstrations in Russia and give the population the impression that it represented the British people as a whole. Benckendorff was invited to Balmoral in September, and on the first evening the king, with rare vehemence, brought up the subject of the proposed deputation, describing it as a 'monstrous procedure' and those involved as 'madmen'.[62] He clearly leaned on those responsible. The Russian government was able to scupper the deputation by refusing entry to the country.

What brought Britain and Russia back to the negotiating table, however, and let the subject of Tibet drop for the time being, was that a crisis occurred concerning the much more important country of Persia. It was the old-old story, but nevertheless serious, and with a new twist. The shah, Muzaffar al-Din Shah, was demanding a loan, but this time Germany, increasingly involved in Persia, was the potential lender.[63] Both Russia's and Britain's positions in Persia were challenged. Vladimir Kokovtsov, the Russian finance minister, recognized that Russia was in no position to offer a loan. Apart from Russia's own financial difficulties, the shah was not creditworthy, and his countrymen were rising up against him. Already Persia owed Russia 33 million roubles (Britain was owed a mere 2 million roubles). It was a financial no-brainer. But, nevertheless, the shah got the money from Russia. Whatever the price tag, Russia was determined to maintain her superior position in Persia. 'English interests are in Afghanistan, ours are in Persia', Benckendorff told Isvolsky.[64] Britain agreed to share in the loan.

There was no avoiding the fact that Persia was the major obstacle to an agreement. Russia had recently won the contract for a telegraph from Meshed in north-east Persia (a British regional intelligence-gathering base) to Sistan in the south-east. To Nicolson, it represented a change in the relative positions of the two countries. Russia was alerted that this had come as a surprise to the British government, and 'we will probably demand a concession to maintain the equilibrium'.[65]

Isvolsky was also under pressure from the ministry of the marine to demand a naval station on the Gulf. As Benckendorff wryly pointed out, what use would that be now that Russia no longer had either a Baltic or Pacific fleet? Such a demand would certainly provoke a rupture in the nascent talks: 'The question of the route to India is one of those rare questions for which England would sacrifice her last warship.'[66] (The Russians did not know that the day after Benckendorff's letter, Grey submitted a memorandum to the king admitting that sooner or later Russia would have to have access to the Persian Gulf, but 'the question of how this should be arranged is likely to remain in abeyance for the present'.[67]) So, as the Russians had expected, it was the question of India and its defence that mattered to Britain, and the Indian government was protesting about the Sistan–Meshed telegraph, calling for the occupation of Sistan. Even so, there was no way that Grey was going to authorize such a risky enterprise.

Both Russia and Britain faced those at home who were opposing an entente. They also had their respective ministers in Tehran to contend with. Nicholas Hartwig, now head of the Russian legation, was an old Persian hand, supporting the Persian court against the British; but, under orders from Isvolsky, in August 1906 he was told to work with the

British. The influential Russian consul general in Tabriz, Ivan Pokhitonov, was known for 'detesting everything English'.[68] The newly arrived Sir Cecil Spring Rice as head of the British legation was the other side of the coin. He had witnessed in St Petersburg Russian military defeat and revolution, and was convinced she would look for compensation elsewhere, as had happened after the Crimean War and the Congress of Berlin. Russia's base in Persia was much stronger than that of Britain, perfect territory for such an action.

The supposedly independent state of Persia, the most affected by Anglo-Russian negotiations, was not consulted on the grounds that it was in the throes of revolution. The shah's position was precarious, and there was no functioning government. Disturbances had erupted in 1905, partly as a result of external factors—Russia's defeat by Japan had aroused traditionalists to resist great power interference, while Russia's constitutional reforms of the same year and the general spread of western liberal ideas encouraged reformers. The strongest impulse to revolution, however, came from within Persia and centred on the hostility of privileged groups—court factions, merchants and above all the religious leaders, the *ulema*—to the expedients to which the government was being driven, in its perpetual need for money.

In July 1906, a tide of protest engulfed the government. A clash between its supporters and opponents led to two *basts* (demands for asylum). Reformers took refuge in the holy city of Qom, while 12,000 to 14,000 merchants found sanctuary in the British legation with help from the *chargé d'affaires*, Evelyn Grant Duff—to Grey's annoyance, as the foreign secretary was anxious for Britain to remain neutral. Russia duly protested that Britain was encouraging the *basts*. At the beginning of August 1906, Muzaffar al-Din Shah succumbed to granting a constitution, including an assembly, the *majlis*, and the reformers returned home in triumph. The constitution was confirmed by the shah at the end of December. Muzaffar al-Din Shah died a few days later, to be succeeded by his son Mohammed Ali Shah, a weak-minded Russian stooge. The new constitution was a recipe for the paralysis of government, and relations between the shah and the *majlis* rapidly deteriorated when Mohammed refused the *majlis*'s demands. Hartwig regarded the constitutional movement as dangerous to Russian interests and applauded and assisted Mohammed Ali Shah's action. Spring Rice advocated practical support for the liberal constitutionalists.

Inevitably, both ministers forcibly objected to the talks between Britain and Russia in 1906. Hartwig insisted that Russia was giving away the fruits of its expensive penetration over many decades. Spring Rice held that British influence had increased during the period of Russia's problems, and that Russia, never to be trusted in his eyes, ought now to be forced into major concessions. Neither diplomat, though Hartwig was well thought of by Nicholas II and Spring Rice had access to Edward VII, was able to sway his minister. Both Isvolsky and Grey held that larger issues were at stake and slapped down their respective diplomats. It was the stance of ministers in St Petersburg and London towards Persia that made a rapprochement possible.

In Russia, the first proceedings of the State Council to discuss an agreement with Britain began on 7 September 1906. Isvolsky stressed that the country faced a choice between a solid guarantee of at least part of Russia's interests, while continued rivalry with Britain could only mean the adjustment of issues to its detriment. Vladimir Kokovtsov, the finance minister, agreed: 'With regard to Persia, the motivation had lain in the striving towards an outlet on the Persian Gulf, which idea had included that of building railways in the south ... If formerly this had been beyond our strength, it was now a sheer impossibility.'[69]

The Russians wanted a settlement but expected British proposals. They were not forthcoming, as Hardinge wrote: 'We have not the faintest idea what the Russians want in Persia and it seems useless to make proposals to them which they will not look at.'[70] Nicolson complained to Grey about Isvolsky: 'During our recent discussions on Persian affairs when I hinted that I should be glad to know in general outlines his views on our future relations in Persia, he looked blankly at me and said that he had no views at all.'[71]

At this juncture, Isvolsky left St Petersburg and embarked on a tour of European cities. This was because of the elephant in the room—Germany. The kaiser had said that he would welcome the settlement of friction between Britain and Russia, but Isvolsky was understandably wary of the volatile Wilhelm II. Russia could not afford to be on bad terms with her powerful western neighbour, and Nicholas II was inherently pro-German. The Russian foreign minister began his tour in Paris, where clearly there was no problem in advocating an agreement with Britain, as it was long-standing French policy. Then on to Berlin, where Isvolsky sought to reassure the German government of Russia's continued friendship. Edward VII noted on a dispatch from the British ambassador in Paris, on 25 October: 'Germany is sure to act against us—behind our back.'[72]

During the autumn of 1906 talks continued over Tibet. In the spring, Britain had backtracked further on the Lhasa Convention by signing a convention with China which recognized Chinese suzerainty over Tibet (without consulting the Tibetans), and allowed China to pay off the 1904 indemnity. Grey hoped that it would put an end to any suspicion of British designs on Tibet, 'which is one of the few places in the world where to leave things alone causes no inconvenience to anybody'.[73] Nicolson was instructed to ask for Russian recognition of Chinese suzerainty and the territorial integrity of the country, while Britain asserted that she had a predominant geographical interest in seeing that Tibet's external relations were not disturbed by another power.

Although the negotiations were conducted in a desultory way, by the end of the year an agreement was reached on Tibet. Britain undertook to abstain from intervention in internal affairs and to withdraw her forces from the Chumbi Valley in 1908. Russia acknowledged that her interests in Tibet were not commensurate with Britain's, notwithstanding the Dalai Lama's spiritual authority over a million Russian Buddhists.

But seven months had elapsed since negotiations began for a full Asiatic agreement, and, for all the goodwill expressed in both Russia and Britain, to have achieved only a settlement on minor Tibet was scant progress.

32

ENDGAME

Alexander Isvolsky insisted that the reason for so little being achieved in 1906 was the obstruction he faced in St Petersburg; he also complained to Donald Mackenzie Wallace about the impatience of Edward VII and Grey.[1] The Russian foreign minister assured Sir Frank Lascelles in Berlin that:

> Earnestly desiring, as he did, to arrive at such an understanding, it was necessary for him to take into account public opinion in Russia, which was still very suspicious of any *rapprochement* between England and Russia. Any attempt, therefore, to hurry on an agreement would probably give rise to difficulties and result in failure.[2]

This was disingenuous of Isvolsky. He knew well that the British government's long-standing desire to settle with Russia stemmed from awareness of the mounting danger from Germany, with its expanding naval programme and increasing involvement in the Ottoman empire and Persia. True though it was that Isvolsky could provide reasons for the dilatory nature of his conduct, it can be suspected that by being so frank about the problems he faced at home, he was using this delaying tactic to extract concessions from the British. In fairness, though, it has to be pointed out that in the last months of 1906 the minister was involved in difficult negotiations with Japan to complete the provisions of the Portsmouth Treaty.

What followed was the epitome of the 'old diplomacy'; negotiations conducted in strict secrecy by a very small number of men. There was, however, a 'new diplomacy' emerging in 1907, in the form of frequent visits to St Petersburg by Russian diplomats based in London, Alexander Benckendorff and Stanislav Poklevsky-Kozzel; and Arthur Nicolson's travelling to London to report home and the dispatch once more of Wallace to Russia to oil the wheels—an early example of shuttle diplomacy.

In February 1907, Isvolsky announced that he was prepared to continue talks, and in the previous month the Russian government had set up an interdepartmental committee to discuss the remaining issues to be resolved between Britain and Russia. Charles Hardinge rightly believed that any meaningful agreement hinged on Persia, and there was optimism in London and the embassy in St Petersburg when the Russian committee set out its terms as regards Persia.

Benckendorff was present in St Petersburg when Isvolsky read the Russian draft proposal on Persia to Nicolson. The line between the zones of influence of the two countries, Russia in the north and Britain in the south-east, was for the Russian sphere to run from Kohsan in the east, dipping south to Yazd, and then through Isfahan to Qasr-e-Shirin in the west. The British government was in general satisfied with the proposed delimitation of the Russian zone, except that in the east they insisted that the Russian government replace Kohsan with Zulficar, so that the Russian sphere did not touch Afghanistan but Russian Turkestan. A neutral zone was to be created south of this, running from Bandar Abbas on the coast, through Kerman, north-eastwards to the Afghan frontier, and encompassing all to the west, south of the Russian sphere. This was already euphoniously called 'the whole of the rest of Persia'. Much was desert and mountainous wasteland. South-east Persia and the Gulf of Oman eastwards constituted the British zone. Nicolson recalled that Isvolsky 'informed me that he had succeeded in winning over the military party to accepting in principle our zone was practically abandoning Seistan to us and was a surrender of what might in certain eventualities be an important strategical position'.[3] The British government had for a long time recognized this: its sphere was small but defensible. The proposed partition of Persia between Russia and Britain was undoubtedly a realistic one.

Grey was restrained on receiving the draft proposal and pointed out that the sphere the Russians claimed was very large and included Tehran:

> This was a matter of very great importance, as the fact that Tehran was in the Russian sphere was bound to increase Russian prestige there. And yet it was at Tehran, the seat of the central government, that any influence we might require would have to be exercised, even in connection with concessions or other matters relating to our own sphere only.[4]

Hardinge, though, was delighted by the Russian proposal and noted that it was less than what the ambitious Curzon had assigned to them, and was particularly pleased that the Russians were not claiming anything on the Persian Gulf.[5]

Both countries had major interests at stake in Persia, but it was the seemingly less tendentious country of Afghanistan that preoccupied the Russians. Isvolsky raised the subject and it seemed prudent not to lose the new momentum towards an agreement. On 23 February/4 March, therefore, Nicolson handed the minister a draft setting out the British position. He reminded Isvolsky that on several occasions in the past Russia had accepted that Afghanistan was outside its sphere of influence. At the same time, he assured the minister that the British government was aware of the inconvenience of the absence of direct communication between Russian and Afghan officials over local and non-political matters. This question would be considered. As the emir himself would have to consent to any arrangements, the British government would need to know what these would be in order to approach Habibullah, who was under British guidance in all his foreign relations.

Nicolson made it clear that the British government would insist that no Russian agents could be sent into Afghanistan. Isvolsky wanted to know what 'agents' meant. All categories, he was told. Another sore point arose from the British demand that the 'bounties in subsidies' given to Russian trade with Afghanistan must be ended.[6] In recompense, Russian traders would be accorded the same facilities as British and Indian traders. The minister promised to reply to all points after he had studied the paper.

Benckendorff was aware that Nicolson was going to set out the British proposals and that they would meet with opposition at St Petersburg. A few days later he wrote to his minister giving reasons for British sensitivity over Afghanistan, as he knew his ministry would baulk at the British demands. The ambassador held that the British position was not properly understood in Russia. People there believed that Curzon's expansionist views were shared by the current government. The previous viceroy's was a 'programme personel, mais nullement un fait'.[7] The British position was weaker than was believed in Russia: 'The relations between the two countries, marked by several wars from which England has gained little, have until recently been unsatisfactory ... In spite of the present improvement ... English suspicion of the Afghans has in no way been overcome.'[8] Benckendorff's dispatch was counterproductive. He who was so fervent in his desire for a rapprochement bolstered his government to take a strong line against the British stance on Afghanistan.

Later in March, the Russians introduced a fresh subject for discussion, but an old chestnut of Anglo-Russian relations. The 'question of the Straits', as Grey recognized, 'had been at the root of the difficulties between England and Russia for the last generation and more'.[9] The foreign secretary believed that Russia's long-held desire for her ships to have egress from the Black Sea was reasonable and would have to be accepted in the near future. But it would not be appropriate to include it in an Anglo-Russian agreement as other states—France, Austria-Hungary, Germany and Turkey—would have to be involved and British public opinion would claim a concession elsewhere. Nicolson feared that dismissal of the Straits question would scupper the talks on Afghanistan, when the aim was for a purely Anglo-Russian settlement of Asian questions. In fact, the opposite happened and he found Isvolsky 'beaming with pleasure' at British support for settling the Straits in Russia's favour at a later date.[10]

The warmer climate in Anglo-Russian relations that month was reflected in the visit of the Russian Dowager Empress Maria Feodorovna to Britain, her first in thirty-four years. She clearly enjoyed seeing her sister, Queen Alexandra, and wrote to her son the emperor: 'How happily we are all living together ... I do wish you too could come over here a little, to breathe another air ... How *good* for you that would be! I myself feel as if I were a different person.'[11] This was followed up by the arrival of a Russian squadron in Portsmouth. The Russian officers and crew, at the king's suggestion, were received in London. The crowds were enthusiastic.

Nevertheless, in the hard world of diplomacy, royal gestures of goodwill did not count in the negotiations over Afghanistan. Two months elapsed from the delivery of the British proposals on Afghanistan before Isvolsky presented the Russian reply. The minister insisted that there were good reasons for the delay. The general staff feared that strengthening the British position in Afghanistan would lead to an aggressive policy against Russia in Central Asia; the minister of commerce objected to the suppression of bounties. To this was added the highly charged political situation in Russia after elections to the second Duma in March 1907, and ongoing discussions with Japan.

Finally, on 15 May, Isvolsky read Nicolson the Russian draft convention. Afghanistan was to remain a buffer state and Great Britain should not annex nor occupy any part of Afghanistan, nor interfere in her internal affairs. It was found unsatisfactory in several respects in London, causing Edward VII 'misgivings'. The king insisted that British hands should not be tied in relations with the emir.[12] In the British counter-draft a month later, the whole form of the convention was recast. The expression 'buffer state' was deleted and alterations made to the proposed Russian article concerning British intervention in Afghanistan, on the grounds that this would confer on the emir too much freedom and thus could threaten the security of the Indian frontiers. Essentially, there was a Russian concern that while London wanted to ensure that British treaties with the emir were observed, and failing this that they could act, on the other hand, Russia would have to forego any right of intervention in the country. Isvolsky rightly pointed out that the prohibition imposed on Russia was absolute, while that imposed on Britain was conditional on the emir's living up to his treaty promises. Afghanistan was proving much more difficult than had been anticipated.

But in early June, it was surprisingly Grey who added a new issue, the question of the Persian Gulf, and this threatened to derail the talks. The foreign secretary felt that for an agreement to be acceptable to British public opinion, the special interests of Britain in the maintenance of the status quo in the Gulf had to be inserted. Isvolsky refused point-blank, fearing that objecting to a terminus for the projected Baghdad Railway would expose him to reproaches from Berlin.

Already enough information had seeped out to alarm the Conservative–Unionist opposition in Britain that too much was being conceded to Russia. The government of India was insisting that British predominance in the Gulf had to be recognized, and the king '[wished] it to be put on record that, according to his view, it is a mistake to give way'.[13] From a different standpoint, British Radicals were outraged at the dissolution of the second Duma in July 1907.

In mid-July, Nicolson decided that he 'had better … run over to London'.[14]

The ambassador remained in London for almost a month, consulting with his ministry and the India Office, and confronting the views of Lord Minto, the viceroy. Minto objected to any discussion with Russia over Afghanistan, and his proposals on receiving the British counter-draft would have effectively sent the negotiations back to square one. However, he and the Indian lobby were steamrollered by John Morley at the India Office. In no uncertain terms, the minister told Lord Minto: 'Please recognize the centre of gravity has changed for good or evil.'[15] The view in London was that vast sums had been wasted in previous years. The monotony of life in the army in India led to a mentality of constantly imagining an impending danger from the north. Nevertheless, Morley, although in favour of resolving disagreements with Russia, was adamant in his opposition to any concessions that would diminish Britain's position in Afghanistan and arouse the emir's suspicions of a third party, Russia, being able to intervene in Afghan affairs. Grey found himself in the middle. Nicolson was anxious to make concessions to the Russians to secure an agreement, and not to jeopardize this overall aim by haggling over relatively minor issues concerning Afghanistan: at the same time Grey could not ignore Morley nor the Indian government. It is a tribute to Nicolson's diplomatic skills that the ambassador persuaded both Grey and Morley to back his position, and, with new proposals in hand, he arrived back in St Petersburg on 12 August.

As ever, the British government feared the kaiser's leaning hard on his Russian cousin and wrecking the Anglo-Russian negotiations. So when it was learned that, after careful concealment, the two sovereigns were to meet in early August at Swinemünde, the spectre of a repeat of Bjørko appeared. But this time Isvolsky and Bülow were present and the Russian minister was able to convince the Germans that nothing detrimental to their interests was at stake in the talks with Britain. Grey reported that he assured Benckendorff:

> I told him we understood perfectly that Russia and Germany being neighbours, it was natural for them to have discussions and communications with each other. We relied on the Russian Government to see that, in any communications which took place, she was not influenced to our prejudice by Germany in matters which affected Russia and ourselves alone.[16]

Once more reassured by the favourable German position, Isvolsky seemed pleased by Nicolson's news about the Afghan concessions, although he expressed reservations about the part of the draft convention dealing with the Persian Gulf. The British government obliged, and agreed to remove any reference to the Gulf from the convention, and to attach a separate dispatch simply reiterating Britain's position. This satisfied Isvolsky, and he informed the ambassador on 22 August that he had the emperor's conditional assent and would recommend acceptance of the British offer to his colleagues. The minister was confident of their approval.

However, the meeting of the Council of Ministers the following day turned out to be quite different from his expectations. Strong opposition was voiced by ministers, who set upon Isvolsky for yielding too much over Afghanistan. The minister argued his case until he was hoarse, but when the meeting broke up with a vote at 2 o'clock in the morning he was in a minority, with only Stolypin and one other supporting him. The distraught minister pointed out to Nicolson that if Nicholas II went along with the minority, which would ensure signature, the majority would do all that they could to hinder execution of the convention. If the emperor went along with the majority, Isvolsky would have to resign.

This Russian brinksmanship cut little ice in London. Grey refused to agree to any changes to the draft convention and Nicolson expressed his government's 'disappointment that an unexpected difficulty has arisen when the negotiations were apparently on the eve of being happily concluded'.[17] Then, for the first time, to focus Russian minds, Grey put on paper the all-important consideration that had lurked behind all the Asiatic deliberations of imperial security:

> His Majesty's Government sincerely trust that the Imperial Russian Government will appreciate that larger issues are indirectly at stake than those directly involved in these Agreements, for it has throughout been the expectation and the belief of His Majesty's Government that an agreement as to their respective interests in Asia ... would so influence the disposition of public opinion in Great Britain as to make friendly relations possible on questions which may arise elsewhere in the future.[18]

This was the crux of the matter.

It worked. 'Nicky ... played up and it was due to his personal intervention that some very serious hitches at the eleventh hour were surmounted without any further concessions from London.'[19] Isvolsky was thus able to persuade his colleagues that the British declaration not to interfere in, nor annex, Afghan territory for as long as the emir honoured his treaty obligations was sufficient guarantee of Russian interests. At the same time, the British government was prepared to drop its requirement for a Russian pledge not to intervene in Afghanistan, and to accede to the demand for consultation. There was also a stipulation which required the Russian government to be notified by the British government that the emir of Afghanistan had consented to the provisions concerning his country.

On 31 August 1907, the Anglo-Russian Convention was signed, the culmination of British aims, since the early 1890s, to end Anglo-Russian antagonism, and to ensure its full import was recognized, Hardinge proposed that it should be signed by Nicholas II and Edward VII. This was done on 3 September, and three weeks later it was published.

Grey was proud of his achievement, and it has been considered by his recent biographer to be 'one of his greatest diplomatic successes'.[20] Grey wrote:

> Russia was to cease threatening and annoying British interests concerned with India ... She was now, once and for all, to give it up. The gain to us was great. We were freed from an anxiety that had often preoccupied British governments; a frequent source of friction and a possible cause of war was removed ... The part of Persia by which India could be approached was made secure from Russian penetration. The part of Persia by which Russia could be approached was secured from British penetration. The gain was equal—on paper. In practice we gave up nothing. We did not wish to pursue a forward policy in Persia ... it is no wonder the Russian Foreign Minister had some difficulty in getting the military authorities in Russia to give up something of real potential value to them, while we gave up what was of little or no practical value to us ... The Persian Gulf was kept out of her sphere, but left in the 'neutral' sphere. Russia gained nothing as regards the Gulf by the Agreement, but her position was not made worse. Even so the Agreement seemed to me one-sided. What we gained by it was real—what Russia gained was apparent.[21]

Nevertheless, he was forced to admit that 'people here do not think that the convention, as an isolated bargain, is a good one; but they will be pleased if it leads to a generally friendly attitude of Russia towards us'.[22]

Isvolsky, for his part, was delighted by the convention, as it represented a stabilized Russia, back as an imperial power on the world stage. Russia needed a period of peace. He left St Petersburg in early September for a holiday in Marienbad (now Marianske Lazne). On 5 September he lunched with Edward VII, who was there taking the waters. The king told the minister that all future problems would be solved easily in a spirit of give and take, now that the ice was effectively broken. He presented Isvolsky with the Grand Cross of the Victorian Order. To a man of the minister's inclinations, this fortified him for the expected hostility at home.

For the Anglo-Russian Convention of August 1907 inevitably provoked praise in some countries, opprobrium and dismay in others.

Grey's cabinet colleagues lauded the foreign secretary. Campbell-Bannerman saw in the convention 'the removal of the danger of an Asiatic avalanche and [it] will make things easier in Europe'.[23] Most Liberal MPs supported the agreement in the belief that it would bring down defence costs, and the foreign office was relieved that the years of Anglo-Russian antagonism appeared to be at an end. Thomas, now Lord, Sanderson, the veteran former permanent undersecretary, expressed his approval that positive and permanent engagements respecting Persia and Afghanistan had been obtained from Russia in place of the previous 'rather fluid assurances' given only in correspondence and conversations.[24]

The Radicals and the Independent Labour Party denounced the agreement as an alliance with autocratic tsardom. Arthur Balfour, leader of the Conservative opposition, and Lord Lansdowne were sceptical of an arrangement that they believed had conceded too much unnecessarily to Russia. For many other Unionists, south-western Persia should have been included in the agreement as this would have provided an additional guarantee of India's security and British dominance in the Persian Gulf. A larger British sphere would, it was argued, also increase British influence in Tehran.

The British press was divided. *The Times*, for so long hostile to Russia, had changed its stance and backed the negotiations. It greeted their successful conclusion, convinced that 'the peace of Asia and the prospect of some eventual reduction of the heavy military burden of India will be worth some sacrifice'. The editorialist was fulsome in his praise, believing that 'it will rank among the most important instruments for securing the peace of the world'.[25] The liberal *Manchester Guardian* took a guarded position, but did not condemn the convention: 'Such agreements are often worth making, but they seldom give sufficient cause for having the bells rung, or for tearing our hair either, and so it is with this one.'[26] The agreement would serve to protect British interests in Central Asia. The two prominent periodicals and opinion formers, *The Economist* and *The Spectator*, were restrained in their support for the convention: *The Economist* conceded that, although for many reasons Russia was an inappropriate ally of Liberal Britain, it made sense to resolve differences with her. For the *Spectator*, the agreement secured the Persian Gulf, but it refused to believe that the convention would have any effect on the balance of power in Europe. The distinguished scholar of Persia, E. G. Browne, devoted much effort to defending Persian sovereignty and opposing the agreement. Henry Lynch, head of Lynch Brothers, with their considerable commercial interests in southern Persia, although a Liberal MP, held forth against the convention in the House of Commons.

Lord Curzon, as expected, launched a broadside against the agreement:

> The Russian convention is in my view deplorable. It gives up all that we have been fighting for [for] years, and it gives up with a wholesale abandon

> that is truly cynical in its recklessness. Ah, me, it makes one despair of public life. The efforts of a century sacrificed and nothing in return.[27]

By the time he was able to take his seat in the House of Lords six months later, the former viceroy's views were of 'purely academic interest'.[28] His 'shrill denunciation' was the 'condensed result of the studies and travels of more than twenty years [before]'.[29] According to Curzon, in Persia the convention surrendered everything of value to Russia and not enough attention had been given to demarcating the spheres. Nothing was gained in Afghanistan; the Tibetan clauses were an absolute surrender. It represented a humiliation for Britain in Asia.

In Russia, Isvolsky acted quickly to pre-empt criticism from within his ministry with a circular letter to civil servants and to embassies setting out the reasons for coming to an agreement with Britain. The finance minister, Vladimir Kokovtsov, told the French that he was 'enchanted' with the accord. Even so, ambassadors Prince Viktor Kochubey in Paris and Count Muraviev in Rome complained openly of Russia's loss of status in Central Asia and Persia. The veteran General Alexsei Kuropatkin, who had played an active role in the Great Game from the early 1880s, through the Russo-Japanese war, praised the convention: 'Russia and England, as Asian powers, should work in conjunction, so as to uphold order in Central Asia and counteract a common menace from the Far East.'[30] The tone of the press turned out to be an agreeable surprise. The Anglophobic *Novoe Vremya* merely regretted that Russia had lost the ability to threaten India, while *Slovo* optimistically believed that the agreement protected Russia from German ambitions.

The Russian equivalent of Curzon came in the form of Sergei Witte. The count, who was inherently Germanophile, had been excluded from the negotiations, and believed that it prevented Russia from annexing Persia and gaining access to Kabul. He was convinced that Afghanistan would be converted into a loaded gun directed against Russia. Historians in the Soviet period took the view that Russia had had her hands tied and gained nothing in return.

France predictably welcomed the rapprochement. It had been the goal of French policy since the signing of the Entente Cordiale three years before that her ally and her friend should resolve their differences. Paul Cambon, the French ambassador in London, believed that Britain had got the better of the agreement.

The official German reaction of studied indifference owed more to diplomatic bravura than a realistic assessment of the convention. The

Germanophile British ambassador, Sir Frank Lascelles, reported that the agreement had, on the whole, been favourably received, yet the press summaries he enclosed showed that the opposite was true. Wilhelm von Schoen, the ambassador in St Petersburg, understood: 'No one will reproach England for such a policy … One can only admire the skill with which she has carried out her plans. These plans need not necessarily be ascribed to any anti-German tendency, yet Germany is most affected by the agreement.' The kaiser was nobody's fool and annotated: 'Yes, when taken all around, it is aimed at us.'[31] In a more typical apoplectic outburst, he believed that Britain 'will become still more unpleasant to us in Europe than before'.[32] The intelligent Kaiser Wilhelm recognized that the balance of power in Europe was transformed by purely Asiatic deals, and that the Triple Alliance had been weakened. In his monarchical megalomania he blamed his dastardly Machiavellian Uncle Edward for being the architect of the encirclement of Germany. It was this view that took hold in Germany in the years that followed. Indeed, it was repeated after the First World War.[33]

The supposedly independent state of Persia, the most affected by the Anglo-Russian Convention, had not been consulted during the negotiations. It was claimed that there was no government. Certainly, the country was in the throes of revolution and the shah's position precarious, but the arrogance of the two powers was inexcusable.

After the agreement was signed, a joint communication informed the Persian government of its existence:

> In signing that Arrangement the two states have not for a moment lost sight of the fundamental principle of the absolute respect of the integrity and independence of Persia. The Arrangement has no other object than that of avoiding any cause of misunderstanding between the Contracting Parties on the ground of Persian affairs.[34]

In Persia, in September 1907, the constitutional struggle raged with Britain and Russia on opposite sides, but Grey and Isvolsky instructed their ministers to cooperate. Hartwig's position, though, was clear—he would have used force to suppress the revolution. He 'seems to have thought that the only way in which the results of Russian diplomacy of past years were to be secured was in the retention, at all costs, on the throne of Mohammed Ali Shah, who … had shown himself thoroughly amenable'.[35]

Although it was not a surprise to him, Cecil Spring Rice wrote to his minister in terms that were little short of insubordination. According to Spring Rice, constitutionalists:

> had been accustomed to look to England for sympathy and support, and they were convinced that England was vitally interested in the maintenance of Persian power. The news of the conclusion of the agreement was a blow to them. However disguised, it meant that Russia had been given a free hand in the North ... and that England had definitely withdrawn her opposition to Russian aggression in return for a share of the spoil.[36]

The minister was correct in recognizing that Britain would bear the odium of the agreement. The violent reaction of Persian constitutionalist politicians and the press was directed largely at Britain. They saw a betrayal of Persia by those they had come to trust; Russia was little mentioned. A strong feeling of indignation was rising against Britain, 'far stronger than that against Russia, who is not accused of disguising her policy or ever having pretended to friendship for the Persian people, or a desire for Persian prosperity and independence'.[37]

The consequences of the 1907 convention are felt today in Anglo-Iranian relations. In his 2013 essay, 'The Myth of "Perfidious Albion": Anglo-Iranian Relations in Historical Perspective', Professor Ali Ansari of St Andrew's University wrote that in the first decade of the twentieth century:

> far from viewing the British with antipathy, Iran's constitutional revolutionaries actively sought British support for their political ambitions, and the British were not averse to providing it ... There seems scant attention paid to Russian behaviour towards Iran both before and after the revolution. Most people would not be aware that Russia (as Lord Curzon would enthusiastically concur), throughout the past two centuries, posed a much greater threat to Iranian sovereignty than the British ever did.

Professor Ansari points out that the Anglophilia that was present in Persia did not wane:

> until the aftermath of the Constitutional revolution, when imperial priorities allowed Russia a free hand to suppress the Constitutionalists ... This sense of disappointment was to grow in subsequent decades and offers a significant clue to the reason why Britain occupies pride of place in the suspicions of Iranians.[38]

Russia had insisted that the stipulations of the convention should not come into force until the Russian government had been notified by the British government that the emir of Afghanistan had consented to them. This constituted the fifth and last article of the agreement.

All did not go as planned. The wily Habibullah was able to thwart the British demand for his signature. Relations between the emir and the British had been strained since his accession in 1901, and it is surprising, given previous experience of Habibullah's irksome habit of incommoding the British whenever possible, that it was not expected that he would not play ball. A messenger was dispatched from Simla with the Afghan text. The emir was on a tour of his country, and when he was reached several weeks later, he retorted that he could not deal with such an important subject until he returned to Kabul. He reached the capital at the end of November, but the year ended without communication from Habibullah.

When he did deign to reply, the emir protested against some of the provisions concerning Afghanistan and tried to seek compensation. The British government refused to be ruffled. At the end of January 1908, the foreign office held that given the slowness of Asians to reply to communications, and the importance of the subject, which necessitated consultation with his advisers, it was not a matter of surprise that he had not replied. Benckendorff, fearful that the convention would be sabotaged by the emir, advised Isvolsky to act as though Habibullah's consent had been given. It is witness to the Russian minister's sincerity that he never attempted to exploit this glaring loophole in the agreement. Almost a year after the convention had been signed, the emir rejected it, but by that time his opinion was of no importance, as Russia had provided clear evidence that she would adhere to the convention.[39]

* * *

There have remained those who believe that the Anglo-Russian Convention had deleterious consequences by dividing Europe into two hostile camps. But these already existed—the Triple Alliance of Germany, Austria-Hungary and Italy, and the opposing Franco-Russian Alliance. What the convention did, by effectively ending the Great Game in Asia, and hence shifting the balance of power in Europe in favour of the Franco-Russian-British entente, was to provide the combination that could defeat the Axis powers of Germany, Austria-Hungary and Turkey in the First World War.

NOTES

1. ENGLAND AND MUSCOVY: THE BEGINNING OF ANGLO-RUSSIAN RELATIONS

1. Richard Hakluyt, *The Principal Navigations, Voyages, Traffiques and Discoveries of the English Nation*, 3 vols. (London, 1907–9), vol. 1, p. 214.
2. Ibid. p. 215.
3. Ibid. p. 274.
4. Ibid. p. 275.
5. Ibid. p. 255.
6. Ibid. p. 242.
7. Ibid. p. 332.
8. Francesca Wilson, *Muscovy: Russia Through Foreign Eyes, 1553–1900* (London, 1970), p. 34.
9. Hakluyt, op. cit. vol. 2, p. 439.
10. Ibid. p. 447.
11. Ibid.
12. Ibid. vol. 3, p. 187.
13. Ibid. p. 196.
14. Wilson, op. cit. p. 48.
15. Quoted in Anthony Cross, *Russia Under Western Eyes, 1517–1825* (London, 1971), p. 7.
16. I. M. Kulishev, *Ocherk istorii russkoi torgovli* (Petrograd, 1923), p. 118.
17. Giles Fletcher, *Of the Russe Commonwealth, 1591, Facsimile Edition with Variants* (Cambridge, MA, 1966), pp. 352–5.
18. Ibid. p. 20.
19. Ibid. p. 116.
20. Ibid. pp. 112–13.
21. Ibid. pp. 113–14.
22. William Shakespeare, *Love's Labour's Lost*, Act V, Scene ii.
23. Jan Hennings holds that the Christian religion united the tsars with western sovereigns; in *Russia and Courtly Europe: Ritual and the Culture of Diplomacy, 1648–1725* (Cambridge, 2016), p. 48.
24. See Chester S. L. Dunning, *Russia's First Civil War: The Time of Troubles and the*

Founding of the Romanov Dynasty (University Park, PA, 2001), for a favourable revisionist view.

25. Maija Jansson, Nikolai Rogozhin et al., eds., *England and the North: The Russian Embassy of 1613–1614* (Philadelphia, 1994), pp. 1–7.
26. Maria Unkovskaya, DPhil dissertation c10354, Bodleian Library, Oxford, 1992, p. 187.
27. Ibid. p. 189.
28. Ibid. p. 236.
29. Samuel Collins, *The Present State of Russia, in a Letter to a Friend at London* (London, 1671), pp. 60–1.
30. Ibid. p. 128.
31. Ibid. p. 148.
32. Ibid. p. 160.
33. Ibid. p. 172.
34. See Paul Dukes, Graeme P. Herd and Jarmo Kotilaine, *Stuarts and Romanovs: The Rise and Fall of a Special Relationship* (Dundee, 2009), for a full account of the life of Patrick Gordon.

2. THE RUSSIAN EMPIRE: PETER THE GREAT

1. From the English translation in the Sutherland Papers in the National Library of Scotland, Edinburgh, quoted in George Barany, *The Anglo-Russian Entente Cordiale of 1697–1698* (New York, 1986), pp. 5–6.
2. J. T. Kotilaine, 'Competing Claims: Russian Foreign Trade via Arkhangelsk and the Eastern Baltic Ports in the 17th Century', *Kritika: Explorations in Russian and Eurasian History* 4.2 (Spring 2003), pp. 279–311.
3. Quoted in M. S. Anderson, *Britain's Discovery of Russia, 1553–1815* (London, 1958), p. 49.
4. Quoted in Anthony Cross, *Russia Under Western Eyes, 1517–1825* (London, 1971), p. 92.
5. Anderson, op. cit. p. 52.
6. B. H. Sumner, *Peter the Great and the Emergence of Russia* (London, 1950), p. 56.
7. Janet M. Hartley, *Charles Whitworth: Diplomat in the Age of Peter the Great* (Aldershot, 2002), pp. 33–104, for a full and excellent account. See also J. M. Price, 'The Tobacco Adventure to Russia: Enterprise, Politics and Diplomacy in the Quest for a Northern Market for English Colonial Tobacco, 1676–1722', *Transactions of the American Philosophical Society* (ns) 51.1 (1961), pp. 1–120.
8. Hartley, op. cit. p. 40.
9. Ibid. p. 41.
10. Ibid.
11. The tobacco trade ended in 1714. See Price, op. cit. p. 81.
12. Hartley, op. cit. p. 68.

13. Quoted in Jan Hennings, *Russia and Courtly Europe: Ritual and the Culture of Diplomacy, 1648–1725* (Cambridge, 2016), p. 224.
14. Although the allocation of countries between the two departments varied slightly from time to time, the general rule in the eighteenth century was that the Southern Department comprised France, Spain, Italy, Switzerland, Turkey and the Barbary Coast and the colonies. The Northern Department was concerned with the remaining countries with whom diplomatic relations were maintained.
15. Holstein was the northernmost territory of the Holy Roman Empire, the region between the rivers Elbe and Eider. Since the mid-sixteenth century the House of Oldenberg had been divided: a senior line held the throne of Denmark; a number of cadet branches were established in various north German territories of which the most important was the Duchy of Holstein-Gottorp. In the latter part of the seventeenth century the political and dynastic connections of the dukes of Holstein-Gottorp with the crown of Sweden had exposed Denmark to the danger of simultaneous attacks to front and rear. That danger had been removed by the collapse of the Swedish empire and the failure of Charles Frederick of Holstein-Gottorp to secure the succession in Sweden on the death of Charles XII in 1718.
16. Francesca Wilson, *Muscovy: Russia Through Foreign Eyes, 1553–1900* (London, 1970), p. 101.
17. Ibid. p. 109.
18. Ibid. p. 111.
19. Nicholas Riasanovsky, *A History of Russia* (Oxford, 1993), p. 240.

3. 'NATURAL FRIENDS'

1. Courland comprised the south-western part of present-day Latvia.
2. Brendan Simms, *Three Victories and a Defeat: The Rise and Fall of the First British Empire, 1714–1783* (London, 2007), p. 234.
3. M. S. Anderson, *Britain's Discovery of Russia, 1553–1815* (London, 1958), pp. 121–2.
4. He was held in captivity in a damp dungeon in the Schlüsselburg fortress until 1764, known by the sinister euphemism of 'Prisoner Number One'. Ivan was probably killed on the orders of Catherine II. Her husband, Peter III, shortly before he was murdered, visited the insane Ivan in 1762. Whether Ivan's mental state was due to his imprisonment is of course impossible to say.
5. Quoted in Simms, op. cit. p. 402.
6. Quoted in David Horn, *Sir Charles Hanbury Williams and European Diplomacy, 1747–1758* (London, 1930), p. 184.
7. Ibid. p. 186.
8. Ibid. pp. 186–7.

9. Ibid. p. 189.
10. Hanbury Williams was naturally *persona non grata* with Elizabeth after the Convention of Westminster in 1756 as she felt that he had duped her, and he was recalled before he was asked to leave. He became insane and died in 1759.

4. CATHERINE THE GREAT

1. Catherine II, *Memoirs of the Empress Catherine II, Written by Herself*, with a preface by A. Herzen (London, 1859). A revisionist view of Peter III is found in Carol S. Leonard's biography, *Reform and Regicide: The Reign of Peter III of Russia* (Bloomington, IN, 1993).
2. *Memoirs of the Empress Catherine II*, op. cit. p. 318.
3. Brendan Simms, *Three Victories and a Defeat: The Rise and Fall of the First British Empire, 1714–1783* (London, 2007), p. 490.
4. James Harris, *Diaries and Correspondence of James Harris, First Earl of Malmesbury*, 4 vols. (London, 1844), vol. 1, p. 160.
5. SIRIO 12, Macartney to Grafton, 11 February 1766.
6. Quoted in Vincent Cronin, *Catherine, Empress of all the Russias* (London, 1989), p. 187.
7. Alexsei Orlov, one of the five Orlov brothers, was probably along with his brother Grigory one of the murderers of Peter III.
8. SIRIO 19/196, Cathcart to Rochford, 16 March 1770.
9. Horace Walpole, *The Letters of Horace Walpole*, 9 vols. (London, 1891), vol. 8, p. 179.
10. Edmund Burke, article in the *Annual Register*, 1773.
11. Quoted in Simms, op. cit. p. 567.
12. *Correspondence of William Pitt, Earl of Chatham*, 4 vols. (London, 1838–40), vol. 4, pp. 298–9.
13. Stanley Ayling, *George III* (London, 1972), p. 247.
14. Harris, op. cit. vol. 1, p. 159.
15. Ibid. p. 212.
16. Quoted in Simon Sebag Montefiore, *Prince of Princes: The Life of Potemkin* (London, 2000), p. 207.
17. Harris, op. cit. vol. 1, p. 298.
18. Ibid. p. 315.
19. Ibid.
20. Sebag Montefiore, op. cit. p. 244.
21. M. S. Anderson, *Britain's Discovery of Russia, 1553–1815* (London, 1958), p. 146.
22. TNA FO 65/20, Whitworth to the Duke of Leeds, 18 February 1791.
23. The foreign office was established in 1782 with one secretary of state in charge of all departments.

24. William Cobbett, *The Parliamentary History of England*, 36 vols. (London, 1812–20), vol. 29, p. 65.
25. Ibid. p. 77.
26. Ibid. pp. 35–6.
27. Ibid. p. 180.
28. Mary Berry, *Extracts of the Journals and Correspondence of Miss Berry, from the Year 1783 to 1852*, 3 vols. (London, 1865), vol. 1, p. 293.
29. Ibid. p. 321.
30. George Rose, *The Diaries and Correspondence of the Rt. Hon. George Rose* (London, 1860), vol. 1, p. 111.
31. Baron Meyendorff, ed., *La Correspondance diplomatique de M. de Staal*, 2 vols. (Paris, 1929), vol. 1, p. 25, Giers to Staal, 8 June 1884.
32. Adam Smith, *An Inquiry into the Nature and the Causes of the Wealth of Nations*, Vol. 1, ed. E. Cannan (London, 1930), p. 238.

5. THE LONG EIGHTEENTH CENTURY: THE DIPLOMATS

1. Anthony Cross, *'By the Banks of the Thames': Russians in Eighteenth Century Britain* (Newtonville, MA, 1980), p. 20. I owe an enormous debt to Professor Cross for his ground-breaking work on Anglo-Russian relations in the eighteenth century.
2. The building has since been demolished.
3. Gleb Struve, 'An Anglo-Russian Medley', *California Slavic Studies* 5 (Berkeley, CA, 1970).
4. Statues of both Florence Nightingale and Sidney Herbert are part of the Guards Crimean War Memorial in Waterloo Place at the bottom of Regent Street in London.
5. Struve, op. cit.
6. Janet M. Hartley, *Charles Whitworth: Diplomat in the Age of Peter the Great* (Aldershot, 2002), p. 55.
7. Ibid. p. 56.
8. Sir George Macartney, *Extracts from an Account of Russia in 1767*, published by Sir John Barrow, Vol. 2 (London, 1868), p. 39.
9. Ibid. p. 36.
10. Ibid. p. 38.
11. Quoted in Jeremy Black, *British Diplomats and Diplomacy, 1688–1800* (Exeter, 2001), p. 132.
12. Ibid. p. 36.
13. Ibid.
14. David Horn, *Sir Charles Hanbury Williams and European Diplomacy, 1747–1758* (London, 1930), p. 22.
15. Ibid. p. 262.

16. Ibid. p. 263.
17. Macartney, op. cit. p. 29.
18. Horn, op. cit. p. 259.
19. James Harris, *Diaries and Correspondence of James Harris, First Earl of Malmesbury* (London, 1844), p. 458.
20. Black, op. cit. p. 35.
21. Antoine Pecquet, *Discours sur l'art de négocier* (Paris, 1737), pp. 33–7.
22. Ian Kelly, *Casanova: Actor, Spy, Lover, Priest* (London, 2008), p. 276.
23. James J. Kenney, 'Lord Whitworth and the Conspiracy Against Tsar Paul I', *Slavic Review* 36.2 (June 1977), pp. 205–19.
24. Horn, op. cit. p. 185.

6. THE LONG EIGHTEENTH CENTURY: WIDER RELATIONS

1. E. R. Dashkova, *The Memoirs of Princess Dashkov*, trans. and ed. Kyril Fitzlyon (London, 1958), pp. 148–9.
2. H. Montgomery Hyde, *The Empress Catherine and Princess Dashkov* (London, 1935), p. 148.
3. Horace Walpole, *Correspondence*, 48 vols. (New Haven, CT, 1938–83), vol. 24, p. 114.
4. Kurakin to Nikita Panin, quoted in Anthony Cross, *'By the Banks of the Thames': Russians in Eighteenth Century Britain* (Newtonville, MA, 1980), p. 251.
5. Simon Sebag Montefiore, *Prince of Princes: The Life of Potemkin* (London, 2000), p. 312.
6. Elizabeth Dimsdale, *An English Lady at the Court of Catherine the Great: The Journal of Baroness Elizabeth Dimsdale, 1781*, ed. A. G. Cross (Cambridge, 1989), pp. 39–40.
7. It was plundered by the Nazis in the Second World War and destroyed at Konigsburg close to the end of the war. A replica was constructed at Tsarskoe Selo between 1979 and 2003.
8. Dimsdale, op. cit. p. 57.
9. Anthony Cross, *St Petersburg and the British: The City Through the Eyes of British Visitors and Residents* (London, 2008), p. 34.
10. Anthony Cross, *By the Banks of the Neva: Chapters from the Lives and Careers of the British in Eighteenth-Century Russia* (Cambridge, 1997), p. 339.
11. Jane Rondeau (later Vigor), *Letters from a Lady, Who Resided Some Years in Russia, to Her Friend in England* (London, 1775).
12. Francesca Wilson, *Muscovy: Russia Through Foreign Eyes, 1553–1900* (London, 1970), p. 115.
13. Ibid. p. 119.
14. Ian R. Christie, *The Benthams in Russia, 1780–1791* (Oxford and Providence, RI, 1993), p. 232.

15. Quoted in Cross, *St Petersburg and the British*, op. cit. p. 101.
16. Betty Kemp, 'Sir Francis Dashwood's Diary of His Visit to St Petersburg in 1733', *Slavonic and East European Review* 38 (1959/60), pp. 194–222.
17. I. Vinogradoff, 'Russian Missions to London, 1711–1789: Further Extracts from the Cottrell Papers', *Oxford Slavonic Papers* (ns) 15 (1982).
18. Nathaniel Wraxall, *A Tour Round the Baltic thro' Northern Countries of Europe, Particularly Denmark, Sweden, Finland, Russia & Prussia* (1775; London, 1807 edition quoted), p. 229.
19. Ibid. pp. 280–1.
20. Ibid. pp. 286–7.
21. Dimsdale, op. cit. p. 66.
22. Sebag Montefore, op. cit. p. 289.
23. William Richardson, *Anecdotes of the Russian Empire in a Series of Letters Written, a Few Years Ago, from St Petersburg* (London, 1784), pp. 37–8.
24. Ibid. p. 197.
25. John Howard, *The State of Prisons in England and Wales, with Preliminary Observations, and Accounts of Some Foreign Prisons* (Warrington, 1777), pp. 77–8.
26. William Coxe, *Travels into Poland, Russia, Sweden, and Denmark*, 4 vols. (1784; 5th edition, London, 1802), vol. 2, p. 188.

7. THE WARS OF THE FRENCH REVOLUTION AND NAPOLEON, PART I: 1793–1807

1. In 1792 the Low Countries comprised the Southern Netherlands, the Austrian Netherlands, today's Belgium and, to the north, the Dutch Republic, the Republic of the Seven United Provinces, sometimes referred to as the United Provinces of the Netherlands. The head of this state was the stadholder William V, Prince of Orange. After conquest by France in 1795 he fled to Britain.
2. Derek McKay and Hamish Scott, *The Rise of the Great Powers, 1648–1815* (London, 1983), p. 284.
3. Hugh Ragsdale, ed., *Paul I: A Reassessment of His Life and Reign* (Pittsburgh, PA, 1979), pp. 24–6.
4. Earl Stanhope, *Life of the Right Honourable William Pitt*, 3rd edition, 4 vols. (London, 1867), vol. 2, p. 405.
5. F. Martens, *Recueil de traités et conventions conclu par la Russie avec les puissances étrangères* (St Petersburg, 1874–1909), vol. 9, p. 425.
6. Alfred Burne, *The Noble Duke of York* (London, 1949), p. 14.
7. James J. Kenney, 'The Politics of Assassination', in Ragsdale, op. cit. pp. 125–46.
8. TNA FO 65/46, Whitworth to Grenville, 18 March 1800.
9. *Morning Chronicle*, 11 and 25 October 1799.
10. N. K. Shilder, *Imperator Pavel I* (St Petersburg, 1897), p. 416.

11. Ibid. pp. 417–19.
12. Leonid I. Strakhovsky, *Alexander I of Russia* (London, 1949), p. 22.
13. James J. Kenney, 'Lord Whitworth and the Conspiracy Against Tsar Paul I', *Slavic Review* 36.2 (June 1977), pp. 205–19.
14. Quoted in Stanley Ayling, *George III* (London, 1972), p. 421.
15. AVPRI f. 133, op. 468, d. 932, Alexander I to George III, 2 May (os) 1801.
16. TNA FO 65/149, St Helens to Hawkesbury, 10 September 1801.
17. VPR 1, pp. 98–9.
18. AVPRI f. 133, op. 468, d. 6070, Alexander I to George III, 10 December (os) 1801.
19. Maurice Paléologue, *The Enigmatic Czar: The Life of Alexander I of Russia* (London, 1938), p. 31.
20. AVPRI f. 133, op. 468, d. 6070, [n.d.] 1804.
21. TNA FO 65/57, Leveson-Gower to Harrowby, 17 February 1805.
22. TNA FO 65/62, Douglas to Hawkesbury, 17 December 1806.
23. TNA FO 65/67, Douglas to Hawkesbury, 9 January 1807.
24. SIRIO 88, Protocol Conference, 14/26 January 1807.

8. THE WARS OF THE FRENCH REVOLUTION AND NAPOLEON, PART II: 1807–1815

1. N. K. Shilder, *Imperator Aleksandr I: Pervyi ego zhizn' i tsarstvovanie*, 4 vols. (St Petersburg, 1897–8), vol. 2, p. 186.
2. Grand Duke Nicholas, ed., *Scenes of Russian Court Life: Being the Correspondence of Alexander I with his Sister Catherine* (London, 1917), pp. 41–2.
3. *European*, August 1808.
4. *Morning Chronicle*, 10 December 1807.
5. TNA FO 30/29, Canning to Granville, 21 July 1807.
6. After a lifetime of living dangerously, d'Antraigues and his wife were murdered by his valet in Barnes in 1812.
7. George III, *The Later Correspondence of George III*, ed. A. Aspinall, 5 vols. (Cambridge, 1962–70), vol. 4, p. 624.
8. Ibid.
9. Paul W. Schroeder, *The Transformation of European Politics, 1763–1848* (Oxford, 1994), p. 331.
10. *The Later Correspondence of George III*, op. cit. pp. 655–6.
11. Lord Granville Leveson-Gower, 1st Earl Granville, *Private Correspondence, 1781–1821*, ed. Castalia Countess Granville, 2 vols. (London, 1916), vol. 1, p. 460.
12. Ibid. vol. 2, p. 130.
13. Ibid. vol. 1, p. 499.
14. Ibid. vol. 2, p. 6.
15. Ibid.

16. William Dalrymple, *Return of a King: The Battle for Afghanistan* (London, 2013), pp. 5–8.
17. *Correspondance de l'Empereur Alexandre I avec sa sœur la Grande duchesse Catherine, 1805–1818* (St Petersburg, 1910), p. 20.
18. Ibid. p. 259.
19. Allan Cunningham, 'Stratford Canning and the Treaty of Bucharest', in *Anglo-Ottoman Encounters in the Age of Revolution: Collected Essays*, Vol. 1 (London, 1993), p. 175.
20. Quoted in Alan Palmer, *Alexander I: Tsar of War and Peace* (London, 1974), p. 226.
21. AVPRI f. 133, op. 468, d. 6262, Alexander I to Prince Regent, 2 July 1812.
22. Ibid.
23. Ibid. Prince Regent to Alexander I, 11 July 1812.
24. Ibid.
25. Dominic Lieven, *Russia Against Napoleon: The Battle for Europe, 1807 to 1814* (London, 2009), p. 152.
26. AVPRI f. 133, op. 468, d. 5591, Lieven to Nesselrode, 4/16 January 1813.
27. Ibid. 21 January 1813.
28. Lieven, op. cit. p. 337.
29. Ibid. p. 295.
30. Ibid. p. 7.
31. Ibid. p. 337.
32. John Bew, *Castlereagh: Enlightenment, War and Tyranny* (London: Quercus, 2011), p. 327. For events from 1813 to 1815, Bew's analysis is first-class.
33. Lieven, op. cit. pp. 469–83.
34. Wendy Hinde, *Castlereagh* (London, 1981), p. 213.
35. Charles Webster, *The Foreign Policy of Castlereagh*, Vol. 1: *1812–1815* (London, 1931), p. 179.
36. Archduke Nicholas, ed., *Letters of the Grand Duchess Catherine* (London, 1916), p. 268.
37. Ibid.
38. AVPRI f. 133, op. 468, d. 6828, Lieven to Nesselrode, 5/17 February 1813.
39. *Letters of the Grand Duchess Catherine*, op. cit. p. 217.
40. AVPRI f. 133, op. 468, d. 6827, Duke of Clarence to the Emperor of Russia, 14 April 1814.
41. Ibid. The Emperor of Russia to the Duke of Clarence, 18 May 1814.
42. Roger Fulford, *George the Fourth* (London, 1949), p. 98.
43. John Gore, ed., *The Creevey Papers* (London, 1963), p. 116.
44. Joanna Richardson, *George IV: A Portrait* (London, 1966), p. 137.
45. Dorothea Lieven, *The Unpublished Diary and Political Sketches of Princess Lieven Together with Some of Her Letters*, ed. H. W. Temperley (London, 1925), pp. 242–3.

46. AVPRI f. 133, op. 468, d. 6848, Nesselrode to Lieven, 5/17 June 1815.
47. Ibid.
48. AVPRI f. 133, op. 468, d. 6506, The Emperor of Russia to the Prince Regent, 30 July 1816.
49. Webster, op. cit. pp. 197–8.
50. AVPRI f. 133, op. 468, d. 6845, Lieven to Nesselrode, 1/13 January 1815.
51. Ibid. J. J. Angerstein to Dmitri Guriev, 18/30 December 1814.
52. Ibid. Lieven to Nesselrode, 5/17 June 1815.
53. Adam Zamoyski, *Rites of Peace: The Fall of Napoleon and the Congress of Vienna* (London, 2007), p. 461.
54. Bew, op. cit. p. 411.
55. Quoted in Hinde, op. cit. p. 233.

9. THE NEW DIPLOMACY: 1815–1825

1. Charles Webster, *The Foreign Policy of Castlereagh*, Vol. 2: *1815–1822* (London, 1934), p. 56.
2. Ibid. pp. 56–7.
3. Ibid. pp. 511–12.
4. Wendy Hinde, *Castlereagh* (London, 1981), p. 269.
5. AVPRI f. 133, op. 468, d. 6857, Lieven to Nesselrode, 6 February (ns) 1816.
6. Ibid.
7. Ibid.
8. TNA FO 65/100, Castlereagh to Cathcart, 1 July 1816.
9. Webster, op. cit. p. 99.
10. TNA FO 95/232, Walpole to Castlereagh, 21 May 1814.
11. TNA FO 65/104, Nesselrode to Cathcart, 27 June 1816 (ns).
12. Webster, op. cit. p. 164.
13. AVPRI f. 133, op. 468, d. 6855, Lieven to Nesselrode, 6 July 1816 (ns).
14. Ibid.
15. Ibid.
16. AVPRI f. 133, op. 468, d. 6567, Lieven to Nesselrode, 11 August 1816 (ns).
17. Ibid.
18. AVPRI f. 133, op. 468, d. 6632, Emperor of Russia to Duke of Kent, [n.d.] January 1819.
19. Ibid.
20. Ibid.
21. AVPRI f. 133, op. 468, d. 6599, Alexander to Duchess of Kent, 28 December 1818 (ns).
22. AVPRI f. 133, op. 468, d. 5423, Duke of Kent to Emperor of Russia, 25 June 1819.
23. Marquess of Crewe, *Lord Rosebery*, 2 vols. (London, 1931), vol. 2, p. 465.

24. From April 1821 he was Marquess of Londonderry, but it is usual to continue referring to him as Castlereagh.
25. Webster, op. cit. pp. 299–300.
26. John Bew, *Castlereagh: Enlightenment, War and Tyranny* (London, 2011), p. 505.
27. AVPRI f. 133, op. 468, d. 6920, Lieven to Nesselrode, 1/13 March 1823.
28. TNA FO 65/142, Canning to Lieven, 15 March 1824.
29. AVPRI f. 133, op. 468, d. 6933, Lieven to Nesselrode, 8/20 October 1824.
30. Ibid. Nesselrode to Lieven, 18/30 December 1824.
31. TNA FO 65/147, Canning to Stratford Canning, 26 February 1825.
32. Ibid.
33. TNA FO 30/29, Canning to Leveson-Gower, 11 March 1825.
34. Dorothea Lieven, *The Unpublished Diary and Political Sketches of Princess Lieven Together with Some of Her Letters*, ed. H. W. Temperley (London, 1925), pp. 95–6.
35. Ibid. pp. 96–7.
36. AVPRI f. 133, op. 468, d. 6941, Lieven to Nesselrode, 18/30 October 1825.
37. See Peter K. Christoff, *The Third Heart: Some Intellectual-Ideological Currents and Cross Currents in Russia, 1800–1830* (The Hague, 1970), for a full discussion.

10. NICHOLAS I

1. The official report, *Vosstanie Dekabristov*, was published in May 1826.
2. AVPRI f. 133, op. 468, d. 6956, Lieven to Nesselrode, 30 January/11 February 1826.
3. Shaun Walker, *The Long Hangover: Putin's New Russia and the Ghosts of the Past* (Oxford, 2018), p. 16.
4. See N. Riasanovsky, *Nicholas I and Official Nationality in Russia, 1825–1855* (Berkeley, CA 1959); T. Schiemann, *Geschichte Russlands unter Kaiser Nikolaus I* (Berlin, 1904); and Peter K. Christoff, *The Third Heart: Some Intellectual-Ideological Currents and Cross Currents in Russia, 1800–1830* (The Hague, 1970).
5. Quoted in Constantin de Grunwald, *Tsar Nicholas I*, trans. from the French by Brigit Patmore (London, 1954), p. vii.
6. Harold Temperley, *The Foreign Policy of Canning, 1822–1827* (London, 1925), p. 214.
7. Ibid. pp. 214–15.
8. TNA FO 65/149, Canning to Strangford, 17 December 1825.
9. TNA FO 65/156, Canning to Strangford, 10 February 1826.
10. TNA FO 65/156, Canning to Strangford, 4 March 1826.
11. TNA FO 65/153, Canning to Wellington, 10 February 1826.
12. Ibid.
13. Temperley, op. cit. p. 220.
14. S. Lane-Poole, *The Life of the Right Honourable Stratford Canning*, 2 vols. (London, 1888), vol. 1, p. 449.

15. Dorothea Lieven, *The Unpublished Diary and Political Sketches of Princess Lieven Together with Some of Her Letters*, ed. H. W. Temperley (London, 1925), pp. 130–1.
16. Sir Henry Bulwer Lytton, *The Life of Henry John Temple, Viscount Palmerston, with Selections from his Diaries and Correspondence*, 2 vols. (London, 1871), vol. 2, p. 37, 4 April 1828.
17. TNA FO 65/175, Dudley to Lieven, 25 March 1828.
18. VPR 3, Nesselrode to Lieven, 17/29 April 1828.
19. F. Martens, 'Étude historique sur la politique Russe dans la question d'Orient', *Revue de droit international et de législation comparée* 9 (1877), pp. 49–77.
20. V. I. Sheremet, *Russko-Turksaya Voina, 1828–1829* (Moscow, 2002).
21. AVPRI f. 133, op. 469I, d. 137, Nesselrode to Lieven, 30 April 1830.
22. TNA FO 65/180, Heytesbury to Aberdeen, 29 June 1829.
23. TNA FO 65/185, Heytesbury to Aberdeen, 11 March 1830.
24. Duke of Wellington, *Despatches, Correspondence, and Memoranda of Field-Marshal Arthur Duke of Wellington*, 8 vols. (London, 1867–80), vol. 6, p. 302. Britain supported Duke Charles of Mecklenburg Strelitz.
25. Ibid. p. 426, George IV to Wellington, 19 January 1830.
26. AVPRI f. 133, op. 469I, d. 121, Lieven to Nesselrode, 15/27 January 1830.
27. Ibid.
28. AVPRI f. 133, op. 469I, d. 137, Nesselrode to Lieven, 15 March 1830.
29. SIRIO 130, p. 36, Nicholas I to Grand Duke Constantine, 6/18 August 1830.
30. Ibid.
31. Dorothea Lieven, *Letters of Dorothea, Princess Lieven, During her Residence in London, 1812–1834*, ed. Lionel Robinson (London, 1902), pp. 33–45.
32. Quoted in Grunwald, op. cit. pp. 111–12.
33. Quoted in R. F. Leslie, *Polish Politics and the Revolution of November 1830* (London, 1956), p. 123. See also Anita Prazmowska, *Poland: A Modern History* (London, 2010), pp. 14–16.
34. SIRIO 132, p. 69, Nicholas I to the Grand Duke Constantine, 8 December 1830.
35. TNA FO 181/84, Palmerston to Heytesbury, 21 March 1831.
36. *Morning Post*, 1 January 1831.
37. *The Times*, 23 December 1830 and 25 January 1831.
38. Ibid. 20 July 1831.
39. Ibid. 17 September 1831.
40. The full list is found in AVPRI f. 133, op. 469I, d. 134a, 7/19 June 1832.
41. *The Times*, 7 January 1832.

11. THE EASTERN QUESTION

1. David Brown, *Palmerston: A Biography* (New Haven, CT, 2010), p. 147.

2. TNA FO 65/200, Palmerston to Durham, 3 July 1832.
3. TNA FO 78/220, Palmerston to Ponsonby, 7 August 1833.
4. Quoted in Charles Webster, *The Foreign Policy of Palmerston, 1830–1841*, 2 vols. (London, 1951), vol. 1, p. 305.
5. Quoted in Jasper Ridley, *Lord Palmerston* (London, 1970), p. 160.
6. Brown, op. cit. p. 131.
7. *Hansard*, House of Commons, 9 July 1833, vol. 19, 437.
8. Sir Henry Lytton Bulwer, *The Life of Henry John Temple, Viscount Palmerston, with Selections from his Diaries and Correspondence*, 2 vols. (London, 1871), vol. 2, p. 199.
9. Ibid. p. 207.
10. *The Times*, 16 March 1835.
11. TNA FO 65/225, Durham to Palmerston, 8 July 1836.
12. TNA FO 65/223, Durham to Palmerston, 3 March 1836.
13. As a result of Vitus Bering and Alexei Chirikov's expedition in the 1730s, Chirikov had established a Russian colony on the west coast of North America in 1741. This became incorporated into the Russian empire in 1799 and the Russian American Company created to administer the territory, plus a monopoly on the lucrative fur trade.
14. The Russo-Circassian War effectively began in 1763 when the Russians began establishing forts to be used as springboards for conquest in the Caucasus. See Oliver Bullough, *Let Our Fame Be Great: Journeys Among the Defiant People of the Caucasus* (London, 2010).
15. TNA FO 65/223, Durham to Palmerston, 19 March 1836; AVPRI f. 133, op. 469, d. 86, Nesselrode to Durham, 9 June 1836.
16. TNA FO 65/225, Durham to Palmerston, 11 August 1836.
17. AVPRI f. 133, op. 469, d. 84, Pozzo di Borgo to Nesselrode, 4 January 1837.
18. TNA FO 65/233, Durham to Palmerston, 12 January 1837.
19. TNA FO 65/251, Clanricarde to Palmerston, 27 January 1839.
20. Ibid. Clanricarde to Palmerston, 17 April 1839.
21. Quoted in Elizabeth Longford, *Victoria R.I.* (London, 1964), p. 116.
22. Viscount Esher, ed., *The Girlhood of Queen Victoria: A Selection of Her Majesty's Diaries Between the Years 1832 and 1840*, 2 vols. (London, 1912), vol. 2, pp. 156 and 158.
23. Ibid. p. 188.
24. Ibid.
25. Ibid. pp. 189–90.
26. Ibid. Palmerston to Clanricarde, 30 April 1839.
27. F. Martens, *Recueil de traités et conventions conclu par la Russie avec les puissances étrangères*, 15 vols. (St Petersburg, 1874–1909), vol. 12, p. 114, Brunnov to Nesselrode, 12/24 September 1839.
28. TNA FO 65/260, Clanricarde to Palmerston, 11 February 1840.

29. Martens, op. cit. vol. 12, p. 125.
30. TNA FO 356/29, Bloomfield to Palmerston, 8 August 1840.
31. Ibid. Palmerston to Bloomfield, 14 August 1840.
32. A. C. Benson and Viscount Esher, eds., *The Letters of Queen Victoria, 1837–1861*, 1st series, 3 vols. (London, 1908), vol. 1, pp. 288–9, King Leopold I to Queen Victoria, 22 September 1840.
33. Ibid. pp. 289–90.
34. Ibid. pp. 311–12, Palmerston Memorandum for the Queen, 11 November 1840.
35. E. Jones Parry, ed., *The Correspondence of Lord Aberdeen and Princess Lieven, 1832–1854*, 2 vols. (London, 1938), vol. 1, p. 18.
36. AVPRI f. 133, op. 469, d. 111, Brunnov to Nesselrode, 7/19 January 1841.
37. AVPRI f. 133, op. 469, d. 114, Brunnov to Nesselrode, 22 October/3 November 1841.
38. *The Times*, 1 May 1841.

12. PERSIA AND AFGHANISTAN

1. TNA FO 60/29, Canning to Wynn, 9 October 1826.
2. Karl E. Meyer and Shareen Blair Brysac, *Tournament of Shadows: The Great Game and the Race for Empire in Central Asia* (London, 2001). A lively and well-documented account of the Great Game.
3. AVPRI f. 133, op. 469, d. 27, Nesselrode to Pozzo di Borgo, 21 December 1835. Count Carlo Pozzo di Borgo was a Corsican friend of Napoleon I who broke with him and later came to England. He became Russian ambassador to France, then Britain.
4. Quoted in Charles Webster, *The Foreign Policy of Palmerston, 1830–1841*, 2 vols. (London, 1951), vol. 2, pp. 842–43.
5. AVPRI f. 133, op. 469, d. 23, Pozzo di Borgo to Nesselrode, 5 May 1837.
6. Webster, op. cit. vol. 2, p. 746.
7. OIOC L/P&S/5/586 vol. 13, p. 88, Secret Committee to Auckland, 25 June 1836.
8. Quoted in William Dalrymple, *Return of a King: The Battle for Afghanistan* (London, 2013), p. 120.
9. An excellent novel set in this period in Afghanistan is Philip Hensher's *The Mulberry Empire* (London, 2003), in which Burnes and Vitevich figure large.
10. AVPRI f. 133, op. 469, d. 129, Pozzo di Borgo to Nesselrode, 24 July 1838.
11. Philip E. Mosely, 'Russian Policy in Asia, 1838–9', *Slavonic Review* 14 (1936), pp. 670–81.
12. AVPRI f. 133, op. 470, d. 60, Brunnov to Westermann, 12/24 September 1872.
13. Quoted in William Habberton, *Anglo-Russian Relations Concerning Afghanistan, 1837–1907* (Urbana, IL, 1937), p. 20.

14. Quoted in Michael Edwardes, *Playing the Great Game* (London, 1975), p. 65. For a full account of the Khiva campaign, see Alexander Morrison, *The Russian Conquest of Central Asia* (Cambridge, 2020).
15. TNA FO 65/258, Palmerston to Clanricarde, 24 March 1840.
16. Lieutenant Arthur Conolly, *Journey to the North of India, Overland from England, Through Russia, Persia and Afghanistan*, 2 vols. (London, 1838).
17. Some attribute the first use to Sir Henry Rawlinson.
18. AVPRI f. 133, op. 469, d. 115, Brunnov to Nesselrode, 21 December 1841.
19. Quoted in Webster, op. cit. vol. 2, pp. 738–9, Palmerston to Hobhouse, 14 February 1840.

13. A FRAGILE FRIENDSHIP

1. Baron E. Stockmar, *Memoirs of Baron Stockmar by his Son Baron E. Stockmar*, 2 vols. (London, 1872), vol. 2, pp. 101–2.
2. A. C. Benson and Viscount Esher, eds., *The Letters of Queen Victoria, 1837–1861*, 1st series, 3 vols. (London, 1908), vol. 2, p. 14, Queen Victoria to King Leopold, 11 June 1844.
3. Royal Archives, Windsor Castle (hereafter RA): RA VIC/MAIN/QVR/1844, Emperor of Russia's Visit, 1 June 1844.
4. Ibid.
5. Benson and Esher, eds., *Letters*, 1st series, op. cit. vol. 1, pp. 17–18, Queen Victoria to King Leopold, 11 June 1844.
6. RA VIC/MAIN/QVR/1844, Emperor of Russia's Visit, 2 June 1844.
7. Ibid.
8. Benson and Esher, eds., *Letters*, 1st series, op. cit. vol. 1, p. 14, Queen Victoria to King Leopold, 4 June 1844.
9. Ibid. pp. 14–15.
10. Ibid. p. 16.
11. Ibid.
12. Ibid. pp. 16–17.
13. Stockmar, op. cit. pp. 106–7.
14. Ibid. pp. 108–9.
15. Ibid. pp. 109–10.
16. TNA FO 65/307, Nesselrode Memorandum, Brunnov to Aberdeen, 26 November 1844.
17. Ibid.
18. AVPRI f. 133, op. 469, d. 89, Peel to Brunnov, 8 May 1845.
19. *Journal de St Petersbourg*, 22 April 1843.
20. TNA FO 65/300, Bloomfield to Aberdeen, 21 September 1844.
21. AVPRI f. 133, op. 469, d. 63, Buchanan to Nesselrode, 19 March 1845.
22. Ibid.

23. AVPRI f. 133, op. 469, d. 91, Nesselrode to Brunnov, 19 May 1845.
24. Bruce Lincoln, *Nicholas I: Emperor and Autocrat of All the Russias* (1978; DeKalb, IL, 1989), pp. 280–1.
25. TNA FO 65/343, Palmerston to Bloomfield, 18 March 1848.
26. TNA FO 65/344, Palmerston to Bloomfield, 14 April 1848.
27. TNA FO 65/345, Palmerston to Bloomfield, 2 September 1848.
28. AVPRI f. 133, op. 469, d. 107, Brunnov to Nesselrode, 29 April/11 May 1849 and ciphered telegram, Brunnov to St Petersburg, 2/14 May 1849.
29. AVPRI f. 133, op. 469, d. 107, Nesselrode to Brunnov, 17/29 May 1849.
30. AVPRI f. 133, op. 469, d. 108, Brunnov to Nesselrode, 17/29 December 1849.
31. Ibid.

14. TOWARDS CRIMEA

1. AVPRI f. 133, op. 469, d. 72, Nesselrode to Brunnov, 7 February 1850.
2. Ibid.
3. AVPRI f. 133, op. 469, d. 69, Brunnov to Nesselrode, 20 February 1850.
4. Ibid. Brunnov to Nesselrode, 21 February 1850.
5. AVPRI f. 133, op. 469, d. 72, Nesselrode to Brunnov, 7 March 1850.
6. *Hansard*, House of Commons, 25 June 1850, vol. 112 [3rd series], 380–444.
7. Metternich retired to Richmond upon Thames and Guizot and Princess Lieven to South Kensington.
8. AVPRI f. 133, op. 469, d. 76, Brunnov to Nesselrode, 19 December 1851.
9. Ibid.
10. AVPRI f. 133, op. 469, d. 78, Brunnov to Nesselrode, 19 August 1852.
11. AVPRI f. 133, op. 469, d. 76, Nesselrode to Brunnov, 2 January 1853.
12. Kenneth Bourne, *The Foreign Policy of Victorian England, 1830–1902* (Oxford, 1970), p. 316.
13. A. C. Benson and Viscount Esher, eds., *The Letters of Queen Victoria, 1837–1861*, 1st series, 3 vols. (London, 1908), vol. 2, pp. 531–2, The Earl of Aberdeen to Queen Victoria, 8 February 1853.
14. Many of Brunnov's dispatches during January and February were published by H. E. Howard in 'Brunnov's Reports on Aberdeen', *Cambridge Historical Journal* 4 (1934), pp. 312–21.
15. Orlando Figes, *Crimea: The Last Crusade* (London, 2010), p. 108.
16. AVPRI f. 133, op. 469, d. 73, Brunnov to Nesselrode, 14 January 1853.
17. David M. Goldfrank, *The Origins of the Crimean War* (London, 1994), p. 153.
18. AVPRI f. 133, op. 469, d. 76, Note of Nesselrode for a dispatch to London, 20 May 1853.
19. Quoted in Figes, op. cit. p. 114, from A. Zaionchkovski, *Vostochnais voina, 1853–1856*, 3 vols. (St Petersburg, 2002), vol. 1, p. 739.

20. AVPRI f. 133, op. 469, d. 75, Brunnov to Nesselrode, 14 September 1853.
21. Figes, op. cit. p. 136.
22. AVPRI f. 133, op. 469, d. 76, Private letter from Nesselrode to Brunnov, 16 November 1953.
23. Ibid. Nesselrode to Brunnov, 28 November 1853.
24. Quoted in Muriel Chamberlain, *Lord Aberdeen: A Political Biography* (London, 1983), p. 490. For detailed analysis of press influence, see Kingsley Martin, *The Triumph of Lord Palmerston: A Study of Public Opinion in England Before the Crimean War* (London, 1963).
25. AVPRI f. 133, op. 469, d. 49, Nicholas I to Queen Victoria, 4 December 1953.
26. RA VIC/MAIN/J/2/8, Queen Victoria, 5 April 1853.

15. WAR

1. RA VIC/MAIN/Y/99/12, Queen Victoria, 31 March 1854.
2. Orlando Figes, *Crimea: The Last Crusade* (London, 2010), p. 252.
3. Hugh Small, *The Crimean War: Queen Victoria's War with the Russian Tsars* (Stroud, 2007), p. 87.
4. RA VIC/MAIN/Y/99, Queen Victoria's Journal, December 1854.
5. A. C. Benson and Viscount Esher, eds., *The Letters of Queen Victoria, 1837–1861*, 1st series, 3 vols. (London, 1908), vol. 3, p. 141, Sir Ralph Abercromby to Queen Victoria, 2 March 1855.
6. Figes, op. cit. p. 322.
7. Benson and Esher, eds., *Letters*, 1st series, op. cit. vol. 3, pp. 141–2, Viscount Palmerston to Queen Victoria, 2 March 1855.
8. Ibid. p. 143, Queen Victoria to Princess of Prussia, 4 March 1855.
9. E. Ashley, ed., *The Life and Correspondence of Henry John Temple, Viscount Palmerston*, 2 vols. (London, 1879), vol. 2, p. 100.
10. For the full terms of the Treaty of Paris, see Michael Hurst, ed., *Key Treaties for the Great Powers, 1814–1914*, 2 vols. (Newton Abbot, 1972), vol. 1, p. 252.
11. W. E. Mosse, *The Rise and Fall of the Crimean System, 1855–71* (London, 1963), p. 33.
12. Sir Horace Rumbold, *Recollections of a Diplomatist*, 2 vols. (London, 1902), vol. 2, p. 242.
13. Ibid. p. 243.
14. AVPRI f. 133, op. 469II, d. 8, December 1856.
15. Herbert Maxwell, *The Life and Letters of George William Frederick, Fourth Earl of Clarendon*, 2 vols. (London, 1913), vol. 2, p. 133.
16. Benson and Esher, eds., *Letters*, 1st series, op. cit. vol. 3, p. 260, Earl Granville to Queen Victoria, 30 August 1856.
17. Edmond Fitzmaurice, *Life of Granville George Leveson Gower, Second Earl Granville, K.G.*, 2 vols. (London, 1905), vol. 1, p. 190.

18. Benson and Esher, eds., *Letters*, 1st series, op. cit. vol. 3, pp. 258–9, Earl Granville to Queen Victoria, 30 August 1856.
19. Fitzmaurice, op. cit. p. 190.
20. Ibid. p. 202.
21. Ibid. p. 205.
22. Ibid. p. 216.
23. Ibid. p. 201.
24. Ibid. p. 213.
25. François Charles-Roux, *Alexandre II, Gortchakoff et Napoléon III* (Paris, 1913), p. 50.
26. Ibid. p. 149.
27. AVPRI f. 133, op. 469 II, d. 72, Chreptowicz to Gorchakov, 3 November 1856.

16. RUSSIA IS NOT SULKING: SHE IS CONSOLIDATING

1. The title of this chapter is taken from Gabriel Hanotaux, *Histoire de la France contemporaine, 1871–1900*, 4 vols. (Paris, 1903–8), vol. 3, p. 93: 'La Russie ne boude pas: elle se recueille.' Hanotaux claims to have heard Count Peter Shuvalov repeating the comment of Gorchakov.
2. AVPRI f. 133, op. 469, d. 100, Gorchakov to Brunnov, 17 January 1859.
3. AVPRI f. 133, op. 469, d. 98, Brunnov to Gorchakov, 9/21 April 1859.
4. Ibid. Gorchakov to Brunnov, 7 January 1860.
5. A. C. Benson and Viscount Esher, eds., *The Letters of Queen Victoria, 1837–1861*, 1st series, 3 vols. (London, 1908), vol. 3, p. 260, Earl Granville to Queen Victoria, 30 August 1856.
6. Ibid.
7. W. E. Mosse, *Alexander II and the Modernization of Russia* (London, 1992), pp. 83–106; Orlando Figes, *The Story of Russia* (London, 2022), pp. 154–60.
8. Mosse, op. cit. p. 108.
9. AVPRI f. 133, op. 469, d. 88, Note, 30 June/12 July 1861.
10. AVPRI f. 133, op. 469, d. 107, Note, 2/14 July 1860.
11. AVPRI f. 133, op. 469, d. 88, Brunnov to Gorchakov, 4/16 February 1861.
12. AVPRI f. 133, op. 469, Note, 23 February 1861.
13. Ibid.
14. Rosamund Bartlett, *Tolstoy: A Russian Life* (London, 2010), pp. 142–3.
15. Edward H. Carr, *The Romantic Exiles* (London, 1933), p. 216.
16. George E. Buckle, ed., *The Letters of Queen Victoria, 1862–1885*, 2nd series, 2 vols. (London, 1926–8), vol. 1, p. 66, Queen Victoria to Earl Granville, Queen Victoria to Earl Granville, 23 February 1863.
17. Ibid. p. 84, Earl Russell to Queen Victoria, 15 May 1863.
18. AVPRI f. 133, op. 469II, d. 86, Brunnov to Gorchakov, 12 May 1863.
19. Ibid. Fond Secret 1863–4, April 1864, p. 463.

20. W. F. Monypenny and George E. Buckle, *The Life of Benjamin Disraeli, Earl of Beaconsfield*, 6 vols. (London, 1910–20), vol. 5, p. 336.
21. Ibid. pp. 336–40.
22. RA VIC/MAIN/H/41, Note for the Queen, 14 April 1864.
23. AVPRI f. 133, op. 469II, d. 79, Brunnov to Gorchakov, 5/17 August 1864.
24. Buckle, ed., *Letters*, 2nd series, op. cit. vol. 1, p. 48, Memorandum of Queen Victoria, 25 November 1862.
25. As the Prince of Wales would become the British sovereign, he could not also succeed to the Duchy of Coburg.
26. AVPRI f. 133, op. 469II, d. 73, Russell to Brunnov, 27 November 1862.
27. Monypenny and Buckle, op. cit. vol. 4, p. 339.
28. There is an excellent account in Jonathan Steinberg, *Bismarck: A Life* (Oxford, 2011), pp. 210–26.
29. This harks back to relations in the eighteenth century.
30. TNA FO 356/32, Russell to Bloomfield, 23 December 1863.
31. The German Confederation was a loose association of states created by the Congress of Vienna to coordinate the economies of separate German-speaking countries. It was briefly dissolved after the revolutions of 1848, but re-established in 1850.
32. AVPRI f. 133, op. 469II, d. 128, Gorchakov to Brunnov, 14 August 1866.
33. The overthrow of the hospodar of the Principalities in 1866 is treated in Chapter 18 on the Eastern Question.
34. Steinberg, op. cit. p. 257.
35. AVPRI f. 133, op. 469II, d. 88, Note of Alexander II, 7/19 February 1861.
36. AVPRI f. 133, op. 469II, d. 67, Queen Victoria to Alexander II, 28 April 1865.
37. Buckle, ed., *Letters*, 2nd series, op. cit. vol. 1, p. 369, Queen Victoria to the Prince of Wales, 16 October 1866.
38. AVPRI f. 133, op. 469II, d. 127, Brunnov to Gorchakov, 7/19 October 1866.
39. Buckle, ed., *Letters*, 2nd series, op. cit. vol. 1, p. 369, Earl of Derby to Queen Victoria, 10 October 1866.
40. AVPRI f. 133, op. 469II, d. 127, Brunnov to Gorchakov, 5/17 December 1866.
41. Buckle, ed., *Letters*, 2nd series, op. cit. vol. 1, p. 428, Earl of Derby to Queen Victoria, 3 June 1867.
42. Ibid. p. 430.
43. F. R. Grahame, *Life of Alexander II: Emperor of All the Russias* (London, 1883), p. 192.

17. MANIFEST DESTINY IN CENTRAL ASIA

1. Alexander Morrison, *The Russian Conquest of Central Asia* (Cambridge, 2020), p. 113.

2. H. Sutherland Edwards, *Russian Projects Against India: From the Czar Peter to General Skobeleff* (London, 1885), p. 267.
3. Ibid. pp. 262–3.
4. The expression 'Manifest Destiny' originated in the United States, explaining the movement westwards.
5. Quoted in Milan Hauner, *What Is Asia to Us? Russia's Asian Heartland, Yesterday and Today* (London, 1990), p. 39.
6. Nicholas Khalfin, *Russia's Policy in Central Asia, 1857–1868* (London, 1964).
7. Quoted in Gerald Morgan, *Anglo-Russian Rivalry in Central Asia, 1810–1895* (London, 1981), p. 96.
8. AVPRI f. 133, op. 469, d. 106, Brunnov to Gorchakov, 23 April/5 May 1860.
9. *Daily Telegraph*, 9 November 1872.
10. A. C. Benson and Viscount Esher, eds., *The Letters of Queen Victoria, 1837–1861*, 1st series, 3 vols. (London, 1908), vol. 3, p. 286, Viscount Palmerston to the Queen, 13 January 1857.
11. Colin Thubron, *The Amur River: Between Russia and China* (London, 2021), pp. 108–10.
12. Khalfin, op. cit. p. 29.
13. Quoted in Morgan, op. cit. p. 93.
14. Letter of Dr Beryl Williams to the author, November 2018. Alex Marshall, *The Russian General Staff and Asia, 1800–1917* (London, 2006), pp. 131–58.
15. Viktor Lopatnikov, *Gorchakov: Vremya i sluzhenie* (Moscow, 2011), p. 13.
16. David MacKenzie, 'The Conquest and Administration of Turkestan, 1860–85', in Michael Rywkin, ed., *Russian Colonial Expansion to 1917* (London, 1988), p. 216.
17. P. A. Valuev (1815–1890), *Dnevnik P. A. Valueva*, 2 vols. (Moscow, 1961), vol. 2, pp. 60ff.
18. Ibid. p. 217.
19. After the Indian Rebellion (Mutiny) and control of India by the British government, the Indian government was headed by a viceroy: the Raj was created.
20. Henry Rawlinson, 'The Russians in Central Asia', reprinted in *England and Russia in the East* (London, 1875), chapter 3.
21. AVPRI f. 133, op. 469II, d. 101, Russell to Brunnov, 16 September 1865.
22. *Morning Herald*, 15 December 1865.
23. Quoted in MacKenzie, op. cit. p. 220.
24. Quoted in Habberton, op. cit. pp. 23–4.
25. Ibid. p. 24.
26. AVPRI f. 133, op. 469II, d. 70, Brunnov to Gorchakov, 2 February 1869.
27. Clarendon to Buchanan, 27 March 1869, quoted in Edmond Fitzmaurice, *Life of Granville George Leveson-Gower, Second Earl Granville, K.G.*, 2 vols. (London, 1905), vol. 2, pp. 407–8.
28. Habberton, op. cit. p. 24.

29. George Villiers, *A Vanished Victorian, Being the Life of George Villiers, Fourth Earl of Clarendon, 1800–1870* (London, 1938), p. 361.
30. AVPRI f. 133, op. 470, d. 75, Gorchakov to Brunnov, 1/13 November 1871, quoted in part as an appendix in Lord Augustus Loftus, *The Diplomatic Reminiscences of Lord Augustus Loftus, 1862–1879*, 2nd series, 2 vols. (London, 1894), vol. 2, p. 283. The full Russian position from 1869 to 1872 is set out in AVPRI f. 133, op. 470, d. 61, Affaires d'Asie Frontieres.
31. AVPRI f. 133, op. 470, d. 61, Affaires d'Asie Frontieres.
32. AVPRI f. 133, op. 470, d. 66II, Gorchakov to Brunnov, 3 December 1871.
33. *Daily Telegraph*, 17 October 1872.
34. *Kaufmanski Sbornik* (Moscow, 1910), vols. 75–76. Morrison, op. cit. pp. 356–62.
35. Supposedly to negotiate the marriage of Alexander II's daughter Marie to Queen Victoria's second son.
36. AVPRI f. 133, op. 470, d. 60, Brunnov to Gorchakov, 24 November/6 December 1872.
37. Loftus, op. cit. p. 97; B. H. Sumner, *Russia and the Balkans, 1870–1880* (London, 1962), p. 28. Brunnov died in 1875.
38. RA VIC/MAIN/H/41/105, Granville Memorandum for the Queen, 25 November 1873.
39. Ibid.
40. AVPRI f. 133, op. 470, d. 85, Shuvalov to Westmann, 15/27 October 1874.
41. RA VIC/MAIN/H/42/47, Lord Odo Russell to the Earl of Derby. Conversation with the Czar, 12 May 1875.

18. THE END OF THE CRIMEAN SYSTEM

1. Stéphanie Burgaud, '1866: Why the Russian Bomb Did Not Explode', *International History Review* 40.2 (2017), pp. 253–72. This article claims that Gorchakov's attempt to abrogate the Black Sea clauses of 1856 marked an explosive change of Russian policy. This is ridiculous. It was known throughout Europe from 1856 that this was a major aim of Russian policy and only a question of when an opportunity arose that would enable Russia to free herself from the trammels of the Treaty of Paris.
2. W. A. Fletcher, *The Mission of Vincent Benedetti to Berlin, 1864–1870* (The Hague, 1965), p. 248.
3. TNA FO 65/802, Buchanan to Clarendon, 16 June 1870.
4. John Morley, *The Life of William Ewart Gladstone, 1809–1872*, 2 vols. (London, 1905), vol. 1, p. 983.
5. Ibid.
6. Ibid. p. 984.
7. Serge Gorianov, *Le Bosphore et les Dardanelles* (Paris, 1910), p. 156.

8. TNA FO 65/805, Granville to Buchanan, 10 November 1870.
9. Morley, op. cit. p. 985.
10. Ibid. pp. 984–5.
11. Ibid. p. 985.
12. AVPRI f. 133, op. 470, d. 83, Brunnov to Gorchakov, 11/23 November 1870.
13. AVPRI f. 133, op. 470, d. 82, Brunnov to Gorchakov, 7/19 November 1870.
14. AVPRI f. 133, op. 470, d. 85, Gorchakov to Brunnov, 24 November 1870.
15. AVPRI f. 133, op. 470, d. 68, Telegram from Brunnov to St Petersburg, 18/30 January 1871.
16. TNA FO 65/820, Rumbold to Granville, 19 March 1871.
17. Quoted in Giles St Aubyn, *Edward VII: Prince and King* (London, 1979), p. 290.
18. Ibid.
19. George E. Buckle, ed., *The Letters of Queen Victoria, 1862–1885*, 2nd series, 2 vols. (London, 1926–8), vol. 2, p. 132, Earl Granville to Queen Victoria, 14 May 1871.
20. AVPRI f. 133, op. 470, d. 68, Gorchakov to Brunnov, 21 December 1873.
21. St Aubyn, op. cit. p. 291. Alfred became Duke of Saxe-Coburg in 1893. He died in 1900. Marie died in Zurich in 1920. Their only son committed suicide in 1897, while their daughters went on to become some of most colourful members of European royalty.
22. Buckle, ed., *Letters*, 2nd series, op. cit. vol. 2, pp. 328–9, Extract from the Queen's Journal, 7 March 1874.
23. Ibid. p. 336, Extract from the Queen's Journal, 13 May 1874.
24. Ibid. p. 338.
25. F. R. Grahame, *Life of Alexander II: Emperor of All the Russias* (London, 1883), p. 229.

19. WAR IN THE NEAR EAST

1. Peter K. Christoff, *An Introduction to Nineteenth-Century Russian Slavophilism* (Boulder, CO, 1991), for a full discussion.
2. Feroze A. K. Yasamee, 'European Equilibrium or Asiatic Balance of Power?', in M. Hakan Yavuz with Peter Sluglett, eds., *War and Diplomacy: The Russo-Turkish War of 1877–1878 and the Treaty of Berlin* (Salt Lake City, UT, 2011). Yasamee advances the unsubstantiated claim that Russia's ultimate ambition was to wrest control of India from Britain. This collection of essays takes an Islamic view of events from 1877 to 1878. Unfortunately, the various authors' necessary knowledge of European diplomatic history is woefully lacking.
3. W. F. Monypenny and George E. Buckle, *The Life of Benjamin Disraeli, Earl of Beaconsfield*, 6 vols. (London, 1910–20), vol. 6, p. 14, Disraeli to Lady Bradford, 3 November 1875.
4. George Buckle, ed., *The Letters of Queen Victoria, 1862–1885*, 2nd series, 2 vols. (London, 1926–8), vol. 2, p. 465, Ponsonby to Derby, 18 June 1876.

5. R. W. Seton-Watson, *Disraeli, Gladstone and the Eastern Question* (London, 1935), p. 41.
6. Ibid.
7. Ibid.
8. AVPRI f. 133, op. 470, d. 78, Telegram from Shuvalov, 15/27 June 1876.
9. Ibid. Shuvalov to Alexander II, 19 June/1 July 1876.
10. AVPRI f. 133, op. 470, d. 80, Shuvalov to Lady Derby, November 1876.
11. Ibid. Shuvalov to Alexander II, 2/14 November 1876.
12. Ibid. Shuvalov to Alexander II, 7/19 October 1876.
13. See Richard Shannon, *Gladstone and the Bulgarian Agitation, 1876* (London, 1963), for a full analysis.
14. Quoted in Philip Magnus, *Gladstone: A Biography* (London, 1963), p. 243.
15. Ibid.
16. Monypenny and Buckle, op. cit. vol. 6, p. 60, Beaconsfield to Derby, 8 September 1876.
17. Giles St Aubyn, *Edward VII: Prince and King* (London, 1979), p. 292.
18. AVPRI f. 133, op. 470, d. 80, Shuvalov to Alexander II, 10/22 December 1876.
19. Andrew Roberts, *Salisbury: Victorian Titan* (London, 1999), pp. 154–68.
20. Ibid.
21. Ibid. p. 160.
22. Monypenny and Buckle, op. cit. vol. 6, p. 111, Disraeli to Derby, 28 December 1876.
23. Quoted in B. H. Sumner, *Russia and the Balkans, 1870–1880* (London, 1962), pp. 251–2.
24. Ibid. p. 252.
25. Salisbury to Lady Derby, late February 1877, quoted in John Charmley, *Splendid Isolation? Britain and the Balance of Power, 1874–1914* (London, 1999), p. 70.
26. Monypenny and Buckle, op. cit. vol. 6, p. 128, Beaconsfield to Lady Bradford, 16 March 1877.
27. AVPRI f. 133, op. 470, d. 36, Decrypt of Wellesley to Derby, 24 January/5 February 1877.
28. AVPRI f. 133, op. 470, d. 35, Decrypt of Loftus to Derby, 14 April 1877. Original emphasis.
29. Frederick Wellesley, *Recollections of a Soldier-Diplomat* (London, 1948), p. 132.
30. AVPRI f. 133, op. 470, d. 70, Derby to Shuvalov, 20 June 1877.
31. Charles Lowe, *Alexander III of Russia* (London, 1895), p. 36.
32. Quoted in Count Egon Corti, *Prince Alexander von Battenberg* (London, 1954), p. 22.
33. AVPRI f. 133, op. 470, d. 81I, Note of Alexander II on telegram of Shuvalov to Gorchakov, 1/13 February 1878.
34. TNA FO 78/2766, Derby to Layard, 19 February 1878.

35. AVPRI f. 133, op. 470, d. 37, Note of Alexander II.
36. TNA FO 78/2766, Derby to Layard, 19 February 1878.
37. TNA FO 78/2810, Layard to Derby, 20 February 1878.
38. TNA FO 65/1049, Dufferin to Salisbury, 11/19 January 1879.
39. S. S. Tatishchev, *Imperator Aleksandr II, ego Zhizn i Tsarstvovanie*, 2 vols. (1903; Moscow, 1996), vol. 2, pp. 440–2.
40. R. Seton-Watson, ed., 'Unprinted Documents: Russo-British Relations During the Eastern Crisis', *Slavonic Review* 6 (1927–8), p. 433.

20. THE WAR WON: THE PEACE LOST

1. Quoted in Sarah Bradford, *Disraeli* (London, 1982). p. 347.
2. W. F. Monypenny and George E. Buckle, *The Life of Benjamin Disraeli, Earl of Beaconsfield*, 6 vols. (London, 1910–20), vol. 6, pp. 306–7, Beaconsfield to Queen Victoria, 31 May 1878.
3. R. W. Seton-Watson, *Disraeli, Gladstone and the Eastern Question* (London, 1935), p. 437.
4. Ibid. p. 348.
5. Ibid.
6. Lady Gwendolen Cecil, *Life of Robert, Marquis of Salisbury*, 2 vols. (London, 1921), vol. 2, pp. 280–1.
7. Prince Bernhard von Bülow, *Memoirs, 1849–1897*, 4 vols. (London, 1931), vol. 4, p. 443.
8. Seton-Watson, op. cit. p. 441.
9. W. N. Medlicott, 'Bismarck and Beaconsfield', in A. O. Sarkissian, ed., *Studies in Diplomatic History and Historiography in Honour of G. P. Gooch* (London, 1961), p. 250.
10. Monypenny and Buckle, op. cit. vol. 6, p. 324, Beaconsfield to Queen Victoria, 21 June 1878.
11. Quoted in Seton-Watson, op. cit. p. 436.
12. Ibid. p. 437.
13. Quoted in Bradford, op. cit. p. 352.
14. Quoted in Seton-Watson, op. cit. p. 503.
15. Quoted in John Charmley, *Splendid Isolation? Britain and the Balance of Power, 1874–1914* (London, 1999) p. 165.
16. Serge Gorianov, *La Question d'Orient à la veille du traité de Berlin, 1870–1878 d'après les archives Russes* (Paris, 1948), pp. 246 and 248.
17. The German theologian Friedrich Jacobi had used the word in the eighteenth century, but in a different context.
18. Andrew Williams's novel *To Kill a Tsar* (London, 2010), provides a vivid account of the revolutionary plots.
19. W. F. Mosse, *Alexander II and the Modernization of Russia* (London, 1992), p. 167.

20. Ibid.
21. TNA FO 65/1049, Plunkett to Salisbury, 6 December 1879.
22. S. S. Tatishchev, *Imperator Aleksandr II, ego Zhizn i Tsarstvovanie*, 2 vols. (1903; Moscow, 1996), vol. 2, pp. 636ff.
23. Charles Lowe, *Alexander III of Russia* (London, 1895), p. 46.
24. George E. Buckle, ed., *The Letters of Queen Victoria, 1862–1885*, 2nd series, 2 vols. (London, 1926–8), vol. 2, p. 202, The Queen's Journal, 13 March 1881.

21. DÉTENTE

1. AVPRI f. 133, op. 470, d. 65, Beaconsfield to Gorchakov, 6 February 1879.
2. Ibid. Gorchakov to Beaconsfield, 30 January/11 February 1879.
3. The Dowager Marchioness of Dufferin and Ava, *My Russian and Turkish Journals* (London, 1916), pp. 11–12.
4. Charles E. Drummond Black, *The Marquess of Dufferin and Ava, 1826–1902: Diplomatist, Viceroy, Statesman* (London, 1903), p. 170.
5. Dufferin, op. cit. p. 115.
6. Ibid. p. 113.
7. Ibid.
8. Jane Ridley, *Bertie: A Life of Edward VII* (London, 2012), p. 230.
9. AVPRI f. 133, op. 470, d. 61I, Lobanov to Giers, 9/21 January 1882.
10. *Novoe Vremya*, 21 September 1882.
11. *Journal de St Petersbourg*, 5 January 1883.
12. Ibid. 14 February 1883.
13. RA VIC/MAIN/H/44/83, Wolseley to the Queen, 24 May 1883.
14. Ibid.

22. THE POGROMS

1. Charles Lowe, *Alexander III of Russia* (London, 1895), p. 19.
2. Quoted in Henri Troyat, *Alexandre III: Le tsar des neiges* (Paris, 2004), p. 5.
3. Lowe, op. cit. p. 20.
4. Edmund de Waal, *The Hare with Amber Eyes* (London, 2010).
5. Dominic Lieven, ed., *British Documents on Foreign Affairs*, Part I, Series A, *Russia 1859–1914*, Vol. 2: *Russia, 1881–1905* (Frederick, MD, 1983), p. 3, Stanley to Granville, 28 May 1881.
6. Ibid. p. 1, Wyndham to Granville, 16 May 1881.
7. *London Illustrated News*, April 1881.
8. *British Documents on Foreign Affairs*, op. cit. p. 1.
9. Lowe, op. cit. p. 207.
10. Spasmodic pogroms continued until 1884.
11. *British Documents on Foreign Affairs*, op. cit. p. 29. Thornton to Granville, 25 January 1882.

12. *The Times*, February 1882.
13. Ibid.
14. Ibid.
15. Ibid.
16. AVPRI f. 133, op. 470. d. 63, Giers to Lobanov, 16 January 1882.
17. Ibid.
18. *Novoe Vremya*, 30 January 1882.
19. *Hansard*, House of Commons, 9 February 1882, vol. 266, 244.
20. See Sam Johnson, *Pogroms, Peasants, Jews: Britain and Eastern Europe's 'Jewish Question', 1867–1925* (London, 2011), for an excellent account of the pogroms.

23. THE PENDJEH INCIDENT

1. Chimkent, the city of Turkestan and Tashkent had been part of Kokand before the Russian conquest.
2. Alexander Morrison, *The Russian Conquest of Central Asia* (Cambridge, 2020), pp. 389–91. Khudayar Khan fled like so many others to British India and died in Peshawar in 1893.
3. Beryl Williams, 'Approach to the Second Afghan War: Central Asia During the Great Eastern Crisis, 1875–1878', *International History Review* 2.2 (January 1980), pp. 216–38.
4. Karl E. Meyer and Shareen Blair Brysac, *Tournament of Shadows: The Great Game and the Race for Empire in Central Asia* (London, 2001), p. 178.
5. Milan Hauner, *What Is Asia to Us? Russia's Asian Heartland, Yesterday and Today* (London, 1992), p. 81.
6. William Habberton, *Anglo-Russian Relations Concerning Afghanistan, 1837–1907* (Urbana, IL, 1937), p. 44n.
7. AVPRI f. 133, op. 470, d. 81II, Gorchakov to Shuvalov, 7 December 1878.
8. AVPRI f. 133, op. 470, d. 58, Disraeli to Gorchakov, Personal letter, 11 September 1878.
9. Meyer and Brysac, op. cit. p. 184.
10. W. F. Monypenny and George E. Buckle, *The Life of Benjamin Disraeli, Earl of Beaconsfield*, 6 vols. (London, 1910–20), vol. 6, p. 1254.
11. George E. Buckle, ed., *The Letters of Queen Victoria, 1862–1885*, 2nd series, 2 vols. (London, 1926–8), vol. 2, p. 641, Extract from the Queen's Journal, 6 October 1878.
12. AVPRI f. 133, op. 470, d. 78, Gorchakov to Shuvalov, 2 January 1879.
13. Ibid. Shuvalov to Gorchakov, 21 January 1879.
14. *The Times*, 8 February 1881.
15. *Daily Telegraph*, 8 February 1881.
16. *The Times*, 12 February 1881.
17. Lytton to Cranbrook, quoted in Martin Ewans, *Afghanistan: A New History* (Richmond, Surrey, 2001), p. 64.

18. AVPRI f. 133, op. 470, d. 78, Gorchakov to Shuvalov, 11 January 1879.
19. Ibid. Shuvalov to Gorchakov, 21 January 1879.
20. AVPRI f. 133, op. 470, d. 80I, Shuvalov to Giers, 27 November/9 December 1878.
21. Ibid. Gorchakov to Shuvalov, 7 December 1878.
22. Merv is today a UNESCO World Heritage Site. General Komarov conducted exploratory excavations in 1885 and published his collection of trophy artefacts in 1900.
23. D. A. Miliutin, *Dnevnik D. A. Miliutina, 1873–1882*, 4 vols. (Moscow, 1947–59), vol. 3, p. 224.
24. Quoted in Gerald Morgan, *Anglo-Russian Rivalry in Central Asia, 1810–1895* (London, 1981), p. 184.
25. Boris Akunin, *The Death of Achilles*, trans. A. Bromfield (London, 2005).
26. Feodor Dostoevsky, *Geok Tepe: Chto takoe Aziya dlya nas?* [Geok Tepe: What Does Asia Mean to Us?], January 1881, in Dostoevsky, *A Writer's Diary*, Vol. 2: *1877–1881*, trans. Kenneth Lantz (London, 1995), pp. 1368–78.
27. Quoted in Meyer and Brysac, op. cit. p. 197.
28. Ibid. p. 198.
29. Ibid. p. 199.
30. Edmond Fitzmaurice, *Life of Granville George Leveson-Gower, Second Earl Granville, K.G.*, 2 vols. (London, 1905), vol. 2, pp. 425–16.
31. Duke of Argyll, *Autobiography and Memoirs*, 2 vols. (London, 1906), vol. 2, pp. 370–1.
32. RA VIC/MAIN/H /45/4, Lord Granville, Note for the Queen, 19 February 1884.
33. Dondukov-Korsakov to Giers, 15 June 1884. Quoted in Baron Meyendorff, ed., *La Correspondance diplomatique de Monsieur de Staal*, 2 vols. (Paris, 1929), vol. 1, pp. 117–22.
34. RA VIC/MAIN/H/45/14, Kimberley to Ponsonby, 5 August 1884. Kimberley had served in the British embassy in St Petersburg in the late 1850s as Lord Wodehouse.
35. RA VIC/H/MAIN/H/45/12, Ponsonby to Kimberley, 6 August 1884.
36. AVPRI f. 133, op. 470, d. 61, Staal to Giers, 17 October 1884.
37. TNA FO 65/1212, Lumsden to Thomson for Granville, 26 November 1884.
38. TNA FO 65/1211, Lumsden to Thomson for Granville, 17 October 1884.
39. *Vedomosti*, 1 February 1885.
40. Quoted in Rose L. Greaves, *Persia and the Defence of India, 1884–1892* (London, 1959), p. 64.
41. AVPRI f. 133, op. 470, d. 68, Komarov to Miliutin, 20 March 1885. The date of 30 March is often cited, but that was the date on which the news arrived in St Petersburg.
42. Ibid.

43. TNA FO 65/1237, Thornton to Granville, 7 April 1885.
44. *Hansard*, House of Commons, 27 April 1885, vol. 297, 865.
45. TNA FO 65/1238, Thornton to Granville, 29 March 1885.
46. AVPRI f. 133, op. 470, d. 66, Staal to Giers, 10/22 June 1887.
47. Lady Gwendolen Cecil, *The Life of Robert, Marquis of Salisbury*, vol. 3 (London, 1931), p. 231.
48. AVPRI f. 133, op. 470, d. 67, Staal to Giers, 5/17 October 1887.

24. THE BATTENBERGS: RUSSIA VERSUS BRITAIN OVER BULGARIA

1. There were doubts as to the legitimacy of the children of Grand Duke Louis II which made Nicholas I reluctant for his eldest son to marry Marie.
2. Quoted in Andrew Roberts, *Salisbury: Victorian Titan* (London, 1999), p. 232.
3. George E. Buckle, ed., *The Letters of Queen Victoria, 1862–1885*, 2nd series, 2 vols. (London, 1926–8), vol. 2, p. 6, The Marquis of Salisbury to Queen Victoria, 12 January 1879.
4. Ibid. p. 16, The Grand Duke of Hesse to Queen Victoria, 8 May 1879.
5. Ibid. p. 27, Queen Victoria to The Marquis of Salisbury, 10 June 1879.
6. Quoted in Count Egon Corti, *Prince Alexander von Battenberg* (London, 1954), pp. 45–6.
7. Ibid. p. 43.
8. Ibid. p. 46.
9. Alexander III to the Prince of Bulgaria, 11/23 May 1881, quoted by Corti, op. cit. p. 67, from the Hartenau Archives. These archives covering the early 1880s were given to the Bulgarian National Museum in the 1920s but have since disappeared.
10. AVPRI f. 133, op. 470, d. 34, Prince of Bulgaria to Captain Polsikov, 29 January 1882.
11. Quoted in George F. Kennan, *The Decline of Bismarck's European Order* (Princeton, NJ, 1979), p. 114.
12. Buckle, ed., *Letters*, 2nd series, op. cit. vol. 2, p. 448, Queen Victoria to Earl Granville, 12 October 1883.
13. Corti, op. cit. pp. 106–7.
14. The question of marriage between Alexander of Battenberg and Victoria dragged on until 1887 and caused much friction involving Bismarck, the crown princess and Queen Victoria.
15. *Pall Mall Gazette*, 31 October 1883.
16. AVPRI f. 133, op. 470, d. 98, Giers, Note, 13 November 1883.
17. AVPRI f. 133, op. 470, d. 68, Staal to Giers, 15/27 November 1885.
18. Ibid. Giers to Staal, 24 October/1 November 1885.
19. Buckle, ed., *Letters*, 2nd series, op. cit. vol. 1, p. 188, Queen Victoria to the Marquis of Salisbury, 25 August 1885.

20. Charles Jelavich, *Tsarist Russia and Balkan Nationalism* (Berkeley, CA, 1958), p. 258.
21. Corti, op. cit. p. 240.
22. George Buckle, ed., *The Letters of Queen Victoria, 1886–1901*, 3rd series, 3 vols. (London, 1930–2), vol. 1, p. 179, Queen Victoria to the Marquis of Salisbury, 22 August 1885.
23. Ibid. pp. 180–1.
24. Ibid. pp. 198–9, Prince of Bulgaria to Queen Victoria, 6 September 1886.
25. Ibid. pp. 229–30. Ferdinand was a grandson of King Louis-Philippe of France and thus also related to the Belgian royal family.
26. Ferdinand declared Bulgaria's independence of Turkey in 1908. He abdicated in 1918 after supporting the Central Powers in the First World War.
27. Quoted in Corti, op. cit. p. 256.

25. THE TSAR PEACEMAKER

1. M. S. Anderson, *Britain's Discovery of Russia, 1553–1815* (London, 1958), p. 234.
2. AVPRI f. 133, op. 467 *Sekretny Arkhiv*, d. 114, Nelidov to Giers, 6 April 1890.
3. Quoted in T. G. Otte, *The Foreign Office Mind: The Making of British Foreign Policy, 1865–1914* (Cambridge, 2013), p. 181.

26. THE TSAR PERSECUTOR

1. The title of this chapter is taken from the journalist Charles Lowe's biography, *Alexander III of Russia* (London, 1895), chapter 8.
2. Richard S. Wortman, *Scenarios of Power: Myth and Ceremony in Russian Monarchy*, Vol. 2: *From Alexander II to the Abdication of Nicholas II* (Princeton, NJ, 2000), pp. 289–90.
3. Alex Butterworth, *The World that Never Was: A True Story of Dreamers, Schemers, Anarchists and Secret Agents* (London, 2010), p. 278.
4. Ibid. p. 277.
5. Ibid. p. 279.
6. Ibid. p. 277.
7. Robert Henderson, 'Russian Political Emigrés and the British Museum Library', *Journal of Library History* 9.1–2 (1991), pp. 59–68.
8. Ibid. p. 62.
9. Ibid. p. 68. The most famous Russia reader, Lenin, was not admitted to the library until 1902.
10. Baron Meyendorff, ed., *La Correspondance diplomatique de M. de Staal*, 2 vols. (Paris, 1929), vol. 2, pp. 93–4, Staal to Giers, 27 July/8 August 1890.
11. *The Illustrated London News*, 20 December 1890.
12. Ibid.

13. Meyendorff, op. cit. vol. 2, p. 128, Giers to Staal, 6 February 1891.
14. AVPRI f. 133, op. 467, d. 64, Staal to Giers, 13/25 December 1890.
15. Quoted in Harold Frederic, *The New Exodus: A Study of Israel in Russia* (London, 1892), p. 171.
16. Ibid. p. 248.
17. Ibid. pp. 250–2.
18. Ibid. p. 191.
19. Ibid. p. 200.
20. A. C. Swinburne, 'Russia: An Ode' (1890), in *A Channel Passage and Other Poems* (London, 1904).

27. PERSIA

1. TNA FO 60/506, India Office to the Foreign Office, 22 May 1889.
2. Rose L. Greaves, *Persia and the Defence of India, 1884–1892* (London, 1959), pp. 14–15.
3. TNA FO 60/405/406/407 deal with the Reuter negotiations.
4. IOR, Minute by Salisbury, 6 October 1874, Persian Correspondence, vol. 81, Political Department.
5. Ibid.
6. TNA FO 60/377, Minute of Napier of Magdala, 4 May 1875.
7. The 1856–7 conflict between Britain and Persia to prevent the latter taking Herat is covered in Chapter 15.
8. Denis V. Volkov, *Russia's Turn to Persia: Orientalism in Diplomacy and Intelligence* (Cambridge, 2018), p. 61.
9. Quoted in Greaves, op. cit. p. 200.
10. TNA FO 65/1246, Salisbury to Thornton, 17 July 1885.
11. TNA FO 60/471, Salisbury to Thomson, 12 August 1885.
12. TNA FO 65/1247, Foreign Office to India Office, 25 July 1885.
13. Sir Ronald Thomson, the British minister, had retired in 1885 and the senior diplomat was the *chargé d'affaires*. Later, Arthur Nicolson as ambassador to Russia was a key figure in negotiating the Anglo-Russian Convention of 1907.
14. AVPRI f. 133, op. 470, d. 115, 7 April 1886 (for Alexander III's comment).
15. IOR, Minutes of a letter on Persia, 25 June 1886, Persian Correspondence 1886, vol. 109, Political Department.
16. AVPRI f. 133, op. 470, d. 36, 20 January 1887; TNA FO 60/492, Nicolson to Salisbury, 20 January 1887.
17. TNA FO 60/498, Salisbury to Nicolson, 3 March 1887.
18. TNA FO 60/492, Nicolson to Salisbury, 4 July 1887; AVPRI f. 133, op. 470, d. 38, 4 July 1887.
19. H. Lyman Stebbins, *British Imperialism in Qajar Iran: Consuls, Agents and Influence in the Middle East* (London, 2016), p. 52.

20. Harold Nicolson, *Sir Arthur Nicolson, Bart, the First Lord Carnock: A Study in the Old Diplomacy* (London, 1930), p. 65.
21. Later Gray, Paul & Co. Today, Gray Mackenzie (part of the Inchcape Group) is active in the United Arab Emirates.
22. Ziegler sold the famous Ardebil carpet to a London dealer who in turn sold it to the Victoria & Albert Museum in 1893 for £2,000.
23. TNA FO 65/1299, Morier to Salisbury, 5 December 1887.
24. Henry Drummond Wolff, *Rambling Recollections*, 2 vols. (London, 1908), vol. 2, p. 331.
25. Baron Meyendorff, ed., *La Correspondance diplomatique de M. de Staal*, 2 vols. (Paris, 1929), vol. 1, p. 64, Staal to Giers, 4/16 December 1888.
26. Ibid. vol. 2, p. 39, Note of Giers, 28 June 1889.
27. RA VIC/MAIN/H/45/133, Paget to Foreign Office, 19 December 1888.
28. Quoted in Greaves, op. cit. p. 132.
29. Meyendorff, op. cit. vol. 2, pp. 43–4, Staal to Giers, 27 July/8 August 1889.
30. Agatha Ramm, *Sir Robert Morier: Envoy and Ambassador in the Age of Imperialism, 1876–1893* (Oxford, 1973), p. 340.
31. TNA FO 65/1379, Morier to Salisbury, 20 November 1889.
32. Meyendorff, op. cit. vol. 2, p. 31, Staal to Giers, 21 June 1889.
33. TNA FO 65/1354, Drummond Wolff to Salisbury, 30 October 1888.
34. *The Times*, 6 December 1889.
35. TNA FO 60/517, Minute by Salisbury, 2 October 1890.
36. TNA FO 60/512, Salisbury to Drummond Wolff, 24 February 1890.
37. AVPRI f. 133, op. 470, d. 33, Note of Alexander III, 24 February 1890.
38. TNA FO 65/1395, Salisbury to Morier, 10 November 1890.
39. TNA FO 60/520, Kennedy to Barrington, 24 October 1890; AVPRI f. 133, op. 470, d. 456, 3 November 1890.
40. In 1892 Drummond Wolff became British ambassador to Spain, a post he held until 1900.
41. Quoted in E. G. Browne, *A Year Amongst the Persians* (London, 1893), p. 52.
42. TNA FO 65/1414, Morier to Salisbury, 4 July 1891.
43. Quoted in Rose L. Greaves, 'British Policy in Persia, 1892–1903, I', *Bulletin of the School of African and Oriental Studies* 28.1 (1965), pp. 34–60.
44. George Curzon, *Persia and the Persian Question* (London, 1892), pp. 593–4.

28. THE ROOF OF THE WORLD: THE PAMIRS CRISIS

1. TNA FO 65/1285, Morier to Rosebery, 7 April 1886.
2. Winston S. Churchill, *Lord Randolph Churchill* (London, 1906), p. 357.
3. Ibid. p. 359.
4. Ibid. pp. 360–2.
5. RA VIC/MAIN/H/45/119, The Queen to the Prince of Wales, 6 February 1888. Original emphasis.

6. George Dobson's articles would later form part of his book, *Russia's Railway Advance into Central Asia* (London, 1890).
7. George Curzon, *Russia in Central Asia in 1889 and the Anglo-Russian Question* (1889; London, 2006), p. 68.
8. Ibid. p. 85.
9. Ibid. p. 101.
10. Ibid. p. 117.
11. Ibid. p. 190.
12. Ibid. p. 10.
13. Ibid. p. 315.
14. Ibid. p. 321.
15. Ibid. pp. 13–14.
16. Quoted in Evgeny Sergeev, *The Great Game, 1856–1907* (Washington, DC, 2013), p. 220.
17. Nicholas II, *Journal intime de Nicolas II*, trans. André Pierre (Paris, 1925), p. 32.
18. George E. Buckle, ed., *The Letters of Queen Victoria, 1886–1901*, 3rd series, 3 vols. (London, 1930–2), vol. 2, p. 664, The Marquis of Salisbury to Queen Victoria, 28 December 1890.
19. Nicholas II, *Dnevnk Imperatora Nikolaya II 1890–1906* (Berlin, 1923), p. 40.
20. Edward J. Bing, ed., *The Secret Letters of the Last Tsar* (London, 1938), p. 47.
21. Quoted in Robert D. Warth, *Nicholas II: The Life and Reign of Russia's Last Monarch* (Westport, CT, 1997), p. 10.
22. Ibid. p. 12.
23. Francis Younghusband, *Wonders of the Himalaya* (London, 1924), p. 180.
24. Ibid. p. 181.
25. Ibid. p. 182.
26. Ibid. pp. 183–4.
27. Quoted in Sergeev, op. cit. p. 217.
28. Ibid.
29. Francis Younghusband, *The Light of Experience* (London, 1927), p. 52.
30. Ibid. pp. 58–9.
31. Ibid. pp. 59–60.
32. TNA FO 65/1415, Howard to Salisbury, 5 August 1891.
33. Baron Meyendorff, ed., *La Correspondance diplomatique de M. de Staal*, 2 vols. (Paris, 1929), vol. 2, p. 155, Staal to Kapnist, 10 February 1892.
34. TNA FO 65/1435, Salisbury to Morier, 1 February 1892.
35. Meyendorff, op. cit. vol. 2, p. 176, Staal to Giers, 30 June/12 July 1892.
36. Note on the Question of Delimitation in the Upper Oxus Territories, 1 July 1892, Secret and political memo, quoted in Garry Alder, *British India's Northern Frontier, 1865–95* (London, 1963), p. 250.
37. Alexander Morrison, *The Russian Conquest of Central Asia* (Cambridge, 2020), pp. 513–16.

38. Colonel Sir Thomas Holdich, *The Indian Borderland, 1880–1900* (London, 1901), pp. 284.

29. THE CELESTIAL EMPIRE AND THE LAND OF THE RISING SUN

1. *The Times*, 30 May 1891.
2. Steven Marks, *Road to Power: The Trans-Siberian Railroad and the Colonization of Asian Russia, 1850–1917* (Ithaca, NY, 1991), p. 126.
3. Quoted in Ian Nish, *The Origins of the Russo-Japanese War* (London, 1985), p. 25.
4. The Prince of Wales wanted George de Staal to succeed Giers, but at the age of seventy Staal considered himself to be too old.
5. Grand Duke Alexander Mikhailov, *Once a Grand Duke* (London, 1932), p. 169.
6. N. F. Grant, *The Kaiser's Letters to the Tsar* (London, 1920), 26 April 1896.
7. OCON 5/2/2, O'Conor to Currie, 12 April 1886.
8. CASR 1/53, Spring Rice to Kimberley, 18 June 1893.
9. AVPRI f. 133, op. 470, d. 59, Giers to Staal, 24 August/5 September 1893.
10. CASR 1/4, De Bunsen to Spring Rice, 28 July 1894.
11. Baron Meyendorff, ed., *La Correspondance diplomatique de M. de Staal*, 2 vols. (Paris, 1929), vol. 2, p. 267, Staal to Lobanov, 5/17 April 1895.
12. Keith Neilson, *Britain and the Last Tsar: British Policy and Russia, 1894–1917* (Oxford, 1995), p. 160.
13. Viscount Grey of Fallodon, *Twenty-Five Years, 1892–1916*, 2 vols. (London, 1925), vol. 1, p. 25.
14. Jennifer Siegel, *For Peace and Money: French and British Finance in the Service of Tsars and Commissars* (Oxford, 2014), p. 25.
15. AVPRI f. 133, op. 467 *Sekretny Arkhiv*, d. 152–8, 16 August 1896.
16. Quoted in David Schimmelpenninck van der Oye, *Toward the Rising Sun: Russian Ideologies of Empire and the Path to War with Japan* (DeKalb, IL, 2001), p. 144.
17. *Edinburgh Review*, January 1896.
18. OCON 6/1/15, Sanderson to O'Conor, 19 January 1898.
19. RA VIC/MAIN/H/48/48, O'Conor to Foreign Office, 30 January 1898.
20. Meyendorff, op. cit. vol. 2, p. 376, Staal to Muraviev, 18/30 March 1898.
21. Ibid.
22. OCON 6/1/15, Sanderson to O'Conor, 13 April 1898.
23. Ibid. 23 March/6 April 1898.
24. For an excellent account of the Boxer uprising see Schimmelpenninck, op. cit. pp. 159–64.
25. AVPRI f. 133, op. 464 *Sekretny Arkhiv*, d. 246, Osten-Sacken to Muraviev, 7/19 January 1900.
26. Quoted in Neilson, op. cit. p. 211.
27. Alexander Isvolsky, *The Memoirs of Alexander Iswolsky, Formerly Russian Minister of Foreign Affairs and Ambassador to France*, ed. and trans. Charles Louis Seeger (London, 1920), vol. 1, p. 20.

28. Quoted in Dominic Lieven, *Towards the Flame: Empire, War and the End of Tsarist Russia* (London, 2015), p. 99.
29. AVPRI f. 133, op. 467 *Sekretny Arkhiv*, d. 208, Lamsdorff to Urussov, 31 January/13 February and 7/20 February 1902.
30. Quoted in Neilson, op. cit. p. 224.
31. Boris Romanov, *Rossiia v Manchzhurii, 1896–1906* (Leningrad, 1928), trans. Susan Jones as *Russia in Manchuria, 1892–1906* (Ann Arbor, MI, 1952); Alexander Galperin, *Anglo-Japonskii Soiuz, 1902–21* (Moscow, 1947).
32. 'Dnevnik A. N. Kuropatkina', KA 2 (1922), pp. 11–12.
33. Sergei Witte, *The Memoirs of Count Witte*, trans. Abraham Yarmolinsky (Garden City, NY, 1921), p. 121.
34. Alexander Savinsky, *Recollections of a Russian Diplomat* (London, 1927), p. 49.
35. BD vol. 2, pp. 222–3.
36. Savinsky, op. cit. p. 52.
37. 'Dnevnik A. N. Kuropatkina', KA 2 (1922), p. 96.
38. Prince Sergei Urussov, *Memoirs of a Russian Governor*, trans. and ed. Herman Rosenthal (New York, 1908), p. 177.
39. Ibid.
40. Lieven, op. cit. p. 100.
41. AVPRI f. 133, op. 467 *Sekretny Arkhiv*, d. 17, Note, April 1904.
42. TNA FO 65/1739, Hardinge to Lansdowne, 28 October 1904.
43. CUL Hardinge Papers 7, Lansdowne to Hardinge, 29 October 1904.
44. *The Letters of Theodore Roosevelt*, ed. E. Morison et al., 8 vols. (Cambridge, MA, 1951–4), vol. 4, pp. 1262–3, 7 July 1905.
45. TNA FO 65/1701, Lansdowne to Hardinge, no. 185, 6 June 1905; from Washington, no. 52, 4 June 1905.
46. TNA FO 65/1726, Hardinge to Lansdowne, 19 August 1905.
47. Quoted in Francis Wcisclo, *Tales of Imperial Russia: The Life and Times of Sergei Witte, 1849–1915* (Oxford, 2011), p. 100.
48. Stephen Gwynn, *The Letters and Friendships of Sir Cecil Spring Rice*, 2 vols. (London, 1929), vol. 1, p. 499.
49. Quoted in Neilson, op. cit. pp. 263–4.
50. Ibid.

30. THE ROADBLOCKS TO AN ANGLO-RUSSIAN RAPPROCHEMENT

1. BD vol. 6, p. 780, Marquess of Salisbury to Mr Ivan Muller, 31 August 1896. A copy of the interview can be found in the Russian archives of 1896.
2. Guildhall speech quoted in Andrew Roberts, *Salisbury: Victorian Titan* (London, 1999), p. 606.
3. BD vol. 6, p. 780, Marquess of Salisbury to Mr Ivan Muller, 31 August 1896.
4. RA VIC/MAIN/H/46/96, Abstract, Sir Frank Lascelles, 9 November 1894.

5. George E. Buckle, ed., *The Letters of Queen Victoria, 1886–1901*, 3rd series, 3 vols. (London, 1930–2), vol. 2, p. 45, Sir Nicholas O'Conor to Queen Victoria, 31 May 1896.
6. RA VIC/MAIN/H /46/112, Sir Frank Lascelles to the Earl of Kimberley, 26 February 1895.
7. Dominic Lieven, *Nicholas II: Emperor of All the Russias* (London, 1993), p. 64.
8. Buckle, ed., *Letters*, 3rd series, op. cit. vol. 3, p. 47, Sir Nicholas O'Conor to Queen Victoria, 31 May 1896.
9. Edward J. Bing, ed., *The Letters of Czar Nicholas II and Empress Marie* (London, 1937), pp. 119–20.
10. Quoted in J. A. S. Grenville, *Lord Salisbury and Foreign Policy: The Close of the Nineteenth Century* (1964; London, 1970), p. 79.
11. OCON 6/1/7, Sir Philip Currie to Sir Nicholas O'Conor, 15 April 1896.
12. CASR 1/30, Charles Hardinge to Cecil Spring Rice, 28 December 1899.
13. Ibid.
14. Sir Sidney Lee, *King Edward VII*, 2 vols. (London, 1925–7), vol. 2, pp. 73–4.
15. Ibid. pp. 75–6.
16. For a full description of events in Chitral in 1895, see Peter Hopkirk, *The Great Game: On Secret Service in High Asia* (Oxford, 1990), pp. 483–501.
17. Ibid. p. 501.
18. Quoted in Keith Neilson, *Britain and the Last Tsar: British Policy and Russia, 1894–1917* (Oxford, 1995), p. 17.
19. Ibid.
20. BD vol. 1, p. 307, Memorandum communicated by the Russian Embassy, 6 February 1900.
21. Abdur Rahman, *The Life of Abdur Rahman, Amir of Afghanistan*, 2 vols. (London, 1900), vol. 2, p. 285.
22. BD vol. 4, p. 519, Memorandum on Russo-Afghan Relations, 14 October 1903.
23. Earl of Ronaldshay, *The Life of Lord Curzon*, 3 vols. (London, 1928), vol. 2, p. 312.
24. Lee, op. cit. vol. 2, p. 280.
25. RA VIC/MAIN/W/44/15, Rough Notes on the Foreign Policy of Russia During the Reign of Nicholas the Second, 5 December 1903.
26. AVPRI f. 133, op. 470, d. 85I, Benckendorff to Lamsdorff, 10/23 March 1904.
27. Quoted in David Schimmelpenninck van der Oye, *Toward the Rising Sun: Russian Ideologies of Empire and the Path to War with Japan* (DeKalb, IL, 2001), p. 31.
28. Quoted in Evgeny Sergeev, *The Great Game, 1856–1907* (Washington, DC, 2013), p. 256.
29. Ibid. p. 255.
30. Quoted in Neilson, op. cit. p. 228.
31. AVPRI f. 133, op. 470, d. 69, Benckendorff to Lamsdorff, 20 March 1903.
32. AVPRI f. 133, op. 470, d. 68, Benckendorff to Lamsdorff, 5/18 November 1903.

33. Quoted in David Gilmour, *Curzon: Imperial Statesman, 1859–1925* (London, 1994), p. 288.
34. AVPRI f. 133, op. 470, d. 85II, Benckendorff to Lamsdorff, 8/21 April 1904.
35. TNA FO 60/566, Memorandum on the Past and Present Policy in Persia, 31 August 1895.
36. Ibid. Private Memorandum on the Situation in Persia, 27 September 1895.
37. OCON 6/2/8, Durand to O'Conor, 17 November 1898.
38. CASR 1/28, Curzon to Spring Rice, 6 November 1898.
39. Stephen Gwynn, *The Letters and Friendships of Sir Cecil Spring Rice*, 2 vols. (London, 1929), vol. 1, p. 281.
40. The customs were placed in the hands of Belgian agents.
41. Quoted in Grenville, op. cit. pp. 300–1.
42. Lord (Charles) Hardinge of Penshurst, *Old Diplomacy: The Reminiscences of Lord Hardinge of Penshurst* (London, 1947), p. 49.
43. Denis Wright, *The English Amongst the Persians: Imperial Lives in Nineteenth-Century Iran* (London, 2001), p. 108.
44. TNA FO 60/731, Hardinge to Lansdowne, 30 May 1901.
45. Quoted in Rose L. Greaves, *Persia and the Defence of India, 1884–1892* (London, 1959), pp. 296–7.
46. TNA FO 60/676, Hardinge to Lansdowne, 9 October 1901.
47. TNA FO 60/645, Hardinge to Lansdowne, 12 October 1901.
48. Jane Ridley, *Bertie: A Life of Edward VII* (London, 2012), p. 374.
49. RA VIC/MAIN/W/43/31, Memorandum by Knollys for the King, 31 December 1902.
50. Quoted in David McLean, *Britain and Her Buffer State: The Collapse of the Persian Empire, 1890–1914* (London, 1979), p. 31.
51. TNA FO 60/677, Hardinge to Lansdowne, 18 July 1903.
52. TNA FO 60/615, Minute by the Viceroy on Seistan, 4 September 1899.
53. Ibid. CAB 6/1, Balfour Memorandum, 20 May 1903.
54. *Novoe Vremya*, 7 May 1902.
55. *Hansard*, House of Lords, Parliamentary Debates, vol. 121, 4th series, 5 May 1903, 1348.
56. Quoted in Firuz Kazemzadeh, *Russia and Britain in Persia, 1864–1914* (New Haven, CT, 1968), p. 444.
57. AVPRI f. 133, op. 467 *Sekretny Arkhiv*, d. 208, Lamsdorff to Urussov, 21 February/6 March 1902.
58. Quoted in Ronaldshay, op. cit. p. 316.
59. Quoted in Lord Newton, *Lord Lansdowne: A Biography* (London, 1929), p. 245.

31. TOWARDS THE ANGLO-RUSSIAN CONVENTION

1. AVPRI f. 133, op. 470, d. 69, Benckendorff to Lamsdorff, 10/23 May 1903.

2. Ibid. 3/16 August 1903.
3. Ibid. 5/18 November 1903.
4. AVPRI f. 133, op. 470, d. 74, 30 May/12 June 1905.
5. *The History of The Times: The Twentieth Century Test, 1884–1912* (London, 1947), p. 383.
6. Ibid. p. 384.
7. AVPRI f. 133, op. 470, d. 69, Précis de mon entretien avec le Roi, 18/31 March 1903.
8. AVPRI f. 133, op. 470, d. 68, Benckendorff to Lamsdorff, 10/23 November 1903
9. Sir Sidney Lee, *King Edward VII*, 2 vols. (London, 1925–7), vol. 2, p. 284.
10. Ibid. p. 285.
11. AVPRI f. 133, op. 467 *Sekretny Arkhiv*, d. 225/226, Lamsdorff to Benckendorff, 15 April 1904; Beryl Williams, 'The Revolution of 1905 and Russian Foreign Policy', in C. Abramsky and Beryl Williams, eds., *Essays in Honour of E. H. Carr* (London, 1974), pp. 101–25.
12. Alexander Isvolsky, *The Memoirs of Alexander Iswolsky, Formerly Russian Minister of Foreign Affairs and Ambassador to France*, ed. and trans. Charles Louis Seeger (London, 1920), p. 20.
13. RA VIC/MAIN/44/198, Prince Louis of Battenberg, Memorandum on his visit to Russia, 28 August 1904.
14. RA VIC/MAIN/45/30, Hardinge to Knollys, 16 October 1904.
15. RA VIC/MAIN/W/45/105, Hardinge to Knollys, 1 February 1905.
16. Ibid.
17. RA VIC/MAIN/W/45/109, Hardinge to Knollys, 15 February 1905.
18. RA VIC/MAIN/W/46/70, Hardinge to Knollys, 19 July 1905.
19. RA VIC/MAIN/W/47/325, Cypher telegram to the British Ambassador St Petersburg, 21 October 1905.
20. CASR 4/1, Spring Rice to Balfour, 13 December 1905.
21. Ibid. Spring Rice to Knollys, 31 October 1905.
22. RA VIC/MAIN/W/47/363, Spring Rice to Knollys, 20 December 1905.
23. CASR 4/1, Spring Rice to Hardinge, 7 November 1905.
24. AVPRI f. 133, op. 470, d. 74, Benckendorff to Lamsdorff, 17/30 March 1905.
25. TNA FO 65/1715, Medhurst to Lansdowne, 2 November 1905; TNA FO 65/1713, Smith to Lansdowne, 2 November 1905.
26. TNA FO 65/1713, Smith to Lansdowne, 2 November 1905.
27. TNA FO 65/1703, Lansdowne to Spring Rice, 6 November 1905.
28. CASR 4/1, Spring Rice to Lansdowne, 9 November 1905.
29. TNA FO 65/1706, Spring Rice to Lansdowne, 7 November 1905.
30. Eliyahu Feldman, 'British Diplomats and British Diplomacy and the 1905 Pogroms in Russia', *Slavonic and East European Review* 65.4 (1987), pp. 579–608.

31. Ibid.
32. Viscount Grey of Fallodon, *Twenty-Five Years, 1892–1916*, 2 vols. (London, 1925), vol. 1, p. 156.
33. The Bund was the General Jewish Labour Union in Lithuania, Poland and Russia, created in 1897. It was a clandestine organization, hardened by many years of struggle against the police.
34. AVPRI f. 133, op. 470, d. 72, Lamsdorff Memorandum, 31 March 1905. For a full account of Benckendorff's efforts, see Marina Soroka, *Britain, Russia and the Road to the First World War: The Fateful Embassy of Count Alexandr Benckendorff, 1903–1916* (Farnham, 2011). She is harsh in her judgement, describing the ambassador as 'naïve' (p. 287).
35. AVPRI f. 133, op. 470, d. 74, Benckendorff to Lamsdorff, 23 May/5 June 1905.
36. Ibid. Benckendorff to Lamsdorff, 30 May/12 June 1905.
37. Paul M. Kennedy, *The Rise of the Anglo-German Antagonism, 1860–1914* (London, 1980), p. 227.
38. Isvolsky, op cit. vol. 1, p. 294.
39. Zara S. Steiner and Keith Neilson, *Britain and the Origins of the First World War*, 2nd edition (Basingstoke, 2003), p. 44.
40. Quoted in Stephen Gwynn, *The Letters and Friendships of Sir Cecil Spring Rice*, 2 vols. (London, 1929), vol. 2, p. 35.
41. In fact it emerged years later that the kaiser's dramatic action in March 1905 was not of his own volition but pressed on him by advisers.
42. Sybil Crowe and Edward Corp, *Our Ablest Public Servant: Sir Eyre Crowe, 1864–1925* (London, 1993), p. 111.
43. Quoted in Alan Palmer, *The Kaiser: Warlord of the Second Reich* (London, 1978), p. 112.
44. AVPRI f. 133, op. 467 *Sekretny Arkhiv*, d. 246, Osten Sacken to Lamsdorff, 24 March/6 April 1906.
45. RA VIC/MAIN/W/48/54, Spring Rice to Knollys, 16 February 1906.
46. Harold Nicolson, *Arthur Nicolson, Lord Carnock* (London, 1937), p. 216.
47. Quoted in Keith Neilson, *Britain and the Last Tsar: British Policy and Russia, 1894–1917* (Oxford, 1995), p. 67.
48. David MacLaren McDonald, in his *United Government and Foreign Policy in Russia, 1900–1914* (Cambridge, MA, 1992), p. 104, takes a contrary view.
49. Quoted in G. W. Monger, *The End of Isolation: British Foreign Policy, 1900–1907* (London, 1963), p. 283. For analysis of the Indian point of view, see Beryl Williams, 'The Strategic Background to the Anglo-Russian Entente of August 1907', *Historical Journal* 9.3 (1966), pp. 360–73.
50. AVPRI f. 133, op. 470, d. 98, Benckendorff to Isvolsky, 8/21 June 1906.
51. Ibid.
52. AVPRI f. 133, op. 470, d. 97, Telegram, 28 June 1906.

53. Quoted in Keith Robbins, *Sir Edward Grey: A Biography of Lord Grey of Fallodon* (London, 1971), p. 160.
54. Nicolson, op. cit. p. 222.
55. RA VIC/MAIN/W/49/91, Report by Sir D. M. Wallace of a conversation with M. Stolypine, 13 August 1906.
56. Nicolson, op. cit. p. 212.
57. Ibid.
58. RA VIC/MAIN/W/49/89, Mackenzie Wallace to Knollys, 11 August 1906.
59. Ibid.
60. RA VIC/MAIN/W/49/98, Mackenzie Wallace to Knollys, 28 August 1906.
61. AVPRI f. 133, op. 470, d. 98, Benckendorff to Isvolsky, 26 August/8 September 1906.
62. Ibid. 28 September/9 October.
63. Mansour Bonakdarian, *Britain and the Iranian Constitutional Revolution of 1906–1911* (Syracuse, NY, 2006), p. 61. This excellent study focuses on British dissent of the Anglo-Russian Convention of 1907, but includes a clear account of events in Persia between 1906 and 1907.
64. Isvolsky, op. cit. vol. 1, p. 368.
65. Ibid. p. 364.
66. AVPRI f. 133, op. 470, d. 98, Benckendorff to Isvolsky, 23 September/6 October 1906.
67. RA VIC/MAIN/W/50/10, Memorandum by Sir Edward Grey for the King, 24 September 1906.
68. Michael Hughes, *Diplomacy Before the Russian Revolution: Britain, Russia and the Old Diplomacy, 1894–1917* (Basingstoke, 2000), p. 149.
69. KA 61, 60ff.
70. BD vol. 4, p. 241, Sir C. Hardinge to Sir A. Hardinge, 7 August 1906.
71. Ibid. p. 242.
72. Ibid. p. 245.
73. Gwynn, op. cit. vol. 2, p. 72.

32. ENDGAME

1. Alexander Isvolsky, *The Memoirs of Alexander Iswolsky, formerly Russian Minister of Foreign Affairs and Ambassador to France*, ed. and trans. Charles Louis Seeger (London, 1920), vol. 1, p. 395.
2. BD vol. 4, p. 247, Sir F. Lascelles to Sir Edward Grey, 29 October 1906.
3. Ibid. p. 275, Sir A. Nicolson to Sir Edward Grey, 19 February 1907.
4. Ibid. p. 277, Sir Edward Grey to Sir A. Nicolson, 7 March 1907.
5. Keith Neilson, *Britain and the Last Tsar: British Policy and Russia, 1894–1917* (Oxford, 1995), p. 283.
6. BD vol. 4, p. 524, Sir A. Nicolson to Sir Edward Grey, 23 February/4 March 1907.

7. AVPRI f. 133, op. 470, d. 88, Benckendorff to Isvolsky, 28 February/11 March 1907.
8. Ibid.
9. RA VIC/MAIN/W/51/49, Sir Edward Grey to Sir A. Nicolson, 19 March 1907.
10. BD vol. 4, p. 283, Sir A. Nicolson to Sir Edward Grey, 27 March 1907.
11. Quoted in Philip Magnus, *King Edward the Seventh* (London, 1964), p. 388.
12. Sir Sidney Lee, *King Edward VII*, 2 vols. (London, 1925–7), vol. 2, p. 570.
13. Quoted in G. W. Monger, *The End of Isolation: British Foreign Policy, 1900–1907* (London, 1963), p. 294.
14. BD vol. 4, p. 551, Sir A. Nicolson to Sir Edward Grey, 14 July 1907.
15. Rose L. Greaves, 'Sistan in British Indian Frontier Policy', *Bulletin of the School of African and Oriental Studies* 49.1 (1986), pp. 90–102.
16. BD vol. 4, p. 297, Sir Edward Grey to Mr O'Beirne, 6 August 1907.
17. BD vol. 4, p. 571, Sir A. Nicolson to Sir Edward Grey, 28 August 1907.
18. Ibid.
19. *The History of The Times: The Twentieth Century Test, 1884–1912* (London, 1947), p. 503.
20. T. G. Otte, *Statesman of Europe: A Life of Sir Edward Grey* (London, 2020), p. 297.
21. Viscount Grey of Fallodon, *Twenty-Five Years, 1892–1916*, 2 vols. (London, 1925), vol. 1, pp. 159–60.
22. Ibid. p. 155.
23. G. M. Trevelyan, *Grey of Fallodon: Being the Life of Sir Edward Grey* (London, 1937), p. 188.
24. Quoted in Rogers P. Churchill, *The Anglo-Russian Convention of 1907* (Cedar Rapids, IA, 1939), p. 327.
25. *The Times*, 2 September 1907.
26. Quoted in Churchill, op. cit. p. 322.
27. Earl of Ronaldshay, *The Life of Lord Curzon*, 3 vols. (London, 1928), vol. 3, p. 38.
28. Ibid. p. 44. For obscure technical reasons this had taken time.
29. Ibid.
30. Dominic Lieven, ed., *British Documents on Foreign Affairs*, Part 1, Series A, *Russia 1859–1914*, Vol. 5: *Russia, 1907–1909* (Frederick, MD, 1983), p. 124.
31. Quoted in Evgeny Sergeev, *The Great Game, 1856–1907* (Washington, DC, 2013), p. 321.
32. Quoted in Churchill, op. cit. p. 318.
33. See, for example, Friedrich Stieve, *Isvolsky and the World War*, trans. E. W. Dickes (London, 1926), p. 13.
34. BD vol. 4, p. 585, Sir Edward Grey to Sir C. Spring Rice, 7 September 1907.
35. TNA FO 371/956, Sir G. Barclay to Sir E. Grey, 10 February 1910.
36. BD vol. 4, p. 591, Sir C. Spring Rice to Sir Edward Grey, 13 September 1907.

37. Ibid. p. 593.
38. Ali Ansari, 'The Myth of "Perfidious Albion": Anglo-Iranian Relations in Historical Perspective', *Asian Affairs* 44.3 (2013), pp. 378–91.
39. In the years following the signing of the Anglo-Russian Convention, the independence of Persia all but vanished, with Russia continuing its aggressive policy. Sergei Sazanov, the Russian minister of foreign affairs, summed up the British position in 1910: 'The London Cabinet looks upon the ... Convention as being important for the Asiatic interests of England; but that this Convention possesses a still greater importance for England from the viewpoint of the policy which is being pursued by England in Europe ... This is a circumstance which we can, of course, exploit for ourselves, as, for instance, in Persian affairs.' B. A. de Siebert and G. A. Schreiner, eds., *Entente Diplomacy and the World* (London, 1921), p. 99. For a full discussion of the post-1907 period, see Jennifer Siegel, *Endgame: Britain, Russia and the Final Struggle for Central Asia* (London, 2002).

SELECT BIBLIOGRAPHY

Manuscript Sources

Arkhiv Vneshnei Politiki Rossiiskoi Imperii, Archive of the Foreign Policy of the Russian Empire [AVPRI].
F 133 The Minister's Chancellery.
F 138 The Minister's secret archive.
F 184 Russian Embassy in London.

The British Library, London.

India Office Records [IOR].
Oriental and India Office Collections [OIOC].

The National Archives, Kew, Richmond, Surrey [TNA]

FO 60 Persia.
FO 65 Russia.
FO 78 Turkey.
FO 371 General Correspondence after 1906.
FO 800 Foreign Office Private Collections, Ministers and Officials, 1824–1949.

Board's Collection

Political and Secret Department.
Home Correspondence L/PS/3.
Secret Correspondence with India L/PS/5.

The Royal Archives, Windsor Castle [RA]

RA VIC Papers of Queen Victoria.
Queen Victoria's Journal is available online at http://www.queenvictoriasjournals.org/home.

Churchill College Archives Centre, Cambridge

O'Conor Mss [OCON].
Spring Rice Mss [CASR].

Cambridge University Library [CUL]

Hardinge Papers.

SELECT BIBLIOGRAPHY

Published Official Sources

British Documents on Foreign Affairs, Part I, Series A, *Russia 1859–1914*, Vol. 2: *Russia 1881–1905*; Vol. 5: *Russia 1907–1909*, ed. Dominic Lieven (Frederick, MD, 1983).

British Documents on Foreign Affairs, Part I, Series B, *The Near and Middle East 1856–1914*, ed. David Gillard (Frederick, MD, 1985).

British Documents on the Origin of the War, 1898–1914, ed. G. Gooch and H. Temperley, 11 vols. (London, 1926–38) [BD].

Hansard. House of Commons, 9 July 1833, vol. 19; 25 June 1850, vol. 112 [3rd series]; 9 February 1882, vol. 266; 27 April 1885, vol. 297.

House of Lords, 5 May 1903, vol. 121.

Key Treaties for the Great Powers, ed. Michael Hurst: Vol. 1, *1814–1870*; Vol. 2, *1871–1914* (Newton Abbot, 1972).

Krasnyi Arkhiv, 106 vols. (Moscow, 1922–41) [KA].

Private Papers of British Diplomats, 1782–1900 (Royal Commission on Historical Manuscripts, London, 1985).

Recueil historique d'actes, négociations, mémoires et traités conclu par la Russie avec des puissances étrangères, 15 vols. (St Petersburg, 1874–1909).

Sbornik Imperatorskogo Russkogo Istoricheskago Obshchestva, 148 vols. (St Petersburg, 1876–1916) [SIRIO].

Vneshniaia Politika Rossii XIX I nachala XX veka, vols. 3–5 (Moscow, 1992–2006) [VPR].

Secondary Sources

Abrahamian, Ervand. *A History of Modern Iran* (Cambridge, 2008).

Alder, Garry. *British India's Northern Frontier, 1865–1895* (London, 1963).

Allworth, Edward, ed. *Central Asia: 120 Years of Russian Rule* (Durham, NC, 1989).

Anderson, M. S. *Britain's Discovery of Russia, 1553–1815* (London, 1958). *The Eastern Question, 1774–1923: A Study in International Relations* (London, 1966).

Anwar, K. M. *England, Russia and Central Asia: A Study in Diplomacy, 1857–1978* (Peshawar, 1969).

Bayly, Martin J. *Taming the Imperial Imagination: Colonial Knowledge, International Relations, and the Anglo-Afghan Encounter, 1808–1878* (Cambridge, 2016).

Becker, S. *Russia's Protectorates in Central Asia: Bukhara and Khiva, 1865–1924* (Cambridge, MA, 1968).

Benson, A. C., and Viscount Esher, eds. *The Letters of Queen Victoria, 1837–1861*, 1st series, 3 vols. (London, 1908).

Bew, John. *Castlereagh: Enlightenment, War and Tyranny* (London, 2011).

Bing, Edward J., ed. *The Letters of Czar Nicholas II and Empress Marie* (London, 1937). *The Secret Letters of the Last Tsar* (London, 1938).

Blake, Robert. *Disraeli* (London, 1966).

Bonakdarian, Mansour. *Britain and the Iranian Constitutional Revolution of 1906–1911: Foreign Policy, Imperialism and Dissent* (Syracuse, NY, 2006).

Bourne, Kenneth. *The Foreign Policy of Victorian England, 1830–1902* (Oxford, 1970).

Bradford, Sarah. *Disraeli* (London, 1982).

Braithwaite, Rodric. *Russia: Myths and Realities* (London, 2022).

Brown, David. *Palmerston: A Biography* (New Haven, CT, 2010).

Buckle, George E., ed. *The Letters of Queen Victoria, 1862–1885*, 2nd series, 2 vols. (London, 1926–8). *The Letters of Queen Victoria, 1886–1901*, 3rd series, 3 vols. (London, 1930–2).

Bullough, Oliver. *Let Our Fame Be Great: Journeys Among the Defiant People of the Caucasus* (London, 2010).

von Bülow, Prince Bernhard. *Memoirs, 1849–1897*, 4 vols., English translation (London, 1931).

Burton, D. H. *Cecil Spring Rice: A Diplomat's Life* (London and Madison, NJ, 1992).

Busch, B. C. *Britain and the Persian Gulf, 1894–1914* (Berkeley, CA, 1967).

Butterworth, Alex. *The World That Never Was: A True Story of Dreamers, Schemers, Anarchists and Secret Agents* (London, 2010).

Carr, Edward H. *The Romantic Exiles* (London, 1933).

Catherine II. *Memoirs of the Empress Catherine II, Written by Herself*, with a preface by A. Herzen (London, 1859).

Chamberlain, Muriel. *Lord Aberdeen: A Political Biography* (London, 1983).

Charles-Roux, François. *Alexandre II, Gortchakoff et Napoléon III* (Paris, 1913).

Charmley, John. *Splendid Isolation? Britain and the Balance of Power, 1874–1914* (London, 1999).

Churchill, Rogers P. *The Anglo-Russian Convention of 1907* (Cedar Rapids, IA, 1939).

Collins, Samuel. *The Present State of Russia, in a Letter to a Friend at London* (London, 1671).

Corti, Count Egon. *Prince Alexander von Battenberg* (London: Cassell, 1954).

Crewe, Marquess of. *Lord Rosebery*, 2 vols. (London, 1931).

Cross, Anthony. *By the Banks of the Neva: Chapters from the Lives and Careers of the British in Eighteenth-Century Russia* (Cambridge, 1997). *'By the Banks of the Thames': Russians in Eighteenth Century Britain* (Newtonville, MA, 1980). *St Petersburg and the British: The City through the Eyes of British Visitors and Residents* (London, 2008).

Crowe, Sybil, and Edward Corp. *Our Ablest Public Servant: Sir Eyre Crowe, 1864–1925* (London, 1993).

Curzon, George. *Persia and the Persian Question* (London, 1893). *Russia in Central Asia in 1889 and the Anglo-Russian Question* (1889; London, 1967).

Dallin, D. J. *The Rise of Russia in Asia* (New Haven, CT, 1949).

Dalrymple, William. *Return of a King: The Battle for Afghanistan* (London, 2013).

Dilks, David. *Curzon in India*, 2 vols. (London, 1970).

SELECT BIBLIOGRAPHY

Dixon, Simon. *Catherine the Great* (Harlow, 2001). *The Modernisation of Russia, 1676–1825* (Cambridge, 2012).

Drummond Wolff, Sir Henry. *Rambling Recollections*, 2 vols. (London, 1908).

Edwardes, Michael. *Playing the Great Game* (London, 1975).

Edwards, H. Sutherland. *Russian Projects Against India: From the* Czar *Peter to General Skobeleff* (London, 1885).

Esher, Viscount, ed. *The Girlhood of Queen Victoria: A Selection of Her Majesty's Diaries Between the Years 1832 and 1840*, 2 vols. (London, 1912).

Ewans, Martin. *Securing the Indian Frontier in Central Asia: Confrontation and Negotiation, 1865–1895* (Abingdon, 2010).

Farwell, Byron. *Queen Victoria's Little Wars* (New York, 1973).

Figes, Orlando. *A People's Tragedy: The Russian Revolution, 1891–1924* (London, 1996). *Crimea: The Last Crusade* (London, 2010). *The Story of Russia* (London, 2022).

Fisher, Alan W. *The Annexation of Crimea by the Russian Empire* (Cambridge, 1970).

Fitzmaurice, Edmond. *Life of Granville George Leveson Gower, Second Earl Granville, K.G.*, 2 vols. (London, 1905).

Fletcher, Giles. *Of the Russe Commonwealth, 1591, Facsimile Edition with Variants* (Cambridge, MA, 1966).

Frankel, Jonathan. *Prophecy and Politics: Socialism, Nationalism, and the Russian Jews, 1862–1917* (Cambridge, 1981).

Fuller, William. *Strategy and Power in Russia, 1600–1914* (New York, 1992).

Geyer, Dietrich. *Russian Imperialism: The Interaction of Domestic and Foreign Policy, 1860–1914* (Leamington Spa, 1987).

Gillard, David. *The Struggle for Asia, 1828–1914: A Study in British and Russian Imperialism* (London, 1977).

Gilmour, David. *Curzon: Imperial Statesman, 1859–1925* (London, 1994).

Gleason, John. *The Genesis of Russophobia in Great Britain: A Study of the Interaction of Policy and Opinion* (Cambridge, MA, 1950).

Goldfrank, David M. *The Origins of the Crimean War* (London, 1994).

Gorianov, Serge. *La Question d'Orient et la veille du traité de Berlin, 1870–1878 d'après les archives Russes* (Paris, 1948).

Grant, N. F. *The Kaiser's Letters to the Tsar* (London, 1920).

Greaves, Rose L. *Persia and the Defence of India, 1884–1892* (London, 1959).

Grenville, J. A. S. *Lord Salisbury and Foreign Policy: The Close of the Nineteenth Century* (1964; London, 1970).

Grey of Fallodon, Viscount. *Twenty-Five Years, 1892–1916*, 2 vols. (London, 1925).

Grunwald, Constantin de. *Tsar Nicholas I*, trans. Brigit Patmore (London, 1954).

Gwynn, Stephen. *The Letters and Friendships of Sir Cecil Spring Rice*, 2 vols. (London, 1929).

Habberton, William. *Anglo-Russian Relations Concerning Afghanistan, 1837–1907* (Urbana, IL, 1937).

Hakluyt, Richard. *The Principal Navigations, Voyages, Traffiques and Discoveries of the English Nation*, 3 vols. (London, 1907–9).

Hall, Coryne. *Queen Victoria and the Romanovs: Sixty Years of Mutual Distrust* (Stroud, 2020).

Harcave, Sidney. *Years of the Golden Cockerel: The Last Romanovs, 1814–1917* (London, 1970).

Hardinge, Arthur. *A Diplomatist in the East* (London, 1938).

Hardinge of Penshurst, Lord (Charles). *Old Diplomacy: The Reminiscences of Lord Hardinge of Penshurst* (London, 1947).

Harris, James. *Diaries and Correspondence of James Harris, First Earl of Malmesbury*, 4 vols. (London, 1844).

Hartley, Janet M. *Alexander I* (London, 1994).

Hauner, Milan. *What Is Asia to Us? Russia's Asian Heartland, Yesterday and Today* (London, 1990).

Hawkins, Angus. *The Forgotten Prime Minister: The 14th Earl of Derby*, 2 vols. (Oxford, 2007–8).

Hinsley, F. H., ed. *British Foreign Policy under Sir Edward Grey* (Cambridge, 1977).

Holdich, Colonel Sir Thomas. *The Indian Borderland, 1880–1900* (London, 1901).

Horn, David. *Great Britain and Europe in the Eighteenth Century* (Oxford, 1967).

Hosking, Geoffrey. *Russia: People and Empire, 1552–1917* (Cambridge, MA, 1997).

Hughes, Lindsey. *Russia in the Age of Peter the Great* (New Haven, CT, 1998).

Hughes, Michael. *Diplomacy before the Russian Revolution: Britain, Russia and the Old Diplomacy, 1894–1917* (Basingstoke, 2000).

Hunczak, T., ed. *Russian Imperialism from Ivan the Great to the Revolution* (New Brunswick NJ, 1974).

Ignatiev, A. *Vneshnaia Politika Rossii v 1905–1907* (Moscow, 1986).

Ingle, H. *Nesselrode and the Russian Rapprochement with Britain, 1836–1844* (Berkeley, CA, 1976).

Isvolsky, Alexander. *The Memoirs of Alexander Iswolsky, formerly Russian Minister of Foreign Affairs and Ambassador to France*, ed. and trans. Charles Louis Seeger, 2 vols. (London, 1920).

Jelavich, Barbara. *Russia's Balkan Entanglements, 1806–1914* (Cambridge, 1991).
St Petersburg and Moscow: Tsarist and Soviet Foreign Policy, 1814–1974 (Bloomington, IN, 1974).

Jelavich, Charles, and Barbara Jelavich, eds. *Russia in the East, 1876–1880: The Russo-Turkish War and the Kuldja Crisis as seen through the Letters of A. G. Jomini to N. K. Giers* (Leiden, 1966).

Johnson, Rob. *Spying for Empire: The Great Game in Central and South-East Asia, 1757–1947* (London, 2006).

Johnson, Sam. *Pogroms, Peasants, Jews: Britain and Eastern Europe's 'Jewish Question', 1867–1925* (London, 2011).

Kaufman, Constantine von. *Kaufmanskii Sbornik* (Moscow, 1910).

Kazemzadeh, Firuz. *Russia and Britain in Persia, 1864–1914: A Study in Imperialism* (New Haven, CT, 1968).

Keep, John. *Soldiers of the Tsar: Army and Society in Russia, 1462–1874* (Oxford, 1985).

Kelly, J. B. *Britain and the Persian Gulf, 1795–1880* (Oxford, 1968).

Kennan, George F. *The Fateful Alliance: France, Russia, and the Coming of the First World War* (New York, 1984).

Kennedy, Paul M. *The Rise of the Anglo-German Antagonism, 1860–1914* (London, 1980).

Khalfin, N. A. *Prisoedinenie Srednei Azii k Rossii 60–90e Gody XIX v* [The Annexation of Central Asia to Russia, 1860s to 1890s] (Moscow, 1965).

Klier, John D., and Shlomo Lambroza, eds. *Pogroms: Anti-Jewish Violence in Modern Russian History* (Cambridge, 1992).

Kuropatkin, A. N. *The Russian Army and the Japanese War*, 2 vols., trans. A. Lindsay (London, 1909).

Lamb, Alastair. *British India and Tibet, 1766–1910* (London, 1986).

Lamsdorff, Vladimir N. *Dnevnik, 1891–1892* (Minsk, 2003). *Dnevnik, 1894–1896* (Moscow, 1991).

LeDonne, John P. *The Russian Empire and the World, 1700–1917: The Geopolitics of Expansion and Containment* (Oxford, 1997).

Lee, Sir Sidney. *King Edward VII: A Biography*, 2 vols. (London, 1925–7).

Lieven, Dominic. *Nicholas II: Emperor of All the Russias* (London, 1993). *Russia Against Napoleon: The Battle for Europe, 1807 to 1814* (London, 2009). *Russia and the Origins of the First World War* (Basingstoke, 1983). *Russia's Rulers Under the Old Regime* (New Haven, CT, 1989). *Towards the Flame: Empire, War and the End of Tsarist Russia* (London, 2015).

Lincoln, Bruce. *Nicholas I: Emperor and Autocrat of All the Russias* (1978; DeKalb, IL, 1989).

Loftus, Lord Augustus. *The Diplomatic Reminiscences of Lord Augustus Loftus, 1837–1879*, 4 vols. (London, 1892–4).

Lopatnikov, Viktor. *Gorchakov: Vremya i sluzhenie* (Moscow, 2011).

Madariaga, Isabel de. *Russia in the Age of Catherine the Great* (New Haven, CT, 1981).

Marks, Steven. *Road to Power: The Trans-Siberian Railroad and the Colonization of Asian Russia, 1850–1917* (Ithaca, NY, 1991).

Matthew, H. C. G. *Gladstone, 1809–1874*, 2 vols. (Oxford, 1995).

McDonald, D. MacLaren. *United Government and Foreign Policy in Russia, 1900–1914* (Cambridge, MA, 1992).

McKay, Derek, and Hamish Scott. *The Rise of the Great Powers, 1648–1815* (London, 1983).

McLean, David. *Britain and Her Buffer State: The Collapse of* the *Persian Empire, 1890–1914* (London, 1979).

Medlicott, W. N. *Bismarck, Gladstone, and the Concert of Europe* (London, 1956).

Meyendorff, Baron, ed. *La Correspondance diplomatique de M. de Staal*, 2 vols. (Paris, 1929).

Meyer, Karl, and Shareen Brysac. *Tournament of Shadows: The Great Game and the Race for Empire in Asia* (London, 2001).

Mikhailov, Grand Duke Alexander. *Once a Grand Duke* (London, 1932).

Miliutin, D. A. *Dnevnik D. A. Miliutina, 1873–1882*, 4 vols. (Moscow, 1947–59).

Monger, G. W. *The End of Isolation: British Foreign Policy, 1900–1907* (London, 1963).

Monypenny, W. F., and George E. Buckle. *The Life of Benjamin Disraeli, Earl of Beaconsfield*, 6 vols. (London, 1910–20).

Montefiore, Simon Sebag. *Prince of Princes: The Life of Potemkin* (London, 2000). *The Romanovs, 1613–1918* (London, 2016).

Morgan, Gerald. *Anglo-Russian Rivalry in Central Asia, 1810–1895* (London, 1981).

Morley, John. *The Life of William Ewart Gladstone, 1809–1872*, 2 vols. (London, 1905).

Morrison, Alexander. *The Russian Conquest of Central Asia: A Study in Imperial Expansion, 1814–1914* (Cambridge, 2021).

Mosse, W. E. *The Rise and Fall of the Crimean System, 1855–71* (London, 1963).

Naimark, Norman M. *Terrorists and Social Democrats: The Russian Revolutionary Movement Under Alexander III* (Cambridge, MA, 1983).

Neilson, Keith. *Britain and the Last Tsar: British Policy and Russia, 1894–1917* (Oxford, 1995).

Nesselrode, Count Karl. *Lettres et papiers du Chancelier comte de Nesselrode, 1760–1850* (Paris, 1904–12).

Newton, Lord. *Lord Lansdowne: A Biography* (London, 1929).

Nicholas, Grand Duke, ed. *Scenes of Russian Court Life: Being the Correspondence of Alexander I with his Sister Catherine* (London, 1917).

Nicholas II. *Dnevnik Imperatora Nikolaya II, 1890–1906* (Berlin, 1923). *Journal Intime de Nicolas II*, trans. André Pierre (Paris, 1925).

Nicolson, Harold. *Sir Arthur Nicolson, Bart, the First Lord Carnock: A Study in the Old Diplomacy* (London, 1930).

Nish, Ian H. *The Origins of the Russo-Japanese* War (London, 1987).

Otte, T. G. *The Foreign Office Mind: The Making of British Foreign Policy, 1865–1914* (Cambridge, 2013). *Statesman of Europe: A Life of Sir Edward Grey* (London, 2020).

Palmer, Alan. *Alexander I: Tsar of War and Peace* (London, 1974).

Pierce, Richard. *Russian Central Asia, 1867–1917: A Study in Colonial Rule* (Berkeley, CA, 1960).

Poliakov, Léon. *The History of Anti-Semitism*, 4 vols. (New York, 1965–85).

Quested, Rosemary. *The Expansion of Russia in East Asia, 1857–1860* (Kuala Lumpur, 1968).

Radzinsky, Edvard. *Alexander II, The Last Great Tsar* (New York: Free Press, 2005). *The Last Tsar: The Life and Death of Nicholas II* (London, 1992).

Ragsdale, Hugh, ed. *Paul I: A Reassessment of his Life and Reign* (Pittsburgh, PA, 1979). *Imperial Russian Foreign Policy* (Cambridge, 1993).

Ramm, Agatha. *Sir Robert Morier: Envoy and Ambassador in the Age of Imperialism, 1876–1893* (Oxford, 1973).

Rawlinson, Sir Henry. *England and Russia in the East* (London, 1875).

Riasanovsky, Nicholas V. *A History of Russia* (Oxford, 1993). *A Parting of Ways: Government and the Educated Public in Russia, 1801–1855* (Oxford, 1976).

Ridley, Jane. *Bertie: A Life of Edward VII* (London, 2012).

Ridley, Jasper. *Lord Palmerston* (London, 1970).

Roberts, Andrew. *Salisbury: Victorian Titan* (London, 1999).

Röhl, John C. G. *Wilhelm II: Der Aufbau der persönlichen Monarchie, 1888–1900* (Munich, 2001).

Romanov, Boris. *Russia in Manchuria, 1892–1906*, trans. Susan Jones (Ann Arbor, MI, 1952).

Ronaldshay, The Earl of. *The Life of Lord Curzon*, 3 vols. (London, 1928).

Roosevelt, Theodore. *The Letters of Theodore Roosevelt*, ed. E. Morison et al., 8 vols. (Cambridge, MA, 1951–4).

Rosen, Baron Roman. *Forty Years of Diplomacy*, 2 vols. (New York, 1922).

Rumbold, Sir Horace. *Recollections of a Diplomatist*, 2 vols. (London, 1902).

Rywkin, Michael, ed. *Russian Colonial Expansion to 1917* (London, 1988).

Savinsky, Alexander. *Recollections of a Russian Diplomat* (London, 1927).

Schimmelpenninck van der Oye, David. *Toward the Rising Sun: Russian Ideologies of Empire and the Path to War with Japan* (DeKalb, IL, 2001).

Schroeder, Paul W. *The Transformation of European Politics, 1763–1848* (Oxford, 1994).

Sergeev, Evgeny. *The Great Game, 1856–1907* (Washington, DC, 2013).

Seton-Watson, Hugh. *The Russian Empire, 1801–1917* (Oxford, 1967).

Shannon, Richard. *Gladstone and the Bulgarian Agitation, 1876* (London, 1963).

Shilder, N. K. *Imperator Aleksandr I. Pervyi ego zhizn i tsarstovanie* (St Petersburg, 1904–5). *Imperator Nikolai Pervyi ego zhizn i tsarstovanie* (St Petersburg, 1903). *Imperator Pavel I* (St Petersburg, 1897).

Siebert, B. A. de, and G. A. Schreiner, eds. *Entente Diplomacy and the World* (London, 1921).

Siegel, Jennifer. *Endgame: Britain, Russia and the Final Struggle for Central Asia* (London, 2002). *For Peace and Money: French and British Finance in the Service of Tsars and Commissars* (Oxford, 2014).

Simms, Brendan. *Three Victories and a Defeat: The Rise and Fall of the First British Empire, 1714–1783* (London, 2007).

Soroka, Marina. *Britain, Russia and the Road to the First World War: The Fateful Embassy of Count Aleksandr Benckendorff, 1903–1916* (Farnham, 2011).

St Aubyn, Giles. *Edward VII: Prince and King* (London, 1979).

Stebbins, H. Lyman. *British Imperialism in Qajar Iran: Consuls, Agents and Influence in the Middle East* (London, 2016).

Steinberg, Jonathan. *Bismarck: A Life* (Oxford, 2011).

Steiner, Zara S. *The Foreign Office and Foreign Policy, 1898–1914* (Cambridge, 1969).

Stockmar, Baron E. *Memoirs of Baron Stockmar by his Son Baron E. Stockmar*, 2 vols. (London, 1872).

Sumner, B. H. *Tsardom and Imperialism in the Far East and Middle East, 1880–1914* (Hamden, CT, 1968).

Tatishchev, S. S. *Imperator Aleksandr II, ego zhizn I tsarstvovanie*, 2 vols. (1903; Moscow, 1996).

Taube, Baron M. de. *La politique russe d'avant-guerre et la fin de l'empire des tsars, 1904–1917* (Paris, 1928).

Temperley, Harold. *The Foreign Policy of Canning, 1822–1827* (London, 1925).

Terentiev, Mikhail A. *Russia and England in Central Asia* (Calcutta, 1876).

Thubron, Colin. *The Amur River: Between Russia and China* (London, 2021).

The Times. *The History of The Times: The Twentieth Century Test, 1884–1912* (London, 1947).

Trevelyan, G. M. *Grey of Fallodon: Being the Life of Sir Edward Grey* (London, 1937).

Urussov, Prince Sergei. *Memoirs of a Russian Governor*, trans. and ed. Herman Rosenthal (New York, 1908).

Valuev, P. A. *Dnevnik, 1877–1884* (Petrograd, 1919).

Villiers, G. A. *A Vanished Victorian, Being the Life of George Frederick Villiers, Fourth Earl of Clarendon, 1800–1870* (London, 1938).

Warth, Robert D. *Nicholas II: The Life and Reign of Russia's Last Monarch* (Westport, CT, 1997).

Webster, Sir Charles. *The Foreign Policy of Castlereagh*, Vol. 1: *1812–1815*, Vol. 2: *1815–1822* (London, 1931–4). *The Foreign Policy of Palmerston, 1830–1841*, 2 vols. (London, 1951).

Williams, Beryl. *Late Tsarist Russia, 1881–1913* (London, 2021).

Wilson, A. N. *Victoria: A Life* (London, 2014).

Wilson, Francesca. *Muscovy: Russia through Foreign Eyes, 1553–1900* (London, 1970).

Witte, Count Sergei. *The Memoirs of Count Witte*, trans. Abraham Yarmolinsky (Garden City, NY, 1921).

Wortman, Richard. *Scenarios of Power: Myth and Ceremony in Russian Monarchy*, 2 vols. (Princeton, NJ, 1995–2000).

Wright, Denis. *The English Amongst the Persians: Imperial Lives in Nineteenth-Century Iran* (London, 2001).

Wyatt, Christopher. *Afghanistan and the Defence of Empire: Diplomacy and Strategy During the Great Game* (London, 2011).

Yapp, Malcolm E. *Strategies of British India: Britain, Iran, and Afghanistan, 1798–1850* (Oxford, 1981).

Younghusband, Francis. *The Light of Experience* (London, 1927). *Wonders of the Himalaya* (London, 1924).

Zaionchkovski, A. *Vostochnais voina, 1853–1856*, 3 vols. (St Petersburg, 2002).

INDEX

INDEX